History of Religious Sectarianism in Russia
(1860s—1917)

Other Pergamon titles of interest

E. ALLWORTH
Ethnic Russia in the USSR: The Dilemma of Dominance

K. P. JAMESON and C. K. WILBER
Religious Values and Development

W. LAUTERBACH
Soviet Psychotherapy

E. A. LIVINGSTONE
Studia Patristica

W. O. McCAGG and B. D. SILVER
Soviet Asian Ethnic Frontiers

R. ROY
Experimenting with Truth: The Fusion of Religion with Technology,
Needed for Humanity's Survival

A Related Journal

HISTORY OF EUROPEAN IDEAS*

Editor: Dr Ezra Talmor

A multidisciplinary journal devoted to the study of the history of the
cultural exchange between European nations and the influence of this
exchange on the formation of European ideas and the emergence of the idea of
Europe

Free specimen copy supplied on request

History of Religious Sectarianism in Russia (1860s—1917)

by

A. I. KLIBANOV

Translated by
ETHEL DUNN

Edited by
STEPHEN P. DUNN

PERGAMON PRESS
OXFORD · NEW YORK · TORONTO · SYDNEY · PARIS · FRANKFURT

U.K.	Pergamon Press Ltd., Headington Hill Hall, Oxford OX3 0BW, England
U.S.A.	Pergamon Press Inc., Maxwell House, Fairview Park, Elmsford, New York 10523, U.S.A.
CANADA	Pergamon Press Canada Ltd., Suite 104, 150 Consumers Rd., Willowdale, Ontario M2J 1P9, Canada
AUSTRALIA	Pergamon Press (Aust.) Pty. Ltd., P.O. Box 544, Potts Point, N.S.W. 2011, Australia
FRANCE	Pergamon Press SARL, 24 rue des Ecoles, 75240 Paris, Cedex 05, France
FEDERAL REPUBLIC OF GERMANY	Pergamon Press GmbH, 6242 Kronberg-Taunus, Hammerweg 6, Federal Republic of Germany

First English edition 1982
Previously published in Russian 1965

Library of Congress Cataloging in Publication Data
Klibanov, A. I. (Aleksandr Il'ich)
History of religious sectarianism in Russia,
1860s-1917.
Translation of: Istoriia religioznogo
sektantstva v Rossii, 60-e gody XIX v.-1917 g.
1. Christian sects—Soviet Union. I. Title.
BR935.5.K413   1982   280'.4'0947   81-12180
AACR2

British Library Cataloguing in Publication Data
Klibanov, A. I.
History of religious sectarianism in Russia,
1860s - 1917.
1. Christian sects - Soviet Union - History
I. Title II. Dunn, Stephen P. III. Istoricheskie
zepiske. *English*
274.7   BR935.5
ISBN 0-08-026794-7

Printed in Great Britain by A. Wheaton & Co. Ltd., Exeter

Contents

Contents

MAPS

From the Author

When Mrs Ethel Dunn, to whose friendly initiative I am obliged for the American edition of my book, asked whether I wished to make any corrections or changes in it, I answered in the negative. I am very far from thinking that the book is above reproach. But additions and changes are justified, I think, when new editions of books (from the points of view of information, source material and textual changes) are published. I hope that the American reader will forgive me, because in return he will receive a book by which he will be able to judge Soviet historiography of religious sectarianism in Russia, and at the same time the scholarly career of the author. To make corrections and additions in a book written long ago would mean to embellish by hindsight the historiography of the question and the scholarly biography of the author, which, of course, should not be done. What has been said does not mean that the author is an opponent of self-criticism. Self-criticism, however, can take various forms. The author chose a positive form, and wrote new books: *Religioznoe sektantstvo v proshlom i nastoiashchem* [Religious Sectarianism in the Past and Today] (1973), *Narodnaia sotsial'naia utopiia v Rossii: Period feodalizma* [Popular Social Utopias in Russia: The Period of Feudalism] (1977), *Narodnaia sotsial'naia utopiia v Rossii: XIX vek* [Popular Social Utopias in Russia: 19th century] (1978), in which I tried to fill in the gaps, and to get rid of the deficiences contained in the book now published in English. In the first book listed above, I wanted to reveal more fully the "mechanisms" which permit us to view sectarian communities as econmic nuclei of a special kind laying out a detour for the development of bourgeois relationships under conditions where serfdom prevailed, and then under those of semi-serfdom. In the second and third books, I tried to illuminate as fully as possible the role of sectarianism in class-wide peasant movements of the 17th-19th centuries. I was interested both in the immediate participation of sectarians in popular uprisings and in their ideological role in the class struggle of the peasantry and socially lower classes of the city.

But in this case, how justified is the work of translation of this book which now becomes available to the American reader? I hope that it is justified. In the first place, the questions considered in later books are reflected (although

vii

incompletely) in the book presented here; in the second place, this book has its own independent character. In it an attempt was made to make order out of chaos, formed by the co-existence of religious sects—which differed in character, arose at different times, and were diffused in dissimilar social milieus, and in geographic and economic regions of Russia distinct from one another. I think that I succeeded in this attempt, even if only in a general way and on the whole, and that I succeeded in showing a kind of single genealogy, if not for all, then at least for all of the most significant religious sects existing in Russia, partly existing today. The succession of basic forms was shown, and the gemmation of religious sectarianism in the course of the historical process and in the struggle of polarizing of forces in the sects themselves, reflecting the objective contradictions of socio-economic and political reality in Russia from the 18th to the beginning of the 20th centuries. On this basis, I revealed the "evolutionary ladder" of the development of religious sectarianism with movement "from above" and "from below", if one takes a reading of the social and historical importance of this or that sect. In other words, the metamorphoses of religious sectarianism in the main phases and steep spires of its development are shown, in my opinion, in their social-historical determinism. I paid great attention to the role of religious sects in the political life of Russia, particularly for the stretch of time at the end of the 19th century to 1917. In a word, the American reader will become familiar with the first and still the only *History of Religious Sectarianism in Russia.*

I am, naturally, happy to meet the American reader, who will now become familiar with a quite interesting and little-known page from the life of pre-revolutionary Russia. Undoubtedly in his mind, there will arise an association with the distant past history of the United States, as these associations arose in me, especially when I studied the occupation of the Amur Region and the Transcaucasus by the sectarians, and their economic activity in Novorossiia and Eastern Siberia. These parallels are given by life itself—and they are instructive.

My books have been repeatedly commented upon by American colleagues, among them Ethel Dunn, whom I deeply respect, and whose scholarly works deserve more attention, and sincere thanks for her work at popularizing Soviet authors. Among reviewers of my books, there were authors undoubtedly well-intentioned, erudite, and apparently convinced that my work would be significantly more effective if I had adhered to a different scholarly methodology. In the given case I can answer my past and future reviewers with the words of Goethe: "The greatest respect that an author can show his readers is to create not what was expected of him, but what he himself considers correct and useful at the given stage of his and the other person's development."

April 26, 1979   A. I. Klibanov

Translator's Preface

When I first reviewed the book which I happily present here to the reader, I wrote: "This is a very important book, impressive by any scholarly standard, and deserving of immediate translation because it makes most other books on the subject of sectarianism appear strikingly inadequate. If the data in it were widely discussed, Russian studies—here and in Russia as well—would never be the same again" (Dunn 1967: 128). My passionate admiration of A. I. Klibanov's "breath-taking mastery of the Marxist formula for the laws of history as they apply to the study of sectarian movements" troubled Henry Roberts as the editor of *Slavic Review*, and it was only five revisions later—after I had added, "After all, a hypothesis does not have to be exhaustive (or even ultimately correct) in order to be useful at a given point . . ." that Professor Roberts yielded and printed my review article, even though I had failed to meet all his objections and answer all his questions.

Finding a publisher for an English translation proved very difficult, and if the book had not become a landmark in my own intellectual development, I might have given up. Many reputable publishers (supportd in this by equally irreproachable scholars) declined to bear the burden of an English edition on the grounds that those who could make use of the data could—and would—read *History of Religious Sectarianism in Russia* in the original Russian. A decade later it was clear that this had not happened, was not happening, and would not happen. Even so, I successfully argued that a translation into English would be useful for anyone unfamiliar with Russia but desiring comparative material in the fields of sociology, and history of religion, cultural anthropology and cultural history, Marxism, and ethnic studies, since the *History* was a major source for studying peasant movements in Russia and for understanding the values adopted by the Soviet regime after the Revolution. I am deeply grateful to the National Endowment for the Humanities for a translation grant in 1977-1978. I also wish to extend my thanks to Pergamon Press for deciding to publish the manuscript as Stephen P. Dunn and I presented it.

After the project was underway, the addition of maps seemed both appropriate and desirable. Since no adequate maps could be borrowed either

ix

from printed sources or from work known to A. I. Klibanov, I asked Adrienne Morgan, a cartographer associated with the Department of Geography at the University of California to draw the four maps included here, from information extracted from the book. I thank her for her patience, and her labor. We tried in these maps to show the spread and geographical distribution of Khristovovers, Molokans, Dukhobors, Baptists and Adventists in the Russian Empire—that is, when Leningrad was still St. Petersburg, and Ordzhonikidze was still Vladikavkaz. If we have not been entirely successful, it is because, as A. I. Klibanov told me, the cartography of Russian sectarianism still awaits a student.

A few words are necessary concerning the format of the book: This is a complete translation, except for a few paragraphs omitted from the pages preceding Chapter One. Stephen P. Dunn (who edited my text) tried to keep editorial notes to a minimum; those that were unavoidable are placed at the end of the chapter in which they occur. There is a glossary which explains words that for one reason or another we decided to leave in the original Russian. The book contains one of the largest source bases on the subject of sectarians in recent times (which was a cogent reason for making it available to students). To minimize the labor involved in footnoting, we adopted scientific style (listing all sources alphabetically by author and chronologically for each author), but the chapter on the Baptists had, in the original, 507 footnotes, and, especially when a citation was repeated, we sometimes weakened and put *ibid.* The list of Literature Cited represents an improvement over the original Russian, since with A. I. Klibanov's help, I was able to supply some dates and titles that were missing.

Not counting the times I have consulted the *History* over the years, I have read the manuscript three times. My admiration for it has, if anything, increased. I offer it to English-reading audiences nearly fifteen years after first encountering it with a single caveat: errors in translation and presentation are mine, but I hope that even if this child of my labor proves cross-eyed, it still has merit. I thank: A. I. Klibanov for his kind words and his responses to queries; Stephen P. Dunn for his editorial skill; Ellen Sheeks for typing the bulk of the manuscript, twice, and Paula Chertok as the latest and last to commit my enthusiasm to paper. Both women, but Ellen Sheeks in particular, by their attention to detail, made the book better than it might otherwise have been.

Aleksandr Il'ich Klibanov began publishing works on sectarians in the late 1920s, concentrating on Adventists and Mennonites. His Candidate of Historical Sciences degree (a Soviet advanced degree for academic personnel) was given in 1935 for a study of "Mennonite colonization of the south of

Russia in the 18th and 19th centuries", according to V. I. Buganov (1977: 273) who also notes Klibanov's early and continuing interest in atheistic propaganda and the formation of a new world-view. Daniel Field, while recognizing the sincerity of this aspect of Klibanov's activity, takes a rather condescending tone toward it (Field 1980: 349-350), but close study of Klibanov's views and works reveals in rather touching fashion the extent to which this great scholar shared the opinion of a significant number of Russian peasant sectarians: if life is to be transformed, a new world-view must consciously replace the old, and it helps immeasurably to be conscious of what the old views really were.

Curiously, Buganov fails to note any publication by Klibanov between 1935 and 1955, a period during which relatively little research into the problem of religious sectarianism was published. Klibanov himself says that of the 380 titles collected by him for the period 1917-1967, 199 were published after 1956 (Klibanov 1970a: 269). It is possible that in his position as senior researcher at the Institute of History, Academy of Sciences, USSR, Klibanov continued to work in the archives. At any rate, he was given the degree of Doctor of Historical Sciences for *Reformatsionnye dvizheniia v Rossii v XIV-pervoi polovine XVI v.* [Reformation Movements in Russia From the 14th to the First Half of the 18th Centuries] (1960). Since 1959, the Institute of History (sometimes collaborating with the Institute of Ethnography) has been sending researchers into the field to study the contemporary status of both old and new sects. Klibanov has not only directed this work by participated in it (see Klibanov 1965, 1970b, 1971, 1974-1975; Klibanov and Mitrokhin 1974, Kozlova 1970, Tul'tseva 1977).

In this *History*, Klibanov says (page 112) that he has no figures on the population increase in Tiflis and Elizavetpol' Guberniias between 1886 and 1897, and this is only one of the problems in writing about sectarians. He declares that "Shtundism is nothing other than a tendentious Church designation for the totality of peasant movements in religious form which developed in the 1860s and 1870s on the grounds of dissatisfaction with the Reform and opposition to the ruling church" (p. 230). Yet it is clear from his exposition to that point that the same can be said of the use of the word "sectarianism". Here and elsewhere Klibanov says that sectarianism was a form of protest in religious guise, but the political aspects are far from obvious in this formulation. Daniel Field, who has analyzed some of the same material (1976) can be excused for having missed the significance of the references to Herzen and Ryndziunskii on page 163, but they provide the key to the tsarist regime's attitude toward sectarians. A series of peasant uprisings in which Molokans (Spiritual Christians) played a prominent part just before and just after the Emancipation showed what the regime felt was a dangerous level of dissatisfaction with agrarian policy. However, the regime's response was not

limited to administrative repression. Spiritual Christians were given the opportunity to resettle in the Transcaucasus and Siberia, and many did so
believing that they were going to find the kingdom of God on earth. The ways
in which the tsarist regime alternately used this millennarian striving and
repressed it is more adequately described in Klibanov's last two books on folk
utopias (1977, 1978), but in a certain sense, Klibanov has, even with the great
depth of his research, only opened the way for this study (see, for example,
Ismail-Zade 1977).

Klibanov begins his *History* by arguing in some detail that Lenin was interested in the problem of sectarianism. When I first set out to translate this section, many years ago, I could not make it seem more than wooden rhetoric,
and more than one publisher suggested that if the manuscript were cut, this
would be an excellent place at which to begin. But that would have been a
fatal error, for I am more convinced today than ever that the study of Russian
sectarianism and of the nature of the Russian peasantry must go hand in
hand, as indeed they have in my work (see Dunn and Dunn 1967, and E. Dunn
1970a, 1970b). I think that Klibanov's work is a significant corrective to
the traditional Marxist view of the peasantry as usually non-revolutionary,
conservative, and passive. And so firmly entrenched is the traditional view
that both Field (1980) and Ryndziunskii (1979) (who can hardly, I think, be
called political co-thinkers) preferred to stress other aspects in their reviews of
Klibanov's books on folk utopias than the political activism of a significant
number of Spiritual Christians (some of whom certainly considered
themselves members of the Russian Orthodox Church).

In my review of the *History*, I said (Dunn 1967: 129) that I thought that
Klibanov's Marxist model broke down precisely at the point of the 1905
Revolution. At that time, I was, frankly, bored by the chapters on Baptism
and Adventism, two sects which spread rapidly after the Edict of Toleration
in 1905, gaining converts from among members of the old Russian sects as
well as among the Russian Orthodox. Klibanov stresses the importance of the
rise of capitalist relationships in the rural areas, and the bourgeoisification of
the sectarian leadership. My own research among Molokans in America
(Dunn 1976, Dunn and Dunn 1977, 1978) leads me to think that outside
pressure from the state is as important as internal theological contradictions
within the sect, and, in fact, Klibanov says much the same thing toward the
end of his book on folk utopias in the 19th century. Describing the fate of Ivan
Grigor'ev's commune, which, as a continuation of the tradition of the Obshchie Molokans, had still been strong enough to outlast the death of the
leader, Klibanov says: "The appearance of exploiters and class divisions in the
commune had sources first of all in relationships lying outside the commune — the surrounding reality — contradictions of which had a decisive effect
on the commune and were fatal" (Klibanov 1978: 264).

The Edict of Toleration in 1905 supposedly allowed sectarian groups the freedom to practice their religious beliefs. In fact the Russian Orthodox Church continued to exercise the right to tell the state who was dangerous, and who was not, in a political or a social sense. The more radical members of Spiritual Christianity (Dukhobors, Molokans, and New Israelites) had either emigrated by the 1905 Revolution or were intending to do so. The point is made more clearly in the books on folk utopias but is still clear enough in the *History* that Spiritual Christians were debating the question, how may life be transformed? Maksim Rudometkin, a spiritual leader of the Priguny, argued with followers of Mikhail Popov, the leader of the Obshchie, that community of property was not called for by divine law (p. 175). Spiritual Christians might, after all, consider that internal spiritual change would have to occur before external changes would be lasting. Klibanov's pages on the Baptists can be read in this light.

In other words, this book can be read for an answer to the question: how is culture changed, and, conversely, how is ethnicity preserved? Molokans and Dukhobors were frequently described in the literature as if they were an ethnic group distinct from the Russians. One Dukhobor author critical of P. V. Verigin, comments that: "It turns out that the Dukhobors are not Russians, but Dukhobors" (p. 110). The extent to which this is true is still a matter of some dispute. Klibanov reports that Dukhobors still living in the Georgian SSR preserve many distinctive traits—presumably ones which set them apart from other Russian groups, and presumably traits which cannot be solely confined to the retention of the Russian folk costume (Dunn 1970a) or to certain archaisms of speech, even though this retention may be conscious, and may be precisely how ethnicity is preserved in a non-Russian environment. A comparison with the Molokans does not reveal the same mechanisms, at least to the same degree. The question is: what sets Russian sectarians apart from all other Russians? In the 19th century, it may well have been their relationship to the means of production and their attitude toward the ownership of land. The description of Molokans in the Amur region is striking when compared with data from other regions of the country. Klibanov calls it a version of American agriculture, and he has several times quoted the negative attitude of Russian observers to this new type of farmer: "Something rigid and coldly calculating breathed from this man. He was entirely taken up in his economic plans and undertakings ... one sensed not a farmer but a 'warrior' ... (p. 194).

In his *History*, Klibanov argues convincingly that the political line of sectarian leaders was what one could expect from the bourgeoisie. He does not seem particularly willing to grant that the continuing development of sectarian communities was possible. In his book on folk utopias in the 19th century, he goes so far as to say that the non-violent approach to cultural change

had been exhausted under the tsarist regime (Klibanov 1978). The surviving
members of Ivan Grigor'ev's commune in Malyi Uzen' (Samara Guberniia)
"accepted the October Revolution as the Last Judgment over the existing
order of forms and considered that snakes and beasts had been put down and
the Kingdom of God established on earth" (Klibanov 1978: 262). However it
is significant that the then leader, I. I. Meshalkin, had substantially modified
Grigor'ev's commune, making it much smaller, and much more exclusive.

I invite the reader of this *History* to follow carefully the logical development
of these sects from essentially traditional peasant to essentially something
else — at least a new type of peasant. I do not consider that Klibanov has said
the last word on the structure of the " 'evolutionary ladder' of the development of religious sectarianism" (see pp. vii-viii of this volume), but I am deeply
impressed by Klibanov's own recognition of the necessity for further study. I
hope, in presenting this book to the public in English translation, that
Klibanov will gain a whole generation of new students.

LITERATURE CITED

BUGANOV, V. I. (1977) Problemy reformatsionnykh dvizhenii i obshchestvenno-politicheskoi mysli
Rossi v trudakh A. I. Klibanova [Problems of reformation movements and the social-political
thought of Russia in A. I. Klibanov's works], *Istoricheskie zapiski* [*Historical Notes*], **98**,
257-275.

DUNN, ETHEL (1967) Russian sectarianism in new Marxist scholarship, *Slavic Review*, **XXVI**,
128-140.

DUNN, ETHEL (1970a) Canadian and Soviet Dukhobors: An examination of the mechanisms of
culture change, *Canadian Slavic Studies*, **4**, No. 2, 300-326.

DUNN, ETHEL, (1970b) The importance of religion in the Soviet rural community. In *The Soviet
Rural Community*, edited by James R. Millar, Urbana, Ill., pp. 346-375.

DUNN, ETHEL (1976) American Molokans and Canadian Dukhobors: economic position and ethnic
identity. In Frances S. Henry (ed.), *Ethnicity in the Americas*, Chicago: Aldine, pp. 98-114.

DUNN, ETHEL and STEPHEN P. DUNN (1977) Religion and ethnicity: the case of the American
Molokans, *Ethnicity*, **4**, 370-379.

DUNN, ETHEL and STEPHEN P DUNN (1978) Molokans in America, *Dialectical Anthropology*, **3**,
349-360.

DUNN, STEPHEN P. and ETHEL DUNN (1967) *The Peasants of Central Russia*, New York: Holt,
Rinehart and Winston.

FIELD, DANIEL (1976) *Rebels in the Name of the Tsar*, Boston: Houghton-Mifflin Co (1980) A far-
off abode of work and pure pleasures, *The Russian Review*, **39**, No. 3, 348-358.

ISMAIL-ZADE, D. (1977) Russian settlements in the Transcaucasus from the 1830s to the 1880s,
Soviet Sociology, **XVI**, 51-77.

KLIBANOV, A. I. (1965) The dissident denominations in the past and today, *Soviet Sociology*, **III**,
No. 4, 44-60.

KLIBANOV, A. I. (1970a) Fifty years of scientific study of religious sectarianism, *Soviet Sociology*,
VIII, No. 3-4, 239-278.

KLIBANOV, A. I. (1970b) Sectarianism and the socialist reconstruction of the countryside, *Soviet
Sociology*, **VIII**, No. 3-4, 383-411.

KLIBANOV, A. I. (1971) Problems in the psychology of religious sectarianism, *Soviet Sociology*,
IX, No. 4, 505-566.

KLIBANOV, A. I. (1974-75) In the world of religious sectarianism: at a meeting of Prygun
Molokans, *Soviet Sociology*, **XIII**, No. 3, 80-93.

KLIBANOV, A. I. (1977) *Narodnaia sotsial'naia utopiia v Rossii. Period feodalizma* [The Folk Social Utopia in Russia. The Period of Feudalism], Moscow.

KLIBANOV, A. I. (1978) *Narodnaia sotsial'naia utopiia v Rossii. XIX vek* [The Folk Social Utopia in Russia. 19th Century], Moscow.

KLIBANOV, A. I. and L. N. MITROKHIN (1974) The schism of contemporary baptism, *Social Compass*, **XXI**, No. 2, 133-152.

KOZLOVA, K. I. (1970) Experience gained in studying the Molokans in Armenia, *Soviet Sociology*, **VIII**, No. 3-4, 318-328.

RYNDZIUNSKII, P. G. (1979) Review of A. I. Klibanov, *Narodnaia sotsial'naia utopiia v Rossii. Period feodalizma, Istoriia SSR* [History of the USSR].

TUL'TSEVA, L. A. (1977) The evolution of old Russian sectarianism (On data From Voronezh Oblast), *Soviet Sociology*, **XVI**, No. 1, 20-48.

January 8, 1981   ETHEL DUNN

**Highgate Road Social Science
Research Station
Berkeley, California**

Introduction

The history of sectarian movements is a component of the history of peasant movements in Russia, to which, as we know, Lenin paid a great deal of attention. As long ago as in 1894, in *Who Are the "Friends of the People" and How Do They Agitate Against the Social Democrats?*, Lenin developed the idea of a revolutionary alliance of the working class and the peasantry, led by the working class, and this great idea directed his interest toward sectarian movements in Russia at the very beginning of his revolutionary activity.

A. A. Beliakov tells of a conversation which Lenin had in May 1890 with two peasant "Shtundists" [proto-Baptists; see p. 229 below]—Amos from Staryi Buian and Erfylich from the village of Kobel'ma. These devout men, like many sectarians, dreamed of "remaking life", "eliminating injustice", "uniting all people in a single fraternal family", and thereby establishing "paradise on earth". They saw as the means of realizing their dream the creation of a "simple faith, with no deceit whatever".

In the course of the conversation, Lenin clearly explained to them the basic Marxist tenet that man's social life determines his consciousness, and that therefore "faith does not change human relations, but, on the contrary, human relations, or more properly economic needs and economic relations, can change any faith." He illustrated his explanation with a number of clear and simple examples, which brought about a change in the consciousness of the sectarians: "Both of them", Beliakov writes, "were as if struck by lightning. They understood that faith is not the essential thing—that faith, like God, is the creation of men." They said: "And we, like fools, have wasted our whole lives trying to remake life through faith. And it's really just the other way around...."

Lenin drew the following conclusion from his talk with the sectarians: "The peasant seeks a way out, struggles, wanders in stale byways of religion, and boldly rejoices when he understands the essence of the matter.... How many such Amoses are scattered in innumerable villages, struggling, seeking a way out, cut off from those who can show it to them! We must unite these forces and drive toward the common goal, not along Narodnik blind alleys and back streets, but along the direct road of Marxism" (Beliakov 1958: 57-60).

1

After 1895, Lenin developed and set forth in a number of articles basic propositions on religious sectarianism as a social phenomenon, on its place in the class struggle, and on the tasks of revolutionary Social Democrats in relation to it.

In the "Draft Program of Our Party," Lenin wrote: "Probably no one will deny the presence of revolutionary elements in the Russian peasantry. We know that there have been peasant uprisings in the post-Reform period against the landowners who govern the peasants, and against the bureaucrats who shield the landowners. We know of agrarian rebellions, murders, and so forth. We know there is growing indignation among the peasants (in whom even the wretched scraps of education they possess have already begun to awaken a feeling of human dignity)—indignation at the wildly arbitrary behavior of that gang of highborn bums who were loosed on them as zemstvo bosses. We know of ever more frequent famines affecting millions of people, who cannot remain passive spectators to such 'difficulties in provisioning'.

"We know of the growth of sectarianism and rationalism among the peasantry, and the appearance of political protest in a religious guise is a phenomenon characteristic of all peoples at a certain stage of their development, and not of Russia alone. The presence of revolutionary elements in the peasantry, thus, in subject to no doubt whatever" (*Lenin* IV: 228). Lenin's statements reveal to us the social essence of sectarianism under the conditions of pre-Revolutionary Russia.

In Western European countries, sectarian movements were widespread at the stage of the decay of feudal-serf relationships, and, being bourgeois-democratic in their objective historical significance, those movements tended to destroy these relationships.

The wide dissemination of sectarianism in Russia dates from the second half of the 18th century. At the end of the 19th century in both the economic and the political structure of Russia, there still remained a great many survivals of serfdom. Lenin wrote: "Given the presence of enormous differences and contradictions in the interests of various classes and groups of the population, the very essence of contemporary society, which is based on a commercial economy, demands the destruction of the autocracy, political freedom, and the open and immediate expression of the interests of the ruling classes in building and directing the state. A democratic revolution which is bourgeois in its socioeconomic nature cannot but reflect the needs of the whole bourgeois society" (*Lenin* XI: 282).

Religious sectarianism in Russia was a peasant movement arising on the basis of contradictions in the feudal-serf structure sanctioned by Russian Orthodoxy. In the form of opposition to the ruling church and its ideology, sectarianism expressed peasant protest against the institutions of serfdom, being thereby one of the tendencies of democratic protest (in the bourgeois sects). In a number of its manifestations, sectarianism in the post-Reform epoch remained a democratic tendency directed against survivals of serfdom.

Having noted the presence of revolutionary elements in the peasantry and having included the sectarians among them, Lenin at the same time warned: "We do not at all exaggerate the strength of these elements, we do not forget the political immaturity and ignorance of the peasants ..." (*Lenin* IV: 228-229). These words of Lenin's are the more applicable to sectarianism, since its political protest appeared in a reactionary religious guise.

Lenin showed with complete clarity that the milieu of the democratic elements was not homogeneous, that class stratification had taken place, and class contradictions developed within it. He wrote: "As for democratic elements within oppressed peoples and persecuted religious bodies, everyone agrees that class contradictions within these categories of the population are rather deeper and stronger than the solidarity of all classes within such a category against absolutism and in favor of democratic institutions" (*Lenin* II: 454).

Even more relevant to sectarianism is Lenin's statement that "it would be rash to put forward the peasantry as the *bearer* of the revolutionary movement, a party would be insane to base its revolutionary activity on the revolutionary mood of the peasantry." Lenin maintained only that "without violating the basic precepts of Marxism and without committing an enormous political mistake, a workers' party cannot *bypass* those revolutionary elements which exist in the peasantry, and not offer support to those elements" (*Lenin* IV: 229).

In *What Is to be Done?*, Lenin forcefully set before the working class the task of being as revolutionary as possible in unmasking the full vileness of the autocracy, particularly "in regard to the harassment of sectarians", the instigators of which he called "gendarmes in cassocks who do the work of the Holy Inquisition" (*Lenin* VI: 70-71).

Lenin repeatedly came to the defense of freedom of conscience, which was violated by tsarism and the church. As early as 1901, in an article written in connection with a speech by Stakhovich, a Marshal of the Nobility from Orel who was incensed at the extremes of religious persecution in Russia, Lenin wrote: "The 'demoralization' introduced into Russian life in general and that of our countryside in particular by arbitrary police action and inquisitorial persecution of sectarianism has gone so far that even the stones cry out!" (*Lenin* V: 337). In 1903, in connection with the promise of Nicholas II to strengthen the basis of toleration, Lenin demanded "the immediate and unconditional legal recognition of freedom of assembly and freedom of the press, and amnesty for all 'political prisoners' and all sectarians. Not until freedom of assembly, speech, and the press is declared will we see the end of this shameful Russian inquisition that persecutes the profession of any faith

and the expression of all opinions and teachings not supported by the state"
(*Lenin* VII: 125).

So that the protest of democratic elements against the force and oppression of
absolutism should be organized and not spontaneous, Lenin demanded "the
cultivation among the Social-Democratic workers of the kind of political
leaders who can manage all the phenomena of this many-sided struggle and
can at the right time 'dictate a positive program of action' to student activists,
dissatisfied zemstvo workers, indignant sectarians, ill-treated teachers [in
zemstvo schools]" (*Lenin* VI: 86).

Lenin pointed out to the Social Democrats the necessity of educating the
sectarians politically, and he considered this a task for the whole Party. The
role of the V. D. Bonch-Bruevich in the fulfillment of this task was exceptionally great: he was the most prominent Marxist student of sectarianism (on
this see Klibanov 1959, Shakhnovich 1963). In a letter to Bonch-Bruevich
dated November 27, 1901, Lenin wrote: "It goes without saying that all information about the persecution of sectarians, including secret circulars about
these persecutions ... interests us extremely; and therefore if you fulfill your
promise to send material we will be extremely grateful to you" (the letter is
kept in the archives of the Institute of Marxism-Leninism, CPSU; quoted
from Kryvelev 1960: 132-133). Political education of sectarians included not
only explaining to them that their position as a persecuted religious minority
was attributable to the absolutism that lay like a yoke on the neck of the
masses, but also familiarizing them with the tasks which the Social-
Democratic Party set in its struggle for the people's revolutionary interests.
Lenin wrote to Bonch-Bruevich: "If you will send the addresses of sectarians
to whom we can send *Iskra* in envelopes, we will regularly send them all
numbers" (Kryvelev 1960: 182-183).

In an article published in 1902, "The Importance of Sectarianism for
Modern Russia", Bonch-Bruevich set forth in general outline his views on the
direction to be taken in Social-Democratic work among the sectarians. He envisaged:

1) the publication of brochures, proclamations, and leaflets;

2) using the connections between urban and rural sectarian organizations
for the distribution of this illegal material in the countryside;

3) the preparation, by means of a systematic distribution of illegal
literature, of the groundwork for peasant revolutionary organizations in the
villages.

To carry out this plan, Bonch-Bruevich proposed that certain Party propagandists and organizers be assigned to work exclusively among sectarians
(Bonch-Bruevich 1902).

Bonch-Bruevich's proposals were in part based on accumulated experience.
In 1900 and 1901, Social-Democratic literature had been sent to sectarians

living in Russia, as well as to those in Europe and America. In 1901, Bonch-Bruevich and V. M. Velichkina (working with D. A. Khilkov and a few others) began publishing anonymous brochures under the title *Narodnye listki* [People's Leaflets]. The foreword to the first number announced that the publication was intended for the broadest strata of the Russian peasantry and the urban workers. The first number was dedicated to the martyrs of the revolutionary struggle for the people; the fourth number contained a militant article entitled "The Russian Weaver Petr Alekseevich Alekseev" and a transcript of Alekseev's speech in court.

"Sectarians", Bonch-Bruevich said in 1903, "willingly took and read the revolutionary socialist literature and distributed it. Comments on the literature were in general highly favorable: the literature was not only pleasing, but as the sectarians wrote, 'opened our eyes to reality' " (Bonch-Bruevich 1959: 178). Moreover, Molokans helped to transport Social-Democratic literature from Turkey and Persia into Russia; the "Novoshtundisty" [Baptists] (and Nekrasovite Old Believers) helped to transport Social-Democratic literature, *Iskra* in particular, from Rumania into Russia across the Danube (Bonch-Bruevich 1924: 22-40).

The question of work among the sectarians was included on the agenda of the Second Congress of the RSDRP. Bonch-Bruevich, in the report "The Schism and Sectarianism in Russia", written on Lenin's instructions and read by Lenin at the 27th session of the Congress on August 23, 1903, declared that it was necessary to isolate sectarians from all those who try to deflect them from the revolutionary struggle or to dissolve their protest into religious ideas of "non-violence" and "self-perfection". Without the removal of class-hostile influences on sectarians, it would be impossible to achieve the task of attracting them to the Social Democrats.

In support of his proposals for Social-Democratic propaganda among the sectarians, Bonch-Bruevich cited the indissoluble connection of these proposals with the whole policy and practice of the Social Democrats. He wrote: "... Comrade Lenin, in his little book *What Is to be Done?*, points out in several places that not only should we not ignore sectarians, but that in our broad Social-Democratic propaganda we must use their frame of mind and the facts of their persecution. *Iskra* has also repeatedly directed the attention of readers to the sectarian question" (Bonch-Bruevich 1959: 177-178).

One had to take account of the fact, Bonch-Bruevich noted, that those of sectarian persuasion who were drawn to the Social Democrats would for a certain time preserve their "purely sectarian peculiarities". But this did not mean that the Social Democrats should enter into any compromises with the politically-immature sectarians or hide from them the tasks and aims of the Social-Democratic Party. "Without forgetting for a minute our demands as Social Democrats", wrote V. D. Bonch-Bruevich, "and our final aims as socialists, and not only not hiding either one, but, on the contrary everywhere propagandizing the bases of class struggle and a proletarian attitude toward the ruling order of things, we, as a Party, reflecting the interests of the purest and the truest democracy, will nevertheless attract all the best forces of the country—all those varied elements of the population whose political consciousness has already come into direct contradiction to the interests of the ruling classes" (Bonch-Bruevich 1959: 186).

Bonch-Bruevich concluded his report with a proposal to publish, under the control of the Central Organ of the Party, a periodical leaflet for sectarians to begin in January 1904. Lenin wrote the text of the resolution on Bonch-Bruevich's report. It was accepted with minor corrections by G. V. Plekhanov. "Taking into account that the sectarian movement in Russia is in many of its aspects one of the democratic trends directed against the existing order of things, the Second Congress calls the attention of all Party members to its work among sectarians, and to its aim of winning their support.

"The Congress directs the Central Committee to take up the question of the proposal contained in Comrade Bonch-Bruevich's report" (CPSU 1954, Part I: 48).

In accordance with the decision of the Second Congress of the RSDRP, a series of Social-Democratic leaflets for sectarians began to appear in January 1904 in Geneva under the title *Rassvet* [The Dawn]. Bonch-Bruevich was its editor, and it came out every month in a printing of 2,000 copies. Over the course of 1904, nine numbers appeared. The journal commented widely on the most important events of the time. It carried articles on the Russo-Japanese War, in which the imperialistic policy of the tsarist autocracy was exposed and the tasks facing the working class in connection with the war explained. The journal paid a great deal of attention to questions of the Russian and international workers' movement and to the strike movement. Survey articles entitled "Among Sectarians" were regularly carried in the journal, which also published articles written by sectarians themselves.

It is noteworthy that *Rassvet* also set the scientific-atheistic education of sectarians as one of its tasks: V. M. Velichkina's informative articles, "On the Scriptures", "What is the Bible, and How and By Whom Was It Written?", and "The Origin of Religious Beliefs in Mankind" were devoted to this question. An article of Nikolai Nilov, "On the Question of Revolutionary Work Among Sectarians", was of considerable interest (Nilov 1904). The author proceeded from the experience of Social-Democratic work among sectarians and expressed opinions and observations which have not yet lost their significance.

While "the Russian proletariat", Nilov remarked, "parts with the church and frees itself from the tutelage of [Russian] Orthodoxy and the influence of religious ideology in general ... the sectarian does not part with his principles so easily." The religious ideology of sectarianism held its followers in stronger bonds than did Orthodoxy, and was a more difficult obstacle to the revolutionary struggle than was the Orthodox ideology. Nilov explained this by saying that sectarianism was a religion "somewhat purified of archaism" and "in one way or another adapted to surrounding conditions", and that the teachings of sectarianism arose from "criticism of the ruling church" (Nilov 1904: 73).

He noted the traits of fanaticism peculiar to the religious psychology of the sectarian. Especially important are the views which he drew from practical work among the sectarians, and on the content of the dialogue with sectarians and the propagandist's preparation for this work. Nilov singled out the special necessity in work among sectarians of the propagandist's training in questions of philosophy and psychology. "I would say that besides the importance of sectarian teachings, the Gospels, and theology, one must have adequate philosophical training, since the sectarian by the very nature of his world-view does not hesitate to dig into profound and very difficult philosophical questions. He becomes a casuist and a scholastic, stubbornly defends his views, and demands basic criticism of them, and the Social Democrat should counterpose to all this special training, solid knowledge, and an understanding of the psychology of the sectarian" (Nilov 1904: 74).

Rassvet was distributed in Russia and abroad (primarily among Russian Dukhobors in Canada).

The appearance of *Rassvet* provoked a violent reaction on the part of the church. In March 1904, the journal *Missionerskoe obozrenie* [Survey of Missions] notified all workers of the Orthodox Mission[1, A] that "as of January of the present year, yet another periodical publication was started abroad for Russian sectarians ... by persons ... interested mostly in the role of political fighters for the interests of the Social Democrats—in other words, without faith or a God, enemies of the church and the Tsar." The missionaries complained that "sectarian leaders from the intelligentsia have decided to lead sectarianism not along the Tolstoyan path of passive resistance to the existing state structure, but along the path of action, i.e. along the path of anarchy and revolution" (*Missionerskoe obozrenie* 1906, No. 6: 764). It is significant that the Tolstoyan *Svobodnoe slovo* [The Free Word] came out against *Rassvet* with an argument identical to that of *Missionerskoe obozrenie*.

The Mensheviks favored the liquidation of *Rassvet*. The journal, being a completely new enterprise for the Party, had its deficiencies, chiefly because experienced Party writers took an insufficient part in it. Five months after the beginning of the publication of *Rassvet*, the Mensheviks raised the question in

---

[1] Let us remember the following statement by Lenin in 1902: "... everyone knows that lately persecution of sectarians has become more brutal, and the formation of the Mission is directly connected with this ..." (*Lenin* V: 338).

the Council of the Party of discontinuing the journal, calling this experiment unsuccessful.

Lenin, while critical of the journal's deficiencies, at the same time spoke decisively against the suggestion by the Mensheviks. In particular, he said: "So far only five months have passed since the beginning of publication. It is possible that the publication can still stand on its feet, especially if other writers come to its aid. Something, at least, has been done: ties among sectarians both in America and in Russia have been extended. Besides this, it should be noted that financially this publication does not lie on the Party's shoulders, since *Rassvet* is published with separate funds. I consider the closing of *Rassvet* premature and propose that the experiment continue" (*Lenin* VIII: 441).

Rassvet continued to appear. Its publication was stopped at the end of 1904. In connection with this there was an announcement from the editor of the journal: "We announce to the public that we have decided to stop publication of *Rassvet,* since the sharp crisis through which our Party is passing demands that we concentrate all our efforts on intra-party work. Under more favorable circumstances we will resume our experiment, which this year has given some positive results" (Bonch-Bruevich n.d.: 69). However, publication of the journal was not resumed. The first bourgeois-democratic revolution which was beginning demanded the concentration of all Party forces on the immediate tasks of the revolutionary struggle. In 1905, Bonch-Bruevich, who directed the journal and in general facilitated connections with sectarians, illegally left Geneva for Russia, for agitation in connection with the calling of the Third Congress of the RSDRP.

Although the foundation of Social-Democratic agitation and propaganda among sectarians was laid down at the end of the 1890s, this task was adopted as a matter for the entire Party only at the Second Congress of the RSDRP. Less than a year and a half after this, the first bourgeois-democratic revolution began in Russia. Naturally, in such a short space of time social-democratic work among sectarians could not penetrate their deepest strata, politically enlighten their consciousness which had been darkened by religion, and paralyze the influence of bourgeois leaders of sectarianism, and also the reactionary influence of Tolstoyan activists.

When Lenin, in the work "A Draft Program for our Party," proposed that Social Democrats support all revolutionary elements of the peasantry, including peasants involved in religious sectarianism, he wrote: "Can these revolutionary elements of the Russian peasantry act as the Western European peasant acted in overthrowing absolutism — this is a question to which history has not yet given an answer" (*Lenin* IV: 229).

With regard to religious sectarianism, the experience of the revolution of 1905-1907 answered this question negatively. While the revolution sobered the minds of many ordinary sectarians, all sectarian organizations of any significance joined forces in these years with the counter-revolutionary bourgeoisie. Lenin foresaw this possibility, when he wrote that "Social Democracy will lose none of its good name or its momentum by this, for it is not Social Democracy's fault that the peasantry did not answer (perhaps could not answer) its revolutionary appeal. The workers' movement goes and will go its way, in spite of any betrayal from the great or petty bourgeoisie" (*Lenin* IV: 229).

The revolution of 1905-1907 put an historic end to sectarianism as a form of social protest by democratic elements.

"There was a time in history", Lenin wrote in 1913, "when ... the struggle of democracy and the proletariat went on as a struggle of *one religious* idea against another.

"But that time is long past.

"Now both in Europe and in Russia *any,* even the most refined, the most well-meaning defense or justification of the idea of God is a justification of reaction" (Lenin XXXV: 93).

But the democratic lower classes of sectarianism remained. They were prisoners of prejudices, slaves of their leaders, victims of priestly persecution and police repression. Social Democracy appealed to them as before.

In December 1905, Lenin in the article "Socialism and Religion" spoke out once more in defense of freedom of conscience, for the definition of religion "as a private matter in relation to the state", for complete separation of the church from the state, for freedom "to preach any religion one pleases or not to recognize any religion at all—i.e. to be an atheist" (*Lenin* XII: 143).

The struggle for freedom of conscience, which included the struggle against religious persecution of sectarians, was also conducted by Social-Democratic deputies from the rostrum of the State Duma. In this connection, we should note the speech of G. I. Petrovskii in the Fourth State Duma, May 3, 1913 in reference to an inquiry about persecutions of sectarians by local government representatives in the provinces:

"Our group", said G. I. Petrovskii, "introduced the urgent inquiry, about which you already know, to the Minister of Internal Affairs on the persecution of sectarians.... This matter brooks no delay. Whatever political party you belong to here, gentlemen, it would seem that on the question of freedom of conscience there should not be two opinions, since the right to freedom of conscience is the most elementary political right." Petrovskii continued: "We, Social Democrats of Russia, have from the very beginning of our existence made the Social-Democratic viewpoint on religion part of our program. Being consistent atheists, we willingly leave heaven, as Bebel has, to the sparrows. We always and everywhere unyieldingly proclaim freedom of conscience" (State Duma 1913: 756-757).

Revolutionary Social Democrats frequently unmasked arbitrary tsarist repressions of sectarians from the rostrums of court sessions as well: "It has been a week since I returned from a great judicial proceeding", wrote Bonch-Bruevich on April 29, 1912, "which took place in the city of Ostrogozhsk in Voronezh Guberniia. There they tried 81 sectarians for their faith.... I had for the first time in my life to act as public defender, and was made deeply happy by the fact that my special knowledge made it possible, and helped the defense to tear from the hands of the prosecution 65 persons who were completely exonerated" (Bonch-Bruevich 1959: 348). Subsequently, Bonch-Bruevich many times took part in proceedings against sectarians, unmasking the falsifications of the tsarist courts.

In the complicated circumstances of political struggle in Russia at the beginning of the 20th century, the Bolshevick Party was the only force showing the sectarians the real path of struggle for liberation from exploitation by the ruling classes, arbitrary police action and violence done to conscience. The Party did everything possible to help the sectarians enter on the path of general democratic struggle, to enlighten their consciousness, and to show that their unification on religious grounds contradicted the basic interests of their unification as workers and exploited people. The Party unmasked the Tolstoyans, and any other figures working among the sectarians, who deceived and lulled their class consciousness with the aid of patriarchal illusions and various religious opiates. It was the only principled and consistent defender of sectarians from the persecution of the tsarist regime, from priest-missionary harrassment and slanders.

The Party's varied activity had a sound scientific basis worked out by Lenin and enriched with the experience of work in drawing sectarians to the Social Democrats.

Lenin's statements on religious sectarianism, and the theoretical and practical experience of Social-Democratic work among sectarians, have key methodological significance for study of all the problems of the history of religious sectarianism in Russia.

Study of the history of religious sectarianism fills in the picture of popular movements in Russia, both in the late feudal period and in the capitalist one, when, in the presence of numerous feudal survivals, the social protest of the popular masses often continued to appear in religious form. Of course, with the growth of the class struggle, the social significance of popular movements expressing their social demands in religious form became ever more special and limited. But the social interests and ideals of the participants in these movements, however obscure the religious language to which they resorted, had not specialized but basic significance.

Marx wrote: "Of course, it is much easier to find by analysis the earthly core of foggy religious concepts than conversely to deduce from the data of the relations of real life the religious forms corresponding to the data. The latter method is the only materialistic, and consequently the only scientific one" (*Marx and Engels* XXIII: 383, note 89). The historian of religio-social movements, by following the method pointed out by Marx (i.e. by studying the roots of these movements in "the relations of real life") thereby shows both the peculiar character of these movements and the common element in them which was part of the working classes' struggle for liberation.

Thus, religio-social movements will be looked at not as a kind of "appendage" which the student of popular movements can safely disregard, but as the product of "the relations of real life", which condition *all* historically known varieties of the struggle for liberation. Without an understanding of the variety and unity of these forms, and of their inter-relationships, which change in the course of history, an integral picture of the history of popular movements is impossible, as a true evaluation of the level of social growth of popular movements at various stages of their history would also be impossible.

The history of religious sectarianism in Russia put its imprint on the attempt at social creativity by its participants, which lay in the channel of utopian social thought and on their searches in the field of political, social, philosophical and ethical questions. However, students of peasant movements of the 17th-19th centuries, as a rule, pay no attention to this form of popular creativity, complaining at the same time of the limited number of sources which characterize the world-view of peasant movements.

The study of the history of religious sectarianism in Russia also has cognitive significance for an understanding of the historically-limited nature of peasant movements in religious form and of the deeply reactionary role which the religious ideology played in them. In the last analysis, as the history of religious sectarianism shows, all democratic movements appearing in a theological integument suffocated in it and were turned into organs of bourgeois reaction.

The task of scientifically constructing a history of religious sectarianism has its difficulties, first of all because the sources on this question have not been sufficiently studied. Numerous sources kept in the central archives (the archives of the [Holy] Synod [of the Russian Orthodox Church], the Ministry of Internal Affairs, etc.), and even more numerous materials kept in local archives (in the archives of guberniia judicial institutions, consistories, etc.), were not accessible to researchers in tsarist Russia. They remain almost unstudied at the present time too, since the study of the history of religio-social movements in Russia is one of the most backward parts of Soviet historiography.

All the same, the pre-revolutionary publications of official sources which we possess, for all their tendentiousness, incompleteness and dependence on the degree of elementary honesty of the publishers, more or less retain their importance for the historian of religio-social movements. In this connection we should name the publications of the civil servants N. Varadinov (*Istoriia Ministerstva vnutrennikh del* [A History of the Ministry of Internal Affairs], Vol. 8, SPb, 1863), F. Livanov (*Raskol'niki i ostrozhniki* [Schismatics and Prisoners], Vols. I-IV, SPb, 1869), V. Val'kevich (*Zapiska o propagande protestantskikh sekt v Rossii i osobenno na Kavkaze* [A Note on the Propaganda of Protestant Sects in Russia and Especially in the Caucasus]), and Bishop Aleksei Dorodnitsyn (*Materialy po istorii religiozno-ratsionalisticheskogo dvizheniia na iuge Rossii* [Materials on the History of the Religio-Rationalistic Movement in the South of Russia]).

The most exhaustive, but also the most tendentious and remote from the basic methods of scholarly publication, are the books of Livanov. He clearly aimed to strike the reader's imagination with the "sensational nature" of the material, seeking a cheap popularity, and at the same time depicting sectarians as inveterate enemies of "the throne" and the church. Many of the materials adduced by Livanov disappeared from the archives, possibly not without his own cooperation.

The London publications of Herzen and Ogarev[B] made a real breach in the secrecy surrounding the policy of the autocracy and the church regarding sectarianism and the Old Belief. On Herzen's and Ogarev's instructions, V. I. Kel'siev published in London: *Sbornik pravitel'stvennykh svedenii o raskol'nikakh* [Collection of Government Information on the Schismatics] (in four parts, 1861-1862) and *Sbornik postanovlenii po chasti raskola* [Collection of Ordinances on the Schism] (in two parts, 1863). These publications had great social importance, since they exposed the arbitrariness and violence practiced by tsarism and the church in their struggle with representatives of the religious opposition.

We must emphasize that for all the importance of the group of official sources for the study of the history of sectarianism, they are by their very nature one-sided. The situation changes in those cases in which the documentation of government and church authorities is accompanied by the literature of the sectarians themselves—their religious and other writings, graphic material, etc.—as "material evidence". In studying the history of religious sectarianism it is necessary to use all available resources, including materials on sectarianism collected by ethnographers, folklorists, economists, statisticians and representatives of other branches of knowledge.

There is no need to speak of the importance of economic-statistical and demographic material as a source for describing the internal processes taking place in sectarianism, and its inter-relationship with the surrounding social environment. While there are economic-statistical and demographic descriptions of the majority of the guberniias of Russia, the places settled by sectarians are not specified in them. However, Dukhobors, Molokans, Subbotniki, Khristovovers of various tendencies, Skoptsy and others, settled, as a rule, compactly and in isolation.

The more peripheral the territories settled by sectarians, the fewer exceptions there were to this rule. Access to economic-statistical and demographic data as a source for the description of religious sects lies through the reconstruction of their geographical distribution, which is achieved by the combined study of official and church sources (local and central), and also ethnographic materials and works.

The following sources served as the basis for my research:

1. Published materials describing the history and world-view of religious sectarianism, and first of all the multi-volume publications of V. D. Bonch-Bruevich: *Materialy k istorii i izucheniiu religioznogo sektantstva* [Materials For the History and Study of Religious Sectarianism] and *Materialy po istorii religiozno-obshchestvennykh dvizhenii* [Materials on the History of Religio-Social Movements]. I repeatedly referred to the documents published in *Materials on the History of the Religio-Rationalistic Movement in the South of Russia* by Bishop Aleksii (Dorodnitsyn) and V. A. Val'kevich's *Note on the Propaganda of Protestant Sects in Russia and Especially in the Caucasus.*

2. Writings by sectarian authors — Khristovovers, Dukhobors, Molokans, Baptists, Evangelical Christians, Adventists — published separately in Russia and abroad, and also in the general periodical press.

3. Manuscript works and documents by sectarian authors in the archives of the Museum of the History of Religion and Atheism in Leningrad, of the Institute of History, Academy of Sciences, USSR, of the Lenin State Public Library, and also those collected by me personally.

4. Works of sectarian folklore, which I used primarily from the publication of T. S. Rozhdestvenskii and M. N. Uspenskii, *Pesni russkikh sektantov-mistikov* [Songs of Russian Sectarian Mystics].

5. Sectarian periodical literature, but especially the journals: *Blagaia vest'* [The Good News], *Blagovestnik* [The Evangelist], *Sektantskii vestnik* [Sectarian Bulletin], *Molokanskii vestnik* [Molokan Bulletin], *Molokanin* [The Molokan], *Khristianin* [The Christian], *Dukhovnyi khristianin* [The Spiritual Christian], *Baptist* [The Baptist], *Gost'* [The Guest], *Seiatel'* [The Sower], *Slovo istiny* [The Word of Truth], *Utrenniaia zvezda* [The Morning Star], *Vestnik khristianina* [The Christian's Bulletin].

6. Ethnographic and ethno-statistical surveys published by V. D. Bonch-Bruevich, A. S. Prugavin, V. I. Iasevich-Borodaevskaia, M. V. Muratov, N. Dingel'shtedt, S. Maksimov, I. E. Petrov, I. Ia. Segal', and others.

7. Economic-statistical works covering the regions and places of sectarian colonization in the guberniias of the Caucasus and in the Amur region.

8. Information emanating from official institutions relating to the description of sectarianism, its statistics, etc., mainly the documentation of the Department of Spiritual Affairs, the Department of Police, the Synod, etc., kept in the corresponding collections *TsGIAL, TsGIAM* and *TsGAOR*.

For reasons set forth partly above and partly in the second chapter, I did not consider it possible to dwell in my work on this or that problem of the history of the Old Belief. I wholly share the opinion of Bonch-Bruevich expressed in the report "The Schism and Sectarianism in Russia" for the Second Congress of the RSDRP: "One of the chief and most persistent confusions leading to great errors and incorrect interpretations is the equating of the Schism, especially its 'militant' variety, with sectarianism, when both the origin and significance of these phenomena in our historical life are essentially different" (Bonch-Bruevich 1959: 153).

I have limited my research, both thematically and chronologically, to the most persistent and widespread forms of sectarianism for that part of their growth from the 1860s to 1917 — i.e., the period of capitalism. However, it was impossible to avoid either an excursus on the earlier history of the sects or a chapter on the genesis of religious sectarianism.

This chronological digression allows us to better understand the processes which took place in religious sectarianism in the period of capitalism. At the same time, it ties the present work to our attempt at the study of religio-social movements in the period of feudalism (Klibanov 1960).

The path to a comprehensive study of the history of religious sectarianism lies through monographic studies of the history of religious sects. I cannot, therefore, undertake more than merely to note the most general contours of this great and complex historical phenomenon. I hope that my attempt will stimulate the appearance of new works in the field under review and will help researchers at the start of their careers.

I am deeply grateful for the advice of P. G. Ryndziunskii, who read my work in manuscript.

I take the opportunity to thank G. S. Lialina — Associate of the Institute of Scientific Atheism, Academy of Social Sciences under the Central Committee, CPSU — for her active cooperation in the finding and primary processing of factual materials, and also for assistance in preparing this work for the press.

Editor's Notes

Note A. This was a special department of the Russian Orthodox Church directed toward the struggle against sectarians.
Note B. Alexander Herzen and his cousin N. P. Ogarev belonged, philosophically, to the so-called Westerners as opposed to the Slavophiles (see Donald W. Treadgold, *The West in Russia and China: Religious and Secular Thought in Modern Times*, Vol. I: Russia, 1472-1917, Cambridge University Press, 1973, pp. 160-161 and *passim*).

The Historiography of Religious Sectarianism

The historiography of religious sectarianism is marked by sharp polemics. This is explained by the character of the object of study: social protest appeared under a religious guise as sectarianism, and the warring classes of pre-revolutionary Russia responded to it on the basis of their interests.

Up to 1917 the bibliography on sectarianism numbered several thousand articles, brochures and books.[1] A great part of this literature was written by leading figures in the ruling church. The obscurantist church-missionary polemic, which provoked planned persecution of sectarians, was elevated by its representatives at the beginning of the 20th century to the level of a "science of sectology".

This "sectology" was unanimously condemned by wide segments of pre-revolutionary public opinion as hopeless obscurantism and was systematically criticised in the entire progressive press.

What kind of "science" this was is shown by the remark of the monarchically-minded A. M. Bobrishchev, author of the once-famous book, *Sud i raskol'niki-sektanty* [The Court and the Schismatic Sectarians]. Describing what, as he says, "is pretentiously called in the polemical literature 'science of sectology' ", Bobrishchev-Pushkin wrote: "... in fact this 'science' is a chaotic conglomeration of raw historical and contemporary material" (Bobrishchev-Pushkin 1902: 137).

In the works of church authors, who wrote much about sectarianism in the 1880s, one still encounters elements of scholarly investigation.[2] Perversion and juggling of facts, unsubstantiated assertions and slanderous inventions, are characteristic of the works of missionaries at the end of the 19th and the beginning of the 20th centuries (Aivazov, Butkevich, Kal'nev, Skvortsov, etc.).

[1] For literature on the sectarian question published before 1900, *see* Prugavin 1887, Sakharov n.d. (1887-1900)

[2] For instance: Rozhdestvenskii 1882: I-III; 1889; Novitskii 1882. Among later works, let us note Dorodnytsin 1909.

15

The Chief Procurator of the Synod wrote in a report for 1905-1907: "Holy Russia knew no sectarianism. The whole believing soul of the Russian man has such affinity with Orthodoxy, is so imbued with the Evangelical testaments, that it would be unthinkable for a Russian to change even an iota of the treasure of the true faith.... This is why sectarianism cannot penetrate into Rus'; it is a phenomenon brought in from outside. Sectarianism is a product of Western European culture, a bridge to unbelief. In this respect it is inimical not only to Orthodoxy but to the genuine nature of the Russian man" (Synod 1910: 159-160). This is the basic "formula" of missionary literature about sectarians in the late 19th and early 20th centuries. Missionaries portrayed sectarians every which way—now as "socialists", now as "foreign hirelings"—and ascribed to them every sort of crime, barbarity and degeneracy.[3]

In using church-missionary literature as a source of information of various sorts on sectarianism, the researcher must have a clear understanding of the highly reactionary class and caste position of its authors, and must check the facts reported by them against all other accessible sources. Along with this, the researcher should take into account the time and the socio-political circumstances in which the various representatives of the Orthodox Church wrote their works, and the presence of disagreements (however limited they may have been) between the Synod and the Missions (these disagreements grew between 1914-1917 and in 1917 led to an attempt by the missionaries to set the Mission against the Synod), and finally, the individual positions of the various Orthodox authors.

A comparatively small literature on sectarianism, written by civil servants—for example, P. I. Mel'nikov (Pecherskii) (Mel'nikov 1862, 1868, 1869), N. Dingel'shtedt (1885), S. D. Bondar' (1911a, 1911b, 1915, 1916)—while tendentious, still is not as clouded a source as the church-missionary literature, and the researcher who has a strictly critical attitude toward the former can extract from it valuable factual data.

Turning from church and governmental literature on sectarianism to bourgeois historiography, we note that its representatives concern themselves comparatively rarely with a study of the question under review. The most important place in the bourgeois historiography of sectarianism is occupied by P. N. Miliukov's essay, "The Growth of Russian Sectarianism" in his *Ocherki po istorii russkoi kul'tury* [Essays on the History of Russian Culture] (Miliukov 1931: 104-165). Miliukov condemned the church-missionary conception of

---

[3] Some of the literary works of Merezhkovskii, Mel'nikov-Pecherskii and Andrei Belyi were not free from missionary obscurantism. Bonch-Bruevich wrote in 1912: "... even such an inveterate opponent of sectarians as the government official Mel'nikov (Pecherskii)—even he had to admit, speaking of ritual murders among 'God's People', that 'there was no instance in which the barbaric crime was completely revealed and juridically proven'. In spite of that, besides Merezhkovskii, Andrei Belyi in the tale "The Silver Dove" [*Serebrianyi golub'*] introduces a ritual murder by Russian sectarians" (Bonch-Bruevich 1912: 273).

sectarianism, according to which "the true Russian could not be a sectarian", and the phenomenon itself was "some alien excrescence of foreign origin" (Miliukov 1931: 104). He refused to trace sectarianism "from the east and the west" and counterposed to this the assertion that Russian sectarianism was "an indigenous and national product" (Miliukov 1931: 105). But sectarianism for Miliukov is not a social but a psychological phenomenon, rooted "in the internal conditions of the psychologial development of the folk" (Miliukov 1931: 104).

Miliukov made the only attempt in bourgeois historiography to understand the history of sectarianism as a law-governed process and to set forth the general scheme of its development.

Interesting and significant in itself, this attempt has a frankly idealistic character: sectarianism evolves, according to Miliukov, under the influence of some world-wide law "of the gradual spiritualization of religion", or in other words, the gradual transformation "of religious ritual into a religion of the spirit" (Miliukov 1931: 105-106). As Miliukov writes it, the history of sectarianism is depicted as a law-governed sequence of religious teachings, which are distinguished from each other by degrees of "spiritualization" of faith. Miliukov's conception of sectarianism is connected with his socio-political world-view. The ideologists of capitalist culture were revolted by the extremes of state-police Orthodoxy, and they connected prospects for preserving the influence of religion on the masses with its "gradual spiritualization".

Miliukov made several observations (on the correlation of the forms of sectarianism, on the philosophical elements in the teachings of religious sects, etc.) which the contemporary researcher cannot ignore, even while remembering that Miliukov was consistent in his idealistic methodology.

Beginning in the 1870s-1880s, there appeared a literature on sectarianism which had a liberal Narodnik tendency and which as time went on evolved into bourgeois liberalism. This literature is represented by I. Iuzov (1881), A. S. Prugavin (1881, 1906a, 1906b, 1907, etc.), V. I. Iasevich-Borodaevskaia (1912), S. P. Mel'gunov (1907-1909, 1919) and a number of lesser-known authors. It was characterized by the idealization of sectarianism, which extended to proclaiming sectarianism the most significant and progressive phenomenon of Russian popular life.

A work on the Schism which caused a stir in its day, *Russkie dissidenty* [Russian Dissidents] — in which the author, the liberal Narodnik I. Iuzov, united the concept of the Old Belief and sectarianism — stated: "The mental and moral peculiarities of our people appeared primarily in the Schism. Therefore a study of the Schism is necessary for everyone in public life who does not wish to fumble and grope in his activities and undertakings" (Iuzov 1881: 5). Since he understands social progress in a purely idealistic way and connects it precisely with the diffusion (in society) of rationalistic ideas, Iuzov presents Old Believers and sectarians as mass disseminators of rationalism (Iuzov 1881: 90, 91).

According to Iuzov's model, ideas of rationalism triumph among the people as a result of the wide diffusion of the Old Belief and sectarianism. At the same time, rationalism did not represent for Iuzov the ultimate in the progressive development of social thought. Along with the mass diffusion of rationalistic ideas thanks to the Old Belief and sectarianism, Iuzov noted a gradual transition to deism by religious proponents of rationalism (Iuzov 1881: 126).

In the same year as Iuzov's book, there appeared an article by A. S. Prugavin, *Znachenie sektantstva v russkoi narodnoi zhizni* [The Importance of Sectarianism in Russian Popular Life]. Also written from a liberal Narodnik position, this work was distinguished by an accent on socio-economic relationships in sectarianism. Prugavin proclaimed that "the Schism, embodied in progressive sects, ... works out ideals of the future and of relations in humanity" (Prugavin 1881: 362). In numerous later works, Prugavin, holding to the basic position of his programmatic article, developed concrete topics from the life of sectarians, for which purpose he travelled much among sectarian communities, established contacts with sectarian leaders and with ordinary believers, and collected their manuscript writings. The basic journalistic direction of the works Prugavin published at the end of the 19th century and the first decade and a half of the 20th century, was expressed in a struggle against church-police persecutions of sectarians and Old Believers, but this struggle did not extend beyond "do-gooder" liberalism.

In the spirit of the ideas expressed by Prugavin in the article mentioned above, P. Uimovich-Ponomarov spoke out in 1886, attempting to show that "there rules with great force among sectarians a restraining and regulating power of brotherhood, which often narrows personal initiative in the sphere of accumulation of individual wealth" (Uimovich-Ponomarov 1886). Citing his study of the life and inter-relations of the sect of "God's People" [Khlysty], whom Uimovich-Ponomarov observed in Orenburg and Buzuluk Uezds of Samara Guberniia, he concluded: "Some of 'God's People' hold back, braking the course of the new economic era *with the employer on top and the wage-worker below* (Uimovich-Ponomarov 1886: 34-35; my emphasis). The mythical sectarian "brotherhood" was elevated to a social ideal, and "communal socialism" of this sort was contrasted to the growth of capitalism in Russia.

The liberal Narodniks' elevation of the social significance of sectarianism to an absolute resulted from their general attitude of repudiation of the revolutionary struggle. The liberal Narodniks contrasted religio-social movements to revolutionary movements, bowing down before the spontaneous elements in popular movements, basing a system on just what was most backward, illusory and utopian in the social consciousness of the peasant masses. The views of the liberal Narodniks had later adherents, who adapted the old doctrines to new conditions.

In the period of the 1905-1907 Revolution and the post-revolutionary period, S. P. Mel'gunov lauded the ideas of the liberal Narodniks. Impressed by the events of the first Russian bourgeois-democratic revolution, Mel'gunov wrote: "The last few years, evidently, have completely changed the previous physiognomy of the mass of the people; popular consciousness has grown beyond recognition. Nevertheless, we must still ask to what degree the instinctive strivings toward a better future, called forth by the socio-economic conditions of the people's life, play a role in contemporary social movements. To what degree are these movements conscious ones?" (Mel'gunov 1919: 231).

Mel'gunov spoke most definitely in favor both of the independent significance of "instinctive strivings toward a better future" and of their "conscious nature": "... the original creativity which distinguishes sectarian movements strikes us willy-nilly in such conditions: here we find elements which relate to the surrounding phenomena of life with rare introspection and self-consciousness; here everything is subjected to careful analysis and criticism, all conclusions are the result of the tortuous work of thought" (Mel'gunov 1919: 231).

Mel'gunov's reasoning echoed the outline of Iuzov's idealistic reflections. Whereas Iuzov connected social progress with the dissemination of rationalism in sectarianism and its natural development into deism, Mel'gunov declared both the triumph of rationalistic ideas in post-revolutionary (1905-1907) sectarianism and the spontaneous development of these ideas into democratic consciousness. In Mel'gunov's presentation, sectarianism played the role of a school for democratic education of the whole people: "The sectarian here was turned into a conscious Russian citizen. And this consciousness was the result not of propaganda but of the action of his own thought" (Mel'gunov 1919: 236). Mel'gunov's judgments were in flagrant contradiction to reality. Post-revolutionary sectarianism was a "school", whose leaders most energetically corrupted the democratic consciousness of their "students". This did not stop the sectarian leaders from calling themselves democrats, as Mel'gunov himself spoke in the name of democracy, as Miliukov and his political sympathizers called themselves "constitutional democrats".

The theoretical constructs of the liberal Narodniks and their intellectual heirs not only failed to introduce fruitful ideas into the scientific understanding of the social nature of sectarianism and its history, but more than that, they were reactionary. However, the abundant factual material they collected, as a rule, from life, deserves attention, since it characterizes the condition of sectarianism much more fully than the materials of government functionaries, not to speak of churchmen.

As for these authors' criticisms of the persecution of freedom of conscience in tsarist Russia, even taking into consideration all that we know about the assumptions on which the criticism was based, public revelation of the arbitrary actions by the church and the police was not without social significance.[4]

The liberal-Narodnik trend in the historiography of sectarianism approaches, although it does not completely coincide with, the literature written by the epigones of the religious teachings of L. N. Tolstoy, the so-called Tolstoyans. The foreign publications of the Tolstoyans—the journal *Svobodnaia mysl'* [Free Thought], edited by P. I. Biriukov in Switzerland, and *Listki Svobodnogo slova* ["Free Word" Leaflets], edited in England by V. G. Chertkov—were filled with articles and materials on sectarianism. Both publications appeared in 1899.

An unrestrained idealization of sectarianism was characteristic of both the periodical and the non-periodical literature of the Tolstoyans; however, the Tolstoyans preferred sectarian movements which arose before the Reform and which were distinguished by the moral direction of their teachings. In contrast to the liberal Narodniks, who still connected the origin and development of sectarianism more or less with the conditions of social and economic life, and even to bourgeois researchers—who, like Miliukov, saw a connection between sectarianism and "popular psychology" (and saw in the development of the former a manifestation of some sort of law of the "spirtualization of faith")—the Tolstoyans were pure subjectivists.

They presented the world-view of sectarianism as the summit of the individual's reflection on life, man and God, and declared it to correspond to the full spiritual freedom of the individual. In Biriukov's words: "Students of sectarianism love to seek the reason for its origin in foreign influence, in economic catastrophes, in political oppression and other external causes, using every means to avoid considering the simple internal basis of this phenomenon—the striving for freedom of the spirit, which is doomed by this freedom to a struggle of light with darkness" (Biriukov, ed. 1905: 3).

The Tolstoyans claimed the role of leading the ideological (and in-so-far as they could, also the organizational) center of Russian sectarianism. They conducted a struggle against the activity of the Social-Democratic Party among sectarians, resorting to all available means of propaganda, and not stopping at political intrigues (Bonch-Bruevich 1959: 111-126).

In the Tolstoyan journals named above, and also in the brochures and pamphlets published by *Svobodnoe slovo*, the researcher will find materials on persecutions of sectarians, letters by sectarians, and their writings. However, the Tolstoyans made every effort to avoid the materials indicating

---

[4] Some of Prugavin's works were banned by the tsarist censorship.

elements of protest among sectarians, their interest in political events, and in general their interest in everything which went beyond the framework of religio-ethical problems.[5]

The study of the bourgeois-liberal historiography of sectarianism, including its more or less remote periphery (extending to the works of the Tolstoyans), aids in understanding the political agreements between the leaders of religious sects and public figures of the liberal bourgeoisie, of which I will speak in the corresponding chapters of my work. But in the center of our historiographic interests is the heritage of journalists and scholars of the democratic camp, who have priority in the study of sectarianism and who made a positive contribution to the scientific understanding of its genesis, its internal contradictions and socio-political role. The democratic journalists and scholars were able to raise the most basic problems in a study of sectarianism, because for all of them, although in varying degree, religio-social movements were a political problem and were looked at in the light of the interests of a consistent struggle against absolutism.

As early as the 1840s, Petrashevskii and his sympathizers turned their "attention to Old Believers and sectarians, considering it possible to use their religiously-formulated protest against the existing order for revolutionary purposes" (Leikina-Svirskaia 1955: 234).

Nevertheless, N. V. Shelgunov was perfectly right in writing: "The question of the Schism, like all other questions of Russian life, had its beginning in the '60s.... That was the time when we looked on the Schism as a social phenomenon and made the first attempts at explaining and ideologically interpreting it. In the primarily political mood of that time the Schism was also explained politically" (Shelgunov n.d.: II, 674).

Thus, A. P. Shchapov, in a number of his works, especially in *Zemstvo i raskol* [The Zemstvo and the Schism] (1862), considered religio-social movements as a form of popular protest against the oppression of the church and serfdom. Schapov as a historian of religio-social movements gave primary attention to the Old Belief. Seeing in the Old Belief of the second half of the 17th and the beginning of the 18th century a form of social protest, he was, however, unable to understand the concrete historical content of the protest in which the participants of Old Believer movements were involved. Shchapov perceived the protest of Old Believers as consciously democratic, whereas in reality spontaneity predominated in this protest, and Old Believers often criticized feudal institutions from the point of view of idealization of patriarchal, pre-feudal social relations.

---

[5] Bonch-Bruevich worked on several issues of *Svobodnoe slova* (from mid-1900 to mid-1902), but as soon as the Tolstoyans found out that in the publications he edited one could hear the voice of sectarians protesting against social oppression, they removed him from work on their publications.

Beginning in the 1860s, A. I. Herzen and N. P. Ogarev became active in efforts to attract Old Believers to the struggle with autocracy and serfdom. Under the auspices of *Kolokol* [The Bell] a special leaflet for Old Believers was published, called *Obshchee veche* [The Town Meeting] (from 15 June 1863 to 15 July 1864).

Kel'siev made an illegal journey to Russia to establish direct ties with Old Believers. In their turn, the leaders of the Polish rebellion of 1863 placed great hopes on Old Believers.

Old Believers, as a rule, did not respond to the summons of the revolutionaries. This is explained by at least two circumstances: in the first place, Old Believers as a whole were not such an opposition force as many revolutionaries of the 1840s to 1860s imagined. In the second place, idealization of the Old Belief kept revolutionary propagandists from seeing the class contradictions which had long ago splintered it into a multitude of factions within which, in turn, class struggle took place.

Kel'siev established ties with the *popovtsy* [priestly] faction of the Old Belief, and what was more, with its hierarchy, at a time when the freshest phenomena in the Old Belief were occurring in its *bespopovtsy* [priestless] wing. "Formerly the *bespopovtsy* movement", writes P. G. Ryndziunskii, "was primarily anti-serfdom; now (in the mid-19th century—A. K.) in the Aristov-Kondrat'ev communities, besides an anti-serfdom mood, an anti-bourgeois one was gaining strength" (Ryndziunskii 1950: 241). *Obshchee veche*, in its appeals to Old Believers, made distinctions neither among the characteristics of factions among them nor between the interests of Old Believer "bigwigs" and the "lesser brethren" subordinate to them.

To a representative of the revolutionary democrats grouped around Chernyshevskii—N. V. Shelgunov—idealization of the Old Belief was alien, no matter what motivated it. He wrote: "At this time, the Polish uprising matured, the leaders of which, both in Russia and abroad, thought to find substantial support both in the politically-motivated part of Russian society and among the Schismatics who, in the opinion of many, represented a solid force if they could be set in motion. Assuming that the political origin of the Schism is correct, this estimate should also be accepted. Schismatics of all persuasions numbered at that time about 10,000,000. Of course this was an enormous force, and reliance on it would have been justified if the Schism had really been what it was thought to be. Although under the agitated political conditions of that time, this interpretation and this estimate were logically inevitable (these days the origin of the Schism is explained by "disorders" within the church), reality did not bear out the expectation and yielded different results" (Shelgunov n.d.: II, 674-675).

Shelgunov's views, as stated in this excerpt, including his sympathetic attitude toward the explanation of the genesis of the Old Belief by "disorders within the church", show the effects of the disillusionment which democratic public figures felt as a result of attempts to use the Old Belief as a force opposed to absolutism. Let us note, however, that Shelgunov by no means explained the failure of Kel'siev's mission by the simple conservatism of the Old Believers: "... to establish ties with them", he wrote, "by promising them pie-in-the-sky was not so easy or simple.... For what could Kel'siev propose to them? What forces stood behind him?" (Shelgunov n.d.: II, 677).

Shelgunov expressed his understanding of the historical essence of the Old Belief thus: "Avvakum, like all proponents of the Schism, was undoubtedly a great force who aroused amazement by his unbending steadfastness, but this steadfastness was not that of conscious thought but that of a steel spring which gives back as much force as is exerted against it.

"In the struggle which Avvakum waged and which his opponents conducted against him, forces of identical content were ranged against each other.... The fight was in defense of various aspects of one and the same order of ideas: two essentially identical forms of superficial piety were being defended, and two identical conservatisms became implacable enemies" (Shelgunov n.d.: II, 866).

Thus, Shelgunov appreciated the strength of Old Believer opposition to the regime, while decidedly denying the role of the Old Belief as the bearer of positive social ideals and giving due weight to the fact that its ideological integument remained Orthodox. On the whole, this was a correct if excessively generalized description, if we take into account the contradictory nature and complexity of the Old Belief and the various persuasions of which it was made up.

In contrast to Petrashevskii and Herzen, Shelgunov's attention was drawn more and more to *sectarianism,* in which opposition to the surrounding order was accompanied by elements of democratic thought which, although it resorted to religious concepts, was already on paths hostile to the Orthodox ideology. Shelgunov wrote: "The Old Believer accepts everything without reflection, without testing it, and therefore he is not only a fanatic but a bigot. The Molokan is a rationalist, and some of the most reflective Molokans will even allow a progressive Molokan faith. Once started on the road of critical thought, the Molokan easily goes ahead, and although he recognizes that what is written in the Gospels is the basis of the Molokan faith, he admits that life moves forward and that religious doctrine should of course change with it.... There is in each Old Believer in greater or lesser degree a Father Avvakum; one always senses in him something wild and even sinister, and his glance is suspicious and distrustful. Perhaps all this has been developed by history—i.e., by the centuries-long persecution and fear under which the Schismatics have lived among us, but one cannot deny that bigotry enters in here" (Shelgunov n.d.: III, 386).

Shelgunov's statements indicate his understanding of the profound difference in historical character between the two basic religio-social movements in Russia — the Old Belief and sectarianism — which has great scientific and political significance.

Idealization of the Old Belief to a significant degree was already in the past for the revolutionary Narodniks of the 1870s, as their propaganda shows. E. K. Breshko-Breshkovskaia, L. G. Deich, V. A. Danilov, I. V. Fesenko and others conducted propaganda work among Molokans, Dukhobors and "Shtundists". But if the direction of their propaganda among representatives of persecuted faiths had changed, the revolutionary Narodniks of the 1870s repeated in another respect the mistakes of revolutionaries in the 1860s: some of them tended to idealize sectarianism, and they gave insufficient attention to the process of social differentiation within it through which elements of a nascent bourgeoisie came to lead the sects. B. S. Itenburg's article, "*Revoliutsionnye narodniki i voprosy religii*" [The Revolutionary Narodniks and Religious Questions] (1963), shows that precisely this group opposed Narodnik propaganda and agitation among the sectarians. Shelgunov's works, showing the appearance in sectarianism of kulaks and large landowning entrepreneurs, are therefore the more significant. In *Ocherki russkoi zhizni* [Sketches of Russian Life][6], Shelgunov introduced the figure of the conquistador of bourgeois farming, giving him the collective name "Tavrian". Who were these Tavrians? "Their religion", Shelgunov writes, "consists in profit, and money is the only god to whom they pray; they exploit the masses with the ruthless, pitiless, cold, calculating heartlessness that is characteristic of the kulak" (Shelgunov n.d.: III, 189). "The Tavrian is 'a pioneer-industrialist after the German-American model' " (Shelgunov n.d.: III, 188), "an aggressor, chasing the Kalmyks from their native Stavropol' and Samara steppes" (Shelgunov n.d.: III, 374), "a buyer-up of land held by landowners or for sale on any basis in the Novorossiia area, who was not frightened off by the high price of land" (Shelgunov n.d.: III, 785).

But how did these heartless money-chasing heroes get the name "Tavrians"? "The Tavrians", Shelgunov writes, "are natives of Tavriia Guberniia and the descendants of Molokans who, at the end of the last and the beginning of this [19th] century were resettled by force or came voluntarily to Tavriia Guberniia.... As sheep-breeders they grew so rich that there was not room for their flocks. Then they dispersed with their flocks over the south of Russia, from Bessarabia to Terek Oblast.... They were transformed into large landlords" (Shelgunov n.d.: III, 188-189). The Tavrian was not only a Molokan. He was, Shelgunov writes, "one of those types created by the Eman-

---

[6] Let us note that Shelgunov in *Sketches of Russian Life* repeatedly criticized the Tolstoyan ideology, and even devoted a special article to it: The Philosophy of Stagnation [*Filosofiia zastoia*].

cipation. This type was formed under the cultural influence of the German colonists of Novorossiia and has common features with the type of Molokan and Dukhobor created by the same German influence" (Selgunov n.d.: III, 785).

The views expressed by Shelgunov on problems of religio-social movements in Russia have parallels in the articles published by M. A. Antonovich and other writers in the journal *Sovremennik* [The Contemporary]. The historiography of sectarianism, in turn, was enriched by the scientific ideas of journalists and writers who followed the best Narodnik traditions. In the early 1880s, the Narodnik I. N. Kharlamov (1854-1887) published a series of works which described the position, ideology and social role of the sects (Kharlamov 1881, 1884a, 1884b, 1885, etc.).[7]

Kharlamov's main general evaluation of sectarianism was given in the article "Idealizatory raskola" [Idealizers of the Schism], which attracted the attention of G. V. Plekhanov. In this article, Kharlamov criticizes the liberal-Narodnik apologia for sectarianism. We must consider it Kharlamov's great scientific achievement to have grasped the inevitability of the development of social contradictions in sectarianism. He wrote: "As long as there is strong religious inspiration in the sect, the morality of the sectarians is raised astonishingly high above the general level. As a result of this elevated morality, their social life is at once improved.... But when the religious ardor of the new sect weakens, the surrounding social structure, and particularly the economic conditions prevailing outside the sect, continue to act on it.... And then look—kulaks have appeared, from among those very people who are the reformers or preceptors of the sect!... There are your 'socio-economic' ideals and strivings for you. And as a result there remains a rich community of egoists over and against the hundreds of small non-sectarian communities living outside, which the sectarian community exploits on principle" (Kharlamov 1881: 24).

Kharlamov attached very great importance to the reactionary influence of religion on popular movements. "The ideal of our Schismatics and sectarians", he declared, "is precisely moral self-perfection for the sake of saving one's soul, of reaching the heavenly kingdom." And what is the relationship of this ideal to the interests of the actual struggle for a progressive social order? With the power of a great public affairs writer, Kharlamov replies: "For more than a thousand years we have heard ardent sermonizing about personal perfection, both for the soul's salvation and for the construction of a better social order. For more than a thousand years life has also assured us that a more just social order has never yet come into being by this means." Kharlamov devastatingly criticized the views of Iuzov and other "idealizers

---

[7] On Kharlamov *see* Smirnov 1896: 144-159.

of the Schism", to the effect that the logic of growth of the religious consciousness of sectarians along the lines of rationalism leads to spiritual
freedom, and hence to social freedom: [...] "... there is a great distance between a philosophy whose last word is personal moral perfection as the means
of reforming society, and science, which is based directly on the idea that
social relations have greater influence on the moral formation of the personality than the latter has on the improvement of social forms.... If we were
to wait for the Schism to travel this long road—even with our help—our teeth
would have fallen out in the meanwhile. [...] Fortunately, social development
does not take a single path; popular thought does not work solely in this (sectarian—A. K.) direction. Little by little, it throws off the yoke of superstition
and begins to seek the real reasons for this evil directly, and of course, more
quickly arrives at the goal" (Kharlamov 1881: 24-26).

Kharlamov is characterized by deep interest in an interpretation of the
phenomena of religio-social life, which he studied, and this is reflected in his
little monographs on the Dukhobors, Shtundists and Stranniki. In turning to
Kharlamov's works, we should remember Plekhanov's remark that "in his
polemic with the 'idealizers of the Schism', he was himself inclined, in the last
analysis, to an idealistic point of view" (Plekhanov 1925: XX, 336), and we
should also take account of Kharlamov's skepticism in evaluating the social
significance of sectarianism.

The works of the leading Narodnik writer Gleb Uspenskii are most important for the student of religio-social movements in post-Reform Russia. His
Melochi putevykh vospominanii [Trifles From a Travel Diary] are remarkable
for their insight and precision in sketching Baptists and Molokans, and his
artistic penetration into the life, psychology and world-view of the post-
Reform peasantry promotes an understanding of the social nature of sectarianism and the socio-economic roots of its ideology. The pages of his famed
Vlast' zemli [The Power of the Earth], which are devoted to familial-marital
relations in the countryside and in particular their connection with
phenomena of accumulation, explain better than anything else the sources of
the asceticism which is so prominent among a number of Russian sects.

Uspenskii's artistic generalizations are excellent material for scientific interpretation in solving the problem of the class of historical phenomena to which
sectarianism belongs. *Trifles From a Travel Diary* contains the following
lines: "... everything is undifferentiated—both nature and people, and
morality, truth, poetry; in a word, a homogeneous tribe, one hundred million
strong, which lives out some sort of collective life and thought, and which is
understandable only in collective form. To separate one person from these
massed millions, let us say even our village elder Semen Nikitin, and to try to
understand him—this is impossible" (Uspenskii 1949: VIII, 204).

Uspenskii's observations were confirmed by Plekhanov, though in a limited way: [...] "There is no 'homogeneous tribe, one hundred million strong' in Russia. But, if taken in proportion, all this is undeniably, completely and strikingly true.... Where there is no internal delineation of the personality, and morality has not lost its undifferentiated character, there is still, properly speaking, neither intelligence, nor morality, nor science, nor art, nor any sort of conscious social life" (Plekhanov 1925: X, 32). The "undifferentiated life", for which Uspenskii himself saw a quick demise, would inevitably yield, in Plekhanov's words, to "European forms of life" (Plekhanov 1925: X, 34).

It is worth noting that the undifferentiated life which provoked Uspenskii's bitter thoughts also attracted the attention of Engels, who gave a precise historical description of it: "In the countryside there is still a semi-communistic community; in the city, cooperative work in an artel', and everywhere collective responsibility, i.e. the mutual responsibility of comrades for each other; in a word, the whole social structure clearly shows, on the one hand, that all salvation is in solidarity, and on the other, that an individual who stands out because of his energy is doomed to complete impotence. The Russian preserves this trait even in war; the compact mass of Russian battalions is almost impossible to scatter; the greater the danger, the more closely they stick together." Engels also wrote at this point that "only on a higher cultural level, on a level of that 'individualistic' development which exists among capitalistic nations of the West" can "the preconditions for the intellectual development of each person in particular" exist (*Marx and Engels* XVI: part II, 350-351).

To what does Uspenskii contrast the undifferentiated life personified by the village elder Semen Nikitin? "It's easier and clearer for me to live in the world", writes Uspenskii, "by living and conversing, not with Semen Nikitin, who is unusually intelligent in terms of received wisdom but has little understanding of his own 'because we are unlettered', but rather with this peasant here, who has the very same beard and so on that Semen Nikitin has; to the question as to why he went over from the Molokans to the Baptists, this man does not respond with the phrase usual in Semen Nikitin's mouth—'you'd know better from books' or 'we're not learned', etc.—but clearly and definitely says: 'Here's why, my friend: I can't understand Christ Molokan-fashion. The Molokans, you know, consider him a human being; they say he was born of flesh; but I *can't* understand that. My head is not willing to understand how such goodness can come from man! Human beings do not have what is in Christ.... That's the very reason I fell away from them.... Here, among the Baptists, my soul feels more at ease. That's why'" (Uspenskii 1949: VIII, 209).

Uspenskii was by no means among the "idealizers of the Schism". In his works we encounter lines condemning social contrasts and various unsavory aspects in the sectarian milieu. And here too, Uspenskii, having introduced the explanation of the "muzhik"[A] who went over from Molokanism to Baptism, feels it his duty to sound a warning: "I will not say that I was particularly enthralled by our sectarians...." But at the same time, he admits, "I constantly and unfailingly felt at ease with them; I was constantly in the society of people thirsting for the conscious life, trying to give meaning to their existence on earth ...; we could carry on a conversation, though not always a brilliant one, about general questions—good, evil, truth—in a language understood by both of us" (*ibid.*).

Uspenskii found no trace in the sectarian world of that social and familial harmony which liberal-Narodnik idealizers enthusiastically ascribed to it. But this world had none of the dullness of the "undifferentiated life". Uspenskii counterposed to the world-view which had its roots in the "undifferentiated life"—in other words, in the survivals of the precapitalist order—a world-view belonging, in Engels' words, "to a higher cultural level", a level of that "individualistic development" which exists under capitalism.

Of course, Uspenskii went only so far. But he indicated the place of sectarianism among the ideological phenomena which historically replaced the system of concepts and ideas arising from the "undifferentiated life".

The Marxist historiography of sectarianism dates from the second half of the 1890s, and its fundamentals were laid down by Lenin (*see* the Introduction to this work).

There is a continuity between Marxist historiography of sectarianism and the attempt by progressive thinkers in the second half of the 19th century to study it. A typical incident: Bonch-Bruevich says that when he arrived in Geneva in 1896 and met with Plekhanov to discuss his intention of studying sectarianism, Plekhanov not only encouraged him but "immediately took Kel'siev's work from the shelves of his library and advised me to read *Obshchee veche,* which was issued under the auspices of Herzen's *Kolokol*" (Bonch-Bruevich 1959: 325-326).

Plekhanov himself was deeply interested in the study of religio-social movements in Russia. In his work, *Istoriia russkoi obshchestvennoi mysli* [A History of Russian Social Thought], he gave a broad description of the history and philosophy of the Old Belief in the second half of the 17th century, and in the 18th.

There are among Plekhanov's writings no special works on sectarianism, but the statements made by him in one connection or other are methodologically significant to a Marxist study of this question. First of all, following Engels' ideas, Plekhanov insisted on a strictly differentiated approach to the study of religio-social movements.

A more or less broad participation in religio-social movements by representatives of socially lower groups is not in itself a criterion of the progressiveness of these movements. Plekhanov contrasts heretical movements in Russia in the 15th and 16th centuries to the Old Belief: "There are schisms and schisms, heresies and heresies. In the north-Russian democratic communities, as we know, the 'heretics' analyzed the essence of the religious teaching; in the Muscovite state they were ready to die for a letter (for 'A')" (Plekhanov 1925: XX, 340). How did Plekhanov evaluate the social significance of the analysis to which the heretics subjected the teachings of the Orthodox Church? He wrote: "In the progressive states of Western Europe, 'religious democratism' was expressed in definite political strivings and served as a stimulus for active thought. We can say almost the same thing of the religious movements which arose in the north-Russian democratic communities" (Plekhanov 1925: 337).

Plekhanov was absolutely correct in his broadly theoretical formulation of how, depending on the social conditions under which mass religious movements develop, in some cases they reflected progressive social interests, and in other cases their 'religious democratism' was combined with intellectual stagnation and was directed toward the historical past.

Plekhanov also correctly contrasts Russian heretical movements to the Old Belief. But one cannot accept the concrete-historical explanation by which Plekhanov, under the influence of Kostomarov's views, connects the progressive nature of heresies with "the free spirit of the north-Russian democratic communities" and the conservatism of the Old Belief with the "despotic" conditions in the Muscovite "*votchina* monarchy". On the contrary, processes of state-formation stimulated the growth of heresies both in Novgorod and Pskov, and in Moscow itself.

Plekhanov followed the principle of differentiating the social character of mass religious movements in studying the Old Belief: "I have said", he wrote, "that there is heresy and heresy, schism and schism. This is also correct, by the way, when applied to the schism within the Old Belief. The *popovtsy* are one thing and the *bespopovtsy* are another. The *bespopovtsy* went much further in their struggle with the official church than the *popovtsy*. In the second half of the 18th century such an extreme sect as the *Beguny* could arise from the *bespopovtsy*" (Plekhanov 1925: XX, 344). This formulation of the problem opens the way for a study of the connection between the Old Belief and sectarianism and of religious forms intermediate between the Old Belief and sectarianism.

Whenever Plekhanov wrote of religio-social movements, he was primarily interested in the problem of their role in the class struggle. He emphatically opposed the then-current idealization of the Schism and showed the untenability of the idealization of the early Schism in Shchapov's work. Shchapov's error, as Plekhanov saw it, consisted in accepting the social motifs in the ideology of the early Schism as "the expression of conscious democratic protests at a time when there was and could be no such protest" (Plekhanov 1925: XX, 326).

Plekhanov repeatedly noted the inability of sectarianism to play an independent role in the Russian emancipation movement and recalled the bitter experience of revolutionaries who tied their political hopes to sectarianism. In the work *A. I. Gertsen i krepostnoe pravo* [A. I. Herzen and Serfdom], Plekhanov introduces a story of Herzen's from 1844 about an uprising of Molokans in one of the volosts of Tambov Guberniia. He wrote: "Peasant uprisings then were not limited to sectarians. It is clear that a disturbance like the one Herzen speaks of in his diary does not yet by any means indicate the peasants' capacity for independent socio-political action. In consequence, our Narodniks, the 'rebels' of the 1870s, made a serious error in pinning their hopes on such disturbances. Life very soon 'disabused' them on that score" (Plekhanov 1925: XXIII, 297-298).

Plekhanov does not get the credit for debunking the idealizers of the Schism. The Narodnik Kharlamov failed to understand the historical limitations of the peasantry—its inability to break by its own strength with religious, patriarchal and all other prejudices and rise to a scientific understanding of social relations. Thus, Kharlamov did not understand that sectarianism was not simply a regrettable error, but a historically-limited form of social protests by the peasants.

This is the course of Kharlamov's characteristically negative attitude toward social movements in religious guise. It goes without saying that Plekhanov fully appreciated the reactionary influence of the religious form assumed by sectarianism. He wrote: "... we can say of all Christian sects, with few exceptions, that most frequently their propaganda deflects human thought from the real sphere into the fantastic and thereby makes its development more difficult" (Plekhanov 1925: XX, 357-358). But Plekhanov did not limit himself to that: "The peasant's thought", he wrote, "is enslaved by 'the power of the earth' and of nature. At best, it can go so far as to create some 'rationalistic' sect but can never rise to a materialistic view of nature, which is the only correct one, to an understanding of *the power of man over the earth*" (Plekhanov 1925: X, 20).

Thus, it was not error itself, not religious delusion, but objective social conditions which limited the peasant's world-view, although his thought protested and struggled to find the way to liberty. Plekhanov evaluated the religious "rationalism" of sectarianism in this way. The formulation of the problem of the necessity of carrying on the work of the Social Democrats among sectarians followed logically from this. Let us remember that Plekhanov took an active part in the drafting of the resolution of the Second Congress of the RSDRP on work among sectarians.

From Plekhanov's conception of religio-social movements as a phenomenon of democratic protest, but in its most historically-primitive form, there follows a methodologically important thought, scientifically valid for contemporary students: "The psychology of Russian popular movements is still insufficiently studied. But we will scarcely err in proposing that the inclination of the masses toward the Schism was in inverse proportion to their belief in the possibility of conquering the prevailing evil with their own strength, and that thus the Schism spread with particular success after the people had suffered heavy defeats" (Plekhanov 1925: XX, 362-363).

The most important representative of the Marxist historiography of sectarianism was V. D. Bonch-Bruevich (1873-1955). To summarize everything that Bonch-Bruevich did in studying sectarianism — a field which engaged his attention for almost sixty years — would require a special historiographic essay.

Throughout our entire work we have turned, in grateful remembrance, to the works of Bonch-Bruevich on sectarianism.

To speak of the most general and the most important — Bonch-Bruevich's approach to the study of sectarianism was determined by the Leninist formulation of the idea of the peasantry as an ally in the revolutionary struggle of the working class, and by Lenin's chief pronouncements on sectarianism. Bonch-Bruevich did not conceive of his role as a student of socio-religious movements outside of concrete revolutionary practice. He set himself the task of carrying the living word of the revolutionary Social Democrats to the mass of participants in these movements.

G. I. Petrovskii wrote of Bonch-Bruevich: "He was one of those researchers who are not satisfied to sit in their studies. Vladimir Dmitrievich sought direct connection with life; he studied the question in all its variety, not only from books, but in contact with those of whom he wrote. Thus, while studying religio-social movements whose roots he saw in the deep social, economic and political contradictions of tsarist Russia, Bonch-Bruevich volunteered to accompany the Dukhobors, who were being persecuted by the autocracy, to Canada" (Petrovskii 1958: 11).

Bonch-Bruevich attributed primary importance to the method of concrete sociological study of sectarianism and used this method extensively in studying sectarianism in Canada (1899); subsequently he made special journeys into sectarian villages in Voronezh, Kharkov and Stavropol' Guberniias, and into the Kuban and Terek areas and the Transcaucasus. While still in Canada, he projected a series of works embracing the history and current status of the sects. Each issue of this series was to contain primary sources with extensive commentaries and an introductory theoretical article.

Busy with extensive and responsible Party work, sometimes in emigration and sometimes in the revolutionary underground and having to overcome every possible difficulty encountered in his scientific work, Bonch-Bruevich showed exceptional singleness of purpose in executing the plan of research outlined: in 1901-1902, he published in London four issues of a series under the general title, *Materials For the History and Study of Religious Sectarianism,* and in Russia, over the period 1908-1916, six more volumes of the *Materials.* Bonch-Bruevich's *Materials* were based on genuine manuscript works written and, as a rule, collected, by the sectarians themselves, and representing an important source for description of the Dukhobors, the Molokans, the Skoptsy, the Old and New Israelites, the Baptists and other sects.

In studying sects like the Dukhobors and the New Israelites, Bonch-Bruevich made a contribution of lasting significance. We have in mind Bonch-Bruevich's numerous articles, and particularly the materials he collected and published on the oral traditions of the Dukhobors, which comprised the so-called "Book of Life" [*Zhivotnaia kniga*], and also the writings of the founders of the New Israelite sect.

The primary significance of Bonch-Bruevich's works consists in the fact that he considered the history of sectarianism in close connection with the class struggle. He explained the multiplicity of sectarian persuasions as the result of social differentiation within sectarianism and the conflict of different class interests. Bonch-Bruevich pointed out the connection between the teachings of this or that sect and the class affiliation and political ambitions of the sect's adherents. He clearly defined what was common for all sects in their political protest and what divided the sectarians: "In spite of all the differences ... in the degree of political consciousness of various groups of sectarians", Bonch-Bruevich wrote, "there is between them that minimum which is common to all sectarians. We think that it can be formulated thus: limitation of the autocratic power in Russia. The declaration of political freedom, which would guarantee to all the inviolability of the domestic hearth, complete freedom of conscience, speech and assembly, and which would give broad self-government to all classes.... We cannot define here, of course, the maximum of these demands, but we will say now that we know of many cases in which sectarian thought strove toward communism and utopian socialism, demanding complete annihilation of private property and contemporary forms of the family and the state" (Bonch-Bruevich 1959: 174).

Bonch-Bruevich also offered an attempt at a scientific classification of sects according to their "socio-political views", which, as he wrote with complete justice, "is diametrically opposed to that (division of sects—A. K.) which is used at the present time in our literature and which has adopted as a criterion that 'mysticism' of the sectarians, 'revelation', 'inner light' or 'gift of the holy spirit' " (Bonch-Bruevich 1959: 165).

Bonch-Bruevich's writings on the question under review number about 150 titles—books, articles, publications and reviews.[8] Everything was included in

---

[8] An exhaustive bibliography is given in Petrovskii 1958.

his scientific field of vision, whether some significant form of sectarianism, or literature on this question, which he always criticized with great care. His works on sectarianism are distinguished by scientific fastidiousness combined with a journalist's passion for unmasking the arbitrary manner in which church and tsarist authorities violated freedom of conscience.

One does encounter in some of Bonch-Bruevich's works and publication of materials, evaluations which overstate the strength of the sectarians' democratic protest, the degree of their "enlightenment", and "awareness". This is true of such fact-crammed generalizing articles as "Znachenie sektant-stva dlia sovremennoi Rossii" [The Significance of Sectarianism for Modern Russia] (1902a) and "Sredi sektantov" [Among the Sectarians] (1902b).

Let us indicate the significance of Bonch-Bruevich's letters in connection with his interest in research on sectarianism, which were partially published in the first volume of the three-volume edition of his *Izbrannye sochinenii* [Selected Works] (1959-1963). Bonch-Bruevich's correspondence shows, on the one hand, the character of the evolution of sectarianism after the Revolution, and on the other hand the fact that in new circumstances the Party continued the stubborn struggle on behalf of lower-class sectarians, succeeding in tearing them away from reactionaries (in a number of places the leaders of religious sects) and drawing them into an ever more conscious and active participation in the construction of the new society.

Among the works of Marxist historians concerned with problems of sectarianism, let us name M. N. Pokrovskii's *Ocherk istorii russkoi kul'tury* [Outline of the History of Russian Culture], on which he worked between 1914 and 1918. Pokrovskii devoted a number of vivid pages of his work to a description of heretical and sectarian movements in Russia. Having considered the question of the significance of sectarianism in the history of Russia, he came to the conclusion that sectarianism, with all its peculiarities, belonged with social movements demonstrating the unity of the basic laws of historical and cultural development of the peoples of Russia and Western Europe.

Pokrovskii wrote: "It is usually said that we in Russia had no Reformation. This is of course true if one understands by Reformation popular movements on the scale of the one in 16th-century Germany, or 16th-17th-century England. But this does not alter the fact that we had and do have Protestant sects; we had and do have Russian popular Protestantism, which did not assume the proportions of a strong historical movement because there did not develop among us the socio-political motifs which, strictly speaking, made the 'Reformation' in the West into a world-historical phenonomenon" (Pokrovskii 1924: 237). Among other statements by Pokrovskii on sectarianism is the highly important one about the existence of an "internal connection" between the religious philosophy of sectarians and their strivings toward bourgeois forms of economy (Pokrovskii 1924: 253).

After the Revolution, much literature by Soviet authors on themes relating to sectarianism appeared.

The preaching and activity of the leaders of sectarianism during the Civil War, which were not loyal and were often openly counter-revolutionary, immediately followed by a policy of collaboration which masked the opposition of the sects to socialist construction, posed a quite definite task for Soviet authors—a struggle against the attempts by sectarian leaders to use the religiosity of ordinary sectarians in their opposition to Soviet power. A massive Soviet literature on sectarians in the 1920s and the early 1930s, which often introduced materials from the history of sectarianism, served this purpose. Let us note the articles of the most important proponents of Soviet scientific atheism, Lenin's associates: Yemilian Yaroslavskii (1925) and P. A. Krasikov (1922), Bonch-Bruevich's pamphlet *Krivoe zerkalo sektantstva* [The Crooked Mirror of Sectarianism] (1922), and also numerous articles and brochures by F. M. Putintsev, B. Kandidov, and others. The most complete idea of the literature of the 1920s criticizing the ideology and activity of sectarianism is given by Putintsev's *Politicheskaia rol' sektantstva* [The Political Role of Sectarianism], published in 1925 and subsequently revised and enlarged into *Politicheskaia rol' i taktika sekt* [The Political Role and Tactics of the Sects] (1935), which still retains much of its significance as a description of the political position of sectarianism in the period of imperialism and the first fifteen years of the history of Soviet society.

Although the literature of the 1920s and 1930s criticizing sectarianism in some cases did not avoid "left-opportunism" and over-simplification, it was distinguished on the whole by a high ideological and political level.

A great contribution to the understanding of processes taking place in sectarianism after the Revolution, and its role under the conditions of Soviet society, was made by the Party meeting sponsored by the Central Committee of the All-Russian Communist Party [Bolsheviks], April 27-30, 1926, and the theses adopted, *Sektantstvo i antireligioznaia propaganda* [Sectarianism and Anti-Religious Propaganda].[9] Works devoted to a scientific study of the history of sectarianism also appeared in the 1920s. Such works are A. T. Lukachevskii's *Sektantstvo prezhde i teper'* [Sectarianism Then and Now] (1925) and N. M. Nikol'skii's chapter on sectarianism in his *Istoriia russkoi tserkvi* [History of the Russian Church] (1930).

In 1929, a leading figure in Soviet ethnography and scientific atheism, Professor N. M. Matorin, established a special seminar for a monographic study of the history and present condition of different religious sects. Participants in the seminar published several monographs and brochures on the Skoptsy,

---

[9] "Sektantstvo i antireligioznaia propaganda" [Sectarianism and Anti-Religious Propaganda] in *Kommunisticheskaia revolutsiia* [Communist Revolution] 1926, No. 12 and *Kommunisticheskoe prosveshchenie* [Communist Education] 1926, No. 5 (26).

Mennonites, Dukhobors and Molokans. In the preface to one of them, Matorin wrote: "The monographic study of different sects in the USSR is just beginning. Many sects were completely ignored, both by the old scholarship and by Soviet anti-religious workers.

"The slanderous works of the clergy and the conciliatory-apologetic works of the Narodniks can at best be used only as material. At the same time, both theoretically and practically, the study of sectarianism is a pressing necessity for us" (Matorin 1931: 3).

However, real progress in the study of sectarianism was noticeable only in the mid-1950s, when the most significant results were achieved by concrete sociological study of it. As the front of concrete sociological study of sectarianism is expanded and its methods improved, the importance of historical study becomes increasingly clear: it protects, as it were, the rear of concrete sociological studies. In fact, at the junction of historical and concrete sociological studies of sectarianism—in other words, by comparing all descriptions of it in the past and today available to the scholar—it becomes possible to give a broad picture of the phenomenon's dynamics, to understand its deepest laws of development and, consequently, through scientific cooperation, to facilitate a more rapid victory in the minds of men over this typical ideological survival of capitalism.

The next vital scientific task in line is a historical study of sectarianism at various stages of the development of Soviet society.

Editor's Note

Note A. *muzhik:* peasant. The word is being used in a pejorative sense.

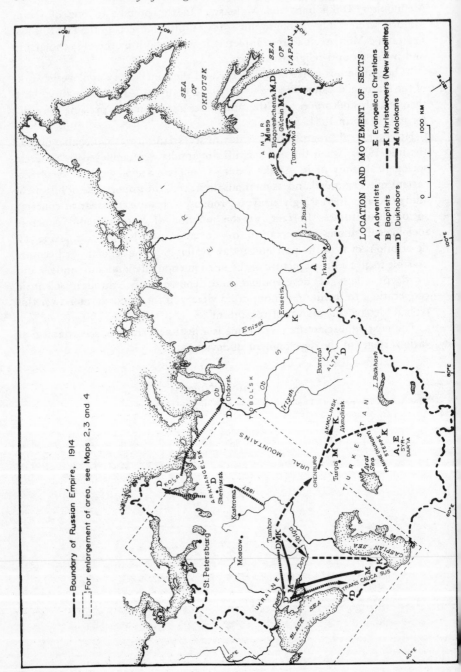

PART ONE

Trends of Pre-Reform Sectarianism and Their Evolution

1

The Origin and Original Forms of Religious Sectarianism

In this history of the class struggle in Russia, as in other countries, there were popular movements which expressed their social protest in a religious form.

In the beginning, these were urban heretical movements. In Russia, they appeared even before the 13th and 14th centuries. In the second half of the 15th and at the beginning of the 16th century, heretical movements were widespread in the largest urban centers of the Muscovite state. Over the course of several decades their leaders collaborated with the Grand Duchy of Moscow which was directing its efforts for the political unification of the Russian lands. This collaboration weakened as the anti-feudal content of the heretical movements became manifest and developed. At the beginning of the 16th century, the heretical movements were suppressed by the common efforts of the Grand Princedom and the Church, fulfilling the wishes of the ruling class of feudal lords. At the beginning of the 16th century, these movements started up again.

This time the most important among them was the heresy of the socially lower classes, a worthy representative of whom was the runaway *kholop* Feodosii Kosoi.

A new wave of popular movements in religious form, known in the literature under the general designation "the Schism", arose in the second half of the 17th century.

If the peasants took no noticeable part in the heresies of the 14th to 16th centuries, by contrast they were the main participants in the Schism, in which the population of the urban settlements also played a significant role. In the second half of the 17th century, religious opposition spread with spontaneous force: "In 1675", A. P. Shchapov wrote, "the priest Kosma, infected with schismatic ideas, fled from Moscow with 20 persons and settled in the Novgorod-and-Northern region ... here, from the seed sown by them, 17

39

schismatic settlements were formed, with a population of as many as 50,000 persons of both sexes.... [I]n Nizhegorod Eparchy, in the Chernoramen forests of Yur'ev and Balakna Okrugs, 35 or 40 years after the first appearance of the weed of Schism, in 1716 there were thought to be as many as 40,000 registered Schismatics alone.

"All the Cossacks of Elets and Iaik, and the greater part of the 20,000 Don Cossacks were infected by Schism ..." (Shchapov 1906: 176).

In the second half of the 17th century, the map of the distribution of the Schism embraced the Pomor'e, the Volga region, the Novgorod-and-Northern lands, the Urals and Siberia: Western and Eastern. Schismatics were also found in Moscow and the surrounding district, in Novgorod and Pskov.

The prominence of protest against the ruling Church in the ideology of the Schism was explained by the enormous influence which the Church exerted on all phases of public life in the 17th century. The Church was a large feudal property-owner: in the 1670s, it already had more than 116,000 peasant households, of which the Patriarch and the higher clergy had about 10,000 households, and the monasteries and churches about 98,000 (Novosel'skii 1949: 122).

The Church kept a careful watch on, and adapted itself to, the new phenomena in economic life. Exploitation in the form of monetary rents was also practiced on the farms of clerical-feudal landowners. In the well-known study by M. Gorchakov, *On The Landholdings of the All-Russian Metropolitans, Patriarchs and Holy Synod,* we read: "The total monetary patrimonial income of the Patriarch, not counting the income of the officials and employees of the Prikaz and of the Bailiffs, amounted to 30,000 a year ...", and "the quantity of income in grain from plowland measured in desiatiny and of quit-rent grain amounted to 9,000 *chetverts* and more" (Gorchakov 1871: 429). In 1667, the income in grain which reached the Patriarch was 12,238 *chetverts* of all kinds of grain, and expenditure of all kinds of grain was 8,880 *chetverts* (Gorchakov 1871: 429, footnote 2).

Thus, in 1667, more than 25% (3,350 *chetverts*) received by the Patriarch constituted reserves for trading operations.

The fact (indicated by sources dating from the 1670s) that hired labor was exploited on monastery farms, along with the labor of serf and dependent peasants, is highly suggestive (Lokhteva 1961: 208-230).

The Church, as a powerful feudal property-owner, resisted the attempts of the nobility and the ruling authorities acting in its interest to decrease the Church's landholdings and its medieval-feudal immunities (Ustiugov and Chaev 1961: 295-329). The Church fought for the position of a state within a state, and in the eyes of large groups of the exploited population personified a hated system of economic and spiritual enslavement.

The exploitation of the labor of hundreds of thousands of peasants subordinate to it was supplemented by the Church with a ramified system of religious taxation, laid on the entire population, the income from which cannot be counted. Financial exploitation fell as a heavy burden on the lower and rank-and-file clergy as well. As N. V. Ustiugov showed, using the example of Velikii Ustiug and Ustiug Uezd which was part of the Metropolitanate of Rostov, the income of the Metropolitan from "the desiatina", "the circuit" and other taxes and collections, doubled between the middle of the 1620s and the beginning of the 1680s (Ustiugov and Chaev 1961: 297). The rapacity of the clerical and monastic feudal landowners was manifested in provocative ways. One of the Tsar's circular letters addressed to the widest audience—the monasteries "of Moscow, near and far, official and unofficial"—contains a general description of the predatory practices of "archimandrites and abbotts and cellarers and treasurers and elders of councils in all monasteries", who "keep with them their children and brothers and nephews and grandsons and give them monastery bread and provisions of all kinds and money from the monastery treasury; and they, the authorities, send out monastery servants to monastery patrimonial estates for wages, and as soon as these servants arrive with wages at the monastery, the authorities and the children and the nephews and the grandchildren take from them indulgences and memorial-feasts, money and wine and honey and martens, and every kind of present; and for whomever does not honor them, seeking vengeance, they arrange great beatings and evictions; they also take from the monastery patrimonial peasants, with cause and without cause, offerings and memorial gifts.... And the authorities also travel to laymen in their houses for feasts, and they carouse, and for this they take with them monastery grain and treasury money" (Akty 1836).

The clerical lords in the 17th century extorted from their charges their last bit of money "with cause and without cause", as they beat their britches "for the living and for the dead" in the 14th century, as they were accused in their time of doing by the Strigol'nik heretics.

As early as the 15th century, the peasants took flight (or transferred from one feudal landlord to another), seeing in this a way of easing their fate.

In the second half of the 17th century, under conditions of complete enserfment, this form of class struggle was reproduced on a wide scale. Among the peasants fleeing from enserfment there were many Schismatics.

Outright insubordination to the Church, mass flight from the lands of lay and clerical lords, was replaced from time to time by open rebellion on the part of Schismatics against the feudal yoke. This was especially clearly expressed in the Solovetskii Uprising of 1668-1676.

Religo-social movements of the second half of the 17th century, their dimensions and characteristics, are made more understandable in the light of

Lenin's characterization of this time: "Only the new period in Russian history (approximately from the 17th century) was characterized by actual merging of all such regions and lands and princedoms in one whole ... it was brought about by increasing exchange between regions, gradually growing circulation of goods, and by the concentration of small local markets into one all-Russian market. Since the leaders and masters of this process were capitalist merchants, the creation of these national connections was nothing other than the creation of bourgeois connections" (*Lenin PSS:* I, 153-154).

Under the stimulus of growing market ties, which covered the country with a network of markets with junctions of all-Russian significance (the Arkhangel'sk, the Makar'ev, the Svena, the Irbit and other fairs), and growing internal trade (with the largest markets in Arkhangel'sk and Astrakhan), the exploitation by lay and clerical lords of the work of serfs in the form of corvée and quit-rent was increased. At the same time, the tax situation of the state peasantry became ever more difficult. The protection of the interests of the ruling class of lords, the most influential part of whom were the nobility, corresponded to the internal policies of the state, based on the development of the principle of serfdom in the Ulozheniia of 1649. The state structure gradually evolved toward absolutism. As N. M. Druzhinin wrote, "the economic backwardness of the majority of the regions was the basis of the establishment of the feudal system: the remote masses of the villages were barely touched by the new economic processes and continued to live in conditions of a closed subsistence economy" (Druzhinin 1958: 200).

However, for all its patriarchal way of life in the second half of the 17th century, the Russian village was not the same as in the 15th and 16th centuries. Now phenomena appeared in the village which outgrew the bounds of a closed subsistence way of life. Out of the mass of patriarchal peasants there emerged an increasingly wealthy trading and artisan elite, which practiced usury and exploitation of hired labor. This was a time, for instance, when the Bosovs—free-holding peasants by origin—became owners of the trading enterprises which served hundreds of traders, when Kalmykov, a former monastery quit-rent peasant, was made the owner of houses and shops in Moscow and Nizhnii Novgorod, and also trading enterprises in many Volga cities.

The ties of the rural population with the cities where the peasants, forced by the lords to pay monetary rent, went to market the produce of their labor, grew stronger. And although an infinitesimal part of the peasantry was transformed into Bosovs and Kalmykovs, although the majority of them remained victims of feudal exploiters and in addition fell into dependence on the Bosovs and Kalmykovs and others like them, having once sampled "city air", the peasants tried with all their strength to become independent producers of goods. Those of them who entered upon this path manifested astonishing keen-wittedness, enterprise, persistence and patience. Along with this the spiritual outlook of the peasants connected with the market changed, and a stay in the city, at times a very extended one, enlightened and broadened their mental outlook.

A study of the religious and social movements of the second half of the 17th century should proceed from the contradictions of Russian reality of this time, bearing in mind the dominance of elements of new social relationships, way of life, and ideology.

The social makeup of the participants in the Schism reflected the contradictions of the social reality of their time, a complicated and variegated picture of clash of inter-class and intra-class interests. In this Schism various groups of peasants took part—serfs belonging to private individuals, free-holding and household peasants, and also the lower clergy, all kinds of elements of the urban population, and even sometimes representatives of Boyar families. Democratic circles of the Schism were united by a common hatred of the ruling church as a tool of class oppression of the serfs.

Underdeveloped social relationships, the fact that new economic phenomena in the 17th century had only begun their history and only a thin stratum of the peasantry was as yet drawn into their sphere, led to an idealization of patriarchal antiquity as a predominant theme in the world-view of the Schism; this was expressed in the opposition of "the old faith" to the "new" Nikonian faith, in a demand for the return to ancient precepts and customs. It would however be an error to ascribe to the Old Belief all forms of religious opposition which constituted the Schism in the second half of the 17th century.

In the religious opposition of the second half of the 17th century we can trace (although at first their influence and sphere of dissemination was limited) trends and tendencies which counterposed to the ruling church not an idealized patriarchal antiquity but ideas having parallels in the teachings of the Russian urban heretical and reformation movement. We have in mind the rejection of the Church, of the whole institution of the spiritual hierarchy and of the basic Christian-Russian Orthodox dogmas preached by the feudal Church. The reformationist ideas revived in the second half of the 17th century were characterized, like the preceding reformationist teachings of the 14th-16th centuries, by religious individualism, combined with elements of rationalism in some cases and with elements of mysticism in others, and opposition to the authoritarianism and formalism of the medieval Russian Orthodox world-view.

As we turn to the concrete characteristics of the reformationist ideas and teachings which arose in the second half of the 17th and beginning of the 18th centuries, we will be convinced that they were not simple repetitions of the Strigol'niki and of the "Judaizers" Matvei Bashkin and Feodosii Kosoi. And at the same time, the characteristic which most clearly distinguishes the reformation movements of the second half of the 17th and the beginning of the 18th centuries from the ones which preceded them is not the ideas which characterized their teachings, but the social composition of the participants of these movements. The reformation movements of the 14th-16th centuries were primarily urban, although peasants played a limited part in them. Reformation movements of the second half of the 17th and the beginning of the 18th centuries were primarily peasant, although urban dwellers played a part in them. Reformation movements arising in the period of developed feudalism grew to the extent that in the cities there appeared and developed the conditions for bourgeois ties. Precisely thus can the urban character of the reformation movements of the 14th-16th centuries be explained. In the 14th-16th centuries, there did not exist in the village the objective conditions for any mass response by the peasants to the heretical preaching of the city dweller.

The very fact that the peasantry resorted in the second half of the 17th century to reformationist ideas was fundamentally new and cannot be explained outside of an understanding of a new phenomenon which can be traced in the socio-economic life of Russia in the 17th century (Klibanov 1963). But while the turning of the peasants to their reformationist ideas was in the 17th century a logical phenomenon, born of the incipient participation of the peasants in bourgeois ties, it was also logical that only a minority of the participants of the Schism paid attention to these ideas. We repeat the words of N. M. Druzhinin: "... the isolated masses of the villages were hardly touched by the new economic processes and continued to live in conditions of closed subsistence economy".

Reformation movements arising under the conditions of the new period of Russian history and disseminated primarily among the peasantry which had been drawn into commodity and money relationships are, collectively, religious sectarianism. Let us trace the origin and first development of sectarian movements.

The initial form of religious sectarianism in Russia is the so-called Khristovshchina. The teaching of the sect served as the rationale for its name, for, according to Dmitrii Rostovskii, the originator of the name, Christ was an ordinary man filled "with the spirit of God", which left open the possibility for any person to emulate Christ. The leaders of the sect, depending on the richness of their "spiritual gifts", were endowed by its participants with the reputation of "Christs", "prophets", and in the case of women "Virgins".

For the first century of its development, Khristovshchina gave rise to two new forms of religious sectarianism. On the one hand we have the Skoptsy movement which appeared in the beginning of the 1760s and gave to the mystical-ascetic teaching of Khristovshchina an extremely fanatical expression. On the other hand there was the so-called Spiritual Christianity which divided at the end of the 1760s into Dukhoborism and Molokanism. Numerous newly-formed sectarian groups arising over the course of the last third of the 18th and the entire 19th centuries in one way or another were in most cases connected with Khristovshchina and Spiritual Christianity.

Let us note one more religious form appearing at the end of the 17th and beginning of the 18th centuries—the Subbotnik movement. Dmitrii Rostovskii and I. T. Pososhkov as early as the first decade of the 18th century listed the Subbotnik movement as one of the branches of the Schism. This tendency, which had its representatives in Dmitrii's Rostov Metropolitanate, quickly won followers, chiefly among the estate peasants.

At the beginning of the 19th century, adherents of the Subbotnik movement were already found in 28 guberniias and administrative regions of Russia. Their number at this time amounted to 15,000-20,000 persons (Rostovskii 1847: 68, 609, 625; Sreznevskii, comp. 1900: 20; Pososhkov 1895: 199; Astyrev 1891: 47).

In 1825, the Committee of Ministers adopted a special resolution directed toward cutting off the spread of the Subbotnik movement with extremely harsh repressive measures (Kel'siev 1863: I, No. 1, 58), which, it should be noted, had no success. With all this, the Subbotnik movement did not give rise in the process of its history to any new forms, and in this sense was not viable. With time, it more and more withdrew into a shell of religious ideas and cult rituals borrowed from Judaism and gradually died "a natural death". By the second half of the 19th century, it was reduced to religious congregations spread out over the entire length of Russia which were cut off from the surrounding population and which did not manifest any interest in questions of public life.

The participants in these communities engaged in petty crafts and trades, and the wealthier of them in money-lending (for example in the Transcaucasus). The Subbotnik religious tendency (also known under the name of "Judaizers") appeared as a peculiar form of social protest of peasants directed against the ruling church. Sources characterizing the history of this tendency, its social composition, and its world-view at all fully have not turned up to this day. Apparently we are dealing with the rather widespread use by democratic elements dissatisfied with the church of motifs of social accusation encountered in the Old Testament literary tradition. Let us recall Marx's words: "Cromwell and the English people used in their bourgeois revolution language, passions and illusions borrowed from the Old Testament" (*Marx and Engels* VII: 120). But from the fact that the sectarian movements arose as a religious form of social protest it does not follow that any religious form of social protest belongs to the group of social phenomena which make up sectarianism. This is well seen in the example of such a vast movement of social protest in religious form as the Old Belief.

It seems to me arbitrary to classify the Subbotnik movement as a form of religious sectarianism. The landlord serfs who broke with the Church and became Subbotniki did not reach in their religiously-formed protest that level of social and ideological development at which the very bases of the feudal religious world were questioned. The Subbotniki rejected the Russian Orthodox Church and the external piety preached by it, but at the same time practiced Judaism with its unlimited power of dogma, complicated rituals and ceremony, and striving toward a literal understanding of the Torah with all that the concept of "Talmudism" embraces.

My encounter with Subbotniki in Rasskazovo Raion of Tambov Oblast during 1959 and in Borisogleb Raion of Voronezh Oblast during 1964 confirmed my opinion that we are dealing with followers of Judaism who give primary importance to its rituals and customary side. It would be natural to suppose that at the dawn of its history the Subbotnik movement was ideologically a more independent tendency than at the present time, when we encounter representatives of the last and already extremely sparse generation of Subbotniki.

Mysticism and asceticism were the most general features characterizing the world-view of Khristovshchina, and for all the changes in the tendency, its adherents preserved them in one degree or another right up to the beginning of the 20th century.

These were religious communities headed by "Christs" and "prophets", prophesying "with the spirit of God", and announcing doctrine which declared the entire surrounding world to be sinful and perishing in sin. To the parasitism and luxury of the ruling classes the religious communities of followers of Khristovshchina counterposed the preaching of severe asceticism down to the rejection of procreation and sexual relations, and even to castration in theory and practice, as was done in the Skoptsy sect which separated out from Khristovshchina. In this asceticism, the disillusioned serfs wished to become aware of, affirm, and show their complete separation from the world of the serf owner, their incompatibility with it. The landowners' serfs henceforth considered themselves "God's people" and during meetings in so-called religious ecstasies brought themselves into a condition of mystical frenzy during which it seemed to them that they experienced the presence of God in themselves.

The sources of Khristovshchina go back to the middle of the 17th century. The Old Believer literature preserves the name of "the marvelous Father Kapiton", whose activity can be traced from the 1630s chiefly in the Vladimir and Kostroma regions. Kapiton's preaching was characterized by a strict asceticism, fulfilling the demands of which a person would suposedly achieve union with God and therefore did not need the spiritual hierarchy and the "sacraments" which it performed. Kapiton acquired the reputation of a prophet "who saw without error into the past and into the future, distant or near" (*Vinograd Rossiiskii* ..., 1. 108 ob.; on Kapiton *see* Smirnov 1898).

According to an Old Believer writer, Kapiton had "many disciples, who emulated his miraculous life" (*Vinograd Rossiiskii* ..., 1. 108 ob.).

We once again encounter Kapiton's disciples and followers in places where Kapiton himself once performed his marvels; in the Old Believer tract, *Poslanie Avraamiia k khristoliubtsu nekoemu* [Epistle of Avraamii to One Christ-Lover], written not later than 1671, we read: "... for Kirik at Plese said to me, a sinner: Kapiton's disciples called his spiritual son into the wilderness, saying: Christ is with us, having descended from heaven, talking with us". To this Avraamii objects: "The good holy fathers taught of this the following: When they tempt you, saying that Christ is in the wilderness either here or there, you should not follow after them ..." (Barskov 1912: 160-161).[1] Avraamii's epistle relates to Kostroma krai (Plessy—i.e., Plessy Volost on the Volga). "Kapiton's disciples" against whom Avraamii spoke were even closer to the ideas of the Khristovshchina than we can judge from the teachings of Kapiton himself: Christ walks with them and talks with them.[2]

Approximately 20 years later the monk Efrosin in *Otrazitel'nom pisanii* [A Letter of Rebuttal] notes directly the appearance among the Kostroma peasants of "foul zealots", namely "icon wrestlers" and "spirit prayers", meaning by the latter adherents of the Khristovshchina doctrine and worship. Efrosin wrote in 1691: "... Everybody likes to call themselves Old Believers, but many among them have been turned to false faiths by this or that scoundrel, like the *Kostroma false Christs* and village dwellers ignorant of city customs, who leave their plows and for the sake of this lead their souls astray, and their false apostles, their devilish disciples and damned prophets, ruinous tempters from Pavlov Perevoz, spirit prayers and icon wrestlers ... saying to pray with the spirit, to cease from prayers, for they supposedly see their soul in themselves" (Pamiatniki 1895: 9-10; my emphasis).

Efrosin's *Letter of Rebuttal* as it were continues and develops the description of "Kapiton's disciples", which was contained in Avraamii's epistle. The persistent geographic localization of the new movement of "Kostroma Christs", which can be traced in all the literary documents mentioned, is worthy of note. Especially important is the direct mention by Efrosin of the peasantry as the milieu in which the new teaching had its adherents, which from the preceding literary monuments could only be assumed.

---

[1] Emphasis mine. Avraamii erroneously ascribes to "the holy fathers" the words of the Gospel: "If anyone says to you ... 'look! Here is the Christ!' or 'there he is', do not believe it ..." (Matthew XXIV, 23).

[2] In one of the songs of the Khristovshchina which has come down to us from the beginning of the 18th century there are the following words: "The Lord God himself, the heavenly tsar himself *along the earth*, our Lord, he walks *equal*, the Lord he is, with *man*, in the flesh the Lord he is in human [flesh] ..." (Aivazov 1915; my emphasis).

Fifteen or 17 years later yet another testimony appeared which left no doubt that the formation of Khristovshchina really flowed from Kapiton's time. I have in mind the testimony of Dmitrii Rostovskii in his *Rozysk* [Investigation]: "... there is a peasant who is called Christ, and honored as Christ, and worshipped without making the sign of the cross. The home of this Christ is in a village called Pavlov Perevoz, on the river Oka, 60 versts below Nizhegorod. It is said that this false Christ was born Turchenin; he has with him a pretty girl, and he calls her his mother, and those who believe in him call her the Virgin. And this girl (or rather, whore) is of Russian birth, from the village of Lantiukhna in Nizhegorod Uezd, the daughter of a *posad* man. This Christ also has 12 apostles, who also go from village to village preaching Christ, as if he were the real one, to simple peasant men and women; and whomever they tempt they bring to him to do homage. This sect called Khristovshchina, although it blasphemes against God's church, does not forbid going to church, kissing the holy icon and the cross and *receiving the priests' blessing*" (Rostovskii 1847: 599; my emphasis).

Dmitrii Rostovskii received this story second-hand from his informant, the monk Pakhomii, who in his turn heard it from "an eyewitness, who saw this false Christ, and was brought to him by a disciple of his for worship" (Rostovskii 1847: 599).

However, the "eyewitness" on whose testimony Pakhomii based his story, and following him Dmitrii Rostovskii himself, did not meet the "false Christ" in Pavlov Perevoz: "This Christ was at that time on the river Volga, in the village called Rabotki, 40 versts down the Volga from Nizhnii Novgorod" (Rostovskii 1847: 599).

Dmitrii Rostovskii's story, although taken at second-hand, abounds in concrete details and is told in a completely realistic spirit. It corresponds to the testimony of Efrosin adduced above, which preceded it, precisely in the description of the preachers who appeared as "false Christs", and as villagers not skilled in "city customs", "who have left their plow".

In the *Letter of Rebuttal* of Efrosin and in the *Investigation* of Dmitrii Rostovskii, the same point of activity of the false Christ is named — the village of Pavlov Perevoz.

On the basis of the historical documents reviewed, a source of folklore origin takes on conviction: the Khristovshchina legend about the (legendary?) founder of the sect — the Muroma peasant Danilo Filippov — in which the latter is called one of Kapiton's disciples. This legend was found by P. Mel'nikov in written form among the documents in the case of the Moscow followers of the Khristovshchina in 1845-1846 and was introduced by him into the scholarly literature (Mel'nikov 1868: 31; Dobrotvorskii 1869: 6-7; Kutepov 1882: 42-44; Barsov 1879: 111). It goes without saying that the episode contained in the legend about how "God the Father" himself was supposedly embodied in the "purest flesh" of Danilo Filippov has cognitive significance only for a characterization of the world-view of the sect under study. But the legend corresponds completely to the historical sources which list the regions of the preaching activity of the founder of the Khristovshchina as Kostroma, Vladimir and Nizhegorod Uezds. The sources available to us do not confirm what we read in the legend about how Danilo Filippov, persecuted on Nikon's orders, was arrested "at the house of Makarii of Nizhegorod", how it was precisely he who first formulated the basic commandments of Khristov-shchina, which included dietary and sexual prohibitions, and also the com-mandment: "Believe in the Holy Spirit!", and how finally, in confirmation of the priority of "the spirit" over "the letter", Danilo Filippov threw into the Volga all the books, both Nikonian and pre-Nikonian.

As the "spiritual son" and successor of Danilo Filippov, the legend names still another Muroma peasant — Ivan Timofeevich Suslov, who supposedly met his "spiritual father" in 1649. According to the legend, Suslov for 30 years (from 1672 to 1702) preached in Moscow, then wandered around for many long years, seeking refuge from persecution, and finally, in 1715, returned to Moscow where a year later he died. If we suppose that at the time of Suslov's meeting with Danilo Filippov the former was about 20 years old, then Suslov died at approximately 85-87 years of age. Khristovshchina oral tradition names Prokopii Lupkin as Suslov's successor. From the materials of an in-vestigation in 1733 of the followers of Khristovshchina, it in fact appears that Prokopii Danilovich Lupkin, who lived in Nizhii Novgorod, a former *strelets,* a participant of the last Azov campaign, and from 1710 a *posad* person in Moscow — did play a prominent role in it in the first two decades of the 18th century.

We can say nothing definite about Danilo Filippov as a historical person. But the opinion of N. M. Nikol'skii that "with Lupkin, apparently, there begins a series of historical personages in Khristovshchina" and that "the ex-istence of Khristovshchina can be traced from documents beginning in 1716" (Nikol'skii 1930: 191), is unfounded. By taking the most cautious attitude toward historical sources, the time of origin of Khristovshchina can be fixed at the second half of the 17th century (precisely from documents — the *Epistle of Avraamii,* and Efrosin's *Letter of Rebuttal).* As concerns I. T. Suslov, at least with him if not with Danilo Filippov (and certainly not with Lupkin), we must start the geneology of historical personages in Khristovshchina. In Pososhkov's *True Mirror* we read: "Christ too had many anti-Christs, and now you have *false Christs like Ivan Suslov* and other such" (Pososhkov 1895, 2: 41; my emphasis).

In those cases where the same features of the history of Khristovshchina are described in written sources and in the legend (geographical localization, characterization of the dogma, Suslov as a public figure), they are close to each other and even coincide. This increases confidence in the real historical events encountered in the legend.

Thus, at least no later than the last third of the 17th century there arose a sect called by its opponents Khristovshchina and later "Khlystovshchina". As appears from the archives of the legal process of 1733, the sectarians themselves called their teaching "Christ's faith" (TsGADA, div. 301, s.u. 313, sh. 299 v.), and we will in future call this religious tendency Khristovoverie. The founders of this tendency and its first disseminators were peasants. The area of dissemination of the early Khristovoverie is also described: this is the region of the non-Chernozem—Kostroma, Vladimir, Nizhegorod, Rostov and Moscow Uezds—where, in distinction to the southern Chernozem regions, there developed a quit-rent system of exploitation, peasant crafts and seasonal migrant labor grew, and where in the first instance we can trace new economic phenomena. It is symptomatic that the sources name as the points of the preaching activity of the founders of Khristovoverie the large trade-industrial village of Pavlov Perevoz, and also the celebrated Makar'ev fair.

In the beginning of the 18th century the area of distribution of the Khristovshchina broadened still further, spreading out over the uezds of Yaroslavl', Uglich, Pereiaroslavl'-Zales'e, Venov, and Kolomna (Nechaev 1889: 160-163). Khristovoverie became quite widespread in Moscow itself, where in the first third of the 18th century congregations of this sect existed in the Ivanovskii, Vorsonof'evskii and Nikitskii nunneries, and in private houses on Vshivaia Hill, in Kochki near the Novodevichii monastery, in Kundrin in the Dorogomilovskii freight-carriers' settlement, beyond the Prechistii gates, beyond the Serpukhov gates, in Shabolovka, and in the Preobrazhenskaia Sloboda (Nechaev 1889: 160-163, 169).

Among the residents of Moscow brought to trial as Khristovovers in 1733, the basic contingent were monastic elements and peasants. The next new trial of Khristovovers in 1745 showed changes in the composition of members of this sect in Moscow: among them 41% were peasants, about 25% monastic elements, and about 16% merchants. The remaining 18% (in round figures) consisted of factory workers, sailors and their children, soldiers' wives and their children, and minor church functionaries. One must take into account the fact that among the monastic elements many were of peasant origin. The ascetic way of life which was demanded by the basic position of Khristovoverie was especially close and acceptable to this element. Of the 17 residents of Petersburg nine were peasants and five were merchants (Nechaev 1889: 163-166).

What sort of peasants were they? "Peasants living in cities", writes N. M. Nikol'skii, "could only be quit-rent peasants or the house serfs of prominent noblemen. The latter, of course, were not inclined to any sect, and the peasants involved in the Petrov affair were, undoubtedly, quit-rent peasants"

(Nikol'skii 1930: 197).[3] Let us add that in those really infrequent cases where house serfs were inclined toward Khristovoverie, they were viewed by the leaders of the sect as an undesirable element. When in 1729 the Platonov brothers — house serfs from the Stroganov house — sought to meet Prokopii Lupkin, the latter through his assistant Vasilii Dement'ev answered that "it is impossible to accept them into the teaching because they are the people of nobles" (OIDR 1887, Book 2: 88). As for those Khristovovers brought to trial in 1745 who lived not in Moscow but in the Uezds (Moscow, Yaroslavl', Uglich, Pereiaroslavl'-Zales'e and Vladimir), the overwhelming majority among them consisted of privately-owned peasants, belonging to monasteries and noblemen (Nechaev 1889: 166).

Thus, the basic ranks of the followers of "the faith of Christ", just as in the case of the Old Belief, consisted of peasants. But in contrast to those Old Believers who fled to the borderlands, and there during the first period turned to slash-and-burn farming or beaver hunting, and to a man cursed urban life, trade, and money, the Khristovovers were among those peasants who streamed from the villages to the cities, taking part in trade and having no doubt of the power of money. Not without reason among the commandments ascribed to Danilo Filippov, there was also the following: "Do not steal. Whoever steals a single kopek will have that kopek attached to the crown of his head in the other world, and when it begins to melt from the fires of hell, only then will that person be forgiven" (OIDR 1887, Book 2: 57). The Khristovovers knew the value of a kopek — precisely that kopek which "grows into a ruble" and by degrees paves the way to personal independence.

Let us note one detail very characteristic for the world-view of Khristovovers. The Old Believers did not have in their religious practice the mystical-ecstatic form of worship of the Khristovovers, and did not enter as the latter did into direct "communication" with the forces "of the Holy Spirit", but many of them believed in the imminent "end of the world", and anxiously awaited it. In 1699, and again in 1702, Old Believers dropped their field work in expectation of "the end of the world". The Khristovovers did not expect or want the world, however sinful they painted it to be, to cease its existence.

With all their mysticism, they were able to look at things realistically and attempted to "get on their feet" precisely in this world and were not especially concerned with the lot awaiting man beyond the grave. As the investigative materials of 1733 showed, Khristovovers prophesied at their meetings: "... there will be fires, and there will be no rain, and therefore God will not give fruit, and ... there will be no end of the world, but as man dies, that will be the end of him" (OIDR 1887, Book 2: 57). It is remarkable that among all the

---

[3] Petrov was one of the leaders of the Moscow Khristovovers undergoing investigation in 1745.

sources from the 18th and 19th centuries from which the researcher can reconstruct the world-view of the sect of Khristovovers both in its early period and later, the materials characterizing the views of the representatives of this sect on life beyond the grave, and in general the other world, are the scantiest. The Khristovovers were clearly making a place for themselves in this world.

What was the social essence of the teaching of the Khristovovers?

In the beginning this was, as we have already noted, a protest against the monopoloy of lay and clerical feudal landlords and serf-owners on wealth and luxury. But the matter was not limited to this. For peasant elements connected with the market and striving to make themselves free and independent commodity producers, asceticism had a quite specific attractiveness that increased with time: it coincided with thrift. Renunciation of alcohol and tobacco, self-denial in food, clothing and all conditions of daily life, the requirement of celibacy, created additional and significant opportunities for accumulation. The social essence of ascetism and its role in the economic origins of the bourgeoisie is explained in the words of Marx: "... So far, therefore, as his actions are a mere function of capital—endowed as capital is, in his person, with consciousness and a will— *his own private consumption is a robbery perpetrated on accumulation ...*" (*Marx and Engels* Vol. 23: 606; my emphasis [Standard English translation from Karl Marx, *Capital,* Vol. I, International Publishers, New York, 1967, p. 592]).

Thrift to the point of miserliness was ennobled and idealized in Khristovoverie as a holy spiritual virtue which elevates man and leads him by way of "abstinence" to God. Marx wrote that in the historical beginnings of the capitalist means of production—and each capitalist parvenu passes individually through this historical stage—the thirst for enrichment and miserliness rule as absolute passions.

And finally, there is another question which we should consider. As rendered in pre-Revolutionary missionary and church literature, the religious practice of the Khristovovers was almost wholly reduced to sexual orgies as an inevitable accompaniment of their ecstatic rites, and also to ritual murder of the babies supposedly conceived as the result of these orgies. This accusation against the Khristovovers, predicated on unhealthy interest and cheap success, and intended to arouse public opinion against them and bring down on them the retribution of state authorities, penetrated into some pre-Revolutionary *belles lettres* (Merezhkovskii, Andrei Belyi).

The sect of Khristovovers, as has been shown, arose at a crucial point in Russian history, which in the 17th century was entering into a new period of its development.

In the crucial periods of social development, parallel with the change in people's general values and views, there is also a change in their attitude toward problems of the family and sex, and toward established traditions in the field. For religious and all other hypocrites, violation of the normal sexual relations which have been customary for centuries seems an infringement on the very bases of morality, and is treated by them as debauchery, decadence, etc. Both the Khristovovers, and the Skoptsy who separated out of them with time, stood out against the traditional bases of the family as sanctified by the Church. But they did this not by declaring anarchy in sexual relations, as church officials described them as doing, but just to the contrary, by way of preaching strict asceticism. This was fanatical, unnatural, and among the Skoptsy outright brutal asceticism, but as we have become convinced, it was a phenomenon born of social traditions, and not of spiritual pathology and the moral corruption of its followers.

Of course, one cannot exclude some cases of sexual debauchery among Khristovovers. In the history of religion we know of numerous cases of sexual crimes committed for religious reasons. But if we speak not of exceptions but of the rule, then the Khristovovers were characterized by the demand for sexual abstinence, which they more or less faithfully followed.

The "confessions" of sexual debauchery and ritual murders made by some Khristovovers during the investigation preparatory to the trial of 1745, as the material published by V. V. Nechaev (1889) showed, were forced, achieved by torture and in the end repudiated by the very people who had "confessed" it. Incidentally, it was precisely these "admissions" which served as the bases for the subsequent provocational accusations advanced against Khristovovers by the priest-missionary literature, and on which some writers relied.

In order to finish our consideration of this question, let us add the following: the mystical-ecstatic practice of Khristovoverie had a social basis. But it also had its psycho-physical side. "Spiritual joy" is a special condition into which Khristovovers brought themselves, experienced and valued by them as the highest degree of bliss, a flaming contact with the world beyond this one. This condition is the same sort of peculiar case as the condition of a man who resorts to alcohol or narcotics.

The effect of spiritual intoxication was achieved by Khristovovers with the help of the system of psycho-physical methods in which a large role is given to "exhaustion of the flesh," by long austerities sometimes lasting several days. Worn out by fasting and concentrated wordless prayer, a man came to a gathering taking place in the deepest secrecy. As if preparing for a holy sacrifice, he was robed in white. The unwinding began. To the rhythmic singing of the Khristovovers sitting on benches, accompanied by rhythm beaten out on their knees, first one and then another believer came out into the "circle of joy" and began to dance.

During collective, and sometimes individual ecstatic dances there occurred glossolalia—disconnected mumbling and cries which were understood as "speaking in tongues", inspired by the Holy Spirit. All this was the "spiritual ecstasy", which sublimated the psycho-physical potential of a person so much that as a result of the ecstatic rituals, their participants, drained of strength and consciousness, fell in a dead faint on the floor, and coming to themselves after some time, believed that they had descended from "seventh heaven". But precisely because the effect of "spiritual ecstasy" required the expenditure of the nervous and physical forces of man, it could not have been implemented if these forces had been allowed to flow into other channels. The claims about sexual orgies of Kristovovers contradict the psycho-physical nature of their religious practice, and, as has already been noted, contradict the facts.

We have characterized in its basic features the religious world-view and cult of Khristovoverie. Let us note that this first large sect which arose from the soil of Russian Orthodoxy, and went a considerable distance in breaking with its dogmas, at the same time preserved external ties with the Russian Orthodox Church. The Khristovovers attended the Russian Orthodox churches, read some church prayers, and retained in their religious practice icons and crosses. In this respect, Khristovovers differed decisively from all subsequent forms of religious sectarianism in Russia. I explain this peculiarity of Khristovoverie in part by tactical considerations on the part of the leaders and followers of this sect, who were attempting to fool the Orthodox vigilance of the clergy, and in part by the historical conditions under which Khristovoverie originated.

If we bear in mind that historically Khristovoverie was the first Russian Orthodox sect, and also that monastic elements played no small role in the original Khristovoverie makeup, it is natural to consider that the dogma of Khristovovers bore the marks not only of the break from Russian Orthodoxy but also bore the marks of the transition from one to the other.

The motivation which is given by contemporary followers of Khristovoverie for their traditional tactics in relation to Russian Orthodoxy is not without scientific interest: "And if you take into account that Jesus Christ went to the synagogue.... He prayed in the synagogues. And they had their own meetings, Jesus Christ and his disciples. And according to his followers—those who followed after him—he went, and that was the kind of meetings they had. And from that time, and not since yesterday—from that time this has been taken" (Klibanov 1961: 239).

Even at the beginning of the 18th century in the world-view of Khristovovers there can be traced changes in the direction of a weakening of mysticism. If the commandment ascribed to Danilo Filippov was "Believe in the Holy Spirit", which is logically connected with the story about the throwing into the river of the church books, both old and new, by Danilo Filippov, then as V. V. Nechaev noted, in the 1720s there appeared among the

Khristovovers adherents of a reconsideration of the negative attitude toward "book-writing" (Nechaev 1889: 170).

In place of the mystical elements in the teachings of Khristovovers there are found signs of the appearance of moral consciousness, the principle of "pure conscience" of man as the genuine sanctuary of faith and vital truth. Vasilii Dement'ev, who was close to Lupkin and himself an exceptional person, wrote of one Khristovover prophetess, Katerina, that she "let fall from her lips ... that all people coming together ... should preserve in themselves pure conscience" (TsGADA, div. 301, d. 6, shs. 242-242 v.).

We connect these occurrences with the course of liberation of the consciousness of participants in Khristovoverie from the mental darkness arising from the conditions of life of the patriarchal peasantry, as new economic relationships penetrated into it.

The Schism in the second half of the 17th century was a gigantic mental laboratory in which there raged, clashed, and gradually separated out, the most various opinions and views, which corresponded to the heterogeneous composition of the participants in the Schism and to the increasingly complex and acute conditions of class struggle in the country. In turn, the Old Belief itself appeared as the arena of a bitter internal struggle. Even in 1669 Avvakum was forced to issue his *Epistle to Christ's Slaves* in which he admonished those whom he considered his fellow believers: "... do not be surprised that there is no agreement among believers" (RIB 1927: 39, column 821).

At that time Avvakum still nourished the hope of uniting believers, and manifested a tolerance for alien opinions that was not characteristic for him: "And that they oppose each other—let it be!" wrote Avvakum, "there truth and justice are more to be found" (RIB 1927: column 822). And finally: "Fight more! I'm not against this" (RIB 1927: 823). But the *Epistle to Father Ion* which appeared approximately 10 years later showed that by this time Avvakum had already finally lost hope of achieving the unity of the participants of the movement which he had aroused. From the *Epistle to Father Ion* it appears that the noticeable changes in Khristovoverie from mysticism to rationalism, if it is permissible to express oneself thus about phenomena of a religious order, are confirmed by rationalistically-nuanced searches also taking place among the Old Believers, which provided Avvakum with the occasion to qualify this kind of Old Believer as "Europeans", "Evangelicals". "Lutherans", and "Calvinists", and in general as heretics (RIB 887-889).

Along with Khristovoverie, lagging somewhat behind it in time, there arose still another phenomenon of social protest in religious form—the so-called Spiritual Christianity, which gave rise at the end of the 1760s to the sects of the Dukhobors and Molokans, and absorbed some representatives of Khristovoverie. Dmitrii Rostovskii's *Investigation* and I. T. Pososhkov's *True*

Mirror, which appeared at the end of the first decade of the 18th century, polemicized in particular with those opponents who can be called early precursors of the Dukhobor and Molokan movements. For example, we learn from the *Investigation* of the existence of zealous "schismatics" who maintain: "It is not necessary to go to churches to pray. Divinity does not live in churches built by hands, *the church is not in boards but in ribs* (that is—Dmitrii Rostovskii explains—not in walls but in the bosom or the heart), and it is in itself sufficient to pray to God in some place other than a church" (Rostovskii 1847: 130; my emphasis).

The Schismatics replaced attendance in "churches made by hands" with secret gatherings, which were held in shacks, "cellars and underground dwellings" (Rostovskii 1847: 149). Some of them preferred solitary prayer to a gathering. They cited Matthew (VI, 6) for this: "... when you pray, retire to yourself, and closing your door, pray to your father in secret" (Rostovskii 1847: 151).

There were also those extreme interpreters of the proposition of a "church not of boards but of the ribs", who considered that thought, insofar as it was embodied in words, was objectified in them, and in a search for an adequate expression of spirituality they arrived at wordless ("mental") prayer: "We were informed recently", Dmitrii Rostovskii wrote, "that some peasant *men and women* in the eparchy have learned from false teachers and false interpreters who have come to them in secret, *and teach others similar to themselves,* that not only should they not go to church to pray, but even in their homes they should not pray as God demands of us before the holy icons with reverential bows even bending the body and the head to the earth: but that one should pray only with the mind in oneself" (Pososhkov 1895: no. 2, 174; my emphasis).

Arguing the adopted method of wordless prayer, "the false teachers" discovered the content of the concept of "the church in the ribs": "In confirmation of this false teaching of theirs, they cite the words of Christ in the Gospel spoken to the Samaritan: true worshippers worship the Father in spirit and truth" (Rostovskii 1847: 351).

The formula of worshipping God "in spirit and truth" was very capricious, if we speak of a religious criticism of the organizational and ideological bases of a feudal Russian Orthodoxy. Potentially this formula contains a denial of sacraments, miracles, saints, icons, holy relics, church ritual and ceremonial, and along with all this of the Church itself with its white and black clergy.[A]

This formula allowed a replacement of the literal understanding of the Bible with an interpretation of it in the direction of "spirit and truth"—i.e., translated from religious language into the language of common sense. In fact, as we can judge from the *Investigation* of Dmitrii Rostovskii, the Schismatics contemporary with him applied the criteria of "spirit and truth" to the Bible itself. Dmitrii Rostovskii spoke out against "schismatics" who do not accept Evangelical history as truth which really happened, but make a parable of it (Rostovskii 1847: 161).

The criterion of "spirit and truth" which the schismatics applied to the Gospels was, in sum, the criteria of common sense. Can the Gospel story of the miracle performed by Christ when he was in the wilderness and fed 5,000 persons, not counting women and children, with five loaves of bread and two fishes, really have taken place? The schismatics answered: "... that did not really happen, but is a parable" (Rostovskii 1847: 351).

What is meant by "parable"? This: "The empty place is the heathen, to whom Christ came, leaving the Jews; the five loaves are the five senses; two fishes, two books: the Gospels and the Apostles ..." (Rostovskii 1847: 351).

The resurrection of Lazarus by Christ was also no miracle. "According to God's word, they say, Lazarus is our mind, conquered by human frailty; the death of Lazarus is [our] sins; the sisters of Lazarus are flesh and the spirit; the flesh is Martha; the spirit is Mary; the coffin is human cares; the stone on the coffin is a stony heart; Lazarus bound with a winding sheet (a shroud — A. K.) is the mind tied with snares (nets, chains — A. K.) of sin; the resurrection of Lazarus is remission of sin (Rostovskii 1847: 351).

One after another the Gospel stories of the miracles of Christ were rejected by the schismatics ("one and another of the miraculous actions of Christ described in the Gospel story ...").

Dmitrii Rostovskii understood that all these discussions led to a general reconsideration of the Christian dogma of the son of God, since with equal success one could declare the incarnation of Christ and his earthly sufferings, etc., to be a parable. The author of the *Investigation* writes that just this view particularly roused him to speak out in denunciation of the schismatics (Rostovskii 1847: 353).

Who were these people who denied the historical reliability of the Gospels and in what milieu did they disseminate their views? Only in passing does Dmitrii Rostovskii note that the propagators of the new views on the Gospels "sow among the *simple people* these their weeds and harm ignorant souls" (Rostovskii 1847: 353; my emphasis).

The exposés by Dmitrii Rostovskii (and Pososhkov) could not refer to the urban heretical circle of Tveretinov, since the latter was discovered only in 1713, i.e. after the *Investigation* and the *True Mirror* were written. It is true that in one of Pososhkov's letters dating from approximately 1705, he reports the existence among the clerks and the posad people of a "new heresy", "for besides works they wish to be saved by faith alone" (Sreznevskii 1900: 28, 30, 31).

However that may be, it was not only clerks, petty officials, and posad people — representatives of urban circles of the population — who shared the views denounced by Dmitrii Rostovskii and Pososhkov. Along with urban dwellers, peasants connected with the city shared these views. Thus, from 1713 to 1717 in Moscow secret religious gatherings, participated in by peasants and posad people, took place in the home of Nastas'ia Ivanovna Zima, the wife of an agent of the land transaction office.

Nastas'ia Zima conducted meetings where she read aloud and interpreted "books", and "in these books it is not written that one should bow to icons and worship and believe bread and wine". She gave evidence at the investigation that "she does not bow to icons and the cross and does not hold them holy, since they are the work of human hands, and she prays to God in spirit and in truth and does not wear Christ's cross and does not make the sign of the cross on herself, and to people who are with her in spiritual union she teaches this, and to the church and to the legends of the church teachers she does not listen and in future will not listen and does not wish to believe in the church sacraments" (TsGADA, div. 371 (Preobrazhenskii Prikaz, sh. 1, pt. 1, d. 925, sh. 62).

In the denunciation of Nastas'ia Zima and her co-thinkers it was confirmed that after the memorial supper for a dead child, "they did not give thanks to God and to the holy icons they did not bow, and bowed to each other among themselves" (TsGADA, *ibid.*, sh. 6 v.). The list of participants of this gathering has been preserved: "The peasant Andrei Anufriev, of the village Pavlov Perevoz, Nizhegorod Uezd, belonging to the Votchina Prince Aleksei Mikhailovich Cherkaskii; the peasant Terentii Ivanov, of the village of Polneva, Yaroslavl' Uezd, belonging to the Stolnik Roman Radionovich Streshnev; Aleksei Filipov, the Stolnik Ignatii Kostomarov's man; Grigorii Liubimtsov, posad man of Kostroma; Ivan Terent'ev, Prince Sergei Alekseevich Galitsyn's man, of the Kostroma Votchina village, belonging to Vasilii Dolgorukov, son of prince Mikhail; ... the peasant Fedor Pavlov; Iakov Artem'ev of Malye Luzhniki; Konstantin Alekseev, Ivan Brogov's man; Kaz'ma Dorofeev, Prince Iurii Iur'evich Odoevskii's man; Gerasim Andreev, blacksmith, of the village of Krasino; Rodion Mikhailov; the widow Avdot'ia, daughter of Nikita, and Nikifor Artem'ev, all of Malye Luzhniki... Ivan Savel'ev, soda maker of the Sloboda, with his wife Akimina; and the peasant's son Ivan Nazar'ev of the village in Yaroslavl' Uezd in the Votchina of Stolnik Streshnev, and also the husband of Nastas'ia, Ivan Zima" (*ibid.*, sh. 2-2 v.). The core of this meeting consisted of the Zima couple, three peasants (Andrei Anufriev, Terentii Ivanov and Aleksei Filipov) and one posad person (Grigorii Liubimtsov).

We will show, if only partially, from the example of the life of Ivan Nazar'ev, a young participant of the Zima congregation, how under the pressure of certain conditions and influences a peasant consciousness critical of the ruling church and its world-view was formed at the beginning of the 18th century.

The biography of Ivan Nazar'ev can be reconstructed without great difficulty from the material of the case of Nastas'ia Zima.

Ivan Nazar'ev, the son of Nazar Demidov, a peasant from the village of Nova in Yaroslavl' Uezd, belonging to the Stolnik Ivan Rodionovich Streshnev, was born in 1689. In 1697, Ivan's father died. Until he was 16 years of age, Ivan Nazar'ev remained in the village in his father's house. Attending the parish church and listening to the Gospel in it, Ivan Nazar'ev "from infancy *by his own reasoning*" came to a recognition of the bankruptcy of church dogma: "... he did not bow to the image of our Lord Jesus Christ and his Virgin mother and the other holy saints painted on the icon."

In 1713, Ivan Nazar'ev with his fellow villager, the peasant Terentii Ivanov, set out for "St. Petersburg to work in the stone works."

The hard labor did not interfere with the intellectual contact of the friends. Terentii Ivanov taught his young comrade "letters ... the knowledge of reading books." In the winter of 1716, Ivan and Terentii went away to Moscow. In the spring and summer, Ivan Nazar'ev wandered around Moscow, feeding himself apparently from casual wages and spending the night under the open sky "in various places ... on vacant lots and on the bridge at the inn."

In the meantime, "autumn and the frosts arrived". Ivan Nazar'ev found "for himself a place beyond the Barbarian Gates, opposite the Vasil'ev Garden in a built-in earthen bulwark". Here he built himself a "cell", where he spent two months "wishing to read the Holy Scriptures in private". Ivan was visited by certain people, who supplied him with books. Information is also preserved about the scope of his reading. They brought him "the Gospels, the Apostles, and the Apocalypse and the catechism in Kievan printing". This latter book, apparently, is the catechism of Metropolitan Petr Mogila, printed in Kiev in 1712 and consisting of three parts, corresponding to the Christian virtues of faith, hope and love.

They valued the book, judging by the fact that "having read it, he, Ivan, gave the catechism to the person who had brought it to him". About the other books brought to Ivan no similar information exists.

The books mentioned, under the conditions of that time, were the only literary-theoretical source against which Ivan Nazar'ev could check the experience of his 27 short, difficult years of life. He was finally confirmed in a negative attitude toward the Church and its teachings. "True worshipers", he maintained, "bow not to the office of the priest *or to the images, but to the spirit*": "he, Ivan, had no priest with him and now (Ivan Nazar'ev gave evidence to this effect in 1717 — A. K.) does not have one, and does not make confession before a priest, but makes confession to the heavenly Father *with the spirit;* he does not and will not partake of the holy sacraments, but supposedly he, Ivan, makes communion with the word of the Gospels, and from this he wishes his salvation, and from communion with the holy sacrament of bread and wine there is no salvation, only simple bread and wine, food and drink created by men."

The hermit was quickly found by the authorities. He was dispatched to the patriarchal clerical prikaz, but the clerical investigators achieved nothing: Ivan Nazar'ev "kept silent". Sent "under charge" to the Andreevskii monastery, he continued to "keep silent". He was transferred to the Don monastery—and he "kept silent". Trusting in the final "silence" of Ivan Nazar'ev and having in full measure demonstrated such a useful quality for the tranquility of the church, the spiritual authorities released Ivan Nazar'ev "to freedom, where he wished to live". Ivan "after that liberation lived in another place in the above-mentioned bulwark, also in a cell, where he continued to study the Gospel. Here his old comrade Terentii Ivanov sought him out. In the spring of 1717, Terentii brought Ivan Nazar'ev to the Zamoskvorech'e district, to Zemskaia Street, to the house of Nastas'ia Ivanovna Zima, 'who reads the Holy Gospels and discusses the word of God in very truth'. Nazar'ev became a participant of Nastas'ia Zima's congregation. On May 22, 1717, 17 days after the arrest of Nastas'ia Zima, Ivan Nazar'ev was taken and given over to torture in the Preobrazhenskii Prikaz" (*ibid.*, shs. 46-47).

Thus, the world-view of the participants of Nastas'ia Zima's circle was characterized by a denial of icon and cross worship, of church legends and sacraments and spiritual authority. The positive basis of their world-view can be considered an understanding of faith as serving God in "spirit and truth", and we know from what Dmitrii Rostovskii wrote that this was the assertion of the rights of common sense veiled in a religious form.

The concept of faith "in spirit and truth" was a religious form of self-assertion of the individual under conditions where the individual was enserfed. And it was no accident that the participants of Nastas'ia Zima's circle "did not bow to icons, but *bowed among themselves to each other*". Thereby they paid tribute to the respect of people for one another which was fixed later, but in the same century, in the custom of mutual bowing adopted in the Dukhobor sect—a custom explained by the Dukhobors from the belief that man is a living icon.

Much in the world-view of the circle of Nastas'ia Zima, especially in the announced primacy of "spirit and truth", makes its participants resemble the followers of Khristovoverie. But differences also existed.

For example, there is no indication of the presence in Zima's circle of mystical-ecstatic worship nor of a requirement of severe asceticism. Secondly, while rejecting the Church tradition, Zima's followers, like their leader, and in distinction to Khristovovers, felt a deep reverence for the Holy Scriptures—especially, as we may judge from the investigative materials in the

Zima case, for the Gospels. This point allows one to see in the participants of the circle early precursors of Molokanism.

Mel'nikov pointed to the connection existing even in the beginning of the 17th century between Khlysty and icon wrestlers" and in confirmation of his conclusion reported the following: "The coiner Maksim Eremeev in private did not bow to icons, but in the presence of people he did bow in order to hide his affiliation with a secret sect. He was a Khlyst, but he was close to the teachings of Tveretinov and to the teaching of Nastas'ia Zimikha. When the barber Foma Ivanov (a follower of Tveretinov) was burned at the stake, Maksim said with pride: 'This is how our people suffer! They do not spare themselves — and they were burned without making the sign of the cross. Nastas'ia Zimikha was briefly acquainted with Maksim, and when she was taken, he became frightened and ran to the Volga, and he was lost ..." (Mel'nikov 1868: 52-53). In the beginning of the 18th century there existed not a few points of contact in the views and interests of various religious tendencies and groups opposed to the Church. Their separation from each other and the struggle for existence between them which then followed became even more apparent in the second half of the 18th century and later.

The data which we have adduced indicate the presence of sectarian tendencies which were more or less formed in an organizational sense and had worked out their dogma, like Khristovoverie, but in other cases, like "Spiritual Christianity", were only at the stage of formation.

The relationship of Khristovoverie to "Spiritual Christianity" from the time that the latter appeared was characterized not by parallel co-existence of these religious formations, but by a progressive development of social protest in religious form changing its aspects with the increasingly complicated social relationships and the development of the class struggle. We noted above signs of evolution in the direction of "Spiritual Christianity" found in Khristovoverie in the first third of the 18th century.

It was precisely former members of Khristovoverie — the peasants Siluan Kolesnikov and Illarion Pobirokhin — who became the heralds of "Spiritual Christianity" at the end of the second third of the 18th century.

Remembrance of the genetic ties with Khristovoverie was retained until the beginning of the 19th century in one of the two basic tendencies of "Spiritual Christianity" — the Dukhobor movement. P. N. Miliukov directed attention to this in his *Outlines of the History of Russian Culture*. He wrote: "... in the Sloboda Ukraine (Khar'kov Guberniia), the Dukhobor movement was also found (like Khristovoverie — A. K.) among Great Russian families who had migrated here from Tambov and Penza Guberniias. The Dukhobors even preserved an apparent recollection of their former affiliation with Khristovshchina — if only we can conclude this on the basis of their statement to the authorities in 1801: "from leaping, from dancing, from devilish hopping (we) have refrained (i.e., this means that earlier they participated in them); for this the world hated us" (Miliukov 1931: 122). But Khristovoverie was not simply transformed into "Spiritual Christianity", thereby facilitating its origin. Khristovoverie continued to develop along its own path, changing form as bourgeois relationships penetrated into the countryside. "Spiritual Christianity" was the ideology of religious opposition to Russian Orthodoxy on the part of those peasant elements which in their economic independence had gone further than the quit-rent peasants who were the main component of Khristovoverie; they were more independent in their relationship to the market and less burdened by patriarchal traditions and prejudices.

Since the development of capitalism in the countryside was in many respects an irregular process proceeding on various levels in various places, it was possible for Khristovoverie to exist along with various tendencies of "Spiritual Christianity", Khristovoverie having passed through a complicated evolution, which is the subject of the following chapter.

The basic center of "Spiritual Christianity" became the Tambov province of Voronezh Guberniia, where at the beginning of the 1760s a fairly numerous group of "Spiritual Christians" was formed and became active. P. G. Ryndziunskii, a student of the anti-church movement in the Tambov area in the 1760s, wrote: "The peculiarity of Tambov province was connected in large measure with its border position between two economic regions of Russia. Adjoining the guberniias of the agricultural center with their strongly-developed serfdom, it on the other side bordered upon regions where large-scale landed estates were almost unknown, including the 'free Don". The lines dividing these two regions passed through Tambov province itself. While, according to the third census (1762), the enserfed population predominated in the northern and central uezds, in the two southern ones, Kozlov and Tambov, where the anti-church movement under review developed, serf peasants were only 33-34% of the entire taxable population and about two-thirds of the population was not personally dependent on landlords" (Ryndziunskii 1954: 159-160).

In the basic contingent of dependent peasants there existed several categories making up a significant group of state peasants, distinguished from the serf-landlord peasantry by a greater degree of economic independence. The position of state peasants, exploited by the serf-owning authorities, was unstable; the boundary separating their position, as formally not enserfed, from that of peasants belonging to landlords, was shaky and broke down in many cases. However that may be, state peasants were better able to manifest economic initiative than peasants belonging to landlords, even if the latter were on quit-rent. This was expressed by the participation of the state peasants in the market, which continued to grow in the second half of the 18th and especially in the beginning of the 19th century. What has been said applies in even greater degree to the category of state peasants called odnodvortsy.

Arising from the descendants of Moscow service gentry, called in the 16th and 17th centuries to plow the eastern and southern borders of the Russian lands, the mass of these small landowners was transferred to the state peasantry at the beginning of the 18th century. However, in relation to the various state burdens (taxation, military service) the odnodvortsy by comparison with other categories of state peasants were in a somewhat more advantageous position and were made equal to them only toward the end of the 18th century. According to the date of the third census (1762), the number of odnodvortsy in Russia exceeded half a million persons.

The Tambov region was an area with a very significant number of odnodvortsy. At the beginning of the 1830s, Tambov Guberniia in number of odnodvortsy occupied second place among the guberniias of the Russian Empire. In the 1760s in Tambov and especially Kozlov Uezds, the number of odnodvortsy exceeded the number of landlord-peasants.

The movement of "Spiritual Christians" in Tambov and Kozlov Uezds was the religio-social offspring of odnodvortsy and consisted mainly of the latter. The world-view of "Spiritual Christianity" developed in this milieu as a rejection of spiritual and any other bondage. The views designated by the participants of the anti-church movement of the 1760s themselves as "Spritual Christianity" was objectively nothing but the religious-moral assertion of the world of new human relationships in which the agriculturalist saw himself and others like him as freed from the fetters and tangles of serfdom and as having entered into the wide spaces of independent labor. In the last analysis, this was a view of society of free goods producers. But subjectively, "Spiritual Christians" were, probably, sincerely convinced that they—their teaching consisted of this—were only preaching the Christianity of apostolic times with its hints of community ownership; they were cleansing "spirit and truth" of such dead layers as icon worship, outward ritual, luxurious meaningless liturgy, superstitious worship of things and of every sort of "holy" object. In a word, the "Spiritual Christians" saw themselves as the champions of "eternal", "godly" truth, desecrated and disfigured by "human legends".

How did they think of this truth? In the last analysis, they saw it in the idea that the immemorial calling and possession of man is work and freedom: "God created man in his own image and likeness, *autonomous,* and he [man] wishes to have his sustenance *with his own hands.*" They saw their truth in collectivism and mutual aid: "... people should have property in common and give to each other without return, because they are brothers." They saw truth in not living in the bondage of external coercion. "The law", they maintained, "was made for the lawless". This meant that one had to trust not external law, but the internal one, i.e. that law which is embodied in the "spirit and truth" of man's reason and conscience. They saw truth, finally, not in bowing before external authority ("idols"), but in man's honoring man, for by this honor he praised God. These were the basic features of the dogma of "Spiritual Christianity", as it is reconstructed on the basis of testimony of participants in the anti-church movement in the Tambov area at the beginning of the 1760s (Ryndziunskii 1954: 172-180).

The demand for man's independence, based on the validity of and the freedom to manifest the forces and capabilities residing in him, was the ideological axis of "Spiritual Christianity", if we free it from its religious wrapping.

As P. G. Ryndziunskii concludes, "the Tambov free-thinkers justified the liberation of people (basically, of course, peasants) from the conditions of existence of slaves, and called for them to liberate themselves from the obligatory service to and dependence on the serf-holding state. Elevating in their own fashion the human dignity of each and every person, they maintained that people could get along without the authorities, supposedly set higher by a supernatural force, and live as free immediate producers of material goods" (Ryndziunskii 1954: 189).

Somewhere around the 1760s or 1770s, "Spiritual Christianity" divided into two tendencies, subsequently receiving the designations Dukhoborism and Molokanism.

The designation Dukhobortsy or Dukhobors had an ecclesiastical origin. At the end of the 17th century, these sectarians were called thus by their accusers in the official Church, who invested the name Dukhobortsy with the meaning that the sectarians were fighters against "the holy spirit" as the third person of the divine trinity. This designation was preserved by the sectarians, who invested it with the meaning that they were fighters for the spirit — i.e., for the revivification of the faith which had died in Russian Orthodoxy, for "spirit and truth".

As concerns the name Molokan, there are several versions of its origin. It is connected with the fact that the sectarians of this tendency, using the Gospel expression, called their teaching "spiritual milk", also that they used milk on "fast days", and finally that for a long time they lived near Molochnye Vody [Milky Waters]. Contemporary Molokans give only the first explanation. At the basis of the world-view of Dukhobors and Molokans lay the concept of "spirit and truth", which arose not later than the beginning of the 18th century and is already known to us, in contrast to Russian Orthodoxy as a religion of dead canons and authoritarian dogmas. For Dukhoborism, as for Molokanism, the concept of "spirit and truth" had in the last analysis (but precisely in the last analysis) one and the same underlying social cause: they were speaking of freeing man from serf dependence, from political and spiritual institutions which kept people in a condition of serf enslavement.

But the depth, breadth, decisiveness and consistency of the social protest, covered on the one hand by the religious forms of Dukhoborism and on the other by those of Molokanism, were not equal, which is explained by the unequal composition of their social bearers.

Consequently, the religious ideology of Dukhoborism on the one hand, and of Molokanism on the other, gave unequal scope for the initiative and activity of their followers. To the rule of the church and its hierarchs, to Russian Orthodoxy as the torture chamber of the thought and will of man, Dukhobors counterposed the concept of God as the active, creative element and force of love, penetrating, even if not to equal depth, each human being—a concept specially formulated by them, thus: "God is man".

Kolesnikov and Pobirokhin, who were mentioned above, preached along these lines as early as the 1760s.

Molokanism counterposed to the authority of the church the authority of the Bible, interpreted, however, not literally, but in "spirit and truth". Thus Molokanism, of which the son-in-law of Illarion Pobirokhin—Semen Uklein—became the head, enclosed the freedom of thought of its adherents within norms limiting their independence on the religious and finally on the social plane. Even so, Molokanism preserved a certain mobility and elasticity of religio-ideological norms, connected both with the wide circle of questions embraced by the material of the Bible (and furthermore, as we know, in a very contradictory fashion), and with the principle of interpreting the Bible in "spirit and truth". The leaders of Molokanism very easily in this or that situation, or in this or that stage of development of the sect, read from the Bible that "truth", and drew from it precisely that "spirit", which most closely corresponded to the developing situation. The reader will find in the corresponding chapters a more complete and detailed characterization of the teachings of the Dukhobors and the Molokans as well as a study of the social causes conditioning the differences in teachings between the two sects.

Khristovoverie, and following it Dukhoborism and Molokanism, were the basic forms of Russian religious sectarianism.

Religious sectarianism appeared as a social movement, born out of the condition of life of a dependent peasantry at that stage of its history, when it slowly but inexorably and with constantly growing force and speed was drawn into goods and monetary relationships.

With all its obscurity and fanatically religious conceptions, early Christianity ideologically strengthened and formed the vital interests of its social bearers. The conditions of public life of the dependent peasantry drawn into commodity and money relationships, made especially relevant to it forms of ideology based in one way or another on the independence and initiative of a person, rewarding his developing initiative, aiding the development of his quick-mindedness and common sense, justifying his attention to the demands and affairs of earthly life, and at the same time freeing man's spiritual world from the tyranny of authorities and dogmas.

That sectarianism was formed on this sort of ideological pathway there is no doubt, just as it is also completely clear that social protest in the form of religious sectarianism was distinguished by primitivism, timidity, inconsistency and obscurity. However reactionary the religious form in which the sectarians invested their social protest may have been in itself, the protest was historically conditioned by the fact of the dominance of the system of serfdom, in which the Church and the ideology it preached continued to play a most important role.

Editor's Note

Note A. In the Russian Orthodox Church, the "black clergy" (from the color of their vestments) are those in the lower orders — up to and including parish priests and members of cathedral staff, who are supposed to be married. The "white clergy" are those who have taken monastic vows; they are celibate — although they may enter after being widowed — and they alone are eligible for appointment to higher ecclesiastical office.

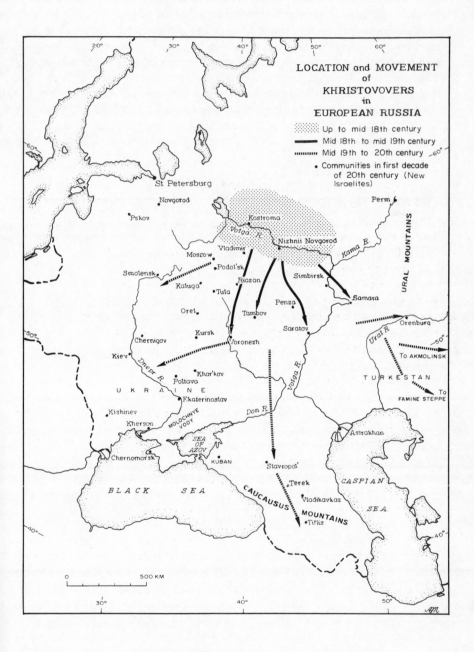

LOCATION and MOVEMENT
of
KHRISTOVOVERS
in
EUROPEAN RUSSIA

Up to mid 18th century
Mid 18th to mid 19th century
Mid 19th to 20th century
• Communities in first decade
  of 20th century (New
  Israelites)

2

The Khristovover Sect ("Khlysty")

1. Contradictions in Pre-Reform Khristovoverie and its Schism at the End of the 1880s and Beginning of the 1890s

The pre-Reform period was a time of great changes in the ideology, internal structure, and dynamics of growth and geography of distribution of the Khristovover movement.

Until the middle of the 18th century this movement was localized in the non-Chernozem provinces of the center and of the upper Volga area — uezds gravitating towards Moscow and Nizhegorod. From the middle of the 18th to the middle of the 19th century, it penetrated into the Chernozem, Tambov and Voronezh Guberniias and in the Volga Guberniias of Samara, Saratov and Simbirsk. From the second half of the 19th century Khristovoverie ever more strongly began to spread into the Northern Caucasus and the Don region, where at the end of the 19th and beginning of the 20th century there developed the most numerous sites of Khristovoverie.

This steady advance of Khristovoverie from north to south, this geographic shift, had a profound socio-economic base: Khristovoverie moved like a shadow following the spread and development of bourgeois [capitalist] forms of economy in Russia. Its rise and original development are noted in non-Chernozem reigons of the center, where the quit-rent system of exploitation predominated, peasant crafts were developed, and the ties of the peasantry with the market and peasant seasonal migrant labor were increasing.

The subsequent history of Khristovoverie was connected with the Tambov area, but now already in equal measure with the milieu of quit-rent peasants and with that of peasant odnodvortsy. On the edge of the 19th-20th centuries Khristovoverie was most widely distributed in the foothills of the Caucasus and on the Don — guberniias where the capitalist system of agriculture predominated. The stream of people moved primarily in this direction, for it was here more than anywhere else that there were developed market grain and animal husbandry farms.

It goes without saying that Khristovoverie was not the same thing at various times and in various economic regions. Even in the second half of the 18th century it began to divide into the Skoptsy movement on the one hand and on the other "Spiritual Christianity". This led to reforms in Khristovoverie which took place in the first quarter of the 19th century in the Tambov area, where the Khristovovers included not a few peasant odnodvortsy and also peasants belonging to the palace and to landlords who had gotten rich.

The serf peasant Avvakum Kopylov of the village of Perevoz, Kirsanovskii Uezd, laid the foundation for a new tendency in Khristovoverie — the so-called Postniki [fasters]. Stengthening the ascetic taboos of Khristovoverie, Kopylov in some degree blocked the transfer of Khristovovers to the Skoptsy movement, which from the second half of the 18th century spread uninterruptedly in the Tambov area, primarily in Morshansk Uezd.

However, it is not his ascetic taboos but his religious innovations — the teaching of the personification of Christ in elect people — which should be considered the chief element of Kopylov's reforms. This teaching was opposed to the concept of the old ideologists of the sect about Christ as the spirit, living in each Khristovover. Inasmuch as the fullness of spiritual perfection henceforth was incarnate in Avvakum Kopylov and in him alone (he declared himself a living Christ), the power of leadership over his co-thinkers was also transferred to him. This was a reform directed toward limiting the democratic traditions and customs inherited from the early times of the development of Khristovoverie.

S. D. Bondar', noting that "the Christological views" of the Tambov Postniki "were sharply distinguished from the views of the old Khristov-shchina", formulated their essence as follows: "The old Khlystovshchina thought of the idea of the incarnation of Christ *collectivistically:* Christ is a spirit which lives in the whole clan, settling in each member of the sect. The sect of Postniki thought of the idea of Christ *individualistically:* Christ is the Holy Spirit, living on earth in *special, chosen flesh.* Thus, for example, the Christ-spirit lives in Avvakum Kopylov, then in his son Filipp and finally in the wife of the latter, Anis'ia Kopylova" (Bondar' 1916: 19; my emphasis).

The Postnik tendency in Khristovoverie won adherents from the old Khristovoverie, found new adherents in Russian Orthodoxy and already in the first post-Reform decade penetrated from Tambov into the neighboring Riazan and Voronezh Guberniias, and also into Saratov, Penza and Simbirsk Guberniias.

But even at the end of the 30s after the death of Avvakum Kopylov, there occurred a schism in the Postnik movement out of which there developed a group headed by Perfil Petrovich Katasonov, a state peasant, who had at one time worked for Avvakum Kopylov, and subsequently grew rich and became a renter of watermills in the village of Afanas'evka, Tambov Uezd. Among the first 15 followers of Katasonov, seven belonged to the merchant milieu, three were state peasants, four were peasants belonging to landlords, and one was a meshchan [tradesman]. Katasonov firmly supported the teaching of Avvakum Kopylov about Christ personified in the elect. On the other hand, he changed a number of food taboos of the Postnik movement, moderated the manifestations of mystical ecstasy during prayer meetings and, without destroying the principle of celibacy, at the same time in some degree legitimized natural relationships of the sexes. The sources note that Katasonov entirely abolished the ecstatic rites.[1]

Whether this was so or not cannot be reliably known, but after Katasonov declared himself to be Christ, it was logical to remove the ecstatic rites, whose sense as for Khristovovers lay precisely in the fact that each one in an ecstatic fit supposedly found Christ in himself. However, the long decades of existence of the practice of religious rites, during which Khristovovers not only experienced mystical joy together, but, what was still more important, recognized themselves equal to each other in Christ, still got the upper hand over the new Christological doctrine.

The ecstatic religious rites in the Katasonov congregations continued, but along with them, the religious importance of the so-called "actions" introduced in Avvakum Kopylov's time increased. Thus, for example, at the prayer-meeting certain participants changed into tattered and dirty clothing, and others into new and clean ones as a sign of disapproval or approval of the way of life of various members of the congregation (VIRA 1961: 265). Wishing to unmask the "spiritual blindness" of this or that sectarian, they bound his head with a handkerchief, etc. (Bondar' 1916: 54-55).

Katasonov's followers saw themselves as a spiritually elect pecple — "Israel", united around their leader — the living Christ — and subordinate to his will. They were, as it were, creating on earth "the kingdom of God", separated from all the rest of society by those special beliefs, ritual, and moral rules which made up the characteristics of their teachings, traditions and way of life. They thought themselves the heirs of the primitive Christians and the continuers of their cause.

Their theological doctrine consisted in the recognition of a spirit, eternally existing, which was absolutely perfect and in this sense "holy", which sometimes penetrated an ordinary person, who bore the name of Christ and became thus the son of the "Spirit" — the son of God. They taught that the Spirit is immortal in a continuous line of elect bearers of whom Perfil Katasonov was considered one. But in distinction to the followers of

---

[1] "That walking or dancing did not exist in Perfil Petrov's (Katasonov's — A. K.) group is shown unanimously by the evidence of all his followers ...", wrote the Tambov governor to the Ministry of Internal Affairs in a secret note of November 26, 1851 (VIRA 1961: 270).

Khristovoverie in its most traditional forms, which considered their union as a "kingdom of God" on earth, consisting of equally valuable and equal "citizens" of this utopian kingdom, the kingdom of the "God" Perfil Katasonov consisted not of "citizens", but of subjects, and the more widely it spread, the higher the role of the newly-established hierarchy, crowned by the figure of the "divine" leader, was elevated.

Precisely that form which was given to Khristovoverie by Perfil Katasonov, especially in the post-Reform 1860s-80s, was most widely distributed in its traditional center: Tambov Guberniia, and after it in Voronezh Guberniia, and also (and this was most symptomatic), it conquered in the 1870s-1880s an enormous new periphery, Rostov-on-Don Uezd of Ekaterinoslav Guberniia, Stavropol' Guberniia, the Don, Kuban and Terek districts.

As S. D. Bondar' writes, "in the 1870s, Perfilov congregations existed already in many settlements and stanitsy of the Northern Caucasus. Then Perfil's sect appeared in the Guberniias of Smolensk, Riazan, Samara and Astrakhan. In the 1880s, the total number of followers of Perfil in all of Russia reached 25,000 persons" (Bondar' 1916: 25).

Although increasingly intense migration processes in the post-Reform period undoubtedly played their role in the diffusion of the Katasonovite movement—in the Kuban region alone (according to the 1897 census) there were slightly fewer than 140,000 emigrants from Voronezh and Tambov Guberniias (Rashin 1956: 75)—the success of this new form of Khristovoverie was primarily attributable to the sermons of Katasonov himself and of his associates, which found a fairly wide response in the countryside. The basic mass of followers of Katasonov were found not in the central, but precisely in the southern guberniias and districts. It was not representatives of the category of "Inogorodnye", so widely represented in the Don, Kuban and Terek regions, but precisely the Cossacks who formed the nucleus of the Katasonovite congregation in these localities. We are faced with the fact that, among the various forms of Khristovoverie existing in the second half of the 19th century, the greatest success fell not to those of its forms whose structure and teachings had in the past been distinguished by elements of democratism, but precisely to those which gave up their democratic traditions.

Thus, the popularity of Khristovoverie in the 1800s-1880s was less and less connected with its significance as a form of political protest of the lower classes of the people, although Khristovoverie remained a movement of direct opposition to the ruling Russian Orthodox Church and obliquely to those socio-economic conditions under which it was the ruling church. As the popular masses of the people not only were more widely drawn into open struggles with the landlords but also felt with growing sharpness the consequences of social differentiation within the peasantry itself, Khristovoverie changed its base from the interests of the socially lower classes to the interests of the bourgeois upper stratum of the peasantry. The reforms of Kopylov and Katasonov were consistent steps in this direction.

Given the large dimensions which the Katasonovite movement assumed and the social and property inequality of its participants, it eventually demanded new forms of organization and centralization. Katasonov broke up the numerous congregations of his followers (there is information that the number of his congregations reached 1,200 (Bonch-Bruevich 1911a: LVI) into districts headed by administering "apostles". Among them emerged Petr Lordugin, administering the Northern Caucasus congregations, Roman Likhachev, administering the Western Kuban congregations and Petr Petrov, administering the Don congregations.

Among the other important figures in the Katasonovite movement there was a certain Kuz'ma, a peasant from Tambov Guberniia, a person of extraordinary mystical exaltation, who was a kind of supreme prophet under Katasonov.[2] A zealous preacher of the new direction in Khristovoverie was the peasant from Voronezh Guberniia, Vasilii Fedorovich Mokshin, who enjoyed great authority in the Voronezh circles of followers of Katasonov and the personal trust of the "Christ" himself.[3]

Thus, Katasonov gave to Khristovoverie traits of a peculiar church organization: a "clergy" separated from the "community" and elevated over it as a spiritual authority holding the masses of ordinary believers in subjugation and exploiting them.

Among the "hierarchy" founded by Katasonov, there were large bourgeois property owners, like for example the "apostle" Egor Matveev, a rich landowner and an important owner of cattle from Medvezh'e Uezd of Stavropol' Guberniia, or the important figure of the Katasonovite movement Stepan Chepakov from Stavropol' Uezd, the owner of large landholdings, or Iosif Eremenko of Kuban Oblast, who became prominent after the death of Katasonov, the founder of a "trading industrial cooperative" in which he and seven other Katasonovites invested capital in the amount of 40,000 rubles and immovable property worth 20,000 rubles. In the masses of the Katasonovite movement there were attempts at an independent social creativity directed at preventing the exploitation by part of the leaders.

In the 1870s, in one of the stanitsy situated in the region of Mozdok, there existed five small Katasonovite communities whose participants combined the conditions of production and daily life and practiced community distribution

---

[2] In the folklore of the Katasonovites, Kuz'ma was sung about along with the founder of the sect himself: "between heaven and earth Perfil lived with Kuz'ma" (Rozhdestvenskii and Uspenskii 1912: 15).

[3] According to a later legend Katasonov designated Mokshin as his successor.

of the products of labor. The families comprising each community lived not in individual houses, but two or three families to a house, combining all valuable property with the exception of the clothes they wore. Fences between the courtyards were taken down, and each of the five communities utilized a vast common courtyard.

It is difficult to say whether each dormitory was a primary economic unit. In any case each community was an economic link in an economic union, formed by five communities. All agricultural work was carried on collectively, and income in kind and in money divided among the communities more or less according to plan.

As concerns the income in kind, it was distributed in the following manner: grain was preserved for the following harvest and in case of a crop failure; part of the grain was set aside for sale; the remaining agricultural produce was used in the community for personal consumption according to the number of mouths to be fed. As concerns the monetary part of the income—i.e., the income derived from the realization of agricultural produce set aside for sale, this did not become the individual property of the community members. The major part of the monetary income received went for the satisfaction of common economic needs (the constructing of farm buildings, and the acquisition of cattle in the case of plague, etc.). The income remaining after the deduction of these sums was sent in part to the treasury of that territorial unit to which the Khristovovers of the given stanitsa belonged, and in part to Tambov Guberniia, where, we may suppose, there existed a central treasury for Khristovovers of the Katasonovite persuasion (Fedoseevets 1881: 37-40).

Communes combining production and daily life were a relatively rare phenomenon in Khristovoverie although the commune just described was not an isolated case. Contemporary with it there existed communes in three stanitsy situated near Ekaterinodar (Fedoseevets 1881: 39).

In the decades immediately succeeding the Reform, communes with their collectivism of property, labor and daily life and distribution served the socially lower classes of Khristovoverie as a means of defense from exploitation by the upper classes, and was an attempt to assert their economic interests in circumstances in which survivals of serfdom predominated.

Materials available to us pertaining to the end of the 19th and the beginning of the 20th centuries contain no information about Katasonovite communes in the regions of Mozdok and Ekaterinodar or anywhere else. It is clear that this social experiment by the lower orders did not stand the test, that communes not only did not prevent the growth of social and economic contradictions in the Katasonovite milieu, but themselves fell victim to these contradictions, like the Dukhobor and Molokans communes, as will be shown in the relevant chapters.

In 1885, Katasonov died, and the contradictions of the movement he led immediately surfaced. The situation created in the Katasonovite movement after the death of its leader was characterized by an eyewitness in the following words: "... There was a terrible commotion. The heads of various guberniias and regions declared themselves leaders, each one saying that the little father, as he (Katasonov—A K.) was called, transferred power to him. And suddenly it was categorically declared that we don't need leaders, his word is in us and we are saved by it ... a kind of set of fiefdoms was formed: in Voronezh Guberniia, Ivan Markov; in Donetsk Oblast, Semen Berezhnov and Ustin'ia Ivanovna; in Tambov Guberniia, Matrena Maksimovna and Avdotia Maksimovna; in the Kuban Oblast, Roman Likhachev; in Stavropol' Guberniia, Iakov Kliushin; in Georgiev, Terek Oblast, Petr Danilovich Lordukhin; in Valdikavkaz, Ivan Fadeev, etc." (Bonch-Bruevich 1911a: vi).

V. F. Mokshin made an attempt to assume the role of the "Christ"—the leader. In the course of almost a decade (the second half of the 1880s and the first half of the 1890s) Mokshin was the most influential of the leaders of the Katasonovite movement. To the Katasonovites of "Old Israel" Mokshin contrasted "New Israel ... powerful, free, liberated from every prejudice, superstition and ignorance" (Bonch-Bruevich 1911a: vi).

Precisely what was the ballast of "prejudices, supersitions and ignorance" from which Mokshin intended to free the Katasonovite movement? Mokshin attempted to introduce "progress" into the Katasonovite movement, making various references to changing circumstances in the surrounding world.

In fact, "progress" as conceived by Mokshin led to further centralization and strengthening of the hierarchical structure of the Khristovover communities, directed against the masses. There followed a distinct limitation of the mystical ideas still preserved in the Katasonovite movement, which allowed the ordinary sectarian to manifest religious creativity, sometimes speaking out at religious gatherings in the role of "prophet", and accusing the leaders of the sect.

This is why, as the contradictions between the upper and the lower strata of the sect deepened, its leaders did not wish to tolerate further the traditions of early Khristovoverie, which they now denegrated as "superstition and ignorance".

Mokshin wished to lead the Katasonovite movement further along the path of bourgeois "progress", to reform it in the spirit of the interests and conceptions of the bourgeois elements which gave the movement its tone. On this path he met not only the competition of other leading figures of the Katasonovite movement, but also the opposition of the lower strata upholding "the old times".

At this time, in the words of the Stavropol' Katasonovites,

> "Israel has strayed from the path
> And bowed down to an idol,
> They moaned, they cried,
> They strove for false Gods,
> Into the chasm, into the abyss they were thrown"
>
> (Bonch-Bruevich 1911a: 588).

In 1894, Mokshin died. In that same year there was a congress of his adherents in Voronezh in which V. S. Lubkov, who had been advanced by Mokshin as his heir, took part.

2. The Reorganization and Centralization of Khristovoverie Along Bourgeois-Church Lines

The New Israelite movement founded by Mokshin, which arose on the basis of the Voronezh organizations of the Katasonovite movement, developed further mainly at the expense of the Katasonovite communities both in the central and in the southern guberniias.

We do not find substantial differences between the social composition of New Israel on the one hand and the Katasonovite movement which preceded it on the other. On the whole, the same social elements determined the face of both movements, but the development of these elements and their interrelationship, of course, did not remain stationary. Direct observation of the life of the New Israelites and contact with them led V. D. Bonch-Bruevich to the followng characterization: "The age-old peasantry, of course, served as the main mass of the New Israelite community. The second most numerous group were elements from the cities and the Cossack settlements: market farmers, hoticulturalists, small tradesmen, artisans and craftsmen, and also railroad workers and white-collar personnel. There were few skilled workers, but there were some. The wealthier elements were also encountered — the owners of large and small bakeries and of small artisan and craft shops and of retail stores of various sizes. But prosperous urban elements in the community were an insignificant minority" (Bonch-Bruevich 1911a: xl-xli).

Let us note especially that "an insignificant minority" among the New Israelites consisted precisely of urban "prosperous elements". The basic contingent of New Israelites were from the countryside, and it included not a few rural magnates and kulaks.

Vasilii Semenovich Lubkov, descended from peasants who had settled in the Uezd city of Bobrov, Voronezh Guberniia, was born in 1869. In 1886, he attached himself to Mokshin's tendency and preached sermons, but was arrested in 1890 and exiled to the Transcaucasus.

At the congress in 1894 to which Lubkov came from exile, he was recognized as the successor "Christ". Lubkov proposed a plan for "a new household management" — in other words, a proposal for the organization of the New Israelite sect — and set about its implementation.

All of Russia was considered the territory of Lubkov's "kingdom of God", divided by him into "seven parts of the world", corresponding to seven local churches, which united the local New Israelite communities. Lubkov administered the seven countries of his kingdom with the help of "archangels" appointed by himself, each of whom in his own country fulfilled the function of supervisor, informing the "Christ" Lubkov about all events in the territories under supervision and comprising the "all-seeing eye of the Christ". Executive functions were implemented by the chiefs of the countries: they were the leaders of the local churches appointed in turn by Lubkov.

The communities formed in each of the given territories of the local church had their "elders", who led the services, carried out rituals, and in various ways looked after the life of the congregation. The "elders" were appointed and removed by the congregation but in both cases with the personal agreement of Lubkov.

Lubkov also had a kind of consultative organ, composed of four evangelists, twelve apostles, twelve prophets and 72 men of apostolic rank appointed by him. It also included seven archangels. With the exception of cases in which Lubkov convened his supreme council, called "the heavenly inspectorate", its members traveled from place to place announcing the will of the Christ to the believers. Each of the apostles and each of the archangels in turn personally served the "Christ" Lubkov — the former for one month a year and the latter for 52 and a quarter days. A special role was set aside for the *blizhnaia* [womanfriend] (mistress) of the "Christ", through whom petitions of the "aggrieved and needy" passed to him. On especially important matters congresses were held. They could take place without the personal participation of the "Christ", but only after his sanction did the decisions of the congress acquire force (Bonch-Bruevich 1911a: lxii-lxxiv; Bondar' 1916: 61).

The pre-Revolutionary student of sectarianism, M. Muratov, who in his time was close to Tolstoyan circles, characterized Lubkov as a person of great "energy and will-power", who was not stopped "by any hindrance" and considered "only his own wishes" (Muratov 1916: 187).

With those personal characteristics and with the help of the organization worked out by him, Lubkov ruled absolutely over the mass of New Israelites. The creation of the new hierarchy in all its important links was already completed by Lubkov by the spring of 1895. Undoubtedly, Lubkov had thought up the approach to the leadership of New Israel and its reorganization even in the period of exile while Mokshin was alive. It was probably then that the candidates were chosen for the "heavenly inspectorate". Lubkov arrived at the congress in 1894 with a plan already prepared for the new organization of the sect. It was also characteristic that the "archangels" were appointed by Lubkov not at the congress in Voronezh but on his return from the Transcaucasus.

Lubkov's reform in its own way considered the growth of internal contradictions in the Katasonovite movement and the internecine struggle of its leaders. The exceptional attention which Lubkov gave to the centralization of power in New Israel and with which he began his activity is in the highest degree indicative. Lubkov did not deceive himself with the hope of seeking ideals and slogans which in and of themselves could have inspired and welded its followers into a unified whole. In the framework of the religious world-view at that time, such ideals and slogans simply did not exist. Lubkov had to replace the unity of believers, which had been seriously undermined by contradictions, with external forms of organization. Essentially, Lubkov completed the formation of Khristovoverie on the basis of a church organization which had already been begun under Katasonov.

Of course, the New Israelite hierarchy was different from the hierarchy of the Russian Orthodox Church. Formally, the elders, the preceptors, had no superiority over the other members of the congregation and in particular did not receive real compensation for their services (Bonch-Bruevich 1911a: lxxiii). And at the same time, it cannot be considered accidental that the attacks on Lubkov by Khristovover activists who considered themselves preservers of Katasonov's precepts were precisely along the lines of accusing the New Israelite hierarchy of simony. "The seducer Lubkov", wrote Fedor Poslenichenko, the head of one of the sects of the "Old Israelite" tendency, "dispenses all prophetic and apostolic ranks exclusively for metal, and trades in the law exclusively in order to receive material advantage" (Ostroumov 1912).

Lubkov did not succeed in his reforms without a struggle. Even in the first years of this reform, one of his followers, Vasilii Grachev, stood out against Lubkov, having drawn away several hundred of Lubkov's followers whom he pronounced "true spiritual Christians". Grachev's followers returned in many respects to the tradition of pre-Katasonovite Khristovoverie (Bondar' 1916: 80-82).

The organizational forms of New Israel, erected on foundations laid out by Kopylov and Katasonov, were only a part of the transformation implemented by Lubkov. It follows that organizational forms alone, however well thought-out they were, could not support the existence of a movement which had thousands of followers in a number of southern, central, and western guberniias of Russia.

Lubkov proposed a re-evaluation of the ideological bases of Khristovoverie but in this field he, as it were, crossed out all those innovations which had been introduced into Khristovoverie by Kopylov and Katasonov.

M. Muratov was quite correct when he wrote, characterizing the new features distinguishing Lubkov's teachings: "He attempted to develop and strengthen rationalistic elements in the views of his followers and did much in this direction: little by little he abolished the fasts, finally repudiated the worship of icons and the carrying out of the rituals of the Russian Orthodox Church, and finally set up an order for ordinary prayer meetings in which all services were reduced to the singing of spiritual songs and the sermons of the preceptors" (Muratov 1916: 187-188).

We have had occasion to note those features in Katasonov's teaching which went in the direction of relieving Khristovoverie of the traditions of the mystical and ascetic dominant in it. In Lubkov's teaching there remained from Khristovoverie chiefly the idea of personifications of Christ, appearing in succeeding generations. This same idea was preserved in Dukhoborism: true, at one time it had adopted this idea under the influence of Khristovoverie. In practice in the New Israelite congregations, cases of various kinds of mystical-ecstatic phenomena were not very rare. Ecstatic religious ritual, "the descent of the spirit", "speaking in tongues", "actions", and fasting—these were the "superstitions" from the weight of which the founders of the New Israel called for people to free themselves, but survivals of which were still strong.

We will consider the internal connection between the actions of Mokshin and then of Lubkov against the mystical-ecstatic and ascetic "superstitions" of Khristovoverie and the spirit of the organizational reforms implemented by Lubkov.

Objectively, Lubkov's organizational reforms were a recognition of the fact that faith in a common ideal and service to it were increasingly losing their significance as a force unifying believers and guaranteeing the internal unity of the community. The ideals of the New Israelites were pale, vague, indefinite. It was not by ideals, but by words about them, that preachers of the lower and upper ranks supported the spiritual life of the New Israelite community. In these conditions the New Israelite movement could not do without strict norms of organization and centralization.

When Mokshin and Lubkov took up arms against "the supersition" of mysticism and ecstasy in Khristovoverie, they were paying a certain tribute of recognition to the success of the education of their day. The owners of large farms, and the owners of shops and craft institutions could not bypass the achievements of technology and agriculture and could not help but be penetrated by the "rationalistic" spirit of the times. As V. D. Bonch-Bruevich noted, among the New Israelites both men and women were predominantly literate (Bonch-Bruevich 1911a: cxxiii).

But the matter was not only and not so much that. Mokshin and Lubkov spoke for purging the religious practice of Khristovoverie of its distinguishing enthusiastic forms at a time when the enthusiasm of the Khristovovers was consistently diminishing. "Spiritual joy" once served Khristovovers as a surrogate for the lack of earthly joys, but it also symbolized the expectation of the imminent approach of a joyous life on earth. This is no longer existed.

D. Konovalov, who studied the psycho-physiology of religious ecstasy in Russian sectarianism, made an acute observation: "... where ecstatic excitation grows weak ... artificial body movements are used with increased intensity, and instead of an exalted seizure of a religious emotion, you get a picture of the stubborn squeezing out of ecstasy" (Konovalov 1914: 123).

Ecstatic excitability in this or that sect, although it had its own neurophysiological apparatus of special interest to the researcher, still depended primarily on the conditions of the time and the milieu, on the peculiarities of these sects as religious and social movements. In late Khristovoverie, religious ecstasy was increasingly reduced to the "squeezing out of ecstasy", and this made the call of the founders of New Israel for putting an end to ecstasy as "a prejudice", "superstition", and "ignorance" especially timely.

Nevertheless, the "rationalism" of New Israel differed in many respects from the "rationalism" characteristic of, for example, the Baptist sect.

Lubkov worked out "a formula of transition" from mysticism to "rationalism," without which he could not count on popularity for his teaching in the wide circles of believers. These were mysteries or, in the terminology of the New Israelite, "co-actions". Mysteries marked all the basic events in the history of the New Israelite movement.

Lubkov instilled in his followers an understanding of the development of the New Israelite movement as reproducing under contemporary conditions the entire cycle of events of evangelical history and, what is more, in the same sequence. Thus, Lubkov carried out the choosing of his evangelists, prophets and apostles which took place in 1895 in the form of a theatrical action under the title of "The Last Supper", in which he himself played the role of Christ. The theatrical action corresponded to the Gospel story and took place in the presence of 800 of Lubkov's followers, but The Last Supper itself was played out, as was fitting, in secret from those present.

For laying out the basis of his dogma Lubkov utilized the Gospel subject of the Sermon on the Mount in a theatrical version. The scene was played on the 20th of October, 1900. The entire "heavenly inspectorate" took part in the ceremony. Lubkov gave a sermon to the New Israelites present, who numbered as many as a thousand persons.

In 1905 in Piatigorsk, Lubkov was the central figure of the mystery of "transfiguration" which was not lacking in irony, having in mind the declaration of loyalty to the regime which Lubkov formed at that time, about which more below. In 1907 there took place a succeeding mystery — "the ascent of

Mt. Zion". Lubkov's entire "household organization" with its archangels, apostles, men of apostolic rank, prophets, his entire "city of God", presented a mystery with a good 1,500 to 2,000 extras, whose roles were given to the ordinary participants of the New Israelite movement.

Such was the new form in which Lubkov paid tribute to the mystical traditions of Khristovoverie, at the same time limiting them in order to make room in his teaching for the "rationalistic" trend of the time.

In the name of his New Israelite followers, Lubkov announced, "We recognize only one thing as deity: the teachings of common sense, which is the spirit of life" (Bonch-Bruevich 1911a: 25). And further: "In the full sense, the day of the Lord will come when the mind of the Christ merges with the spirit and with the free thought of men ..." (*ibid.*). Hence: "... each word read which speaks of supernatural events and phenomena which are higher than human understanding (Lubkov is speaking of the Gospels and other "holy" books — A. K.) must be brought into agreement with the good sense of the mind of Christ" (Bonch-Bruevich 1911a: 48-49), i.e., "be subjected to careful rational study" (Bonch-Bruevich 1911a: 49). The basis for a "rational study" of the Bible is provided, Lubkov continues, by the fact that "in the written holy books there are errors, since they have gone through multi-volume combinations, translations and transcriptions by countless human hands and minds, and therefore many articles can by no means be recognized as God-inspired writings ..." (*ibid.*).

The appealing to "common sense", even to "the free mind of man", acquired in the system of dogmatic beliefs of the New Israelites the highest significance. The small and middle bourgeois property owners, living by all sorts of calculations, both in their households and by way of trade, valued "sobriety of judgment", and freely attributed self-sufficient significance to their own internal world. For the circle of ordinary New Israelites, the appeal to reason served the interests of the negation of external authority, of the struggle against deprivation of rights, against economic and spiritual enslavement. However much pre-Revolutionary researchers of sectarianism counterpose mystical sectarianism to rational, in reality the Khristovover mystics even at the beginning of the 18th century adopted the criteria of "common sense" in their critique of Russian Orthodoxy.

As the ascetic prohibitions of old Khristovoverie were eliminated among the New Israelites, and various forms of the manifestation of religious ecstasy were crowded out of their religious practice, they came close in their religious views to Dukhoborism. At a time when a large mass of Dukhobors, persecuted by the Autocracy and the Church, left Russia, the New Israelite movement developed in the guberniias of the south, center and west of Russia as a kind of new edition of Dukhoborism. The following sociological experiment conducted by V. D. Bonch-Bruevich in 1910 deserves attention:

"In order to be completely convinced in fact," wrote V. D. Bonch-Bruevich, "of the similarity of views of New Israel and the Dukhobors, I proposed when setting out for the Kholodno Dukhobors that a New Israelite accompany me.... This sociological experiment was highly important, since in the encounter of representatives of these two oldest sects in Russia, I hoped conclusively to establish the degree of similarity and difference of the tendencies they practiced" (Bonch-Bruevich 1911c: 239).

The meeting organized by Bonch-Bruevich between the New Israelites and the Dukhobors showed that representatives of these tendencies "at once began to talk, to explain complicated questions in completely similar Aesopian language, so close together and so clearly, that it was as if they had always lived from year to year and from day to day inseparable from one another" (Bonch-Bruevich 1911a: xxv).

It is possible that in the encounter organized by Bonch-Bruevich, "there came together representatives of two independent broad popular organizations, who not only had never seen one another *but had almost never heard of one another*" (*ibid.;* my emphasis).

However, as a rule, the leaders of New Israel were knowledgeable people. In November 1909, representatives of the Taganrog, Rostov-on-Don, Ekaterinodar and other New Israelites presented a "Report" to the Synod, in which they categorically maintained that "the sect of New Israel has nothing at all in common with the Khlysty but rather has close fraternal ties with the Dukhobors who once migrated from Russia to Canada" (TsGIAL, div. 796, f. 190, s.u. 59, sh. 29). The "Report's" authors, as follows from its subsequent text, indignantly and hotly denied the Khristovover origin, as if they had to vindicate their descent from Adam and Eve against the assertion of their descent from ape-like ancestors.

It is characteristic that, as distinct from the leaders, the lower ranks of the New Israelite sect felt solidarity with representatives of other sectarian groups as being similarly exploited by the ruling church. At the turn of this century, a song evolved among them:

"The evil hairy priests
Make frequent collections in the households;
Whoever gives them little—
They call 'Dukhobors'.
By their frequent collections in the households
They wiped the thresholds with their tails;
Whoever would give them little—
They called 'Khlysty'.
These priests in the households
Knocked on all the doors;
Whoever would give them little—   (Rozhdestvenskii and
They were called 'Molokans'."   Uspenskii 1912: 338)

Let us note — although this does not diminish the lack of principle shown by the authors of the "Report" — that their appeal to the Synod was called forth by the fear that being equated with the "Khlysty" would deprive the New Israelites of the right to legalization according to the Ukaz of October 17, 1906.

Study of the relationship of the New Israelite movement to Dukhoborism has great scientific interest from the point of view of recognition of the regularities of development of sectarianism. As we know, those who adhered to Khristovoverie at the end of the 17th and the beginning of the 18th century were mainly quit-rent peasants in the non-chernozem regions of the center of Russia. Though they were connected with the market and gradually drawn into commodity and money relationships, they were not in an independent relationship to the market, since they were serfs bound to the noblemen by quit-rent. Khristovoverie served them as a form of social protest against external dependence, and as a peculiar ideology of self-assertion as free producers. But among the peasant *odnodvortsy,* as factual data relating to the mid-18th century show, Khristovoverie was not adopted as a religious form of social protest. Odnodvortsy were distinguished from quit-rent peasants by the fact that they were not personally dependent on the landlord, being (like all categories of state peasants, to which the odnodvortsy also belonged) feudally dependent on the serf regime. And still, as N. M. Druzhinin wrote, "The system of extra-economic constraint on state lands never took the form of property rights and, in spite of the arbitrariness and force of the crown administration, was combined with a *recognition of the personal freedom of the peasant, his right to independently dispose of his labor*" (Druzhinin 1958: II, 572; my emphasis — A. K.).

The odnodvortsy were significantly more independent in their relationship to the market than the quit-rent peasants. We noted above that in this milieu in the middle of the 18th century "Spiritual Christianity" developed, soon splitting into Dukhoborism and Molokanism.

In the middle and second half of the 18th century, Dukhoborism, Molokanism and Khristovoverie co-existed, but the social base of the latter gradually altered and narrowed. "Until recently", N. M. Druzhinin wrote, "little attention was paid in the historical literature to the enormous proportion of this category (state peasants — A. K.) of rural producers: gradually growing in number, it at the beginning of the 1890s comprised 45% of the peasant population of European Russia" (Druzhinin 1958: II, 571).

By the beginning of the 19th century, Khristovoverie, having steadily lost its original base, was crowded out by Dukhobors and related tendencies of "Spiritual Christianity".

During the period of the Reform, the process of crowding out of Khristovoverie by other forms of sectarianism sped up significantly. There were ever more eloquent instances indicating the extent to which Khristovoverie continued to exist only at the price of gradual renunciation of those traditions which at one time characterized it as one of the manifestations of democratic protest, even if expressed in a fantastic-mystical form. The reforms of Kopylov and especially Katasonov convince us of this. In the 1880s, Mokshin already came out with an open demand that Khristovoverie be freed from "prejudices, superstition, ignorance", and Lubkov distinguished one kind of Khristovoverie from another to such an extent that there is significant reason not only to note the parallel between New Israel and Dukhoborism contemporary with it, but to consider New Israel as it was described in the literature, as New Dukhoborism (Kuntsevich 1912: 33-36).

However, New Israel was not a simple repetition of Dukhoborism — the more so since Dukhoborism did not remain unchanged. For all the common features between the two movements under discussion, there existed differences both of creed and of an organizational character. For example, as distinct from Dukhoborism, New Israel had no principle of dynastic inheritance of religious power, requiring that the succeeding Christ be the "flesh and blood" offspring of the former one. New Israel was distinguished from Dukhoborism by "modernism" of the internal structure, which made it close in some degree to the organization of Baptists, Adventists and Evangelical Christians. Everything in New Israel which represented the traits of a bourgeois-reformed church organization (with the stamp of Khristovover mysticism) relates to this: namely, a spiritual hierarchy, the presence of a dogmatic exposition of the foundations of the faith (*Kratkii katekhizis osnovnykh nachal very Novoizrail'skoi obshchiny* [A Short Catechism of the Basic Foundations of the Faith of the New Israelite Congregation], written by Lubkov in 1905), well-developed norms of ritual[4] and religious practice.[5] But this was an underdeveloped bourgeois church.

3. Social and Political Problems in Khristovoverie at the Beginning of the 20th Century

New Israel did not completely break with the democratic traditions proceeding from those forms of old Russian sectarianism which evolved on the basis of the contradictions of the social order marked by serfdom. In the world-view of the sect, for example, there was none of the fatalistic dogma of

[4] Special, even if simplified, rituals accompanied birth, marriage and burial.

[5] Mysteries, a festival calendar, including the "Great Festival" — May 30th to June 1st, in honor of Lubkov's return from exile; the festival of "the descent to earth of the holy city of Jerusalem" — February 3rd; the festival of "the Sermon on the Mount of our Lord Jesus Christ in the 21st century" — October 20th; the festival of the "transfiguration" of Lubkov — October 1st (see Bondar' 1916: 72).

Baptism, dooming man to the blind role of a tool of divine predestination.

It was not divine predestination, but the determination by man himself (formulated in religious terms, of course) of daily tasks and their ultimate implementation which remained the guiding idea of the New Israelites, inherited by them from earlier Khristovoverie and shared with Dukhoborism and Molokanism. The concept of the "kingdom of God" on earth was the religious manifestation of this idea.

V. D. Bonch-Bruevich, the first Marxist student of Russian religious-social movements, was profoundly correct when he wrote of New Israel: "... the building of 'the kingdom of God' here on earth is proclaimed — and this is the fundamental tenet, and the most continuous and passionate striving of all of Israel (i.e. of all of Khristovoverie — A. K.). In force, unconditional nature, and importance to the sects of 'spiritual Christianity' from ancient times and in our days — it is equalled only by the principle of the eternal and continuous nature of Christ" (Bonch-Bruevich 1911a: liv).

The teachings of the overwhelming majority of the tendencies of old Russian sectarianism were formed as more or less vividly expressed peasant religio-social utopias of "the kingdom of God", created by the believers themselves and always and solely here on earth. Just as behind the peasant reasoning about "God's earth" there stood the attempt to take away land from the landlord, so behind the peasant reasoning about the kingdom of God on this earth there stood the attempt to implement on earth their peasant kingdom. "Look not at the words", wrote V. I. Lenin, "but at the essence. The peasant wants private property and the right to sell land, and words about 'God's kingdom' and so fourth — this is only an ideological cover for the desire to take land from the landlord" (*Lenin* XIII: 28).

Not being able to ignore the will of the ordinary New Israelite or to disdain the most vital democratic traditions of early Khristovoverie, Lubkov announced: "The kingdom of God on earth — this is the basic thought of the entire teaching of Jesus Christ.... The Kingdom of God — this is a just, moral, perfected life for people on earth, awakened by Christ the Savior and based on his eternal justice" (quoted in Bonch-Bruevich 1911a: 27).

Lubkov criticized the Russian Orthodox-Christian doctrine of Divine Providence: "The happiness of people will only begin when they say that Olympus is empty and they will cease to raise their heads to call for mercy and damnation from above but will begin to construct a better, freer life here on earth among people, among a fraternal family ..." (Bonch-Bruevich 1911a: 16).

Lubkov gave his teachings a Christian-socialist shading. He wrote, for example: "Christ's mission on earth is not yet finished. For he came to earth only to lighten the sorrow and suffering of people, to construct here on earth a rational and beautiful life. He wanted everyone to become brothers and all peoples to flow into one godly family where there would be neither ruler nor slave and nothing would rule over the people except his holy, wise will" (Bonch-Bruevich 1911a: 15).

This series of utterances by Lubkov could be expanded. First of all, they give an idea of the questions and interests which agitated the poorest segment of the New Israelites and which the leaders of the sect could neither evade nor keep silent about.

But if we look not at the words but at the actions, Lubkov's utterances turn out to be social demagogy, and his "Christian socialism" compatible with open monarchism.

In reality "the kingdom of God" of the New Israelite was a religious organization dominated by wealthy peasant-Cossack elements, who bought up and rented the land of the local population and landlords and preferred a free-enterprise farming type of economy to all others, including bourgeois-cooperative farming. We have the coinciding testimony of Bonch-Bruevich and M. V. Muratov, who had occasion to observe directly the economic life of the New Israelites. "The New Israelites", wrote Bonch-Bruevich, "did not conduct a communal economy. Each lived for himself...."[6] M. V. Muratov gives us the following observations:

"The New Israelites, in the mass, did not consider a communistic society necessary, and, although they spoke with sympathy of those times when, in the words of the Acts of the Apostles, believers held everything in common, they, however, reacted with mistrust to attempts to create that system in our day" (Muratov 1916: 191). The concept of "the kingdom of God" on earth of the laboring lower classes and of the bourgeois upper classes of the New Israelite sect were diametrically opposed.

We may judge of this from the biography of S. A. Sushkov (February 1905 — May 1910), who wrote: "... I from time to time came to the conclusion that life or the kingdom of God consisted not only in faith in God but in common union, in brotherhood" (Bonch-Bruevich 1911: IV, 296). By "a common union" Sushkov meant an economic union of New Israelites on a communal basis, not doubting that this was indeed the true "kingdom of God" on earth of which Lubkov spoke so much and so eloquently. Sushkov became a fervent propagandist for his idea and as a first duty brought it forward "among the already recognised people of Israel", but did not encounter any support: "... [the people] who had means did not want to listen to me and with disdain pushed aside my suggestion" (Bonch-Bruevich 1911a: 297). As for the religious leaders of the sect, "the elder brothers in the faith ... insistently suggested that

---

[6] Bonch-Bruevich 1911a: lxxv. Bonch-Bruevich noted the high standard of living of the New Israelites compared with the surrounding population, connecting this with the New Israelites' practice of mutual aid.

my appeal was nothing other than propaganda serving to undermine the well-being of all of Israel" (*ibid.*).

Sushkov's preaching did not have any significant response among the lower classes of the sect either, although they were in sympathy with the idea of a cooperative in and of itself. The lower ranks of the sect looked realistically at things and did not strive to cooperativize their poverty, but to make the capital of the rich common property: "... and although some poor peasants seemed to agree, it was with the proviso that stronger ones should join. And if they saw that the entire brotherhood consisted exclusively of poor peasants like themselves, they immediately refused" (*ibid.*).

Two of Sushkov's friends, one of whom was a railroad guard, and the other "earned his living as a daily laborer and at the same time sowed a desiatina of grain" (Bonch-Bruevich 1911a: 298), supported him. A cooperative was soon set up uniting seven poor peasant families.

But Sushkov's idea consisted in the reconstruction of the social life of all of New Israel, and he began to struggle for it. He succeeded in issuing severa! hundred copies of a little book he had written entitled *Gore tem, kotorye nazyvaiut zlo dobrom i dobro zlom* [Woe to Those Who Call Evil Good and Good Evil]. As Sushkov explained, "The title was chosen because my preaching about common brotherly life was considered evil coming from stupid people" (quoted in Bonch-Bruevich 1911a: 299). It is highly significant that protest against economic inequality was connected by Sushkov with protest against giving the New Israelite movement the form of a church with a ruling spiritual hierarchy and external ritual. Explaining the reasons according to which the "elder brothers" persecuted him as "a heretic and profaner of life" and subjected him to boycott, Sushkov did not let pass the opportunity to say: "... when meeting with these leaders, I had occasion at times to note that although they stood at the head of the people, they themselves were turning aside from the path of truth to mere rituals of life, which they considered as perfection, and they suppressed by their power the truth which Christ brought" (*ibid.*).

In the atmosphere of boycott and persecution created by the leaders of New Israel, the economically weak "commune" could not survive and was disbanded by Sushkov himself. Its participants returned to the community of New Israelites, and Sushkov himself publicly repented of his actions, forced to this by the leaders of the sect.

The leaders of New Israel had their own sociol-economic and political ideals, foreign and deeply hostile to the social creativity of the masses and their struggle with the institutions of serfdom and the institutions of tsarism and to their anti-capitalist protest.

These leaders had something to guard against the exploited lower classes of the sect, and they well understood that the organization created by them to rule over the lower classes was supported in the last analysis by the general conditions of landlord and bourgeois rule. The political ideology of the upper stratum of the New Israelite movement was manifested with complete clarity in the period of the revolution of 1905-1907.

As early as May 1905, in Rostov-on-Don, the leaders of New Israel called a general congress which was supposed to unite the upper stratum of the sect around a definite political platform, and also to systematize the religious views and strengthen the organizational basis of the sect. The leaders of the New Israelites expressed their positive social and political program in decidedly clouded fashion, confining themselves to expressing a desire for "betterment of the life of the Russian people, and also renovation and rebirth to a better life for all mankind", and immediately cancelling out this wish: ".. this should be done by reform, according to the Tsar's will, and by enlightenment, but not through mutiny and blood-letting" (Bonch-Bruevich 1911a: 120). The entire meaning of the declaration of "attitude toward the state structure", which was part of the "catechism" adopted by the congress, from which we took the texts quoted above, consisted precisely in condemnation of the revolutionary movement and demonstration of servility before tsarism: "We, true sons of the Tsar and the Fatherland, perform all religious rituals called for by law, and also military service; we respect authority, we need the protection of the law from violence and injustice; we do not belong to any mutinous party whatsoever; according to our dogma any rebellion against the state structure and sedition are abhorrent to the Lord ..." (*ibid.:* 120).

The reactionary nature of these political declarations is highlighted by the fact that at the May General Congress of Zemstvos, which corresponded in time with the congress of the New Israelites, the liberal bourgeoisie also raised its voice for the urgent convening of "popular representatives". Precisely at this time the New Israelite leaders called themselves "true sons of the Tsar and the Fatherland", and called upon the mass of their followers to do likewise.

Having set a course for legal self-determination as a church organization, prepared to co-exist with other organizations of similar type, including the Russian Orthodox Church, the congress adopted *A Short Catechism of the Basic Foundations of the Belief of the New Israelite Congregation.* At that time there appeared a council decision, formulating generally obligatory norms of New Israelite theology for their followers. It is noteworthy that among the theological sections of the *Catechism,* which discuss "the primeval and everlasting God", "of the descent of Christ on earth", a place was found for recognition as "holy" not only of the Old and the New Testaments but also of "explanations [of them] according to the interpretation by the holy fathers" (TsGIAL, div. 821f, f. 133, s.u. 133, sh. 141).

The Manifesto of October 17, 1905, was enthusiastically welcomed by Lubkov: "At the dawn of a new era! All hail freedom! Remember, friends, this freedom was achieved with great labor and much blood of the innocent was spilled"—thus the head of New Israel addressed his fellow believers.

The Manifesto of October 17 exhausted the understanding of the New Israelite leaders of freedom, but they were by no means sure of the solidarity of the New Israelite rank-and-file with them. This uncertainty was expressed in the following words of Lubkov's appeal: "Now I ask *all you followers of free Israel* to know how to use the freedom you have been given; *do not use it evilly, and do not mix with evil and ignorant actions* this pure and sweet freedom" (Bonch-Bruevich 1911a: 54fn; my emphasis—A. K.).

The time for action by the New Israelite leaders came with the Manifesto of October 17th. They made an attempt to broadcast their movement, putting themselves at the head of all Khristovover groups and completing the establishment of Khristovoverie on the bases of a bourgeois church organization. Five weeks after the publication of the Manifesto (November 25, 1905) there was distributed *Vozzvanie Novoizrail'skoi obshchiny* [An Appeal of the New Israelite Congregation] to all "the elders of Israel" in which they were invited to gather for a congress. The appeal was addressed to all activists of the Khristovover movement.

The congress was conceived precisely as a unifying "congress of delegates of the various dogmas and groups of Israelite congregations", as "the first all-Russian council of holy Israel" (Bonch-Bruevich 1911a: 170). The leaders of New Israel were attempting to find a common line with other activists of Khristovoverie, to overcome the differences existing in their own movement (Bonch-Bruevich 1911a: 169), and if they succeeded, "to organize an all-Russian Christian union" (Bonch-Bruevich 1911a: iv, 170).

The initiative of the New Israelite leaders did not meet with sympathy on the part of representatives of other Khristovover tendencies. Two centuries earlier, dispersed and having neither hierarchs nor catechisms, the Khristovover congregations were distinguished by a unity of world-view and practice. They were united by common class interests, and by belonging to one and the same stage of development of their movement. Now there was neither a common world-view nor common class interests. The congress which was held on February 3, 1906 in Taganrog represented only New Israelites. At the congress the leaders of more than 200 congregations took part, and there were a total of about 450 delegates. They represented New Israelite congregations of the Don, Kuban and Terek oblasts, Stavropol', Ekaterinoslav, Khar'kov, Voronezh, Tambov, Kaluga, Riazan, Samara and Kiev Guberniias, and the Transcaucasus (Bonch-Bruevich 1911a: 161).

Speaking at the congress, Lubkov once more appealed to the "elders" and to "the people of Old Israel", to "unite in a new union of Christ".

The congress reviewed the question of "the contemporary situation in Russia". In the resolutions adopted, the participants unanimously declared that they wished "that all freedoms promised from the height of the throne be introduced into life by the Tsar himself, who had promised to introduce them by reform and education but not by mutinous movements and blood-letting" (Bonch-Bruevich 1911a: 164). The congress resolved "not to adhere to any extreme party or union" i.e. to no kind of left party (Bonch-Bruevich 1911a: 3). *A Prayer for the Tsar and our Adored Monarch* was composed in the spirit of the congress's resolution (Bonch-Bruevich 1911a: 163).

The leaders of New Israel were at one with the counter-revolutionary bourgeoisie. The fact that the congress in Taganrog was not so much a representative congress as a council of hierarchs of New Israel (they made up half of the people gathered) made it all the easier to obtain unanimous approval of the congress's loyalist resolutions.

New Israel's leaders could count on their pro-monarchist course being supported in a number of local congregations, primarily in the congregations in the Don, Kuban and Terek regions, settled by Cossacks, who basically at that time still supported tsarism.

The overwhelming majority of New Israelites remained aloof from the revolutionary struggle of 1905-1907. The Ministry of Internal Affairs in a report to the Over-Procurator of the Synod on August 16, 1907, reported that, for example, in Stavropol' Guberniia, "the New Israelite sectarians, according to the uezd police superintendent, behave themselves with great reserve, and in reality there cannot be noted among them manifestations of teachings accompanied by a danger to public morality and peace" (TsGIAL, div. 796, f. 190, s.u. 65, sh. 5-6).

And still, the revolution of 1905-1907 left deep traces in the consciousness of the ordinary New Israelite and facilitated the further demarcation between the upper and lower strata of New Israel. It is difficult to suppose that after the revolution of 1905-1907 the mass of New Israelites preserved the illusion on the basis of which there appeared at one time a story about a "tsar-liberator", killed by the priests. We do not have concrete data as to how revolutionary events were interpreted among rank-and-file New Israelites. Let us note, however, that among Khristovovers in Khar'kov Guberniia in the period between 1905-1910 there appeared a song about justice, in which the Tsars were no longer contrasted to the clergy—they were condemned equally with the clergy as persecutors of social and any other justice:

> "There's no room for justice anywhere
> Under heaven in the whole wide world.
> The archpriests and the tsars,
> Having seized justice and brought her to court [say]:
> 'Why has she come here
> To ruin our kingdom,
> To open eyes to the world,
> To take away our kingdom?'

....

> You, archpriests and tsars,
> Send justice to heaven,
> Yourselves rule the world,
> Until your end comes
> And a crown to those who love justice."

(Bonch-Bruevich 1910: 104)

Thus tsarist illusions were gradually overcome even among the mass of peasants belonging to the Khristovover movement. It is symptomatic that in Khar'kov Guberniia—not until 1910, it is true—an incident occurred in which, as we learn from the report of the Khar'kov governor, "the New Israelites allowed themselves offensive expressions relating to the imperial majesty, criticized in the presence of peasants the actions of the government, propagandized for non-payment of taxes and for refusal to fulfill military obligations" (The Section of Manuscript Collections of the Institute of History, Academy of Sciences, USSR [ORF], Sector Ts, Div. VI, d. 11).

Lubkov and the activists of New Israel surrounding him could not buy off the lower classes of the sect with Christian-socialist rhetoric, especially after they showed themselves open defenders of the Autocracy. On the other hand, for all their hostility to the revolutionary movement, from which they sought the protection of the Autocracy, they as bourgeois property owners were hindered by survivals of serfdom in the agrarian structure of Russia. In this contradictory situation, bourgeois elements of New Israel sought every sort of "bypass". The organization of New Israel itself as a kind of state within a state had the significance of such a "bypass", primarily in that its "constitutional" structure gave these elements additional opportunities to develop bourgeois-entrepreneurial initiative and at the same time to inoculate the lower classes with new illusions to take the place of the old.

Lubkov's efforts at resettlement went precisely in this direction, striving to create new settlements of New Israelites in the border regions of Russia where survivals of serfdom were less strongly felt, and where the "constitutional" structure of New Israel could operate more effectively.

At the beginning of the 1890s, Lubkov organized the resettlement of part of the New Israelites to Central Asia (the Hungry Steppe). This attempt had an adventurist character, since neither had the conditions of resettlement been studied nor had there been the necessary economic calculations. Resettlement in the Hungry Steppe led to the ruin of the settlers and gave an impulse to the open action of some of the New Israelites against Lubkov's dictatorship. As papers from the Department of Spiritual Affairs explained, "In the New Israelite community in the *sloboda* of Shiriaeva, Bogucharskii Uezd in Voronezh Guberniia, one of Lubkov's former followers, Endovitskii, under the influence of Lubkov's unsuccessful resettlement adventure, began to preach that Lubkov's spiritual mission on earth as leader of the New Israelite sect was already finished.... Endovitskii's preaching met with sympathy among many members of the Shiriaeva New Israelite community. Another part of the community, which remained true to Lubkov, separated and excluded Endovitskii and his co-thinkers. The movement called forth by Endovitskii, however, did not acquire large dimensions" (TsGIAL, div. 821, f. 133, s.u. 91, sh. 15).

The unsuccessful attempt at resettling the New Israelites in the Hungry Steppe did not stop Lubkov from implementing a mass resettlement of his followers in the Transcaucasus after the revolution of 1905-1907. Beginning with 1908, about 5000 New Israelites traveled there. The leaders of the sect collected large sums of money among their adherents, with which they acquired, partially as private property and partially by rent, vast and fruitful lands in the Transcaucasus. In the New Israelite settlements which were formed there were both farms of industrial type and elementary forms of bourgeois cooperative economic units. The settlement of Elizavetinskii, where Lubkov settled, became the factual administrative center of the settlers. From here Lubkov ruled his kingdom of God, regulating the relationships of the New Israelites, who, both in economic disputes and in civil and everyday matters of governmental administration, appealed to Lubkov's power, to adjudicate and settle them according to the "laws" of New Israel. In a short space of time, the New Israelites succeeded in setting up a life in the new places which externally presented a picture of economic prosperity.

In 1912, Bonch-Bruevich visited the resettled New Israelites: "... I again along with several New Israelites set out for the village of Zelenoe Pol'e, situated in the depths of Kakhetiia, not far from the city of Signakh. This was a new settlement built only two and a half years ago on purchased fertile land. It is striking in its picturesqueness, prosperity and good maintenance" (Bonch-Bruevich 1912: ms., sh. 5).

Bonch-Bruevich noted the high technical level of equipment of the New Israelite farms, who "worked the land with the most modern equipment having steam threshers, steam mills, numerous plows, disc harrows, etc." (*ibid.*).

From the settlement of Zelenoe Pol'e, Bonch-Bruevich traveled to the settlement of Katasonovo, Borchalinskii Uezd, Tiflis Guberniia. "This settlement also was founded not long ago on lands purchased by the New Israelites", he wrote, "not far (7 versts) from the city of Bashkichet. The settlement is a large one. well-constructed, with an enormous tilled area; the majority of the settlers live in the community" (Bonch-Bruevich 1912: ms., sh. 7).

Behind the external facade of economic prosperity of the New Israelite settlements there were hidden the characteristic phenomena of bourgeois disintegration—the enrichment of a few, the impoverishment of others—although the social and property inequalities and class struggle among the New Israelites were blunted by the forms of material mutual aid which they practiced. The imposition of restrictions on and direct persecution of both those who remained in the old places and of the resettled New Israelites by the tsarist authorities and the ruling church continued. Under these conditions, Lubkov in 1910 conceived a plan for replacing the unjustified resettlement policy with one of emigration and transporting his followers to South America, where he hoped to find those conditions of economic, political and religious freedom which corresponded to his ideals as a leader of New Israel. Wherever he happened to be, Lubkov unceasingly wished to found on earth the kingdom of God, as he understood it, in concert with the leaders of the New Israelite sect. With this aim, he and a certain Mishin, who occupied a position of "first-born in Israel", set out for Uruguay. What motivated Lubkov in his plans for emigration? The persecution of New Israelites by Tsarism and the Church? The failure of the socio-economic experiments in the Transcaucasus and the mood within the New Israelite congregations? Apparently, both.

In October 1910, the Viceroy of the Caucasus published a circular, *O deiatel'nosti posledovatelei sekty 'Novyi Izrail'* [On the Activity of Followers of the Sect of New Israel], on the basis of which six New Israelite communities were closed in the Kuban region alone between December 1910 and May 1911. In 1911, a number of New Israelite communities in Terek and Stavropol' regions and in Khar'kov Guberniia were closed (Bonch-Bruevich 1911b).

At the same time, one must recognize a share of truth in the conclusion of M. V. Muratov, who wrote: "... in 1910, when Lubkov finally firmed up his intention to take his followers out of Russia, the New Israelites had relative freedom of religious worship.... It was impossible even to compare their position in 1910 with what they had to endure before legalization" (Muratov 1916: 188-189).

Lubkov's decision called forth a contradictory reaction among the New Israelites. For many of them it meant a severe spiritual struggle between love of country and fear of the arbitrary actions of the tsarist and clerical authorities. The New Israelites in the community of Tauz Station on the Transcaucasian railway told Bonch-Bruevich: "When we become convinced that we can no longer live in the fatherland, that our homeland is not a mother to us but a stepmother—only then can we decide to leave Russia, where we were all brought up and nourished, where all our kin live, where our people and our language stretch from one end of the country to the other. There, in an alien land, we will be as in the slumbering forest[A] and homesickness for the motherland will always be part of us" (Bonch-Bruevich, ms., 1912: sh. 9).

At the same time a definite role in the attitude of the working masses of the

New Israelite movement towards Lubkov's plan was played by the utopian ideas rooted from ancient times in the consciousness of the peasantry, as for example about the mysterious and beautiful Belovod'e, where there was no "theivery and robbing and other things abhorrent to the law", where people "did not have a secular court; spiritual authorities ruled the nations and all people", where "every earthly fruit existed; the vineyard sprang up and the grain fields yields fortyfold" (see the detailed and very interesting study by K. V. Chistov 1962).

The popular fantasy of Belovod'e was situated on an island in the "ocean-sea", somewhere in the vicinity of the state of "Opon" (apparently Japan). Hundreds and hundreds of peasants over the course of the entire 19th century set out for distant wanderings in search of Belovod'e, not discouraged by any privations. The last of the known attempts to find Belovod'e was made by a group of Ural Cossacks in 1898. The utopian story about the kingdom of God on earth was nevertheless more sober: "paradise" had to be created by people themselves, it demanded action and not a search for a ready-made "paradise". But both forms of utopia coincided. Approximately in the very years when the Ural Cossacks wrote the last chapter in the history of the search for Belovod'e, there evolved among the New Israelites, under the fresh influence of the resettlement of the Dukhobors, songs about "the American Tsar", the enemy of the priests and the protectors of sectarians, and about how "the Americans heartily honor God and settle them (sectarians—A. K.) on convenient land" (Rozhdestvenskii and Uspenskii 1912: 337, 339).

In the view of many rank-and-file New Israelites, Lubkov's emigration adventure presented itself as a departure under the guidance of the "leader" for a new Belovod'e, the road to which this time lay across the "ocean-sea", but now in directly the opposite direction from the state of "Opon".

Lubkov made an agreement with the Uruguayan government to allow the entry of the New Israelites, who were offered the opportunity to obtain as private property or by rental virgin lands lying along the river Uruguay approximately 400 kilometers from Montevideo (Muratov 1916: 180).

The resettlement of the New Israelites began in 1911-1912. It continued up to 1914 and was broken off by the beginning of World War I.

In all, about 2000 New Israelites resettled in Uruguay, which comprised, I suppose, not less than 10% of the total number of the followers of the sect.

What did Lubkov take away to Uruguay and what did he leave in Russia? He left his sect, which was facing the same but even deeper contradictions under the stimulus of which twenty years earlier it separated out from the Katasonovites. "The ship of Israel", as the sectarians called their religious union, although it was newly outfitted, was wrecked once more, and the first to run from the ship was its captain.

In 1914, among data on the growth of New Israel, there also appeared the opposing testimony of the Ekaterinoslav eparchial missionary Afanas'ev: "The New Israelite sect, which was very prominent within the boundaries of the Ekaterinoslav eparchy after 1905, last year was almost completely silent. The waning of the sect began in 1912" (Afanas'ev 1915: 30).

The New Israelites who followed Lubkov to Uruguay found themselves under conditions in which the relationship between the bourgeois upper stratum and the working lower clases of the sect were not complicated by those restrictions and persecutions to which their society was subjected daily in tsarist and Russian Orthodox Russia. Here opportunities were also broader for the practice of a bourgeois economy, which was hindered in Russia by survivals of serfdom. The facts show that for this reason the internal contradictions among the resettled New Israelites developed more fully.

Let us characterize briefly the condition of other forms of Khristovoverie in the first fifteen years of our century. The Katasonovite movement continued to exist, represented by approximately fifteen sects numbering from several dozen followers (for example the sect of Ekaterina Egur'eva in Medvezh'e Uezd, Stavropol' Guberniia) to several thousand followers (for example the sect of Aleksandra Lodurgina, who had communities in Stavropol' Guberniia, in the Kuban and Terek Regions). Between these very small and very large Katasonovite sects there were the sects of Fedor Mal'kov, Tikhon Belonozhkin, Moisei Vel'mozhnii, Fedor Poslenichenko, and others numbering 100, 300, 500 or 800 each. The socio-economic contrast among the Katasonovites at this time reached its extreme.

In 1914 a certain P. Pechelkin, who separated from the Katasonovites, published an article under the title *Kniazi mira sego* [The Princes of This World] (*DKh* 1914, No. 3: 52-53). This article gives us an idea of the social make-up of, and the social relationships which characterized, the Katasonovite sects on the eve of World War I. We see peasants beaten down by need and arbitrary rule, who "sincerely believed that a harvest or crop failure depended on the will of the god who stood over them". Above them there was a stratum of wealthy peasants who used the borrowed power of "those who lived among them or worked for them", and on "Olympus" there was "the person in whom 'God was shut up' ", the owner of hundreds of desiatiny of land, an exploiter collecting quit-rent in money and in kind, not stopping at corvée when it came to it, and reinforcing his spiritual authority with "godly" socks on the jaw.

The Katasonovite sects had become ossified; their participants were blindly subordinate to their "prophets" or "Christs", and having become frozen in the traditional concepts of the Katasonovite movement, they did not even enliven their existence by religious disputes. Nevertheless, they showed an interest in the events of social and political life. Along with the power of the leaders and the forces of tradition, they were united (and their ossified religiosity also enlivened) by their common position as people persecuted by the clergy and the government administration. This fact partially explains the paradox which S. D. Bondar' observed during his meetings with the Old Israelites. "It is remarkable", he wrote, "that among some branches there exists a fear of freedom of conscience.... Freedom of conscience, which implemented the principle that sectarian gatherings should be public, is for many Old Israelites a dangerous thing, since it leads and has already led many of the 'faithful' to 'secularization' ". This mood is expressed in one of the Old Israelite songs:

"Turn, Israel, toward my path,
Look, Israel, at your stupidity;
Once you were a warrior for my truth,
And now you have set out for your own ruin.

Your fasts, your tears, where are they?
They have drowned, in sins and vices.
You all prayed for freedom,
And when freedom came—it did you no good"

(Bondar' 1916: 56)

The development of class struggle in the country, expressed in 1905-1907 in the bourgeois-democratic revolution, opened sectarian eyes to the reactionary nature of sectarianism, but for many participants of these movements, "insight" was limited to that concrete form of the movement in which they took part. Their sense of social protest was dissatisfied with the given concrete form of religion, but not with the religious form in general.

The sectarians climbed an agonizingly long stairway of new religious formations in their search for justice in life. They scanned and invented dozens of recipes for religious "salvation", but by this they found nothing and could not find anything. Many of them, because of oppression and backwardness, were already no longer searching, having given themselves over to the will of the religious leadership, and been turned into meek victims of the exploiting elements which made up the upper classes of the sect.

This in general was the condition of the Katasonovite sect, whose followers apathetically looked at the events happening around them ("You all prayed for freedom, and when freedom came, it did you no good").

Of course, in a number of cases the Katasonovites freed themselves from their religious chains, some in order to break with sectarianism as a whole, and others only in order to break with Khristovoverie.

In the three decades after the Katasonovite movement fell apart, all its branches constantly declined in numbers. The Katasonovite movement decayed in all respects and was gradually reduced to nothing.

As I have already written, the Katasonovite movement was based on the

Kopylov movement—a Khristovover sect, whose followers called themselves *Postniki*.

While the center of the Katasonovite movement moved in the Reform era to the southern guberniias, and its periphery included the inner and western guberniias of Russia, the Postnik movement became strong in Tambov Guberniia, where it was concentrated in Kirsanov, Borisogleb, and Tambov Uezds. In time the Tambov Postnik movement put out branches in Syzran' Uezd, Simbirsk Guberniia; Atkar Uezd, Saratov Guberniia; and Penza Uezd (near Penza) (Bondar' 1916: 24). There were congregations close in doctrine and structure to the Tambov Postnik movement in the beginning of the 20th century in Khar'kov (Mironenko in Bonch-Bruevich 1910a) and Ekaterinoslav (Iasevich-Borodaevskaia 1912: 282 *et seq.*) Guberniias. The Postnik movement in general kept its local significance, differing in this both from the Katasonovite and from Lubkov's movements. S. D. Bondar', citing data from a first-hand study of Postnik congregations in 1911-1912, wrote that "the total number of Postniki does not exceed 3000 persons" (Bondar' 1916: 24). But this does not include Postniki in Khar'kov and Ekaterinoslav Guberniias; small groups, it is true.

A characteristic feature of the Postnik Khristovovers was a comparatively high level of material well-being, which of course did not exclude the presence among them of poor and exploited persons. "All of them [the Postniki—A. K.]", wrote Bondar', "are wealthy in the highest degree. Their homes and farms in Kirsanov and Borisogleb Uezds of Tambov Guberniia are the best and exemplary—particularly compared with the farms of the miserable local Russian Orthodox masses, with their large families" (*ibid.*).

As the Tambov eparchial missionary M. I. Tret'iakov revealed, "When the city of Syzran' burned, the Khlysty from the village of Perevoz in Kirsanov Uezd collected for those of their fellows who had been burned out 1000 rubles in money and 500 rubles in goods. The Inzhavin Khlysty collected more than 5,000 rubles in money and 2,000 rubles in goods. The same quantity was donated to the Syzran' Khlysty by the rich Khlysty of Rasskazovo, Tambov Uezd" (Tret'iakov 1911: 171).

It is not without interest to add to Tret'iakov's information that in the village of Perevoz, Kirsanov Uezd, there lived according to data of the Ministry of Internal Affairs for 1909, 127 "Khlysty" (Postniki) (TsGIAL, div. 821, f. 133, s.u. 21, shs. 78-95). According to the same source in the same year, 112 Khlysty (Postniki) lived in the village of Rasskazovo. Among the Tambov Postniki there were very wealthy men. In the summer of 1959, the Subbotnik Ia. A. Zhitenev from the city of Rasskazovo in Tambov Oblast recalled in conversation with us: "I. A. Eremin was well-known among the Postniki; he had a large parcel of forest and a wharf for lumber, and he had a farmstead in the village of Pavlovka in the Rzhaksa region. The Postnik

Panferov was a lumber merchant, and he had a large house with a cupola, where the Postniki gathered to pray" (VIRA 1961: 221).

Iasevich-Borodaevskaia, observing the Postnik-Khristovover movement in Ekaterinoslav Guberniia, by the way, wrote: "The folk evolved the belief that a sectarian lay down a stone for a 'spell', and in the morning finds ... bread and as much money as needed" (Iasevich-Borodaevskaia 1912: 234).

As Iasevich-Borodaevskaia wrote of the Khristovovers in the village of Petrovka, Ekaterinoslav Guberniia, "many of the Khlysty are *very* wealthy people; their barns are filled with stacks of grain, in the 'meadows' there are haystacks, in the corrals cattle being fattened, and in the shed well-fed horses are tied up; the internal furnishings of the huts speak of complete material well-being" (Iasevich-Borodaevskaia 1912: 239-240; my emphasis). The researcher ventures the assertion that "among sectarians there are no poor" (Iasevich-Borodaevskaia 1912: 234). But she contradicts herself when, enumerating the stimuli facilitating the union of Khristovovers, she writes: "the 'ship' serves as a refuge in all misfortunes and disasters: if the cattle die (so not everyone has "fattening cattle" in the corrals—A. K.), if there is nothing with which to plow the land (and everyone does not have well-fed horses tied up—A. K.), if it is necessary to pay taxes (and not everyone is a very wealthy person—A. K.)—for everything there is fraternal support. The sectarians never allowed their 'brothers' to be birched for non-payment of taxes, to be put in jail, or to have to sell their fattening cattle" (Iasevich-Borodaevskaia 1912: 233).

Thus, among the Khristovovers whose belief and way of life Iasevich-Borodaevskaia studied, there was no "equality of the rich", but there was inequality, as among other peasants, with this difference, however—that in the Khristovover congregation a system of material mutual aid operated, and this material mutual aid was at least sufficient so that need did not turn into misery. Among the Postniki, as a rule, there were no beggars.

The Postnik communities in the second half of the 19th and the beginning of the 20th centuries were in large measure economic rather than religious fellowships. Their dogma, as was explained above, stood opposed to that of the Russian Orthodox Church, but the significance of the Postnik movement as a form of religious and social opposition was highly conditional: its followers kept their social protest to themselves. They were little excited by ideological interests, but in following the religio-ethical principles of the Postnik movement they were strict, and the firm control of their leaders was supplemented by mutual control.

Iasevich-Borodaevskaia justly points out that "the rules of this community are extremely severe. Any offense drew punishment in the form of prostrations to the ground and fasts, sometimes exhausting to the point of fainting" (Iasevich-Borodaevskaia 1912: 234).

In a conversation with us which took place in the summer of 1959 in the city of Rasskazovo, Tambov Oblast, one of the Postniki, a 75-year-old man, told us that in former times, for violating the vow of chastity, the "criminal" was not allowed to attend gatherings of the congregation for two years (VIRA 1961: 240). This was because the religio-ethical norms of the Postnik movement were intertwined with the economic norms they adopted. The Postniki built their material well-being on the single basis at their disposal in the society contemporary with them — the appropriation of the labor of others. But they also had their own methods tested in practice, which facilitated the acquisition of wealth.

Celibacy freed their budget from expenses so burdensome to the budgets of peasants with many children. The Postnik prohibitions on wine and tobacco had the same significance. Not having formally broken with the church, the Postniki were not freed from expenses for the clergy.

But the Postniki did not have to spend money on weddings and christenings, and the expenses for funerals were significantly less among them than among peasants with large families, especially if we keep in mind the high death-rate in the pre-Revolutionary countryside. For instance, in Voronezh Guberniia, from the data of budget studies in 1894-1896, in a peasant household with an allotment of up to five desiatiny, expenses for religion were 554 rubles, of which 310 rubles were expenses for weddings, christenings and burials (Grekulov 1963: 126). If we consider the small families of the Postniki, it develops that among them budgetary expenses for the church were reduced to a minimum. The Postniki had no expenses for vodka, but according to data from a study of peasant budgets in Likhva Uezd, Kaluga Guberniia, in peasant households with allotments of more than 3 desiatiny, expenditures on vodka even exceeded fees paid to the clergy (Grekulov 1963: 130). The ascetic prohibitions of Khristovoverie were consciously evaluated by its followers as a means of curtailing the expenditure side of their budgets.

Even at the beginning of the 19th century, Bishop Feofilakt gave a characteristic explanation of the reasons leading one village sexton from Kaluga Guberniia to enter the congregation of Khristovovers: "... the sexton Petr Semenov, of the same village of Kniaz'-Ivanov. He has belonged to the so-called Khristovshchina sect since Shrovetide of 1802 ..., he agreed to be in it because this Khristovoshchina sect teaches one not to drink wine and not to have sexual relations with one's wife, *which appealed to him, for he, a sexton, is exceedingly poor, and the raising of children and the use of spirits would have ruined him completely*" (Vysotskii 1915: 188; my emphasis — A. K.).

The connection of Khristovover asceticism with the very simple economic calculations of the peasant can be traced over the entire course of the history of the sect. In the 1880s, the Voronezh Khristovovers repeated for the writer

E. Markov,[7] who visited them, the explanation which the Bishop of Kaluga, Feofilakt, was given by the village sexton Semenov many decades before. The leader of the congregation, whom Markov calls Miron Ivanov, said: "The other day one came to me (a peasant who was not in the sect — A. K.): he says, Ivanovich, take two desiatiny from me — But I take land for a year for 7 rubles. Listen, brother, I tell him, if I take it what profit will you have? Here you will take 7 rubles, carry them to the tavern, and for two desiatiny at least 60 rubles of grain will be taken out of your own hide; so that tavern will cost you not 14 but 60. You'd do better to have patience and give up your foolishness. The land will stay with your little children, and you yourself won't go barefoot.... Well, when you make an appeal to conscience — he began to think like us — look, he became a man" (Markov 1887: 14).

Thus the Khristovover leader explained the economic significance of Danilo Filippov's commandment — "drink no alcohol" — to a poor man who came to him. In the same spirit Miron Ivanov spoke of the other ascetic taboos of Khristovoverie: "... I know well: in a year each person needs our poor seven rubles for tobacco. But for seven rubles I tell you, a peasant can pile up a desiatina, so that tobacco costs him not seven but thirteen rubles in a year."

Finally, about weddings: "We now have a wedding, what a joy — we drink a little tea, we sing very nicely. Others go to complete ruin, when a wedding occurs they throw away 200 or 300 rubles on vodka alone, but we hold the very best wedding for 50 rubles."

Miron Ivanov summarizes his opinions as follows: "The matter is not in teaching but in life ... how we'll live in the other world and what will be there, man will never know.... But we have to live on this earth, we really know this. We should build a heavenly kingdom here on earth, among people, so that there will be a paradise and God will live in man" (Markov 1887: 15, 17, 18). Among the things required by the Khristovovers for a "paradise", built among people, was a peasant budget in accordance with his needs.

The religious and everyday lifestyle of Khristovoverie served the interests of accumulation. Hence the stern regulation of the way of life and behavior of its members by the community, reminiscent of guild regulations.

We have still to speak of Khristovover communities continuing in the imperialist stage of social development[B] of Russia the traditions of 17th-18th-century Khristovoverie. Among the various sects surrounding them at the end of the 19th and the beginning of the 20th centuries, these residual phenomena of early Khristovoverie played no role whatever.

The origin of the Kopylov movement, then of the Katasonovite, and then of Lubkov's movement, was conditioned by the fact that the basis in socio-

---

[7] Markov describes a congregation including Khristovovers from the village of Staraia Khvorostan'ia and the settlements of Anoshkino, Badeevka and Solovtsy in Korotoiak Uezd of Voronezh Guberniia (see Rozhdestvenskii 1899: 593).

economic conditions, which at one time gave rise to Khristovoverie, was being broken up piece by piece. Pre-Revolutionary researchers, studying the history of Reform-era sectarianism, as a rule, did not single out the earliest form of Khristovoverie among its other forms. One of the few exceptions is the work by S. D. Bondar', whom I have cited repeatedly, and who established that followers of what he calls the "original" form of Khristovoverie were to be found in Kazan, Kaluga, Riazan, Tambov, Ekaterinoslav, Khar'kov, Tavriia and Baku Guberniias, and in the Kuban and Terek Oblasts, and that their main mass was concentrated in Samara Guberniia (Bondar' 1916: 7).

The status of the form of Khristovoverie under review as the original one is extremely relative. It is worth noting that the original territory of Khristovoverie — the regions centered on Moscow, Vladimir, Iaroslavl, Kostroma, and Nizhni, Novgorod — have in recent times been free from traditionally-oriented Khristovovers. The guberniias and regions listed by Bondar' are primarily zones of diffusion, and not of original spread of Khristovoverie, which appeared in these places only in the 19th century, partly as a result of migration movements directed from the center to the south of the country, and in part as a result of state-church persecution. Of the guberniias listed by Bondar', only Tambov and Kaluga had Khristovover congregations in the 18th century. But in these guberniias, as in Orel and Tula Guberniias, not mentioned by Bondar', Khristovoverie appeared only in the middle and second half of the 18th century.

Considering that in the second half of the 18th century the social base of the original Khristovoverie changed and consistently declined, I assume that followers of traditional Khristovoverie yielded to followers of reformist Khristovoverie. There is no doubt that this was precisely the case in the guberniias of Tambov, Ekaterinoslav, Khar'kov, Kherson, Tavriia and Baku, and in the Kuban and Terek Oblasts. In Kaluga Guberniia, in Tarussa Uezd, there existed Khristovover communities, apparently of a traditional persuasion. These communities suffered great losses as a result of the trial in 1895 of their leaders and participants (Sokolov 1897). Then, after some years, in about 1900 there appeared groups of New Israelites in two villages of Kaluga Uezd (Zharov 1912). Of Samara Guberniia alone, we may definitely say that traditionally-oriented Khristovovers predominated on its territory. This did nothing to change the numerical relationship of the followers of the "original" and reformed types of Khristovoverie.

These considerations allow us to answer the question about the size and total number of Khristovovers in Russia in the first decade and a half of this century. In the course of the preceding exposition, it appeared that during this time, New Israel, having swallowed up a significant part of the Old Israelites, exceeded in number the Old Israelite groups remaining in opposition to them. How many followers did New Israel have? At the 1906 congress of New Israelites, 200 congregations were represented. In 1911, 9 registered congregations of New Israel had 2045 members (Synod 1912).

In addition to this there existed unregistered congregations of New Israelites, about whose number we can only guess, judging again according to the number of congregations represented at the congress of New Israelites in 1906.

Proceeding from what we have set forth, on an average each registered New Israelite congregation had 200 followers. But let us assume that these registered congregations were in fact unions of a number of local congregations. We are led to this thought by the fact that each of the 9 registered congregations had one special building for prayer, with 40 permanent rooms for prayer meetings. Probably, these 40 buildings for prayer give an idea of the number of local congregations united in the 9 registered ones. In this case, 2045 registered followers of New Israel were distributed in 40 congregations, which is an average of 50 persons in one congregation. Thus the average number of followers in a New Israelite community was not more than 200 and not less than 50. Accepting that the number of New Israelite congreations did not decline from 1906 (probably it even grew in the period from 1906 to 1909; from 1910 governmental restrictions on the New Israelites increased), we receive the maximum number of New Israelites—200 × 200 = 40,000 persons, and the minimum number—200 × 50 = 10,000 persons. I assume that at the beginning of the emigration movement among the New Israelites there were as many as 20,000 of them.

At this time in the Old Israelite group, there were not more than 15,000 persons. I recognize as real the data of S. D. Bondar' about the followers of the Postnik movement, whose number he determined as 3,000. The total number of followers of reformist Khristovoverie approximated 40,000. As has been already shown, followers of traditional Khristovoverie yielded to followers of reform Khristovoverie. As a total, we conclude that the number of followers of Khristovoverie numbered in the tens of thousands, and considering the inevitable errors in calculation, I consider that it did not exceed 100,000 persons.

As concerns the geographical distribution of Khristovoverie, using the mutually supplementary data of the yearly reports of the Over-Procurator of the Synod (for 1907-1914) and the statistical data collected by the Ministry of Internal Affairs in 1909, it develops that there were Khristovover communities in more than 30 guberniias and oblasts: Akmolinsk, Vladimir, Vladikavkaz, Voronezh, the Don, Ekaterinoslav, Enisei, Kaluga, Kishinev, Kiev, Kursk, Orenburg, Orel, Penza, Poltava, Podol'sk, Perm, Petersburg, Riazan, Samara, Saratov, Smolensk, Stavropol, Tambov, Tavriia, Tiflis, Tula, Khar'kov, Kherson, Chernigov and Chernomorsk.[8]

Editor's Notes

Note A. Russian: *v dremuchem lesu*—a stock phrase in folk speech. The forest is said to "slumber" because it is uninhabited and for the most part untravelled.

Note B. In formal Marxist terminology, imperialism is the final phase of the development of capitalism, in which the economies of individual countries are integrated into a world-wide system, importing raw materials from underdeveloped "colonial" areas and exporting finished products to them.

[8] Reports of the Over-Procurator of the Synod (1907-1914): see the tables on the departure from Russian Orthodoxy and the return to Orthodoxy of Khristovovers: Khlysty, Old Israel, New Israel; see also TsGIAL, div, 821, f. 133, d. 21, shs. 2-386.

3

The Dukhobor Sect

The Dukhobor sect lost in a comparatively short time its significance as a form of ideological protest influencing any large stratum of the population opposed to the ruling church and the serf order. This was one of the peculiarities of the Dukhobor movement in comparison with other sectarian movements of the 19th and beginning of the 20th centuries.

Whereas Khristovoverie over the course of more than 50 years (from the end of the 17th to the middle of the 18th century) occupied a leading place in sectarianism, Dukhoborism even in the first stage of its origin and development shared influence on circles of the population opposed to Russian Orthodoxy with the same Khristovoverie, with Molokanism which appeared and flourished in the second half of the 18th century, and to a significantly smaller degree with the Skoptsy movement. However, from the 1760s to the beginning of the 19th century, Dukhobor preaching found a relatively wide response chiefly among various categories of state peasants. In this space of time, it acquired thousands of followers, primarily in Voronezh (especially in its Tambov provinces), then in Ekaterinoslav, Khar'kov, Tavriia, and finally in Astrakhan, Samara, Penza and Riazan Guberniias.

From the end of the 18th to the beginning of the 19th century, increase in the Dukhobor sect became less and less significant, its religio-social ideas lost their popularity, and the sect continued to exist primarily thanks to the natural growth of the families of its followers. Undoubtedly, both the exceptionally severe court actions against the Dukhobors at the end of the 1760s and in the beginning of the 1770s and in the 1790s, and also the extralegal persecution of them, impeded the spread of the Dukhobor movement.

However, the Autocracy and the Church persecuted with no less cruelty other sectarian groups contemporary with Dukhoborism, while they still won from the Church ever-new adherents both in the second half of the 18th century and in the second half of the 19th century.

Molokanism, which at that time was especially successful in competing with

Dukhoborism, differed from it in being less radical. It did not in general deny the Church dogma of the Trinity, did not completely deny Church teaching on the sacraments, kept prayer for the dead, and in complete contrast to Dukhoborism, based its world-view not on "inner revelation", but on the Bible. It is no accident that precisely among the Molokans at the end of the 1820s there appeared the so-called Don persuasion, which, in Bonch-Bruevich's apt expression, "played among the Molokans the role of Edinoverie for the Old Believers or the Uniates for the Russian Orthodox and the Catholics who once lived in Poland" (Bonch-Bruevich 1959: 294). Molokanism was also distinguished from Dukhoborism by the lesser degree of expression of social motifs in its teaching.

However paradoxical it may seem, it was just these peculiarities of Molokanism which accounted for its success compared to Dukhoborism: with the development of the class struggle, sectarianism ever more lost its significance as a form of democratic protest by the popular masses.

Having arisen approximately ten years before the peasant war led by Pugachev,[A] the Dukhobor movement was disseminated in the situation which followed the defeat of the peasant war. It goes without saying that the ideology of Dukhoborism, although democratic, scarcely answered the mood of those elements of the peasants and Cossacks who had fought under Pugachev's banner, and who later in the first half of the 1790s, were participants in the anti-serfdom disorders in more than half of the guberniias in Russia. As concerns the wealthy peasants, who were occupied with buying up goods and trading, and who had industrial enterprises and often supplemented the ranks of the meshchane and other urban strata, the "moderation" and "sobriety" of the Molokan teaching answered their mood better than the amorphous world-view of the Dukhobors, which was not without elements of a sort of pantheism, and had even in some respects broken with Christianity.

The forms of Dukhobor opposition to serfdom could not answer the desires of the lower social classes of the countryside, especially after they began to recover from the consequences of the defeat of the peasant war in 1773-1775. On the other hand, the social upper classes of the countryside, since they were developing into a peasant bourgeoisie, worked out their own religious forms of anti-serfdom opposition less "sharp" than Dukhoborism.

Tsarism, after failing to achieve its goal of liquidating Dukhoborism by means of repression at the beginning of the 19th century, attempted to localize it, and to a certain degree succeeded, in the presence of objective conditions which limited the diffusion of this movement. Measures for resettling the basic contingent of Dukhobors from Voronezh, Tambov, Ekaterinoslav and Khar'kov Guberniias are connected with the name of Alexander I (this was in the spirit of his policy of an external show of liberalism), and they were shifted from places of exile to Mariupol' Uezd in Novorossiisk Guberniia, where they were settled on fertile land along the Molochnaia River (Ministry of Internal Affairs 1858: 23-25, 28-32). This resettlement was implemented in stages and lasted from 1804 to 1816.

Not less than 4,000 Dukhobors lived in Molochnye Vody at the end of the resettlement project. We have data from approximately this time about 2,300 Dukhobors who were settled at an unknown date in Akhaltsikhe Uezd, Tiflis Guberniia (*Letopisi* 1861: 6-7).

Among the first settlers in Molochnye Vody there were also Spiritual Christians from Tambov, known to us from investigative materials characterizing their way of life and thought in the middle of the 1760s (see above, pp. 63-64). These were representatives of the older generation of Tambov Spiritual Christians (from the 60s), their children and grandchildren. They brought with them their customs, based on the conviction that "people should have property in common, and give to each other without asking return, because they are brothers." This social principle was the more important for the majority of Spiritual Christians who had resettled from various places to Molochnye Vody, because the original system on the previously uninhabited lands demanded collective efforts.

In a memorandum titled *Nekotorye cherty o obshchestve dukhobortsev* [Some Features of Dukhobor Society], written in 1805 from direct observations (by Senator Lopukhin?), we read the following about the Dukhobors in Molochnye Vody: "The most respected virtue in Dukhobor society is fraternal love. Among them there is no [private] property but each considers his farmstead as a common one." This was the same "virtue" which the Tambov Spiritual Christians announced in the 1760s, and which they, in their words, practiced.

How extensive was this "virtue" in the social and economic life of the Tambov Spiritual Christians?

I assume that the property belonging to the Tambov Spiritual Christians remained in the hands of each individual owner, who was at that time under the control of the religious community in the sense that the community saw to it that the rule "to give to one another without return" was in fact implemented. In Molochyne Vody, the principle of fraternal love developed further: "When they resettled in Molochnye Vody, they ... put all their belongings there in one place, so that now they have there a common treasury, one common herd, and in two settlements, two common grain stores; each takes from the common property everything he needs" (*Letopisi* 1861: 7).

Did this collectivism of consumption affect collectivism of production?

The public treasury and storehouse of grain could be formed by voluntary or obligatory contributions in money and in kind from individual owners.

However, the testimony of one source that the Dukhobors "put all their belongings there in one place" allows us to suppose that the Dukhobors also had a common source for tools. "The Dukhobors lived (in Molochnye Vody—A. K.) as a community having vast plowland in common ..." wrote V. D. Bonch-Bruevich (1959: 289). Let us note in this connection the curious detail contained in the memorandum of 1805 cited above: "In Molochnye Vody, three and even as many as five large families lived together in one large *izba*" (*Letopisi* 1861: 8). What made it necessary for the Dukhobors to set up in a new place a building adapted for three or even five large families to live together? These were not temporary barrack-type buildings. Were not these "large izbas" of the Dukhobors dormitories like those which several decades later were put up in Popov's commune, which was formed from Saratov Molokans exiled to Baku Guberniia? In Popov's commune, as we will see in detail below, they built large izbas intended for several families with 30 to 50 people (this is what three to five large families means).

But the fact is that in Popov's commune each such dormitory was a primary production nucleus—a "work" party, uniting its activity with other work parties like it in the same village.

One way or another, not all the resettled Dukhobors based their economic life on collectivism. It is characteristic that the author of the 1805 memorandum says, for example, that not everyone had common grain stores—just two settlements in Molochnye Vody. Also characteristic is his remark that "their (the Dukhobors—A. K.) occupations were the usual ones, according to callings, whatever they happened to be. Thus, the trader traded and the farmer farmed, but since a large part of them are farmers, their basic occupation is agriculture; in some ways they even prefer this noble occupation to all others" (*ibid.*).

"A special public house", where the "public funds" were kept, and where travelling "lay administrators" stopped and lived "at the expense of the community", was common to all Dukhobors, resettled or in process of resettlement. This was the so-called Orphans Home. In the course of time it was elevated to the role of a religious, administrative and economic center for the Molochnye Vody Dukhobors.

At first the social order among the Dukhobors in the process of resettlement was marked by democratic structure. They had neither religious hierarchies nor administrative authorities. "In their meetings", we read in the memorandum of 1805, "they teach the word of God to each other. Any could speak of what he knew for the edification of the brothers" (*Letopisi* 1861: 6). The rights of women were not limited, "for they say, women also have intellect—and the light is in intellect" (*ibid.*). As concerns the institutions of power, in the words of the author of the memorandum, "in their society there are no *starshchiny* at all, who would administer and direct the society; but the society is ruled by everyone and by each one" (*Letopisi* 1861: 8).

Miliukov considered the memorandum an "idealization" of the way of life and morals of the Dukhobors (Miliukov 1931: 162). It is possible that its author was silent about negative phenomena among the Dukhobors or simply had not penetrated thoroughly into the life of the Dukhobor settlers. But primarily Miliukov himself took a hostile attitude toward the experience of social creativity of the people. Over the entire course of pre-Reform sectarianism we can trace an attempt "to solve" the root contradictions of social life by means of various social utopias in local conditions of this or that religious community. The short-term success of these attempts each time only made the picture of the subsequent destruction of sectarian communes, and the development and the sharpening of social contradictions in them, stand out more starkly. This is what happened in the case of the Molochnye Vody Dukhobors.

Soon after the resettlement of the Dukhobors, the son of Illarion Pobirokhin, Savelii (who took his mother's name of Kapustin), counting on the wealthy elements, arrogated to himself unlimited power over the sectarians. As Bonch-Bruevich wrote, "the chief bearer and establisher of power in the Dukhobor community was their leader, Savelii Kapustin, who, by the way, worked mightily to implant in the consciousness of the Dukhobors the concept of one-man rule and the creation of a dynasty of Dukhobor leaders ... at one of the general congresses of the Dukhobors there was confirmed the text of a psalm which he himself wrote, where the chief of the Dukhobors was elevated to the holy rank of leader. Under Kapustin the man himself became the victim of this text" (Bonch-Bruevich 1959: 290).

Kapustin formed a "council of elders". The Dukhobor authorities began to disburse public funds at their own discretion. By the 1820s, "fraternal love" remained only a memory in the minds of ordinary Dukhobors exploited by the "brother" owners of cattle and land of various degrees of wealth. Kapustin and the "elders" committed every kind of repression on ordinary believers.

With the rise in the 1830s and 1840s of the anti-feudal movement and the strengthening of reaction, the policy of the Autocracy toward the Dukhobors changed.

From 1841 to 1845 the resettlement of Dukhobors from Molochnye Vody to the Transcaucasus was implemented. About 1,000 settlers remained, who preferred a renunciation of Dukhoborism to a renunciation of the accumulation of wealth, and returned to Russian Orthodoxy. From the 1840s, the Dukhobors lived in compact settlements in the Transcaucasus. As in the period of their stay at Molochnye Vody, they led here an isolated life, not allowing strangers among them and making no attempt to disseminate their teaching among the local population or among other Russian settlers.

I. L. Segal', the secretary of the Elizavetpol' Guberniia Statistical Committee, speaking from personal observation of the life of the Transcaucasian

Dukhobors, wrote: "The Dukhobors lived separately from schismatics of all other sects.... The spirit of proselytism was alien, and at the same time, they were sharply distinguished from schismatics of other sects, and did not allow mixed marriages; they entered more willingly into relationships with the natives than with schismatics of other sects.... All other schismatics lived mixed" (Segal' 1890).

In particular one of the barriers which served to isolate the Dukhobors from the surrounding population was their ritual regulations, which with time acquired a growing significance in the religious practices of Dukhobors.

In the article *Obriady dukhobortsev* [Rituals of the Dukhobors], Vladimir Ol'khovskii (a literary pseudonym of V. D. Bonch-Bruevich) wrote: "the largest mass, brought up exclusively in the Dukhobor milieu ... looks at ritual as something absolutely essential, without which one cannot live, and for which one may sacrifice everything, including one's life.... And here, in this mass, this ritual is an impenetrable Chinese wall between the external world and members of the Dukhobor community ..." (Bonch-Bruevich 1905: 269).

The Dukhobors were not only a religious and ritual group. They worked out their customs and traditions, a peculiar form of male and female costume, a system of raising children, etc., and in a certain sense evolved into an ethnic group. In the words of one of the Dukhobor figures who settled at the end of the 19th century in Canada, S. F. Rybin, "They (the Dukhobors—A. K.) have turned their sect into a nation. When they meet an unknown person they ask: and who might you be? I am a Dukhobor, one answers. Ah, a Dukhobor. And I thought you were Russian. It turns out that the Dukhobors are not Russians, but Dukhobors" (Rybin 1952: 3).

In the life of the Dukhobor communities—the country of "Dukhoboriia", as the Dukhobors conceived their religious union—the many-sided influence of the surrounding milieu, to which the Dukhobors were connected primarily by economic ties, interfered. But as much as this was at all possible, the Dukhobors worked out and insisted upon their way of life in economic and family matters. To the degree to which, among the influences of the surrounding world, this could be achieved, they strove toward the realization of their religious and social ideas and toward the creation as they understood it of "the kingdom of God" on earth.

The history of Dukhoboriia as an attempt to create a religio-social utopia—the construction in the world of socially contradictory artificial social organizations based on a Christian understanding of brotherhood, equality and love—has great cognitive interest. This was a concentrated experiment, to one degree or another characterisitic for all the basic groupings of Russian religious sectarianism, which arose and developed on the basis of contradictions in the feudal-serf system. It led (like the experiments of all other sects) to results directly opposite to the interests and desires of ordinary participants of the sectarian movement.

1. Economic Development and Social Contradictions in Dukhobor Settlements

The resettlement of the Dukhobors in the Transcaucasus was centered in Akhalkalaki Uezd of Tiflis Guberniia. Some time later part of them resettled in Elizavetpol' Guberniia and in Kars Oblast.

By the middle of the 1880s, there were the following settlements of Dukhobors in the Transcaucasus and Kars Oblast, as shown in Table 1.

TABLE 1

I. Tiflis Guberniia Akhalkalaki Uezd (Source: *Sbornik* 1899, Appendix 1: 10-11)

village	total inhabitants
1. Bogdanovka	779
2. Goreloe	1277
3. Efremovka	689
4. Orlovka	979
5. Rodionovka	780
6. Spasskoe	658
7. Tambovka	504
8. Troitskoe	657
TOTAL	6323

Borchalinskii Uezd (Argutinskii-Dolgorukov 1897: 278-279, 290-291)

1. Armasheni	255
2. Bashkichet	406
3. Karaklis Russkii	148
TOTAL	809
Total for guberniia	7132

II. Elizavetpol' Guberniia Elizavetpol' Uezd (Abelov 1887: 212-213)

village	total inhabitants
1. Novogoreloe	446
2. Novospasskoe	202
3. Slavianka	1426
4. Novotroitskoe	203
Total for guberniia	2277

III. Kars Oblast, Kars Okrug (on January 1, 1894) (Bochkarev 1897: 505-508, 512-513)

1. Gorelovka	472
2. Kirillovka	602
3. Spasovka	817
4. Terpenie	886
5. Novopokrovka	550
6. Troitskoe	269
Total for oblast	3396
GRAND TOTAL	12,805

Besides this, about 200 Dukhobors lived in Erevan Guberniia and quite small groups of them were found in Terek Oblast, and in Dagestan (*Raspredelenie* 1902).

The information in the table on the number of Dukhobors is confirmed by the results of the census of 1897 (*ibid.*). According to census data, there were 3,344 Dukhobors living in Kars Oblast (in our table, from data of 1894, 3396). Against the 2,277 Dukhobors living in Elizavetpol' Guberniia, the census of 1897 numbered 2,867 persons. The increase in the number of Dukhobors by 590 persons, i.e. approximately by 26%, can be completely explained by natural increase in the population over eleven years, which in this case amounts to an average of 2.4% per year.

As against 7,132 Dukhobors living in Tiflis Guberniia in 1886, the census of 1897 lists 8,613 persons. The increase in Dukhobors by 1,481, i.e. approximately by 20%, in turn is within the boundaries of the natural growth of the population.[1]

However, according to V. A. Sukhorev, the Dukhobors (before emigration) were more numerous, thus: in Tiflis Guberniia, 11,800; in Elizavetpol' Guberniia, 4,000 in Kars Oblast, 5,000 — and in a total more than 20,000 persons (Sukhorev 1944: 58-59). These data are close to G. V. Verigin's , who wrote in 1896: "Our community in the Caucasus consists of about 20,000 persons" (Verigin 1935: 181).

The table given shows that about 60% of the resettled Dukhobors lived by 1886 in Akhalkalaki and Borchalinskii Uezds of Tiflis Guberniia. If we add Stepanov's data on the number of Dukhobors who lived at the beginning of the 1880s in Kars Oblast, which he said was 1,924 persons,[2] then it turns out that about 60% of the resettled Dukhobors were in Akhalkalaki Uezd of Tiflis Guberniia alone. This increases the significance of study of the economic life of the Akhalkalaki Dukhobors in order to characterize the economic activity of the entire mass of resettled Dukhobors.

Kh. A. Vermishev, who studied the settlement of the Akhalkalaki Dukhobors in the middle of the 1880s, came to the conclusion that "the Dukhobors are distinguished by incomparably greater well-being than the surrounding population" (Vermishev 1886: 43). Vermishev wrote: "... the Dukhobors are both absolutely and relatively the best-supplied with land in the uezd ..." (Vermishev 1886: 23).

Let us turn to the statistical data. The following table (Table 2) compiled from *Sbornik statisticheskikh dannykh o zemlevladenii i sposobakh khoziaistva v piati guberniiakh Zakavkazskogo kraia* [A Collection of Statistical Data on Landholdings and Farming Methods in Five Guberniias of

TABLE 2

Population (in 69 villages of the uezd)	39,141
including Dukhobors (in 8 villages)	6,323
Landholdings (in des.)	90,937
including among the Dukhobors	32,085
Cattle	56,864
including among the Dukhobors	11,483
Sheep and goats	152,310
including among the Dukhobors	64,886
Horses	10,573
including among the Dukhobors	7,075

[1] According to the data adduced by V. K. Iatsunskii, the average yearly natural increase of the population from 1867 to 1897 was 2.4% in Novorossiia, 3.5% in the North Caucasus (Iatsunskii 1957: 217). Unfortunately we have no corresponding data for Tiflis and Elizavetpol' Guberniias in the period 1886-1897 which interests us.

[2] In Kars Oblast in 1881 there were the Dukhobor settlements of Troitskoe, Kirillovka, Spasovka, Terpenie and Gorelovka in which 1,924 persons lived (Stepanov 1882-1883: 189-191).

the Transcaucasian Region] shows the absolute and relative significance of the Dukhobor farms in the economy of Akhalkalaki Uezd from data collected in 1886 (*Sbornik* 1899, Appendix 1: 10-11).

The Dukhobors, who were approximately 16% of the population of the uezd, concentrated in their hands in rounded figures 35% of the land area (plowland, meadowland and pasture), 20% of the cattle (cattle of the Cherkass breed), 43% of the sheep and goats (fine-fleeced sheep of the "Shpanka" [Merino] breed), and 70% of the thoroughbred horses. At a time when the average landholding per head among the population of the uezd was 2.32 desiatiny, among the Dukhobors it was 5.07.

A concentration of land and livestock holdings was also characteristic for the Dukhobors of Elizavetpol' Guberniia and Kars Oblast. We have data on landholding, animal husbandry and field crops in three settlements of Dukhobors in Elizavetpol' Uezd of Elizavetpol' Guberniia (out of four), namely Novogoreloe, Slavianka and Novospasskoe. In these villages, the average landholding per head of the population of Elizavetpol' Uezd was 4.58 desiatiny. The Dukhobors in these three villages (their residents were only 4.4% of the population of the uezd) held about 26% of the sheep and goats, 10.5% of the cattle, 17% of the horses, and 7% of the pasture, meadow and plowland of the uezd (calculated from data published in *Sbornik* 1899: 212-213). Comparing the relative meadow and pasture land with the plowland among the Akhalkalaki and Elizavetpol' Dukhobors, it turns out that whereas among the Akhalkalaki Dukhobors, plowland made up only 20% of the landholdings and 80% of the meadow and pasture, the Elizavetpol' Dukhobors had 50% of the land under the plow. This testifies to the animal-husbandry emphasis of the economy of the Akhalkalaki and the grain-and-animal-husbandry emphasis of the economy of the Elizavetpol' Dukhobors.

The greater supply of land and working stock allowed the Dukhobors to grow significantly bigger crops than could be achieved by the local population which suffered from lack of land and exhausted soil. A characteristic example: "In the Dukhobor village of Kirillovka (Kars Okrug — A. K.)", wrote S. Zavorov, "of 1,060 desiatiny, about 150 des. or 14% were under grain, but in the neighboring Turkish village, of 488 des. of useful land, 170 were sown to grain or 35%. The latter figures show that if among the Russian population one and the same plot of land could be sown to grain every eight to ten years, among the the neighboring natives after a year of planting could rest only one, and more rarely, two years" (Zavarov 1899: 178-179). Agriculture among the Dukhobors was marked by a high level of technical equipment which had no comparison with the working of the land by routine tools which the local population used. Vermishev wrote that "the Dukhobors ... are very eager seekers for every possible technical improvement", and he added as an aside the following: "There is no doubt that the telegraph, the railway and other improvements of our century enjoy their attention" (Vermishev 1886: 49). Twenty years later, I. E. Petrov, who studied specially the economic position of the Dukhobors, witnessed the high technological level of agricultural labor among the Elizavetpol' Dukhobors, who specialized as we noted above in grain farming: "Almost every farm has an iron plow and several harrows. The total number of plows among the Dukhobors in Slavianka is 121, in Novo-Gorelovka 37, and in Novo-Spasovka, 20. There are 339 harrows in Slavianka, 103 in Novo-Gorelovka and 64 in Novo-Spasovka. The plows are acquired from Tiflis shops, one of which opened a branch in Slavianka. The price of the plow, depending on the model, is 35 to 50 rubles. Several owners acquired winnowing machines and cockle collectors. In Slavianka there were 39 winnowing machines and 3 cockle collectors" (Petrov 1906: 190).

The Dukhobors, especially the Elizavetpol' ones, put part of their land to market gardening. It is worth noting that market gardening became an important economic item in precisely those Dukhobor villages which were close to the railroad; this is evidence of the market character of the truck farming of the Dukhobors. According to data published by I. L. Segal' in 1890, three Dukhobor villages in Elizavetpol' Uezd (Slavianka, Novo-Troitskoe and Novo-Spasovka) and two Molokan villages (Mikhailovka and Borisy) harvested yearly as much as 45 to 50 thousand puds of potatoes (Segal' 1890). The products of truck farming—potatoes, carrots, cabbage and beetroot—were sold on the local market at a very good price, and a significant portion of the potatoes were carted out for sale in Tiflis (Segal' 1890).

Grain-growing also had market character and brought the Dukhobors many times more income than truck gardening. A recent investigator of the peasant economy in the Transcaucasus, V. D. Mochalov, came to the correct conclusion, highly important for our study, that: "the most market-oriented grain production in Georgia and Azerbaidjan was in the farms of the German colonists and the Russian sectarians (the Dukhobors, Molokans, Baptists, etc.), who as a rule were much better supplied with parcels of land than the local native population" (Mochalov 1958: 152). According to V. D. Mochalov's data, the Dukhobors of Slavianka, Novo-Gorelovka, Novo-Spasovka and Novo-Troitskoe supplied "the Kedabek copper-smelting plant located nine versts from it (Slavianka—A. K.), at which the number of workers and white-collar personnel numbered as many as two or three thousand persons.... At the same time the peasants of the other Azerbaidjan villages, which surrounded the factory, not only did not have a surplus of grain for sale, but could hardly satisfy their own needs for it" (Mochalov 1958: 153).

But the largest source of income for the Dukhobors (in Tiflis and Elizavetpol' Guberniias and Kars Oblast) was fine-fleeced sheep. Making a comparison between the sheep-raising of the Kars Dukhobors and the neighboring Kurds, V. P. Bochkarov noted that whereas among the Kurds, shearing from the sheep reached 4.5 pounds of wool and was valued at 4.5-5 rubles a pud, the shearing from a sheep on Dukhobor farms was 6 and more pounds and was valued at 6-7 rubles a pud (Bochkarev 1897: 433). The Kars Dukhobors traded in wool and sheep.

The sheep-raising operation of the Akhalkalaki Dukhobors, considering that there were as many as 65,000 sheep in 1886, must have been directed toward the market.

Data on the head of sheep in the economy of the Elizavetpol' Dukhobors are contradictory. According to some data, there were more than 27,000 sheep, but in I. L. Segal''s opinion, which is accepted by A. L. Masalkin, there were as many as 50,000 sheep (Segal' 1890; Masalkin 1893b). These authors state that the Elizavetpol' Dukhobors yearly marketed 35-40,000 rubles of wool and 12-15,000 rubles in sheep. Through the mediation of Armenian jobbers, the wool produced by the Elizavetpol' Dukhobors appeared on the Moscow and Nizhegorod markets (see Segal' 1890 and Masalkin 1893b).

V. P. Bochkarev, summing up his observations of the economic activity of the Kars Dukhobors, wrote: "Judging from official comments, which it is impossible to suspect of partiality, and finally, from all other circumstances, one must agree that Dukhobors indubitably are the best and most productive part of the population in the region" (Bochkarev 1897: 370). Vermishev gives a description more or less close to this for the Dukhobors in Elizavetpol' Guberniia.

In fact, by the 1880s, the Dukhobors created a progressive animal husbandry and grain economy, exceeding in wealth, productivity and technological sophistication the economy of the native local population.

On the basis of what socio-economic relationships did the Dukhobor economy develop? It developed on the basis of exploitation of and theft from the economically-dependent mass of Dukhobors, including a stratum of poor farmers, supplemented by permanent and seasonal hired laborers from among the native inhabitants of the Transcaucasus and Kars Oblast, on the part of large-scale stock-breeding farmers and landowners.

Contrary to the opinion, widespread through the efforts of liberal-Narodniks, about the artel organization of the Dukhobors, Vermishev categorically asserts: "... the Dukhobors must in any case be considered individualist". They were deeply imbued with individualism of economic behavior and lifestyle, the basic principle of which was entrepreneurial initiative, fired by selfish material interests. "Personal profit, personal labor and skill", Vermishev wrote of the Dukhobors," in their opinion should not be wasted by fecklessness, and therefore each Dukhobor, having become independent, strives absolutely to separate himself out and to live on his own grain and to test his strength in everyday matters" (Vermishev 1886: 44). This is the remark of an impartial, but if anything sympathetic, student of the Dukhobors who directly observed their economic life and mutual relations. According to the same testimony, the Dukhobors not only strove to carry on individual operations, but were in principle opposed to cooperative economic forms: "nothing similar to communal life, or any memory of productive cooperatives can be observed among them. They even deny the possibility of such societies, since in these communities, they think, lazy people would surely live on the labors of industrious ones." Vermishev writes that the Dukhobors felt "antipathy to communal life and communal labor" (*ibid.*). Thus, in their economic practice and in their world-view, the Dukhobors were at this time the direct opposite of their distant predecessors, who in laying down the bases of the movement proclaimed: "People should hold property in common and give to one another without return, because they are brothers" (Ryndziunskii 1954: 178). For a very long time, exploitation and competition had divided "brothers", and made them enemies to each other. In all the sects, relations between fellow believers in the last analysis evolved on the basis of economic dependence and exploitation of the lower ranks by the upper. However, whereas, for example, among the Khristovovers and the Mennonites, the upper classes, having resorted to open forms of exploitation of labor, preferred to use hired labor from outside the community, in the Dukhobor milieu this "squeamishness" was abandoned. "The Dukhobors", Vermishev writes, "do not consider it a sin, as other sectarians do, to keep laborers" (Vermishev 1886: 44). In the Dukhobor milieu, the institution of hired labor was firmly fixed.

Vermishev, having been in his travels around Tiflis Guberniia a witness to the horrifying misery of its native inhabitants, apparently correlated these impressions with observations on the life of the Dukhobors, when he wrote: "Even so-called idlers (Dukhobors—A. K.) live as hired laborers, and having a certain income, do not produce a depressing impression by their poverty and submissiveness" (Vermishev 1886: 43).

But a more exact idea of the Dukhobor poor was given by the reminiscences of an Akhalkalaki Dukhobor from the village of Efremovka, S. F. Rybin: "The wealthy ate wheat bread", he writes, "and the poor barley" (Rybin 1952: 327). One must remember that barley—that part of it which was left over from sale on the market—was used as fodder for horses.

The working conditions of agricultural laborers in Dukhobor settlements were exceptionally difficult: "Wealthy Dukhobors unceremoniously enslaved their impoverished brothers—they kept them as workers, paying 25 rubles a year and giving clothes and food. The hired laborers worked from dawn to dusk: in summer 16 hours. In extreme poverty, even such remuneration was considered as alms" (Rybin 1952: 3).

In other cases, hired labor cost the boss more. This depended on the age, stamina and ability of the worker. I. N. and G. S. Zibarov, who were well-known among the Dukhobors and who settled in Canada, shared with Dukhobor young people their recollection of life in Russia: "We have to say something about wages too, how we earned a kopek—there a capable young man of thirty worked a whole year for 40 or 50 rubles from dawn to dusk ..." (Malov 1949: 211).

According to the contemporary Canadian Dukhobor historian P. N. Malov, social inequality and exploitation were characteristic phenomena in the Transcaucasian Dukhobor villages in the 1860s (Malov 1949: 26). The reminiscences of the Dukhobor Vasilii Pozdniakov relate to this time or a little later: "... in my memory there was a time when many brothers, having become wealthy, began to abandon our former teachings, they began to drink wine, to smoke, and began to separate out, and each owned his property individually" (Bonch-Bruevich 1901: 7). Among the hired laborers there were numerous representatives of the impoverished and homeless local population (the Tatars, Kurds and Armenians), both men and women (Verigin 1935: 27; Zavarov 1899: 232).

Besides the institution of hired labor, other forms of economic dependence existed in the Dukhobor milieu. Thus, for example, the soil conditions which existed in the place where the Akhalkalaki Dukhobors lived made unfulfillable demands on the poor farmers: to work the land with a plow demanded a team of five to six horses with four workers (Vermishev 1886: 41). As a rule a large part of the Dukhobors were forced to enter into relationships of bondage with rich property-owners who loaned them tools and means of production, which the poor peasants paid back with work on the owners' lands (Vermishev 1886: 41-43). Forms of dependence based on money-lending were also widespread. The poor, entangled by debt, were ruined. The Dukhobor Vasilii Pozdniakov, whom I have just cited, wrote: "Many even went so far, having given each other loans, as to demand the return of debts" (Bonch-Bruevich 1901: 7). I. E. Petrov, who studied the farms of the Elizavetpol' Dukhobors, asserted that "among the Dukhobors there are many debts" (Petrov 1906: 193). According to his data, the size of the minimum debt among the Dukhobors in Slavianka and the surrounding villages was 25 rubles, but debts in the amount of 150 to 350 rubles predominated, and in seven cases, the debt amounted to 1,000 rubles (Petrov 1906: 193). Every possible form of economic dependence and coercion was supplemented by outright acts of thievery on the part of rich people in relation to the mass of Dukhobors. Vermishev made the observation: "... among the Dukhobors there is no recognition of a crime against the property of a friend" (Vermishev 1886: 43).

In fact, the entire economic might and administrative power of the large livestock-owners and landowners impressed the mass of Dukhobors with a holy respect for private property. As concerns pastureland, whose area measured thousands of desiatiny and formally belonged to the Dukhobor communities in joint use, the crimes of the rich people against this kind of "property of a friend" were systematic. "... In Russian settlements", N. A. Abelov wrote, "and especially among the Dukhobors, we see that public pastureland was fearfully exploited by rich people who had many cattle. Their numerous herds, even before the beginning of winter, trampled down the public pasture ... leaving the land bare for the cattle of the poor people.... With the beginning of warm days, the herd of the wealthy again hurried to the public lands, where they spent the summer if there was even the smallest possibility of feeding there" (Abelov 1887: 39).

In order to give an idea of a large Dukhobor farm in the 1880s, we will briefly characterize the farm of the Verigin family from the village of Slavianka, Elizavetpol' Uezd, well-known among the Dukhobors. Judging from the words of G. V. Verigin, this was an average farm. "Our parents did not live that richly but also not poorly", he wrote (Verigin 1935: 21). Verigin was the owner of a 3,000-head herd of sheep, 100 cattle and 70 horses, a water-mill with 2 sets of millstones, and a craft shop. The Verigin farm used hired labor. G. Verigin tells of a visit in September of 1886 to Slavianka by Peter Verigin, who played an important role among the Dukhobors: "... he (Peter Verigin — A. K.) wished to look at all our holdings ... he looked at everything and said: "Well, you here are only supervisors ... but your workers work hard for you.' He pointed them out to us. The workers were from among the Tatars of the poorer class; there were married men, yearly workers and every sort. There were twelve of them. Among them there were also women" (Verigin 1935: 26-27).

Supplementing the description of the size and make-up of the Verigin farm and the forms of exploitation adopted on it, let us add the testimony of S. F. Rybin, who illustrated the practice of the stealing of common land by the rich Dukhobors: "The family of Vasilii L. Verigin was especially distinguished among the wealthy Dukhobors for its cruelty.... Having enormous herds of rams, they unceremoniously trampled down the meadow which was designated for the use of all the residents of the village of Slavianka. To the requests and complaints of their brother Dukhobors that they should not spoil the harvest of grass, they responded with laughter or threatened beatings ..." (Rybin 1952: 5).

We showed above that the Dukhobors created a high-productivity animal-husbandry and grain economy, distinguished by technological sophistication and high marketability. But the "kingdom of God" which they introduced into the Caucasian and Kars lands turned out under close scrutiny to be founded on the most ordinary principles of capitalist domination. The sources of well-being of rich Dukhobor property-owners was the exploitation of hired and other economically dependent labor.

Bourgeois economic principles permeated the entire structure of familial living and property relationships among the Dukhobors. Dukhobor families as a rule were 1.5 to 2 times smaller than the neighboring Armenian, Georgian and Kurdish families. Property divisions and redistributions took place in them periodically: "The Dukhobor does not like to live in a large family", Vermishev says, "where his personal zeal, personal dignity and personal work are completely diffused in the economic activity of the entire family" (Vermishev 1886: 44). The attitude toward women had the obvious character of an attitude toward a commodity on the labor market. The inability of a woman to work, even if conditioned by illness, served as sufficient basis for divorce; in this case the woman's property which she had brought to the family of the husband was returned to her and, most cynically, the woman received a monetary account reflecting her work expenditure in the husband's family, on the basis of the standard yearly payment for one hired woman laborer (Vermishev 1886: 47).

The Dukhobors (like other sectarians) were among the pioneers and pathfinders of the bourgeois entrepreneurial system in the agriculture of the Transcaucasus. They had experience at conducting a market economy, which had been accumulated by them and their ancestors over the course of many decades of their stay in the Tambov area and in the areas of Ekaterinoslav and Khar'kov, and then in Molochnye Vody, where some of them had not only market but even capitalist operations.

The beliefs of the Dukhobors, in turn, corresponded to their interests of commodity producers, ideologically strengthening and blessing individualism, facilitating the growth of personal initiative, enterprise, economic quickness and thrift. They brought to the Transcaucasus not only a definite economic experience and convictions giving religious sanction to this experience, but also significant cash on hand accumulated in Molochnye Vody. With all the difficulties which they experienced in the period of resettlement and initial construction in the Transcaucasus, this time remains in the memory of Dukhobors, in the words of their historian, "a period of rest" (Sukhorev 1944: 60).

Thanks to all this, the Dukhobors resettling in the Transcaucasus quickly succeeded in making a start in the market and then in the bourgeois development of their farms.[3] But this was not all. The Dukhobors created and in

---

[3] We must remember that among the sources of the quick wealth of the Dukhobors, military transport was of some importance in 1878. Dukhobor transport served the needs of the standing army in the Caucasian theater of the Russo-Turkish war. Several "dynasties" of large bourgeois property-owners in "Dukhoboriia" date from this time. It was precisely after the war of 1877-1878 that the flow of Dukhobors from Akhalkalaki Uezd into Kars Oblast increased. Most of those settling in Kars Oblast were "wealthy owners of large herds, who were cramped in their villages and were involved in the general tendency toward the development of stock-breeding" (Vermishev 1886: 23).

practice worked out forms of organization which served to make their economic activities successful. At the base of this organization there lay the principle of mobility of monetary funds and exploitation of the advantage of large operations over small ones. The Dukhobors founded in the village of Goreloe, Akhalkalaki Uezd, Tiflis Guberniia, the so-called Orphans Home, modeled on the Orphans Home founded during the stay in Molochnye Vody. "This institution", writes P. Malov, "was a kind of public treasury or aid fund, consisting both of capital on hand and of various operations and properties.... The entire capital of the Orphans Home was made up by voluntary contributions by the Dukhobors themselves and served as a source of support in any disaster ... and in general in all cases of need.... The Orphans Home and everything connected with it was considered common property and was under the direction and at the disposal of the Dukhobor leader. The Orphans Home was also the main residence of the leaders and their families, and also the center of all spiritual and material treasures" (Malov 1949: 23).

The Orphans Home was essentially a bank, whose capital consisted of systematic deposits by the entire Dukhobor population, acting in the peculiar role of moral stockholders, and completely dependent on their leaders, who united in themselves a divine hypostasis with the hypostasis of a financial magnate. This was a bank, financing the entrepreneurial activity of large owners of cattle and grain operations, facilitating vast transactions for the acquisition of land tracts, which were considered common property but in fact, as has already been shown, were trampled by the wealthy livestock-owners to the detriment of the interests of the poor peasants. We may judge of the financial capabilities of the Orphans Home from the fact that in 1886 its capital was valued at more than half a million rubles. At this time the Orphans Home also owned plowland, pastureland, horses, sheep, goats and cattle. The Orphans Home had branches in various places, where regular deposits were made by Dukhobors calculated on the basis of from 20 pounds to a pud of grain per head of population (Vermishev 1886: 44). It follows that the actual owners of the Orphans Home, interested both in its existence and in the bulk of its capital, should be obliged in some measure to spend the accumulated wealth on the needs of the basic mass of Dukhobors. This was expressed mainly in subsidies, issued to the Dukhobors in case of natural disaster — cattle plague, fires, etc., and also in various forms of philanthropy.

Mutual aid, in which wealthy elements also took part, was relatively widely practiced among the Dukhobors. There were instances in which well-to-do Dukhobor farmers plowed the land of a poor Dukhobor with the help of draft animals and agricultural tools which they owned. Vermishev notes: "... the rich man did not dig between himself and the poor man that deep gulf which was so characteristic for the rest of the life of the population" (Vermishev 1886: 43).

We have already shown how deep the "gulf" between various social strata of the Dukhobors was, but the capital of the Orphans Home and its branches, which was at the collective service of the rich men, permitted them from time to time to soften the bite of the social contradictions among Dukhobors with handouts. Encouraging "mutual aid" among Dukhobors served the same goal of creating the illusion of social harmony, and the appearance of respect for the collectivist traditions of the earlier period of Dukhoborism.

The founding of the Orphans Home dates, apparently, from the second half of the 1840s. The so-called agricultural funds were introduced taking into account the experience of the Orphans Home in the 1890s in Tiflis Guberniia. These were public funds formed by a collection of grain from the peasants (up to 20 pounds of grain from a worker) and designated, in the words of its initiators, "to support the independence of the countryside, and to awaken in it creative agricultural forces" (Zertsalov 1916: 4). This meant first of all financial support of "strong" peasants, in order to help them to develop into capitalistic farmers. "Agricultural funds" were issued to acquire technology and land, to improve the breed of cattle, and also for help in natural disasters. They primarily served those peasants who already conducted a market economy, and the ruling stratum counted on acquiring allies in the village by encouraging the spread of this entrepreneurial system. Not for nothing was the Tiflis governor Shervashidze among the initiators of "agricultural funds", since he in particular deserves notice as the constant sympathizer and supporter of the Dukhobor bosses of the Orphans Home and for the bloody reprisal unleashed in 1895 on the defenseless Dukhobor poor.

For all that distinguished the Orphans Home from "agricultural funds", the latter proceeded from the same economic principles and served the same aims as the Orphans Home. Capitalist-oriented economists saw the future of agricultural funds in their being transformed from the possession of individual villages into a fund for the whole guberniia under the title of "The Tiflis Peasant Mutual Agricultural Bank" (Zertsalov 1916: 14) and, thus, a powerful financial organization being placed into the hands of agricultural entrepreneurs. Just such a function was served by the Orphans Home within the narrow boundaries of the Dukhobor villages.

The economic activity of the Orphans Home was periodically supplemented by the formation of "brotherhoods" of the wealthier Dukhobors, who united to rent land (primarily hayfields and pastures) from outlying landowners and peasants. As Vermishev discovered, "the Dukhobors leave only pasture in common use, and the hayfields they hasten to divide among the members of the brotherhood, in accordance with the participation of each of them in the payment of the rent" (Vermishev 1886: 23).

Let us turn to a description of the organization of power in "Dukhoboriia". The institutions of power worked out here were in no way democratic. At their head stood a leader of unlimited power (before 1886 the leader was Luker'ia Vasil'evna Kalmykova—"Lushechka"). The leader implemented power over the Dukhobors from his "palace residence" in the village of Goreloe. Here Kalmykova was repeatedly visited by the viceroy of the Caucasus and the higher members of the Caucasian government administration; several of them used the monetary "services" of Kalmykova.

Under the leader of the Dukhobors there was a consultative body, which met irregularly and consisted of the wealthiest and most influential Dukhobors, who were designated "elders", although there were no age requirements whatever for membership in this group. A so-called *ataman* of the Orphans Home was "chosen" to direct its economic and administrative activity. The post of *starshina* of the Orphans Home existed and had great significance, but I have not succeeded in determining his function. It is known that the external ties of the Orphans Home, for example with the uezd, gubernatorial and state administrations, was primarily within the competence of the *starshina*.

The Orphans Home also had a peculiar kind of military organization—the Dukhobor "Cossacks". The existence of this organization originally was connected with the hostile mutual relations which existed between the Dukhobors and the surrounding local population. P. Malov writes: "... the enormous farms and great quantity of cattle were a constant temptation for the warlike local population.... It was necessary to guard their property, and thus, little by little the Dukhobors began to carry weapons ... often bloody dramas were played out and murders even occurred on both sides" (Malov 1949: 25-26).

The Dukhobor historian is not objective. In fact, who was defending himself from whom? Were not the pastures of the local population damaged by the Dukhobor livestock-owners? Did the Dukhobors not trap their neighbors in obligations of debt-bondage in the form of loans in money and in kind? Did they not seize or acquire for very little the lands and pastures belonging to the native residents?

The Dukhobors were assigned a role in the colonization plans of tsarism. Let us cite the statement of the Tiflis governor Shervashidze: "They (the Dukhobors—A. K.) ... made all the local population respect them and on the far boundary it seemed they raised the Russian banner high. Spreading out over three guberniias among the miserable native population, their flourishing villages were pleasing oases, and on the political side, were staging points for the Russian cause and influence in the region" (Borozdin 1907: 175).

Most probably the Dukhobor Cossacks were called upon to guard by one or another means the land taken from "the warlike native population". That is the way it was in the 1840-1860s. But in the 1880s, mounted Cossacks, armed with sabres, daggers and revolvers, under the command of local chiefs, existed in a number of Dukhobor villages, carried out military training and were subordinate to the overall command of "the sergeant-major"—Peter Verigin, who stood in a special relationship to the Dukhobor leader.

The Dukhobor leader surrounded himself with an aura of imperial authority. A visit by him to Dukhobor villages was like a tsar's progress. G. Verigin left a description of the journey of Luker'ia Kalmykova to the village of Slavianka: "During her visits no one remained at home to look after the house. News of her arrival spread rapidly to all the villages and everyone who could make it hurried to travel to Slavianka to meet her. The first encounter was set up about 30 versts away. In front were the leaders on horses, 12 men, and then everyone who could, both from Slavianka and also from other villages, traveled about 8 versts beyond the boundaries of their lands. She was always met with bread and salt and the singing of psalms, and when her carriage was a verst away, the entire people was set in motion. On the one hand there was joy and on the other an attempt to put everything in order" (Verigin 1935: 24).

The designation "Dukhoboriia" was of course arbitrary; it served the sectarians to distinguish their circle from the rest of society. But if we allow this arbitary designation, Dukhoboriia was a monarchy and not a republic. It was a bourgeois-theocratic state, existing in an empire controlled by the nobility and the bourgeoisie. Ordinary Dukhobors were obliged to be absolutely submissive to their theocracy, and Vermishev had full reason to state: "There was not a single case in which a sectarian (Dukhobor—A. K.) complained of the decision of his judge" (Vermishev 1886: 45). Any serious "disobedience" brought with it a boycott of the disobedient person, and his ruin.

Patriarchal conceptions of power prevailed in the Dukhobor villages, under conditions of arbitrary rule which did not stop at the law of the fist.

The motto of Dukhoborism is that man "is a marvelous, wonderful creation of God."[4] How did it turn out in practice? V. Pozdniakov left a description of the administrative life in Dukhobor settlements in the 1880s: "Once V. Verigin was chosen volost starshina, and he at once paid back the people subordinate to him in such a fashion that they many times repented of having chosen for themselves an executioner. He never went anywhere away from home without a whip. As soon as anyone said something he didn't like, he got the whip across the forehead (man "is a marvelous, wonderful creation of God"!—A. K.). Whoever didn't see him, didn't take off his hat, and did not bow to him—also got the whip (man "is a marvelous, wonderful creation of God"!—A. K.). Riding on horseback in the villages, if he saw the smallest mess next to anyone's house, he called the owner of the house, and used the

---

[4] Bonch-Bruevich 1909: xvii. He characterized as one of the most important propositions of the Dukhobor teaching, the following: "Only man, for the sake of man, lays the foundation of the knowledge of all life, and therefore everything proceeds from man and is contained in man—man 'is a marvelous, wonderful creation of God'."

whip. It got so bad that people began to hide when he rode along the streets ..." (Pozdniakov 1914: 108). S. F. Rybin relates how Luker'ia Kalmykova "made young children whip drunkards with switches in public, and meanwhile said: 'You didn't listen to the spirit, so now listen to the switches' " (Rybin 1952: 7). The rights of the "spirit", enforced by public whippings!

The economic enslavement and social oppression of the masses of Dukhobors were supplemented by ignorance, superstition and prejudice. In the 1880s in the Transcaucasus, literate Dukhobors constituted an exception. Village communities of Dukhobors subscribed to the newspaper *Kavkaz* [The Caucasus], which rare literate people read aloud to their fellow villagers. Every sort of spell and witch-doctoring was in use.

The situation changed very slowly. At the beginning of the 1900s, of 392 male Dukhobors of Elizavetpol', there were 272 literate ones, but, as the researcher Petrov wrote, "The literacy of men was limited in large part to the ability somehow to put their names on papers, and somehow to make out what was written" (Petrov 1906: 187). Of 857 Elizavetpol' Dukhobor women, not one was literate. True, at that time the Dukhobors opened schools in the Elizavetpol' settlements, served by three teachers (*ibid.*). The illiteracy of the Dukhobors distinguished them from other sectarians in the Transcaucasus—the Molokans and Baptists. This was caused not only by socio-economic, but also by religious reasons. In distinction to the Molokans and Baptists, who based their teaching on the interpretation of the Bible, and studied it in detail, the Dukhobors counterposed inner revelation to the Bible, and on the basis of the New Testament expression, "the letter killeth, but the spirit giveth life", declared the letter outside the law, for which they paid with complete illiteracy. Even with "living revelation", the situation among them was very bad. Children and young people learned by rote the psalms which made up the famous *Living Book,* without understanding their content at all. No live sermons were preached. From Bonch-Bruevich's personal observations, "the ritual flowed into a definite form, taking the place of the usual church religious ritual, often losing all meaning, but preserved by tradition" (Bonch-Bruevich 1905: 269).

Drunkenness and smoking were widespread among the Dukhobors.

Such were the socio-economic conditions, the cultural backwardness, the intellectual stagnation and moral decline hiding behind the facade of material well-being in Dukhobor settlements.

This was also the price which the mass of Dukhobors paid for the flourishing farm operations of their fellow believers—the owners of livestock and land. "The Dukhobors were an entire world in miniature", S. F. Rybin wrote of his fellow believers, "They had their gods in the person of their leaders, their aristocracy, wealthy families and their opposites, the poor, their slaves" (Rybin 1952: 3).

From the very beginning, the religio-social utopias of the Dukhobors were nothing other than a clouded anticipation of bourgeois social relations. The attempts to bring these utopias to life ended with the only thing they could end with—the establishment of a system of bourgeois relationships among the Dukhobors themselves. The Dukhobors facilitated the dissemination of bourgeois forms of economy in the Transcaucasus, successfully using the additional possibilities given them by the peculiarities of their organizational structure, morals and teaching. In this sense, the role played by them in the Transcaucasus was objectively progressive. But the Dukhobor world was made up of contradictions. What seemed to the Dukhobors a struggle for the building of the kingdom of God on earth in reality was a deception and self-deception. Among the mass of Dukhobors, a social protest matured, this time pointed not against the ruling church as a tool of enslaving serfdom, but against their own leaders, who turned the religious organization and teaching of the Dukhobors into a weapon of bourgeois class rule.

2. The Class Struggle in the Dukhobor Settlements and the Emigration of Some of Them to Canada

On December 15, 1886, Luker'ia Kalmykova died without leaving an heir. The dynastic line of leaders was broken. At this time there belonged among the people close to Kalmykova: her brothers—the elders Mikhail and Ignatii Gubanov; the ataman of the Orphans Home, I. V. Baturin; Kalmykova's favorites, the starshina Aleksei Zubkov, Sergeant Major P. V. Verigin, A. F. Vorob'ev; and Mariia Tikhonova, Luker'ia Kalmykova's confidante.

Peter Verigin, who had the role of protégé in Kalmykova's lifetime, and Aleksei Zubkov, who was influential among the Dukhobors, had the trust of their wealthier circles and had extensive ties with the government administration in the Caucasus, were the most serious contenders for the vacant "throne". Zubkov understood that he had no formal rights to inherit the power and property of Kalmykova (the Orphans Home with its capital was entirely in her name). In the struggle for power he made a wager on subsidiary figures—either on the brother of Kalmykova, the characterless Mikhail Gubanov (it was after all a collateral line), or on Mariia Tikhonova, a faceless woman whom many Dukhobors considered a "saint", the receptacle of "the divine spirit of Kalmykova". In both cases the factual ruler of Dukhoboriia would be Aleksei Zubkov himself.

On the 17th of December, Kalmykova's funeral was held, and on the same day Zubkov, Baturin and Mikhail Gubanov demanded that Verigin leave the Orphans Home. With this Mikhail Gubanov was named the heir of the property of the Orphans Home. Verigin obeyed, but began energetic activity against Gubanov and his adherents. Gubanov was declared an expropriator of the public property of the Dukhobors—the Orphans Home. In reality, the public ownership of the capital of the Orphans Home was a fiction. Juridically this capital was Kalmykova's private property, factually in joint use by the wealthier strata of the Dukhobors. But in the eyes of a wide mass, who were under the heel of a homegrown aristocracy, Verigin was immediately transformed into an apostle of "justice", the defender of the Dukhobors not only from Gubanov's encroachments on the Orphans Home, but in general from the oppression and thievery of the all-powerful rich.

January 26 was declared a memorial day for Kalmykova and a day for announcing the new Dukhobor leader. Both sides prepared for the event, each according to his means and possibilities. Verigin attempted to enlist the widest possible support among the Dukhobors. Zubkov and Gubanov turned to the police. On January 26, the Dukhobors gathered in Goreloe. Prince Sumbatov, the Akhalkalaki Uezd police superintendent, arrived, accompanied by police officers. After completion of the memorial ritual, one of the oldest Dukhobors, Makhortov, proposed that those gathered bow to the new leader—Peter Verigin. As Rybin writes, "a large part of the crowd fell on their knees in the snow, but a small part remained on their feet" (Rybin 1952: 13). That very day, Verigin was arrested, and then sent into exile (first in Shenkursk, Arkhangel'sk Guberniia, then on the Kola Peninsula, and then in Obdorsk, Tobol'sk Guberniia). Several of Verigin's most fervent followers were also exiled, Makhortov among them.

Verigin's exile set off a wave of unrest in the villages of the Tiflis, Elizavet-pol' and Kars Dukhobors, and facilitated the final division of the Dukhobors into two parties: the Small—Gubanov's adherents—and the Large, Verigin's adherents.

If we rely on the testimony of Grigorii Verigin, the total number of adherents of the Large Party reached approximately 11,000 persons, whereas the total number of adherents of the Small Party was approximately 2,000 (Verigin 1935: 31).

A special agent of the Synod, V. Skvortsov, who visited the Dukhobor settlements in 1895, reported that the number of Verigin's adherents reached 6,000 persons (3,000 in Tiflis Guberniia, 1,000 in Elizavetpol' Guberniia, and 2,000 in Kars Oblast) (Skvortsov 1899: 320). The discrepancy between Grigorii Verigin's and Skvortsov's testimony is not as significant as it would seem at first glance. In fact, when Skvortsov visited the Dukhobor settlements, a fairly significant compromise party had separated out, headed by A. F. Vorob'ev and receiving the designation of the Middle Party. Although in both the Large and Small Parties there were elements of very different social and property position, basically these were one party for the rich property-owners and another for the poor. P. Malov tells of a certain Ponomarev, first attaching himself to the Small Party: "... Ponomarev was one of the rich people and, it was said, a very proud man. He had at first reacted negatively to the Dukhobor reforms in the Caucasus, more because poor people, or, in his opinion, beggers, figured most prominently in these movements" (Malov 1949: 70).

We will not dwell on the complicated upheavals of the struggle of the representatives of the Large and Small Parties for the inheritance of the property of the Orphans Home. In the last analysis, thanks to malicious litigation, bribes, and graft by Gubanov and his adherents, a legal vindication was achieved of their rights to the possession of the capital of the Orphans Home. At the same time, Mariia Tikhonova was proclaimed spiritual leader of the Dukhobors by the Small Party.

This struggle had, however, a sobering influence on the consciousness of the mass of Dukhobors: it showed clearly the antagonism between the interests of the rich and the poor, and made public the connection existing between the privileged Dukhobors and the tsarist administration.

The Small Party won in the "small" struggle for capital, but the Large Party waged a great struggle for the social and economic interests of the poor, against the large property-owners and the representatives of the Autocracy in the Caucasus who supported them.

The social movement of the Dukhobors, being an open manifestation of the social contradictions in their midst, was distinguished by the stubbornness of its participants. The name of Verigin became for them a symbol of their cause, completely independent of Verigin's own aims and mode of thought.

In exile, Verigin made contact with the remaining activists of the Large Party on the spot and transmitted directives to them in both written and oral form. In the first letter, dated March 6, 1888, Verigin called upon the Dukhobors of the Large Party of "go without a murmur along the path where the gates are sown with sharp and prickly thorns", cautioning: "I fear and am frightened by your weak and meandering spirit". However he himself manifested genuine "weakness of spirit": "Do not quarrel and do not offend those who offend you, but pray for them ..." (Bonch-Bruevich 1901).

Some time later, there followed a new letter from Verigin, containing motifs and, as Bonch-Bruevich established, literal excerpts from L. N. Tolstoy's essay, *Tsarstvo bozhie vnutri vas* [The Kingdom of God is Within You]. Following the ideas of Tolstoyan "Christian anarchism", Verigin in his letter called upon his followers not to submit to any human laws and directives. He reproduced in his letter texts from Tolstoy's "Kingdom of God", in which the latter cited the famous American publicist William Lloyd Garrison, a representative of the philosophy of "spiritual anarchism" (Parrington 1962: 416; see also 410-420).

Verigin's letter facilitated the formation of the ideology of Dukhobors on the move. Their protest over the course of the first few years of the existence of the Large Party was directed primarily against the Small Party of the rich. Even at that time slogans about equality of property received currency among the Dukhobors of the Large Party, but in the foreground stood complete economic, social and familial demarcation from the adherents of the Large Party, and if possible, territorial separation from them. In the words of the governor Shervashidze, between 1886 and 1892 "relations between the parties sharpened to the point where a petition was initiated to divide the Goreloe rural community into two communities—Goreloe proper, where it would be possible to domicile all Dukhobors of the Small Party, and Spasskoe (from the villages of Spasskoe, Orlovka, Bogdanovka, Efremovka, Tambovka, Rodionovka and Troitskoe), for the Dukhobors of the Large Party ..." (Borozdin 1907: 187). By 1893 this division finally was implemented. We can judge the significance for the Dukhobors of the bases for this division from the fact that it touched not only their property interests but also family and kin relationships. Marriages were dissolved in cases where men and women belonged to opposing parties; married couples divided the children. "Cries, groans, murmurs", Rybin writes, "were heard like an ominous echo in all the villages" (Rybin 1952: 15).

But the struggle of the parties which had been formed in Dukhoborism, although openly social in character, did not pass into revolutionary action of the poor against the rich. The rupture of contact with the rich to the point of territorial demarcation from them was the first step on the path by which the Dukhobors of the Large Party finally arrived at the decision to leave Russia. Whatever sacrifices this path demanded, it went along the line of least resistance: the leaders of the Large Party did not struggle to dictate their will to their opponents. They preferred to lead their followers from the field of battle. Long before the leader of the Large Party arrived at the decision to take his followers to Canada, Verigin (in 1890) brought forth the idea of resettlement from the Transcaucasus somewhere in outlying guberniias of Russia. On Verigin's instructions, Ivan Konkin, who was close to him, visited several guberniias of Eastern Siberia and the Far East with this aim. But his mission ended in failure (Verigin 1935: 55). This happened several years before the Dukhobors of the Large Party entered into open conflict with the Autocracy.

Thus, the plan for resettling the Dukhobors out of the Transcaucasus was the result of the development of total contradiction among them. Subsequently, when the internal struggle in Dukhoborism was complicated by the interference of the tsarist authorities, the leaders of the Large Party implemented an idea thought up long before.

The emigration of the Dukhobors to Canada was not only a result of their conflict with the Autocracy, but was a consequence of two social wars which the lower ranks of the Dukhobor sect conducted as they could, in view of their level of social development.

The path of the struggle which the leaders of the Large Party pointed out was marked by utopianism. They could break with their fellow believers and exploiters, and territorially divide from them, but outside the revolutionary struggle, neither in Russia nor in Canada nor anywhere in the world was there any exit from the contradictions which held the small Dukhobor world in a vise.

The leaders of the Large Party called their followers not forward but back to the legends of primitive Christianity, as they described their fancies. In 1893, Verigin formulated a new program for the Dukhobors and with his emissaries, Ivan Konkin and Vasilii Ob"edkov, sent it to the Transcaucasus. This program consisted of the following basic positions:

1. Exploitation of hired and any other dependent labor is incompatible with Christianity;

2. Property inequality is to be annihilated by an equal distribution of property of the rich among the poor with the voluntary agreement of the rich;

3. Stimuli leading to the accumulation of wealth are to be abolished, from which follow: a) limitation of the size of the farm so that it only fulfills the needs of simple reproduction of the conditions of life, which demands maximal "simplification" of the way of life of believers (lifestyle, dress, etc.); b) the ending of marriages, and abstention from sexual relations by those already married, so that the growth of the family would not make necessary supplemental means for its upkeep;

4. Service in the military, being connected with force, is incompatible with Christianity (Verigin 1935: 58-60).

This program deserves attention first of all because it shows the connection between the movement of the Dukhobors in the second half of the 1880s and in the 1890s, and the exploitation of the lower ranks by the upper in the Dukhobor sect. The strong side of this program was the protest against property inequality and social oppression. At the same time Verigin's program was marked by a complete inability to understand the causes of socio-economic inequality and to find the real means for struggle with it. One is easily convinced that this program in its decisive points corresponds to the religio-social teachings of L. N. Tolstoy and was formed under his immediate influence. Like Tolstoy's teaching, it was dictated by patriarchal reaction to the victorious development of capitalist relations in the countryside, which brought to the small farmer new forms of economic oppression, ruin, beggary and transformation into a proletariat. Verigin's program was reactionary-utopian.

Society, according to this program, would be freed from contradictions at the price of the ruin of the society itself. Did not Verigin put forth the return to savagery and degeneration of humanity as a condition for the implementation of the kingdom of God on earth? In turn, society was freed from the exploitation of labor at the price of cessation of labor itself. It is true that the program under review speaks of its limitation. But it is impossible not to connect the thought about limiting labor with the subsequent judgments by Verigin about "the illegitimate multiplication of people", as a result of which "man lives where he should not live at all, where his life is unsuitable and difficult".

From Verigin's Malthusian judgments it follows that through limitation of the number of people and curtailment of the consumption of each person, the rest of them gain increased possibilities for satisfying their vital needs from the natural produce of the earth, by resorting to a simple gathering economy. Such a condition of humanity—the condition of animals—is Verigin's Kingdom of God. In a letter to Iziumchenko dated January 1, 1896, Verigin wrote: "Although I have said that spiritual perfection needed companions —work and self-denial—I do not put work at the basis of life" (Bonch-Bruevich 1901: 39). Verigin put self-denial at the basis of life as the maximum possible limitation of all natural conditions of the life of a person, which included sexual abstention: "A large saving is effected with restraint, and daily bread appears of itself (i.e. without labor—A. K.) in that house where self-denial dwells" (Bonch-Bruevich 1901: 44).

How to achieve the miracle of spontaneous appearance of bread on the tables of idle people? "I assume the possibility of a counsel", Verigin wrote, "of not working physically and being satisfied.... There is so much grain that one need only stop being greedy. The land, freed from the violence of human hands (this relates to work according to Verigin—A. K.), would begin to be filled with everything that it gave to our ancestors ... eating moderately, humanity would have enough of everything edible for a hundred years, from what there already is; after a hundred years, the earth would be completely reclothed and enter into its original state. And humanity along with the spiritual growth that Adam and Eve lost would receive a natural earthly paradise" (Bonch-Bruevich 1901: 44).

This was a preaching of return to the wild, to a primitive condition of the earth and man together. Verigin's preaching, although it embodied the anticapitalist protest of the small property-owner, remained in some things an echo of that morality against which it was protesting. Was not self-denial the prescribed virtue which the capitalist suggested to the laborer, while appropriating his labor: you are greedy, and therefore you are poor!

Verigin's preaching relieved the capitalist of responsibility for the poverty of the working classes: the matter was mainly that "at the present time there are so many people that one should be rid of them". People themselves were responsible for the fact that life is difficult: they "multiplied illegitimately"!

On December 10, 1893, Verigin's emissaries set out from Shenkursk in Arkhangel'sk Oblast to the Transcaucasus in order to announce to the Dukhobors of the Large Party the will of their spiritual leader.

The situation in the Dukhobor settlements had become increasingly tense — the enmity of the Small and Large Parties had grown. On the other hand, Verigin apparently took account of the existence of disagreements among his adherents: even in the first letter he expressed the fear that several of them had a "weak and meandering spirit". Soon life showed that among his followers there were many people inclined to compromise with the Small Party. Verigin's epistle furthered both the split between his adherents and a social definition of the trends within Dukhoborism. As we might expect, "the apple of discord" was the point of the leader's program devoted to the equalization of property.

The poor paid no attention whatever to the fact that Verigin conditioned this equalization on the voluntary agreement of the property-owner. The poor demanded the unconditional distribution of property. They devoted themselves to the new doctrine of self-denial with enthusiasm. The abandonment of smoking and drinking was supplemented by a prohibition of meat. The Postnik movement spread. Marriages were not contracted, and those already married henceforth considered themselves as "brothers and sisters". A feverish exaltation prevailed, seizing some of the rich and a significant number of the moderately wealthy Dukhobors. The division of property was begun. In the words of an eyewitness there occurred "the reconstruction of life with personal family property turned into public property.... They built public shops for various crafts: cabinetmaking, blacksmithing, shoemaking, tailoring, metalworking ..." (Bonch-Bruevich 1901: 108 [from N. I. Dudchenko's reminiscences]).

These events unfolded in the winter of 1893-1894 in all the Dukhobor settlements, although with unequal intensity. Great upheavals began among the Dukhobors of Kars Oblast and Akhalkalaki, while the Borchalinskii Dukhobors, for example, manifested less interest in the events which were occurring. At this time, A. F. Vorob'ev, who was once close to Kalmykova and who in the beginning sympathized with the Large Party, acted. The situation was right for uniting the mutually hostile Dukhobors and leading them on a new basis. Verigin was far away; the adherents of the Small Party, not to speak of their leaders, had earned the hatred and boycott of the basic mass of Dukhobors. With a broad invocation of Kalmykova's name, Vorob'ev demanded a return to the traditions of her day and declared Verigin's new ascetic teachings contradictory to them (Rybin 1952: 18-19).

But of course the question of whether to prefer meat to vegetables or vegetables to meat was not the sticking point of the disagreement between Vorob'ev and Verigin. We must suppose that Vorob'ev was sincere when in his declaration to the gubernatorial authorities he explained: "The new teachings (Verigin's — A. K.) began to appear among us two years ago (i.e. in 1893 — A. K.). Vereshchagin, Vasilii Verigin (Peter's brother) and Konkin were most active in their dissemination; it is their fault that a disagreement has occurred among us; it arose first because of the division of property, since many of us, i.e. of those who remained with the second party (the Large— A. K.), refused to take part in this division, finding it unwise; then there followed disagreements on other questions, and at the beginning of the present year, we finally separated" (Borozdin 1907: 222).

The Large Party split into a party of Vorob'ev's adherents, called the Middle Party, and a party of those who remained true to Verigin. The latter exceeded the Vorob'evites in number. Along with the old designation for Verigin's followers there was added the additional designation of "Postniki". The coincidence with one of the trends in Khristovoverie in the given case is not without some internal sense. We had occasion to note in the Khristovover movement at the end of the 19th and the beginning of the 20th centuries phenomena similar to Dukhoborism. We can now note in the Dukhobor movement at the end of the 19th century phenomena going back to Khristovoverie. In the first case the limitation of asceticism, mysticism and exaltation ideologically accompanied change in the very social character of Khristovoverie, developing along the path of transformation into a bourgeois church body. In the second case there occurred a directly opposite process.

It is noteworthy that the class solidarity of those who were fighting went beyond the bounds of religious and national separatism: "Other nations", writes G. Verigin, "the Molokans, the Armenians and the Moslems, seeing this division, also turned to us for help; they were also provided with whatever we could give" (Verigin 1935: 65).

The incidents which Verigin speaks of are confirmed by the testimony of other Dukhobors (Pozdniakov, Rybin, Sukhorev, Malov) and the testimony of lay authors (Muratov etc.). But several wealthy Dukhobors who had affiliated with the Postniki, not being able to suppress their own property-owning natures, resorted to deceit, and hid and covered up their wealth from the poor.

As P. Malov writes, "the division was not carried out completely in Russia. A division was carried out between individual families and then among villages. But such a complete equalization did not occur between residents of one guberniia and another.... In addition to this, instances were found in which some people did not give exact figures for the division and hid part of their resources.... When they resettled in Canada, there was from the very beginning a significant difference betwen immigrants from one guberniia and another ...; it is true that they avoided speaking of this difference, but the injustice of this phenomenon was all too evident to everyone" (Malov 1949: 65). Some of their new leaders also had designs on the public property of the Dukhobors; when the Kars followers of Verigin built their Orphans Home in the village of Terpenie, Vasilii, the brother of the exiled Verigin, was domiciled in it, but he was soon evicted on the order of the leader, and the poorest family in the village, that of one Petr Dorofeev, was installed in the Orphans Home (Rybin 1952: 23).

We noted that in the statement to his followers sent to the Transcaucasus at the end of 1893, Verigin spoke out for a boycott by them of military service.

The Dukhobors' struggle against their own rich people could not help being entwined with the struggle against the Autocracy. A secret government agency conducted systematic observation of the events occurring in the Dukhobor villages, and representatives of the administration openly appeared at Dukhobor meetings. Konkin, Verigin's emissary, on arrival in the Transcaucasus, was not allowed by the authorities into Kars Oblast, but immediately arrested and exiled. In 1894, on the coronation of Nicholas II, the Dukhobors in the village of Terpenie in Kars Oblast refused as a sign of protest to take the oath of allegiance. At this time Verigin's usual emissaries arrived with their orders, first to call for refusal for continued service in the army by those already in it, and secondly to stage an anti-militarist demonstration—the burning of weapons in the possession of Dukhobors.

How sincere was Verigin in his resistance to Autocracy? Let us grant that he followed the natural development of the movement, without which he could not remain in his role of leader. Following Verigin's directive, several dozen Dukhobors refused service in the army, for which they were inducted into disciplinary battalions where they were subjected to insults and tortures. Nine men among them were tortured to death.

On June 29, 1895, on Peter Verigin's birthday, the Dukhobor Postniki in Tiflis and Elizavetpol' Guberniias and Kars Oblast burned the weapons in their possession. The burning of weapons in Kars Oblast occurred without excesses; in Elizavetpol' Guberniia the authorities carried out mass arrests among the Dukhobors; in Tiflis Guberniia, Cossack detachments were sent into the villages of Akhalkalaki Uezd and carried out a bloody massacre on a crowd of almost 2,000 Dukhobors. The reprisal was supplemented by destruction of property lasting several days, and by the raping of women.

On the same day, June 29, 1895, Governor Shervashidze summoned representatives of the Middle and Postnik Parties for talks. Vorob'ev and his co-thinkers who accompanied him, coming into the governor's presence "bowed low, and requested that they not be confused with the Postniki ... demanded the total execution of the schismatics, as bandits who did not deserve to live" etc. (Borozdin 1907: 194).

The representatives of the Postniki refused to come when called, and were brought in a body of 24 persons to Shervashidze by the police. Their conduct was completely opposite to the grovelling behavior of Vorob'ev and his companions. In their speech there appeared something quite new, disturbing to the governor, who was used to servility. "They entered without bowing, without greeting, with disdainful smiles on their mouths.... I was extremely surprised by the appearance of these Dukhobors, so unusual to me, but I was yet more astonished when they began to talk ...; the representatives of the Postniki carried on a conversation with me using expressions so impolite that, not considering it possible to give the real expressions here, I set down the general sense of what was said" (quoted in Borozdin 1907: 195-196).

In fact, in Shervashidze's characterization the Dukhobors are presented not so much as sectarians, proponents of "non-resistance to evil", but rather as representatives of the poor, strong with the spirit of class hatred for the exploiter, their titular patron and defender.

The tsarist authorities answered the anti-militarist demonstration with the resettlement of more than half of the Postniki from their homes. According to Bonch-Bruevich's data, "4,300 persons were exiled from their dwellings and settled in the fever-ridden valleys of Kakhetiia and Kartaliniia" (ROBIL, div. 396, sh. 147). Those who were exiled were not allowed to sell their movable property. Making use of the disaster which had overtaken the Postniki, their former "brothers", mainly the Vorob'evites, bought up cattle and horses for very little.

In the journal *Rabotnik* [The Worker], printed in Geneva by the Union of Russian Social Democrats and published under the editorship of the group "Liberation of Labor", there was a report, "News From Russia", devoted to the barbaric resettlement of the Dukhobors: "This disgraceful story deserves to have more attention paid to it. It reveals to us a terrible Asiatic despotism which is completely unthinkable in a civilized country" (Biulleten' 1924: 25).

Events as they developed in the Dukhobor settlements in 1895, chiefly the mood of the participants of the Postnik Party, disturbed Verigin.

P. V. Verigin's closest helpers—I. E. Konkin, F. G. Vereshchagin and V. V. Verigin—were incarcerated at this time. The Postniki were in significant degree left to themselves, and their movement took a turn not foreseen by Verigin and politically unacceptable to him.

Not being able to deal with a movement which by the flow of events was at the point of slipping out of the path of non-resistance, Verigin turned for help to the Tolstoyans. In a letter to the Tolstoyan E. I. Popov dated January 8, 1896, Verigin wrote: "The main thing I am concerned about for my people is that by an effort they should be turned as peaceful and meek as possible. If you are willing, settle in Elizavetpol' Uezd, in the village of Slavianka.... You would have an assignment from me—to advise all there who know me not to get angry and mutter against the government that it persecutes them" (Bonch-Bruevich 1901: 56-57). In a letter dated December 4, 1896 to the Dukhobors in prison, Verigin expressed himself still more clearly: "The government must be convinced that we are not as harmful as it thinks" (Bonch-Bruevich 1901: 100).

On the same day, Verigan sent a letter to the Dukhobors of the Large Party, who were finding a profound difference of interests between him and his rank-and-file adherents: "Did the Lord God leave you any livestock?" Verigin asked. "There must have been a little something left from the calamity and the auction sale?" (*ibid.*). But the expression of sympathy for the misfortune of the people served Verigin only as an excuse to develop his basic idea, contained in the following: "Not long ago I read in the newspaper, in *Moskovskie vedomosti* [Moscow News] how you were ordered to sell horses and cows. It was written that some sisters took iron forks, and did not let them, as the paper wrote, into the horse barns. I don't believe this. If that really happened, it's bad: you can argue peaceably with words, but do not give your hands over to an evil will, otherwise it will come to a real war ..." (*ibid.*).

Yes, Verigin did everything possible to convince the government that the ideas he preached were "not as harmful as it thinks".

There was a fundamental difference between the interests of the leaders of the Large Party and the poor who participated in it. How symptomatic for the mood of the Dukhobor masses was the case which served as the theme of Verigin's letter? Were the fears expressed by him about the possibility of "a real war" between the poor and their enslavers and persecutors justified? What occurred at the end of the 1880s and the middle of the 1890s in the Dukhobor settlements was a social war between the lower ranks of the Dukhobor sect and the united forces of the rich and the tsarist regime. If this war remained one-sided insofar as only one side — the one holding the power — used the means of armed force, Verigin and his helpers were first of all responsible for this, having clouded the consciousness of the poor by teaching "non-resistance to evil".

But in the course of the class struggle, the religious covering of the movement wore thin. Verigin had cause to consider serious instances of armed resistance to the authorities expropriating the property of the Dukhobors. Evidence of the readiness of the Dukhobors to adopt means of armed struggle against the rich, if it came to that, is the reaction which took place in the ranks of the Small Party when it learned of the collection of weapons by Dukhobors. The last thing the Small Party expected was that the weapons were intended for burning, and it prepared to repel an armed attack by its opponents. "Gubanov's party", writes S. F. Rybin, eyewitness and participant of the movement, "learning of this collection of weapons ... sounded the alarm to the government. An accusation was made: 'The Large Party intends to fall upon us with weapons in their hands!...' The government, of course, knowing well what enmity there was between the parties, took the alarm seriously and immediately summoned a detachment of soldiers from Aleksandropol' under the leadership of the general, Prince Mikhail Ameridzhibi, with whom while in exile (Rybin meant the resettlement of his family in Gori

Uezd—A. K.), I happened to become acquainted.... He told us how his solders marched all night to defend the Gubanov party from an attack which didn't happen" (Rybin 1952: 20).

The Small Party was deceived about the real purpose of the collection of weapons among the Dukhobors of the Large Party, but rang the alarm, since, being their immediate neighbors, they could not help knowing about their intentions. But—and this is the main thing—the Dukhobors themselves, occupied with the collection of weapons, by no means imagined what purpose it would serve. Among Bonch-Bruevich's unpublished works there is a very important testimony: "I personally heard from many Dukhobors in Canada that on the occasion of the well-known anti-militarist demonstration of the burning of weapons, having received instructions to go to a definite place with weapons in their hands, dressed in 'death clothes', they said farewell to their households with the 'distant obeisance', as was done among the Dukhobors when they went on a journey not knowing what would happen to them and whether they would return home. We didn't know why we were called. We took guns, took other weapons, and went to the assigned place. We were prepared for anything: both an attack on us and our resistance" (ROBIL, div. 369, typescript).

The burning of weapons by the Dukhobors, dictated by Verigin, had of course significance as an anti-militarist demonstration, but at the same time, this was a disarming of the Dukhobors at the very moment when the class struggle among them was taking increasingly acute forms.

We have been able to acquaint ourselves with the views of Verigin and their evolution in the letters to the Dukhobors in 1888, the programmatic appeal transmitted through emissaries in 1893, and the letters of 1896. This evolution consisted first of all in the fact that as his followers were brought into active class struggle, Verigin's reactionary "sociology" swallowed up the motifs of socio-political protest contained in his letters and appeals preceding the events of June 1895. What Verigin wrote in 1896 objectively brought his position close to those of the Small and Middle Parties, called for an agreement with the Autocracy, and aimed at the curbing of the struggle of the Dukhobor lower classes.

The evolution of the views of the ordinary participants of the movement went in the opposite direction.

Following the events of June 1895, the special agent for the Synod, V. Skvortsov, was sent to the Dukhobor villages. He experienced the same thing that happened to Shervashidze during his encounter with the Dukhobor Postniki on June 29, 1895. During Skvortsov's meeting with the Dukhobors in the village of Spasskoe, Kars Oblast, the Dukhobor Ivan Vasil'evich Podovinnikov "with a loud laugh shouted: 'Brothers and sisters, let's hear what song the Starling sings!' "[B] (Rybin 1952: 21). The conversations were heated.

Skvortsov asserts that he made on-the-spot literal transcriptions of what the Dukhobors said. Apparently, Podovinnikov was Skvortsov's most active interlocutor. As Verigin writes, "In Spasskoe village in Kars Oblast, Ivan Vasil'evich Podovinnikov in conversation spoke with him (Skvortsov—A. K.) seriously about the attitude toward the sovereign and all authority, to which he could not give a correct answer. When he [Podovinnikov] departed, he [Skvortsov] wrote down his name, and what do you think! After some time Podovinnikov was sent to Zanziguri Uezd, Elizavetpol' Guberniia—a place with the worst climate in the Transcaucasus" (Verigin 1935: 108-109). Podovinnikov's exile preceded incarceration: "Soon after Skvortsov's departure, Podovinnikov was arrested and put in prison" (Rybin 1952: 21).

The statements by Podovinnikov and his comrades give and idea of the awakening political consciousness of the Dukhobors. Here is what they said about land: "The land is God's; it is created for all equally. Ownership is theft. The princes and the landlords have robbed the people in owning so much land.... There should be no division of land: let each own as much land as he needs" (Skvortsov 1899: 321). They sarcastically asked Skvortsov: "Did the Emperor create the land, that he calls it imperial?" (*ibid.*). Calling for the brotherhood of peoples, they declared: "To us, all are brothers—the Russian emperor and the Persian shah and the Turkish sultan and the German king" (*ibid.*); the Dukhobors understood this brotherhood as based on an equal participation in labor by each person. "The officials and the peasants are all brothers and should be equal; let everyone take to the plow", they declared (Skvortsov 1899: 320).

Skvortsov described the views of the Dukhobors on political power as "extremely anarchistic", but the Dukhobors' decisive negation of political power related to the tsarist form with its whole hierarchy of bosses and laws. "The bosses and the brigand are all equal—they have the same trade", the Dukhobors said (Skvortsov 1899: 321). But they made a distinction between "bossing" and "governing", as is clear from the following note by Skvortsov: "In France, they say, the son of a bootmaker governs; whomever the people elects should rule the country ..." (Skvortsov 1899: 320). Skvortsov also interrogated the Dukhobors about whether they considered the tsars "God's anointed". He wrote of this: "Concerning tsars as God's anointed, the Dukhobors expressed themselves so rudely and sacrilegiously, that we delete this phrase" (*ibid.*).

The spirit of peasant democratism breathes from the transcriptions by Skvortsov of the utterances by Dukhobors close to the party of the poor, in spite of the religious prejudices of the latter. In the article "Lev Tolstoi—kak zerkalo russkoi revoliutsii" [Leo Tolstoy—A Mirror of the Russian Revolution], Lenin wrote: "The attempt to demolish the ruling church and the landlords and the landlords' government to their foundations; to anninhilate all the old forms and dispositions of land tenure; to cleanse the earth; to create in place of the police-and-class state a communal life of free and equal small peasants—this desire runs like a red thread through each historical step of the peasantry in our revolution, and there is no doubt that the ideological content of Tolstoy's writing corresponds considerably more closely to this peasant striving than to the abstract 'Christian' anarchism, as the 'system' of his views is sometimes labelled" (*Lenin* XVII: 211).

The opinions of the Dukhobors belonging to the Large Party, like their entire struggle, lay along the lines of these peasant strivings.

I share Bonch-Bruevich's opinion: "To rouse the Dukhobors to some action, if the ruling group had wanted to do so, would not have been difficult" (ROBIL, div. 369, typescript). But the ruling group, and primarily P. V. Verigin himself adopted (not without pretense) the "Christian anarchism" of the Tolstoyans, and in the last analysis were not far from the ideals of reactionary-bourgeois liberalism. It used religious prejudices, its own personal influence, and finally the services of the Tolstoyans for the moral and political disarming of its followers—which, by the way, was supplemented in most timely fashion by the act of physical disarmament of the Dukhobors on June 20, 1895.

The resettled Dukhobors, who were in an unaccustomed climate without means of subsistence and mercilessly exploited by the native inhabitants for whom they went to work—died off. During the years spent in resettlement, the Dukhobors lost about half of their number. They beseiged the governmental chain of command with every possible appeal to improve their lot.

The movement led by Verigin was in a cul-de-sac. Fettered by principles of non-violence and self-sacrifice, it was in effect given over by its leaders to the vengeance of capitalist bosses from the Small Party and the Autocracy. Its most active elements, permeated by democratic ideas, perished in Kakhetiia and Kartaliniia.

In these extremely contradictory and complicated circumstances, Verigin in August 1896 addressed a letter to the Empress personally, petitioning for permission for the Dukhobors to settle as a compact group in some guberniia of Russia, and guaranteeing that if permission were granted, the Dukhobors would assume all state taxes in return for freedom from military obligations. Failing this, Verigin requested permission for the Dukhobors to go abroad—for instance to England or to America.

At this time the Tolstoyans—V. G. Chertkov, P. I. Biriukov, I. M. Tregubov, D. A. Khilkov etc.—with Tolstoy's active personal participation mounted a vast campaign in Russia and abroad for the mitigation of the lot of the Dukhobors. The appeal *Pomogite* [Help Us] was written and distributed, calling for action by the Dukhobors and unmasking the governmental persecution of them, which led to repressions against Chertkov, Biriukov and

Tregubov. Finally, in May 1898, the Ministry of Internal Affairs agreed to the departure of the Dukhobors from Russia. With the aid of English and American Quaker organizations and with the material support of Tolstoy, who donated the royalties for the novel *Resurrection* for the resettlement of the Dukhobors, four groups of Dukhobors set out for Canada between December 1898 and April 1899. In all, as many as 7,500 persons emigrated: 1,100 Elizavetpol', 3,100 Kars and 3,300 resettled Dukhobors (Pozdniakov 1914: 93). Bonch-Bruevich and his wife, V. M. Velichkina, accompanied the last transport to Canada.

Even though the basic contingent of those emigrating were poor, some representatives of wealthy Dukhobors, the adherents of the Large and Small Parties, took the opportunity to resettle in Canada (*Svobodnaia mysl'*, October 1899: 5). The large landowners were following a goal of effective use of their capital in Canada, where a bourgeois-democratic structure, with no survivals of serfdom, prevailed.

Here are characteristic figures: the 3,300 Dukhobors of the Large Party who had been resettled brought to Canada 30,000 rubles — the sum which they were given when they sold their property. Average figures tell little, but let us still compare them in relative terms: for each person in this group of Dukhobors, there was a beggarly sum — approximately 9 rubles. The property realized by the 3,100 Kars Dukhobors was a sum of 150,000 rubles, which rounds out to 48 rubles per person. Finally, the Elizavetpol' Dukhobors numbering 1,110 persons got at least 100,000 rubles from the sale of their property, which in round figures was 91 rubles per person.

For the first group of Dukhobors the average data given are really characteristic, since in the places of resettlement, the people were in equally miserable conditions. As concerns the Elizavetpol' and Kars Dukhobors, the majority of them had little property, and the lion's share of the sum named belonged to a small group of property-owners.[5]

Thus, the Dukhobors went away from the exploitation of their rich "brethren", from the persecution of the Autocracy, full of hope for the establishment of "justice" in their midst as they settled in the new place. But in reality, some of them brought large sums of money, and others brought nothing but themselves as workers. On arrival in Canada the Dukhobors were given the chance to change their funds into Canadian money. The exchange accounts were a clear demonstration of the material insecurity of the Dukhobors. But the sums which individual Dukhobors had, like it or not, to

[5] The data on the money given to the Dukhobors from the sale of the property is taken from the article by V. Pozdniakov, *Pravda o dukhoborakh* [The Truth About the Dukhobors]. There he says that the Dukhobors took with them to Canada public capital in the amount of 52,000 rubles (Pozdniakov 1914: 93).

take from their secret pockets were worth tens of thousands of dollars in exchange.

The Dukhobors then considered this fact as yet another bitter remembrance of the disagreements of their recent past. But, alas, it symbolized the future: social contradictions—the "old Adam" which, it seemed to the Dukhobors, they had shaken off and left forever in Russia—set out with them over the ocean unseen. On Canadian soil, the old Adam was not slow to reveal his presence.

In December 1902, P. V. Verigin, released from exile, arrived in Canada.

3. Dukhoborism in Russia at the Beginning of the 20th Century

Although the Dukhobors who migrated to Canada comprised the smaller part of the Dukhobor population of Tiflis and Elizavetpol' Guberniias and Kars Oblast, "Dukhoboriia" ceased to exist with their departure. The remaining majority of Dukhobors were not bound by a unity of goals and interests under whose sign their community could still exist as some kind of special world, even when the development of social contradictions made increasingly evident the utopian nature of their religio-social ideals. One way or another, it was precisely the religio-social utopianism of the lower ranks of the Dukhobor sect which supported the existence of "Dukhoboriia".

It is necessary to remember that these utopias—and herein lay their strength—had material roots. The elements of cooperation which marked the internal structure of the Dukhobor community, and which weakened over the course of time, were called forth by the desires of the peasants who were attempting to become independent commodity producers and to be confirmed in this position.

Without consideration of these interests, the genesis of the Dukhobor movement is inexplicable, as is that of a number of other Russian sects arising from the soil of the contradictions of the serf system. These interests in their day created the solidarity of the participants of the Dukhobor movement, each of whom understood the needs of the other because these were his own needs, and each of whom made his own contribution to mutual aid in money, kind and labor, mutual responsibility and mutual moral support. The attitudes of solidarity in early sectarian communities were ideologically fixed among their participants in the consciousness that they were "the chosen people", and their communities were scattered across the earth as outposts of "the kingdom of God".

The development of capitalism in Russia in the 19th century gave rise to a relatively thick layer of bourgeois peasants, for whom the situation of simple commodity producers was a long-past stage, and consequently, old forms of religious sectarianism were an anachronism.

In the new social and economic circumstances there arose new forms of sectarianism and reformed old ones. We have had occasion to trace the latter from the example of the evolution of the Khristovover movement in the second half of the 19th and the beginning of the 20th century, and in particular from the example of the internal struggle in Dukhoborism, which received its characteristic religious framing.

With the departure to Canada of the major part of the adherents of the Large Party, Dukhoboriia ceased to exist precisely because the remaining Dukhobors were dominated by bourgeois property-owners, including large ones toward whom the remaining adherents of the Small and Large Parties gravitated. These entrepreneurial elements became increasingly characterized by an interest in multi-faceted business connections going far beyond the boundaries of the Dukhobor community—toward every kind of contact and contract on the side, which were dictated by the needs of the capitalist development of the economy. The Dukhobors in general did not make any effort to renew the religious union which was split by contradictions and falling apart. Not so long before, non-Dukhobors had been refused "visas" to live within the boundaries of Dukhobor villages. I. E. Petrov, who visited Dukhobor villages in Elizavetpol' Guberniia in March 1905, already established that among their residents, 271 persons were not Dukhobors, and what was highly significant, 172 of them were Baptists (Petrov 1906: 187).

The missionary Terletskii noted in 1908 that "Dukhoborism, which up to now has been marked by relative steadfastness, is beginning to waver and to lose its followers. Some are turning to Baptism, and some to Russian Orthodoxy" (Terletskii 1911: 24). He maintained that the Dukhobors "are in a transitional state—at the crossroads so to speak, and, looking around, are wondering where they should go; it is possible that if we do not turn them toward Russian Orthodoxy, they will go to Baptism" (*ibid.*). It is true that Terletskii based his opinion on Dukhobor groups in Khar'kov and Ekarterinoslav Guberniias—i.e. outside of Dukhoboriia, where external influences had easier access to them. Concerning the Khar'kov Dukhobors, Terletskii wrote that even "in the last quarter of the century they merged with the Shtundists and the Baptists ...; partly they went over to Molokanism and even into the Khlysty movement" (*ibid.*). The success of the Orthodox mission among the Dukhobors was modest, even though a certain tendency for Dukhobors to convert to Russian Orthodoxy was noted at the beginning of the 20th century. According to the reports of the Over-Procurator of the Synod, the number of cases of conversion of Dukhobors grew: for 1907-1908, 24; for 1909-1910, 70; for 1911-1912, 103 cases. But for 1913-1914, 33 such cases were noted (data taken from the reports of the Over-Procurator of the Synod for 1907-1914). At the same time, it is characteristic that instances of conversion of Dukhobors to Russian Orthodoxy did not relate to the Transcaucasian

Dukhobors, but to those who lived in the central, northern and eastern guberniias.[6]

Dukhoborism was really at the crossroads, but neither Baptism nor Molokanism, and even less Russian Orthodoxy, succeeded in enticing the Dukhobors. Those of them who remained no longer travelled the paths of religious searching.

The destruction of Dukhoboriia was the destruction of the Dukhobor "cause" — of everything that characterized this tendency as one of the forms of the democratic movement. But for its wealthy elements, there was no necessity to reject its religious doctrines, which were subject to adaptation to bourgeois interests, in at least the same degree as Russian Orthodoxy or the Old Belief, which were eagerly professed by numerous representatives of the bourgeoisie. However, limited attempts to revive Dukhoborism took place.

These attempts, which proved unsuccessful, originated with those Dukhobors who became the next victims of exploitation by the rich. Social contrasts among the Dukhobors at the beginning of the 20th century were no less acute than at the end of the 19th. The thirteen-year period (1886-1899) of acute internal struggle in Dukhoborism reflected negatively on the level of material well-being of the mass of Dukhobors. The greatest decline was observed in their Akhalkalaki settlements. We have succeeded in getting only statistical data characterizing the lowering of the level of material well-being for the Elizavetpol' Dukhobors. The population in Dukhobor Slavianka, Novospasskoe, and Novogoreloe in Elizavetpol' Guberniia in 1905 was at the 1886 level (if we consider the "alien faith sector", which we described above), and was 2,060 persons (in 1886, 2,074 Dukhobors lived in these villages); both animal husbandry and agriculture in these settlements were at a lower level than in 1886. Over the twenty-year period, the head of cattle alone grew approximately by 6%; horse-breeding stayed at the same level, and the head of small stock — the chief item of Dukhobor income — declined by almost 30%.

For this same time, the Dukhobors' wealth in land decreased, judging from the fact that the average landholding per head of population (in desiatiny) was, in 1905, 4.99 in Slavianka, 8.0 in Novospasskoe, 3.0 in Novogoreloe, against 6.62, 11.77 and 8.0 respectively in 1886 (see the absolute figures for 1905 in Petrov 1906: 188-189; the absolute figures for 1886 are from *Sbornik* 1899: 212-213).

The decrease in landholdings, as well as the significant decrease in the head of sheep and goats, testified to the material difficulties of the Dukhobor population, since the upper strata not only kept but strengthened their economic position during this time.

[6] With the exception of 10 cases of conversion of Dukhobors to Russian Orthodoxy, which took place in 1909 on the territory of the Georgian Exarchate.

When Bonch-Bruevich visited the Akhalkalaki Dukhobors in 1910, he became convinced of the flourishing condition of the economy belonging to the wealthy farmers. In the village of Orlovka, whose residents were adherents of the Middle Party, Bonch-Bruevich was met by the notorious A. F. Vorob'ev and P. P. Verigin. "... We set out to look at the Dukhobor economy", Bonch-Bruevich writes. "In the granaries there is much grain; in the back yards there are cut stacks of hay and straw.... The large horse and cow barns at once show us that animal husbandry is the chief branch of the Dukhobor economy. They brought out to us the studs standing in the horse barn.... The Dukhobors have for many years running taken first prize at agricultural exhibits in Tiflis for remarkable specimens of working, riding and trotting horses" (Bonch-Bruevich 1911c: 248).

Along with commercial horse-breeding at the beginning of the 20th century, commercial cheese-making appeared in the Dukhobor settlements, and the operators in the course of time took over production and sale. "Over the last decade the Dukhobors have set up magnificent cheese factories", Bonch-Bruevich writes. "At first the factories were in the hands of Germans. But now the Dukhobors themselves have learned cheese-making and make marvelous Caucasian-Swiss cheeses.... Earlier, selling through middlemen, the Dukhobors lost a lot on the sale of cheese, but since 1909, they have begun to sell the cheese themselves in large lots in Moscow and Petersburg.... These factories belong to a private company of Dukhobors, but when the new enterprise was fully operative, its initiators wished to turn it into a cooperative (which would not in the slightest have changed the capitalistic character of these enterprises — A. K.). At the present time they have made the factories show a profit, which is added to reserve capital" (Bonch-Bruevich 1911c: 246).

The managers of commercial horse-breeding, sheep-breeding and agriculture set the tone among the Dukhobors: "... more and more a chasm is formed between the rich and the poor ...; there is a dependent situation of workers and bosses, and complete discord in the community ...", wrote Bonch-Bruevich in 1910 (Bonch-Bruevich 1911c: 249).

Bonch-Bruevich also visited the settlement of Goreloe — the center of the adherents of the Small Party, who were, by the way, without leaders: Gubanov and his helpers in the robbery of the Dukhobors had long since gone away somewhere to the inner guberniias of Russia, taking with them the capital of the Orphans Home (Nikol'skii 1930: 245). What did Bonch-Bruevich find in Goreloe? He wrote: "... they are almost all dead, they live in the old days and on memories.... They are Dukhobors only in dress and name and everything typically Dukhobor has left them irrevocably" (Bonch-Bruevich 1911c: 249).

By the beginning of the 20th century, Dukhoborism was a kind of "Old

Belief" within sectarianism. Only dead traditions—"dress and designation"—remained at its disposal. If in the past, the vitality of Dukhoborism was uniformly conditioned by its ties with the struggle of the working classes, now these ties no longer existed, which led to an apathetic attitude on the part of the Dukhobors to the significant social events taking place in the country. Even the Russian Orthodox missionary Terletskii, zealously standing watch over the interests of the Church and the Autocracy, wrote: "How much the sect of the Dukhobors is distinguished by conservatism is evident from the fact that the imperial Manifesto of April 17, 1905 made no impression on the Dukhobors, and did not call forth among them that increased effort and vitalization of internal life which is noted now in the rest of sectarianism" (Terletskii 1911: 24).

Dukhoborism was dead. But the Dukhobors, who had borne on their shoulders the basic weight of the struggle in the period 1886-1899 and were in Canada, were not indifferent to the events of the Russian revolution of 1905-1907. After the Manifesto of April 17, 1905, the question arose in Dukhobor emigré circles of the possibility of return to the motherland. Being far from the events of the political struggle in Russia, the Dukhobors placed their hopes on the promises of freedom in the tsarist Manifesto. On the other hand, even the first years of emigration had brought the Dukhobors disillusionment, both with bourgeois-democratic freedoms in Canada, and with the implementation of their own religio-social ideals.

At the end of 1906, a delegation of Dukhobors arrived in Russia, consisting of six persons headed by P. V. Verigin (Popov 1907: 4). In Petersburg, P. V. Verigin had a meeting with Stolypin and other ministers. In Verigin's words, "the Minister for Internal Affairs spoke by telephone with the emperor about our arrival, and about the Dukhobors. The emperor regrets very much what happened to the Dukhobors, and would be very glad if the Dukhobors re-emigrated to Russia. I asked whether there could be unoccupied land. The government mentioned the Altai Okrug in Siberia. I know that this place has a fairly mild climate" (P. V. Verigin's letter to Canada, dated March 16, 1907; see Rybin 1952: 109). Moreover, Stolypin promised Verigin that if the Dukhobors returned, they would be free from the obligation of military service (Popov 1907: 4).

Why was the matter dropped? Nicholas II and his ministers gave permission for the return of the Dukhobors; they promised to free them from military service, and to give them land in the Altai region; even the climate in the projected place of settlement satisfied Verigin. The tsarist Manifesto also satisfied Verigin, and he said of it at the time to his acquaintance G. Klochkov in Petersburg: "The Manifesto will not facilitate the revolution but prevent it. It is a saving Manifesto. It is exactly against revolution and not for it" (see Malov 1949: 572, Klochkov's description of Peter Verigin in Petersburg).

The only trouble was the Verigin did not believe in the real ability of the "saving Manifesto", as he called it, "to save" the ruling classes from revolution: "From P. Verigin's speeches", Klochkov wrote, "it was quite clear that he sensed the coming storm in Russia" (*ibid.*).

Verigin described the events in Russia in a counter-revolutionary style in a letter sent to the Dukhobors in Canada: "The disorder in all of Russia is great; everyone throws bombs at the officials, shoots revolvers, kills with daggers—in a word, does whatever he can. The anti-government party—revolutionaries—do this, in order to remove the monarchical regime and set up a parlimentary Duma.... From its side the government now by no means thinks to give up easily; all Russia is declared in a state of martial law, and almost all governors are allowed the right of summary judgment. For the slightest attempt on an official's life, people are immediately shot or hanged" (Rybin 1952: 109). In Verigin's mind the revolution was senseless terror, against which the "poor" Autocracy used bullets and the gallows in self-defense. In March 1907, Verigin and his fellows left Russia: "From Sevastopol' we sailed across the Black Sea to Constantinople; there, beyond the border, we all breathed more freely from the Russian disorders" (*ibid.*).

The return of the Dukhobors from Canada did not take place. On the contrary, at the end of 1905, about 200 Dukhobors, who were in Yakutia where they had been exiled by the tsarist government in the period between 1897 and 1900, emigrated from Russia to Canada (on the Dukhobors sent to Yakutia *see* Safronov 1961: 129-135).

All during the time after the emigration of the Dukhobors to Canada there arose among them no noticeable movement of protest either against the Autocracy or against the capitalist property-owners who continued to exploit the ordinary Dukhobors. Dissatisfaction existed, but it was expressed as a cultural and a temperance movement, in which chiefly Dukhobor young people took part, as noted by Bonch-Bruevich in his article *U zakavkazskikh dukhobortsev* [Among the Transcaucasian Dukhobors], which we have cited. The First World War in 1914-1918 again placed before the Dukhobors the delicate question of participation in military service. But this time they did not dare to make an anti-militarist demonstration and silently bowed to the law. From the beginning of the war to April 1, 1917, there were 837 cases of sentencing by military judges of persons who refused military service on religious grounds. There were 16 Dukhobors among them, and in the Caucasian military district there was not a single case in which Dukhobors were accused of refusal to serve in the army (*see* the figures cited by Putintsev 1935: 96-96).

The events of the second bourgeois-democratic revolution attracted the attention of Dukhobor emigrés in Canada toward Russia. "The Russian revolution of 1917 made a strong impression on the life of the Dukhobor communalists", P. N. Malov writes. "The Dukhobors gave enormous significance to the Russian revolution.... In meetings they often sang Russian popular and revolutionary songs, like *Otrechemsia ot starogo mira* [We Renounce the Old World], *Ot pavshikh tverdyn' Port-Artura* [From Those Fallen at the Stronghold of Port Arthur], *Vpered, tovarishchi, stupaite* [Step Forward, Comrades], and many others" (Malov 1949: 113). But the upper and lower classes of Dukhobors evaluated revolutionary events differently. For Verigin, for example, the revolution was embodied in the bourgeois Provisional Government which had been formed, and whose existence settled all his political doubts. By March 23, 1917, Verigin telegraphed the Ministry of Internal Affairs of the Provisional Government: "Dukhobors numbering 1,000 persons wish to return to Russia as good farmers and horticulturalists" (Sukhorev 1944: 152). But the bourgeois Provisional Government did not need farmers or horticulturalists, but rather soldiers to continue the war "to a victorious end", while the Dukhobors insisted on being free from military service. The Provisional Government failed to act on Verigin's telegram.

The newspaper *Russkoe slovo* [Russian Word], published in New York, informed its readers on April 2, 1917 of the Provisional Government's refusal to grant Verigin's request (*ibid.*), which did not keep the leaders of the Dukhobor community in Canada from sending an appeal to Petrograd on April 30, 1917, which began with the words: "Hearty congratulations on the new government of all the Russian people. Glory to God in Heaven and peace on earth" (Malov 1949: 239). The appeal further said: "We beg all those on whom it depends that Nicholas himself, and also the entire Romanov family, and all former ministers, and also the obsolete false clergy ... if they bow their rebellious heads before the truth—all without exception be mercifully spared death. And judgment should be left to the will of God" (Malov 1949: 240). This was a proposal to give amnesty to the Autocracy and to the Church which had served it. Did it come from the principles of Christian love of peace? Whatever the origin of this proposal, essentially it was directed at the reduction of the class struggle and at preventing the further development of revolutionary events in the country. S. F. Rybin published the text of the political program preserved in his personal archives, composed by Verigin and dated November 1917. This program, which begins with the words: "Necessary reforms in Russia after the war", is reduced to the following basic points:

1. Stopping of the export of raw materials and the development by every possible means of industrial production, with simultaneous transformation of industry into a "popular-state" activity, and with dispersion of it outside cities;

2. The maximal reduction of taxes;

3. The transformation of the army into a volunteer one, and the proclamation of political neutrality;

4. The creation of a volunteer militia for the preservation of internal order;

5. The maximum curtailment of the "urban system", looking toward the complete liquidation of cities (Rybin 1952: 226).

Such points of Verigin's program as tax reduction, the end of military conscription and the proclamation of a policy of neutrality, were aimed at attracting the sympathy of the workers. But Verigin completely bypassed the question of the political structure under which his program would be implemented. This question did not arise for him because he was assuming the existence of the bourgeois Provisional Government. Verigin's political platform was to be implemented under the bourgeois social order, under which the army and bodies responsible for internal order were weapons of the class rule of the bourgeoisie, independently of the principle of their recruitment. His "popular-state" industry, for which according to the program all native raw materials were destined, would be nothing but capitalist industry united in state monopolies. Yet there had been a time when Verigin called his followers to the simple gathering of the fruits of the earth, seeing in these occupations the basis for the rebirth of an earthly paradise. Industrial-capitalistic development in the progressive countries of the American mainland determined anew Verigin's concept of earthly paradise. It is true that Verigin proposed to relocate industry from cities to rural localities and to set a course for the gradual liquidation of cities. Verigin's bucolic capitalism was a necessary tribute to the patriarchal prejudices of many of his followers.

Twenty-two years before this time there had occurred the conversation between the Dukhobor Podovinnikov and the Synodal official Skvortsov, which I described above. Podovinnikov and his comrades spoke most of all about the land (a question completely bypassed by Verigin in his program). They said that the princes and landlords who ruled the land thereby robbed the people, since land "was created for all equally". They demanded a system in which labor should prevail, and the administration belong to those elected by the people. This also was a program, but a democratic one in contrast to Verigin's program, which was bourgeois in content and demagogic in form.

I have not succeeded in finding the utterances of the Dukhobors who remained in Russia, from which I could have judged the responses which the events of the bourgeois-democratic revolution of 1917 had among them.

The more businessmen appeared among the Dukhobors, the rarer the public figures became. Whether these businessmen belonged to the Small or Large Parties, they shared with the Russian bourgeoisie their class-political position. Among the Dukhobors of the Middle Party, P. P. Verigin—the son of P. V. Verigin—was respected. By tradition, A. F. Vorob'ev also exercised influence. P. P. Verigin in 1905 (accompanied by Vorob'ev) and again in 1906 visited the Canadian Dukhobors. He in no way distinguished himself by activity among the Dukhobors remaining in Russia, and was satisfied with external homage and also the primitively conceived "blessings" which were brought to him in abundance in his position of inheritor of "the spirit", and possibly the power of P. V. Verigin, who ruled the Canadian Dukhobors.

According to data relating to 1909, there were about 13,000 Dukhobors in Tiflis and Elizavetpol' Guberniias and in Kars Oblast (TsGIAL, f. 133, d. 21, shs. 241, 272). Besides this, there were Dukhobor settlements with a total number of about 2,000 residents in 1909 in Voronezh, Samara, Kiev, Irkutsk, and several other guberniias and in the Amur region (TsGIAL, *ibid.*, shs. 147, 222, 277, 282, 298). By 1917, the geography of the Dukhobor settlements had not changed. Considering that among the Dukhobors the teachings of other sects had no very great success, and considering the natural growth of the population, we may hypothesize that by 1917 there were 17,000-20,000 Dukhobors in Russia.

Editor's Notes

Note A. The rebellion in 1773-1775, led by Emel'ian Pugachev, a Don Cossack, was intended to depose Catherine the Great, and achieved considerable success in the eastern part of the Empire.

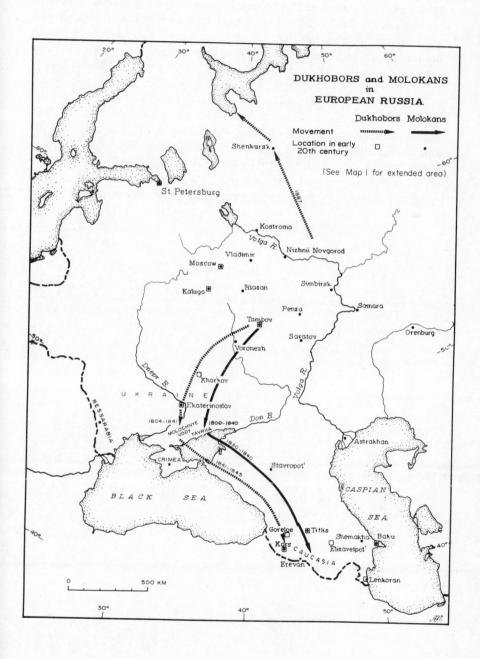

DUKHOBORS and MOLOKANS
in
EUROPEAN RUSSIA

Dukhobors   Molokans

Movement

Location in early
20th century

(See Map I for extended area)

4

The Molokan Sect

1. Basic Trends in Molokanism

In the literature on the history of religious sectarianism, a parallel study of Dukhoborism and Molokanism has become traditional. This tradition, which was formed in the works of pre-Revolutionary authors, was taken into consideration by Soviet researchers as well. In the opinion of N. M. Nikol'skii, "between the one and the other sect there is much in common, and the small differences are explained by a not quite identical social composition and by different conditions of life" (Nikol'skii 1930: 200). And further: "Uklein's followers worked out a doctrine and an organization extremely similar to the Dukhobor one ...; to distinguish one from the other of these closely connected sects is hardly convenient or possible" (*ibid.*).

Nikol'skii's opinion of the close connection of Dukhoborism with Molokanism is elaborated by the observations of P. G. Ryndziunskii about the movement of so-called Spiritual Christians which arose among the peasant *odnodvortsy* in the Tambov area in the 1760s. Ryndziunskii sees Dukhoborism and Molokanism as products of differentiation taking place in Spiritual Christianity as early as the second half of the 18th century (Ryndziunskii 1954: 157, 190-191). I can agree that there is much in common between Dukhoborism and Molokanism, but I cannot agree with the suppression of specifics about either movement with the assertion that only "small differences" separate them and that their individual study "is hardly convenient or possible". For a comparative study of Dukhoborism and Khristovoverie, in its turn, convinces us that there is much in common between them, which was partially shown in the preceding chapter.

In fact, Dukhoborism was genetically and ideologically connected with Khristovoverie, but these tendencies differ both in time of origin and in social composition, and do not coincide even in what relates to the mystical elements of their world-views. Comparing the teachings of Dukhobors and Khristovovers, Nikol'skii notes: "... the Dukhobor 'spirit' is not some wild intoxication during some ecstatic ritual, but rational study and judgment. It is apparent that such a 'spirit' should give completely different practical advice" (Nikol'skii 1930: 202). Dukhoborism was akin to Khristovoverie not in the ecstatic dissolution of man in "spirit", but in the presence in the teaching of both sects of a peculiar pantheistic world-view, of an idea of the spilling over into the "nature of the word" of spiritual wisdom, grace and love. In the teaching of the Dukhobors, the pantheistic mysticism of the Khristovovers acquired a rationalistic nuance.

We have something quite different in the teaching of the Molokans. They renounced from the very beginning the pantheistic motifs which were covered up, among the Khristovovers and the Dukhobors, by Christian forms; their teaching was Christian theism, merely freed from church-canonical forms. Dukhobors designated as "spirituality" some universal principle of the understanding of life, corresponding to the nature of the deity; they distinguished three types of spiritual bases—memory, intellect and will, which they called God the Father, God the Son and God the Spirit. This was their "trinity". When P. V. Verigin was required to formulate the Dukhobor concept of God, he, following every tradition, wrote: "God is life and participates in everything existing.... Understanding God as life itself, essential and the same in everything which appears, we should not fear bodily death.... Man is part of one whole in the world. We also understand God as love, with whose help everything existing is maintained" (Sukhorev 1944: 207).

Molokanism, from the time when we learn of its teachings from so-called ritual books, which were current even in the time of Semen Uklein and his closest disciples, based its understanding of God on the Bible. In Miliukov's words, "The basic Christian dogma of Uklein's followers could not be interpreted allegorically. They remained true to the Russian Orthodox interpretation of the doctrine of the Trinity" (Miliukov 1931: 131). For the Molokans, God was a God in three persons, in which the "Son" and the "Holy Spirit" were considered the same as the "Father", even if not completely equal to him in "divine properties".

Both the trinitarian and the Christological doctrines of Molokanism were closer to Russian Orthodoxy than to Dukhoborism. Christ in the teaching of the Molokans was the son of God, immaculately conceived by the Virgin Mary, and not a spiritually perfect, deified person.

If for the Khristovovers and Dukhobors, the Old Testament and New Testament books had no binding significance, and the chief source of their faith was revelation, for the Molokans the Bible had the authority of the sole inspirational source of faith, and knowledge of the Bible served as the most important witness to the religious perfection of the believer.

Like the Khristovovers and Dukhobors, the Molokans in their views proceeded from "the equality of the sons of God", holding to the ethic of "good works" and—more or less—to the idea of building "the kingdom of God" on earth; but the demand for equality and community of property was far less popular among them than among the Dukhobors. This demand, as will be shown below, arose in the Molokan milieu also, but only as a rebuff by the poorest strata to the exploiting, large-property-owning elements of the sect. Various kinds of social institutions had less significance in Molokanism than in Dukhoborism.

Molokanism rejected the ruling church and its ideology as a weapon of serf rule, but did not go as far as Dukhoborism in denying the institution of the Church itself, assigning great significance to the preceptors (presbyters), from the very beginning working out its religious norms and fixing them in written books of ritual. For the Molokans, the ideal standard of religious structure, at least in ideas, was represented by the Christian church and its teaching before the era of ecumenical councils, which "perverted Christianity". All these are not "small differences", but—within the boundaries of the developing forms of religious sectarianism—fundamental distinctions demanding historical study and explanation. Molokanism arose as a result of the rift and subsequent struggle between Semen Uklein and his adherents on the one hand, and on the other Illarion Pobirokhin and those Dukhobors who remained true to his teaching. The Molokans later rejected communion with the Dukhobors.

In 1817, the military governor of Kherson, in connection with the arrival of Molokans from Orel Guberniia in Melitopol Uezd of Tavriia Guberniia, reported to the Minister of Internal Affairs that "the Molokans, asserting there that the Dukhobor sect maintained by the Melitopol settlers is completely different from their Molokanism, declared to the governor of Tavriia that for this reason they could not live in the same villages with these Dukhobors, and the latter completely refused to accept the Molokans into their society as a different sect" (quoted in Livanov 1872: III, 468). According to the Molokan author A. I. Stoialov, Uklein "taught his followers to believe as the Bible taught, and rejected everything that was not literally expressed in it" (Stoialov 1870: 299). Uklein's appeal to the Bible was intended in the beginning as not so much a denial of the Orthodox Church organization and canon as part of the struggle against Dukhoborism: "Directing his teaching against the Dukhobors", Stoialov continues, "whose faith in the power of the spirit clearly contradicts the Holy Scriptures, Uklein did not reject faith in inner enlightenment, but strictly subordinated himself to the letter of the Scriptures and took from this belief (in "the power of the spirit"—A. K.) the importance it had among the Dukhobors ..." (*ibid.*).

Translated from the language of religious conceptions, to take from the belief in "the power of the spirit" that "importance which it had among the Dukhobors" meant to limit the democratic significance of the Dukhobor teaching. Molokanism, for all its anti-clericalism, was a variety of Christian theism, which put an end to those vague pantheistic ideas which made the earlier Dukhoborism not simply a phenomenon of anti-clerical protest but also an instance in the history of free thought, born in the peasant milieu. What, concretely, did the assertion of the power of the spirit mean in the period of origin of Dukhoborism? A representative of Spiritual Christianity in the 1760s, Kirill Petrov, declared to his judges: "He does not wish, he says, to be in the sovereign's service, because God created man in His image and likeness, autonomous, and he wishes to gain his daily bread with his own hands. The people should have common property and give to each other without return, because they are brothers" (Ryndziunskii 1954: 178).

P. G. Ryndziunskii, from whose work we have borrowed these words by Kirill Petrov, which are full of human dignity, writes: "The doctrine of the autonomous nature of man, which completes the system of views of the anti-clerical circle of *odnodvortsy,* gave it pronounced traits of humanism.... At the same time the humanism [of these views] lacked features of individualism. The followers [of this system] were, on the contrary, characterized by ideas of collectivism, which was due to their social nature — to the fact that their views developed not among the urban bourgeoisie but in the circle of the feudally exploited peasantry" (Ryndziunskii 1954: 189). He concludes: "This was a distinctive kind of *peasant humanism,* genuinely democratic in character" *(ibid.).* This is what was meant by the Dukhobor beliefs in the powers of the spirit which Molokanism set out to limit.

N. M. Nikol'skii called attention to the "not quite similar" social composition of Dukhoborism and Molokanism in the last half of the 18th century, pointing out that at this time Molokanism, spreading in the peasant milieu, enjoyed success (as distinct from Dukhoborism) "particularly among the small urban meshchane and craftsmen" (Nikol'skii 1930: 200).

Let us add that even in the early stage of development of Molokanism, merchant elements took an active part in it. One of Uklein's successors was the Morshansk merchant S. A. Shvetsov, who, "not satisfied with the title of mayor and with the medal he had received, petitioned to be made an honorary citizen" (Varadinov 1863: 355). According to a Molokan historian, who, I think, exaggerates, Shvetsov was "one of those persons who was as important as Uklein among the Molokans" (Samarin, ed. 1928: 30).

Shvetsov wrote an exposition of the Molokan teaching in the course of which he did not fail to repeat, following the ritual books which had appeared earlier—"we pray ourselves, for all persons, for the Tsar and for all those like him in power" (Varadinov 1863: 351). The figure of Shvetsov is indicative for the characterization of the social elements which over time acquired decisive influence in Molokanism.

Let us turn to factual data describing the differences in the social composition of Dukhoborism and Molokanism, which were already clearly fixed in the first quarter of the 19th century. According to the data of the Ministry of Internal Affairs for 1825, in Russia (with the exception of Kurland and Riazan Guberniias, the Kerch-Enikal' borough, and the Omsk and Don regions) there were 23,207 registerd Dukhobors. Of these, 17,763 (7,258 men and 10,505 women)—i.e., more than 76%—belonged to "free classes", and to the class of serf peasants 5,444 (2,651 men and 2,793 women), i.e. more than 23% (Varadinov 1863: 225-226). These figures are extremely eloquent, since they show that the social face of Dukhoborism was determined precisely by representatives of "free classes".

Among the representatives of the free classes making up three quarters of the participants of the Dukhobor movement, representatives of the urban classes—merchants and meshchane—were almost entirely lacking. This entire group of Dukhobors was made up of state peasants of one or another category. Dukhoborism, having arisen as a movement of state peasants (odnodvortsy), continued to develop chiefly in this social milieu, while at the same time being supplemented by people from the serf peasantry. As concerns Molokanism, its mass base was in the countryside and, once again, among the state peasants, but in distinction to Dukhoborism it put down roots in the merchant and meshchan circles of the city.

The archives of the Ministry of Internal Affairs contain valuable information allowing us to judge both the dissemination of Molokanism in the cities and the great significance of merchant elements. Even in 1816, the civil governor of Simbirsk noted that the sect of Molokans in his guberniia "had significantly increased ..., finding many followers from the trading class of people (i.e. the merchants—A. K.) and townspeople. Both are for the most part wealthy people and therefore have influence on others" (Varadinov 1863: 498).

The testimony of the governor of Tambov shows among precisely which strata the Molokans attracted their followers in the second half of the first decade of the 19th century—i.e., just at the time when in Morshansk, Tambov Guberniia, "our" mayor Shvetsov was giving a Molokan sermon: "In the city of Tambov, the merchant Fedor Ivanov Malin has been a Molokan since 1817, the meshchanin Ivan Dmitriev Popov since 1819, the meshchanin Efim Efimov Trunilin since 1817, the merchant Gavriil Ivanov Sorokin since 1817, and the merchant Petr Alekseev Loskutov since 1818; in the village of Rasskazovo, Mrs. Postnikova's (quit-rent—A. K.) peasants, Ivan Semenov Khomutkov since 1818, Zakhar Trofimov Kazakov since 1820, Nikita Larionov Lapinov since 1819; in the village of Soldatskaia Vikhliaika, Tambov Uezd, the odnodvorets Matvei Timofeev Korobov since 1813; in the village of Mordvinovka, Kirsanovskii Uezd, Iuda Feofanov Kunitsyn since 1815" (Livanov 1872: IV, 220-221). Of ten residents of Tambov represented in the lists, who converted to Molokanism in the period from 1813 to 1820, three were merchants, two were meshchane, two landlord peasants, one an odnovorets and one of unknown origin—probably a state peasant.

In the first quarter of the 19th century, a Molokan congregation arose in Odessa. It was made up of "merchants, meshchane, and other residents of the city of Odessa (56 families), and 37 families from other cities living in Odessa; on top of this, police investigation discovered 17 merchants and meshchane in the Molokan sect, but they, being absent on business matters, remained unquestioned" (Livanov 1872: III, 516). Precisely these merchant-meshchan elements occupied command positions in Molokanism by the beginning of the 19th century. In Dubrovskii Posad of Saratov Guberniia, among Molokan "interpreters"—i.e. those whom we would now call the activists in the sect—seven were merchants of the third guild, and three meshchane (Livanov 1872: IV, 403). We have general data describing the participants of the Molokan sect in Saratov Guberniia in 1842.

Among the 9,553 Molokans counted in the guberniia there were: 436 merchants (4.6%), 581 meshchane and craftsmen (6%), 3,683 state peasants (38.6%), 2,922 crown peasants (30.5%), 1,650 serf peasants (17.3%), and 281 freed serfs (3%) (Varadinov 1863: 495). Thus, more then 10% of the Molokans of Saratov Guberniia were urban, and of these, 4.6% were trading bourgeoisie. In turn, among the state and crown peasants there were quite a few rich property-owners. Which crown peasants willingly became Molokans is shown by the example of the crown peasants Maksim and Petr Bolotin (village of Novoe Ust'e, Morshansk Uezd), who had a stone house, a stone barn, a number of enterprises, a windmill, a factory (whose product is not stated); besides this, in 1819 "various people were indebted by more than 15,000 rubles" to these peasants (Livanov 1872: IV, 217).

An idea of the role of elements of the trading and industrial bourgeoisie among the Molokans is given by the governmental instructions of February 13, 1837, according to which Molokans were forbidden: "1) to be inscribed into the merchant guilds, other than those in which they were previously inscribed, and from these it is forbidden to transfer to higher guilds"; 2) to transfer to a city community from a peasant one, "even if they have received freedom from the landlord," and "for those inscribed in an urban community ... [to transfer] to other communities" (the prohibition described in the second point did not relate to Molokans living in the Transcaucasus—A. K.); 3) "to have Russian Orthodox people as servants in the home, in factories and other production facilities" (Ministry 1858: 241-242). In 1842, there followed a decree signed by the tsar, denying Molokans and Dukhobors from among the odnodvortsy "the right to acquire peasants from people equal to them" (Polnoe Sobranie Zakonov: XVII, 27).

On March 15, 1847, the governmental instruction of February 13, 1837 was affirmed in categorical form, forbidding Molokans to use the labor of Russian

Orthodox persons. Apparently, the experience of the past decade showed that the Molokans had found means to recruit workers from the Russian Orthodox poor, against the state prohibition. "Molokans under no circumstances", it was stated in the new instruction, "are to have in their factories and enterprises people of Russian Orthodox persuasion, neither as servants nor as workers, and the Molokans themselves on the same basis are not to take service in homes or for bosses of Russian Orthodox persuasion" (Ministry 1858: 469).

The sum of these data attests that the Molokan movement had a wider and more complex base than the Dukhobor one, differing from the latter first of all by the participation in it of the trading bourgeoisie of the city, and also of meshchan elements.

Considering the great significance which merchant elements and representatives of the nascent peasant bourgeoisie acquired in Molokanism, the question of the character and tendencies of the ideological influence which they had on the masses of their followers becomes extremely important. Suggestive in this respect is a document in which the Tambov Molokans—the large merchants Fedor and Ivan Sorokin and 15 other persons (merchants and meshchane)—appealed on April 6, 1819 to the governor of Tambov. In their appeal, they requested that the sect be legalized by the state and the Russian Orthodox clergy prohibited from interfering in the sect's internal affairs. The governor, as his first duty, turned to the police, who "reported to the governor that among the petitioners there were in service to the municipality by election: the merchant Fedor Malin in the Tambov criminal court as judge, the meshchan Ivan Popov in the City Duma as councillor, and Igor Oparin as price-setter ..." (Livanov 1872: IV, 225). The attempt to secure state legalization of the sect expressed by the large merchant class and its trusted and recognized representatives, it goes without saying, presupposed a limitation of the differences existing between the religious views of Molokanism and the official doctrine of Russian Orthodoxy.

N. Varadinov, who showed himself a thoughtful student of the archival documentation on the Old Belief and sectarianism kept in the Ministry of Internal Affairs and relating to the first half of the 19th century, came to the significant conclusion: "The Molokans of Tambov, although they remained true to their doctrine and spread it gradually, became much more cautious in their actions; many of them, especially those of the merchant calling, began to fulfill the rituals of the Church and had thier icons in the home ..." (Varadinov 1863: 639). Such was the line taken by merchant elements in Molokanism.

Peasant circles of the movement stood at the opposite extreme, not wishing to fold the ideological banners of opposition to the ruling church and the system it defended. "On the contrary", Varadinov continues, "the Molokans of Ranenburg and Zarai Uezds of Riazan Guberniia, numbering about 500 persons of both sexes, did not take part in even the most important rituals of the Church; they showed complete disgust with it and openly preached their heresy" (Varadinov 1863: 639).

At a time when Khristovovers still preserved the unity of their communities on the basis of the traditions of Danilo Filippov, Suslov and Lupkin, and the Dukhobors assembled group after group in Molochnye Vody in hope of implementing their religio-social ideals away from state and Church authority, in Molokanism there was found a tendency to constitutionalize the movement along bourgeois-church lines and to seek its state legalization on this basis. The price of such concessions by the leaders of the Molokan movement was to put the sect under the cloak of state law, as shown by the appeal of the Molokan presbyter Dirin from Mikhailovskaia *stanitsa* in the region of the Don Cossack Host to Alexander I. Dirin in his appeal to the "highest name", made in 1811, called himself the representative of all the Molokan congregations in the region of the Don Host. He affirmed loyalty to the throne and willingness to take oaths, and recognized "the necessity of the sacraments" accepted in the Russian Orthodox Church (Livanov 1872: III, 513, 514).

This was the platform of the Molokans who formed the so-called Don branch, in which a leading role was played by representatives of the Cossack authorities and of the wealthy Cossacks. Many of them had the officers' ranks of *sotnik* [a squadron commander] and *esaul* [Cossack captain]. The Tambov Molokans who were asking the governor to legalize their society could have had no platform significantly differing from that given by Dirin.

At the beginning of the 19th century there was a universal tendency of the bourgeois leaders of Molokanism to come to agreement with the Autocracy by supporting the existing system and adapting the Molokan dogma to Russian Orthodoxy. This tendency expressed not only the monarchical sympathies of the large property-owning elements of Molokanism, but also their struggle for their economic interests, since their trading and industrial activity suffered from discrimination.

In both respects, the appeal by the leader of the Samara Molokans, Akinfii Grachev, made around 1814 to Benckendorff,[A] is highly indicative: "From ancient times, according to the legends of the ancestors, I have confessed the evangelical Christan faith ... saying prayers to Our Lord Jesus Christ for His Imperial Majesty and his most holy house and the most holy ruling Synod (! — A. K.) according to the ritual of the early Christians and quietly and zealously fulfilling state obligations and public obligations for sixty years of my life ... I have asked to be confirmed in our religion and to call our faith evangelical ..." (Livanov 1872: IV, 421). And further: "Cast your all-powerful eye on a little member of the fatherland, who has a family of 11 males and is experiencing difficulties in his livelihood from pressure by the police ..." (*ibid.*). Grachev asked for permission "to call himself *a Christian of the evangelical faith*" (Livanov 1872: IV, 422).

Of all the sects arising as a result of the contradictions of the serf order and expressing opposition to serfdom, precisely in Molokanism was there first defined a tendency forming into a bourgeois-Protestant type of church, ready to serve the Autocracy.

However, the government of Alexander I left unanswered the petition of bourgeois elements of Molokanism. Their appeals only served as an excuse for increased police and Church surveillance of the spread of the Molokan teaching. This did not diminish the activity of the preachers of the "evangelical faith", who spread their ideas not without success at the beginning of the 1820s among Molokans resettled, like the Dukhobors, by the government from Tambov, Voronezh, Samara, Astrakhan and other guberniias into Berdiansk Uezd of Tavriia Guberniia.

The presbyter A. I. Stoialov from the village of Novo-Vasil'evka (Tavriia Guberniia), "a Cossack cavalier of the Order of St. George", as he proclaimed himself in the press, wrote in 1870 of the Don persuasion: "This dogma can with all justice be called the dogma of evangelical Christians, and not of Molokans as it is called in reproach. And it can in no case be called harmful, as the Russian Orthodox do, probably not knowing the essence of this teaching" (Stoialov 1870: 304). Stoialov wondered: "Why does not a beneficent government allow these Spiritual Christians to set up houses of prayer with tables for books and benches for sitting according to their simple teaching, so close to the simplicity of the Gospel?" (Stoialov 1870: 305).

Turning to the history of Molokanism in the 1820s, Stoialov reports data valuable to the researcher about how the Molokans who held to Uklein's teaching "dreamed of being free from every external fleshly obligation, but with the failure of their claims to receive freedom, they undertook, on the example of the Don persuasion, to correct the articles of false teaching on which Uklein based his hopes" (Stoialov 1870: 308). Not finding any response among the ruling circles, the adherents of the evangelical tendency in Molokanism remained true to their loyal and religiously moderate views, and tried in every way to broaden the sphere of their influence. This fact shows that we have before us not a simple example of monarchical servility of the bourgeois upper classes of Molokanism, but a thought-out and refined expression of their class interests. The evangelical movement, precisely by its refinement, disturbed many representatives of the bourgeois upper classes of Molokanism, which, although they shared, with various reservations, its political sympathies and evangelical-Church tendencies, feared opposition from the lower classes of the sect.

Molokanism—and this is its chief distinction from Dukhoborism—was a form of religious ideology, corresponding to the interests partly of those social elements who strove to be in the position of independent commodity producers, but mainly of those who, having passed this stage, were already confirmed as representatives of bourgeois forms of economic behavior.

Hence the "moderation" of the Molokans, their "sobriety" not only in relation to the intoxicating mysticism of the Khristovovers, but also in relation to the religio-social utopias which inspired the Dukhobors. Hence their satisfaction with demands that the church be made less expensive, and that its organization, ceremonial and ritual be simplified. Hence, finally, the relative indifference, characteristic of the Molokans, to various forms of social creativity, which were present in Khristovoverie and Dukhoborism.

The various kinds of economic mutual aid, coordination and regulation, implemented by the religious community in relation to the activity of its members, although present in Molokanism, had secondary significance there. This is understandable: the beginning of social self-organization, traceable in Khristovoverie and more completely in Dukhoborism, had primary significance for those social elements which were striving to achieve an independent relationship to the market, to increase the productivity of their subsistence operations, and to set them on the path of commodity-and-money relationships. In parallel fashion, the interest of these elements in forms of social self-organization weakened — the coordinating and regulating functions of the religious community became a burden to them. The history of Khristovoverie and Dukhoborism in its late stages shows that this was so. Molokanism *began* where Khristovoverie and Dukhoborism *left off*.

In the course of historical development, features distinguishing Dukhoborism and Molokanism became increasingly apparent, and the ideological foundations which were common to them related to the 1760s and 1770s, when these tendencies emerged from "Spiritual Christianity".

What were the ideological foundations which give a basis for considering Dukhoborism- and Molokanism-related religio-social movements? Let us turn to the so-called ritual book of Uklein, which unfortunately has not come down to us as written by the author himself.

"The basis of the moral life of the true Christian", we read in the ritual book, "should be perfect freedom and independence of any human laws and constraints. There should not be power over people in whom Christ's teachings have settled. The lay authorities are beneficent on earth and put there by God, but put there only for the sons of the world; but the Lord said of Christians: they are not of this world as I am not of this world ...; therefore, for Spiritual Christians, who are not of the world, lay authorities are not necessary ...; fulfilling God's commandments, they have no need of human laws ..., which contradict the teaching of the word of God. Thus, they should avoid slavery to landowners, wars, military service, and oaths, as things not permitted by the Scriptures. And as it is impossible openly to oppose the government and not fulfill its demands, Spiritual Christians reflecting the first Christians, can hide from it, and their brothers in the faith are obliged to accept and hide them ..." (*Pravoslavnyi Sobesednik* 1858: 55-56).

It is not difficult to be convinced that in spite of the qualification about the beneficence of the lay authorities, we are dealing in the given instance with the religious theory and sanction of passive means of resistance to the serf-owning state and the serf-owner, tested by the peasantry in long experience of class struggle and partly expressed in flight from the feudal landowners. But as the upper stratum of the Molokan movement turned away from the democratic principles of early Molokanism, and then broke with them entirely, these principles were guarded by the lower classes of the sect, and were held dear by them, since they corresponded to their interests. This was the chief hindrance in the way of dissemination of their teaching by the preachers of the Don branch of Molokanism, as a result of which this branch remained a union of the minority of the Molokan movement.

The 1820s were a time of acute religious disputes between the adherents of the Don persuasion and the rest of Molokanism. An increasingly profound gap appeared: there was an increase in the influence of the adherents of the Don branch on those bourgeois elements in Molokanism who were not prepared to manifest solidarity with them openly, and at the same time opposition from the lower ranks of the sect increased, both to the Don persuasion and to the ruling upper classes of Molokanism in general. At the beginning of the 1830s, there occurred open action by ordinary participants in the movement against the leaders, who had renounced the democractic ideology and attempted to enclose the movement within church forms with the hegemony of the emergent "clergy" over the "layman", and with obligatory dogma and norms of thought prescribed for the layman. This action only laid the foundations for open forms of struggle by the lower classes against the upper, which continued over the whole 19th century, and spilled over into the 20th century.

In the middle of the 1830s, disturbances seized a number of Molokan villages in Samara, Astrakhan and Tavriia Guberniias. "Prophets" appeared here, teaching that the end of the world was approaching, and picturing this as retribution on the "sinful" and as the prelude to the millennial kingdom of the "righteous". Both those Molokans who refused to follow the teachings expounded by the prophets, and all representatives of non-Christian faiths and "pseudo-Christian" faiths, such as for example Russian Orthodoxy, were relegated to the ranks of the sinful.

A Tambov Molokan, Luk'ian Sokolov, who had fled to Bessarabia from Siberian exile, proclaimed the approaching end of the world in 1836. He preached widely among the Molokans in favor of their resettlement on Ararat so that there, among the chosen, the new Jerusalem would be set up.

An analagous message was preached by the Astrakhan Molokan Terentii Belogurov, who declared himself the prophet Elijah. Among the Molokans of Tavriia and Saratov Guberniias, the preaching of Fedor Bulgakov (known among the Molokans as David Evseevich) about a thousand-year kingdom of the chosen found a response.

The success of chiliastic and eschatological preaching among ordinary Molokans can be correctly understood only against the background of the general upsurge in the popular movement against serfdom at the beginning of the 1830s. In the central, southern and northern guberniias there occurred popular uprisings, to which the governmental chain of command gave the title "cholera mutinies"; mass actions against the landlords occurred in the Ukraine; At the beginning of the 1840s among state and serf peasants there arose a new wave of anti-serfdom actions, which seized the central guberniias and the Middle Volga region, in which it occurred in the form of so-called potato riots. Thousands of peasants from Kursk, Voronezh and Sartov Guberniias, fleeing from the yoke of the serf-owners, moved to the Caucasus, to the southern and southeastern borders.

Representatives of the poor and middle classes in Molokanism took part in the spontaneous resettlement movement, which was one of the forms of class struggle against serfdom. Bishop Iakov, who occupied the see of Saratov in 1832-1847, was an eyewitness to these events. He testified that "in 1833 among the Molokans a strong movement started everywhere. In enormous lines of carts they stretched out from various guberniias to the Caucasus ...; as future citizens of a godly city of Jerusalem soon to be established, the Molokans went with solemnity and joy to the New Land ...; often they loudly sang psalms[B] and various religious songs under the open sky" (*Pravoslavnyi sobesednik* 1858: 301). This was the time when there were obscure rumors among the peasants about "freedom" which would supposedly be given to all who settled on the borders. Bishop Iakov could observe that "the Russian Orthodox peasants among whom the Molokans lived were agitated.... Many Russian Orthodox were so insecure in their faith that, taking up the Molokan heresy, they left the motherland and together with the wandering heretics went to seek the new Jerusalem" (*Pravoslavnyi sobesednik* 1858: 352).

The eschatological and chiliastic ideas, of course, covered up the eyes of the participants of the new movement, turning them aside from the main movement of class struggle against serfdom. But however the paths of the participants in the "cholera mutinies" and potato riots of the 1830s, and the representatives of religious forms of social protest contemporary with them diverged, they were all peasants, hating the serf-owners and every kind of exploiter. In any case, the preachers of the end of the world and the beginning of the millennial kingdom and, still more, of community of property, reckoned with the democratic interests of their followers and reflected them in their own fashion.

The democratic content of the preaching of the ideologists of the new movement in Molokanism belongs to the common struggle of the peasantry against serfdom, as distinct from everything that was sectarian in it, and had particular limited significance. The student of the ideology of the anti-serfdom movement of the peasantry in the first half of the 19th century only impoverishes the description of it by not taking into account and duly evaluating the democratic motifs contained in the sermons and compositions of the religious and social accusers, who spoke out in the 1830s-1850s, particularly among the Molokans. A collaborator of Sokolov and Bulgakov, Maksim Rudometkin, a native of the village of Algasovo, Morshansk Uezd, Tambov Guberniia, in epistles from prison directed to his followers, prophesied: "Let us all remember the beginning of God's last judgment, which will soon unexpectedly fall on the Russian tsar like that which unexpectedly fell on the Egyptian tsar Pharaoh.... This is why I dare to point here and now to that example of the most evil of Pharaohs — directly to the Russian tsar drunk with blood" (Samarin, ed. 1928: 451). Rudometkin prophesied the "ruin" of the tsar and "his damned progeny", who "all together will burn in the heavenly fire and all together will go directly into the burning lake, together with the devil in eternal torment" (*ibid.*).

He warned believers and unbelievers alike that "eleven o'clock of heavenly time has struck", that there have already appeared prophets (Rudometkin himself first of all), before whom "the whole earth trembles and even more the darkly evil proud military detachment of Antichrist, or to say it more directly, his innumerable impious army, and equally those like it — all rich people, city-dwellers, merchants, nobles, and also those following them, all God-forsaken left-handed simple children of the world" (Samarin, ed. 1928: 343). Under these conditions, instances were possible in which Molokans did not stand aside from the participation in peasant uprisings, which once attracted Herzen's sympathetic attention (Herzen 1919: 322-323). Thus, at the beginning of the 1840s, the Molokans Popov and Panferov became important participants in the movement of state peasants in Borisogleb Uezd of Tambov Guberniia. In Ryndziunskii's opinion they "belong to those leaders of the movement who, although they stubbornly acted against the authorities, tried to act chiefly by peaceful means ..." (Ryndziunskii 1955: 326).

The widest scope for the preaching of the new prophets was achieved in the place of Molokan colonization, in Erevan, Baku (Shemakha), and Elizavetpol' Guberniias. The formation of religious parties in Molokanism took place half a century before the Dukhobor movement split into the hostile Large and Small Parties. The profound social contradictions distinguishing the Molokan movement were the basis for the earlier manifestation of open struggle between the upper and lower ranks of the sect than had been the case in Dukhoborism. It is characteristic that the religio-social slogans which gave form to the action of the Molokan lower classes, partly anticipated the religio-social slogans which in the second half of the 1880s united the adherents of the Large Party in Dukhoborism.

As a counterweight to the forced regementation to which the Molokan upper classes subjected the way of life and thought of the rank-and-file believers, the prophets who appeared among the Molokans spoke out with a validation of "spiritual freedom", as inalienably belonging to the believers from the "fact" of the descent upon the apostles of the "Holy Spirit" during Pentecost. They declared that the "outpouring of the Holy Spirit" on the believers was constant, which supported the assertion that those in whom the action of the Holy Spirit manifested itself were the enunciators of "divine truth"—as distinct from the leaders, whose mouths had long ago become dumb for preaching the word of God, and their hearts turned to stone.

The sermons of the prophets, among whom Sokolov and Bulgakov were marked by special eloquence, ignited a religious ecstasy in their followers, similar to that religious ecstasy which seized Verigin's followers in the mid-1890s.

We know that during the Cossack massacre of the Dukhobors in the village of Bogdanovka on June 25, 1895, their religious exaltation reached such heights that "they 'saw' Verigin on one of the clouds floating by, blessing their heroic deed". In order not to let the religious exaltation among them decline, the Dukhobors resorted to exhausting fasts and adopted every possible ascetic prohibition. Precisely in this intense psychological atmosphere among the followers of the Large Party there occurred the distribution of property and the reorganization of the structure of life on the bases of apostolic "communism".

Something similar took place in Molokanism as well. In the words of the prophet Bulgakov, "In 1833 there occurred an awesome phenomenon among our brothers—a strong outpouring of the Holy Spirit, influencing by miraculous means many persons given over to the will of God. At this time there was a famine, but they set up a common sum, food, clothing, and so forth, dividing it up among all according to need. Many prophesied about the end of this age, the coming of the last judgment of Christ: sinners would all perish, but the righteous would remain to rule with Christ on earth for a thousand years" (Samarin, ed. 1928: 80).

The kingdom of Satan was to be replaced on earth by a kingdom of God, but what kind? What was the order which would distinguish it precisely as "divine"—i.e. a kingdom ideal in structure? Opposition to the reactionary upper classes of Molokanism seized on various social elements of the sect, and this opposition was divided in its answers to this cardinal question. We cited above a segment from a work by Bulgakov, from which it appears that his contemporaries, close to him in spirit, had a common treasury and distributed foods and clothes, "among all according to need". Bulgakov will have it that this was a purely practical measure, due to the fact that "at the time there was a famine". But in reality among the Molokans there were both proponents in principle of communalization of property, labor, distribution and way of life, and opponents in principle of this means of solving social contradictions. Bulgakov himself was among the latter, which did not stop him from salting his compositions with attacks against the greed of the rich, and declaring decisively: "He who acquires wealth unjustly is a usurer and a servant of idols" (Samarin, ed. 1928: 112).

Among the socially-heterogeneous participants of the movement Bulgakov represented the interests of the middle layer of peasants, who suffered from the violence of serfdom and the Church and the economic dependence in which rich people, who had seized power in the Molokan communities, put them; at the same time, these peasants possessed property and attempted to defend their interests in the struggle with the rich.

Bulgakov prepared his followers to enter into the "kingdom of God", but he described it only in general terms. He was taken up by the struggle with opposing tendencies in Molokanism, but chiefly he believed that God's miracle would be achieved before he succeeded in telling of it with his mortal pen. But when 1836 passed and the miracle did not occur, all that the prophets could do was to capture the imagination of the believers with the desired pictures of the coming kingdom.

Rudometkin did this. He pictured in his works a kingdom of God situated on a square of land beyond whose boundaries remained the "Gogs and Magogs" — "false Christians," "unbelievers," all those who did not follow his teaching. In the center of the square there was a city. Surrounded by twelve courtyards and four towers (each building had three storeys), there stands a seven-storey palace, built of precious stones, topped by a roof of pure gold, over which an inextinguishable fire burns. The streets of the city are paved with marble. The seven-storey palace was picked as the residence of Rudometkin himself, who created for himself the title "Tsar of the Spirits and Leader of Zion's People". In the three-storey palaces, united by a common roof, were the residences of 12 tsar-priests — i.e., clergy subordinate to Rudometkin — and 12 prince-courtiers: a tsar is after all a tsar! And the remaining people spiritually subordinate to Rudometkin were also promised houses built "of the wood of fruit trees and stones of hewn marble".

Rudometkin did not avoid the pressing needs of the people ruled by him in the thousand-year kingdom, and even was concerned to give them items of luxury. As concerns the latter, they were both valuables which appeared as tribute from kingdoms where the "Gogs and Magogs" ruled, and gold and silver dishes which "God's people" were prudent enough to take out of the churches before they settled in the promised land. "God's people" would use the precious metal "however they saw fit; perhaps the shoes of all our horses would be universally gold and silver". For the satisfaction of the pressing needs of the population in Rudometkin's kingdom there would be driven in a herd of "every sort of livestock, which would have neither size nor number", and the soil on the promised land would be of unhead-of fertility.

But even so, the fields here would need working and the stock tending. There would be every sort of household chore. In a word, the "Tsar of the Spirits" was faced with the problem of organization of labor in the future kingdom. And here he decided to make a generous concession to the Mohammedans and to settle them also in the promised land as objects of exploitation, within a pale of settlement—along its four boundaries, it is true. "They themselves (the Mohammedans—A. K.)", Rudometkin wrote, "will be our servants and breadwinners forever and their wives will be the servants and wetnurses for our children, everywhere with bows to them to the earth" (Samarin, ed. 1928: 361).

Having written a plan for the kingdom of God on earth, Rudometkin in his imagination never went beyond the bounds of social relations based on exploitation and force. Let us add that he envisaged punishments for those who opposed the order he set up. The measures were severe: "And whoever opposes this union of ours, he will perish either by being driven across the boundaries under the shadow of eternal confinement, or will soon die the death of the 'electric' sun" (Samarin, ed. 1928: 363).

Rudometkin's project was not as fantastic as it seems at first glance. Let us remember Dukhoboriia, which had existed for a long time before Rudometkin wrote his essays. The center of the promised land of Dukhoboriia, its Zion, was the village of Goreloe where in a stone palace—if only a two-storey one—the Orphans Home, there was the residence of Luker'ia Kalmykova, also a kind of empress of the spirits and leader of the people of Zion. Kalmykova had her tsar-priests—her "elders" and prince-courtiers—Zubkov, Vorob'ev, Verigin and others. There were also in Dukhoboriia fertile fields and countless livestock, and with them "Mohammedans" from among the Dukhobor poor, and real Mohammedans from among the native local population—the "servants and breadwinners" of the rich.

Dukhoboriia with its social and life-style contrasts was the earthly prose of that kingdom of God which Rudometkin chose as the subject of his apocalyptic poem.

In expectation of a "miracle", the followers grouped around Sokolov, Bulgakov and Rudometkin preserved among themselves a condition of ecstasy with the aid of a religious practice which in part repeated that of the Khristovovers and in part anticipated the ritual of Christians of the evangelical faith—the Pentecostals. Here there was prophecy under the outpouring of the Holy Spirit, and babbling "speaking in tongues", and a special form of ecstatic religious ritual—solo and group jumping—the consequence of religious excitation, which the believers saw as a manifestation of the action of the Holy Spirit in man.

The adherents of the tendency in Molokanism under review called themselves "Spiritual Christians-Pryguny". At the price of an overburdened nervous system on which the Pryguny operated with artificial means, they brought themselves into a pathological state, in which, it seemed to them, they left their "bodily envelopes" and sought to elevate their "spiritual essences".[1] Thus they prompted heaven, which was slow to send down the kingdom of God, painted for them by their leaders in blinding color.

From the Pryguny movement in Molokanism, let us turn to another movement headed by the peasants Evstignii Iakovlevich Galiaev and Mikhail Akinf'evich Popov, which had been given the name of the Obshchie sect.

The researcher has at his disposal an extremely limited number of sources from which it would be possible to begin a study of the history of the Obshchie. The basic source remains the works of the Obshchie which describe their teaching published by V. Tolstoi in 1864 (V. Tolstoi 1864: 93ff).

Polemical epistles written by F. O. Bulgakov (Samarin ed. 1928: 132-140) supplement somewhat Tolstoi's publication. The observations of N. Dingel'shtedt (Dingel'shtedt 1885), S. Maksimov (1867), and Gleb Uspenskii (1949: 302 ff) have great value, since these authors were directly acquainted (at various times) with the activists and participants in the Obshchie sect, with its economic set-up and way of life.

These observations supplement each other, since their subject is one and the same process taking place in the Obshchie. At the same time the observations of the authors named above relate precisely to those forms of social organization which were the subject of the work published by Tolstoi. We have no reason to doubt the high quality of these observations as a source, with all their differences in depth and perspective of characterization.

The reminiscences and observations characterizing the milieu of the Obshchie, written in 1914 by Mikhail Saiapin and published in the first and second issues of *Ezhemesiachnyi Zhurnal* [Monthly Journal] for 1915, are a special case.

The author was born and grew up among the Obshchie and was the grandson of A. I. Saiapin, Popov's successor in the post of leader of the Obshchie. For a number of years, Mikhail Saiapin taught in a Ministry [of Education] school in the village of Nikolaevka—the place where the Obshchie were concentrated—but broke with their teaching, while at the same time remaining

---

[1] "... If the Darochichag Zionites (the Pryguny—A. K.) had not been visited by the Holy Spirit for a long time, they attempted to call it forth by acts of fanatical asceticism. They did not take any food or water at all for four or five days" (N. D. 1878: 420).

deeply devout. He accumulated a large mass of memories and observations, and he was quite familiar with the oral legends of the Obshchie and with their writings.

However, Saiapin did not possess the methods of a scientific researcher. He used legend equally with historical testimony and his observations and recollections are not unmarked by the desire to settle accounts with the milieu to which he once belonged. One must take account of this and of the religiously-limited world-view of the author in turning to his essay as a source for information about the Obshchie sect.

The beginnings of the activity of the founders of the Obshchie, Galiaev and Popov, date from not later than 1833, when Galiaev gave Popov a work titled *Articles of the Common Faith* (Articles of Faith of the Obshchie Doctrine) (Tolstoi 1864: 93). This work was a plan for the construction of life on the basis of the obligatory nature of labor and community of property, and, in the opinion of its authors, revived the example of the life of the apostles.

Mikhail Popov supported his convictions with action—he distributed his property among the poor and with great success preached a new doctrine in the Molokan villages of the Trans-Volga. The Molokans in the villages of Tiagloe Ozero (at the end of the 18th and the beginning of the 19th century about 500 Molokans lived here) and Iablonnyi Ovrag unanimously adhered to Galiaev's and Popov's teaching.

Galiaev and Popov acted in an atmosphere of exaltation which seized the Molokan and partly the Russian Orthodox population in the rural localities of Saratov and Samara Guberniias, to whom he preached the imminent end of the world. Tying a kerchief across his shoulder, Galiaev went around the villages, and hoisting an image of a cherub which he had drawn, he called out: "Repent, brothers, the days for the last repentance are approaching, and there will be no other repentance" (Varadinov 1863: 346). At this time Popov distributed a piece of writing consisting of Gospel texts, and called upon the peasants to sign it: in the face of the approaching judgment of God it made some sense to inscribe oneself in a society of "the faithful". What was this writing? I assume that this was the Articles of the Obshchie Faith (Varadinov 1863: 346-347).

Galiaev's and Popov's activity took place in an apocalyptic atmosphere, was warmed by it and needed it. The teaching disseminated by Galiaev and Popov was so new, and called for such a decisive renunciation of the entire existing system of relationships, that only in an atmosphere heated by an expectation of extraordinary events could it receive a lively response and collect around itself a following of any size.

But chiliasm and eschatology played a role by Galiaev's and Popov's teaching extremely different from the one which it played in the teachings of Sokolov, Bulgakov and Rudometkin. The latter rested their hopes on a miracle and limited themselves to the acquisition of more and more converts to their faith. Galiaev and Popov also hoped for a miracle, but this was, as it were, in the background of their teaching, and in the foreground was faith in the possibility and necessity of building an earthly Jerusalem, anticipating the approaching heavenly Jerusalem.

How Popov understood the relationship between the Jerusalem which he and his co-thinkers were supposed to build (which he called "the temple", "the refuge", "the camp of salvation", and "the righteous village"), and the "heavenly Jerusalem", is evident from his subsequent epistle: "The righteous know", Popov wrote, "that they are in a refuge, in a temple, and the temple is in them. The first temple is the camp of salvation, the righteous village; the second temple is your soul. The righteous preserve both these temples in purity and chastity as the Bride awaiting the Bridegroom. Our Bridegroom is about to descend from the clouds and enter into us and with Him the Mountain Jerusalem. So the heavenly is combined with the earthly and every visible part of our flesh will be transformed and freed from bodily slavery for a thousand years. Our earthly dwelling will be blessed and bathed in light forever" (quoted in Saiapin 1915: I, 67).

Forseeing the beginning of the millennial kingdom of Christ, Popov, like chiliasts contemporary with him, called for a cleansing from "filth", but—and this was the originality of his teaching—not only from the filth of moral defects, but primarily from that of the defects of the social structure. And the millennial kingdom in Popov's view was not a kingdom of the ideally virtuous, but an ideal projection of the Articles of the Obshchie Faith, its perfect expression and entirely earthly triumph. Precisely thus, in Popov's understanding, the heavenly was united with the earthly.

Let us describe the social and Church-religious structure of the Obshchie, using mainly the Articles of the Obshchie Faith.

Acceptance into the community and departure from it were voluntary. He who desired to enter publicly declared agreement with the principles of:

(1) community of property;

(2) equalization;

(3) respect for the collective will.

He supported his declaration by transfer to the community of the property which belonged to him. A special commission carried out an inventory and evaluation of the entrance contribution. Departure from the community was free, regardless of the motives for it; more than that, the Articles of the Obshchie Faith envisaged material guarantees for this. The one who left the community was paid a monetary share. Its size did not correspond to the actual cost of the contribution which he had brought on entering the community. The one leaving the community was paid a median arithmetical share—i.e., a sum which expressed the ratio of the total cost of the entrance contribution to the number of members of the community. Since those who entered brought unequal contributions to the community, actual deviations on this or that side of the median arithmetical share were equalized by a recalculation of surpluses over it at the expense of those whose cost of real contribution was lower than the arithmetical average. But the wealth created by the work of the members of the community remained as the inalienable property of all those who continued its work.

The right of return of the actual cost of the contribution was preserved, in all probability, for cases when departure from the community was motivated not by some concrete circumstance, but by a rejection of the teaching of the Obshchie itself.

The basic production unit in the Articles of the Obshchie Faith was called the party, and consisted of several families living in one house. Since marriage was considered indissoluble, man and wife could not live in different parties (depending on the size of the house, a party consisted of 30-40-50 persons) (Dingel'shtedt 1885: 46). The party was simultaneously the primary religious organization, called the *domestic church*.

The parties of each individual village formed an *assembly church*. Immovable and movable property, tools and the means of production were the joint property of the assembly church. It granted to each party the rights of use of farm buildings, dwelling space, tools, production inventory, land, garden plots, orchard plots, cattle, shops, subsidiary enterprises, mills, etc. There was an institution of chief supervisors who administered the work of several parties. In turn, the chief supervisors were subordinate to the guardian in whose power and responsibility the production and economic activity of all the assembly churches and parties which had been formed were placed. The laboring income of the parties formed the so-called Common Fund. Part of the Common Fund, remaining after payment of obligations, taxes, and general expenses in the village, was given to the party and distributed equally among its members, according to their number.

Along with the basic monetary fund, the Common Fund, there existed the Table Fund — an aid fund, formed from voluntary contributions by believers. This fund was subject to double-entry bookkeeping. It was disbursed on the simple declaration of a believer experiencing need. The sum received was to be returned, but without any interest. There existed a peculiar idea of "spiritual interest". The believer receiving aid was obliged to fast. If the debtor was unable to return the sum received, he could "cover" it by a fast calculated at a day of fasting for a ruble of debt. Depending on the size of the debt, it was considered possible to distribute the number of fast days demanded from the debtor among a group of believers, with their voluntary agreement. Each party was headed by a supervisor, also called the household or earthly supervisor. He was answerable for the organization and productivity of labor of the members of the party, for the completion of tasks, and for the size of income sent from the party to the Common Sum.

Each evening the supervisor, according to the economic assignments received from the officials of the assembly church, gave production assignments to the members of his party, being obliged to include himself in the work detail. Each party had a sequential number, which was not fixed, and which designated the place occupied by it on the ladder of seniority of parties making up the given assembly church. The seniority of the party was determined by the amount of income contributed by it to the Common Fund. According to the amount of income, the party was given a sequential number: first, second, third, etc. The same principle of seniority determined the position of the assembly churches, which, depending on the economic achievement and income received, were designated as the first, second, etc. assembly churches.

Along with the supervisor in the party, there were:

(1) an assistant supervisor;

(2) a household (or earthly) female supervisor, who shared with the male supervisor his functions in relation to women in the party;

(3) the female food supervisor, answerable for production of food items, their quality, quantity and equal distribution among the members of the party;

(4) the general female supervisor who fulfilled the function of linen-keeper. However, she had charge only of items of female clothing and shoes. Male clothing and shoes were kept by the male supervisor of the party. In general, outer clothing, shoes, cloth for sewing clothes and domestic utensils were the joint property of the party.

The post of party supervisor was changeable. A supervisor who manifested good capabilities in the organization of labor of the members subordinate to him and who made the operations entrusted to him profitable, received advancement, becoming the chief supervisor, or even the guardian. On the other hand, a negligent or incompetent supervisor was subjected to measures of moral influence, and when such were unsuccessful he was removed from his post.

Schools with a five-year course of study where reading, writing, arithmetic and singing were taught existed under the assembly churches. Study was obligatory for all children, boys and girls, who had reached seven years of age, and took place *jointly*. In the summertime there were no lessons. The children took part in the completion of production assignments. They gathered together at festivals to repeat the material covered during the school season.

The school functioned not only as a place of study, but also as an organization of students with a distribution among them of "officials", corresponding to the scale of church organization of the Obshchie. Thus, the school combined study with the education of the students in the spirit of the Articles of the Obshchie Faith, and accustomed them to the organization of social and church life envisaged in the Articles.

Textbooks and paper were paid for from the Common Fund.

As we have shown, communalization of means of production and tools was the basis of the social order set up among the Obshchie. But there coexisted with this elements of a private economy. Thus, for example, the female half of the population — only after finishing public work, it is true — was allowed to carry on small household production intended for sale, such as spinning, weaving and embroidery.

Members of the community got and kept as their own property various valuables from relatives who did not hold to the teaching of the Obshchie. Finally, the Table Fund was a fund specially designated to serve the sphere of private interests of the community members.

The church structure had exceptional significance for the whole life and activity of the community.

The economic administration of the party was under the leadership and control of a church administration consisting of three levels: the administration of the house churches; standing over them, the administration of the assembly churches; and the higher church government, which stood over the assembly churches and was made up of a council of 12 apostles, headed by a "tsar of the faith of the Obshchie". The general church was governed by officials: the judge, the sacrificer, the supervisor, the seer, the one who prays, the one who administers the sacraments, the one who thinks, the one who speaks, and the "member."[C] The officials had assistants. This administrative structure characterized first of all the structure of the assembly church, but within the house church there existed approximately the same "officials". The office of judge was the chief one. The judge controlled and regulated the activity of all other officials. The church supervisor (of the house church) supervised the activity of the party supervisor and his auxiliary apparatus, and if the party supervisor was to be removed, his word, apparently, was decisive.

The officials of the assembly church were keepers and distributors of the Common Fund, which was not entered in the account books. The Common Fund was directly in the keeping of the supervisor of the assembly church, but its solvency was reviewed by higher officials of the assembly church. They had the right to sanction the ways in which the Common Fund was used.

The system of the hierarchy was exceptionally ramified and encompassed all the members of the sect. Even its ordinary participants fulfilled some, even if very small, official function. Each believer (at least this tendency can be guessed) was seen as an intersection of one or another line in the hierarchical network which embraced the community as a whole. This system guaranteed a common mutual control, whose threads proceeded from the judges. Not only control of higher officials over lower ones was envisaged, which was, for example, the function of the "members", but of lower-ranking members for higher ones, which was the function of the "seers".

Exceptional significance was attributed to confession, the receipt of which was the function of the ones who administered the sacraments.[D] While the person administering the sacraments supervised deeds, the thinkers had the function of observing utterances, and moreover of discovering whether "sinful" thoughts had not arisen in the minds of members of the community. All officials together bore the obligation to observe the behavior, discipline and mutual relations of the leaders, down to the mutual relations of parties to a marriage. Over all members of the community, officials and ordinary persons, stood the leader of the community, called not without reason "the tsar of the Obshchie Faith". His authority and power as a person in immediate and constant communication with God was considered divine.

An element reinforcing the organization of the community was the order of religious life set up in it. In the community there were special buildings (with benches for sitting) for religious meetings, in which "the Holy Scriptures" were read and interpreted, and specially trained singers sang psalms. There were regular prayers four times a day, concluding with general kissing symbolizing the brotherhood of believers. Along with the account books in which the operations of the Table Fund were recorded, there was a written registration of prayers, fasts, good deeds of believers, and religious singing they had done. These notes, apparently, were publicly read during religious gatherings.

Without going into the details of the religious teachings of the Obshchie, let us note that they colored the entire sphere of social interests of the Obshchie and their day-to-day structure.

In the teaching about the coming kingdom "of the third testament" — "the testament of the holy spirit", which calls up an association with the historical-theological conceptions of Joachim of Flora — Popov gave exceptional significance to revelation and prophecy. A believer's capacity for mystical exaltation was highly valued and opened the way to official rank.

The sermons of the best-known "prophets" were written down in a book entitled *The Third Testament. The Gospel of the Holy Spirit.* Let us cite a characteristic excerpt: "As long as you see among you people who are in the Spirit, taking part in spiritual gifts, your joy will not dry up and weaken in tears and in merriment. Listen to your gifted ones and go the ways pointed out by them. Preserve those who prophesy and the men who see" (Saiapin 1915: I, 67).

The religious practice of the Obshchie registered the external manifestations of ecstasy, in which state movement arose so that by ecstasy it could, so to speak, be aroused repeatedly as a conditioned reflex.

A half-century after the origin of the Obshchie sect, an eyewitness observed: "The common work took place with the singing of sobbing psalms, broken by weeping for the perishing world. Weeping was replaced by stormy joy over one's own salvation ... triumphant songs broke forth, the spirit descended on the 'gifted', and prophesying and speaking in tongues began ... people laughed in ecstasy, were bathed in tears, sang, stamped their feet, waved their hands and kissed like drunken people. This is a picture of the prayer meeting of the Obshchie, which has been before my eyes since early childhood" (Saiapin 1915: I, 68).

Let us sum up the factual data characterizing the teaching of the Obshchie.

The basic principles expressed in the Articles of the Obshchie Faith arose as a protest of the lower ranks against the yoke of serfdom and the appearance of increasing stratification. It was part of the idea of utopian socialism. "This was a real phalanstery", N. M. Nikol'skii wrote of the Obshchie commune, "which would have made Fourier himself ecstatic" (Nikol'skii 1930: 206).

Under conditions in which the realization of the teachings of the Obshchie was not objectively possible, and the limited material basis could not but hinder their social beginnings at every step, the organization of power among the Obshchie was an attempt to overcome just this contradiction: the extremely ramified and graded superstructure literally was designed to bear the basis.

This was not a viable attempt. In turn, mystical exaltation as a means of supporting the solidarity of the Obshchie could not give a continuous effect. Neither stood the test of time.

About 1840, Popov, Galiaev and their associates were exiled from Saratov Guberniia for their activity and settled in Lenkoran Uezd of Baku Guberniia. Popov immediately organized a small commune in the new place and headed it. But this was a continuation of the experiment, the beginning of which was laid in the old location of Popov's activity. When Popov's Saratov adherents sent to him an emissary, the latter in a letter sent to the homeland told of Popov's commune, not as of a new beginning, but as a testimony of his fidelity to the old cause, which was not shaken by any trials.

Here is what the emissary wrote: "Our elders live in one izba, all thirteen together; they have gotten three horses ... they plow the land with them in turn, but together. They live in great need, but do not think to part; better to lie in the damp earth from our misfortunes, than to destroy our common cause. Mikhailo Akin'tich (Popov — A. K.) rules them.... The life of our elders is very hard, but just look at their cause and you won't want to leave; everything in the faith and according to our law.... Besides this existence one does not need to wish for more" (Maksimov 1867: 12).

The Obshchie commune functioned in Saratov Guberniia according to the

Articles of the Obshchie Faith: among those exiled to Baku Guberniia there was one A. I. Saiapin, who had the title of supervisor, and six other persons whose surnames are unknown to us, who were his assistants (Saiapin 1915: I, 69). Let us remember that the function of the supervisor included the leadership of the primary production collective—the party. The fact that Saiapin had six assistants makes it highly probable that he had the title of chief supervisor—i.e. that he led several production collectives.

The small congregation grew, by the addition of both Popov's Saratov followers and followers of Sokolov and Bulgakov, whom Bulgakov was forced to try to persuade of the "non-correspondence" of the Articles of the Obshchie Faith with "Scripture". Disorder arose among Bulgakov's adherents. "You began with the spirit", Bulgakov addressed them, "and you end with the flesh: you say—we are Mikhail Akint'evich's (Popov's—A. K.), others that they are Semenushka's (Semen Uklein's—A. K.), and others say—we are Isai Ivanovich's and Luk'ian Petrovich's (Sokolov's—A. K.). Who are Mikhail (Popov—A. K.) and the others? They are only servants" (Samarin, ed. 1928: 137).

The stumbling block in Bulgakov's differences with the Obshchie was the basic principle of the latter—common property. Bulgakov wrote, polemicizing with the Obshchie: "Concerning public property, let us look at Abraham our father, how he separated from Lot, but there is no divine prohibition of this anywhere, neither in the law and commandments, nor in the New Testament.... Now I want you and myself to go by the necessary laws of the Holy Scriptures, not laying on ourselves a self-willed angelic service and burden, not demanded from us by divine law" (Samarine, ed. 1928: 133).

Soon a community gathered around Popov, whose population was distributed in ten izbas, and it continued to grow. Then there followed the expected blow from the government. In 1844, Popov was exiled to Eastern Siberia and settled in a village near Minusinsk. This was a severe test for the Obshchie. It is true that Galiaev, who had great influence among the Obshchie, remained in the Molokan village of Vorontsovka. Still more important were the ties which were set up between them and Popov. From his place of exile Popov sent the Obshchie epistles, and from time to time money for the Table Fund; sometimes these sums exceeded 100 rubles.

The news coming from Lenkoran Uezd, where Popov's co-thinkers were (the villages of Nikolaevka and Andreevka), could hardly have pleased him. It is true that Popov had quite a few co-thinkers. In 1854, there were 645 of them in Lenkoran Uezd. (About 200 of Popov's followers were in Saratov Guberniia, and also in places of exile in Enisei and Tomsk Guberniias) (Dingel'shtedt 1885: 55.) But these were no longer those people who preferred "rather to lie in the damp earth from their misfortune" than to destroy the "Obshchie cause", as the messenger once wrote of the handful of originators of the commune. Among the Obshchie social and property differentiation occurred and deepened, leading to a division between ordinary believers in the earthly circle, and "heavenly" circles consisting of "officials" contrasted to them. The latter not only ruled over the earthly ones, but appropriated their labor. There existed besides a circle of "the underworld", as the persons who were excommunicated from the church were called (Saiapin 1915: I, 68). Such an evolution is not to be explained, of course, by the fact that the community lost its founder and leader.

The Obshchie commune did not by any means stand apart from the surrounding social ties, in the first instance monetary ones. Its economy was not isolated or of a subsistence character. The basic and auxiliary funds of the commune—the Common and Table Funds—were monetary. Trade, loans and credit, and rental operations of the commune were done by its leaders. But as we have already noted, the participation of ordinary commune members in commodity and money ties, even if in limited dimensions, was not prohibited. All these ties fed the property-owning interests above all of those elements who, by their position in the commune, had access to public goods, and could connect the prospects of their material success more with the possession of private property than with fidelity to the principle of community of property. A vicious circle was formed: to support the bases of communal property and collective forms of labor in those objective conditions in which the commune existed, it needed a hierarchy, but the hierarchy, as the commune developed economically, cooled to the principles of community of property, was permeated by private property-owning interests, and gradually grew into a parasite on the labor of ordinary commune members.

S. Maksimov, who visited the Molokan settlements in Lenkoran Uezd in the mid-1860s, was told by old Molokans who were sharing memories 25-30 years old at that time: "Even in his (Popov's—A. K.) day, matters did not go very well among them: the healthy ones worked, but there were naked people and beggars; the elders lay on their sides, hiding and saving little bits of money. Some commanded, but matters got no better; others, like oxen, hauled water for the elders. They began to get angry and complain a lot. At first they got nowhere: they got excited for nothing. They decided to separate, to live separately in their own houses: that worked" (Maksimov 1867: 20). These recollections are not without exaggeration—the Molokans doing the remembering belonged, after all, to a movement hostile to Popov, but the phenomenon itself was noted correctly.[2]

As the commodity-and-money connections destroyed the commune, in parallel fashion the attitude toward it on the part of the local population

---

[2] Bulgakov, whom we have mentioned a number of times, unmasked the parasitism and the power-seeking of their church hierarchy in many epistles written between 1843 and 1845 and addressed to the Obshchie (*see* Samarin, ed. 1928: 132-141).

became more tense. On the initiative of their leaders, the Obshchie embarked on a path of land seizures similar to what the Transcaucasian Dukhobors had done. I. A. Saiapin, who was (in 1860?) a judge in the Obshchie commune, gave an order to the commune members "to plow a large part of the Tatar lands. The Tatars who had been peaceful until now ... reached for their clubs; the first battle occurred but the Russians were victorious ... they had a military organization, and the judge himself (Saiapin—A. K.) commanded them. In this battle three Russians and about two dozen Tatars were killed, not to speak of the wounded. And no complaints helped the Tatars: the Russians kept the rice plantations and the plow land" (Saiapin 1915: I, 73).

Similar sorties were repeated more than once.

At the beginning of the 1860s the Obshchie organization, as Popov and Galiaev had founded it, fell apart.

Of what Popov and his followers had begun, only the treasury of reciprocal small credit—the Table Fund, which had once played a secondary role in the commune—remained. The former communards continued to call themselves Obshchie, but they had individual farms, and their common treasury was designed precisely to give support to individual owners. Where previously the source for forming and supplementing the Table Fund was voluntary contributions ("sacrifices") by believers, now the Table Fund was formed by an obligatory tithe of the income, which the Obshchie were to pay in money or in kind. The Obshchie told Maksimov: "... Our rules are such that we support each other strongly: every tenth ruble of profit is common. Every tenth pud of threshed grain is also common. A hundred puds of threshed grain, and 10 are common; if someone has 1,000 puds in profit, 100 puds are poured into the common granary which Mikhailo Akint'ich himself built" (Maksimov 1867: 17). The tithe established among the Obshchie naturally allowed the treasury to be supplemented by sums exceeding those which could be formed by voluntary contributions. Under these conditions the activity of the treasury could exceed the bounds of small credit—someone would hardly be interested in it if he had brought to the treasury 100 puds of grain.

The public treasury built by Mikhail Popov's hands had become the seat of operations, having the aim of facilitating the development of private property; it was a miniature replica of the Dukhobor Orphans Home. S. Maksimov wrote: "Aid went without distinction to the well-off and to the poor.... Instead of a bank they had a sack, which on important occasions of public need was empty and silent" (Maksimov 1867: 23). But even in this new form, the cause founded by Popov continued to be the center of attraction for his followers coming from various points in the Transcaucasus to their "Mecca"—the village of Nikolaevka—and receiving from the local authorities permission for "all Transcaucasian Obshchie to settle in one place" (Maksimov 1867: 12).

At the beginning of the 1880s, Gleb Uspenskii visited Nikolaevka. The interest he showed in the Obshchie, about whom he wrote that "this sect is truly remarkable" (Uspenskii 1949: 302), is understandable. Uspenskii met in Nikolaevka with old men who had personally known Popov "in the period of the most genuine communistic order — common work, common dining halls, common property" (Uspenskii 1949: 304). How everything that Uspenskii saw contrasted with this past! "At the present time, Nikolaevka is a fairly large village", he wrote, "by no means reminiscent of that phalanstery of which, so it seems, its founder dreamed. There are rich houses here, and there are poor ones, and there are hovels. Equality in the means of life and property is no more. There are neither public dining halls nor common work: each works for himself with the labor force he has in his family" (Uspenskii 1949: 305). Of the social institutions Uspenskii found the Table Fund and the granary (*ibid.*). A meeting with I. A. Saiapin shocked Uspenskii: the grasping leader of the Obshchie complained of the liberalism ... of the state starosta, to whose authority he appealed for physical punishment of various erring believers (Uspenskii 1949: 308-309).

In spite of the fact that the Obshchie sect did not so much exist as drag out an existence, the number of its participants with time even grew a little.

By 1909, there were 958 Obshchie (TsGIAL, div. 821, f. 133, s.u. 21, shs. 294-296) as against 654 in 1854. In 1910, the Synodal authorities, still under the influence of the recent revolutionary years, reported on the Obshchie sect to the Ministry of Internal Affairs: "Rationalistic sectarianism ... is infected with ideas of cosmopolitanism, and some of the individual rationalistic sects — like, for example, the Obshchie or the Obshchie faith — even with ideas of socialist and communist teachings of the West ..." (TsGIAL, div. 796, f. 190, s.u. 146a, sh. 81).

But this characterization for a very long time had nothing in common with reality. One need not possess any insight in order to conclude as M. Saiapin did in his article: "... To describe the life of the Obshchie for the past 10 years (1904-1914 — A. K.), a life which has occurred before my eyes — is both very difficult and very uninteresting: almost all the time one has to dig around in petty details and in rubbish, which is all that these sobered-up ecstatics live by.... Nikolaevka is now a quiet backwater, where everything vital has perished ..." (Saiapin 1915: II, 69).

Thus, the Obshchie sect completed the circle of its development.

Let us return to the Pryguny movement in Molokanism.

We have already noted that the ideologists of the Pryguny movement, like for example Bulgakov, took from the very beginning a negative attitude toward the movement headed by Popov. Bulgakov's successor — Maksim Rudometkin — as is clear from his plan for a "kingdom of God" on earth, held views opposed to Popov's teaching. However, his preaching had great success.

In the pre-Reform years, it attracted many Molokans. Thus, for example among the Molokans in Erevan Guberniia in the second half of the 1850s, more than 50% became Rudometkin's followers (Liaister 1912: 9). The kingdom of God somewhere near Ararat of which he preached, his curse on the "Russian tsar drunk with blood", reflected in their own fashion the ripening revolutionary situation in Russia at the end of the 1850s and the beginning of the 1860s: its characteristics were both the peasant revolts in 1855 in the Kiev area, and the mass resettlements in 1856 of peasants from Ekaterinoslav and Kherson into the Crimea in the hopes of receiving there "land and freedom", and the armed uprising of the Georgian peasants in 1857, and the increasing revolutionary-democratic movement.

But even at the beginning of the 1870s, the ideology of Rudometkin's followers had undergone great changes. In the eyes of his closest successors, Alexander II was not "drunk with blood", but a "blessed" tsar. When Alexander II visited Tiflis in 1871, the Lenkoran Pryguny, neighbors of Popov's followers, prepared to present the emperor with welcoming verses:

> "O our great Tsar,
> Most gracious sovereign,
> Renowned and mighty hero,
> Sovereign Alexander the Second!
> In Russia he freed the peasant
> And universally was not forgotten.

(N. D. 1878: 410)

The social figure around which the Pryguny movement oriented itself was the well-to-do peasant, basing rights on "fields and sowings", "granaries with grain", "good work animals and domestic livestock" in the face of the serf-owners, and defending his economic independence from the inroads of the rich people, who were the upper stratum of the Molokan movement.

The Prygun verses of 1871 reflected servility toward the monarch and an attempt to attract his favorable attention. The point is that the Prygun movement of this time had acquired its own elite, vying in prosperity with the leading circles of other groups in Molokanism.

At the end of the 19th and beginning of the 20th centuries there was among the Pryguny a stratum of large property-owners — possessors of flocks, herds, and grain farms. A struggle developed between the upper and the lower strata, in which the upper stratum counted on the support of the government administration, as also occurred during the struggle between the Small and the Large Parties in Dukhoborism. The internal struggle in the Pryguny movement had an ideological form: the upper stratum increasingly departed from the mystical-ecstatic motifs, under whose sign the Pryguny movement had once emerged as a special group in Molokanism. As for the lower ranks, they not only insisted on the earlier traditions, but came out in opposition to the military draft, and openly demonstrated a hostile attitude toward militarism.

Under circumstances of conflict both with their own leaders and with the Autocracy, ordinary participants of the Pryguny movement, stimulated by the example of the Dukhobors, began to prepare for emigration from Russia. A story was circulated about a supposed prophecy by Rudometkin of "the flight into refuge" by his followers at the turn of the present century. Pryguny, living at this time in Erevan, Baku, Tiflis and Elizavetpol' Guberniias, and in Kars and the Transcaspian Oblasts, beginning in 1900, sent messengers and written requests to Petersburg, seeking permission to travel abroad. Some Molokans who did not belong to the Pryguny movement took part in these petitions. From 1901 to 1911, more than 3,500 Pryguny emigrated to California. The basic emigration by Pryguny was from Kars Oblast, Erevan Guberniia, and the Transcaspian Oblast. These were basically "agricultural workers, tillers of the soil, stock-breeders and craftsmen, who loved work and avoided idleness and gain from easy endeavors" (Samarin ed. 1928: 753).

A. F. Liaister, who published in 1912 a work on the Transcaucasian Pryguny based on data from personal observation, wrote: "... I was often in villages which still had remnants of the Pryguny movement and frequently visited Pryguny prayer meetings. They all occur without 'the Spirit' and differ little from Molokan meetings" (Liaister 1912: 14). And further: "At the present time they (the Pryguny — A. K.) number not more than 600 persons of both sexes in Erevan Guberniia. The thrift and wealth in which they now live, having forgotten Rudometkin's call to live 'like the birds in the sky', sharply distinguish them both from other sectarians in Erevan Guberniia ... and from the local peasant population" (Liaister 1912: 17-18).

In order to conclude the survey of the basic groups formed in Molokanism from its beginning in the 1770s to the 1830s, let us mention a group of Molokans formed by Sundukov — a Saratov follower of Uklein — who got the name of Molokan Subbotniki. This group celebrated the Sabbath [Saturday], adhered to the Old Testament food taboos, and in respect to their teaching were an intermediate form between Molokanism and the Subbotnik movement.

Thus, by the 1830s, internal contradictions were marked in all aspects of Russian sectarianism — Khristovoverie, Dukhoborism and Molokanism. This was the consequence of the social differentiation taking place in the peasantry, which formed the basic cadre of sectarianism. But neither Dukhoborism nor Khristovoverie nor other forms of sectarianism gave such early and clear examples of internal contradictions and schisms arising from them as Molokanism, which fragmented by the first half of the 19th century into the Don, Subbotnik, Prygun and Obshchie tendencies.

Not one of the groups named was the leading and predominant one in Molokanism. The basic mass of Molokans, gradually being eroded by various persuasions, continued during the second half of the 19th century to adhere to the basic religious positions set forth by Semen Uklein. After the separation from Molokanism of a number of groups, particularly after a significant contingent of Molokans went over to the Prygun movement as a result of the preaching of Sokolov, Bulgakov and Rudometkin, the remaining majority of Molokans (primarily those living in the Transcaucasus) began to call themselves the Steadfast Molokans [Postoiannye].

2. Economic Development and Social Contradictions in Molokan Settlements

Of all the movements which made up Russian sectarianism, Molokanism was the most numerous. Only in the first decade of the 20th century, when Molokanism was clearly on the decline, did Baptism become equal to it, if we are referring to the totality of all its groupings and varieties.

The geographical distribution of Molokanism was also the broadest of any sect. In the work *Sektantstvo i staroobriadchestvo v pervoi polovine XIX veke* [Sectarianism and the Old Belief in the First Half of the 19th Century], V. D. Bonch-Bruevich wrote: "The spread of the Molokans in the first half of the 19th century was enormous. They not only settled Stavropol' Guberniia, not only lived in the Crimea, but also lived as entire villages in Tambov, Voronezh, Samara, Saratov and Astrakhan Guberniias; they settled in large numbers in Siberia, the Transcaucasus, Central Asia and on the most distant eastern borders of the Russian state, and everywhere passionately preached their doctrine" (Bonch-Bruevich 1959: 295).

In studying the reasons for the wide distribution of Molokanism even in the first half of the 19th century (which continued into the second half), we must note a common feature which related to the reason for the spread of many other sectarian movements.

Molokanism arose and developed as one of the religious forms of social protest directed against the ruling church, the Autocracy and serfdom, which explains the success of the Molokan preaching. But we have become convinced of how complicated and contradictory was this very opposition, which split in the first half of the 19th century into tendencies corresponding to the interests of the various social groups participating in Molokanism.

The spread of Molokanism from its original site — the central chernozem guberniias — into the guberniias of the Volga region, and also into the southern, eastern and far-eastern borderlands of the state, in turn facilitated the system of Church-police persecution to which the Molokans, like the Khristovovers, Dukhobors and other sectarians, were subjected. This system of Church-state persecution included forced group exile of Molokans from the central and Volga guberniias to the borderlands. But in the geographical spread of Molokanism yet another reason played an important role, the effect of which can be followed in the history of this sect far more strongly than in the history of Khristovoverie and Dukhoborism (due to the peculiarities of the social composition and character of Molokanism). Among the participants of Molokanism over the entire 19th century and the beginning of the 20th century, the number of Molokans in the guberniias of the center reached 13,400 persons (Tambov, Voronezh, Riazan, Vladimir), in the Volga guberniias 28,400 (Samara, Saratov, Astrakhan, Nizhegorod and Simbirsk), in the Caucasus 21,300 (Tiflis, Erevan, Kars Oblast), and finally in the Far East 28,400 persons (Amur Oblast) (I am adding up statistical data from the Ministry of Internal Affairs for 1909; TsGIAL, div. 821, f. 133, d. 21, sh. 386). We encounter the fact of transfer of the basic centers of Molokanism into the Volga area, and from there to the Caucasus and the Far East. As concerns the Volga guberniias, the spread of Molokanism there is explained both by the success of its preachers, who actively disseminated their doctrine in the villages and cities of these guberniias among the native population lapsing from Russian Orthodoxy, and by the settlement here of Tambov, Voronezh and Riazan Molokans beginning in the 1780s.

In the Caucasian guberniias and in the Amur region, where at the beginning of the 20th century not less than half of all followers of Molokanism were concentrated, the native population which adhered to non-Christian religion responded less than moderately to Molokan preaching, while this preaching had no effect among Dukhobors, Subbotniki, Khristovovers and other sectarians who lived in neighboring villages to Molokan ones in Caucasian guberniias and the Far East.

Forced resettlements of Molokans into the guberniias mentioned were not so numerous as to lead us to the statistical data cited above, even if we took into account the optimal percentage of natural growth of the Molokan population. We are dealing with a relatively broad resettlement movement, the direction of which is quite definite: the Molokans emigrated from guberniias in which their land allotment was on the average not more than 15 desiatiny into guberniias of the Volga region, where they could receive allotments of 30 desiatiny, and from there into Amur region, which opened the prospects for Molokan farmers to have allotments of 100 desiatiny. The same considerations drew Molokans to the Caucasian guberniias (for example, among the Molokans in Vorontsovka, Borchalinskii Uezd, Tiflis Guberniia, there were in the 1880s quite a few property-owners with allotments of from 200 to 350 desiatiny); besides they counted on finding here favorable conditions for maintaining large sheep farms.

Of course, in the migratory flow directed toward the Volga area, the

Caucasus and the Far East, there were also Molokan poor, who suffered from exploitation and land shortage, and who attached themselves to the resettlement movement in hopes of bettering their economic position. These hopes, as a rule, were not realized, and the lot of the Molokan poor in the new places most often remained lack of land and exploitation. The resettlement of ordinary Molokans in the new lands was facilitated by the larger Molokan landowners. To relocate large farms in new places made no sense for their owners. They preferred to expand their farms in the old places by taking over additional pieces of the land of neighboring rank-and-file Molokans, offering the latter credit foɪ resettlement in the borderlands — with encumbering conditions, of course.

I quote one of the surviving descriptions of Molokan farms in Tavriia Guberniia, relating to the beginning of the 1860s: "... they (the Molokans — A. K.) have achieved remarkable success in sheep-breeding. Many of their herds ... are managed by the rules of rational improvement of the breed. Thus, the Mazaev brothers, who have about 30,000 sheep, the Zakharovs, the Ivanovs, the Mamontovs, and many others have in general thoroughbred heavy-fleeced merino sheep, numbering 6,000 to 15,000 head" (Filibert 1870: 292-203). The large livestock-owners — the founders of the Mazaev and Zakharov dynasties, well-known in Molokanism, and others — felt the need to broaden the pasturelands and an especially acute need for laborers. They bought up privately-owned land and rented state lands on a broad scale along all the periphery of Tavriia Guberniia and beyond its boundaries, but not farther than "beyond the Kuban into the Black Sea region" (Filibert 1870: 293).

The work force in these regions was made up of peasant seasonal migrant laborers, who had come from the northern guberniias to the south of the country in search of wages. However, as we remember, there existed state restrictions connected with serfdom, preventing the Molokans from using the labor of Russian Orthodox peasants.

Anna Filibert, insisting that the Mazaevs, the Zakharovs and other large property-owning Molokans, equally with other "persons of alien faith" — the Mennonites, the Herrnhüter, and the Reformationists — should have the right to exploit hired labor, wrote: "All workers for the most part arrive as artels, in the majority from the northern guberniias of Russia, and all farm owners who are in any way substantial have to resort to their aid. The Molokans, the wealthy farmers, lack this possibility and are driven to the extreme of hiring as shepherds Tatars from Kazan Guberniia ..." (Filibert 1870: 295). In addition, the Molokan property-owners found means of making use of the labour of Russian peasant migrants as well; to judge by what Anna Filibert says, "the police actively persecute Molokans who they say detain Russian Orthodox workers ..." (*ibid.*).

With the passage of time, limitations on Molokans using the hired labor of Russian Orthodox peasants were relaxed.

The make-up of the resettlement movement of Molokans was determined, not by the Mazaevs, the Zakharovs and others like them, but by the poor, and in large measure persons who already had a minimum accumulation, which allowed them to act in their new places of residence on their own "fear and risk".

Let us study the economic development and social contradictions in the Molokan villages from the example of the largest center of Molokan colonization in the Amur region. I consider this example especially characteristic: precisely in the Amur region, Molokanism found the freest conditions (of all those possible in semi-serf Russia) for the structuring of their life on the basis of the faith, traditions, and social and ethical bases to which they adhered.

The resettlement of Molokans into the Amur region began in 1859, when Molokans—natives of Tavriia and Samara Guberniias—founded on the right bank of the Zeia River the village of Astrakhanka (Priamur'e 1909: 110). In 1865 (and later in 1892 and 1893), Molokan settlers from Tomsk, Tambov and Samara Guberniias settled in the village of Andreevka in Ivanovka Volost of Amur Guberniia (Grum-Grzhimailo 1894: 489). In the 1870s, Molokan settlers from Tambov, Samara, Voronezh and Tobol'sk Guberniias settled in the villages of Tambovka and Gil'chin, in Gil'chin Volost of Amur Guberniia (*ibid.*: 494-495). In the 1880s, Molokan settlers from Tambov Guberniia settled in Gil'chin Volost, in the villages of Tolstovka, Chuevka and Zharikovo (*ibid.*: 495-496). In the 1890s, Molokan settlers from Samara Guberniia settled in Gil'chin Volost, in the village of Verkhne-Urtui (*ibid.*: 497). Besides this, Molokan settlers continued to come from Tambov and other guberniias to the villages of Gil'chin, Chuevka, Andreevka, etc.

According to the data of G. Vvedenskii, who headed the resettlement project in Iuzhno-Ussuriiskii Krai, the Molokans and Dukhobors up to the 1880s were half of the rural population of the Amur region (Priamur'e 1909: 110). In the 1890s, the Russian rural population of the Amur region was 51,320 persons (Grum-Grzhimailo 1894: 526). Vvedenskii's information apparently is close to the truth. In particular it confirms K. Litvintsev's observation; he wrote in articles about the Amur sectarians published in 1887: "... it would not be an exaggeration to call the city of Blagoveshchensk a Molokan city, as many do" (Litvintsev 1887: 550).

The resettlement movement of Molokans in the Amur region, thus, was not limited to rural localities, which is understandable if we consider the significant merchant-meshchan stratum of the resettlers. K. Litvintsev characterized the occupations of the Blagoveshchensk Molokans in the following manner: "Among the Molokans living in the city, all attention is consumed with buying and selling.... Their trade is primarily small, on the guild certificates for the second and third ranks; many, by the way, conduct large trading operations in meat and grain, which unfortunately are monopolized exclusively by them. Many, having made timely purchases of grain and oats, sell them from barges in Cossack stanitsy as far as Nikolaevsk, from which operations they make large profits. In general, compared to the Russian Orthodox population of Blagoveshchensk, the Molokans are the wealthiest class ..." (Litvintsev 1887: 550-551).

The occupations of Molokans in Nikolaevsk-on-the-Amur were more or less analogous. "The Molokans", we read in Litvintsev, "trade in large quantities of salted and dried fish—the ket—which they themselves bring to Nikolaevsk-on-the-Amur" (Litvintsev 1887: 552).

Litvintsev's description of the occupations of the Molokans settled in the cities of the Amur region date from a time when their trading activities overshadowed their entrepreneurial activities in the field of industrial production. During the 1880s and especially the 1890s in the cities of the Amur region, industrial production developed—flour-milling, lumbering, and the cheese-making industry, many of whose plants were the property of Molokan capitalists. The Molokans Alekseev, Voblikov and Saiapin had in Blagoveshchensk a flour-milling operation, whose equipment cost 132,000 rubles, and their yearly production in 1896 amounted to 643,030 rubles (Berezhnikov 1898: 43).

Unfortunately, I have not succeeded in finding materials characterizing the conditions of labor at the enterprises in Blagoveshchensk which belonged to the Molokan entrepreneurs. In order to fill this gap, at least in part, I will use the impressions of the Molokan author D. V. Zaitsev, who visited the weaving enterprise belonging to the Molokan S. I. Zheltov in the traditional center of Molokanism—the village of Rasskazovo in Tambov Guberniia: "The apartment of the factory-owner", Zaitsev wrote, "was decorated European-fashion, with soft furniture and electric light ... from the surroundings, one sensed that people here lacked for nothing and lived far from all cares and anxieties, blessed by fate" (Zaitsev 1909b: 45).

Let us move now from the apartment of the factory-owner "furnished in European fashion" to his factory: "A large two-storey building housed two dozen different operations with a variety of different special machines and hand looms. More than 300 persons, more than half of them women and adolescent girls, worked at the factory. Life within the factory was the usual picture of modern industrial labor: dark, awkward cells, humming and shaking with heavy machines, and near them dirty, sweaty people with thin, often yellow faces. These people were chained all day to the machines; it was particularly depressing to see the girls, for the most part thin and faded before their time.... The people at the factory come mostly from Rasskazovo and are for the most part brothers [i.e. Molokans—Tr]" (Zaitsev 1909b: 45-46).

For a ten-hour day, the monthly wages at the factory of a Molokan capitalist were: for a weaver, from 10 to 18 rubles; for a machinist, from 15 to 20; for women workers from 4 rubles, 69 kopeks to 6 rubles, 50 kopeks; and for adolescent girls from 4 rubles, 10 kopeks to 4 rubles, 68 kopeks (*ibid.*: 46). Exploitation of female and child labor was an important part of the income of the Molokan capitalist, since a large part of his workers were women and adolescents.

The Blagoveshchensk Molokan property-owners, in addition to commercial and in a number of cases industrial enterprises, had large landholdings. These Molokans were characterized by the desire to unite in their hands the production, processing and sale of agricultural produce. The landholdings of this category of property-owner were made up of virgin lands, the so-called isolated farms (these were often based on shares), and also purchased and rented land.

In the first half of the 1890s, the Molokans in Ivanov and Gil'chin Volosts of Amur Oblast had 42 isolated farms (on which 103 households with a population of 800 persons lived). The area of the isolated farm was 25,060 desiatiny of garden, hayfield and plowland, with the latter category being almost 70% of the total area. On these farms, there were 1,680 horses (the overwhelming majority working ones), 340 bulls and oxen, 121 camels, 823 cows, and 917 sheep and goats (*see* the Appendix, Table 1). These were large farming operations, some of them having, as we have already noted, co-owners, but it is necessary to take full account of the economic significance of the fact that the co-owners of the farms had large amounts of capital invested in other forms of landed property, and in trading operations, and in some cases in industrial enterprises.

In 1901-1903, the well-known liberal figure, the author of works on the resettlement question, A. A. Kaufman, visited the Molokan villages and isolated farms, and left notes in which he clearly depicted the images of "Russian Americans"—the Molokan farmers of the Amur region (Kaufman 1905).

Let us visit with Kaufman the isolated farm of Epifanii Lankin and his co-owners Tulupov, Evdokim and Trofim Lankin: "We enter into the first delapidated izba—old man Tulupov's, one of the 'first residents' of the isolated farm; he is a stocky, strong old man, of pure peasant aspect; a simple peasant courtyard with a big barn for machines.... Besides a share in the common property, Tulupov has besides two plots of land, one of 120 and another of 150 desiatiny; he sows about 70 desiatiny—the sowings are always the same: wheat, oats and Chinese beans. Tulupov immediately wanted to brag to us about his machines: he led us into the barn, where there were three plows with seats, horse rakes, a sheaf binder, a thresher, and a drill seeder" (Kaufman 1905: 79-80).

From Tulupov's courtyard let us go to the house of Evdokim Lankin, who has, besides a share in the same farm as Tulupov, an additional 900 desiatiny of land: "A luxurious urban house, an enormous courtyard, several large storehouses, a big barn with agricultural equipment and machines; he is building a steam mill with a 15-horsepower locomobile" (Kaufman 1905: 80).

Highly characteristic of the figure of Molokan bourgeois businessman was the other Lankin, Trofim: "Trofim is a stocky man, with the face of a meshchan and crafty penetrating eyes, who for the most part lives in the city and only travels to the farmstead; like the majority of wealthy Molokans he carries on large trading operations along with his farm—increasing quantities of various supplies to the mines; and in 1900 he earned neither more nor less than 12,000 rubles bringing military cargo to Tsitsikar and other points involved in the military situation in Manchuria.... Trofim has less land than Evdokim: he has, besides a share in an artel, only 600 desiatiny, but he sows more—as much as 100 desiatiny ... he subscribes—presently without special success, by the way—to improved varieties of wheat and oats; he is getting ready to set up a stud farm and is building a tannery" (Kaufman 1905: 80-81).

Visiting the isolated farms one after the other reveals in general terms a similar picture of bourgeois-farmer prosperity. Of Nikifor Bolotin's farm, Kaufman says that "the latter's economy is one of the best known in the region" (Kaufman 1905: 82). In fact: "... 80 desiatiny of land, 150 Molokan desiatiny of plowland, four plows with seats, three sheaf binders. The Bolotins' pride is their horse farm of 25 to 30 mares of local breed with Tomsk studs; the horses are bought up in Blagoveshchensk and in the villages for 300 rubles and more apiece. The cattle are also good, but of local breed, without any attempt to improve them from outside" (*ibid.*).

The merchants and meshchane among the Molokans kept close ties with agriculture and in case of failure of trade went into the ranks of rural owners. Kaufman relates: "Beyond the river we see the village of Zharikovo (Molokan—A. K.), drowning in gardens and groves. They call it Bankrotovka [bankrupt], my companion says—a Molokan merchant from Blagoveshchensk goes bust and inscribes himself as a peasant in Zharikovo; how many of them have already inscribed themselves so" (*ibid.*).

The Molokan merchants, entrepreneurs and farmers were a leading force in the urban Molokan communities and also had great influence on the social life of the cities of Amur Oblast. Workers for zemstvo organizations in the Far East, summarizing their observations on the activity of Molokan farmers, wrote: "By reason of his material success, the householder has great weight in the rural society and a powerful voice in the rural skhods [gatherings]. Along with other rich people, he conducts the affairs of the community. The usual rural story develops, imprinted for generations in the proverb—'don't fight

with the strong....' The strong allow themselves methods of seizure, relying on
... their impunity and irresponsibility to their ordinary fellow villagers and
community members" (*Priamur'e* 1909: 374).

In Blagoveshchensk, the Molokan mechant class played an active role in
bodies concerned with urban government, and occupied important positions
in financial organizations. "... They (the Molokans—A. K.)", Litvintsev
wrote, "fulfilled the obligations of counselors in urban public adminstration
and have the position of chairmen for trade in the city public bank" (Litvintsev
1887: 559-560). The Molokan merchants used their social position to secure
the most advantageous conditions for trade and the bourgeois
entrepreneurial system for the most flexible maneuvering among all kinds of
limitations and encumbrances of the system of serfdom. "As counselors of the
urban public administration", Litvintsev wrote, "the Molokans are a highly
steadfast force, as one discovers in evaluating important public questions and
especially when electing a new head.... If the highest civil authority, which
there for some reason ("for some reason"!—A. K.) always stands for the
aristocrats, doesn't interfere in the public administration, the party of
democrats or the small tradespeople on whose side the Molokans also stand,
always wins out" (*ibid.*: 560).

Let us turn now to the socio-economic phenomena characterizing the
Molokan village. Let us note first of all that in the first half of the 1890s, differences in the supply of land, working stock and cattle between Molokan and
non-Molokan villages was not to be observed, although in the latter, the
development of productive forces proceeded relatively more slowly than in the
former.

For one non-Molokan peasant household in Gil'chin Volost, on an average
there were: 188.3 desiatiny of land, 5 horses, 3.6 cows, 9 sheep and goats. For
one Molokan peasant household in Gil'chin Volost there were on an average:
180 desiatiny of land, 8 horses, bulls and oxen, 3 cows, and 6 sheep and goats
(*see* Appendix, Table 1).

The large supply of land of both groups is noteworthy. However, the
relative amount of land in crops was small, and the means of cultivation
backward: the presence of large land areas permitted the Molokans not to
spend money and labor on its proper cultivation and, having used one parcel
for plowland, to abandon it and go to another in order to work a new plot,
etc. In Grum-Grzhimailo's words, "because of a desire for enrichment the
Molokan left behind him only weeds and simply robbed present and future
generations for the sake of personal profit" (Grum-Grzhimailo 1894: 543).

Other testimony corroborates this. "... The enterprises of the local
peasants", we read in the book *Priamur'e* [The Amur District], "both the
agricultural and the industrial, have the character of seizure and theft; each
strives to seize as much as he can, to extract everything possible, caring

nothing at all for the interests of others, or for the future" (*Priamur'e* 1909: 604).

However, even in the first half of the 1890s, with approximately the same large supply of parcels of plowland for the peasant, the relative amount in crops in Molokan villages was significantly greater than in the non-Molokan. If in the non-Molokan villages of Ivanovka Volost out of 65,860 desiatiny of plowland, 8,021 were sown—i.e. 12.3%—and in the non-Molokan villages and isolated farmsteads of Gil'chin Volost out of 40,886 desiatiny of plowland, only 1,626 were sown—i.e. about 4%—in the Molokan villages of Gil'chin Volost out of 38,150 desiatiny of plowland, 8,916 were sown, i.e. 23.4%, and in 42 Molokan isolated farms in Ivanovka and Gil'chin Volosts out of 17,204 desiatiny of plowland, 4,309 were sown, i.e. 25%.

The production of grain among the Molokans had a capitalist commodity character—and not only the isolated farms but in the Molokan villages—with all the phenomena of stratification and exploitation of hired labor belonging to capitalism.

Pre-Revolutionary statistics were based almost exclusively on averages, but it is still remarkable that whereas each peasant household in the Amur district (1908 data) marketed an average of 16.7 puds of grain, the peasant household of Amur Oblast, in which the Molokans were concentrated, put on the market 238 puds, i.e. 14 times more. There were also "variations by groups: from surpluses of 39.4 puds to deficits of 469.1" (*Priamur'e* 1909: 721). We may say with certainty that the greatest amount of marketable grain was from the Molokan villages and isolated farmsteads.

The system of agricultural production in Molokan villages can be defined as capitalistic first of all by the fact of exploitation by the large property-owners of hired labor. Grum-Grzhimailo directed attention to the fact that in Molokan villages of Gil'chin Volost (Tambovka, Tolstovka, Gil'chin) "very many plowed from 100 to 120 desiatiny, and even frequently 180 desiatiny, these being Molokan desiatiny (100 × 40)" (Grum-Grzhimailo 1894: 543).

The so-called Molokan desiatina—4,000 square sagenes—was 1.66 state desiatiny. Above we noted that on an average per Molokan household in Gil'chin Volost, there were 180 desiatiny of land—farmstead, hayfield and plowland. But if in the villages of this volost there were farmers—and "very many" at that—whose single parcel was 100 to 200 Molokan desiatiny, and there were numerous farmers whose parcels were 180 Molokan desiatiny (or, calculated in state desiatiny, 166-199 and 299), then it becomes clear how much these average figures concealed the actual picture of property and social inequality existing in Molokan villages.

Grum-Grzhimailo's data are confirmed and amplified by Kaufman, who visited in particular Tambovka and Tolstovka in 1901-1903. Noting the relative "equality" in the level of wealth of the population of Tolstovka compared to other Molokan villages, Kaufman states that at a time when some "sow 90 or 100 Molokan desiatiny, others sow only 15 to 20 of the same" (Kaufman 1905: 76). Kaufman saw another picture in Tambovka: "Material prosperity in Tambovka is less uniform than in Tolstovka; quite a few farmers sow more than 100 Molokan desiatiny, and many of the Tambovka Molokans, living as before in the village and working the allotted plot of land, own parcels of purchased land. But there are also poor people who sow 2-3 desiatiny and some who have no sowings at all" (Kaufman 1905: 78).

In the light of data adduced by Grum-Grzhimailo (1894) and Kaufman (1901-1903), the data of the resettlement official Tarnovskii become very convincing; he wrote in a report for 1897: "In an economic sense, the position of the peasant resettlers in general is satisfactory, and in particular in almost all villages of Amur-Zeia Volost; as concerns other volosts, in more than half of the villages there are approximately 60% wealthy—primarily in villages settled by sectarians; the remaining 40% live poorly; of them a third have as good as no farming operation or household equipment, and therefore tend to wander around, having no steady position locally" (*Priamur'e* 1909: 138).

The poor, who according to Tarnovskii represented about 40% of the population in sectarian villages, sowing, as Kaufman observed, 2-3 desiatiny, and some having no sowings, made up a reserve of those deprived or almost deprived of the means of production of labor. This labor force, however much it "tended to wander around", could not get away from exploitation and economic dependence on large property-owners. However in the 1890s and even at the beginning of this century, the broadest contingent of exploited persons in Molokan villages were, on the one hand, Russian settlers in the first years of settling in, gold-mine workers who had left the mines for one reason or another, and soldiers on indefinite leave, and on the other hand the local non-Russian poor.

Grum-Grzhimailo wrote of the Molokans: "The main contingent of workers is made up of newly-arriving settlers. Many of them in the first years of their settlement live as laborers for the old settlers; as wages, the employer offers the worker the use of 1 or 2 desiatiny of land for sowing; they sometimes also offer him ownership of a horse or a cow as part of his wages" (Grum-Grzhimailo 1894: 543). The wages of an agricultural worker were paid by the Molokan bosses both in natural form and in money, and in the latter case was up to 25 rubles per month (with the boss providing food) and from 1 ruble to 1 ruble, 25 kopeks per day (at haying).

The Molokan property-owners were especially eager to hire the non-Russian poor as workers, considering their miserable state and the low price of their labor. Thus in 1908, in Tolstovka, such a hired farm laborer received per month from 15 to 17 rubles, whereas the Russian poor farm laborer was paid up to 25 rubles; in Gil'chin for day labor during haying the non-Russian was paid 80 kopeks and the Russian received from 1 ruble to 1 ruble, 25 kopeks (*Priamur'e* 1909: 430).

In 1908 in Gil'chin and Tambovka, the non-Russian poor were the main contingent of agricultural labor, plowing hundreds and hundreds of "Molokan" desiatiny. They occupied a very large place among the agricultural laborers working the fields of property-owners in the village of Tambovka (*Priamur'e* 1909: 429).

The Gil'chin Molokan property-owners cynically said of these people: "Estimable people! So docile, so docile, and so industrious that it's astonishing!" (*Priamur'e* 1909: 361).

The gradual transfer to advanced forms of land use and the introduction of agricultural technology were connected with the development of Molokan economies. As Grum-Grzhimailo showed, "the enormous plots of land also called forth a strong spread of agricultural machines, particularly harvesters, which can be encountered in great quantity and of the most advanced types in each Molokan village" (Grum-Grzhimailo 1894: 543).

In the first decade of the 20th century, sowing in particular was mechanized in Molokan villages. While in the Amur region at this time "the most widely used method of sowing" was "the usual hand method", and while "in Ussuriiskii Krai sowing machines in peasant economies were a quite rare phenomenon", in the central chernozem region of Amur Oblast "and particularly on Molokan farms, there are many sowing machines, and in such villages as Tambovka, Gil'chin and Tolstovka, almost no method of sowing other than by machines was encountered. Broadcast sowers of various types are so common here that local shops even exist (in Tolstovka) to manufacture them" (*Priamur'e* 1909: 460).

The mechanization of all kinds of agricultural work in Molokan villages was characteristic even at the end of the 1890s and at the beginning of the 1900s. As Kaufman wrote after a visit to Molokan villages and farms in 1901-1903, "in point of tools and machines, Tolstovka and neighboring Tambovka are not far behind the very richest privately-owned isolated farms; in both there are farmers who have machines worth 4,000 and 5,000 rubles; everyone who is a little wealthier has gone from relatively cheap to expensive plows with seats; the majority have row-sowers and sorters...; in Tolstovka, even in 1900, 12 sheaf-binders were operating ...; 12 farmers have threshers, and one of them is adapted to the locomobile of the steam mill ..." (Kaufman 1905: 177).

Like the large land parcels, the basic mass of agricultural technology belonged to the rich farmers and served them as a means of economic enslavement of the poor. "But while in the old settlements of the entire Amur Oblast in general, there was exclusively machine harvesting with simple reapers or sheaf-binders, and in the Molokan villages there were only the latter, this does not yet mean that all householders in the village possessed these machines (as we noted above, in Tolstovka and Tambovka, there were large property-owners who had agricultural machines worth 4,000-5,000 rubles — A. K.). Many harvested with the machines of others, renting them for a certain sum" (*Priamur'e* 1909: 469).

Gradually with capitalist development of agriculture in the Molokan villages in Amur Oblast, the means of land use also changed. While plowing was relatively small-scale, predatory use of land succeeded completely: "to seize everything that was possible" from a plot and go on to another was not difficult. But with the appearance and rapid growth of large grain operations, "nomadic" agriculture yielded to "settled", intensive agriculture. Simultaneously, the struggle for land intensified, as did encroachments by large landowners on the land allotment of small farmers; redistributions of land became a common phenomenon, and land became the object of purchase and sale and every sort of rental transaction. Simultaneously in the first decade of the 20th century in a number of Molokan villages, the farmers went over on a large scale to a system of land use close to the three-field. In 1907, in Tambovka "of 13,000 desiatiny of useful land, 7,047 desiatiny, i.e. more than half ... were under short-term fallow and sown" (*Priamur'e* 1909: 391). In the same year the landowners in Chuevka went over to a three-field system proper, and the following year the farmers of Tolstovka followed their example (*Priamur'e* 1909: 388).

We can trace the economic evolution of the Molokan villages for a quarter of a century, namely from the first half of the 1890s, when Grum-Grzhimailo described them, to 1917, when *Poselennye itogi sel'sko-khoziaistvennoi perepisi v Amurskoi oblasti* ... [Village-by-Village Totals of the Agricultural Census in the Amur Region ...] was compiled (Poselennye 1918). In *Village-by-Village Totals* ... there is a detailed description of the economies of Tambovka, Zharikovo, Gil'chin, Verkhne-Urtui, Tolstovka and Chuevka, which were almost entirely Molokan when Grum-Grzhimailo described them.

At the time the *Village-by-Village Totals* ... was compiled, the villages of Chuevka, Tolstovka, Tambovka and Zharikovo had been transferred from Gil'chin Volost to Tambovka Volost. Only the Molokan settlements of Gil'chin and Verkhe-Urtui remained in Gil'chin Volost. The small village Parunova, which was in Gil'chin Volost and consisted entirely of Blagoveshchensk meshchane, had ceased to exist by the time of the census. Finally, the Molokan village of Novo-Aleksandrovskoe figures in the *Village-by-Village Totals* ..., and had been founded a little later in time than Grum-Grzhimailo's description.

We will compare the indices relating to the Molokans of Gil'chin Volost in the make-up of their villages as described by Grum-Grzhimailo with the indices of the *Village-by-Village Totals* ... relating to the make-up of Molokan villages separating from Gil'chin into the new Tambovka Volost with the remaining Gil'chin and Verkhne-Urtui in Gil'chin Volost (*see* Appendix, Table 2).

On this territory, the Molokan population, including the isolated farms, in the mid-1980s was 3,135, living in 429 households (farms). By 1917, there were 10,676 persons, living in 1,122 households. In other words, with an increase of population by 340%, the number of farms grew by 261%. We unfortunately do not have information about the number of hired laborers in Molokan villages of Gil'chin Volost in the 1890s. By 1917, among the Molokan population of Tambovka and Gil'chin Volosts, the number of permanent hired laborers was 1,325 men and women. Besides the permanent contingent of farm laborers, the Molokan property-owners exploited the labor of seasonal workers. From which contingent did the permanent and temporary agricultural laborers working on the farms of Molokan property-owners come? In the 1890s and in the first decade of the 1900s these were mainly non-Russian and non-Molokan Russian populations — new settlers, gold-miners, and soldiers who had served their terms.

At the time of the 1917 census there had grown up among the Molokan population a stratum of people deprived of means of production and tools of labor, or who had them in minuscule quantities, and were forced to sell their labor. We know from *Village-by-Village Totals* ... that of the total number of 1,122 economies, 989 possessed land. Thus 133 were without land. We know also of the presence in the total number of 105 without sowings, 95 who had no stock, 45 who had no working stock, 50 without cows, and 151 without agricultural tools. Before us is a socially-differentiated countryside, having on the one hand rich and wealthy property-owners and on the other poor people and agricultural laborers.

In the 1890s, the land of the Molokans of Gil'chin Volost was almost exclusively *allotment land* and was 74,140 desiatiny.

By 1917 the land (allotment, rented, purchased) of the Molokans who had left Gil'chin Volost and who had transferred to Tambovka Volost was 101,200.4 desiatiny — i.e., had grown approximately by 36%, in spite of the growth of the number of farms by 261% for this period.

The possibilities for development of Molokan agriculture on a broad scale significantly decreased at the beginning of the 1900s. The further development of agriculture could proceed primarily by a redistribution of the available land fund, by reassignment, renting, and purchase and sale of land. In the landed property of the Tambovka-Gil'chin Molokans of Amur Oblast, according to the 1917 census, allotment land was 49,961 desiatiny (48.4%), rented 30,894 (30.5%), and purchased, 20,366 desiatiny (20.1%).

The make-up of the property of the Tambovka-Gil'chin Molokans already attests to the significant forward movement occurring in their land relationships over the course of a century — land became a commodity.

The proportion of plowland in crops increased sharply (in the 1890s the Molokans had used only 25% of it). Of the 92,162.3 des. of plowland belonging to Molokans of Tambovka and Gil'chin Volost in 1917, 64,392.9 were sown, 21,257.2 were under short-term fallow, and 6,512.2 long-term fallow. In practice by 1917 all the plowland belonging to the Molokans was used for grain production which, as we showed, was done in capitalistic fashion. Among the Molokans there were farm laborers, poor people, a considerable stratum of prosperous farmers and large land-owning farmers. Among the latter, there were 77 residents who possessed on top of the allotment and rented land, 5,703 desiatiny of purchased land. There were also wealthy bourgeois renters: 26 households in the village of Gil'chin, on top of 10,439 des. of allotted land, rented an additional 9,432 des. These were essentially commercial farms, in which there were 70 permanent workers alone. On these 26 farms there were 1,836 horses, 1,427 cows and 2,295 sheep and goats.

Let us isolate now (*see* Appendix, Table 3) from the total number of Molokan farmers in Gil'chin and Tambovka Volosts, the group of farmers who lived on isolated farms. According to the census of 1917, 104 such farmers owned 14,662.4 des. of purchased land; in addition 70 persons rented 11,718.2 des. (the farmers themselves rented out 1821.2 des.).

Thus, 70 owners of isolated farmsteads and 26 rich householders of the village of Gil'chin rented in total approximately 20,000 des., i.e. about 65% of all land which the Tambov and Gil'chin Molokans rented. From this it follows that rent among the Molokans was primarily entrepreneurial.

Continuing the description of the group of farmers we have isolated, we see that among 1,788 persons inhabiting these farms, 441 were permanent workers. The farms were excellently supplied with draught animals: there were 2,268 horses. There were also cattle, sheep, and goats in great numbers, but animal husbandry in general was not industrial.

The high technological level of the operations of the Molokans of Tambovka and Gil'chin Volosts (*see* Appendix, Table 4) is striking.

We have an opportunity to become acquainted with the psychological type of Molokan bourgeois "conquistador" in the Amur region. One of the zemstvo workers—Tikhon Pozner—transmitted his impressions about a meeting with a young Molokan farmer from the village of T. (Tambovka, Tolstovka?): "A conversation began. It was not very interesting. Something rigid and coldly calculating breathed from this man. He was entirely taken up in his economic plans and undertakings. Conversations turned exclusively around business deposits, 'taxes', 'turnover', the renting of hayfields, Tomsk stallions, Russian cows, and similar things ... one sensed not a farmer, but a 'warrior', a fighter for existence, a passionate entrepreneur, a hero of profit, which possessed all his being and which for the moment (and perhaps forever) had swallowed up the man in him. For some reason there emerged more and more a type of stock-market gambler, who today would be a farmer, tomorrow a trader, and in case of success would risk borrowed money and build in Blagoveshchensk bath-houses, open a hotel, sail steamboats along the Zeia and the Amur" (*Priamur'e* 1909: 660-661).

Just such figures of predatory bourgeois businessmen ruled unhindered in the Molokan movement at the end of the 19th and the beginning of the 20th century. They did in fact build enterprises in Blagoveshchensk, and opened steamship companies to transport commercial loads. I have had occasion to speak of the role which Molokan businessmen played in the economic life of the cities of Amur Oblast in the 1880s. At the turn of the century, parallel to the development of Molokan grain farms, the influence of the Molokan entrepreneurs on the economic life of the cities of Amur Oblast intensified.

In 1910, the Evangelical Christian newspaper *Utrenniaia zvezda* [Morning Star], published in Petersburg, was visited by I. V. Alekseev, a representative of a very large Blagoveshchensk firm, the trading house of V. Alekseev and Sons (a Molokan family with milling and lumbering enterprises and a steamship line on the Amur).

Alekseev the elder, a peasant settler who had arrived with his family in the 1870s in the Amur region, possessed just those properties of a warrior and a hero of profit which Tikhon Pozner saw in one of his young interlocutors from the village of T. As the editorial board of the newspaper *Utrenniaia zvezda* reported on the basis of conversation with I. V. Alekseev (*UZ* I/22/1910: 3): "The Molokans are the basic element of Blagoveshchensk and many other cities and villages of Amur Oblast. They are at the head of all branches of economic and public life of the region. The steamship companies, the lumber trade, flour-milling, cheese-making, and the financial institutions are organized and directed by them."

Let us pause to consider that part of Alekseev's conversation with the journalists which characterizes his economic views as a representative of the interests of the monopoly bourgeoisie: "You know", Alekseev said, "that the question of the trade and industrial crisis is fashionable on the Amur now.... Let's take, say, flour-milling operations in our Amur region. One large local mill has already suffered bankruptcy and stopped payment; those millers who remain are in very poor shape" (*UZ* IX/26/1914: 2). The reasons for this crisis, as Alekseev's bourgeois consciousness conceived it, consisted in the fact that "the mills are too big for the region: nine of the largest mills, with all the rollers working, can process up to 30,000 puds of grain a day into fine flour, but the region cannot consume this amount, and local grain is insufficient" (*UZ* IX/26/1914: 2).

What did Alekseev propose for a way out of the crisis? He maintained: "In the first place, the idea spontaneously presents itself of forming a cartel or a syndicate — if one can so call millers.... In the second place the flour-milling crisis could be solved by seeking external markets for surplus Amur flour" (*UZ* IX/26/1914:3).

Let us not bypass those motives which made Alekseev an enthusiast for the resettlement movement in Amur Oblast. "As an entrepreneur I cannot help being interested in resettlement ...", Alekseev remarks. "The large peasant population is needed by local trade and industry, because in the first place it is a good market for the distribution of goods, and in the second place only the population of the countryside gives local tradesmen and industrialists a sufficient quantity of free working hands" (*ibid.*).

Alekseev's opinions repeat in all their basic positions the ideas of the well-known memorandum by Stolypin[E] about the organization of the resettlement project in Siberia; there are even the Stolypin ideas about a struggle for external markets, and the export to them of Siberian (including Far Eastern) wheat.

L. B. Beliavskaia, summing up a study of the socio-economic consequences of the Stolypin policy in the Far East, writes:

"The Amur Oblast, the granary of the Far East, can be considered typical for this region of the country. In the Far East on the eve of 1917, more than half of the peasants were poor farm laborers. Here capitalism in agriculture had developed intensively, which was facilitated by the absence of large landed estates and the existence of squatters' rights, which were used by the "hundred-desiatiners"—the old settlers who adopted advanced agricultural tools and machines, and also hired labor, constantly supplemented by the flow of settlers.... The profound differentiation of the peasantry prepared the ground in the Far East for intense class struggle, directed both against the tsarist officials and against the kulak class" (Beliavskaia 1962: 145).

This description can be applied with full justice to the social relationships evolving among the large Molokan landowners and the Molokan and non-Molokan poor. A special study of private property in land in Amur Oblast, conducted in 1910 and embracing about 70% of all privately-owned land, showed that the proportion of Molokans among landowners was at that time about 68% (Trudy 1913: 23, 30).

Among the Molokan old settlers we see pioneers of capitalist landowning in Amur Oblast, who in time became the basic group of capitalist landowners in this region. They were a bulwark of tsarism and reaction, in spite of a religious world-view different from Russian Orthodoxy. They personified the capitalist slavery and the political yoke of tsarism to which the mass of poor and laboring elements of the peasantry of the Amur region, among whom there were quite a few Molokans, was opposed.

I have shown in very general outlines a picture of capitalist development in Molokan villages in Amur Oblast, and the social stratification in them.

To what degree was the course of economic development, which we have traced using the example of Molokan villages in Amur Oblast, characteristic for Molokan villages in Baku, Erevan, Tiflis, Elizavetpol', Tavriia Guberniias, the Volga and central chernozem guberniias, the Don and Kars Oblasts—in a word, for other large centers of Molokanism?

One of the most honored and prestigious congregations among the Postoiannye Molokans was the one in Vorontsovka, Borchalinskii Uezd, Tiflis Guberniia. It can be called the religious center of pre-Revolutionary Molokanism. This village was founded in 1846 and was formed by Molokans exiled from a number of Great Russian guberniias. In 1847, the settlers rented from Prince Makarii Orbeliani 5,250 des. of land. In 1870 the Vorontsovka Molokans had purchased from Orbeliani all the land they had rented and about 2,000 des. of land and 1,000 des. of forest in addition.

Twelve years later, 59 Vorontsovka Molokan families purchased from Prince Vakhtang Orbeliani more than 3,300 des. of land. These purchases cost the Vorontsovka Molokans about 109,000 rubles (Eritsov 1887: 473). In the middle and second half of the 1890s—i.e. only a little later than when Grum-Grzhimailo described the villages of the Amur Molokans—272 Molokan households in Vorontsovka had private property amounting to 14,622 des. of land, and rented an additional 1,500 des. They had at this time 1,461 oxen, 778 horses, 1,335 cows, and 1,775 sheep (Argutinskii-Dolgorukov 1897: 304-305, 316-317). A. D. Eritsov, in a work published in 1887, justly noted that "the Vorontsovka Molokans set the first examples for the acquisition of private lands ..." (Eritsov 1887: 473).

The Vorontsovka Molokans were the pioneers of farming in the guberniia: in the 1880s many of them held from 200 to 350 des. of their own land (*ibid.*). Other Molokans in Tiflis Guberniia followed the Vorontsovka Molokans. At the end of the 1880s, Molokans from the village of Novo-Pokrovka acquired lands from Tiflis landlords and founded on them the village of Novo-Mikhailovka. In the second half of the 1880s, 40 Novo-Mikhailovka Molokans owned 1,580 des. of purchased land and rented an additional 789 des. Their farms had 240 oxen, 80 horses, 160 cows and 200 sheep (Argutinskii-Dolgorukov 1897: 40).

The Vorontsovka and Novo-Mikhailovka Molokans conducted large grain operations. Both the Amur Molokan farmers and the Molokan property-owners of Tiflis Guberniia used agricultural technology widely on their holdings. "The working of the fields", A. M. Argutinskii-Dologorukov writes, "is carried out here almost exclusively with improved equipment. At a time when many villages still plow with the ancient wooden plows, in Vorontsovka there are as many as 160 plows of the Guenier, Howard and Ransolls systems, around 10 threshers with horse-drawn carts, a great many cornhuskers and sorters, hayers, harvesting machines, and much else which other villages cannot expect to have for decades. Recently in Vorontsovka there have appeared 4 shops issuing on the spot plows with improved systems. Vorontsovka supplies many villages, even distant ones, with these plows" (Argutinskii-Dolgorukov 1897: 99-100).

The shops for constructing plows in Vorontsovka successfully competed with equivalent trade and industrial enterprises in Tiflis. I do not know what quantity of the grain production of the Vorontsovka Molokans—especially oats, which they sowed in significant quantity—was put on the market, but from their hayfields (7,678 des.) the Vorontsovka Molokans yearly sold in markets beyond the boundaries of Borchalinskii Uezd 100,000 puds of grain (Argutinskii-Dologorukov 1897: 114). An important source of income of the Vorontsovka Molokans was commercial carting, serving the market needs of Tiflis, Kars, Aleksandropol', Erevan and Vladikavkaz (Argutinskii-Dolgorukov 1897: 39).[3]

The village of Vorontsovka increasingly acquired the aspect of an urban settlement: "The small huts on the edges of the villages", Argutinskii-Dolgorukov wrote, "are quickly replaced with beautiful one- and two-storey houses with large windows and decorated with balconies and other trappings of urban life. The architecture of the houses, the mass of shops, the lively movement on the streets, and in particular the internal furnishings of the houses, make one forget that one is in a village with 272 households, more than 100 versts from the nearest city" (Argutinskii-Dolgorukov 1897: 38).

However the prosperity of the Vorontsovka and Novo-Mikhailovka Molokans and many others in the Caucasus, the flourishing appearance of their villages was nothing more than the facade of their social and economic life. In fact, their economy was distinguished by the development of productive forces, which separated them not only from among the surrounding Russian Orthodox population, but also from the neighboring Dukhobors. But to the same degree, the Molokan villages were distinguished from Russian Orthodox and Dukhobor ones by the depth of social stratification and contradictions.

The superiority of Molokan villages over Russian Orthodox and Dukhobor ones in terms of economics and way of life was nothing other than a difference in the level of development of capitalist relationships: the Russian Orthodox village, bound up in survivals of serfdom, lagged behind the Dukhobor one, which developed in the direction of commodity capitalism, just as the latter lagged behind the Molokan village which was on a higher level of capitalist

---

[3] Commercial carting was one of the primary and constant sources of the enrichment of Molokans, who specialized in transporting trade goods in almost all the Caucasian guberniias. Moreover, as V. P. Bochkarev reports of the Molokans in Kars Oblast, the latter, "not limiting themselves to the role of freight-carriers ... sometimes take upon themselves the buying of goods in large trade centers and the distribution of them to small tradesmen: they are, so to speak, wholesale peddlars.... Formerly, when there were still no railroads in the Transcaucasus, the Molokans conveyed goods over routes from Vladikavkaz to Erevan, from Baku to Tiflis and Elizavetpol', frequently to Tabriz and even to Erzerum" (Bochkarev 1897: 369).

development. This was the crux of the matter, and pre-Revolutionary economists and statisticians came in their own way to an understanding of this, encountering evidence of differences in the prosperity of the Orthodox, Dukhobor and Molokan peasants.

A. M. Argutinskii-Dolgorukov, noting the smaller degree of social and property differentiation in Orthodox villages by comparison with sectarian ones, pondered the connection of this phenomenon with survivals of serfdom in the Orthodox village (Argutinskii-Dolgorukov 1897: 37). He drew attention to the fact that by comparison with the Molokans, among the Dukhobors "the external conditions of their life do not hit one in the eye; there are no multi-storey houses here ..., for there is not that difference in prosperity of fellow villagers which is to be noted in Vorontsovka" (Argutinskii-Dolgorukov 1897: 41).

The Vorontsovka Molokans made wide use of hired labor. Argutinskii-Dolgorukov wrote: "The Vorontsovka Molokans can be called agriculturalists only by stretching the point, since they are little occupied with field work, preferring to resort to hired labor" (Argutinskii-Dolgorukov 1897: 39). In the guberniias of the Transcaucasus, the sectarian villages were the first to breed the exploiter-kulak type. "Neither solidarity nor concern for the interests of the *mir*", he continues in his description of the Vorontsovka Molokans, "is found among them, and as might be expected, the kulak class, a phenomenon still new here, develops noticeably with each passing year" (*ibid.*).

Whether we turn, following the description of the Amur and Caucasian Molokan villages, to the villages of Molokans in Tavriia Guberniia or in the guberniias of the chernozem center, we find the same picture of the development of capitalist agriculture, with accompanying social differentiation of Molokans into capitalist bosses, and the poor and proletarianized elements. Thus, one of the largest Molokan villages in Tavriia Guberniia was Astrakhanka (Berdiansk Uezd), which played in economic terms approximately the same role as Vorontsovka in Tiflis Guberniia. In Astrakhanka in 1912 there were about 7,000 residents, including numerous landowners, whose yearly turnover in good harvest years amounted to half a million rubles (Kremenskii 1913: 47). Astrakhanka had two steam rolling mills, a casting factory, and workshops for making winnowing-machines, the largest of the shops belonging to the Molokans Bolotin, Krugov and Koloskov. The yearly production of winnowing-machines amounted to 10,000 and was marketed in Siberia, the Caucasus and the central guberniias. The Molokan author P. Kremenskii described Astrakhanka in the following words: "The population has good wages, is neat and satisfied and literate; the village has 4 zemstvo schools, a bank and a post-and-telegraph office. In a word, a happy Arcadia for the Russian peasant" (Kremenskii 1913: 48-49).

However, Astrakhanka was "a happy Arcadia" only for the bourgeois property-owners among the Molokans. There developed in the village a real class struggle between the bourgeois upper classes and the poor, on whose land the large owners encroached. The latter thought up at the end of the 1890s a plan for resettling their "poor" brothers from Tavriia Guberniia to Orenburg Guberniia, in order to lay hands on their land and to "round out" their own holdings. The largest Molokan property-owner, Zakharov from the village of Astrakhanka, took the initiative in this matter. In the 1890s, Astrakhanka had about 4,500 residents, whose property consisted of a little less than 10,000 desiatiny.

The operation thought up by Zakharov was implemented on the pretext of "assuring land ... to posterity" (TsGAOR, div. 102, General Division of the Department of Police, 1898, 12, pt. 2, sh. 5 v.)—i.e. the future generation of Molokans. In 1890 and 1893 there were acquired "more than 13,000 des. of land in Orenburg Guberniia with the aim of gradually settling on them the Molokan poor. This operation took place with the help of the Peasant Land Bank and on the initiative of several large landowners among the householders of Astrakhanka ... who spent their money on this and, drawing their fellow villagers into the matter, which required expenditures of more than 270,000 rubles, they took the management of the purchased lands into their hands" (*ibid.*, sh. 5-6 v.).

The land acquired in Orenburg Guberniia turned out to be unsuitable, as a result of which the plan based on the resettlement of indigent residents of Astrakhanka was broken off. The initiators of the affair, Zakharov and others, who held 13,000 des. in Orenburg Guberniia, turned them into a source of income and began to "give out land in parcels on the spot for rent and for the pasturing of cattle" (*ibid.*, sh. 6). Now this was done on the pretext of seeking means of extinguishing the loan received from the Peasant Bank. In reality, the borrowed sums were used by Zakharov and his plenipotentiaries in Orenburg Oblast as they saw fit. Moreover, Zakharov obtained a resolution by the community "on the separation from the land allotments of the residents of Astrakhanka of 2,200 des. and the conversion of them to quit-rent, the income of which could supplement the sums lacking for payment to the bank for the Orenburg land" (*ibid.*, sh. 6-6 v.).

The operation with the purchased Orenburg land serves as a typical example of a large capitalist speculation, of which the indigent Molokans became the victims. Although as a whole the plan of resettling poverty-stricken Molokans on Orenburg land did not succeed, in the first decade of the 20th century in Aleksandrovsk Uezd of Orenburg Guberniia there still existed a Molokan settlement bearing the name "Astrakhanka" (TsGAOR, div. 579, f. 1, s.u. 2580, sh. 1).

Soon after the collapse of the plan of resettlement of Molokans from

Astrakhanka to Orenburg Guberniia, the bourgeois upper classes of Molokanism conceived a plan for resettling indigent elements of the sect in Semipalatinsk Oblast, again dictated by the direct interests of capitalist exploitation and profit. "Several years ago", the Molokan author Andrei Bolotin wrote in 1905, "when our capitalist brothers felt crowded living in Russia, they rented in Semipalatinsk Oblast an enormous parcel of Crown land, something more than 100,000 des., for 6 kopeks a des., as I remember. In order to have cheap, and if possible free labor, they set a goal of recruiting tenants from among their brother villagers at a rental of neither more nor less than a third of the corn harvest. They well knew that the hungry brothers would go after such bait; they were promised protection with this, and they were promised a cheap share-rental such as they did not have at home. This would cost the resettlers from 7 to 10 rubles per des., and not a single capitalist brother, inviting tenants to him with a prospect of 1,000% profit, blushed with shame" (Bolotin 1906: 8). We do not know how the "capitalist brothers" realized their plan. According to official statistics, by 1909 about 200 Molokans lived in Semipalatinsk Oblast (TsGIAL, div. 821, f. 133, d. 21, sh. 386).

The phenomenon of stratification and disintegration in the mass of the peasantry belonging to the Molokan sect developed universally, in large and small communities, progressively growing and reaching the sharpest possible contrast. In the Molokan village of Marfinka, Taganrog Okrug, Don Oblast, beginning with the mid-1890s, the land hunger continued to increase, and the victims were the ordinary peasant Molokans. "The land quickly slipped from their hands and finally decreased to such a point that the grain-grower could not feed himself and was doomed to a half-starved existence", we read in a report from this village (Marfinka 1909: 35). It is true that the Marfinka Molokans (along with the Russian Orthodox living in the village) bought up land from the local landlords and over the course of a number of years gathered in their hands up to 8,000 des. of purchased land, which would have been 8 des. per person, if the Molokans had adhered to the legacy of equality under whose banner their movement had once arisen. In reality, the mass of Molokans dragged along in a "half-starved existence", and the purchased land was concentrated in the hands of the village bourgeoisie, like the Tsapin-Sheshnevs, who had 3,000 des., the Kovalevs who acquired 1,000 des., the Seleznevs, who bought up 1,000 des., etc. (Marfinka 1909: 33).

In the large village of Mazurka, Novokhoper Uezd, Voronezh Guberniia, out of 800 households, 35 were Molokan and of these, 12 owners engaged in trade and crafts, one of the householders had a handicraft shop, and three were the owners of steam mills. "... Our brotherhood", they wrote from this village in 1909, "has ceased to stand guard over Spiritual Christianity; good works and love for one another have gradually cooled and been replaced by concern for oneself and not for the general good" (Khmyrov 1909: 19).

I confine myself to the concrete facts adduced above, which characterize the economic growth of the Molokan settlements and the social contradictions in them. Making a general summary of the half-century stay of the Molokans in the Transcaucasus, A. I. Masalkin noted in 1893 that, as was occurring "among the native residents of the Transcaucasus", among the Russian settlers there was observed "a gradual mobilization of land in the hands of several wealthy and influential individuals, which leads to the formation of a class of peasantry and agricultural workers with little land" (Masalkin 1893a).

A more generalized picture of the development of Molokanism from the Reform era to the beginning of the 20th century was given by Andrei Bolotin in an article published in 1906: "In the reign of Alexander II, Molokans received the right to rent and acquire as property large land parcels", he wrote, "At the same time, the pale of settlement was eliminated.

"Among the more affluent Molokans there appeared a desire to proceed from small-scale to large-scale agriculture. From this time we can date the beginning of the decline of material well-being and of the high-minded patriarchal system, and along with this, the beginning of the development of a class of capitalists ...; sheep-breeding passed into the hands of a few well-off people; the majority—small farmers—continued to sow grain. But grain-growing with each year lost its attraction. The land quickly slipped from their hands, the parcels continued to decline in size and finally reaching the point where the worker couldn't feed himself and was doomed to a semi-starved existence.... Many, naturally, went over to new forms of economic behavior—to crafts—and many began to seek their fortune elsewhere" (Bolotin 1906: 7).

This eloquent picture of class contradiction in Molokanism is drawn by a Molokan author, and nothing other than the bitterness of these contradictions roused Bolotin to take up his pen.

The Reform epoch gave only a new and very strong impetus to the development of class contradictions in Molokanism. I showed their beginning in the Molokan milieu at the turn of the 19th century. The dissolution into factions which occurred in Molokanism in the first half of the 19th century, and which I described above, was the religious expression of the social contradictions developing in it.

In Molokanism, the "middle" strata of the peasantry were represented more broadly than in Khristovoverie and Dukhoborism, and from the very beginning there was a relatively high proportion of bourgeois elements in Molokanism. Molokanism owed its diffusion primarily to these social forces, especially in the last pre-Reform decades.

The factions arising in Molokanism in the first half of the 19th century, however, did not erode the basic nucleus of the sect. In the Reform epoch, the social contradictions seized and set in motion the entire mass of Molokans.

The material which I adduced to describe the economic development in Molokan villages and the social contradictions in the Molokan milieu, shows that in the second half of the 19th century and at the beginning of the 20th, Molokanism was faced first of all with its own internal problems. The contradictions of capitalist development, and the calamities which capitalism brought, immediately personified in the bourgeois upper strata ruling in Molokanism, were the reality which confronted Molokans with new ideological problems. The old Molokan teaching, which criticized the state church, its clergy and ideology, gradually lost its former significance. Despotic Russian Orthodoxy and its subservience to the serf owners were and remained hated by the Molokans, but in the Caucasian guberniias, in Siberia, in the Far East, and also in the guberniias of the chernozem center and the Volga region, the mass of ordinary Molokans suffered from capitalist exploitation and aggression by their fellow believers immediately and on a daily basis.

The new conditions in which the Molokan mass found itself refracted (and at a sharp angle) the general contradictory conditions of the development of capitalism in Russia during the Reform era. It follows that the soil of capitalist contradictions fertilized religious ideas differing from those which arose on the soil of the contradictions of the epoch of serfdom, although these latter were by no means removed. Religious, ethical and social conceptions which made up the Molokan teaching during its original development could not serve even as the starting-point for the ideological formulation of the internal struggle at that level of development in Molokanism, when the relationships between the lower and the upper strata of the sect received the express character of relations of capitalist rule and subordination.

In these conditions, a complete "change of landmarks" became inevitable, a change of all ideological principles and organizational bases which characterized not only Molokanism but sectarianism in general as a religious form of the democratic movement, as a phenomenon of anti-feudal protest in a religious integument.

Baptism accomplished this "change of landmarks".

3. Molokanism at the Beginning of the 20th Century

Even though Molokanism in tsarist Russia was a persecuted faith, its bourgeois upper strata invariably supported monarchism and all the basic directions of tsarism's internal and external policy. We have already noted all the loyalist declarations which the representatives of the Don branch of Molokanism made in the very beginning of the 19th century, and which were shared by the merchant elements in Molokanism not belonging to the Don group. We are interested in the political line of the Molokan upper strata in the period of imperialism, but it has traditions of its own which are worth remembering if only because the latest representatives of Molokanism themselves cite these traditions in seeking from the Autocracy whatever concessions interested them.

I cite a document which contains valuable historical information — a letter from Molokans in the village of Astrakhanka, Orenburg Guberniia, addressed in 1913 or 1914 to the leader of the Kadet party, P. N. Miliukov. "You know that the Molokans in Tavriia Guberniia during the Sevastopol' war[F] acted quite selflessly," the authors of this document wrote. "They delivered provisions in the heat of battle, prepared bandages, gave up their dwellings to the wounded, and themselves remained without housing (there is an imperial scroll [about this]).

"During the Russo-Turkish war,[G] the Caucasian Molokans helped to provide transport and deliver provisions" (TsGAOR, div. 579, f. 1, s.u. 2580, sh. 3).

The authors of the letter were silent about the enormous profits which they, like the Dukhobors, gained from provisioning the army and from military transport.

"Who, knowing our Transcaucasian Molokans", A. I. Masalkin asked in the newspaper *Caucasus* in 1893, "can say that they still openly, or even secretly, profess in theory their views on the law, authority, etc., as it was originally formulated among them?" Masalkin comes to the conclusion that Molokanism had completely lost "the inner meaning of their teaching in the field of social questions", and he concludes, "the Caucasus had this sobering effect on their utopian views on full brotherhood and equality, and on the absence of bureaucratic offices etc." (Masalkin 1893a: 3).

Given the leading position which various bourgeois entrepreneurs occupied in Molokanism, any sort of utopias concerning the kingdom of God on earth was long ago crowded out of the circle of social and religious concepts of Molokanism, which by no means attests to the coincidence of the social views of the upper and lower strata of the sect.

In this respect a more exact description of the mood in Molokanism is contained in the report of the Chief of Civil Administration in the Caucasus for the Ministry of Internal Affairs, Sipiagin, dated December 28, 1901. The Chief gave weight to the influence of the Tolstoyan propaganda on some of the Molokans, citing "disturbed" elements among the Molokan group, which had once separated from the basic mass of Molokans, such as, for example, the Pryguny, etc. The Chief at the same time reported, in full agreement with Masalkin's description: "The sectarians who remain true to the old Molokan persuasion are marked by correct behavior and fulfill unquestioningly all government orders and demands, even taking a critical attitude toward the part of the sectarian population which is disturbed" (ORF, sector "Ts", div. VI, d. 10, sh. 43).

The bourgeois upper strata of Molokanism supported tsarism in the Russo-Japanese War, being aware that the course of military events had an immediate influence on the exacerbation of the political circumstances in the country. As the newspaper *Utrenniaia zvezda* reported in an article devoted to the Amur Molokans, "during the Russo-Japanese War the Molokan community responded with contributions to the Red Cross and so forth", and what was especially remarkable: "At the end of the war, the Molokans organized charity on a broad scale for the returning soldiers, giving out hundreds of puds of grain and provisions. As a result, in Blagoveshchensk there were no riots or excesses" (*UZ* January 22, 1910). In the letter by Molokans to P. N. Miliukov already cited, direct military service by Molokans is noted: "... each Molokan willingly goes as a soldier. They conduct themselves in model fashion in the service. It is a rare person who does not achieve the rank of non-commissioned officer. In the Japanese war many were inducted into the ranks of brevet-corporal and brevet-staff officer" (TsGAOR, div. 579, f. 1, s.u. 2580, shs. 3-3 v.).

One of the most important and most reactionary figures in Molokanism — Z. D. Zakharov, whom we have already mentioned in connection with the speculation regarding purchase of Molokan lands in Orenburg Guberniia — in a personal appeal to the tsar in March 1909 sought for Molokans the right to enter the ranks of non-commissioned officers. He characterized Molokans as recommending themselves as zealous military campaigners; "We are unutterably proud that we have no one who hid from military service, no deserters, almost no one who was fined. On the contrary, our soldiers often received promotions, and the majority went home as non-commissioned officers and sergeants-major"; and then Zakharov reported about some Molokans who had been the personal bodyguards of Alexander II and Alexander III (TsGIAL, div. 821, f. 133, s.u. 133, sh. 74).

The Molokan upper strata shared with the bourgeoisie profound hostility to the revolutionary struggle of the people, at the same time soliciting concessions from the Autocracy precisely on this basis. The bourgeois leaders of the Tiflis Molokan community in 1905 wrote: "In the anxious time we experienced, when our dear fatherland was overtaken by a great misfortune — the difficult war with Japan, the debilitating struggle with internal disorders, when some strata of the population of Russia manifested their demands by way of all kinds of strikes and mutinies — we as true sons of Russia, completely sharing all griefs and misfortunes of our dear fatherland, thought it better to announce our needs by way of what is legal and just ..." (Otchet 1907: 5).

The Molokan reactionary ideologists tried in every way to convince the Autocracy of the Molokans' detachment from the revolutionary events of 1905. One of them, who signed with the initials "S. B." a sentimental obituary on the death of the Kadet leader Karaulov, admitted that "many sectarians are interested in" politics (S. B. 1910: 68), but at the same time cited with enthusiasm Karaulov's speech in the Duma: "In the revolutionary days, in the days when the homestead was afire, sectarian hands did not touch it" (S. B. 1910: 80). The religious ideology of sectarianism, in this instance Molokanism, in fact paralyzed the will of its ordinary participants. The well-known ideologist and public figure in Molokanism, N. F. Kudinov, both affirmed the fact of isolation of the basic mass of Molokans from participation in the events of the revolution of 1905-1907, and pointed to one of the important reasons for this: "Spiritual Christianity, having lived through all tests, by its internal conviction did not attach itself to the basic mass popular movement; it stood aside" (Kudinov 1913: 43-44).

The bourgeois industrialists and farmers who adhered to Molokanism held in the years of the Russo-Japanese War and in the years of the first Russian revolution a number of monarchical demonstrations, which were an external expression of the daily policy which they pursued among the Molokan masses. The more the class struggle intensified in the country, the more dissatisfaction and opposition to the exploitation and force grew in the mass of ordinary Molokans, and the more unconditionally the Molokan factory-owners, entrepreneurs and farmers came out in support of the bourgeois-noble empire.

The wave of monarchical demonstrations by the Molokan bourgeoisie rose especially high in the years of the first imperialistic war [1914-1917]. During Nicholas II's stay in Tiflis, he was introduced to two Molokan deputations: one from the representatives of the city community headed by M. I. Pigarev, and the other from Vorontsovka — the champion of Molokan bourgeois farming in the Transcaucasus — headed by S. K. Zhabin.

Speeches were made: "Your Imperial Majesty", S. K. Zhabin declaimed to Nicholas II, "... under the patronage of Almighty God, under the protection of the rule of Your Imperial Majesty, and with your wise governors, we live happily in the Transcaucasian region" (Anon. 1914: 4).

Zhabin was a man of "business" and, welcoming Nicholas II, did not avoid mentioning "the wise and intelligent councillors for governing the distant Caucasus in the person of our highly respected Count I. I. Vorontsov-Dashkov and his faithful helpers and servants" (*ibid.*).

The speech of the next orator, M. I. Pigarev, was again in the spirit of monarchical servility: "We Molokans are your true sons, great sovereign. Accept our loyal feelings and love for you, sovereign, in the days of our motherland's severe test" (Anon. 1914: 5). As the Molokan author, who described this scene of loyalist outpourings by the Molokan activists, says, "the sovereign emperor thanked the Molokans heartily for their love and loyalty and for the feelings they expressed" (*ibid.*).

A year later in the palace of the viceroy in Tiflis a scene full of symbolism was played out, whose participants were on the one hand the Grand Duke Nikolai Nikolaevich and his retinue, and on the other nine Vorontsovka and Novo-Mikhailovka Molokans headed by the notorious S. K. Zhabin. The latter gave "His Imperial Highness" a Bible and an exposition of the faith of the Molokans (*Tiflisskii listok* [Tiflis Flyer], X/1/1915).

Molokan preachers in the years of the imperialistic war inflamed chauvinist passions and, in unity with the counter-revolutionary landlords, the bourgeoisie and their servants, helped to delude the people, sowing the illusion that the victory of the Entente would be the final victory over the war. "... Do you wish that war continue ...," rhetorically exclaimed the well-known Molokan ideologist V. A. Danilov, "or that this will be the last war? If you wish the first, help Germany and her allies, but if you wish this to be the last war, go and demand of you governments that they subscribe to the Triple Entente.... Two great peoples, the Mongolo-Finnic-Slavic and the Anglo-Saxon, cannot submit ... and give their religious soul over to the pagan despotism of Wilhelm and the secret strivings of the Masons" (Danilov 1916: 11).

N. F. Kudinov, the "progressive" figure in Molokanism, spoke in the same spirit: "... may every punishment rain down on the head of the second Herod-Pilate, Wilhelm II" (Kudinov 1914: 117).

We find a summary of the mood of the Molokans in connection with the events of the first imperialistic war in the note "on the military service of Molokans (1915-1917)" compiled in the Ministry of Internal Affairs: "The War Ministry receives in the places most settled by Molokans the very best responses about the service of Molokans to state interests by way of immediate service in the military, as a consequence of which the question is even raised about a review of the prohibition existing until recently against accepting Molokans into the officer corps" (TsGIAL, div. 821, f. 133, s.u. 213, sh. 41). Initiative in the question of inducting Molokans into the rank of officer, which came from a number of Molokan activists, met with the complete support of the War Ministry and somewhat limited support from the Ministry of Internal Affairs: "From his side, the Chief of the Ministry of Internal Affairs, Prince N. B. Shcherbatov ... supported a change in the negative attitude toward inducting Molokans into the rank of officer, recognizing that such a prohibition should be left in effect only in respect to followers of the Molokan sects of 'Pryguny', Obshchie and Tolstoyans, and Subbotniki" (*ibid.*).

Raising the question of making Molokans officers undoubtedly gave an impetus to measures adopted by tsarism in 1905 which weakened the narrow caste principles on which the officer corps was recruited: in 1910 the caste limitations on admissions to military school were abolished. It was in the spirit of these policies that representatives of the War Ministry and Ministry of

Internal Affairs acted, favoring a positive resolution of the questions of allowing Molokans to enter the ranks of officers. But even so the question was not solved, because of the unceasingly hostile attitude of the Synod toward this measure.

In describing the political course adhered to by bourgeois circles in Molokanism, whose most "left" representatives occupied positions of Kadetism, one must note their militantly hostile attitude to Marxism and the Bolsheviks.

One of the most active workers for the Molokan journal *Dukhovnyi khristianin,* D. Zaitsev, published in 1914 slanderous and chauvinistic articles, in which he pictured Marx's teaching as one of the components of the ideology of violence put in the service of pan-Germanism. Zaitsev wrote of Marx: "... The famous German brought to the world as some sort of revelation the very same principle of violence, but with a different sauce" (Zaitsev 1914: 7). In essence Zaitsev's article anticipated the Black-Hundred fable about the Bolsheviks as "German spies". Zaitsev found most hateful of all the ideas of the Communist Manifesto about international solidarity of the proletariat and about expropriation of the expropriator. "Weaklings unite and support the strong", Zaitsev screamed, "suppress them and take everything that belongs to them, and on this solemn occasion the apostle of violence even published a famous manifesto ..." (*ibid.*).

Another Molokan figure, V. A. Danilov, published in the pages of the same journal an article in which he wrote insultingly about the speech of the Bolshevik deputy of the Duma, G. I. Petrovskii: " 'We are atheists'...; our comrade Bebel said: 'heaven we leave to the sparrows...'. Thus in the State Duma, deputy Petrovskii began his speech" (Danilov 1914: 54; *see* Petrovskii's speech in the Introduction to this book, p. 9).

Danilov led an attack against proletarian atheism: " 'We are atheists', Petrovskii proudly announces ... why this phrase? Who asks them about their belief? Who is interested in Bebel's atheism and that of his followers?" And furthermore: "The phrase cited from Bebel is remarkable in that heaven is left to the sparrows but there are other birds capable of flying high" (Danilov 1914: 57). In the next sentences of Danilov's article the reader learned: "The sufferings of some (Danilov is speaking of the proletariat — A. K.) are the soil on which the power and pride of others grow" (*ibid.*).

Danilov's article is an example of the tired bourgeois slander on the revolutionary proletariat and its leaders.

The social disintegration of Molokanism, and its domination by bourgeois-exploiter elements, led broad strata of Molokans to deep disillusionment with "the teachings of the ancestors". On the one hand, one observed the non-participation of believers in the affairs of the religious community and a moral decline in the prayer meetings; in these circumstances Baptist and later

Adventist preachers operated successfully. On the other hand, in the Molokan communities, protest was coming to a head; sometimes it was still wrapped in a religious form, but most frequently it was expressed in open social accusations directed against exploitation and spiritual dictatorship by the bourgeois upper strata of the sect. This phenomenon was a new one, and it widened, the social criticism directed against the Molokan capitalists sometimes reaching a high level of generalization, and attacking political and any other kind of collaboration between the leaders of the sect and the blood-stained tsarist regime.

The awakening political consciousness of the ordinary Molokan was directly connected with the developing revolutionary crisis at the beginning of the 20th century, and with the first bourgeois-democratic revolution in Russia. The revolutionary struggle liberated increasingly large numbers of Molokans from religious ideology. But in those still numerous cases in which religious prejudices preserved their power, the Molokans, if they did not go over to other sects, remained Molokans only by inertia and by tradition. Under these circumstances the disintegration of the Molokan movement began, symptoms of which were present even in the 1880s and grew rapidly in the 1890s and beginning of the 20th century.

Assessing this time, the Molokan figure N. F. Kudinov wrote: "Baptism spread across Russia with such rapidity that it seemed this avalanche would sweep away Molokanism....

"The chief task of their preachers (Baptists—A. K.) was to raid as often as possible Molokan congregations, where they reaped an abundant harvest.... And when the Molokans made a spirited effort to repel the Baptist attacks, the latter had already gained the chief positions" (Kudinov 1913: 39-40). From their side the Baptist activists, basing themselves on the success of their preaching among the Molokans, prophesied for Molokanism an inevitable and quick ruin: "... what will happen to the Molokans?" we read in one of the articles published in the journal *Baptist,* "... we can assume that they are moving with quick and certain steps toward annihilation, like a tree whose roots have long ago dried up, standing without being of any use: neither shade nor fruit, only memories" (Baptist 1912: 11).

The missionary who spoke at the Fourth Missionary Congress in Kiev in 1908 also came to the conclusion that "Molokanism is a sect which is disintegrating and dying; whoever comes will take it; now the Shtundists are coming with sermons to the Molokans and seducing them into their sect" (Pribavleniia 1908: 1893).

Information reaching the Ministry of Internal Affairs at the beginning of the 20th century confirmed and supplemented the picture of the disintegration of the Molokan movement. According to data coming from Vladimir Guberniia, "at their (Molokan) prayer meetings lately one can encounter only old men and old women; the young people are either indifferent or infected with atheism.

"The most intensive activity in the propaganda of their own faith is shown by the Shtundo-Baptists" (TsGIAL, div. 821, f. 133, s.u. 21, sh. 108 v.).

Analogous information also came from Saratov Guberniia: "Molokanism is beginning to fall apart. According to missionaries, among Molokans lately one observes an indifferent attitude toward questions of faith, a cooling toward attendence at prayer meetings, especially among the younger generation, and transition to Baptism and even unbelief" (*ibid.*, sh. 143).

Recruitment to Baptism at the expense of the Molokans did not account for the entire drain from the Molokan ranks, part of whom entirely broke with religion. N. F. Kudinov, in a sketch devoted to the history of the Molokans, maintains that in the last analysis Molokanism succeeded in beating back the attacks of Baptism (Kudinov 1913: 43-46). At the beginning of the second decade of our century, the transfer of Molokans into Baptism apparently slowed down a little, which is to be explained partially by responsive measures introduced by the leaders of the Molokans, but chiefly by the deep internal contradictions of Baptism itself, which were developing and becoming manifest after this time. But long before this, deep within Molokanism there arose a group akin to Baptism.

In the first half of the 1880s, i.e. approximately at the time to which the data on economic development and social contradictions in Molokan villages which we have cited relate, there arose the so-called Neo-Molokanism—a religious group named, probably not by accident, by analogy with New Mennonitism, which arose at the beginning of the 1860s in Mennonite colonies. New Mennonitism, or the Mennonite fraternal congregation, was a Baptist group in Mennonitism. But Neo-Molokanism, or Christians of the Evangelical Faith, was a group of Baptist type in Molokanism.

The leader of Neo-Molokanism was the richest bourgeois property-owner, already known to us, Z. D. Zakharov, subsequently a member of the Third State Duma. The village of Astrakhanka, Berdiansk Uezd, Tavriia Guberniia, became the center of the new group. Having arisen on the basis of the Don branch of Molokanism, which is itself highly characteristic, the Zakharov group attracted to its ranks many adherents of the Don branch in Tavriia Guberniia.[4] At the beginning of the 20th century it also had congregations in the Kuban and Terek regions, in Stavropol', Orenburg, Samara, Vladimir, Khar'kov and Moscow Guberniias.

Like the Don branch, Zakharov's followers recognized the sacraments of

[4] "... In Berdiansk there are three enormous Molokan colonies—Astrakhanka, Novo-Vasil'evka and Shavkoi (Astrakhanka and Shavkoi contain primarily Molokans of the Don group) with 10,000 Molokans (of more than 11,000 in the whole guberniia—A. K.), half of whom were attracted to Baptism or Neo-Molokanism" (Vortovskii 1911).

baptism (which was done with water), communion, confession, marriage and extreme unction. But in distinction to the Don branch, as is clear from documents of the Ministry of Internal Affairs, "they are close in their dogmatic teachings (in the teaching on sin, justification, etc.), in their liturgical structure and in the internal organization of the congregation to the Baptists and the Evangelical Christians" (TsGIAL, div. 821, f. 133, s.u. 181, sh. 42).

The transformation of a number of congregations of the Don branch into Zakharovite ones, on the one hand, testifies to how much the dogma of Baptism and its church structure were "nurtured" in Molokanism, even independently of the preaching of Baptist missionaries, and on the other hand shows on what flank of the Molokan movement the earliest raids by Baptism appeared.

The organization led by Zakharov was centralized. Its highest organ was the All-Russian Evangelical Christian Committee, headed by Zakharov and maintaining ties with the World Evangelical Union. An activist from this Union, the theologian Zhak [Jacques], who spoke Russian, was sent for by Zakharov from Germany and placed at the head of a theological school founded in Astrakhanka for training personnel as evangelical "evangelists". The World Evangelical Union, and Zakharov's organization connected with it in a dogmatic sense were close to Baptism. Within the bounds of Protestant religious principle "Evangelical Christianity" attempted to reconcile Lutheranism with the Reformationist faith.

In a socio-political sense, the organization of Christians of Evangelical Faith was an organ of bourgeois reaction, not masked by any liberal phraseology. According to the remarks in 1910 of the vice-director of the Department of Police, Zubovskii, "Zakharov himself is known as a convinced monarchist" (*ibid.*, s.u. 213, shs. 3-3 v.).

In the *Short Rules of the Faith* worked out by Zakharov there were formulated not only dogmatic-Church positions akin to Baptism, which in any case enter into the concept of rules of faith; there were also introduced into the Rules of Faith absolute support of tsarism and categorical condemnation of "those who do not submit to authority": "Our faith orders us to submit to authority, threatening God's anger to those who do not, as a criminal whom God commands that we resist.... We consider ourselves obliged to submit to the laws of the government, since according to Scripture, 'the heart of the tsar is in his (God's) hand, and therefore all laws proceeding from the sovereign are written under the influence of Divine Providence for the good of the people" (*ibid.*, sh. 4).

The political position of the leaders of the Evangelical Christians was closest to the Octobrists. The tsarist manifestos of April 17 and October 17, with their religious and constitutional "freedoms", were seen by Evangelical Christians as written under the influence of Divine Providence.

In the heat of the events of the first bourgeois-democratic revolution there was held a regular congress of Evangelical Christians, at which along with delegates from the communities, representatives of the German and Swedish evangelical mission attended. The congress sent a telegram to the chairman of the Council of Ministers, Stolypin: "As a result of the Emperor's decree from the 17th of this October, we, deputies of the Evangelical Christians from various places in Russia, gathered in the village of Astrakhanka, pray to the Lord God and humbly ask you to place at the feet of the Tsar—God's anointed—our loyal feelings" (Zhurnal 1906: 16).

Further there followed expressions of complete solidarity with the fraudulent tsarist manifestoes of April 17 and October 17: "We also express complete hope that the tsarist government will succeed in implementing in life the will of the sovereign, expressed in full measure in the manifestoes of April 17 and October 17" (*ibid.*).

In conclusion they expressed affection and sympathy to Stolypin personally in connection with the attempt on his life: "We express our complete sympathy and joy that the Lord spared you from the fearful danger of August 12th" (*Zhurnal* 1906: 16).

The hangman Stolypin was the political hero of bourgeois businessmen from the All-Russian Evangelical-Christian Committee. On his side, he was not without sympathy for the leaders of the Molokan movement: in the ideas of his counter-revolutionary agrarian policy there loomed the living model of Molokan kulak farming.

Stolypin's telegraph in response to Zakharov—"I sincerely thank the deputies from the Evangelical Christians for the kind sympathies expressed to me (*Zhurnal* 1906: 16)—may have been an act of courtesy, of course, not without political overtones. But the testimony we gain from the journal *Sektantskii vestnik* [Sectarian Herald] is remarkable: "We recall the very favorable comment about the Amur Molokans by the deceased P. A. Stolypin; after it the viceroy of the Caucasus spoke of us more loudly and more forcefully" (*SV* 1913, No. 5: 1-2).

The organization of Evangelical Christians did not have great success in Molokanism. Its sphere of influence was limited primarily to followers of the Don branch, and many of them followed after the Baptist preachers.

However, the leaders of Molokanism had no political differences with Zakharov. The material adduced above, characterizing the political positions of the leaders in Molokanism in the period of the Russo-Japanese War, the revolution of 1905, and World War I, attests to the similarity of interests and views of the leading circles of Molokanism, which did not exclude differences among them on questions of political tactics.

The differences between Zakharov and the other leaders of Molokanism were limited to the field of religion and, in particular, reflected the struggle for the leadership of Molokan movement. At the same time, the attempt to restructure the Don branch on the bases of Evangelical Christianity showed the bankruptcy of this attempt to block the inroads of Baptist preaching among the Molokans by various dogmatic concessions to Baptism.

Baptism was the most successful but by no means the most formidable adversary of the Molokan leaders.

However much the minds of ordinary Molokans were bound up in religious fetters, the course of the class struggle could not help but weaken the religious chains of Molokanism, and moreover could not help stretching and tearing the religious integument of the sectarian movement in general. The social contradictions in Molokanism, which became especially intense at the end of the 1880s and the beginning of the 1890s, revealed themselves under the conditions of the beginning of the proletarian stage in the liberation movement in Russia. The maturing revolutionary crisis in Russia at the beginning of the 20th century, which permitted the bourgeois-democratic revolution, not only intensified the pressure by the lower classes of Molokanism on the upper, but multiplied instances showing the awakening and growth of class-political consciousness among ordinary Molokans. The revolution of 1905-1907 gave especially strong impetus to this. Among ordinary Molokans the question became more acute of what had to be done "in order to free the poor brothers from the power of the rich?..." (Pankratov 1906: 11).

The most varied answers were given to this question, including those in the spirit of Christian socialism, whereby it was proposed that the rich people "be asked to mend their ways", that "common fraternal treasuries be organized to help the brothers", that "a store of grain be set up in each community to give to improverished brothers to seed their fields" (*ibid.*). It was proposed that all this be done "on the example of the Apostles and the Christians of their time" (*ibid.*).

Of course such proposals are interesting only because they clearly show that from the question of how to "free the poor brothers from the power of the rich" there was no longer any escape. But we must also note something else. In an article, "Zadacha soznatel'nykh molokan" [The Task of Conscious Molokans], published in the journal *Molokanskii vestnik,* young people were warmly urged to struggle with the "mental somnolence" of ordinary Molokans, "due to which the capitalists hold the brothers in their golden exploiting hands", and to take a militant attitude "toward every deficiency in the life around us — a life whose rulers are *autocrats of every kind and aspect*" (*MV* 1906, No. 4-5: 50).

True, this appeal was still made in the framework of a religious ideology, and Molokan youth was called to struggle against compulsion by the capitalists "in the spirit of Molokanism". Yet the *content* of the quoted article, which was a kind of program document, contradicted "the spirit of

Molokanism" and the policy of its bourgeois activists, including the liberals. The Molokan leaders were stamped with eternal shame as capitalists bowing and scraping before blood-stained tsarism.

While some Molokans organized various forms of demonstration of monarchical fealty on the occasion of the tsarist manifestoes of April 17 and October 17, others were aware of the demagogic maneuvers of tsarism and its servants, including Molokan ones. In the article cited, we read: "How strong the power of the capitalist Molokans among our brotherhood now is ..., we may judge from the following incident which occurred in the city of Baku. After the miserable sop to all sectarians, and in particular to the Molokans, of 'freedom of worship' in the form of the manifesto of April 17, our moneybag ringleaders, feeling an upsurge of 'patriotism', decided—decided, I say—to set out for the proclamation[H] square in the city and there hold a triumphal prayer service" (*MV* 1906, No. 4-5: 52).

While some Molokans supported the imperialistic Russo-Japanese war in every way and sought religious justification for it, others unmasked the servility and hypocrisy of their bourgeois leaders. Continuing his description, the author of the article cited unmasked the "moneybag leaders": "Soon a wide area was dammed up by our brotherhood, and here, on a spot which is still shameful for Molokans, the moneybag leaders, drawing a mass with them, placed a shameful stain on our brotherhood. People with the Gospels in their hands approved murder here.

"They asked the love of God to give the victory to Russian weapons.

"They asked that the Japanese forces be destroyed, i.e. they asked that the Russians kill as many Japanese as possible" (*ibid.*).

The author of the article spoke out further against "autocrats of every kind and aspect", beginning with the autocrat on the Russian throne and ending with the little autocrats who served him. He unmasked the bloody provocations of tsarism, which sowed national dissention among peoples: "... our capitalist ringleaders did not hesitate to behave servilely and bow as representatives of Molokanism before those whose hands were stained with Armenian and Tatar blood. They shamefully pressed the bloody hands of the executioners of the poor Russian people. They dragged the Molokan mass to the same place" (*ibid.*). In the presence of similar utterances expressing the mood of the progressive part of the ordinary Molokans, the leaders of Molokanism could not help acknowledging that the religious rope, with which they had succeeded in dragging the mass with them, might break. Of course, the article "The Task of Conscious Molokans" has a religious tint; Tolstoyan motifs in particular creep into it. And still, analyzing its content, we can see its connection with information from those official documents in which it was said that among Molokan young people there had appeared religious indifference and even cases of unbelief and atheism.

One must admit that after the mass of Molokans began debating the question of how to "free the poor brothers from the power of the rich", and the connection of the interests of Molokan capitalists with blood-stained tsarism was publicly announced, the articles in the Molokan journal *Dukhovnyi khristianin* [The Spiritual Christian], directed against Marxism and in particular against proletarian atheism, not only characterized the general class-political positions of the leaders in Molokanism but had the concrete aim of struggle with the growth of class-political consciousness of its lower classes.

Those representatives of the ordinary Molokans who admitted that their capitalist ringleaders shamefully pressed the bloody hands of tsarist executioners of the poor Russian people could not be fooled by the bankrupt ideas of traditional Molokanism, or by the ideas of Evangelical Christianity, or by those of Baptism. In these conditions an attempt was organized to renew the religious ideas of Molokanism, to take away from it what was compromised in any case, and what could call forth only the condemnation of its progressive elements.

At the end of the 1890s, on the initiative of A. S. Prokhanov, the brother of I. S. Prokhanov (the former a prominent figure in Baptism, and later the organizer of the Union of Evangelical Christians), there was founded a Society of Educated Molokans. The program of the Society envisaged "unification of educated sectarians on the grounds of that world-view which would exclude any contradiction between religion and science, and which would lead them to mutual harmony" (*MO* X/1899: 310). If such a union succeeded, its next task would be "the transformation of traditional (i.e. popular) sectarianism with the help of this scientific but religious world-view" (*MO* X/1899: 311).

Faced with religious indifference, which had seized the ordinary Molokans, especially young people, and with cases of outright breaks with religion, the Molokan leaders began to sow the illusion that religion and science were compatible. They openly abandoned those ideological positions which they had in fact lost in the course of development of social life and the progress of science. They were forced to make concessions, if only to save the very idea of God, if only to remain standing on the last bastions of fideism.

Astronomy and geology destroyed the story of the divine origin of the solar system and the earth, and the founders of the Society of Educated Molokans proclaimed, "We recognize that the world was created and is governed with the help of natural laws, and not by miracles. On the question of the origin of our solar system and the earth, we follow the scientific achievements of astronomy and geology. We reject the authority of the Bible on this question" (*MO* X/1899: 311-312).

Darwinism destroyd the Biblical story of the origin of man—the founders of the Society of Educated Molokans were prepared to flirt with Darwinism too: "On the question of the origin of man and organic substances on the earth, we follow the science of biology: we hold to the teaching of Darwinism, until a more conclusive theory will be discovered. We do not accept the authority of the Bible on this question" (*ibid.*: 312).

In order to preserve the idea of God in their followers, A. S. Prokhanov and his co-thinkers were ready to throw the Bible overboard entirely for a new teaching constructed by them: "We maintain that man in searching for truth should be guided first of all not by faith in the Bible, but by his own personal judgments, i.e. by experiencing with his intellect every truth before adopting it. Therefore we reject the literal divine inspiration and authority of the Bible which usually serves the sectarians as a criterion—i.e., a measure and an infallible touchstone for discerning any truth" (*ibid.*: 311).

A. S. Prokhanov described the society he organized as "a religious godless (!—A. K.) sectarian society" (Letter by A. S. Prokhanov dated February 2, 1900, TsGAOR, div. 102, pt. 2, sh. 19). It follows that the program of the Society included nothing "godless", however radical the judgments of educated Molokans about the leading role of opinion in the search for truth and the test of truth by intellect may seem at first glance.

In fact, *how* did educated Molokans propose to research the truth, by means of *what* epistemology? The program of the Society of Educated Molokans contained an exhaustive answer to this question and at once removed any doubt as to the religious character of the new doctrine being propagandized: "In questions of the possibility of knowledge and truth, we hold to Kant's critical direction" (*MO* X/1899: 312). As we know, setting forth in *The Critique of Pure Reason* his epistemological theory, Kant unambiguously wrote: "I should have to limit the field of knowledge in order to make room for faith" (Kant 1915: 18). The whole thing came down to this—the educated Molokans did not renounce faith in favor of knowledge, but on the contrary attempted to save faith from the inroads of knowledge. In the struggle to preserve the idea of God they turned to theories fashionable at the end of the 19th century among the German and Austrian bourgeois intelligentsia, who renovated Kant's criticism and on this basis elevated their religious goldlessness, awarding the championship to the Russian God-building philosophers, the followers of the empirio-criticism of Mach and Avenarius.

Denying the divine origin of the solar system of the earth, life and man, "the educated Molokans" affirmed the existence of the single and indivisible God, the immortality of the soul, and recognized "prayer as an expression of our dependence on the deity" (*MO* X/1899: 312).

How did the educated Molokans unite these incompatible propositions? The answer lies in a quotation from the critical direction of Kant. For Kant, God was not the immediate sculptor of the world, but the creator of conditions under which the world subsequently developed in a natural, historical process. The new teaching could not leave aside questions "of the origin of the family, property, society and the state", but secured full freedom in deciding these questions by making a vague reference to the necessity to "follow the progress of the science of sociology and social economy" (*ibid.*).

Judging from A. S. Prokhanov's letters, the ideas of the Society of Educated Molokans found some response among representatives of sectarian student youth. However, the attempts to bring the Baptists over to its side, as A. S. Prokhanov tried to do, and also attempts to find means of "compromise on religious grounds between our rationalistically-inclined sectarian young people and the traditional fanatical-superstitious sectarians", had no success at all. In the Society of Educated Molokans there was only a small group consisting of representatives of the bourgeois intelligentsia and the students. The Society did not deal with a single one of the tasks for which it was created and did not unite either educated or uneducated Molokans, still less sectarians in general. Nevertheless its adherents did not cease their activity, travelling throughout the Molokan communities and preaching the ideas of "the religion of knowledge". They worked out a fund of ideas adaptive to science, to which some Molokan preachers willingly turned after the Great October Socialist Revolution as well. The attempt to form a Society of Educated Molokans was not an isolated one, but constituted one of the links in the chain of efforts undertaken in certain circles of Molokanism in order to save the movement from complete collapse. Bourgeois-liberal elements of Molokanism made up such circles, who, in the tense internal situation developing in the sect and in its own way reflecting the development of class struggle, attempted to take the Molokan movement into their hands.

The most important figure of this circle was N. F. Kudinov, who led the so-called progressive movement in Molokanism. Placing his hopes on the younger generation of Molokans, Kudinov worked out a program for the "renewal" of Molokanism, which in a religio-philosophical sense was close to some ideas of "the educated Molokans". Thus for example, like the latter, Kudinov preached that "the universe is eternal and history is endless" (Iakovlev 1913: 20).

Kudinov's program embraced a much wider circle of questions than did that of the educated Molokans and, chiefly, it was immediately connected with the internal struggle taking place in Molokanism. Kudinov spoke out against the leaders of Molokanism contemporaneous with him, citing in the process the disastrous position of its ordinary members, whose real needs were essentially alien to him.

The fact was that "the elders" — the religious leaders of Molokanism — were a hierarchy shot through with corruption, who had earned the hatred of the lower classes of the sect and who had implanted the discipline of the stick. "The elders" were a tool of the large bourgeois Molokan business-men — open monarchists countering the opposition from the lower classes of the sect by means of economic pressure on them, religious compulsion, and finally reprisals against dissatisfied elements, using for this purpose their connections with the civil authorities.

These were elements who in their social position and political views were close to the Octobrist[1] bourgeoisie. They attempted to keep Molokans outside politics, education and culture, considering that however the non-religious interests of the latter were expressed, they were fraught with unforeseen consequences threatening the existing order in the sect. They preached, inculcated and preserved the ideals of patriarchal Molokanism, enclosed in the sphere of religious traditiohs under their authoritarian rule.

The solemn All-Russian Congress of Molokans devoted to the centenary of the sect in Russia, supposedly completed in 1905, was conceived under this sign of conservative traditions.

"The elders" and their factual bosses, thus, dated the centenary of their sect not from the time when Semen Uklein acted and Molokanism bore the first plentiful sacrifices for its opposition to the ruling church, but from 1805 — the date when the name of the sect appeared in the official state decrees. The Congress was not at all conceived as a forum for the collective assessment of the problems facing Molokanism. It was supposed to manifest a wide demonstration of Molokan loyalty, as opposed to the revolution taking shape in the country. The elders prepared the Congress, inviting not only the best-known representatives of capital, religious figures of their stripe, but also highly-placed officials of the tsarist administration.

To the policy of the elders and the large bourgeois businessmen who stood behind them, which had brought Molokanism a massive loss of followers, Kudinov and his co-thinkers presented a more flexible policy. Like the educated Molokans who had taken from Molokanism what in the field of their religious conceptions factually was lost anyway, the progressive Molokans, counting on the awakening class-political consciousness of the Molokans and their religious isolation, which was weighing them down, condemned sectarian exclusivity and called Molokans to "progress", and even to participation in public life. Kudinov and his co-thinkers made "progress" their policy just as the elders made "the patriarchal system" theirs.

What was the essence of the policy of "progress" proclaimed by Kudinov? This was a policy of bourgeois reaction in the mask of progress. The "progressivists" legitimized the right of Molokans to an education in order to bring them closer, for example, to the ideas of "educated Molokans". They legitimized the participation of Molokans in public life in order to be able to lead them in it. Kudinov and his co-thinkers personified the bourgeois-liberal direction in Molokanism. They prepared for the upcoming Congress and for taking from the elders priority in the leadership of the Molokan movement.

In a letter distributed to his co-thinkers, Kudinov advanced the demand that the spiritual hierarchy of the Molokans be reformed at the forthcoming Congress. "... Lately", he wrote, "the positions of presbyters and preceptors have been occupied primarily by rich people without talent, who have won honored places for themselves as preceptors by hospitality and bribery" (Platonov 1905: 4).

Kudinov wanted to "lay the foundation at the Congress for the opening of a seminary for preparing preceptors and presbyters" and "to institute in all Molokan congregations proper accounting for all monies spent for philanthropic purpose" and "to found a public treasury on the basis of mutual aid" (*ibid.*). As an important task of the Congress he proposed "that means for general education of Molokans be sought by opening schools in all villages where Molokans live...." The education planned by Kudinov in the schools was not so much secular as religious. In it there should be obligatory teaching "of the law of God, according to the articles of faith of Molokans, in order that our posterity not be threatened with decline and complete religious and moral dissolution ..." (Platonov 1905: 3).

Kudinov gathered a majority of participants of the Congress who sympathized with his plan, in connection with which he appealed to his co-thinkers: "It is desirable that people be sent to the Congress who stand higher both by education and according to moral life than those who have gained priority by force of wealth ..." (Platonov 1905: 4).

The All-Russian Congress of Molokans opened on July 22, 1905, in the notorious Vorontsovka — the citadel of their capitalist agriculture. A special ark, erected in honor of the high government administration invited to the Congress, was decorated with the initials of Alexander I and Nicholas II. The Congress opened with a prayer for the Tsar. Telegrams and letters expressing the loyalist feelings for Nicholas II were read. However, the jubilee celebration and monarchical demonstration were somewhat clouded for the organizers of the Congress by Kudinov's speech, which supported his adherents at the Congress. Kudinov disclosed the project of a reform, noted in his pre-Congress letter to his co-thinkers. He proposed that Molokanism be given a legal-Church character (in the spirit of Protestantism), that a ritual and dogma common to all congregations be set forth, a catechism of Molokan teaching be published, a school of Molokan theology be opened, a "spiritual-moral journal and newspaper" be published, a regular procedure for the election of church officers be established on the basis of bourgeois democracy, and that a yearly All-Russian Congress of Molokans be called. Kudinov paid special attention to the organization of schools, circles, choirs and "cultural" organizations for youth.

In general, Kudinov borrowed the organizational forms worked out in Baptism, in order to transplant them on the soil of Molokanism, not changing the religious doctrine of the latter in this transfer. But however characteristic was the fact that in the time under review all forms of sectarianism could no longer exist as voluntary societies of co-thinkers and needed external forms of church organization, Kudinov's argumentation for his projected reform was still more characteristic. This argumentation deserves attention precisely because it characterizes the acuteness of the internal contradictions in Molokanism, the decline and disorder in it to which Kudinov was forced willy-nilly to testify, and for the reduction of which he prepared his organizational-Church testimonies. "Our brotherhood", he said at the Congress, "has everywhere fallen very low, especially in the large industrial cities, where the general flow of contemporary life has seized hold of our brotherhood.... The communities are disintegrating, the meetings sparsely attended.... In our society there is no sort of organization, all spiritual-public power has been seized by a small number of members of the congregation, distinguished either by capital or by qualities of a negative character ..." (Platonov 1905: 10).

Kudinov had to call things by their names, in order to be heard not only at the Congress, where the majority were his opponents, but—and this was more important for him—beyond the bounds of the Congress, in the local congregations where he and his co-thinkers were organizing Molokans around themselves. Kudinov counted on drawing sympathy among the middle strata of Molokanism who were dissatisfied with the dominance of the capitalist moneybags in the congregations; he hoped to win the trust of the lower ranks of Molokanism by acting in the role of their defender from the exploitation and violence of the rich people. "The capitalists", he continued in his speech, "surround themselves with persons of especially rude morals, and this small circle of people suppresses all the remaining smaller brothers and young people. Thus, they remove from influence on public affairs nine-tenths of the members as if they had no right at all to speak.... All, even the most important questions and public affairs, are decided at the arbitrary discretion of a few leaders" (Platonov 1905: 11).

Kudinov's speech called forth sharp disagreements at the Congress; however, the leaders of the Congress succeeded in burying his concrete proposal. It was ruled "on the advice of the elders" that Kudinov's proposals would be taken up at the next Congress, which it was proposed to call with a restricted membership—namely, one consisting "only of representatives of the congregations" (Otchet 1907: 43).

The leadership positions in Molokanism thus remained occupied by the "elders". Nonetheless, Kudinov's influence on the local Molokan congregations increased, especially in the central regions and in Tavriia Guberniia.

Both before and after the 1905 Congress, Kudinov preached in the spirit of the political ideas of Kadetism. Complaining that "the men who trade in oil—rich businessmen like N. M. Kashcheev—constantly hold back the noble impulses and good intentions of the Molokans" (Kudinov 1905: 85), he at the same time praised those capitalists who, "possessing millions", did not set themselves up against the ordinary members of the congregation and preserved toward them the external traits of "brotherhood" and "equality" (Kudinov 1905: 36).

Busying himself with the extension to Molokans of equal rights with representatives of the religions recognized by the Autocracy, Kudinov unceasingly presented himself as an adherent of the Autocracy and bowed and scraped before it. Thus, he servilely wrote that in 1905 "the government, having become convinced of their (the Molokans'—A. K.) complete harmlessness in a political sense, permitted them to publish their own journal, the monthly *Dukhovnyi khristianin* ..." (Kudinov 1913: 44). In 1913, Kudinov, with the aim of begging from the Autocracy juridical sops in favor of the Molokan sect, published in honor of the 300th anniversary of the House of Romanov the book *Spiritual Christians. Molokans,* in which he wrote: "... I have taken upon myself the labor of compiling a short historical sketch in honor of the 300th anniversary of the founding of the House of Romanov, under whose reign and sceptor Spiritual Christianity developed and became strong" (Kudinov 1913: 4). These were words full of lies and monarchical servility.

Dissension continued in Molokanism. Throughout their congregations there travelled various more or less well-known preachers, each of whom claimed to possess the ultimate truth and all of whom presented themselves as reformers and leaders of Molokanism. A certain Danilov, who appeared frequently in the pages of *Dukhovnyi khristianin,* preached the "religion of knowledge" in the congregations; D. V. Zaitsev preached the unification of Molokanism with Tolstoyanism; M. I. Kalmykov convinced Molokans of the approaching end of the world and the beginning of the millennial kingdom etc., etc. (Iakovlev 1913: 20-21).

Along with Baptism, Adventism began to spread among the Molokans, ultimately confused by the dissension among their leaders, in the second decade of the 20th century; it was successful among the communities of Kars and Akmolinsk Oblasts, Elizavetpol', Tiflis, Erevan, Baku and other guberniias (Semenov 1913: 33, 34; *see* also *DKh* 1909, No. 2: 63). The success of the Adventist teaching among the Molokans was charateristic as an index of the disillusionment which seized them in the face of social contradictions. They had long ago lost faith in the Molokan kingdom of God on earth; they expected nothing further from the "Divine Providence" preached by the Baptists and now placed their hopes on a miracle alone—the coming of Christ—to free them from need, oppression and exploitation. Perhaps an even more characteristic phenomenon was the preaching of an Adventist nature which appeared among the Molokans themselves, as, for example, the preaching of Kalmykov, mentioned above.

And yet, although Molokanism was in decline, it remained the most widespread sect even at the beginning of the Great October Revolution. Its basic sites, as is clear from statistical data collected by the Ministry of Internal Affairs in 1909 and 1916, which in general agree with the data reaching the Synod from the Eparchial Reports, were in Amur Oblast, Tiflis, Samara, Saratov and Tambov Guberniias, Kars Oblast, Astrakhan, Voronezh, Erevan, Bessarabia, Riazan and Stavropol' Guberniias, in the Don Host region and Turgai Oblast. Smaller centers were in Penza, Simbirsk, Enisei, Nizhegorod and Vladimir Guberniias.

The statistics for the last years of pre-Revolutionary Russia are extremely unclear. Kudinov wrote in 1913 that Molokans "in Russia now number more than a million souls of both sexes" (Kudinov 1913: 4). These data are subject to much doubt, the more so because Kudinov in the first half of the 1920s easily counted 2 million Molokans, although it is known that after the October Revolution their number significantly declined. Even with a very indifferent attitude toward the events of their religious life, it is difficult for example to imagine that out of a million Molokans counted in 1913 by Kudinov, their basic organ — the journal *Dukhovnyi khristianin* — had in 1913 only 690 subscribers of which 568 were paying ones (Editorial 1914: 85-86).

Taking account of the phenomenon of mass transfer of Molokans to Baptism noted by all the sources, it is hard to believe in the existence of a million Molokans, considering that Baptists at this time numbered not more than 100,000 (excluding the Baltic area) and a highly significant part of them were people who had come to Baptism from Russian Orthodoxy.

According to official statistics, Molokans of various groupings in the first decade of the 20th century numbered about 200,000. These data seem to me underestimated, but closer to reality than Kudinov's. We must consider that Molokans basically lived in compact settlements, which made it easier to count them. The chief targets of Church-government persecution of sectarians at this time were, first, the so-called fanatical sects (primarily the Khristovovers) and, secondly, sects of Baptist type, in view of their manifestation of vitality and successful preaching among the Russian Orthodox. The church author who wrote in 1906 in the *Tambovskie eparkhial'nye vedomosti* [Tambov Eparchial News] (1906, No. 10: 552) was right in his own way when he concluded: "The danger to Russian Orthodoxy from 1,500 Baptists is greater than from 8,000 Molokans." This was of course accurate not for Tambov Guberniia alone.

Of course, bureaucratic considerations, like the preservation of Russian Orthodoxy's prestige, led to a clouding of the true picture of the distribution of Molokanism. There were more Molokans than were shown by the official statistics but many fewer than their apologists reported.

Let us sum up. Pre-Reform sectarianism arose as a religious form of social protest, mainly along the peasant masses, directed against the ruling feudal-serf relationships. The religious form in which this protest was wrapped was conditioned by the dominance of feudal-serf relationships, under which a religious ideology was the prevailing one. Social protest was the earthly core of an ideology which took a fanciful, fantastic form first in Khristovover, then in Dukhobor, and finally in Molokan religious doctrine. Hence the significance which was given in these teachings as distinct from Russian Orthodoxy to man, his conscience and intellect, his personal ethics and activity and his ability to implement with his own strength the kingdom of God on earth. All this the ideologies of old Russian sectarianism owed to the peasant democratism of their participants.

The doctrine of the "kingdom of God", which people were to build on earth by their own efforts, was a religious reflection and expression of the strivings of democratic elements, struggling against the feudal-serf violence sanctioned by the authoritarian religion of Russian Orthodoxy. This struggle corresponded to the objective course of dissolution of the feudal-serf structure, which inspired its participants and gave them strength and confidence. But as capitalist relationships expanded their bridgehead in society, the kingdom of God, whose inception the sectarians dreamed of, turned out to be the kingdom of spontaneous market relationships.

In the competitive struggle of Baptism with all forms of old Russian sectarianism, the first thing to be scrapped was the idea of the kingdom of God on earth, and in general all the conceptions of old Russian sectarianism which proceeded from the ethic of "good deeds", from trust in the moral and intellectual strength of man: in their religious form they did not stand up to the test of social practice.

Baptism contrasted with old Russian sectarianism, and particularly with Molokanism, precisely in the foundations of its religious philosophy and not on any questions of ritual or ceremonial practice (for example, "spiritual" or "water" baptism); this is rather clearly presented by the ideologists of the pre-Reform groups in sectarianism. "According to Baptist teaching", wrote the Molokan D. V. Zaitsev, "Christ ... now brings about in us *every good wish and desire;* Satan however breeds in us evil and sly thoughts; *we people seem to have nothing to do by our own will and efforts*" (Zaitsev 1909a: 23 [emphasis in original]). Zaitsev continued: "... according to Baptism, man is some kind of pocket puppet on a string which is alternately pulled by either a good or a bad operator, and according to their desire the puppet moves his limbs; in a word, Baptism *denies man's free will* and this is its first basic deplorable error, for according to the Bible, man was created free.... Freedom of will is the basic dogma of the teaching of Spiritual Christians" (*ibid.* [emphasis in original]).

Zaitsev correctly formulated the basic idea of Baptism, while at the same time not at all understanding that nothing other than the rule of the blind, destructive forces of capital had perverted man into "a pocket puppet on a string". The small farmers, the poor, and the proletarianized elements of pre-Reform sectarianism long ago lost faith in the fruitfulness of their efforts and the viability of their ideals.

It is true that the farmers, entrepreneurs, businessmen and usurers who played such an important role in Molokanism, as in other sects of pre-Reform origin, were in turn "pocket puppets": they were not immune to crises, losses, ruin and bankruptcy.

Coming from different directions, both the lower and the upper classes of pre-Reform sectarianism, particularly Molokanism, arrived at the idea of predestination.

Looking at Baptism as the religious product of bourgeois social relationships we can now evaluate the process of change in Khristovoverie, in Dukhoborism and finally in Molokanism, traced by us earlier, as a kind of "Baptization" of them, beginning long before the appearance of Baptist missionaries in Russia.

We can say that in the 19th century the very course of development of the social life of Khristovoverie, Dukhoborism and Molokanism (insofar as their adherents did not break with religion) attracted them to Baptism, which was expressed in the limitation of creativity and religious initiative by believers, the attempt at codification of religious views, the growing significance of the ritual side of religious practice and of religious ceremonial, and finally in the appearance of a religious hierarchy in the sects and the broadening of its functions and rights. In essence all this was a turn in the direction of Baptism and corresponded to the process of social differentiation which had taken hold of pre-Reform sectarianism, and to the expanded role of bourgeois elements in its leadership.

Social motifs were silenced in sectarianism; ever more frequently groups of believers split off, reviving for a time the social traditions of early sectarianism in new communities. But if not in the social, then at least in the religious sense, Khristovoverie and Dukhoborism and Molokanism had not yet broken with the bases of their teaching: formally, they all continued to give divine significance to the internal world of man and denied the doctrine of "Divine Providence" blindly ruling people, which was accepted in Russian Orthodoxy.

The change of landmarks, as we have already said above, brought only Baptism, although its doctrine of Divine Providence was not a copy of the Russian Orthodox one. Molokanism stood closer than other sectarian groups to Baptism, and therefore at the end of the 19th and the beginning of the 20th centuries, almost half of "today's" Baptists consisted of "yesterday's"

Molokans. The soil for the success of Baptist teaching among the Molokans was prepared by social contradictions, which were manifested earlier in Molokanism and developed more widely and deeply than in other directions of old Russian sectarianism. The peculiarities of the world-view of the Molokan sect were connected with this; that world-view contrasted to the blind, superhuman Providence of Russian Orthodoxy, not the "spiritual clair-voyance" of man, as was customary in the Khristovover and Dukhobor sects, but the Bible, which it adopted as an immutable code of faith.

In any case, the distribution of Molokanism, which had primacy over other sectarian groups, and the phenomena of social and ideological stratification within other sects which we have traced, attests that in the 19th century in old Russian sectarianism the bourgeois-reformationist tendencies predominated over the popular-reformationist ones, which led at the end of the 19th and the beginning of the 20th centuries to the logical victory of Baptism.

Replacement of Molokanism by Baptism was the final act of transforma-tion of the democratic movement in religious form which sectarianism once was, into a bourgeois-Church organization of Protestant (Reformationist) type.

Editor's Notes

Note A. Minister of Internal Affairs under Tsar Alexander I.

Note B. In the Molokan tradition the term "psalm" (Russ. *psalom*) refers to any Biblical text set to a specific traditional melody and usually sung in polyphonic style.

Note C. Russian: *chlen;* this official may have had charge of the sex lives of male church members, since M. A. Saiapin's grandmother retained remnants of this function among women (*see* Saiapin 1915).

Note D. Russian: *tainiki;* literally "keepers of secrets".

Note E. P. A. Stolypin. Prime Minister from 1906 to 1911 and author of a major agricultural reform directed at turning Russian peasants into modern European or American-type farmers.

Note F. That is, the Crimean War.

Note G. Of 1878.

Note H. An elevated place near the main governmental buildings, apparently; but the Russian *lobnoe mesto*) suggests that executions also took place there, and the description which follows implies that Molokans may have been punished there.

Note I. A major pre-Revolutionary political party which supported Stolypin's policies.

LOCATION of SECTS
in
EUROPEAN RUSSIA

A Adventists (1880 - 1914)
B Baptists (1880-1890)
E Evangelical Christians
(1910 - 1914)

PART TWO

Trends of Post-Reform Sectarianism and Their Evolution

5

Baptism, Evangelical Christianity, Pentecostalism

1. The Distribution of Baptism in the 1860s-1880s

The appearance of Baptism was preceded by a broad religious movement among the peasantry, the so-called Shtudism. It arose in the first years of the Reform era and is not equated with any one definite form of sectarianism.

Shtundism appeared in the general stream of the peasant movement of the first Reform-era years but in circumstances of the collapse of the revolutionary situation of 1859-1861. Externally it was expressed in the mass formation in the peasant milieu of circles for studying the Bible, which had a spontaneous character.

Struggling at any cost to represent Russian Orthodoxy, which was undermined by contradictions, as being one with the people, the Church unceasingly declared any deviation from Orthodoxy to be the product of "insidious" foreign propaganda. This time as well, the Church saw in the wide interest in the Bible manifested by the peasants in the 1860s the influence of German religious brotherhoods of the late 17th and early 18th centuries, in which special hours were set aside to study the Bible; hence these brotherhoods received the name of Shtundists, from the German *Stunde* — hour.

The translation of the Bible into Russian dates from the 1860s and 1870s — several centuries after Luther and Hus translated the Bible into the national languages, which served at the time as a mighty force for the development of the Reformationist movement in the Czech lands and Germany. In Russia the translation of the Bible did not come from below but from above: the Bible in the native language did not issue from the hands of reformers but from the hands of serf-owners in veils. We should remember in this connection the decades-long struggle of the Church against the translation of the Bible, and furthermore against any wide distribution of it even in Church Slavonic.

229

The interest manifested in the Bible in wide circles as early as the beginning of the 19th century is attested to by the fact that the Bible Society founded in 1812 (the Russian branch of the British and Foreign Bible Society) brought out 15 editions of the Bible from 1817 to 1823. In 1822, the Psalter was printed in Russian and went through 100,000 copies in two years. Next a number of Old Testament books were translated into Russian, but were not permitted to circulate.

In the first years of the reign of Nicholas I, the Church obtained the liquidation of the Bible Society, unleashed repression on its translators and collaborators, and — a fact extraordinary even in the dark history of the Church — burned the published edition of the Pentateuch in Russian translation. In 1860-1861, the New Testament was finally published in Russian translation, and over the course of the 1860s and 1870s the books of the Old Testament. This became possible only due to the emancipation movement. The desperate efforts of the Church to prevent the translation of the Bible into Russian is explained by its fear of the possibility that the people would turn the Bible against the Church.

Let us remember Feuerbach's words: "Each epoch reads from the Bible only itself; each epoch has its own home-made Bible" (Feuerbach 1955: 264). Let us remember the experience of Weitling, who published the famous *Gospel of the Poor Sinner.* The Shtundist movement was an attempt to create a home-made Bible, which should serve as a means of validating and religiously sanctifying the interests of the new mass readership from among the peasantry. But the more massive this readership was, the more various were the interests in whose name it undertook the study of the Bible. This variety of interests was determined primarily by the different conditions under which the Reform took place, as well as those consequences which it had for different groups of the peasantry in different regions of the country. Therefore Shtundism is nothing other than a tendentious Church designation for the totality of peasant movements in religious form which developed in the 1860s and 1870s on the grounds of dissatisfaction with the Reform and opposition to the ruling church.

Above we characterized the new phenomena which occurred in old Russian sectarianism and were especially clearly manifested in the Reform era. But Shtundism signified a new wave of relgious movements in the Russian Orthodox milieu, a new splitting-off from it of believers, particularly peasants, and one to which the Russian Orthodox Church was highly sensitive.

N. M. Nikol'skii, noting that the designation "Shtunda" covers "not homogeneous phenomena, but heterogeneous sects in various localities of Russia" (Nikol'skii 1930: 239), distinguishes the leading tendencies in its make-up — the Biblical Christians or (according to the official terminology) the Great Russian Shtunda, and the Spiritual Christians or (according to the official terminology) the South Russian Shtunda. Nikol'skii places the sect of the peasant Vasilii Siutaev, which arose at the end of the 1870s in Tver Guberniia, in a group similar to the South Russian "Spiritual Christians" (Nikol'skii 1930: 240-244).

"These three sects", Nikol'skii writes, "do not however exhaust those organizations which are known under the name of Shtundism. So-called Shtundo-Baptism was extremely widespread in the south of Russia" (Nikol'skii 1930: 244).

Siutaev's movement and groupings related to it — Spiritual Christianity and also the movements of the "Nemoliaki" [those who do not pray], "Neplatel'niki" [those who refuse to pay taxes] and "Luchinkovtsy", which developed in the Urals and the region around the Urals — although highly characteristic for the state of mind of the Reform-era peasantry, are episodic. A distinguishing feature of this group of sects was social protest, just barely covered with a religious draping. For those peasant elements who decided, as was done in 1865 by the Sarapul' Nemoliaki in Viatka Guberniia, on direct struggle against the slicing-up of land allotments and the thievish buying of them, there was no need at all for a religious mask. As regards the fidelity of the Nemoliaki themselves to their religious ideas, much can be explained by the feeling of depression which seized them when their action was put down by force of arms and their best representatives were thrown into prison or scattered in places of exile.

The new conditions created by the development of capitalism in Russia significantly differed from those social and economic conditions at the end of the 17th and the first half of the 18th centuries, in which sectarianism arose as a religious form of social protest proceeding from the peasant milieu. During the Reform-era development, social protest gradually separated from its religious form. On the one hand this was a path from religion to an open social struggle. In the beginning it meant only that the believers no longer connected the implementation of their social interests with faith and gradually recognized their interests not as religious but as social, and conducted a struggle for them. This still did not have to mean a break with sectarianism and with religion. The social consciousness of believing peasants was purified only in the course of class struggle.

But the further the social demands of the peasantry went, broadening the front of its struggle against the landlords and then against the kulak group, the more apparent it became to them that sectarianism was incapable of arming them with any effective or even suitable slogans. The spread of sectarianism was accompanied by the gradual extinction of motifs of social protest in it.

Only the least conscious peasant could be attracted to the new Reform-era groupings in sectarianism. The popularity of the latter at this time was in large measure the popularity of their religious and not of their social ideas. Religious ideas were transformed into an end in themselves. This was a path from struggle to religion, from protest to disillusionment, and this demanded the restructuring of former religious views adapted in one way or another to social protest. For its followers persecuted by the authorities and by circumstances, sectarianism was intended to serve as a relgious refuge—an earthly outpost of the heavenly Canaan. Baptism did this.

Baptism was the main group of the so-called South Russian and Great Russian Shtunda. Originally, the largest and most influential center of Baptism was formed in the South and Right-Bank Ukraine.[A] In the 1860s and 1870s, Baptist groups appeared in the following settlements of Kherson Guberniia: Osnova, Ignatovka and Riasnopole in Odessa Uezd; Ignatovichi, Sharzhinka and Nikolaevskoe in Anan'ev Uezd; Konstantinovo in Gur'ev Uezd; Iavkino in Kherson Uezd; Liubomirka, Krivoe Ozero, Karlovka, Oboznovka, Ignatovka, Lelekovka, Lysaia Gora, Nikolaevka, Pomoshnaia, Peschanyi Brod and Glinianoe in Elizavetgrad Uezd (Rozhdestvenskii 1899: 55-75). The most important leaders and active preachers in these groups were the peasants Efim Tsimbal, Ivan Riaboshapka, Mikhail Ratushnyi and Gerasim Balaban.

At this same time, Baptist groups appeared in the following settlements of Kiev Guberniia: Plosskoe, Rozhki, Chaplinka, Popovka, Kosiakovka, Kuchkovka, Veselyi Kut, Popruzhnaia, Malaia Berezianka and Zhidovskaia Greblia in Tarashcha Uezd; Boriarka, Votylevka, Vinograd and Shubiny Stavy in Zvenigorod Uezd; Skibentsy and Brilevka in Skvir Uezd (Rozhdestvenskii 1899: 55-98). The most important leaders and propagandists of Baptism in Kiev Guberniia were Gerasim Balaban, already mentioned, and also the volost clerk from the village of Chaplinka, Ivan Liasotskii.

At the beginning of the 1870s, Baptist groups arose in Podol'sk Guberniia, and in the second half of the 1870s in a number of villages of Ekaterinoslav, Tavriia and Bessarabia Guberniias.

Simultaneously with the centers of Baptism in the settlements of the Right-Bank and Southern Ukraine and independent of them, a center of Baptism was formed in the 1860s in the guberniias of the Transcaucasus and Northern Caucasus.

At the end of the 1870s around the Baptist congregations in Tiflis and Novo-Ivanovka (Elizavetpol' Guberniia) there were grouped several daughter congregations, the so-called stanitsy: namely, in the village of Vorontsovka in Borchalinskii Uezd and in the city of Gori, Tiflis Guberniia; in the village of Chukhur-Iurt, Shemkha Uezd; in the village of Andreevka, Lenkoran Uezd; in the villages of Novo-Saratovka and Novo-Mikhailovka in Elizavetpol' Uezd; and in the village of Mikhailovka, Kazakh Uezd, Elizavetpol' Guberniia. Baptist groups also appeared in the 1870s-1880s in the Terek region, in the cities of Vladikavkaz, Mozdok, Georgievsk and Groznyi, in the stanitsy of Pavlodol'skaia, Zakan-Iurtovskaia, Troitskaia, Novoterskaia and Alekuiskie Khutora (Val'kevich 1900: 197-128). Among the Baptist figures in the Caucasian guberniias the most important were V. G. Pavlov, N. I. Voronin, D. I. Mazaev, G. I. Mazaev and V. V. Ivanov.

Finally, a third site of Baptism arose in St. Petersburg. Even in the 1870s the preacher I. V. Kargel' had begun activities, and at the end of the 1870s and beginning of the 1880s a Baptist congregation arose. The evangelical teaching disseminated from Petersburg in the middle of the 1870s by the large landowner and colonel of the guard V. A. Pashkov was close to Baptism. This teaching, in an aristocratic Petersburg salon, partly thanks to the evangelical preaching of Lord Granville Radstock, was energetically disseminated by Pashkov by means of mass-scale printed propaganda and preaching in meshchan and worker circles of St. Petersburg, and also among the peasantry, primarily those who lived on Pashkov's estates. In the second half of the 1880s there were Pashkovite followers in Tver, Tula, Iaroslavl, Moscow, Tambov, Nizhegorod, Samara and Olonetsk Guberniias (Terletskii 1891: 75-89). Around 1890 in Petersburg among the Pashkovites, I. S. Prokhanov and G. I. Fast, who held to Baptist ways of thinking, were especially active (Val'kevich 1900: 158-161).

The Baptist sites mentioned above which formed over the course of the 1860s and 1870s differed among themselves. In the guberniias of the Transcaucasus and Northern Caucasus and in Tavriia Guberniia, the major part of the followers of Baptism came from Molokans. According to Val'kevich, who wrote at the end of the 1890s, "in the Transcaucasus there is not a single Molokan settlement where the Baptist sect has not built itself a solid nest ..." (Val'kevich 1900: 125). According to the same author, "among the individual parts of the Transcaucasus, Baptist propagandists' greatest success was in Baku Guberniia, as a consequence of the numerous Molokans who made up almost 43% of the entire Russian population of the guberniia ..." (*ibid.*).

According to Val'kevich, the total number of Baptists in the Transcaucasus and North Caucasus at the end of the 1880s barely exceeded 2,000 persons. But from the time when in the second half of the 1870s connections were made between the Baptists of the Caucasus, the Ukraine, the north-west and central guberniias of the country, Baptist organizations of the Caucasus began to play a primary role. It was precisely these organizations which contributed the best-known figures of the Baptist movement in Russia and concentrated power in their hands.

The genetic connection between Molokanism and Baptism, most clearly traceable in the Caucasus, explains the reason for the special position occupied in the Baptist church by representatives of the Transcaucasian and

North-Caucasian Baptists. Baptist communities in the Caucasian guberniias were close in social composition to the Molokan ones out of which they arose.

The emerging Baptist church included large, and even very large, representatives of capital. To the latter category belonged the brothers Dei and Gavriil Mazaev, heirs of the Molokan millionaire I. G. Mazaev, who died in 1897. In time Dei Mazaev became the leader of the Union of Russian Baptists and Gavriil Mazaev the treasurer of the Union.[1] A prominent Baptist missionary, the leader of one of the Tiflis congregations, the editor of a collection of spiritual songs, *Golos Very* [The Voice of Truth], was N. I. Voronin — a Molokan by birth, and a prominent representative of the Tiflis trading bourgeoisie. V. G. Pavlov also came from the Molokans, and belonged to a wealthy Tiflis family (Val'kevich wrote of him that "he is indisputably the most prominent of the Baptist missionaries" [Val'kevich 1900: 79]), and so did the merchant S. A. Prokhanov, the leader of the Vladikavkaz Baptists and member of the Baptist Missionary Committee (the father of I. S. and A. S. Prokhanov). There was a whole group of persons of Molokan birth (Mamontov, Stoialov, Fefelov) who did not occupy very responsible positions in the Baptist hierarchy but enjoyed great personal influence, thanks to their capital and connections with business and official circles. Of one of them, T. I. Fefelov, we know for example that he was the keeper of the post on the Tiflis-Aleksandrov post road, the owner of several houses in Tiflis, and his wealth was estimated at several hundred thousand rubles (Val'kevich 1900: 122).

Wealthy property-owners were to be found among the Baptists concentrated in other guberniias of the country, but as a rule these were peasants who were the first generation of the rural wealthy. As regards the movement into Baptism of the bourgeois upper strata of Molokanism, these were no longer representatives of the rural bourgeoisie. If Gurii Pavlov and Stepan Prokhanov were still simple businesspeople, solid urban dwellers, their children Vasilii Pavlov, Ivan and Aleksandr Prokhanov belonged to the bourgeois intelligentsia polished in Western-European fashion. Ivan Prokhanov studied (in 1889-1893) in the St. Petersburg Technological Institute, and upon graduating he went to England where he entered the Baptist University College in Bristol. His brother Aleksandr Prokhanov, after attending Derpt University, graduated from a theological course at the Protestant Faculty in Paris. Vasilii Pavlov, like the Prokhanovs, was fluent in several foreign languges and received a theological education in Germany in the Hamburg missionary seminary.

But the Pavlov and Prokhanov families did not belong among the large

[1] "The Mazaev brothers rented in the regions of the Don and Kuban Hosts, and in the guberniias of Tavriia, Stavropol, Tambov, Samara and others, tens of thousands of des." (Aleksii 1908: 688).

bourgeois property-owners. The most substantial group of property-owners in Baptism were the dynasties of Mazaev, Stoialov, Mamontov and others, who traced their capitalist geneology to the Molochnye Vody period in the history of Molokanism.

Having gotten rich and increased their wealth in the pre-Reform era, first in Molochnye Vody and then in the Caucasus, many of these property-owners personified in the second half of the 19th century a page in the pre-Reform history of the Russian bourgeoisie. In their economic activity they adapted themselves to co-existence with the serf economy and functioned with profit to themselves under the hegemony of the serf system.

In the pre-Reform period, as P. I. Liashchenko wrote, "only a very small stratum of the trading bourgeoisie went over into the ranks of the industrial bourgeoisie and was interested in the 'free' production relationships between the capitalist entrepreneur and the worker. A large part of the bourgeoisie — that is, the merchant-trading, the small and large rural and urban bourgeoisie — connected their trading profits and interests with the serf economy and the trading exploitation of the serf producers" (Liashchenko 1956: 573).

Though they occupied in the 1870s-1880s a leading position in Caucasian Baptism, the bourgeois upper strata were not a unified whole. Among them there existed a patriarchal Molokan wing, headed by the Mazaev brothers, which by reason of the weight of its capital enjoyed the most influence; another wing consisted of their lesser brothers in capital, not burdened by traditional ties with serf production, who had received education and tasted the fruits of Western-European bourgeois civilization, such as for example the Pavlovs, the Prokhanovs and others like them.

We have already shown that the Caucasian center of Baptism was not numerous. This is explained by, among other things, the fact that the possibilities for the growth of Baptism here were limited: the main reserve for it in the Caucasian guberniias were adherents of Molokanism and other sects, which made up almost a majority of the Russian population of the Caucasus. Baptism attracted to its side representatives of the small German colony which existed in the Caucasus. As for the basic mass of the native Caucasian population, although there were numerous persons of Russian Orthodox faith among them, the Baptist mission to them had very modest success.

From the 1860s to the 1880s Baptism had its greatest success in the guberniias of the Right-Bank and South Ukraine. Whereas in 1871 in Elizavetgrad Uezd of Kherson Guberniia, by official data, there were 224 Baptists (Aleksii 1908: 123), according to the same data by 1881 there were 998 of them here (Aleksii 1908: 276). Whereas in Kherson Guberniia as a whole in 1875 there were 1,546 Baptists (Aleksii 1908: 246), by 1881 there were in the same territory 3,363 (Aleksii 1908: 276).

The development of Baptism proceeded still more rapidly in Kiev Guberniia. By 1873 in Tarashcha Uezd of this guberniia (in the villages of Chaplinka, Kuchkovka, Popovka, Kosiakovka and Plosskoe) 112 persons called themselves Baptists (the followers of Mikhail Ratushnyi, who was baptized in 1871) (Aleksii 1908: 165-166). And by 1881 in these villages there were already 693 Baptists and on top of that an additional 13 settlements with 641, a total of 1,334 persons (Rozhdestvenskii 1899: 135). Baptists were represented in 35 points in Kiev Guberniia in 1884 and in 95 points in Kherson Guberniia in 1886 (Rozhdestvenskii 1899: 145-149). The sources which we use are either official (the statistics of the guberniia administration), or ecclesiastical and, without doubt, underestimate the real number of Baptists present in the given places.

Thus, in 1881 in a memorandum of the Kherson governor to the Novorossiisk governor-general, the number of Baptists in Kherson Guberniia was put at 3,363 (Aleksii 1908: 276), but in his note sent to the Ministry of Internal Affairs in the same year, he said that in Kherson Guberniia there were 2,147 Baptists (excluding Aleksandriia Uezd, in which according to guberniia statistics for 1881 there were 141 Baptists). The higher the department to which statistical information on sectarians was sent, the lower was the number of sectarians.[2]

Summing up the first dozen years of the spread of Baptism in Russia, A. Rozhdestvenskii wrote: "From the time of its official discovery the sect in a little more than a dozen years spread into 6 uezds of Kherson Guberniia, 7 uezds of Kiev Guberniia, 3 uezds of Volhynia, and 3 uezds of Mogilev Guberniia; and then into the 8 following guberniias: Podol'sk, Ekaterinoslav, Minsk, Chernigov, Tavriia, Bessarabia, Poltava and Orel; and into the region of the Don Host" (Rozhdestvenskii 1899: 147-149).

The above-mentioned centers of development of Baptism (Rozhdestvenskii details the spread of Baptism along a wide periphery, at the center of which were the Kiev and Kherson areas) coincide with the geography of the most rapid development of capitalism in Russia around the time of the Reform.

---

[2] Aleksii 1908: 264. In the sources from which I have taken the statistical data about the spread of Baptism, it is sometimes called Baptism but more frequently Shtundism. The first leaders of the Kherson and Kiev Shundists—Tsimbal, Ratushnyi, Rybalka, Riaboshapka, Khlystun, and I. Liasotskii—were Baptists. V. I. Iasevich-Borodaevskaia, one of the most erudite of the pre-Revolutionary students of sectarianism, wrote: "Baptism from the very beginning was a native element in the religious movement in Kiev Guberniia, as we may judge both from the primary sources and from the survivals of this movement which at the present time have grown and strengthened ..." (Iasevich-Borodaevskaia 1912: 166).

In the 1860s-1870s Baptism was in the process of being *founded* and of course did not at once take on clear forms of Baptist organization and religious ideology, and in addition, contradictory tendencies were found in it at the very beginning of its formation. All this played its role in the appearance of that confusion of concepts which was characteristic of Church authors who wrote of Baptists as of Shtundists.

Baptism appeared among the population of those guberniias where new bourgeois relationships were formed earliest and most clearly. These were primarily the guberniias of the Right-Bank and South Ukraine and the non-chernozem guberniias of the center of the country. In the latter, as was stated above, Baptism was disseminated in the 1880s in the form of the Pashkovite movement, which in the 1890s was transformed into Evangelical Christianity. In the guberniias of the Caucasus, Baptism developed basically at the expense of the Molokan population, among whom bourgeois relationships, with all their attendant contradictions, also evolved.

No less characteristic was the fact that Baptism spread into Tambov, Kursk, Orel and Penza Guberniias — i.e. into the chernozem agricultural center of the country — only with great delay and extremely slowly by comparison with its development in the Caucasian guberniias and the Kherson, Kiev and Ekaterinoslav areas. For example, in Tambov Guberniia, Baptism began to spread only in the late 1880s and early 1890s, and its success at that time was much more modest than in Kiev Guberniia in the 1860s and 1870s.

The whole point was that the chernozem guberniias of the center were the stronghold of large-scale land tenure based on corvée. Corvée peasants comprised more than 70% of the peasants of these guberniias. The landed estates specialized in the production of "gray grains",[B] for which there was no demand on the foreign markets; internal market ties were relatively undeveloped, and peasant non-agricultural occupations were quite insignificant.

Baptism existed where capitalism existed, where the countryside gave rise to a kulak elite at the expense of the impoverishment and pauperization of a large part of the peasantry.

One of the microregions of Baptism, distinguished by the especially fast pace of its spread and also by the variety of groups there, was Tarascha Uezd of Kiev Guberniia. This uezd was set apart from all others in the guberniia, even in pre-Reform times, by the depth of the social stratification of the peasantry. According to the property inventories on landed estates, in 1845 45% of the peasants of Tarashcha Uezd (the so-called pedestrians) had no working stock at all; next there came a group of peasants who not only did not have draft animals but did not even sow grain. Some of them, the "market gardeners", had cottages and small plots of land in truck gardens and flax. Others — the "landless peasants" — had neither cottages nor truck gardens. This group comprised 33% of the entire peasant population of the uezd. And finally there came a group of so-called team and half-team peasants. The first were peasants who owned not less than two bullocks, and the second those who owned a bullock or a horse. Team and half-team peasants were 22% of the peasant population of Tarashcha Uezd.

Let us compare these indices with the corresponding average indices for

Kiev Guberniia. In the guberniia 30% were team and half-team peasants and 55% were "pedestrians", while market gardeners and landless peasants were 15% (Funduklei 1852: 306). In Tarashcha Uezd, thus, there were twice as many poor peasants and paupers as in any other uezd of Kiev Guberniia.

These categories of ruined and improverished peasantry were described in detail in the report of the Tarashcha Zemstvo district police officer, who reported in 1861 to the Kiev governor-general in connection with the peasant uprisings in the uezd (in the village of Litvinovka) that the peasants "are very poor and have almost no working stock so that primarily the fields are worked in half-shares by the free people who live in the village ... taxes are extracted from them (the Litvinovka peasants—A. K.) with particular firmness, and with beatings in addition, so that they, not having time from the continuous excessive corvée obligations to work at hired labor for the money needed to pay taxes, are forced to sell part of their last small stock" (Leshchenko 1959: 169).

Such was Tarashcha Uezd, in which the number of Baptists grew for the decade 1871-1881 (the first Baptists appeared in the uezd in 1868) from 112 to 1,334 persons.

In the pre-Revolutionary literature on the history of the Shtunda, as a rule great significance is given to the fact that even in the 1850s and 1860s, Baptism in the form of the so-called New Mennonitism appeared in the Mennonite colonies in the south of Russia. By the efforts of the preachers of New Mennonitism—Willer, Neufert, Unger and others—Baptism was spread among the Russian population of Kherson, Tavriia, Ekaterinoslav and other guberniias.

In the somewhat peculiar form of Neo-Mennonitism, Baptism in fact spread in the Mennonite colonies of the southern guberniias of the Ukraine at least a decade before it appeared among the Russian population.

The preachers of Neo-Mennonitism were partly the purveyors of religious influence among the Russian peasants who worked for hire in the Mennonite colonies. "All the prominent original propagandists of the Shtunda— Ratushnyi, Balaban, Riaboshapka and others—" Aleksii writes, "either worked for the Germans or lived in close proximity to them for a long time" (Aleksii 1909: 268).

Neo-Mennonitism was the product of a very intense struggle in the Mennonite colony, which developed on the basis of profound bourgeois stratification and sharp contradictions (Klibanov 1931: 63-80).

As bourgeois relationships became stronger in the agriculture of the Russian villages of the Kherson, Ekaterinoslav and Tavriia areas, a certain stratum of their population became receptive to Baptism.

The genuine fatherland of Baptism was capitalism. This of course was not understood by Bishop Aleksii, the author of the most detailed study of Baptism in Russia among all that was written about the sect by historians of church and official tendencies. However he at least understood that "we have no basis for accusing all German colonists in general of desiring to Germanize the Russian population by seducing them into their faith. In particular this should be said about the German Mennonites, to whom as far as we know proselytism is completely foreign" (Aleksii 1909: 210).[3]

Bishop Aleksii (A. Ia. Dorodnitsyn), the author of the book *Religiozno-ratsionalisticheskoe dvizhenie na iuge Rossii vo vtoroi polovine XIX stoletiia* [The Religio-Rationalistic Movement in the South of Russia in the Second Half of the 19th Century], and the large collection of source materials, *Materialy dlia istorii religiozno-ratsionalisticheskogo dvizheniia na iuge Rossii vo vtoroi polovine XIX stoletiia* [Materials for the History of the Religio-Rationalistic Movement in the South of Russia in the Second Half of the 19th Century], was concerned from the beginning of the 1880s with gathering materials for the history of Baptism. For over a quarter of a century he was the anti-sectarian missionary in the eparchies of Kherson and Ekaterinoslav and gained experience, even if of a very specific kind, of immediate observation of sectarianism both in the cities and in rural localities. He repeatedly met (including unofficially) with sectarian activists, conducted correspondence with them, attributed special importance to the manuscript work of the sectarians themselves, and collected it, drawing from the local archives materials characterizing the history, dogma and religio-social life of sectarianism (Aleksii 1908: i-vi).

In outlook Aleksii was a real "serf-owner in a veil", complaining about the penetration of bourgeois relationships into the countryside, which was breaking up the patriarchal unity of the peasants so dear to him — in particular the peasant commune with its joint responsibility — a process which Aleksii saw as one of the reasons for the spread of the sectarian teachings he hated so much. For all this, he did not falsify facts, and attempted to preserve a formal objectivity in relation to the facts.

All that has been said allows us, critically and within limits, of course, to use the concrete observations and material collected by Aleksii. We have used them and others in studying the question of the social composition of the Baptist movement in the 1860s-1880s.

The social make-up of the participants of the Baptist movement differed in some of its features in its Caucasian, Ukrainian, and what we may conditionally call its Great Russian centers, referring in the latter case to Baptism in the northwest Russian guberniias and the non-chernozem guberniias of the

---

[3] The anonymous author of the pamphlet *Chto podgotovilo pochvu dlia shtundizma* [What Prepared the Soil for Shtundism], published in 1875 in Kiev, in spite of its Russian Orthodox frame of mind, places the development of Shtundism in direct connection with the consequences of the Reform and denies the view of it as a product of German Protestant propaganda.

center. Baptism in the Caucasian guberniias grew almost exclusively at the expense of Molokans and was forced to accept the Molokan heritage in the form of social contradictions between the upper and lower strata. There were also some Molokan conceptions and traditions in religion and lifestyle in this heritage.

A more important question is that of the social makeup of the Baptist congregations in the Ukraine, since it was precisely here that its most massive base was formed. Let us turn to the sources relating to the question.

Bishop Aleksii, looking at the reasons for the "deviations" from Russian Orthodoxy, considered that "possibly the strongest factor in the weakening of the religio-moral bases in the Russian Orthodox population of South Russia, which in turn facilitated the growth in it of various sectarian errors, was the *landlessness* of a significant part of the Russian Orthodox population in the guberniias of the Novorossiia region" (Aleksii 1909: 196). Under the "landless class", which was in his judgment the basic nutrient medium of Shtundism, he subsumed the category of the so-called *desiatinshchiki*. This was a large category of agriculturalists who did not have parcels of land and were not formally enserfed, made up basically of Great Russian and Belorussian peasants who had fled their former homes because of poverty and lack of land. The desiatinshchiki did not belong to the rural communes, were registered in the meshchan class and could transfer from landowner to landowner. The situation of this category was characterized by their dependence on the large landowners from whom the desiatinshchiki were obliged to rent parcels of plowland, pastureland, and finally dwellings.

Masses of desiatinshchiki could be encountered in the guberniias of Bessarabia, Tavriia and Kherson, and were also present in Podol'sk and Ekaterinoslav Guberniias (Aleksii 1909: 88). At the end of the 1870s they made up 20% of the population of Odessa Uezd in Kherson Guberniia (Missionary 1891), and around 1890, 25% of the total population of Kherson Guberniia (Aleksii 1909: 88). The desiatinshchiki were a pauperized and proletarianized group of the population having neither property nor a homestead, who often migrated from place to place in search of a piece of bread. In Aleksii's words, "the oppressive rentals brought the desiatinshchiki to horrifying poverty." "A cluster of dugouts scattered in disorder, settled deeply into the earth", he writes, "courtyards without trenches,[C] overgrown with tall weeds, half-ruined barns, made of dung and for the most part not having any sort of roof—these are the characteristic features of the dwellings of the desiatinshchiki ..." (*ibid.*).

Let us supplement the observations made by Aleksii on the social composition of the basic mass of participants in the Baptist movement in Kherson and Ekaterinoslav Guberniias with the analogous observations of A. D. Ushinskii in Kiev Guberniia.

A. D. Ushinskii worked as an anti-sectarian missionary and, like A. Ia. Dorodnitsyn (Aleksii), attempted to penetrate, insofar as this was at all possible within the bounds of his world-view, into the basic causes for the growth of Baptism. With the aim of studying the Shtundist movement, he visited first in 1875 and then in 1881 Tarashcha and other uezds of Kiev Guberniia. The results of these travels, during which Ushinskii met with the main figures and ordinary participants in Shtundism, were his works *Verouchenie malorusskikh shtundistov* [The Teachings of the Little Russian Shtundists] (1884) and *O prichinakh poiavleniia ratsionalisticheskikh uchenii shtundy* [On the Causes of the Appearance of the Rationalistic Teachings of the Shtunda] (1884).

Comparing the make-up of the Shtundists in the German colonies and the Russian settlements of the Kiev area, Ushinskii came to the following conclusions: "... in economic and social terms, the Russian community of Shtundists makes a contrast with the Germans, since the former consist primarily of poor people—landless peasants, free tenants and meshchane; that is, the rural proletariat ...' (Ushinskii 1884: 39). Reflecting on the question of the political character of the movement he studied, Ushinskii did not come to any definite conclusion, but he noted that "this sect, primarily of the rural proletariat, is always and everywhere receptive to communistic teachings ..." (Ushinskii 1884: 40).

The fact that Ushinskii became acquainted with Shtundism directly at the place of its growth, and had in his hands the names of more than 1,500 Shtundists living in the villages of Kiev Guberniia (Ushinskii 1884: 25-27), increases our trust in his observations.

Finally, according to V. Skvortsov, who spoke at the Second Missionary Congress in 1891, "the overwhelming majority of followers of Shtundo-Baptism by economic position are the poorest of their fellow villagers, since of the Shtunda we may justly say that this is the proletariat of the people, deprived, dissatisfied, hoping from the sect for an improvement in their material way of life as a people" (Missionary 1891: 30).

Let us check, insofar as this is possible, the testimony of Church figures against the testimony of Baptist activists contemporary with them. Let us cite the description of a meeting of Baptists in the village of Usokh, Khar'kov Guberniia, made by the traveling Baptist preacher V. V. Ivanov in 1883: "In the evening the congregation gathered and I gave a sermon. This people is striking for its poverty and for the primordial state of our Russia. The men in homespun white shirts and breeches. The women also in a single white homespun shirt and red cloth skirt.... Any sort of luxury is lacking here.... This congregation knows about redemption and the blood of Christ; the men and women pray from the heart and the children pray too. The simplicity of Christ is evident here" (Val'kevich 1900: Appendix 4, p. 5).

Can we extend the description given by Ivanov of the Baptists in the village of Usokh to other groups of Baptists?

From a Baptist document *O sbore na missiiu* [On Collection for the Mission], relating to 1884, we receive characteristic information describing the milieu in which the Baptist leaders competed. "A good example", we read in this document, "was given by the sister of the Novo-Vasil'evskaia church, among whom several designated for the Lord the income from one chicken; i.e., the eggs produced by the chicken in the course of the year were sold, by which 37 rubles were collected" (Aleksii 1980: 11).

Like the Novo-Vasil'evka sisters setting aside eggs for the Lord, the sisters from the congregation in Tambovka (Kuban Oblast), using a fund donated by the Tiflis Baptist E. V. Beklemisheva, knitted stockings, sewed shirts, and from the money received from the sale of their produce, "gave part to the poor and propertyless" (*ibid.*). Who were these poor and propertyless? Primarily Baptists.

The fact that the "poor and propertyless" drew the close attention of the disseminators of the Baptist teaching is affirmed by the following casuistic utterance of one of the Baptist orators in 1879: "... several brothers have expressed the thought that the money donated for the mission would be more usefully distributed to the poor. I can by no means agree with this, because by donating money to the poor we can only give aid to their bodies, but not to the soul, and spiritual aid is more important than physical" (Val'kevich 1900: Appendix 1, p. 35). Finally, in one of V. V. Ivanov's letters from 1894, we find a generalized description: "Looking at all these communities (Baptist — A. K.) from the material side, it is worth noting that they *almost all consist of the poorest class of people* and the majority of brothers are in need of subsidies in order to deal with their economic affairs and to be free from old debts ..." (Val'kevich 1900: Appendix 3, pp. 26-27).

I conclude that the broadest strata of the Baptists consisted of representatives of socially lower classes. In this there was no distinction between the Baptists and any other of the old Russian sects. But both Baptist and Russian Orthodox Church sources agree that the mass of recruits of Baptism came from the most deprived part of the socially lower classes, from the proletarianized peasants, deprived of the means of production and often not having a dwelling.

However, Baptism consisted not of lower classes alone but also of upper classes. We are already acquainted with the most prominent of their representatives in the Caucasian guberniias. In the Ukraine, however, among the circle of leading activists and propagandists of Baptism, we do not encounter either "millionaires" or "hundred-thousanders", as, for example, Mazaev and Fefelov; we do not encounter the scions of bourgeois families, who received advanced philosophical training in the seminaries and colleges of Germany,

England and France, as, for example, V. G. Pavlov, I. S. and A. S. Prokhanov.

Who were the first leaders of Baptism in the Ukraine according to social position? In March 1885, the Kherson governor made a report to the Ministry of Internal Affairs concerning the most important organizers and propagandists of Baptism in his guberniia, with a view to taking repressive measures against them. In the governor's report these people (20) were named (Aleksii 1908: 325). Some time later, the governor demanded of the uezd district police officers that they present a description of the 20 "propagandists of Shtundism" named by him whose activities were developing in the districts entrusted to the police officers. From the responses of the police officers of Kherson, Odessa and Elizavetgrad Uezds relating to January-February 1885, the social affiliation of 19 leaders and disseminators of Baptism is revealed, whose activity was not limtied to any one uezd of Kherson Guberniia; among them were the basic organizers and missionaries of Ukrainian Baptism — Mikhail Ratushnyi, Ivan Riaboshapka, Trofim Khlystun, Ivan Rybalka, Aleksandr Kapustian and Gerasim Balaban (Aleksii 1908: 327-334).

Let us cite the information describing the social and property situation of the leaders and propagandists of Baptism in the Ukraine:

1. Mikhail Ratushnyi "has a parcel of land of 5.5 des. and besides that 20 des. acquired by purchase from the community, which is encumbered in the Kherson Land Bank; a stone house, five head of working stock and four working horses" (Aleksii 1908: 329);

2. Ivan Riaboshapka "has his own garden and farm, to wit: a cottage, two smithies, two barns costing 400 rubles, a horse-drawn thresher, 4 horses, 3 cows and 4 head of non-working stock; besides his parcel, he rents 3 des. of land" (Aleksii 1908: 330);

3. Trofim Khlystun "lives on his own farmstead.... His property consists of 250 des. of land and various items of movable property worth 2,000 rubles" (*ibid.*);

4. Ivan Rybalka "has his own garden and farm consisting of two cottages with outhouses and a threshing barn valued at 500 rubles, a horse-drawn threshing machine, two pairs of bullocks, a pair of horses, a cow, 8 head of non-working stock and 30 head of sheep" (Aleksii 1908: 331);

5. Aleksandr Kapustian "has a parcel of land of 1.75 des., 2 stone houses, 2 head of large cattle and 4 working horses" (Aleksii 1908: 329);

6. Gerasim Balaban "has 334 des. of his own land which is encumbered in the Kherson Land Bank, a stone house and two attached dugouts, 79 head of cattle, 18 sheep and goats, 18 working horses and 2 colts" (Aleksii 1908: 328);

7. Ivan Skirko "has 70 des. of his own land with a house and other buildings, domestic cattle and other property" (Aleksii 1908: 327);

8. Andrei Bukhovitskii "has a parcel of land, a garden and also a windmill, 4 horses, a cow and various other enterprises" (Aleksii 1908: 328);

9. Evstafii Gora "has ... 70 des. of land with buildings and a farm" (*ibid.*);

10. Petr Griva "lives ... poorly. All his property consists of a pair of horses and a cart" (Aleksii 1908: 331);

11. Stepan Budnichenko "has a garden and a farm, to wit: a cottage with outhouses, costing 35 rubles, a pair of bullocks, a cow and 15 sheep" (Aleksii 1908: 332);

12. Zakharii Gorobets "has a parcel of land of 5.5 des., a stone house, 2 working horses and 2 colts" (*ibid.*);

13. Anton Strigun "has a parcel of land of 1.75 des., a stone house, 15 head of working cattle, 4 sheep and goats and 2 working horses" (Aleksii 1908: 329);

14. & 15. Andrei and Grigorii Umskii had "two houses, a mill, a mortar and a churn" (Aleksii 1908: 333);

16. Andrei Sychev "sows grain; his farm is insignificant" (Aleksii 1908: 332);

17. Fedor Taran "has his own house, garden and farm" (Aleksii 1908: 334);

18. Daniil Tarasenko "has his own house and garden, sows grain and is considered a wealthy peasant" (*ibid.*);

19. Nikolai Pukhovoi "owns several parcels of land, working and non-working stock, and is considered a wealthy householder" (Aleksii 1908: 333).

From the basic group of the first organizers and missionaries of Baptism, 16 persons belonged to the kulak class (in some cases very well-off) or were wealthy peasants; 3 were poor peasants.

With their stone houses, landholdings, agricultural tools, mills and working stock they were the complete opposite of the basic contingent of Baptists, in particular the desiatinshchiki mentioned above, who in the literal sense had neither house nor home, and whose dwellings Aleksii compared "with a snake's nest" (Aleksii 1909: 88).

Among the Baptists in the guberniias of the Ukraine there undoubtedly existed representatives from the middle strata of the peasantry, both craftsmen and urban meshchane, but the social image of Baptism was determined on the one hand by the wealthy kulak elite and on the other by the proletarianized peasantry.

Thus, Baptism in its social make-up represented the final results of the bourgeois distintegration of the countryside. "The disintegration of the peasantry", Lenin wrote, "developing its extreme groups at the expense of the middle peasantry, created two new types of rural populations. The common characteristic of both types is the commodity-and-money character of the economy" (*Lenin*: III, 168).[D]

Two new types of rural population determined the composition of the religious organization of Baptism and, however abstract the religious ideas were, under the external sign of which the Baptist movement gathered together and was built, the ideas were an expression, although a fantastic one, of the laws of development of a commodity-and-money economy — the "common characteristic" of the two new types of rural population.

But before going to a description of the social essence of the religious ideas of Baptism, we must still explain the conditions, the social milieu, the peculiarities of the spread of Baptism in the north-western and central Great Russian guberniias.

In contrast to the guberniias of the Caucasus and the Ukraine, where the ideas of Baptism from the very beginning had roots among elements of the bourgeoisie and the proletarianized middle strata, in Petersburg the first success of Baptist preaching took place in the salons of the higher aristocracy of the capital. Here Baptism passed through its formative stage in the form of evangelical preaching. In the mid-1870s, evangelical preaching gathered its hearers and worshippers in the parlors of princes and counts — V. A. Pashkov, M. M. Korf, A. P. Bobrinskii, V. F. Gagarina, etc. I have in mind the evangelical preaching of Lord Granville Radstock, which he began in Petersburg in 1874.

Let us use N. S. Lekov's description of the milieu of Radstock's St. Petersburg admirers. "So: let us suppose that we are in a company of distinguished persons", Leskov writes, "gathered for a sermon which is to be given in the evening in a high-society Russian private home.

"The gathering is fairly large, but ladies are much more numerous than men, among whom there are noticeable several military people and two generals in dress uniform.... No colorful or even slightly frivolous attire is permitted. The military men are in their uniforms and the civilians in black frock-coats" (Leskov 1877: 188).

We will omit Leskov's descriptions of the behavior of the "ladies and gentlemen" expecting the preacher. But now "downstairs a bell is heard; the hostess jumps up and whispers: 'He has arrived' — and runs to meet him. General movement: all settle in their places, and he comes in" (Leskov 1877: 196). After a short prayer, Radstock gives a sermon, the leitmotif of which is " 'the salvation' of man for 'eternal life', for which a person must lose himself in the recognition of his impotence, *deserve* 'salvation' and be penetrated by *faith* that he is *already* 'saved', thanks to the redeeming sacrifice of Christ" (Leskov 1877: 199-222).

With the help of Count Pashkov and Count Korf, the ideas preached by Radstock crossed the thresholds of high-society houses and penetrated into the milieu of artisans, meshchane, workers, the lumpen proletariat and also the peasant population. Both the oral sermons of Pashkov and his followers, and especially the printed propaganda, served this purpose.

In 1875, the Pashkovites (Radstockists) found a journal with a spiritual and moral slant—*Russkii rabochii* [The Russian Worker], whose publication lasted until 1886. In 1876 (three years before he was converted to Baptism in Switzerland), Korf with the consent of the Ministry of Internal Affairs founded the Society for the Distribution of Spiritual-Moral Readings, which began energetic press activity. This society published and distributed in enormous quantity mass popular pamphlets, both by mail and by special traveling booksellers. Some titles were distributed free and some for a sum which varied from a grosh[E] to six kopeks. In the words of G. Terletskii, "the success of the propaganda of the Society for the Distribution of Spiritual-Moral Readings was enormous: the pamphlets were distributed quickly both in Petersburg and in the interior of Russia ... "(Terletskii 1891: 93).

The journal *Russian Worker* and the pamplets of the society founded by Korf were especially widely distributed in factories and public schools. These publications, clumsily adapted to folk speech, revealed a complete lack of knowledge of worker and peasant life, propagandized to the mass monarchical-meshchan ideals, and printed every kind of sentimental story with obligatory moralizing endings. They were directed primarily toward preaching the same idea on which Radstock spoke in the salon described by N. S. Leskov: man should direct all his thoughts toward salvation, know that no efforts of his own could save him, and believe that he was already saved thanks to the redeeming sacrifice of Christ.[4]

However unexpected the attention of the St. Petersburg aristocracy to the evangelical preaching of Radstock, and then their attempts to popularize this preaching among the masses of the people might seem, both can be completely explained by the conditions of public and political life in the 1870s. This was a time of an upsurge of social movements, which flowed in 1879-1880 into a revolutionary situation. Peasant and Cossack uprisings became more frequent in the country. The revolutionary Narodnik movement became active. In the very year when Radstock began his preaching, the mass "going to the people", which embraced dozens of guberniias, began. But most importantly the 1870s were a time of upsurge of the workers' movement. Precisely in St. Petersburg in the first half of the 1870s there occurred mass strikes and uprisings by workers, which broke out with new strength in 1878-1879. Between these two waves of the strike movement, there occurred in 1876 the famous Kazan demonstration.

---

[4] Let us cite the opinion of A. S. Prugavin, a well-known pre-Revolutionary student of sectarianism, on the pamphlets of the Pashkovite publishing house: "The ideas of these publications were marked by extreme fogginess, cloudy mysticism, and constant appeals to heaven. All these pamphlets were filled to overflowing with judgments about the vanity of earthly life and its interests, about the great joy which awaited people beyond the grave, about the necessity of always and unceasingly striving toward heaven, and moving away from this sinful world, drowning in evil and injustice, etc., etc." (Prugavin 1904: 151-152).

In 1871, revolutionary circles in St. Petersburg welcomed the red banner of the Paris Commune. In the 1870s, the red banner appeared on squares in St. Petersburg. Organizatons of the working class arose—the South Russian Union of Workers and the Northern Union of Russian Workers. Tsarism was distraught, varying from extreme repression to liberal indulgence, calling on "society" for help in the struggle against the revolutionary movement. Mortally frightened by the growth of the workers' movement and the general upsurge of the democratic movement in the country, the aristocracy resorted to a tested means of consolation—religion. Activists in the "high-society Schism" very soon realized that the light narcosis they experienced from Radstock's preaching could be used successfully in heavier doses for the moral disarming of the masses of the people rising to struggle. Then an attempt at broad evangelization of the population was launched, and this aim was served both by the preaching of the Pashkovites and their mass press production, as well as their philanthropic institutions, free dining halls, etc., etc.

In the given instance the Russian aristocrats only followed in the footsteps of the English bourgeoisie. Barely recovered from the revolution of 1848-1849 in a number of countries of Europe, still in fear of their own workers' movement (in spite of the failure of the Chartists in 1848), the English bourgeoisie set to the evangelization of the people. "If the British bourgeoisie", Engels wrote, "was convinced even earlier of the necessity of holding the plain people in religious bonds, then how much more strongly should it feel this necessity after everything it had experienced ... it continued to spend from year to year thousands and tens of thousands for the preaching of the Gospels to the lower classes. Not satisfied with its own religious apparatus, it turned to 'Brother Jonathan', the greatest entrepreneur in the field of religious speculation, and imported from America the revivalism of Moody, Sankey and others like them" (*Marx and Engels:* XXII, 314). On the wave of the revivalist (awakening) movement in the United States, Baptism grew strong and flourished.

Pashkov's activity was directed toward rousing in the masses of the people a kind of revivalist movement, conceived as a way of directing revolutionary energies into a religious channel.

The frank admission of I. P. Kushnerov, one of the veterans of Russian Baptism, on the role of the Pashkovites in the 1870s, which he made in 1905, is highly indicative: "This group (the Pashkovites—A. K.) began in the highest strata of Russian society in Petersburg at the beginning of the 1870s. As we know, during this time of the rule of terror and the increased activity of revolutionary parties, there were people in high society who looked with horror at the chaos of philosophical, political-economic and literary theories which were then swirling about, devouring each other, and bringing with them an irreconcilable hostility of classes and struggle of parties. On the one hand the desire for inspiration in their unsatisfying personal lives, and on the other the attempt to find a well-constructed spiritual world-view, led them to the same thing that the peasants of South Russia (the Baptists—A. K.) arrived at, i.e. to a reading of the Gospels.... In the Gospels they discovered a counterweight to the surging wave of various negative ideas of that time, and firm foundations for legality, morality, and the salvation not only of their own souls but of the state and of society from the storm of spiteful struggle and hatred of mankind" (Kushnerov 1905: 4-5).

In 1905, Kushnerov wanted to convince the tsarist regime of the usefulness of Baptism and collected in his memory everything that Baptism had to its credit in the struggle with the revolutionary movement. We will return again to Kushnerov's statement.

Radstock's teaching, accepted and disseminated by Pashkov and his circle, contained the same basic ideas as Baptism, namely the concepts of "original sin", "Divine Providence", "redemption in the blood of Christ"; besides this, the Pashkovite movement had its own peculiarities both of an ideological and an organizational nature. In the guberniias of the Caucasus and the Ukraine, Baptism increasingly took on the character of a successor religious formation, replacing earlier varieties of sectarianism and from the very beginning developing along the lines of a church.

The activity of the Pashkovites was not directed toward forming a religious corporation which would by its origin multiply the number of existing religious sects in Russia. It had the aim not so much of finding external forms for coordinating the activity and disciplining the minds of its followers, as of awakening religious enthusiasm, of stimulating in the people "revivalism"—that paradoxical religious formation of "awakening" known in the history of the United States when people sleep with their eyes open.

With these aims, Pashkov and his circle could not stand, for example, on the dogmatic positions of personal predestination—i.e., that doctrine of predestination according to which salvation is the destined lot of the elect alone.[5] The predestinarian position was close to the feeling of many leaders of the Baptist movement in the guberniias of the Caucasus and the Ukraine, who advanced the task of their churches precisely as churches of "the elect", directed by the order of Divine Providence.

Assuming that the people had the quality of being "the bearers of God", and that one had only to find and open the valve controlling it and it would spring to the surface and set the people in motion, the Pashkovites were concerned with propagandizing their religious slogans, and not with the creation of a new religious hierarchy on the local level. On the contrary, in the development of Baptism in the guberniias of the Caucasus and the Ukraine

---

[5] Concerning the salvation of people in Pashkov's belief system it was said: "I believe that the Lord Jesus Christ is the only savior for sinners", and "that everyone who believes in Him will certainly be saved" (Aleksii 1909: 313).

the question of the creation of a religious hierarchy, its position and its rights, took on ever-increasing significance.

However, both the Pashkovites and the Baptists took hold of one and the same "valve" in order to open an exit for the religious feelings of people. In what did the peculiarities of these new ideas consist which took hold in several differing versions among certain strata of the population of the Caucasian, Ukrainian and Great Russian guberniias? These ideas came down at the crucial point to an anti-humanistic teaching about man, his significance and destiny.

The place of man in captialist society was different than in the preceding feudal one. Precisely this question of the place of man in life was the central point at which Baptism undertook a revaluation of values. In the religious teachings of early Khristovoverie, man was given the possibility of being like God in his spiritual qualities. The Khristovovers looked on themselves as living Christs, and then transferred this view to their leaders, considering themselves "living temples", in which the spirit of God dwelt. To the Dukhobors, whose leaders also played the role of Christ, man was "a marvelous wonderful creation of God". The Molokans had no Christs but considered the person who accepted their teaching as the possessor of "spiritual wisdom".

Each sect in its own way held to views asserting that wisdom, will and the moral feeling of man (the believer) were an inborn essential quality of humanity, which man can and should develop, and build life as a kingdom of God on earth. These views reflected the democratism of the participants of the early sectarian movements, their certainty in the final victory over the forces of evil, by which they understood the ruling church and all those institutions of serfdom to which the Church gave its blessing.

In Baptism these views were reconsidered. Man was considered neither a temple of God nor a wonderful marvelous creation of God, nor the bearer of spiritual wisdom. Mikhail Ratushnyi asserted that "man by nature is spiritually blind—i.e. he does not see his own sins and defects" (Aleksii 1908: 478), and that "all people without distinction as to nation or faith are under the power of sin, and in spite of all religious ceremonials and rituals must eternally perish if within man there does not occur that important change called ... repentence or rebirth ..." (Aleksii 1908: 477).

But Aleksii thought that the author of this statement of belief was Karl Bonekempfer—"Ratushnyi's original preceptor and leader in the errors of Baptism" (*ibid.*).[6] In any case, Ratushnyi held to this confession of faith and

---

[6] Karl Bonekemper (Bonekempfer), an evangelical preacher, was born and received a secondary education in Russia. Bonekemper received his theological training in America. He returned to Russia in 1867 and lived in the German colonies of Rorbakh, Odessa Uezd, and Neidorf, Tiraspol' Uezd, Kherson Guberniia. In 1877, he emigrated to America (*see* Rozhdestvenskii 1889: 59; Val'kevich 1900: 40-41 etc.).

cited it verbatim in letters—for example the one sent in 1873 to his co-thinker Liashkov (Aleksii 1908: 188-190).

The thought of original sin burdening man penetrated the statement of belief composed for Baptists from Russian Mennonite colonies by the founder of the Baptist mission in Germany, the merchant Johann Oncken, who visited Russia in 1869. This statement of belief was published in German in 1872 (Aleksii 1908: 495), and some time later it appeared in Russian translations and was distributed among Baptists. Most probably its translator was V. G. Pavlov.[7] "... Since all men", we read in the statement of belief, "came from Adam's seed, they ware made to partake of the same fallen and completely damaged nature, since they are conceived and born in sin" (Aleksii 1908: 497).

If we turn from the Ukrainian and Caucasian Baptists to the Baptist movement as it was formed in the Great Russian guberniias and use for this purpose the statement of faith distributed among the Pashkovites, we encounter the following: "I believe that mankind in his natural condition is deprived of holiness and is quite corrupt.... I believe that man because of his corruption must be born from on high in the spirit, and without this spiritual birth no one can be saved" (Aleksii 1909: 313).

Beyond the Baptist idea there stood a philosophy: if man by nature is sinful, if his nature is corrupt, can man rely on himself in his thoughts, desires and actions? Can the human race derive strength within itself for the construction of life if, beginning with Adam and Eve, original sin from generation to generation is transmitted like bad heredity? The philosophy of the Baptist confession of faith basically devalued man.

In Oncken's confession of faith, it was said that people because of their "completely damaged nature" were "servants of anger, *completely unable and unwilling to do any good, but capable of and inclined to any evil*" (Aleksii 1908: 497). In the tract *Obrashchenie k cheloveku greshnomu* [An Appeal to a Sinner], of which [Aleksii] says that "this pamphlet was widely distributed in manuscript among the Baptists (of the Kherson and Ekaterinoslav areas—A. K.): they use it to seduce the Russian Orthodox into their sect" (Aleksii 1908: 511), ideas of the substantial impotence of man received especially complete expression. In this essay it was asserted: "You cannot justify yourself to God if even in front of people you are unimpeachable.... You are unjust and therefore you cannot inherit the kingdom of God.... You are guilty and you cannot smooth over your guilt.... You cannot give any ransom for your soul.... Neither your fasts nor psalms

---

[7] In November 1873, V. G. Pavlov wrote from Tiflis to V. V. Ivanov: "We still have no books of 'confession of faith', but recently we ordered *A History of the Baptists* and *A Confession of Faith* in German sent to us from Odessa; as soon as we receive the *Confession of Faith*, I will translate it into Russian and then will try to send it" (Val'kevich 1900: Appendix 5, p. 4).

nor prayers nor your charity, however pleasing they are to God, can of themselves smooth over your sins ..." (*ibid.*).

All this contradicted the world-view of pre-Reform sectarianism, in which the ethic of good deeds stood as one of the crucial concepts. The former followers of Khristovoverie, Dukhoborism and Molokanism, transferring to Baptism, re-evaluated ideas which had not justified themselves, since "the ethic of good deeds", alas, had not led to the construction on earth of the kingdom of God, but to precisely the opposite — in the places of compact settlement of Khristovovers, Dukhobors and Molokans, exploitation and violence ruled.

Man was dethroned, and in the foreground of the Baptist teaching there appeared the concept of "Divine Providence", which stands over man, an indivisible and inscrutable ruling power. But Baptism addressed its preaching to people and could not leave unanswered the question of the relationship of Divine Providence to man.

If man could win the favor of Divine Providence by his own efforts and sacrifices, he would not be the powerless victim of sin. A way out was found: Baptism gave exclusive significance to the concept of the redemptive sacrifice of Christ for the sins of all — former, present and future — people.

Christ in Christianity is the son of God, and to take into account his sacrifice for people was purely a familial right and an affair of the divine family, since it did not lay on it any obligation to people: the sacrifice was made for them and not by them.

Faith for Baptism is faith in the redemptive sacrifice of Christ as necessary and sufficient for salvation. Salvation, thus, is a gift — under circumstances, true, in which the individuality of man clearly is not taken into account; on condition that man pay for "salvation" precisely with his individuality, the bargain is called a gift ("you are being given salvation free ... because with *your* deeds you cannot justify yourself before God's justice") (Aleksii 1908: 512).

The idea of omnipotent Divine Providence and, correspondingly, the impotence of man's own efforts in the matter of salvation, is central to Baptism. In some cases it was given an extreme expression, in which salvation was declared not to be open at all, even though one might acknowledge oneself as nothing, and Providence as omnipotent, and believe in the redemptive sacrifice of Christ.

The direction which became basic in Russian Baptism — Baptism proper, in distinction to Evangelical Christianity (Pashkovism) — held the view that God destines some people for "salvation" and others for "damnation". Oncken's confession of faith, which did not suffer any essential change over the entire history of Russian Baptism, stated: "... those persons from the ruined race of man, who in the course of time really must acquire redemption, are also chosen by the Father ... their names are written in Heaven and they themselves are given over into the hands of the Redeemer ... as His people.... These people are destined for eternal life in Jesus Christ.... Such a divine determination is unchangeable and set forever ..., so that those to whom it applies—the chosen ones—cannot be torn from the hands of Christ ..." (Aleksii 1908: 499).

In the given instance, the very appeal for faith in the redemptive sacrifice of Christ is the result of the age-old divine predestination.

Thus, it was not the denial of the hierarchical structure of the ruling church, its ritual and ceremonial, sacraments, veneration of icons and relics that was the exclusive feature of Baptism. In this, Baptism coincides with the teachings of the majority of sects which preceded it. And recognition of the Bible as the sole authority in questions of faith and life was not peculiar to Baptism alone. The Bible occupied the same position in Molokanism, for example. The specific feature of Baptism was not even the so-called Last Supper, the breaking of bread in remembrance of Christ's sacrifice.

The ritual of water baptism "of those who have come to believe", having achieved maturity, belongs to a relatively narrow circle of religious organizations. Baptists immersed their neophytes in water face-up. But in this respect they are not original. Newly-converted Adventists are immersed in water in the same way.

Basic to the world-view of Baptism is the teaching of the omnipotence of Divine Providence and of salvation achieved only by faith in the redemptive sacrifice of Christ.

What is the social essence of the religious doctrine of Baptism?

In Engels' definition, "any religion is nothing other than a fantastic reflection in people's heads of those external forces which dominate them in their everyday life—a reflection in which earthly forces take the form of unearthly ones" (*Marx and Engels:* XX, 328).

In the process of historical development, forms of exploitation change—the external forces dominating people, and their fantastic reflections, change along with them.

In comparing the religious movements which arose because of the contradictions of the feudal-serf system with those arising out of the contradictions of capitalist society, and in explaining the differences existing between them, we must take into account the following.

The basis of the class hegemony of the feudal lords and the economic dependence of the peasants on them was large feudal property in land. The acquisition of additional produce was accomplished by the feudal lords by way of extra-economic compulsion, which manifested itself in the most direct and obvious form as rent in labor—the so-called corvée. Social relationships in feudal society were relationships of personal dependence. "If the landlord did not have direct power over the person of the peasant", Lenin wrote, "he would not be able to make a person who was in possession of land and was operating his own farm, work for him" (*Lenin:* III, 159).[F]

Class relationships in feudal society, precisely because they appeared in the form of personal dependence of the peasants on the feudal lords, were naked relationships of dominance and subordination.

Marx wrote: "Personal dependence here (in feudal society—A. K.) characterizes the social relations of production just as much as it does the other spheres of life organized on the basis of that production. But for the very reason that personal dependence forms the ground-work of society, there is no necessity for labor and its products to assume a fantastic form different from their reality.... No matter then what we may think of the parts played by the different classes of people themselves in this society, the social relations between individuals in the performance of their labor appear at all events as their own mutual personal relations, and are not disguised under the shape of social relations between the products of labor" (*Marx and Engels:* XXIII, 87-88).[G]

In accordance with this, the anti-feudal opposition, appearing in religious form, expressed primarily protest against personal dependence, against the dominion of one man over another. Not without reason did a text from the epistles of Paul become enormously popular in the heretical movements of the Middle Ages: "You are bought for a high price. Do not make yourselves the slaves of men". The inspiration of the sectarian teachings which arose in pre-Reform Russia was the criticism of Church organization and ideology as *authoritarian.*

The resolutions of ecumenical and local councils, and in general all canonical and patristic writings which were used by the Church to justify feudal dominance, were denied, and the strongest argument advanced by the sectarian oppositon in criticism was that all this was "*human* invention". Here we have the same motif—"do not make yourselves the slaves of men". The veneration of icons, of the remains of saints' bodies, and of every conceivable holy relic, was denied on the same basis. The ecclesiastical hierarchy and the Church structure were subjected to criticism and denied, in turn, on the supposition that the original church founded by Christ was marked by simplicity of structure and an absence of ecclesiastical power, and that church institutions and the power of the clergy were a very late "human invention".

People dependent on lay and clerical feudal lords, having entered into one or another sect, called themselves "God's people", and affirmed their individual freedom as "temples of the living God", meaning by this a right to social freedom; they maintained, as the Tambov Spiritual Christians in the 1760s did, that "God created man in His image and likeness as autonomous ..." (Ryndziunskii 1954: 178).

In other words, *the protest against the enslavement of man by man* was central to the ideology of early sectarianism.

The dominance of earthly external forces over man in bourgeois society was different. Here there were no longer relationships of personal dependence, and in place of extra-economic compulsion on the immediate producers, carried out directly by the feudal lords and their overseers, there came the incomprehensible, "suprasensory" and even more powerful force of economic compulsion. The structure of social relationships was not blanketed in mystical shadows; "the social relationships between individuals in the performance of their labor" appeared not "as their own mutual personal relations", but were "disguised under the shape of social relations between the products of labor". Henceforth "man ceased to be the slave of man and became the slave of *things*" (*Marx and Engels*: I, 605).

The secret of the transformation of the products of people's labor into commodities and the dominion of commodities over people—a faceless dominion not subject to control, not dependent on people's conscious individual activity—which is to say, the secret of economic compulsion, received religious explanation in the fearful dominion of Divine Providence, which played with the fates of people, incomprehensible in its supernatural will, blind and deaf to the sufferings, needs, activities and entreaties of a humanity defeated by "original sin". But if man *recognized* himself as an impotent marble spinning in the roulette wheel of "Divine Providence", this was considered participation in the secret, as the first step to salvation, and therefore as a sign of election.

Baptism was a typically bourgeois variety of Christianity, and not only because in the last analysis the doctrine of Divine Providence was the religious parallel to the natural action of the law of values, which threw some into the ranks of the chosen and other into the ranks of the condemned, and regulated social production and the circulation of commodities.

Baptism was a bourgeois variety of Christianity also in its attitude toward everyday practice. The sectarian doctrines preceding Baptism demanded from their followers an ethic of good deeds, since only by adhering to this and becoming perfect in it could man justify himself as the bearer of the spirit of God, of divine wisdom, etc. At that time the ethic of good deeds included, for example, asceticism, which served to condemn the luxury and wealth of lay and clerical feudal lords. To the extent to which the peasant was turned into an independent commodity-producer, and then into a bourgeois property-owner, sectarianism increasingly divided into upper and lower strata; the ethic of good deeds became a weapon of the lower classes in the struggle against the corvée system, usury and money-grubbing, against the privileged position of the upper classes. The wealthy and kulak elements among the Khristovovers, Dukhobors and Molokans clearly did not go along with this ethic.

Baptism did not count the ethic of good deeds among the "paths leading to God". No virtues and no righteousness had any significance in terms of man's salvation, as Baptist dogma proclaimed with total clarity. Salvation depended on Divine Providence, which thus as it were took *on itself* responsibility for the earthly activities of its favorites.

In making a distinction between salvation and deeds, Baptism freed the hands of its followers for trade, entrepreneurship, and in general any kind of worldly activity. As we know, the cradle of Baptism was England—a classic capitalist country. Engels said ironically of the religiosity of the English: "The English are the most religious people in the world and at the same time the most irreligious; they are more concerned about the other world that any other nation, but at the same time live as if there were nothing more for them than earthly existence; their hope of heaven does not hinder them at all from believing equally strongly in 'the hell of not earning money' ".[8] To those who earned money, Baptism forgave their sins in advance, and promised them, like those who did not earn money, "free salvation".

These were the basic ideas of Baptism, and they were the more quickly disseminated, the more rapidly the peasants, meshchane and artisan groups of the city were drawn into the sphere of capitalist relationships. Around the 1880s-1890s, Baptism had smaller or larger groups of adherents in the eparchies of Astrakhan, Vladikavkaz, the Don, Ekaterinoslav, Kishinev, Kiev, Kursk, Mogilev, Minsk, Moscow, Nizhegorod, Novgorod, Orel, Orenburg, St. Petersburg, Pskov, Podol'sk, Polotsk, Poltava, Riazan, Samara, Saratov, Stavropol', Tavriia, Tambov, Tver, Kar'kov and Kherson (Missionary 1891: 28), and also in Siberia and the Far East. By 1891, according to eparchal statistics, the eparchies of Kiev and Kherson—i.e. the original sites of Baptism—had approximately 5,000 Baptists each.

Let us note that in 1884 in Kiev Guberniia there were 2,000 Baptists (Rozhdestvenskii 1889: 136, 149), and in Kherson Guberniia, if we follow the data of reports by the Over-Procurator of the Synod for that year, 3,000. But apparently the data on the widening of the circle of villages in which Baptist groups appeared are of greater cognitive value than the figures adduced on the absolute numerical strength of Baptism. In 1884, there were Baptists in 95 settlements in Kherson Guberniia (Rozhdestvenskii 1889: 149). By 1891, 167 villages in Kherson Guberniia had Baptists (Missionary 1891: 27). The rapid dissemination of Baptism to new sites is striking. By 1891, the

---

[8] *Marx and Engels:* I, 601. Engels was interested in the situation of Baptism in England. Reviewing the question of the spread in England in the 1850s of "skepticism in religious questions", Engels wrote: "… it has come to a state in which agnosticism, although it is not yet considered 'a first-class thing', like the English state church, still stands in point of respectability almost on the same level with the Baptists and in any case a rung higher than the Salvation Army" (Marx and Engels: XXII, 302).

Astrakhan eparchy had about 2,500 Baptists, and the Kishinev about 3,000 (Missionary 1891: 28).

Parallel with the growing success of Baptist preaching, beginning in the 1870s, the organizational structuring and strengthening of Baptism was taking place, and this in turn facilitated its dissemination. During the 1870s personal contacts among its activists in various guberniias of the country were established, and close contacts were maintained between Russian Baptist figures and Baptists in German colonies in Tavriia and Ekaterinoslav Guberniias, and in the regions of the Kuban and the Don Host. Apparently Baptist congregations existing in the German colonies had prestige among Russian Baptists both by virtue of their connections with foreign Baptist missions and because of the dogmatic and theological training of their preachers.

On the basis of the Baptist congregations existing in the German colonies, a conference of Baptists was held in 1882 in the colony of Rikenau, with 64 delegates from the German congregations and 18 Russian delegates representing the Baptists of Tavriia, Kherson, Bessarabia and Tiflis Guberniias, and Terek Oblast. Among the Russian delegates were A. M. Mazaev, M. T. Ratushnyi, A. S. Kapustian, T. O. Khlystun, G. M. Kushnerenko and I. T. Riaboshapka.

This activity of Baptist missionaries resulted in Baptism having, around the 1880s-1890s, compact groups of adherents in more than 30 guberniias of Russia. The Russian Orthodox Church was powerless even to localize, let alone to halt, the impact of the Baptist mission.

Since they were powerless in the ideological struggle with Baptism, the reactionary clergy resorted to settling political scores with them.[9] They frightened the Autocracy with the bugbear of Baptism's "revolutionary" nature.

In a letter to the governor of Kherson dated November 12, 1884, Nikanor, Bishop of Kherson and Odessa, wrote that "the Shtunda, in the very principle of its teaching, undermines the very root, not only of the Church, but of the whole system, both social and governmental" (Aleksii 1908: 321). He demanded the unleashing on the Shtunda of the whole weight of state repression, and even forecast a still more terrible fate for the Autocracy than for the Church if it failed to implement reprisals against the Shtunda on a nation-

---

[9] The reaction on the part of some representatives of the lay administration to the attempts of the Church to deal with the opposition movement by means of judicial and police repression is curious. The procurator of the Odessa court wrote not without sarcasm to the Ministry of Justice in January 1875: "... among the pastors of the Russian Orthodox Church, there has not been for a long time the necessary stimulus for action on the conscience of their spiritual charges by way of persuasion, reasoning and the example of their own lives, if they can rely for implanting the truth of the Russian Orthodox faith on the obligatory cooperation of district police officers, and for holding their parishioners in the lap of the Orthodox Church, on the threat of severe criminal punishment for apostasy" (Aleksii 1908: 237).

wide scale. "Will it be much use", he wrote, "if you exile two or three Shtundists and the remainder go on as before? But I think that all existing regimes established by God should defend themselves.... Of course it may be said that even France, moving toward the destruction of its faith and church, still continues to live. But the question is, is this life or only a death agony? Even so, the altars remain and will remain, but the thrones of every dynasty have been overturned. Is it proper for our authorities to go the same way?" (Aleksii 1908: 323).

But even earlier, the Autocracy, in the person of Alexander III, adopted a course of the broadest and most decisive persecution of Baptism. Concerning the report of the Kiev governor on the state of the guberniia in 1881, in which, among other things, mention was made of the growth of Shtundism, Alexander III wrote: "A very serious question. Call to the attention of the Ministry of Internal Affairs and the Over-Procurator of the Holy Synod". But further in the governor's report there followed that supposedly the Shtunda teaches that natural wealth, including the land, is common property, and denies taxes, obligation and obedience to authorities. "Almost socialism", wrote the frightened tsar. At the same time, Pobedonostsev, having shortly before this assumed the post of Over-Procurator of the Synod, forwarded to Alexander III reports by Kiev priests in which they wrote of the connections of the Shtundists with the socialists. "We must certainly direct very serious attention to these sects", Alexander III once again demanded (Aleksii 1908: 279-281).

What, in reality, was the social and political role of Baptism at the stage of its founding and original development in Russia? If we exclude Church sources and turn only to documents of the local administration, it develops that the followers of Shtundism had no connection with socialism and in general were peaceful loyal subjects of the tsar.

In the report of the Elizavetgrad district police officer to the governor of Kherson dated July 13, 1883, we read; "Judging by the way of life of the Shtundists of Elisavetgrad Uezd, we must suppose that they have not yet been permeated by a spirit of socialism, for property equality does not exist among them, and the farm of each individual person is recognized as his own property, and no one without the agreement of the owner has the right to use alien property as he sees fit" (Aleksii 1908: 291).

An even more definite description of the mode of thought and behavior of the Shtundists is contained in the report of the Odessa district police officer dated May 14, 1883: "Observations and inquiries conducted among clergy and other persons living in places settled by Shtundists and also of the local village authorities did not reveal that ideas of socialism have appeared among the Shtundists. While recognizing themselves as equal and spiritual brothers to all, they scrupulously and submissively carry out all orders and decrees both of all governmental officials and organizations and of local police and village authorities; they fulfill conscientiously and carefully all public obligations: like others, they go on inspections, accompany those arrested, fulfill the sewer and apartment obligations; and there are even many Shtundists elected by communities to the post of rural starosta, and civilian police deputies" (Aleksii 1908: 287).

Descriptions of the frame of mind and social behavior of the Baptists, contained in these official sources, are confirmed by those descriptions which the Baptists themselves gave. Baptists in the village of Ingul, Kherson Uezd, appealed on February 16, 1886 to the governor with a request to preserve their right to gather in the house of prayer which had been forbidden them by the local police authorities. In their request they wrote: "... on every holiday we gather in the house of prayer to pray to the Most High for the prosperity of our father and patron, the great monarch Alexander III ..." (Aleksii 1908: 335). At the end of the appeal, they declared: "The Baptists do not belong to the category of those sects which are persecuted by the government; we are believers in Christ the Savior, like the Russian Orthodox, also loyal to our monarch like the Russian Orthodox, and do not belong to any evil corporations; we fulfill the obligations put on us by the state and society, work with sweat on our brow for a piece of bread, live quietly and peacefully, and praise God in a Christian ritual" (Aleksii 1908: 336).

The request which we cite is characteristic not only as an example of the Baptists' expressions of loyalist feelings. It is especially interesting for the idea expressed in it that the Baptists because of their world-view are truer and more useful subjects of the tsar than the Russian Orthodox. The Baptists pointed to themselves as more *solvent* subjects of the state than the Russian Orthodox peasants: "The Russian Orthodox drink up in taverns the coin gained by the sweat of their brows, become unable to pay state and community obligations, and are finally beggared. We however do not slop around in taverns, and with the coin from our labor, after first obeying Holy Scripture's command to 'give to Caesar that which is Caesar's', we satisfy state obligations and then concern ourselves about our needs" (Aleksii 1908: 335-336). Further the Baptists wrote of the many mendicant and indigent Russian Orthodox peasants, contrasting them to themselves, who did not have "paupers and idlers". They stated that the courts were filled with cases of crimes against property by Russian Orthodox peasants, while the Baptist congregations themselves see to "the morality of our brothers", and the "unrepentant" are expelled from their midst. Finally they maintained that the conversion of Russian Orthodox to their church transforms a man in the sense that he becomes a solvent, useful, and faithful servant of the state: "If then a right-thinking Russian Orthodox voluntarily unites with our brothers, even if he has been an immoral person, he can only reform, and having returned to the lap of the real truth and love of mankind, he will be a good family man, a useful member of society, a worthy son of the fatherland, and loyal to the throne" (Aleksii 1908: 337). We can hardly doubt that the appeal of the Baptists in the village of Ingul was written by their leader. This is shown by the content, style, and language of the appeal. It was signed by one Luka Diskant, who, "because of the illiteracy" of the 18 remaining Baptists in the village of Ingul, signed their names with his hand (Aleksii 1908: 337). Did these illiterate people think as Luka Diskant did? It is doubtful.

When we speak of the loyalism of the Baptists, and of their negative attitude toward social struggle, we have in mind the result of the influence of the religious ideology of Baptism on its ordinary adherents. But however great this influence was on the ordinary mass of Baptists, it could not stifle the contradictions between the lower and the ruling classes.

Let us turn now to the earliest evidence we have. This is a memorandum submitted in 1867 to the governor-general of Novorossiisk by the Kherson landowner Znachko-Iavorskii, and devoted to a sketch of the history and causes of Shtundism, about which Znachko-Iavorskii wrote as a first-hand observer. The landowner was afraid of the Shtunda, strove for its extirpation, and was inclined to a realistic expression of the conditions facilitating its appearance and dissemination. He wrote: "... the Shtundists acquire a mass of followers both among Christians who consider 5.5 des. too little, and among the Germans, who, having gotten wealthy and multiplied, are not satisfied with 60 des. per family given to them when they settled in Russia. Both the former and the latter have the thought in the back of their heads that if land belonging to the state and to the landlord becomes part of the general distribution, they will get a little more" (Aleksii 1908: 63).

Znachko-Iavorskii thought that distribution of land was communism, and the teaching of the Shtundists, the attractive idea of the distribution of the land, was nothing more nor less than ... communistic. "Communism is the bait with which Shtundists catch neophytes", Znachko-Iavorskii wrote. "Here are a number of conclusions by which the Shtundists explain communism. Jesus Christ, they say, suffered for the entire human race, and consequently his love for all is equal; if Christ's love for all persons is the same, then the goods of this world should be divided up among all living people" (*ibid.*). The latter, it is clear, was what the landowner feared most of all.

We do not have to speak of the untenability of Znachko-Iavorskii's characterization of the teachings of Shtundism. Shtundism was not an ideology of struggle of the peasant, robbed by the Reform, for the distribution of estate and government lands. It was the ideology of those who despaired of success in the struggle against landowners, and was a means of religious self-deception. But contrary to everything that Baptism taught, there lived in the minds of its ordinary followers, distantly but still ineradicably, the hope for a better earthly life, and whether they admitted to themselves or not, this hope was dearer to them than heavenly Canaan.

But while the upper strata of Shtundism held power in their hands, the landowner Znachko-Iavorskii could moderate his fear for the fate of his estate. Not without some penetration, he noted the idea of fatalism in the doctrine which he qualified as communistic, and duly evaluated the reactionary influence of fatalism on the consciousness of ordinary believers. "It is much more difficult", he wrote "to explain the fatalistic direction which has also developed in significant degree in this sect.... It seems to me that the reason why fatalism is maintained in the Shtundist sect is that the chief leaders, knowing that on the basis of communistic principles, Russians with their expansive natures are capable of starting various disorders and the whole thing may be discovered earlier than they desire, have deliberately brought in fatalism here: 'You', they say, 'do your usual business, and this important matter (the division of the land) will be done by itself; what is to happen cannot be avoided.' In general, in my view", Znachko-Iavorskii concluded, summing up his life experiences, "the Shtundist sect has more political and economic than religious significance" (Aleksii 1908: 63-64).

Thus, even in the period of establishment of Baptism, internal contradictions and opposition of the basic interests of the lower and upper strata are marked in it, which did not escape the notice of a bystander, even if he had his own interests, as, for example, Znachko-Iavorskii did.

2. Social Contradictions in Early Baptism

Even in the first decade of the existence of Baptism in Russia, the communities were led by representatives of the rural bourgeoisie, who did not let their positions as presbyters, preachers and deacons hinder them in any way from being traders and usurers, and from resorting to various means of exploiting dependent labor. These were typical representatives of the kulak and wealthy parts of the peasantry, of whom Lenin wrote: "Free money, received in the form of pure income by this peasant group, was turned either to trading and usury operations, so exorbitantly developed in our countryside, or under the right conditions — invested in purchase of land, improving the economy, etc." (*Lenin*: III, 169).[H]

In the 1870s, one of the questions which most agitated the Baptist community was the widespread practice of usury among them. In 1879 a case involving an accusation of large-scale usurious operations against N. I. Voronin became very well-known in Baptist circles (and even led to a temporary division among them). This case was brought by the then leader of the Tiflis Baptist congregation, V. G. Pavlov, and it is indicative for a description of the morals of the Baptist leaders and especially for the profound influence of money-lending, trading, and entrepreneurial capital on the relationships developing in the congregation.

V. G. Pavlov came to Baptism under the influence of N. I. Voronin, for whom he worked as a steward. Having distinguished himself in Baptist circles for energy and theological literacy, Pavlov on his return from Germany in 1876, became a preacher in the Tiflis congregation, being prompted to assume leadership both by a special opinion developing in him on the paths and forms of Baptism and by a love of power. The implementation of Pavlov's plan was hindered by other claimants to the role of leaders of Baptism — first N. I. Voronin, then D. I. Mazaev. To the capital and authority of an elder, which Voronin possessed, Pavlov counterposed his popularity as an erudite and eloquent preacher, and his skill in intrigue, as a result of which he won a victory over his competitor, even if an incomplete one.

In December 1879, Pavlov, at a meeting of the Tiflis Baptist congregation, accused Voronin of usury and hypocrisy. In Pavlov's words, Voronin "against his own conviction, which he had forcefully maintained at previous conferences here and openly declared to all — that no one should be charged any interest whatever — had become a shareholder in a money-lending company under the name of the Kasumov & Co. Trading House, which was occupied mainly with making loans at high rates of interest, in which company he invested 1,000 rubles, and sits on the loan committee, so that before making a loan to anybody at interest, they ask his opinion" (Val'kevich 1900: Appendix I, p. 40).

From Pavlov's report we see that the question of usury had been raised earlier among the Baptists, and that usury as such was condemned. This does not mean that other forms of using monetary capital called forth vocal condemnation in Baptism — quite the contrary, as Voronin demonstrated, declaring in his defense that "he did not know the aims of this company, that he had invested money there not to receive interest but to receive profit from trading operations which this trading house intended to undertake" (Val'kevich 1900: Appendix 1, 41).

The attitude toward money-lending dependence led to clear conflicts in the Baptist milieu. This found direct confirmation in Pavlov's words on the Voronin affair: "... Voronin had upset other brothers, maintaining that to take any interest at all from anyone at all was sinful, on account of which no little bitterness occurred among the brothers ..." (*ibid.*).[10]

---

[10] Pavlov achieved Voronin's excommunication, but Voronin gathered his co-thinkers and formed a second Baptist congregation. He had supporters in the Vladikavkaz and several other congregations, and as a result, Pavlov, under pressure from Vornin's adherents, was forced to review the decision of his congregation and reinstate Voronin. However, after the scandalous affair connected with Voronin's participation in the Kasumov Trading Company, his authority was shaken. Less successful for Pavlov was his struggle with D. I. Mazaev, whose millions did their work and paved his way to the post of leader of the Union of Russian Baptists.

No public condemnation or prohibition could remove the practice of money-lending from the Baptist milieu, as was shown by the special ruling on "interest" by a conference of Baptists in Novo-Vasil'evka five years after the Voronin affair: "The conference decided: any member of our church who gives money to a poor person must not charge interest in any case; whoever gives someone money for trade or other investment should not charge more than six percent" (Aleksii 1908: 582)

The Baptist congregations kept control of the economic activity of their members. For instance, not long before the Voronin affair, the Tiflis congregation reviewed the case of the Baptist Treskovskii, who had previously been excluded as an insolvent debtor ("for lying and making debts frivolously") (Val'kevich 1900: Appendix 1, p. 40). The congregation stood guard over the interests of "sacred private property" and punished "crimes" against it with the highest measure of punishment which is possessed—excommunication. Treskovskii was enmeshed in debts and explained that "he had long ago recognized his crime", but "was in such a situation that he could not pay the debts", He was reinstated in the congregation with the proviso "that he begin to pay his debts", and the congregation was to "ask him whom he owed, and to list all his debts" (*ibid.*).

Thus, the congregation mobilized means of religious and moral influence on its members in order to guarantee a course of economic activity making it possible to insure its bourgeois elements against losses. The matter was not limited, as we saw, to the use of religious and moral means of influence. The congregations (of course not all to the same degree) were economic organizations placed at the service of the bourgeois upper strata. A special economic institution, created around the 1880s-1890s in the Tiflis Baptist congregation and bearing the title of "Church-Economic Council," was particularly characteristic in this regard. In the charter of the Council of the Tiflis Baptist congregation we read (point 8):

"On the Council is laid the obligation to look after all the members of the congregation in their economic life.

"Note: not entering into small everyday affairs, but only to look after certain enterprises of the members—only those under the jurisdiction of the Council, as when, for example, a certain member of the congregation undertakes an unsuitable enterprise which he has neither the wit not the position nor the capital to carry out, as a consequence of which he may suffer a loss or be completely ruined ..." (Val'kevich 1900: Appendix 1, pp. 65-66).

Having assumed the right to control over the economic affairs of the members of the congregation—and wide rights, inasmuch as they included fundamental recommendations on economic policy—the Church-Economic Council, as deputy for the congregation, took upon itself both consultative and material-financial obligations. The latter came down to monetary subsidies to those members of the congregation who, acting in accordance with the will of the Council, suffered losses in their trade and entrepreneurial affairs.

I cannot help being interested in the question in whose class interests the Church-Economic Council of the Tiflis Baptists existed and acted, but no less interesting is the general picture which emerges from all the documentation adduced. The Treskovskii and Voronin cases, the rulings devoted to money-lending capital, the institution of the Church-Economic Council in the Tiflis Baptist congregation—all this transports us into a world of "heartless cash", into the world of competition.

The economic organization functioning in the Tiflis congregation was a kind of attempt by bourgeois elements to bend in their direction the stubborn lever of economic success, using for this purpose the peculiarities of the Baptist church stucture. The Church-Economic Council, as its charter unambiguously indicates, sanctioned the entrepreneurial activity of those of its elements who had "intelligence, position and capital" on their side. But to sanction, as the charter makes clear, meant to finance the property-owner in a case where his enterprise was threatened by lack of profit or bankruptcy. In other words, the congregation acted in the role of an organ which with its funds insured the entrepreneur against a chance disaster on the market. However, the economic "governor" thought up by the bourgeois upper strata of Baptism—"the rich brothers"—inevitably had to act as a force which did not ameliorate, but on the contrary, made the contradictions more acute, and as a weapon used by some rich brothers against others, and by them jointly to put pressure on ordinary Baptists.

The establishment of Baptism as a church with a powerful hierarchy at its head, with the suppression of rights and initiative of ordinary believers, and with economic dependence of the lower strata on the upper, called forth protest which took on an ideological shape.

The indignation of the lower classes was directed against the power of the leaders and all external forms of organization of Baptism, its ritual, and everything that characterized it not as a movement based on the equality and independence of its participants, but as an organization maintained by external church discipline. Questions raised at a number of conferences of Baptists—on allowing communion with believers close to Baptists—seem to have purely dogmatic significance, whereas in reality the question was whether ritual had a primary or secondary significance in Baptism.

Likewise, the question of the limits of the power of the presbyter in the congregations, which was reviewed in Novo-Vasil'evka, was a question of what their internal structure should be—hierocratic or democratic. Persons with differing research interests making observations among the Baptists noted even in the second half of the 1870s the separation of the upper strata of Baptism from the lower.

When A. D. Ushinskii arrived in Tarashcha Uezd in 1881 for conversations with Shtundists, they summoned their leaders, who at that time were settled in Kherson Guberniia—Gerasim Balaban, Pavel Tsibul'skii and Semen Velichuk. "However", Ushinskii writes, "in conversing with these three former preceptors of theirs, I did not note in them either that energy which distinguished their followers or that knowledge of Scripture which is so remarkable among their present presbyters. It seemed to me that these once zealous leaders of the sect, having become rich and, as they say, grown fat in prosperity, have lost their energy and ceased to concern themselves with Holy Scripture" (Ushinskii 1884: 29).

Emel'ianov, having chosen as the subject of his study "rationalism in the south of Russia", and having visited in the latter half of the 1870s the sites of rationalism in the Ukraine, very definitely testifies both to the split between the upper and lower strata of Shtundism and to the internal struggle which was beginning in it. He came to the conclusion: "Almost all the first teachers of the Little Russian [Ukrainian] Shtunda, fearing lest the rejection of Russian Orthodox rituals go too far and touch the rituals of the Shtunda itself, attempted to put a seal of silence on the mouths of their followers relative to the chief points of the Shtunda, in order that during the meetings no one spoke a word against 'the breaking of bread, water baptism and the elder brother' ..." (Emel'ianov 1878: 225).

The ideological protest of the lower classes, as is clear from Emel'ianov's observation, was directed against the hierarchy and ritual in Baptism.

In order to describe the mood which was increasingly taking hold of the ordinary mass of Baptists, let us cite a letter dating from the latter half of the 1870s, which was a platform of opposition by the lower strata to the upper:

"I report to you, brothers, about the affairs of an elder brother ... he took money from the treasury for the needy and bought with it a cup and cloth for the table.[1] This custom is stolen from the Russian Orthodox Church, and they say to us that we should accept it as holy. But this is an idol and it should not be so! I also will tell you of the water baptism.... All this is only a snare and the elder brother wants to tie us up in it. He has already put a heavy burden on us—two rubles from a brother per year and one from a sister for his travels among the brothers. But in the Gospels it is said, do not take with you money or unnecessary clothes when you go to preach the word of God. That's a Christian brother for you, and an elder one too! And water baptism helped him. One yoke isn't enough, so he places another on us. Should there be princes and priests among us, as among the pagans, when Christ himself said that among you it will not be so ... but our false brother ... calling himself God's creature, attempts to rule over the same sort of creatures as he himself is, and attempts to draw weaker persons into the sins of idolatry and by this to kill not only their bodies, but also their souls ..." (Emel'ianov 1878: 212-213).

It is difficult to say whom the unknown author of this accusatory letter had in mind—perhaps Mikhail Ratushnyi. In any case in his protest he comes to a profound generalization: "One yoke isn't enough for him so he lays another on us."

In the eyes of the ordinary believers, representatives of the peasant poor who had gone over to Baptism, the new teaching and the new church were like "a new yoke", like a twin to the Russian Orthodox Church, even if unrecognized. The author of the letter was able to look at the root of things, when in the following manner he unmasked his elder brother: "Several years ago he had only one horse, and now he already has twenty of them: he wears new clothes and a good hat, has two watches, buys tobacco and smokes, puts his hands in his pockets, and walks through the bazaar with a cigarette in his lips, as if he were a real idol, for heaven's sake! This is how the treasury helped him, the cup and the water baptism—these three ropes on the whole world. He intends to come to you to perform the marriage cermony, but when he comes, read him my letter before the entire congregation. I have already read him a lecture before witnesses, saying that he's not doing a good thing, but he scolded me with unseemly words, so that I will hand him over to the church, and you too, wherever you can, let the churches know of the crimes of the elder brother.... I will soon be among you and bring you a living letter—the living word—and I will fight with the beasts" (Emel'ianov 1878: 213).

The author of the letter entered into battle with "the beasts", and the appeal to join him in his struggle was heeded. In the second half of the 1870s among the Baptists of Kiev Guberniia—earlier in other places—a schism occurred in Tarashcha Uezd and a sect emerged whose head was the shepherd Iakov Koval' (was he not the author of the letter?). And precisely as happened in the 1880s in Dukhoborism, the leaders called for the government's help to suppress their rebellious brothers. According to Emel'ianov: "Mikhailo Ratushnyi and Vasilii Komarov (a Baptist leader who subsequently returned to Russian Orthodoxy—A. K.) resorted even to accusations against the new brothers who supposedly preached 'policy', i.e.", Emel'ianov adds, "rose up against the kulak behavior of the elder brother" (Emel'ianov 1878: 225).

The sect headed by Koval' and derived not from Russian Orthodoxy but from the Baptist church, had its original site in the village of Chaplinka, Tarashcha Uezd, but very soon its followers appeared in all the uezds of Kiev Guberniia where there were Baptist groups. In 1881 A. D. Ushinskii counted more than 1,000 of Koval''s adherents, which was approximately two thirds of the total number of Baptists present at that time in Kiev Guberniia (Ushinskii 1884: 25-27). Koval's sect rejected the hierarchical structure and ritual present in Baptism and placed at the head of its teaching the concept of the Holy Spirit as the invisible leader of believers, which communicated directly with them and used their mouths to announce its will. Both Ushinskii and

Dorodnitsyn, who wrote after him, equate Koval''s teaching with Molokanism.

Koval''s teaching has features common to all the teachings of religious tendencies of Russian pre-Reform sectarianism, but is most of all reminiscent of Khristovoverie, beginning precisely with the fact that it counterposed to state Russian Orthodoxy the concept of the spirit descending on the believer and the believer immediately communicating with the spirit. I wish to note the primary position which the third person of the Christian trinity—the Holy Spirit—attained in the sect headed by Koval'. The fact is that successive sectarian groups arising out of Baptism, including the so-called Christians of Evangelical Faith—the Pentecostals (and, by the way, some of Koval''s followers called themeselves "evangelical Christians")—went in their teaching in the same direction and gave the Holy Spirit priority over the Father and the Son.

The teaching of the spirit allowed Koval''s followers to contrast the church as an institution to the church as a gathering of believers. "We believe", Koval' wrote in his statement of faith, "that our Savior has one church, which is ruled by the Holy Spirit, but invisibly" (Ushinskii 1886: 188).

This teaching allowed the rejection of the church hierarchy, ritual and ceremonial: "We believe that the church is composed of believing members, precisely those gathered in the name of our Lord Jesus Christ. When we gather in the meeting, all the believers come together face to face, according to the teaching of the teacher, the Apostle Paul, who says: '... well, brothers! When you come together, and each of you has a psalm, or a lesson, or an utterance in tongues, or a revelation, or an interpretation, let all this be for edification. Thus, we are not conducting ... religious ceremonies" (Ushinskii 1886: 184).

Koval''s teaching left no room for the concept of the power of Divine Providence. "We wish", Koval' wrote, "to be filled with the fullness of God, since we believe that ineffable grace was granted to every believer ..." (Ushinskii 1886: 186). Thus the teaching of pre-Reform sects about man as a temple of God and as the bearer of spiritual wisdom was reinstated.

Koval''s movement in general had a local character and over the course of the 1880s died out. This occurred partly as the result of Church-police repression, to which its participants were subject, and partly because of disillusionment with the leader of the movement himself, who had besmirched himself by an improper act (he embezzled public funds), but chiefly because the ideas proclaimed by Koval' leading back to the ancient forms of religious protest, could not unite in any stable or long-term way the peasant poor, who in their indignation against Russian Orthodoxy and Baptism gave vent to hatred of landlords and rural rich people. Koval''s teaching yielded no slogans besides religious ones.

Meanwhile, at the end of the 1880s and once again in Tarashcha Uezd of Kiev Guberniia, there arose a new movement among the Baptists headed by the cooper from the village of Tarashcha, Kondratii Malëvannyi, who had been converted to Baptism from Russian Orthodoxy in 1884. This time the movement was not so local and short-term and, apparently, attracted Koval''s former adherents.

Malëvannyi's teaching absorbed the basic idea of his predecessor Koval' — the priority of the Holy Spirit — but Malëvannyi did not stop at that. On the one hand, he took the path of mystically deepening the teaching of the Holy Spirit, and on the other gave his preaching a social-accusatory coloring.

V. I. Iasevich-Borodaevskaia, who visited Tarashcha and other uezds of Kiev Guberniia when Malëvannyi's movement was still quite new, left verbatim transcripts of her conversations with Malëvannyi's followers, from which it is clear that they equated Orthodoxy and Baptism: "This is a yoke, and that is a yoke, for the Russian Orthodox faith is an old faith, which our grandfathers and great-grandfathers bore, suffering a yoke, and among them (the Baptists) there are authorities in front of them who will not let their people go back (hold them strictly)" (Iasevich-Borodaevskaia 1912: 146).

One must respect the depth of Iasevich-Borodaevskaia's unknown informant's thought. He not only characterized Baptism in the best possible way, by calling it a yoke, but with exceptional accuracy and eloquence showed the peculiar nature of Baptism as a new yoke replacing the yoke of Russian Orthodoxy suffered for long generations by grandfathers and great-grandfathers. That "there are authorities in front of them", including authorities in vestments embroidered with crosses, was nothing new for the unfree peasant; what was new was the situation in which "in front are the authorities who do not let their own people go back".

In Iasevich-Borodaevskaia's words, the Malëvannite movement grew out of Baptism "by gradually throwing off the oppressive yoke of hierarchical formulas, rituals and frequent regimented meetings" (Iasevich-Borodaevskaia 1912: 129). Malëvannyi's dispute with the leaders of the congregation to which he belonged apparently began with his criticism of the ecclesiastical nature of Baptism, as a result of which in 1890 he left the congregation with a small group of co-thinkers.

From the testimony of one of the women followers of Malëvannyi relating to 1891, matters stood thus: "... the Baptists began to hate him and even wished Malëvannyi to be excommunicated from the church, because he accused them of improper actions, and then the martyr Malëvannyi explained to the church that whoever wished, brothers and sisters, should come with him ...'; another four families agreed to this proposition, and things went on like this for five or six months; they praised the Lord separately from the Baptists, and in the month of October 1890, God gave the martyr Kondratii a sign to spend time in fasting and prayer" (Biriukov, ed. 1905: 8; *see also* Zhikarev 1909: 3).

As a religious leader, Malëvannyi could not counterpose to Baptism anything but a faith in revelation, in direct communication of man with God, which needed neither intermediaries nor ritual and ceremonial, nor dogma and prayer formulas. More than this, he shook the authority of the Old and New Testaments in the minds of his followers.

His contemporary and follower, whose name we have not been able to learn, maintained that, besides the prophet Elijah, there existed not a single one of those prophets who are falsely considered the authors of the corresponding book of the Old Testament. As concerns the New Testament the situation with it is the same as with the Old: "... there were no apostles or evangelists" (ROBIL, Chertkov Collection: Poslanie Neizvestnogo [The Epistle of an Unknown], typescript, p. 8). At the center of Malëvannyi's teaching was the concept of the spirit dwelling in the believers. He appealed to his followers in an epistle dated February 18, 1900: "... believe that the spirit of God lives in you as a supreme authority and reason not of this earth, but heavenly, which is given to each of you according to his measure, as is pleasing to his will, in order that everything should be divine and not human, for everything human is finished and Christ's kingdom is beginning ..." (ROBIL, Chertkov Collection: Poslanie Malëvannogo iz Kazani 18 Fevralia 1900 g. [Malëvannyi's Epistle from Kazan', February 18, 1900]; typescript, p. 2).

Malëvannyi's followers called their leader Christ, and his teaching "the true Christian faith", and they wrote that this faith "began to exist in 1892 and that they, the Malëvantsy, are its first heirs" (The Epistle of an Unknown, p. 5). They did not suspect that Malëvannyi's religious preaching in all its basic positions only repeated at the end of the 19th century a doctrine which arose among the Khristovovers not later than the end of the 17th century, and since then was repeatedly revived both in the 18th century (among the Dukhobors) and in the first half of the 19th century (among the Prygun Molokans). Thus, by the time Malëvannyi was active, among the ideas of religious sectarianism the entire store of possible combinations and permutations was already exhausted.

Malëvannyi introduced into his sect a religious practice which in turn repeated that of the Khristovovers. There was fasting, ecstatic dances, jumping, and "speaking in tongues". Malëvannyi's unknown follower, whose text we cited above, describes the first prayer meeting, which took place in Malëvannyi's home, at which Malëvannyi's was declared Christ. Malëvannyi, having been beaten by the police not long before his "epiphany", lay in his bed and spoke so that "it seemed a great river was flowing". The brothers who had been called to Malëvannyi — i.e. Baptists — "were much embarrassed, and thought he had gone crazy, but others knelt and prayed. Then those who were praying also began to speak in other languages and cried, 'Christ has been born!' and they began to wave their arms and jump to the very ceiling. Thus it continued three days" (The Epistle of an Unknown, p. 2).

In 1892, Malëvannyi was arrested and incarcerated on a certificate falsified by state doctors, in an insane asylum in which he spent many years. He continued, overcoming all obstacles, to lead his followers; their number grew, and they were found at the beginning of the 20th century not only in Kiev Guberniia, but here and there beyond its boundaries in Kherson and Minsk Guberniias, and in the city of Nikolaev.[11]

The Social Democrat A. P. Raevskii succeeded in penetrating into the hospital where Malëvannyi was kept. "He said to me", Raevskii wrote, "that people had put him in the hospital without realizing what they had done, and that soon the heavenly kingdom would begin on earth ... when everyone would be equal and there would be then neither enemies nor their victims, neither rich nor poor. He said to me that the end of the world was approaching and that people should prepare themselves for a renewed life when a new order would begin on earth" (Raevskii 1904: 21).

As is clear from Raevskii's reminiscences, which reveal the reprisals of the priests and police against Malëvannyi, the latter revived the old sectarian idea of the imminent triumph on earth of the kingdom of God, together with the mystical doctrines and religious paractice of Khristovoverie.

What would be the kingdom of God on earth? Malëvannyi apparently did not go further than the abstract ideas of equality, justice, etc. His follower, Ivan Lysenko, perhaps not in accordance with the way of thought of Malëvannyi himself, called for a renunciation of private property and even organized in the village of Trubovka a commune which united 80 persons (Putintsev 1935: 456-457).

The religious creativity of sectarians was literally turning over without catching. But there were aspects of Malëvannyi's preaching which testified to glimmerings of political consciousness among sectarians.

The 1880s, as we know, were a time of frequent peasant disturbances, in the Ukraine as in other regions of the country, which went as far as direct armed clashes with the authorities. In letters from his place of incarceration, Malëvannyi appealed to his followers: " ... the world is seduced by earthly passions. The first [people] are [those] given over to the desire to be rich: this is the first beginning of evil; they corrupt themselves with large amounts of money and demand praise from their poor brothers who are enslaved by them.... The Lord calls them rude bandits and robbers of their poor rural and urban brothers.... All these are called ancient bands, bandits who in old times gathered in the thick woods and beat their brothers and took away their

[11] According to data from the Department of Police relating to 1916, the total number of Malëvannyi's followers reached 2,000 persons (Special Section of the Department of Police 1916, s.u. 132, sh. 66 v.).

lives ..." (Biriukov 1905: 18; compare Iasevich-Borodaevskaia 1912: 156 ff.).

From antiquity Malëvannyi proceeded to modern times: "But now they have become cleverer and gather in the capital cities and in the ports, and in the guberniia cities, and even in the villages and hamlets, and they have robbed the whole people and made them beggars and half-dead. All of them are called beasts and monsters; this is kike-ishness; they sold Christ for 30 pieces of silver and Russia for millions" (Biriukov 1905: 18; Iasevich-Borodaevskaia 1912: 156 ff.). What is characteristic in this clearly accusatory document directed against monetary capital, against the rich, is the critique of political and any other instruments of rule—"dishonest judges", "monasteries and churches", "insane asylums", and also "drinking establishments" and "public places", by the help of which the rich corrupt the people, and finally "theaters and circuses", which Malëvannyi in turn added to the means of perverting the minds of the people (Biriukov 1905: 18; Iasevich-Borodaevskaia 1912: 156 ff.).

As Bonch-Bruevich notes, Malëvannyi's followers were connected with the peasants in the village of Pavlovka, Sumi Uezd, Khar'kov Guberniia, who destroyed a Russian Orthodox church on September 16, 1901, and then entered into unequal struggle "with the police, the shop-owners, the meshchane and the rich people of the village" (Bonch-Bruevich 1959: 103).

Malëvannyi's movement had quite a few followers and went beyond the bounds of its original site, but this was still a local, even if comparatively persistent, phenomenon in sectariansim. This recurrence of the ideas of early Khristovoverie had at this time no foundation, and therefore it was an insignificant, although in its way instructive, episode. It is instructive as an example of the opposition of the lower classes which existed in the Baptist movement and was expressed in different forms, but in its major tendency was directed (and this is shown by the example of Malëvannyi's movement) toward a general protest against the power of monetary capital.

The reconciliation of the ordinary working masses of the Baptists with their bourgeois leaders, in a common recognition of divine predestination which ruled over the world, was illusory. The example of Malëvannyi's movement shows what was the only remaining form of religious protest against Baptism, and at the same time shows its profound atavism. In other words, the development of social life and of class struggle pushed the ordinary Baptists to protest, but this protest could triumph only on the grounds of political struggle. Of course, Malëvannyi did not admit this, but in paying tribute to religious and mystical superstitions, and reflecting the peasant hatred of rich people and serf-owners, he made his "spirit" the bastion of threatening social accusations.

In the 1880s, a wave of dissatisfaction with the church administration in Baptism swept over all the places in which it was found. F. Savel'ev from the

Baptist congregation in the village of Chukhur-Iurt, Baku Guberniia, wrote in 1886 to A. M. Mazaev: "We beg you, pray for us to the Lord, that he might spare us from the attacks and divisions; it is apparent that Satan does not cease his attacks from all sides ..." (Val'kevich 1900: Appendix 5, p. 15). In 1889, a certain Filatov reported to A. M. Mazaev on the "sad situation" created in the Baptist congregation in the village of Andreevka, Baku Guberniia: "Satan has fallen on us and with his poisonous blow has cut off from our ranks several members." Apparently Satan's blows about which Filatov wrote already dated back some time, since, turning to current events, Filatov continued: "And now he (Satan—A. K.) has mounted his new attack, and his arrows rain down like hail; the church now suffers a trial by fire" (*ibid.*).

It develops that "Satan" was entrenched in the Baptist congregation in Akush, and in its midst there appeared brothers whom the author of the letter described as "having fallen away from the church and having denied all Baptists" (Val'kevich 1900: Appendix 5, p. 33). In 1888, a certain Krizunov of the Lenkoran Baptist congregation informed Mazaev of the excommunication of "one brother, Stepan Lan'kin" who denied the divinity of the Savior and rejects *Golos very* [The Voice of Faith] (a collection of Baptist hymns—A. K.), and has begun to slander all brothers and sisters" (Val'kevich 1900: Appendix 5, p. 22). From St. Petersburg, the Pashkovite Bezzubov wrote to his adherents in Elizavetpol' Guberniia of events occurring at the end of the 1880s in the local congregation: "... we have had a division within the St. Petersburg church. Now some belong to the same reform as you and Mazaev do" (meaning D. I. Mazaev—A. K.).

What was the "Mazaev reform" which called forth "division within the St. Petersburg church"? Bezzubov writes: "They elected presbyters by all those rules that Mazaev has ... the majority were for the presbyters ... and this Kargel', one of the chief Baptists, introduced our brothers to the rules, and dismissed Christ, the chief pastor.... This is our third year of this division" (Bezzubov's letter was written at the end of 1890—A. K.) (Val'kevich 1900: Appendix 5, p. 38).

Bezzubov did not write to the Elizavetpol' brothers accidentally. Agitation was occurring among them there in connection with the rules introduced by the leaders of the Union of Baptists headed by Mazaev, and Bezzubov encouraged opposition elements: "I hear of your agitation in a spiritual matter and hurry to help you.... Dear brothers, is Christ not enough for you? And it is difficult to be with Him.... Have you forgotten that where there is a decree, there is lawlessness?" He appealed: "Remain firm in the freedom which Christ has given you ..." (Val'kevich 1900: Appendix 5, p. 34).

The views which Bezzubov developed had no mystical tinge and did not contain elements of social accusation, but at individual points they agreed with the views of Koval' and Malëvannyi. In Bezzubov's eyes, Baptism as it was formulated by Mazaev was like a state church, the reverse side of Russian Orthodoxy itself. "Where is it written", he exclaimed, "that members of the body of Christ should seek in addition to belong to another church, which is not Christ's but belongs to the State, and in which there is abomination before the Lord!" (*ibid.*). And again: "Do not subject yourself again to the yoke of slavery; why were you chased out—because you did not wish to submit to injustice (i.e. to the Russian Orthodox Church—A. K.)? And again you have sought to belong to the same injustice, the same yoke, but differently, the same form, only inside out" (*ibid.*).

In the 1880s, in the Baptist congregations of the guberniias of the Caucasus and the Ukraine, instances were noted of the conversion of believers to Adventism, which in its turn attests to their disillusionment with both the doctrine and the hierocratic order of Baptism.

We noted above that in the top stratum of Baptism, consisting of representatives of the bourgeoisie, there were elements of unequal wealth, position and traditions. Here there were represented very large property-owners, of Molokan background and accustomed to exploiting the proletarianized poor, the serf and semi-serf producer, such as for example the Mazaev and Stoialov families, and others; and families less wealthy than those like the Pavlovs, Prokhanovs and the like, who were permeated by the ideas of Western bourgeois democracy; and finally, representatives of the peasant bourgeoisie who were beginning to succeed, like Ratushnyi, Riaboshapka, Rybalka and others, who only yesterday had been indigent or impoverished peasants.

As class contradictions in Baptism deepened and became more apparent, among its leaders there appeared adherents of more liberal rules than those which Mazaev and his group introduced. I. S. Prokhanov and his adherents blocked the path of Mazaev's missionaries, who attempted to place under their influence the followers of the Pashkovite movement, and themselves spoke, not without success, before congregations belonging to the Union of Russian Baptists.

V. G. Pavlov now gained the opportunity not only to confront a possessor of millions with his personal authority and foreign theological training, but to frighten him with the increasing dissatisfaction of the lower strata. Liberal phraseology was characteristic of Pavlov even at the beginning of his activity as a Baptist preacher. Thus, in November 1873, in a letter to V. V. Ivanov, he developed the idea of the need for freedom of opinion in Baptism, including the critical appraisal of the decisions of the organs of church (Baptist) power. "Of course", Pavlov wrote, "in disputed questions you can appeal to the whole church ... but you simply cannot blindly and unconditionally adapt and submit to the decision of the whole church. No! And the decision of the whole church should be tested in the same way as the opinion of one person" (Val'kevich 1900: Appendix 5, p. 7).

At the end of the 1880s and the beginning of the 1890s, Pavlov, adopting the goal of pacifying the lower classes and earning for himself and his co-thinkers leading positions in Baptism, spoke out in criticism of "the rich". For example, he wrote in 1892: "I have a very unfavorable opinion of the Tiflis congregation: with the acceptance of the rich, many have begun to toady to them, and their voices prevail over all others in everything" (Val'kevich 1900: Appendix 5, p. 53). A year before this, Pavlov made analogous complaints to his fellow believer, V. P. Burov, who was at the time in London. Burov's answer to Pavlov was not consoling: among the English Baptists, as among the Russians, the power of the moneybag ruled. Burov answered: "... and really, whereas in Russia, among a relatively young Christanity, faith in brothers who are more or less well-to-do is required, in England this is demanded: the authority of money influences in equal measure the poor in all countries, and high position also carries influence" (Val'kevich 1900: Appendix 5, p. 46).

Pavlov spoke out against the fawning of the rich before the tsarist authorities who were persecuting the Baptists; of course in doing this he did not exceed the bounds of legality and good order. While in exile in Orenburg, he wrote in November 1891 to the Tiflis congregation: "I advise all brothers to make yet another appeal to the Ministry of Internal Affairs, and explain that the local police forbid you to hold public prayer services in spite of the law of May 3, 1883.... If you write the appeal, it is necessary that all members, rich and poor, sign, an not evade or refuse.... Oh, where is the spirit of the first Christian martyrs!" (Val'kevich 1900: Appendix 5, p. 49).

But however much Pavlov condemned the rich, and however much he called for "the spirit of the first Christian martyrs", his position was different in principle from that of Koval', Malëvannyi and even Bezzubov. Pavlov was by no means the spokesman for the thoughts of the socially lower classes of Baptism. He was the champion of the interests of the bourgeois-liberal elements in it.

Bezzubov, in accordance with the circle of his ideas could put the question: "... does God demand that we, in his body (i.e. in the circle of believers — A. K.), make a structure and an order?" And he answered: "Of course not. We cannot rule the body, of which Christ is the head; He builds Himself from us" (Val'kevich 1900: Appendix 5, p. 34). But Baptism would not be Baptism without government, structure, rules — i.e. without church organization by power of a spiritual hierarchy.

If for Koval', for Malëvannyi and for Bezzubov also, the starting point of theology was the New Testament expression: "Where the spirit of the Lord is, there is freedom", then Pavlov refined it thus: "God is a God of order and structure" (Val'kevich 1900: Appendix 5, p. 5), and in this respect was in full agreement with Mazaev. Whereas the New Testament expression cited by Malëvannyi served as the ideological integument for a protest against monetary capital and its ruling institutions, Pavlov's God of order and structure served as a confirmation of capital and as a weapon of its political hegemony. Pavlov declared—and of course Mazaev agreed with him on this—"While we live in this life, we have need of the power of government, which punishes evil-doers and rewards those who do good. But with the coming of Christ there will be no need for any sort of power ... then there will be the end of everything which is in this world; then laws will end, which God has set up in this life.... Then Christ will disband every government" (Val'kevich 1900: Appendix 5, p. 6).

The implementation of worldly justice, to which Malëvannyi, as his medieval predecessors had also done, gave the fantastic form of the building of a kingdom of God on earth, Pavlov firmly put off until ... the second coming.

These were the contradictions and the ideological forms corresponding to them which characterized the complicated picture of the relationships between the lower and the upper classes in Baptism, and the group disagreements in the Baptist upper strata. This picture became more complicated in the late 1880s and early 1890s, which were marked by the beginning of the proletarian stage in the Russian liberation movement. Under the circumstances of the maturing revolutionary crisis in Russia at the beginning of the 20th century, the role of Baptism as an active instrument of bourgeois repression became quite evident.

3. The Spread of Baptism at the Beginning of the 20th Century. Evangelical Christianity

According to the Ministry of Internal Affairs, by 1916 there were 114,652 Baptists in Russia, including 47,864 converts from "non-Orthodox" faiths (TsGIAL, div. 821, f 133, u. 23, sh. 6).

The statistics for 1916 repeat the data published by the Ministry of Internal Affairs in 1912, reflecting the number of adherents of Baptism as of January 1, 1912 (Statistical 1912).

In what measure do these statistics for January 1, 1912, correspond to reality? In 1910 one of the leading figures of Baptism in Russia, V. Fetler, published statistical information about this sect (Fetler 1910). Fetler's statistics were incomplete. One hundred and forty-nine Russian congregations and 147 of German, Latvian and Estonian Baptists were included—296 congregations in total—but the number of Russian Baptist congregations at that time was significantly greater, as Fetler himself in his publication warned.

We do not know the total number of Baptist congregations in Russia as of 1912. According to the statistics of the Ministry of Internal Affairs, there were, by 1912, 89 congregations with 14,926 members; besides, mention is made of 99,726 Baptists united in congregations not officially registered. If we conditionally assume that registered and unregistered congregations had on an average similar numerical strength, then proceeding from the data adduced, there were in Russia 590 unregistered congregations, a total of 679. In the Baptist journal *Gost'* [The Guest], managed by V. Fetler, V. Gedeonov reported that in Russia "according to the latest data there are 839 Baptist congregations ..." (Gedeonov 1914: 271).

If we turn to Fetler's statistics which list as of January 1, 1910, 147 Russian Baptist congregations with 10,935 members (including children, 19,507 persons), and 149 German, Latvian and Estonian—with 26,126 members (in total in these latter "the number of persons considered Baptists", Fetler writes, "is 49,690"), it should be noted that the gap in Fetler's statistics is precisely in the Russian Baptist communities. In V. Pavlov's article, published in 1911 in the journal *Baptist*, we read: "About the number of members in Russia, we have exact information only about the German Baptists, who number more than 25,000" (V. P. 1911: 370). As we see, Pavlov confirms Fetler's data on the number of German Baptists.

What is the relationship of the data contained in the Baptist sources which describe the number of Baptists to the data reported by the Ministry of Internal Affairs? This latter source named 47,864 Baptists who had converted to this sect from other faiths, according to which "the number of souls considered Baptists" (Germans, Latvians, Estonians) was equal to 49,690 persons. From the fact that Fetler did not have exact statistical data on the Russian Baptists, it does not follow that he did not have an approximate idea of them. As *Russkoe slovo* [Russian Word] reported in July 1913, Fetler in conversation with the director of the Department of Spiritual Affairs, Menkin, "declared that at the present time there are a little less than 100,000 Baptists ..." (*Russkoe slovo* 1913, No. 171).

The prominent Baptist figure, Stepanov, speaking at the European Congress of Baptists in Stockholm, asserted that in Russia there were 100,000 members of Baptist congregations (*B* 1913, No. 7, p. 87). This apparently does not contradict the data given at the end of 1914 by Gedeonov, who reported that the total number of "parishioners" in Baptist congregations approached 200,000 (Gedeonov 1914: 271). The number of "parishioners" naturally exceeded the number of members of Baptist congregations, since to "parishioners" could be added so-called attenders, who had "turned" but were not yet "christened in the faith", and finally some people who visited Baptist prayer-meetings with some regularity.

We now come to the conclusion that the statistical data of the Ministry of Internal Affairs, according to which in Russia at the beginning of 1912 there were about 67,000 Baptist of Russian nationality and about 48,000 Baptists of non-Russian nationality (in total about 115,000 persons), give an approximate idea of the real number of Baptists in Russia.

The notation in the statistics of the Ministry of Internal Affairs that for 1905-1911 the additions to the ranks of Baptism amounted to 25,000 persons, deserves special attention. In other words, 23% of the total make-up of Baptism over the course of half a century entered this sect during the short period of time from 1905 to 1911 (Statistical 1912).

In 1911, V. V. Ivanov wrote: "In Russia this large movement of Baptists began with 1905, when God granted us religious freedom. Before this time we Baptists were suppressed. With 1905 there began an era in the history of Baptism which we can call the era of open storm. Under the influence of Baptist attacks in many places there occurred significant changes" (Ivanov 1911: 69). Whom did the Baptists "storm"? As at the beginning of their history, they stormed the old Russian sects, primarily the Molokans and also the Russian Orthodox.

After the first flow of "converts", more significant than in the time preceding 1905 (for 1905-1907 the transfer to Baptism was made, according to data from the Ministry of Internal Affairs, by about 8,500 persons), the leading organs of the Baptist church established (in the summer of 1907) a special Baptist missionary society with a staff of traveling missionaries and an independent budget. Along with the centralized missionary organization, missionary activity was undertaken on a large scale by local Baptist organizations.

In order to give an idea of the activity of missionaries, let us cite the yearly reports of the missionaries I. Savel'ev and M. Iashchenko, who for 1907-908 (the reporting year) traversed 12,801 versts by railway, 2,479 versts by water, 1,744 versts on horseback, and gave 410 sermons (Baptist Missionary 1909: 5, 11). The local missionaries were in their turn very active. One of them, having set out on a missionary trip on December 18, 1911, reported that by February 12, 1912, he had visited 15 villages and baptized "247 souls from among the Molokans and the Russian Orthodox" (*B* 1912, No. 5, p. 29). Another missionary wrote: "In Siberia the joyful Gospel news was disseminated successfully ... now beginning from Omsk to Vladivostok, in every city and every station there are brothers" (*B* 1911, No. 3). A single Baptist congregation in Astrakhanka (Tavriia Guberniia) between 1909 and the beginning of 1914 "turned" to Baptism 729 Russian Orthodox (*B* 1914, No. 7-8, p. 23).

The funds for the mission were accumulated mainly from the donations of local congregations. The central organs and local congregations of the Baptist church possessed large sums of money, parts of which were also spent on the mission. Thus, in 147 congregations of German, Latvian and Estonian Baptists, the sum of all contributions was in 1909, 128,074 rubles (Fetler 1912).

The training of qualified missionary personnel for Baptism was conducted in the Baptist seminary in Hamburg, which 42 students from Russia finished before 1911, and also in the Berlin Bible school and the Hausdorf seminary (TsGIAL, div. 821, f. 133, d. 196, sh. 27). The immediate aim of the mission was to attract the population to the Baptist church and to polemicize with representatives of non-Baptist faiths. However, the Baptist missionaries in practice also combatted revolutionaries and atheists. For instance, from the report of the missionary Savel'ev we learn that on the Ostrovskoe khutor he "had a conversation with atheists", whom he supposedly "reduced to silence" (Baptist Missionary 1909: 5). The missionary Iashchenko reported that during his visit to Alupka he "had occasion to battle with the revolutionaries" (Baptist Missionary 1909: 10).

Baptist propaganda was furthered by the publication of a mass literature and journals (*Baptist, Slovo istiny* [Word of Truth] and *Gost'*).

Thus, in the course of 1910 alone 104,000 copies of the journal *Baptist* were issued (*B* 1910, No. 52, p. 1). According to the editor of the Baptist journal *Gost'*, each number had about 20,000 readers (*G* 1914, No. 5, p. 91).

The rapid and significant growth of the number of followers of Baptism occurring from 1905-1906 in significant degree was connected with the legalization of the Baptist church, achieved as a result of religious "freedoms", the organization of its missionary affairs, secured with personnel and funds, and an energetically pursued and supported and relatively wide press propaganda.

However, the matter is not only and not so much this. The beginning of the 20th century was marked by an industrial crisis, especially acute in 1902-1903, and replaced by a depression which lasted until 1907. From 1901 to 1903 as many as 3,000 factory enterprises were closed, and the number of workers from 1901 to 1903 declined by more than 150,000 persons. The standard of living of the population declined sharply under the influence of the crisis, not only in the industrial centers but in the countryside, ruined by the landlord and the kulak, and experiencing severe crop failures in 1901 and 1907. The calamities of unemployment and crop failure, poverty and hunger, were added to the calamities experienced by the people during the Russo-Japanese War. Lenin wrote of the feelings of "horror and despair" arising from the war: "The churches are once again filled with the people—the reactionaries exclaim. 'Where there is suffering, there you have religion', the arch-reactionary Barrés says. And he is right" (*Lenin*: XXI, 251).

Another reactionary was also right, the Estland baron and Baptist Vol'demar Ikskul', who wrote in 1907: "I see the preparatory wisdom of God in the difficulties experienced now by Russia. Infantile freedom is always born with blood-letting. The change is too great, the contrasts are too immeasurable for this to happen without struggle and blood-letting, but pacification is beginning. Many families are lamenting the loss of a loved member of their circle, killed in the war or in revolutionary uprisings. Many factories have collapsed because they could not satisfy the demands of the workers. Many workers remain without food for themselves and their families. All these people need help and comfort, and who can comfort them like Jesus? They are prepared for news of Him. The hand of the Lord uses calamity as a strong plow for breaking up the soil of the heart to accept the divine seed" (*B* 1907, No. 2, pp 8-9).

Whatever the Baptist figures said about the preparatory wisdom of the Lord, on their own terms they understood that the roots of religion are social, and had already calculated what spiritual interest they would receive from war, unemployment and famine. The victims of exploitation by capitalists and landlords turned to Baptism. Petty-bourgeois elements, frightened by revolution, also turned to it. A. F. Shirobokii from Michurinsk, who entered Baptism in 1907, remembers the revolutionary years 1905-1907 thus: "Each was busy in his own way. Some became revolutionaries but I joined the Baptists" (Bograd 1961: 114). A certain "Brother Timofei" from Enesei Guberniia wrote in the journal *Gost'* of his turn to Baptism: "I turned to the Lord in February 1908. A former Social Democrat, like other artisans, seeking the truth only among others and for others, I by this tormented both others and myself ..." (*G* 1911, No. 5, p. 78).

An idea of I. A. Malakhova's seems to me deserving of attention: she notes that in Tambov Guberniia "the basis of the growth of sectarianism at this time was the 'moderate' and 'reliable' opposition to tsarism and the Church, corresponding to the policies and interests of the bourgeois elements which at that time led the majority of sectarian congregtions in Tambov Guberniia. For these elements the ideology of Baptism served as one of the forms of social self-awareness" (Malakhova 1961: 82). In fact, during the time under review, changes were taking place in the social base of Baptism, which now carried its summons to those strata of the peasantry which were involved in the Stolypin agrarian reform.

According to Malakhova's data, in the Tambov area in 1906 there were 1,500 Baptists, in 1909, 1,800, and in 1915, 2,500 (Malakhova 1961: 81). The rapid growth of Baptism in Tambov Guberniia caused consternation in Church and government circles. In the explanation of the governor of Tambov to the Department of Spiritual Affairs "about the propaganda of Baptism in the guberniia" (February 1912), the reason for this is connected with the Stolypin reform: "As a consequence of the land reform in Tambov Guberniia, *otrub* agriculture has appeared. The settlement of small property-owning peasants in isolated farmsteads has reflected very unfavorably on their religious and moral condition. As a result of the new conditions of life, they have been forced to settle far from churches and schools.... For the sectarians, there is opened complete freedom of propaganda on these isolated farms ..." (TsGIAL, div. 821, f. 133, s.u. 194, sh. 217a).

At the same time as in Tambov Guberniia, Baptism developed in the Steppe region (Akmolinsk and Semipalatinsk Oblasts). In May 1913, the growth of Baptism in the Steppe region was the object of discussion at a meeting of the Council of Ministers. A special study commissioned by the Ministry of Internal Affairs affirmed: "... Baptism is, as everywhere in Russia, threatening in its spread in the region" (TsGIAL, div. 1276, f. 17, s.u. 263, sh. 220). The settlement of the Steppe region, and in general the guberniias of Asiatic Russia, was one of the significant links in the agrarian policy of Stolypin. It pursued the aim of purging European Russia of uneasy peasant elements in opposition to the Autocracy, and of transforming them in the places of settlement into *edinolichnyi* farmers with kulak isolated farms. At the end of 1915 in the guberniias of Asiatic Russia there were about 12,000 edinolichnyi, otrub and khutor farms (Dubrovskii 1963: 399).

Baptism spread in the Steppe region with success which frightened the supporters of the system of serfdom in the years marked by a rise in agriculture, the spread in the region of sown area and the intensification of agricultural production which occurred in direct connection with the development of capitalist forms of economy. The sown area in the Steppe region in 1911-1913 grew by comparison with the area under cultivation in 1901-1905 by 62.7% (Liashchenko 1956: 276).

Researchers for the Ministry of Internal Affairs wrote: "Quite exceptional conditions for growth are found in the Steppe region by the most dangerous and militant representative of sectarianism — Baptism.

"Left to themselves as a result of that same deficiency of control by both lay and spiritual authorities on the spot, Baptist settlements, large, firmly organized into independent units, with excellent material security thanks to the mutual aid developed among the sectarians, have in fact the possibility to freely conduct their activity among all the populated points surrounding them" (TsGIAL, div. 1276, f. 17, s.u. 263, sh. 223).

In 1912, there were more than 8,000 Baptists in the Steppe region. This was a well-run organization, possessing a staff of missionaries. The head of the entire Baptist movement here was the "local capitalist, a large landowner and sheep-breeder, the well-known author of the Baptist prayerbook, G. I. Mazaev, who is one of the most zealous and active disseminators of this sect in Russia.... Special traveling preachers are commanded by him at his personal expense in cities and villages ... they have from him a permanent salary (TsGIAL, div. 821, f. 133, s.u. 285, sh. 197).

Siberia and the Far East were also regions of significant spread of Baptism. Thus for instance in the Synodal statistics, the defections from Russian Orthodoxy to Baptism for 1907-1914 in Omsk Guberniia yield 6% of the total number of those who defected in all the guberniias of the Empire.[12] In the Amur region, according to data of the Ministry of Internal Affairs for 1909, there were about 4,000 Baptists (TsGIAL, div, 281, f. 133, s.u. 21, sh. 386). Thus, increase in the ranks of Baptism occurred in significant degree through the expansion of the Baptist church in newly-missionized border territories, which were involved in capitalist development.

Relatively new territory for Baptism were the guberniias of the chernozem center—for instance Tambov, where the first significant successes of Baptism were gained precisely in the years of implementation of the Stolypin reforms. Baptism continued to grow in the ancient centers of its development— especially the Kiev area. According to the data of Synodal statistics, defec- tions from Russian Orthodoxy to Baptism for the period between 1907 and 1914 (I do not use these statistics in absolute form because of their obvious conscious distortion), the Kiev area contributed 22.5% of the entire mass of conversions to Baptism and was first of all the guberniias of the Empire in this respect (Reports of the Over-Procurator of the Synod for 1907-1914). Let us note that in terms of the amount of privately-owned land, according to the decree of November 9, 1906, Kiev Guberniia was far ahead of all guberniias of European Russia. Whereas in these guberniias the ratio of privately-owned land to the total area of land in allotments was 14%, in Kiev Guberniia it was 50.7% (Dubrovskii 1963: 574-576).

The missionary preaching of the Baptists was consciously directed to the khutor dweller. In a report of the Baptist Missionary Society, we read:

"In Orenburg Guberniia there are many khutora, for example the Solomonovskii, Levonskii, Raskidnoi, Novo-Aleksandrovskii, Bogodarskii, the Pashkov settlement, Riabtsev, Chernev, Pravoliskii, Kievskii and others on which Ukrainian brothers have settled from the southern guberniias— Kherson and others. All these khutora Brother Sigitov visited with the Nizhnegumbek presbyter, Brother Levontii Trifonovich Pchelintsev. During this visit they had a meeting for the first time in the settlement of Vasil'evka, in which there were as many as 30 visiting brothers and 300 attenders, who for the first time heard the joyful news of salvation in Christ" (Baptist Missionary 1909: 23).

As the capitalist development of the regions of the Right Bank and South Ukraine served as the basis for the original dissemination of Baptism, so a strong new impetus to this dissemination was given by the time when in Lenin's words "the serf landlords with all their might, at a pace increased to the utmost, conducted a *bourgeois* policy, taking leave of all the romantic

---

[12] Reports of the Over-Procurator of the Synod for 1912-1914; Nagornov 1910: 326. ("Judging from the reports", A. A. Nagornov writes, "the results of the work were brilliant: there were great awakenings, conversions and unions with Christ's church ... individually, by the dozens and by the hundreds.")

illusions and hopes for the patriarchal nature of the peasant, *seeking* allies from the new bourgeois elements of Russia in general and rural Russia in particular" (*Lenin*: XX, 329 [emphasis in original]).

Baptism received recruits from new bourgeois elements. The figure of the khutor dweller, who gained fame as an independent and enterprising farmer, earning the trust of the government administration, and, thanks to wealth and connections forcing the local priest to "bite his tongue", becomes increasingly prominent in it. The journal *Baptist* published letters like these:

"From the Gaikin khutor, Don Host region.

"May 6, 1913, in our khutor by permission of the authorities there were elections for the village ataman, and a Baptist was elected, the Cossack noncommissioned officer Zakhar Andreevich Kundriukov, and all cried 'Bravo, bravo, now we will have an exemplary ataman' " (*B* 1914, No. 13-14, p. 21).

Z. A. Kundriukov, a khutor dweller, a Baptist and a village ataman, was the classic type of ally of the landlord-serfowners from among the new bourgeois elements.

By comparison with the social makeup of Baptists in the 1880s and 1890s, at the beginning of the 1900s the proportion of urban elements in it had increased. Congregations of Baptists were organized and grew in Baku, Odessa, Rostov-on-Don, Nikolaev, Sevastopol, Moscow, St. Petersburg, Kronstadt, Kerch', Warsaw, in a number of cities of the Urals, Western and Eastern Siberia, the Baltic area and the Far East, although the basic and clearly predominant contingent of Baptism as before was the rural population.

Let us note that in the industrial centers, the Baptist church everywhere made efforts to attract workers to its ranks. From the report of the chief of the St. Petersburg security force (1915) which contained a survey of the number and make-up of the visitors to Baptist prayer-meetings, it appears that visitors to them numbered 800-850 persons in total, "primarily of the working class and in insignificant number from the intelligentsia and students in higher educational institutions" (ORF Institute of History, Sector "Ts", Division VI, d. 11, shs. 51-53). In addition to this, prayer-meetings were held "in house No. 53, apartment 7, on Predtechenskaia Ulitsa, whcih was composed of Baptists from the working class" (*ibid.*, sh. 53).[13] Not long before the beginning of World War I, Baptist sermons were preached in factories in Perm, "in

---

[13] Many of the workers who were influenced by Baptism were connected with agriculture; these were seasonal workers. From the data of the Ministry of Internal Affairs describing the religious organizations in Vladmir Guberniia, for example, the following emerges: "The sect of Shtundo-Baptism appeared since 1906 in Gorokhovetskii Uezd; the followers of this sect ... are primarily workers, who have gone away to work in St. Petersburg and in the south of Russia. The main leader of the Baptists in Gorokhovetskii Uezd is considered the peasant from the village of Klokovo, Kozha Volost, Efrem Semenov Andrianov, who lives at the present time in his village but earlier went to St. Petersburg to work as a boiler-maker; according to rumor, he is a member of the St. Petersburg Evangelical congregation" (TsGIAL, div. 821, f. 133, s.u. 21, sh. 108).

the factories and mines of Ekaterinoslav Guberniia", "among workers in railroad shops in Konotop ..." (TsGIAL, div, 821, f. 133, d. 196, shs. 99-99, v. 100), in factories in Kovno, where "yearly, German artisans and workers arrive from East Prussia to work in Kovno and other populated points of the guberniia, and to bring with them the seeds of Baptism and zealously sow them primarily among persons who have professions similar to theirs" (Contemporary 1910: 3), in Berdiansk and Melitopol (Vortovskii 1911: 12, 13).[14] In a report to the Department of Spiritual Affairs (January 1914), the director of the Department of Police summed up: "The main contingent of followers of Baptism is composed primarily of the lower classes of the population — peasants, workers, artisans — but in recent times one notes the appearance of sympathy for Baptism also among the intelligentsia" (TsGIAL, div, 821, f. 133, s.u. 195, sh. 314 v.).

In his time Bonch-Bruevich notes that "propagandists of Baptism" were not distinguished for selectivity and "attracted to themselves positively everyone whom they could" (Bonch-Bruevich 1959: 179). However, of all the classes and strata to whom the Baptist mission was addressed, it (like any other sectarian preaching) had minimal success among the working class. Here the Baptist position did not hold. Several hundred workers, who visited the prayer-meetings of the St. Petersburg Baptists, represented an insignificant handful of the St. Petersburg proletariat. It was the same in other cities.

Tolstoyan correspondence allows us to judge the attitude of workers towards sectarians (in practice towards Baptism and its varieties, since other forms of sectarianism were very little represented in the cities at the beginning of the 20th century).

In 1903, Tolstoyans in emigration appealed to their followers in St. Petersburg, asking them to test the ground concerning the possibility of disseminating sectarian ideas among the workers. Thus, on one and the same day, April 29, 1903, the Tolstoyan Tregubov wrote letters to his emissaries in St. Petersburg — V. P. Makarov and O. K. Klodt: "... how firmly disseminated are violently revolutionary ideas and actions among the St. Petersburg workers? .... Are there many sectarians among the factory and shop workers? Which faith predominates among them? Are there many among them who believe in nothing at all?" (Tregubov's Letter to Makarov, April 29, 1903, ROBIL, Chertkov Collection). And again: "... probably among the sectarians there are those who favor a violent overthrow. Do you not know such sectarians?" (Tregubov's Letter to Klodt, April 29, 1903, Chertkov Collection).

---

[14] Vortovskii's next observation is highly indicative: "A special sectarian missionary point was set up in the city of Berdiansk. Several German Baptist workers and the Russian Timoshenko were settled here. These people began to carry on active Baptist propaganda among the working population but had no success".

The answers of Tregubov's correspondents have not survived. But from the content of Tregubov's letter to Klodt from August 10, 1903, we learn that the answers were received and they were murderously disillusioning to the Tolstoyans: "Thanks for the information", Tregubov wrote to Klodt, "it is a pity that there is only one Christian per 1,000 (i.e. sectarians in the under-standing of Tregubov and his correspondents — A. K.) for 999 heathens!... We will not live to see the kingdom of God!... It's enough to make you lie down and die!..." (Tregubov's Letter to Klodt, August 10, 1903, ROBIL, Chertkov Collection). Now Tregubov wished to know whether at least "Chris-tian" literature was current among the workers: "It would be interesting to know whether truly Christian (i.e. Tolstoyan and in general sectarian — A. K.) tracts enjoy great demand among the workers? Or are they all nourished by heathen literature? If only one out of 1,000 reads Christian literature, that's horrible!...." (*ibid.*).

But Tregubov put his question purely rhetorically. He understood very well that the workers were turning away from sectarian literature just as from sec-tarianism itself. And Tregubov wondered whether there was not a change in the landscape? He wrote: "Perhaps we have gone to extremes: we speak all the time of the spirit, but of the flesh with disdain.... Should we not change our tactics a little bit? Should we not learn from those who are nourishing ten times as many workers? Probably they are answering demands better than we are.... We should become a little heathen ..." (*ibid.*).

This is how the matter of dissemination of sectarian ideas among the workers stood in 1903 — i.e. before the experience of large-scale class battles of the proletariat during the revolution of 1905-1907.

The urban Baptist congregations were made up primarily of petty-bourgeois elements. Summing up extensive experience in studying sectarians, Bonch-Bruevich wrote in a report to the Second Congress of the RSDRP, that the Baptists attract "their followers for the most part from among the petty-bourgeoisie of the cities, surburbs, trading villages, urban settlements, large and small villages, from this entire meshchan and more or less well-to-do peasant group ..." (Bonch-Bruevich 1959: 169).

Representatives of large capital were the ruling force in Baptism. In the 1870s and 1880s their power was disseminated primarily in the Baptist con-gregations and groups in the Caucasian guberniias. Athough they really kept the deciding word in the affairs of the entire union, they were forced at this time to take account of the immediate leaders of the Baptists of the Right Bank and South Ukraine — representatives of the rural bourgeoisie. It is clear that between the Mazaevs, Fefelovs and Voronins on the one hand, and the Riaboshapkas, Rybalkas and Balabans on the other, there existed a dif-ference in position, interests, mode of thought, traditions, etc.

At the begining of the 20th century, although the stratum of rural bourgeoisie in Baptism grew noticeably, particularly in the years of the Stolypin reform, its role changed. The rural bourgeoisie became the transmitters of the will of the elder brothers in capital—the owners of large landholdings, trading firms and factories. The latter, with some exceptions, took no formal part in the leading organs of the Baptist church, but they exerted an influence on the entire life of the congregations.

Let us use the description of these elements in Baptism contained in an article by Pavel Pavlov (the son of V. G. Pavlov) under the significant title "Bogatstvo tserkvi" [The Wealth of the Church]. Pavlov begins his article by demonstrating that "the increased growth of capital is observed throughout the entire modern world, in spite of the various disasters which overtake this or that country" (Pavlov 1914: 345). The fact of "the growth of capital" in spite of any unfavorable conditions in all the countries of the world should, according to Pavlov, show believers that this phenomenon is inevitable and cannot be opposed by anything, any more than the force of "divine predestination". Then Pavlov demonstrates "an increase in economic and productive forces of our country", "the growth of wealth and its accumulation", "in spite of all external hindrances" (*ibid.*). Now the world-wide inevitability of the accumulation of capital is extended to Russia.

"The Russian Baptist congregations", Pavlov writes, "have among them some members who have millions, and particularly in the northern Caucasus and in the Transcaucasus, Baptists who have provided from among themselves sturdy workers for the evangelical cause, are also well supplied with material goods. Siberia also has strong representatives of capital among the Baptists. The writer of these lines personally knows congregations whose preceptors can say: 'Today I preached to two million rubles'. But however high these figures seem, they are rather lower than reality, although certainly it is not so easy to establish people's real wealth" (*ibid.*). Still not convinced that the ordinary believers would agree with him and approve the capital of their brothers, Pavlov supplements the justification of the Baptist holders of capital by the fact that their capital was, as it were, the property of the church: "God has lately given his people gold and silver. Almost unlimited wealth is at the disposition of the church, wealth given to it by the great giver of 'all blessings and perfect gifts' " (Pavlov 1914: 345).

We have described the social make-up of the Baptist church as it was at the beginning of the 20th century and as it remained on the eve of the Great October Socialist Revolution. For all the external successes which accompanied the development of Baptism over this period of time, it not only did not overcome the internal contradictions characteristic of the original period of its history in Russia, but became the arena of still deeper and sharper class contradictions, which the religious integument of the Baptist movement could neither remove nor hide.

A congress in Novo-Vasil'evka in 1884 and subsequent congresses served to unite Baptists from Caucasian and Ukrainian guberniias into one church, and also united Baptist congregations scattered in various guberniias of Russia. But the branch of Baptism founded by Radstock and Pashkov continued to exist. Pashkov, who was forced to emigrate in 1884 and died in Paris in 1902, continued to maintain connections with groups of his followers.

Gradually, ideological influence on these groups, organizational leadership of them, and finally activity directed to increasing them and creating new groups, passed over to an editorial committee composed of Fast, mentioned above, and the Prokhanov brothers, which published the journal *Beseda* [Conversation]. *Beseda* was published from 1890 in Russia. In 1894-1896, its publication was transferred abroad. The journal was the organ of the "Evangelical Christians" (a designation subsequently attached to a religious movement growing out of Pashkovism and headed by I. S. Prokhanov). Tolstoyans (particularly D. A. Khilkov) took part in it, along with Baptists, and its editorial board strove to unify all religious tendencies on the basis of a sort of doctrinal minimum, reduced to a recognition of the authority of the "Scriptures" and faith in the redemptive sacrifice of Christ. The editorial board acted in the spirit of Pashkov's ideas, in spite of the failure of the attempt he made in 1893 to achieve agreement among the sectarian groups.

I. S. Prokhanov was an especially ardent adherent and champion of the idea of uniting the basic groups of Russian sectarianism into one religious and social movement. As early as 1896 he published an article in the journal *Beseda* devoted to the international congress of the Evangelical Union in London, in which he propagandized the idea of "the unity of Christians", and presented the activity of the Union, which united representatives of the Episcopal, Presbyterian, Lutheran, Methodist and Baptist churches, as worthy of "an enlightened world" (Val'kevich 1900: Appendix 3, pp. 120-121). Upon his return to Russia, Prokhanov in the late 1890s carried on energetic propaganda for his ideas of unification, traveling around the congregations which supported his ideas, and also preaching these views among the Baptists. In the beginning, Prokhanov did not strive for formal centralization, either of the congregations which he had inherited from the Pashkovites, nor from those he "acquired".

Let us note that even in the 1880s tendencies toward unification with the Pashkovite movement were rather strong in Baptism, which was to be explained by the growth of contradictions in Baptism, and the growing dissatisfaction of its lower classes because of the arrogance and cupidity of the upper classes. Open manifestations of sympathy for the Pashkovite movement were cut off in Baptism when it was headed by Mazaev. However, as internal contradictions in it became more acute, cases became more frequent of individual and group transfer of Baptists to the Pashkovite movement, or, as it was called in the 1890s, Evangelical Christianity. The organization of Evangelical Christianity, which was not formally centralized, and the minimal significance which Evangelical Christianity gave to a hierarchy at the beginning stage of its development, and finally its dogma, according to which the possibility of "being saved" belonged not to "the chosen", but to *all* believers — in the presence of this difference in the levels of "democratism" there occurred a significant drain from Baptism to Evangelical Christianity.

For all this, Evangelical Christianity was a branch of Baptism; it adhered to the views of the direction developing in international Baptism and bearing the title of "general" or free Baptists as distinct from the "private" or strict ones. The Union of Russian Baptists headed by Mazaev shared the views of the private or strict Baptists. "At the present time", S. D. Bondar' wrote, "the general and private Baptists are two religious tendencies inhabiting one and the same church society. The general Baptists hold Arminian views, while the private ones remain Calvinists. The general Baptists have 'open' breaking of bread [that is, communion] — i.e., allow participation by persons who have not been christened in Baptist fashion but who declared themselves believers. Private Baptists admit to the breaking of bread only persons 'who have received baptism in the faith'. As a consequence of this, the general Baptists are also called free Baptists; the private Baptists are called strict Baptists. The Russian Evangelical Christians (Prokhanov and others) count themselves among the free Baptists" (Bondar' 1911: 4).

Evangelical Christianity grew quickly, having social roots in common with Baptism, and it became a competitor, the more fearful for Baptism because in large measure it grew at Baptism's expense. Reviewing the periodical press of the Baptists, the protocols of their congresses, and finally the correspondence of Baptist leaders preserved in the archives, we everywhere encounter one and the same motif — the Evangelical Christians are enticing the Baptists!

In order to leave this question, let us turn to a note from the report of the special agent, Kologrivov, to the Ministry of Internal Affairs concerning the congress of Baptists in 1911: "The basic if not the only hindrance to the unification of the Baptists with the Evangelical Christians was almost unanimously declared by the speaker to be the manifestation by the latter of a hostile attitude toward Baptists. At the congress it was stated (by V. V. Ivanov) that many of the congregations of Evangelical Christians were founded by persons excommunicated or expelled from Baptist congregations, and that these excommunicants (fugitives) in general find the most fraternally joyous acceptance in Evangelical Christian congregations, while such a situation seems to have the full approval of the head of the Evangelical Christians, Prokhanov" (TsGIAL, div. 821, f. 133, s.u. 285, shs. 182-183 v.).

Evangelical Christianity grew out of the social contradictions of capitalism, particularly as these contradictions developed among the Baptists. According to statistical data from the Ministry of Internal Affairs, the total number of Evangelical Christians in Russia was about 31,000 persons (*ibid.*). There were almost 3.5 times fewer Evangelical Christians than Baptists, but at a time when among Baptists there were approximately 48,000 Germans, Letts, and Estonians, and the Russians numbered about 67,000 people, the Evangelical Christians were almost exclusively Russian (29,988 out of 30,776) (*ibid.*). Thus, within the Great Russian and Ukrainian guberniias, there were approximately two times fewer Evangelical Christians than Baptists.

Let us turn to a description of the composition of the membership of Evangelical Christianity. One is struck by the comparatively greater proportion of urban elements in Evangelical Christianity, originating in St. Petersburg and having there a significant number of followers (by 1912 there were about 4,500 Evangelical Christians, 931 Baptists and 145 Adventists in St. Petersburg [Statistical 1912]). By 1910-1914 congregations and groups of Evangelical Christians were found in Baku, Warsaw, Moscow, Nikolaev, Odessa, Sevastopol (*ibid.*), Novgorod, Kazan, Pskov (TsGIAL, div. 821, f. 133, s.u. 198, sh. 61 v.), Feodosiia, Yalta, Alupka, Simferopol (*ibid.*, s.u. 181, sh. 6), Ekaterinoslav, Mariupol', Rostov-on-Don, Aleksandrovsk (Afanas'ev 1915: 25, 26), and many other cities.

As we see from the report of the vice-director of the Department of Police to the Ministry of Internal Affairs, April 14, 1910, on the results of a trip to Tavriia Guberniia, "the contingent of the Evangelical Christians in Tavriia Guberniia is composed exclusively of plain people — workers, artisans, janitors and domestic servants; not a single completely intellectual J person is included in their ranks" (TsGIAL, div. 821, f. 133, s.u. 18, sh. 166). An official of the Department of Spiritual Affairs who visited a small prayer meeting of Evangelical Christians on Vasil'evskii Island in Petersburg in 1908, wrote in his report: "Twenty three persons attended, almost all workers. A worker preached who explained in his sermon the third chapter of the Gospel of John concerning the necessity of the inner rebirth of man through the spirit" (*ibid.* s.u. 164, sh. 19).

According to data of the Ministry of Internal Affairs of a more general nature than the preceding, the Evangelical Christians "conduct propaganda among the peasants in the villages, and in the cities among gate keepers, kitchen help, parlor maids, cab drivers, small craftsmen, and others" (*ibid.* s.u. 21, sh. 276).

There were few workers among the Evangelical Christians. It is true that the Pashkovites began their activity by publishing a journal, *Russkii rabochii* [Russian Worker]. The factory-owners themselves drew the workers into Evangelical Christianity. In 1900, "the Moscow factory-owner F. Savel'ev began to hold in his house meetings for reading the Holy Scriptures.... The appearance of Pashkovism in the holy city of Moscow produced quite a bit of commotion. Skvortsov (the missionary—A. K.) was immediately sent there as a skilled physician against this spiritual infection. Skvortsov himself appeared at a meeting ... and declared to Savel'ev that ... if the meetings continued, he would close the factory ..." (*Svobodnoe slovo* [Free Word], 1903, No. 4, p. 19). However, meetings held by Savel'ev in the factory were not popular: "Several men and women gathered" (*ibid.*). Not workers but artisans, craftsmen, low-ranking white-collar workers, and domestics were the basic contingent of the urban congregations of Evangelical Christians. In 1908, the Evangelical Christians published a journal, *Seiatel'* [The Sower], directed toward a mass readership. In its direction it was somewhat reminiscent of the journal *Russkii rabochii.* It contained small easy stories about various persons who had "been converted" to the faith, and about the salutary consequences, not only spiritual but also worldly, which faith brought to those who were "converted".

The tales were usually spiced with a fairly large dose of sentimentality and were distinguished by their "prettiness". I studied the professions of the heroes of these stories from issue to issue—they were the popular "heroes" of Evangelical Christianity. Who were they? A postman, a housemaid, a young telegraph operator, a stone-cutter, a salesgirl at a bakery, servant in a hotel, the wife of a metal-worker, a boot-maker, a laundress, several blind people, a woman student, an unmarried woman, a workman in a factory, the wife of a factory worker, a salesperson in a shop, a needy teacher in a secondary school, a nurse, a young clerk, an artisan (engraver), a soldier, a recruit, a worker for a watchmaker, a tailor and his apprentice, a cabinetmaker, and (much more rarely) a kind master, a rich trader, a landowner, and finally, a prisoner (*Seiatel'* 1903, No. 2-46).

Evangelical Christianity, following a tradition inherited from the Pashkovite movement, preserved its ties with the St. Petersburg aristocracy. In a report compiled for the Department of Police by civil servants in the Department of Spiritual Affairs (May 1916), we read of the second St. Petersburg congregation of Evangelical Christians: "The congregation has the patronage of highly placed persons, such as: Princess Gagarina, Her Highness Princess Paskevich, Princesses Lieven and Bariatinskaia, Chertkov, the heirs of Pashkov, etc." (TsGIAL, div. 821, f. 133, s.u. 198, sh. 60 v.). In the Russian Evangelical Union organized by Prokhanov in 1908—the unifying organ of Protestant religious groups—the chairman was Prince A. P. Lieven, and the deputy chairman Baron P. N. Nikolai (Evangelical 1912: 1). Both in Baptism and in Evangelical Christianity the leading role was played by representatives of industrial, agricultural and trading capital. Among the readers and subscribers of the newspaper published by Prokhanov, *Utrenniaia zvezda* [Morning Star], there were factory-owners, representatives of trading firms, and "large and medium-scale landowners of Russia" (*UZ* X/29/1910: 1).

Urban elements were represented in Evangelical Christianity in rather greater degree than in Baptism, but the basic part of its followers consisted of peasants. The largest sites of this organization were in Kiev, Ekaterinoslav, Stavropol, Kherson, Khar'kov, Samara, Vladimir, and Kursk Guberniias (Statistical 1912). The sites of the distribution of Evangelical Christianity by comparison with the Pashkovite movement had moved noticeably southward, stopping, however, at the Northern Caucasus.

As once Baptism had spread into the ancient centers of Molokanism, so Evangelical Christianity followed on the heels of Baptism. Evangelical Christianity aimed its propaganda at the urban lower classes. Therefore the leaders of Evangelical Christianity were forced to adopt a liberal position in questions of faith, organizational structure, and also those questions which were advanced by social life. At the same time, beginning with Pashkov, Evangelical Christian leaders aimed at the development of as mass a religious movement as possible, which in turn demanded flexibility and cleverness in political and religious matters.

In the relevant section of this work we will look at the program of religious reformation in Russia, prepared by the Evangelical Christian leaders, who were bourgeois politicians devoid of any sense of reality. One way or another, the Evangelical Christian variety of Baptism was its liberal-bourgeois variety.

From the time of origin of Evangelical Christianity, both its leaders and the leaders of the Union of Russian Baptists undertook repeated attempts at convergence and even union: "At the Baptist congresses at Rostov-on-Don (in 1902) and in Tsaritsyn (in 1903) there was a union of Baptists with Evangelical Christians; then the Baptist union organization bore the name of the Union of Evangelical Christian-Baptists. Several congregations of Evangelical Christians entered into it, but not all" (TsGIAL, div. 821, f. 133, d. 193, sh. 66).

Despite what would seem to have been mutual agreement, the union of Evangelical Christianity and Baptism did not occur. Both sides returned repeatedly to questions of unification (in 1908, 1911, 1912 and 1913), set up "unification committees", but could not unite and on the contrary became even more disunited, heaping on each other every possible accusation. On the eve of the Great October Revolution, in May 1917, a Baptist delegation, sent to a congress of Evangelical Christians in order to work out the conditions for a union, carried on regular debates with their "brothers". As a result it was agreed "to begin (for the how-many-eth time! — A. K.) the activity of a unification committee", in order to prepare a constituent congress of both organizations, on condition that the Union of Baptists agree to this (Manuscript Division of MIRA, K. VIII, f. 1, s.u, 24, sh. 3 v.). But several years after the Great October Revolution, Prokhanov solemnly swore: "I will not die until I step over the corpse of the Baptist organization", and the leaders of Baptism publicly called the Council of Evangelical Christians "a house of prostitution" (Klibanov 1928: 16).

Between Evangelical Christianity and Baptism there existed differences in dogma and church organization; there was rivalry and personal enmity between the leaders of both movements. But in the last analysis the differences lay in the socio-political field: Evangelical Christianity was oriented toward the liberal bourgeoisie, toward the social ideas and political direction of Kadetism, while the Union of Russian Baptists, although there was a liberal element in it, was led by inveterately reactionary elements, politically close to the positions of the Right-Octobrist bourgeoisie.

Meanwhile, Prokhanov's attempt to keep Evangelical Christianity within the bounds of more or less regulated independent activity of its participants ended in failure. The slogans of religious reformation could not stir any large portion of the people, who had undergone the experience of the bourgeois-democratic revolution and had their class consciousness enriched. These slogans were incapable of unifying the participants of Evangelical Christianity themselves and did not kindle any enthusiasm among them. In these circumstances Prokhanov took the only possible path for the preservation of his organization—he rebuilt it as a bourgeois Protestant church. In 1907 and 1908 there occurred congresses of Evangelical Christians, and in 1909 their All-Russian Congress was called. At these congresses, the institution of presbyter was given legal status. In the congregations there appeared ranks of various degrees of spiritual elder. The organization was given a centralized structure crowned by the All-Union Council of Evangelical Christians, headed by Prokhanov. Norms of dogma were worked out and reduced to writing.

In 1913, Prokhanov published in St. Petersburg *A Short Exposition of the Beliefs of Evangelical Christians*. Dei Mazaev rubbed his hands and remarked approvingly in the journal *Baptist* on the beginning of the recovery of Evangelical Christians from the "childish disease" of democratism. At the Congress of Baptists in 1911, the speakers called Prokhanov to Canossa[K]: "Almost all speakers said that the union of Baptists with Evangelical Christians could be implemented only if the Evangelical Christians joined the Union of Baptists. S. Stepanov on this score expressed the conviction that sooner or later this union would take place.... Evangelical Christians, the speaker said, have already accepted Baptist doctrine on presbyters, whereas not long ago they denied the very name for them. In any case, it's not for us to come to them" (TsGIAL, div. 821, f. 133, s.u. 285, sh. 182). As we know, neither a merger nor a unification occurred. But Evangelical Christianity was finally constituted as a church.

Both Baptist churches—the Union of Russian Baptists and the All-Russian Union of Evangelical Christians—were ideologically and organizationally connected with the world Baptist church and enjoyed its finanacial support. Figures in Russian Baptism and Evangelical Christianity (especially

Prokhanov) repeatedly visited Baptist churches in Germany, England, and the U.S.A., and translated and published in large editions the writings of Western European and trans-Atlantic theologians of Baptism.

In 1905, a delegation of Russian Baptists, headed by Dei Mazaev and V. V. Ivanov, took part in the World Congress of Baptists in London. In 1909, the protocols of the Congress were published in Russian Baptist publications (Ivanov and Mazaev 1909). In 1911 a delegation of Russian Baptists took an active part in the World Congress of Baptists in Philadelphia. Prokhanov, who was still busy at this time with the organization of the All-Russian Union of Evangelical Christians, could not take part in this congress. This time Pavlov and Fetler, who had been schooled on the Western European model, took part in the Russian delegation.

The delegation was received by President Taft of the United States. V. Fetler related that President Taft "welcomed each delegate and shook his hand. I had the honor to give the President a book in English on God's work in Russia, and in the book, by the way, he wrote this line: 'God bless you and keep you ...'" (Fetler 1911: 195).

The Union of Russian Baptists entered the World Union of Baptists. At the congress in Philadelphia the Union of Evangelical Christians joined the World Union of Baptists, and Prokhanov was chosen in absentia as vice-president of the World Union of Baptists. The administrative leaders of the Union of Russian Baptists were very much offended at Prokhanov's election, which bore, by virtue of his absence at the congress, a demonstrative character. Prokhanov's election was explained by the fact that he had close personal connections with the ruling figures of English and American Baptism and was known in their circles as a convinced partisan of the social and political system of these countries, and by the fact that the liberal-bourgeois direction given by Prokhanov to Evangelical Christianity was to the taste of foreign leaders of Baptism. Evangelical Christians not without foundation declared to Mazaev: "Do you know, dear Dei Ivanovich, that Evangelical Christians are much closer to Baptists in England and America than you and your tendency?

"At one of the congresses of your people you thought up some sort of senior presbyters. But do you know, my dear, there was never any such thing among American and English Baptists during all their history, for this fundamentally contradicts the principle which is so dear to them, autonomy (independence) of churches?" (Letters 1916: 89).

I do not have any systematic data on the financial support which the Baptist churches in Russia received from the World Union of Baptists and from individual foreign Baptist churches.

At the congress in Philadelphia, Pavlov appealed simultaneously to the souls and to the pocketbooks of American and British Baptists. "We turn our gaze to our trans-Atlantic and British brothers", he wrote, "in order that they help us in our battle for the cause of Christ. We appeal like the Macedonian in the vision of the Apostle Paul: 'Come and help us' " (*B* 1911, No. 31).

According to the data of the Department of Spiritual Affairs, large amounts of money were collected at the congress in Philadelphia for the building in Moscow of a prayer house and seminary for Baptists. In England there existed a Russian Evangelical Society which materially aided Baptists preaching in Russia. Fetler in 1916 reported to this Society concerning the sums which he had already collected in America, and those which he was intending to receive in England for the "House of the Gospel in Petrograd". Fetler wrote on this account that "the union of England with Russia serves to significantly broaden religious freedom...."

One of the most vexing questions for the student of the history and condition of religious organizations in pre-Revolutionary Russia is their statistics. What was the number of followers of Baptism and Evangelical Christianity in Russia on the eve of the Great October Socialist Revolution? I assume that the statistical data of the Ministry of Internal Affairs, stating that by 1912 there were 115,000 Baptists and 31,000 Evangelical Christians, give only an approximate idea of the number of followers of these churches. How did the dynamics of these numbers change in succeeding years? For the period 1912-1916, they changed in unequal degree.

According to the reports of the Over-Procurator for the eight-year period from 1907 to 1914, defections from Russian Orthodoxy to Baptism numbered about 20,000 persons, of whom 9,900 defected to Baptism during the five-year period 1907-1911 and for the three-year period 1912-1914, 10,300 (Reports of the Over-Procurator of the Synod for 1907-1914).

According to the same source, defections from Russian Orthodoxy to Evangelical Christianity for the years 1913-1914 alone numbered 2,728 persons (Report of the Over-procurator of the Synod for 1913-1914). These data, of course, do not allow us to judge the real growth in numbers of followers of Baptism and Evangelical Christianity, both because of the deliberate distortion in the sources and because the increase in Baptism and Evangelical Christianity did not take place only at the expense of Russian Orthodoxy. At the same time there were cases of return to Russian Orthodoxy of those who had defected, numerous cases of conversion from Baptism to Evangelical Christianity and back, and finally, cases of rupture with all of them. The growth of Baptism and Evangelical Christianity remains a fact, fixed by Synodal statistics, and noted in a number of articles and notes published in 1912-1914 in the Baptist and Evangelical Christian press.

The situation changed in the 1914-1916 period. In the years of the First World War, under circumstances of the growth of chauvinistic moods and increasingly arbitrary political action in the country, the breakup of many Baptist and Evangelical Christian congregations was accomplished. All the Baptist congregations in the jurisdiction of the governor-general of Odessa, and in

Kherson and Tavriia Guberniias, were closed. Some Baptist congregations were closed in Ekaterinoslav Guberniia. Baptist congregations were closed in Kazan, Astrakhan, Pskov, Revel', Kronstadt, and Aktiubinsk ("List of Closed Evangelical Christian/Baptist Congregations", Typescript, collection of author). More than 20 important leaders and preachers of Baptism were exiled ("List of Exiled Members of Sectarian Congregations 1914-1916", Typescript, collection of author). Many ordinary Baptists and Evangelical Christians were victims of arbitrary judicial and police action.

Even so, the total number of members in Baptist and Evangelical churches, which was in 1912, according to approximate data, 150,000 persons, had grown by 1917. If we accept the pace of growth in numbers of the followers of Baptism in the years of religious "freedom", and even take into account the fact that not only for the years 1912-1914, but also during 1915-1917, they maintained the same pace of growth, we come to the conclusion that the churches of Baptists and Evangelical Christians had in 1917 not less than 200,000 followers.

4. The Internal Struggle in Baptism and Evangelical Christianity. The Pentecostals

The changes noted above which had occurred in the social make-up of Baptism, the increased proportion of bourgeois property-owners, both the representatives of more or less large agricultural, industrial and trading capital, and those of the rural bourgeoisie, led to a strengthening of the contradictions and the growth of conflict between the upper and lower strata in Baptism. New recruits from the socially lower classes of the city and the country, and from petty-bourgeois elements, continued to enter Baptism, while its old personnel from the ranks of ordinary believers, who had become convinced of the discrepancy between Baptism and their interests and strivings, broke with the Baptist church and in the majority of cases went over to Evangelical Christianity. It was precisely the ordinary believers who left Baptism, the representatives of the urban and rural poor. This is what Dei Mazaev had in mind when he called the Union of Evangelical Christians "the refuge of every sort of rabble" (Letters 1916: 71).

At the beginning of the 20th century in all large Baptist congregations, especially the urban ones, there was not a trace of the patriarchal way of life which had marked the situation of the Shtundist congregations in the 1860s and 1870s. There was no trace either of the atmosphere of mutual aid and trust which at the very beginning of Baptism's existence made it attractive to the Kiev, Kherson, Ekaterinoslav and other peasants, oppressed by need, forgotten by the landowners, rich men, rural administrators and police authorities.

Now matters had proceeded so far that the editors of the journal *Baptist* were forced to write a special appeal to "rich brothers and sisters": "Do not lead these 'little ones' into temptation with your luxury; given them an example of simplicity, industriousness and modesty. Rich sisters, your costumes are not worse than the costumes of your worldly sisters. In your costumes there is as little decency and modesty as they have.... Prayer-meetings have begun to be turned into exhibitions for costumes" (*B* 1912, No. 16, pp. 5-6).

Somewhat earlier V. V. Ivanov had addressed an open letter to believers: "Many have put hundreds and thousands in banks as surplus capital, and it's terrible to think that believers wear gold in their ears and on their fingers, pay a hundred rubles and more for wedding and holiday dresses, and unceasingly chase after Paris fashion like worldly people" (*G* 1911, No. 5, p. 81).

Of course, the leaders of Baptism were not inclined to reveal the social contrasts irresistably growing in their midst. These contrasts were fairly well characterized in a polemic with the leaders of Baptism by the Molokan activist, M. I. Kalmykov, even in 1906. I am using Kalmykov's testimony, since he knew the Baptist milieu from personal experience.

After what P. Pavlov wrote of the Baptist millionaires of the Northern Caucasus, Transcaucasus and Siberia, what V. V. Ivanov wrote in his open letter, and what the editors of the journal *Baptist* wrote in the appeal to the "rich brothers and sisters", one can place complete trust in the testimony of Kalmykov concerning the Baptists:

"There are millionaires among them who sit importantly in the meetings and poor people who settle themselves in corners in rags.... One believer has 5,000 desiatiny which he will give to no one free. Whether there is a harvest or not, give him his rent; if there is no money, sell the last cow. Let the children starve and die. Let your body be naked in frost. Let your cabin go without heat, it's not his affair. And the result is that these believers live like brothers, but only brothers like Cain and Abel, with the sole difference that Cain killed his brother in an instant and these kill their brothers gradually, sucking from them the last drop of blood. What kind of brothers are these when they drown in gold and another suffers from hunger? Yes, they are brothers in the faith, but in love and in life they are not brothers. For the rich man it is advantageous to show that belief is the foundation and that through faith one is saved, but what about the poor man?" (Kalmykov 1906: 7-8).

And as it was in Baptism in the second half of the 1870s and in the late 1880s-early 1890s, when the ordinary believers, led by Koval' and in another case by Malëvannyi, attempted to free themselves from "the new yoke", as they called Baptism, so at the beginning of the 20th century ordinary believers repeated the attempt to free themselves from the "new yoke" which had become heavier and heavier. But the actions of ordinary Baptists against the leaders now took place under the conditions of a ripening revolutionary crisis and then of the first bourgeois-democratic revolution in Russia.

While in Malëvannyi's teaching the elements of social protest were in fantastic union with elements of religious mysticism, a combination of mysticism with social protest was uncharacteristic of the ideology of the lower classes of Baptism, who reacted against their bourgeois leaders at the beginning of the 20th century.

As will be shown below, ordinary Baptists and Evangelical Christians, reacting against their leaders, attempted to resurrect and renew the mystical ideas of Koval' and Malëvannyi. But only in very insignificant degree did they renew in this the genuine and passionate social and political accusations of Malëvannyi. The frequent cases of conversion of Baptists to Aventism also marked a return to mysticism.

The drain from Baptism to Evangelical Christianity was accompanied ideologically by a critique of the hierarchical structure of Baptism, but was limited as a rule to this. On the other hand, among ordinary Baptists, social protest was expressed which, although it started from a critique of the dictatorial order in Baptism, was not however accompanied by conversion to any other new religious teaching. Among ordinary believers, both Baptists and Evangelical Christians, even if they had not yet overcome their religious world-view, an interest in revolutionary ideas was noticeable. However much the leaders of Baptism attempted to close off the interests of ordinary believers, however narcotic its ideas, the class consciousness, the social life and the liberation struggle of the proletariat exploded in the isolated milieu of the followers of Baptism, Evangelical Christianity and other religious groups. The leaders of Baptism had now to concern themselves not only with the struggle with their numerous religious competitors. Their spiritual peace was much more disturbed by the penetration of revolutionary ideas among ordinary believers.

The congress of representatives of Baptist communities which took place in June 1903 in Tsaritsyn, devoted a special item in its decisions to "the dangerous intellectual ferment" expressed in "the distribution of brochures of an anti-state tendency", and imposed the obligation on leaders of the congregations "in case of use of the above-mentioned harmful publications among our brothers to oppose in every way their circulation among the brotherhood and to subject the guilty parties in this respect to immediate exclusion" (Putintsev 1935: 28).

What was between the lines of this protocol? Among Tregubov's papers there are preserved excerpts from a letter written, in his words, by "a former Baptist": "If you wish to live on the earth you'll have to defend yourself from the most ravenous predators—the mighty people of this world. Everything indicates that people, in the final analysis, should defend themselves, otherwise people will never be free from these rampant predators. Two thousand years have already passed since non-resistance to evil was preached, and to this day nothing has been done. If somewhere there is some freedom, it was achieved with the blood of the people" (Tregubov's Letter to Biriukova, December 4, 1902, ROBIL, Chertkov Collection). In a letter dated May 11, 1903, to the

Baptist I. D. Liasotskii, Tregubov wrote: "... I know that among the Evangelists there is sympathy for the revolution" (Tregubov's Letter to Liasotskii, May 11, 1903, ROBIL, Chertkov Collection). In a letter dated May 7, 1903, to E. N. Ivanov who had broken with Baptism, Tregubov showed that supposedly "progressive socialists have renounced violence", and advised Ivanov to read "the second chapter of the essay by Professor Isaev, 'The Socialism of Our Day', and the last chapter of the essay by Professor Masaryk of the University of Paris, 'A Critique of Marxism'... " (Tregubov's Letter to Ivanov, May 7, 1903, ROBIL, Chertkov Collection).

Cases of the awakening of the class-political consciousness of ordinary Baptists, Evangelical Christians, Adventists and representatives of old Russian sectarian groups, were not numerous. The class consciousness of the sectarians, even those who had departed from the religious path, often continued to be clouded by this or that idea in the spirit of Christian socialism. But such awakenings occurred, and they represented an unusual phenomenon for the sectarian milieu — unusual in the sense that this time I am speaking not of some new religious searches, even if connected with social protest. I am speaking of ideological searches on *non-religious* paths, although this, of course, did not happen at once.

The leaders of Baptism could not help thinking about these new incidents in their midst, independently of how frequent they may have been. They could not help recognizing that in new social circumstances, the dissatisfaction of believers independently of the forms in which it was expressed, potentially threatened not only the caste but also the class interests of the zealots of the Baptist church.

How could the leaders of Baptism answer the increasingly acute contradictions and class dissension in the congregations, the awakening interests of ordinary believers in the events of class-political struggle? By excluding the rebels from the church and still more deeply isolating believers from the life surrounding them? Such a path was possible and the Tsaritsyn congress of Baptists in 1903 took it.

However, draconian measures could neither liquidate the dissatisfaction of believers with the structure of religious life set up in the Baptist church, nor extinguish the awakening socio-political interests among them.

The internal struggle in the Baptist congregations was conducted around the division of believers into clergy and laymen, into big and little brothers. Ia. Demikhovich, who joined Baptism at the very beginning of the 1900s and subsequently became an Evangelical Christian, wrote of "the most important thing" in "the internal life of Baptist": "The presbyters and their deacons, former artisans, have long since left their workers' benches and live at the present time on salaries received for preaching activity, that is, have become hired 'servants of the word of God', for which they once sharply criticized the Russian Orthodox and Catholic clergy" (Demikhovich 1914: 137). G. Savel'ev wrote in the journal *Baptist* about the dissension in the congregations as a universal phenomenon and named as its reason "the unequal social position and conditions of life", which "divide all brothers into two different categories of people ..." (Savel'ev 1912: 14).

In 1915, a group of members of the Tiflis Baptist congregation appealed in a letter to "all Baptist congregations and individual Baptist brothers in Russia", which characterized in the following manner the situation which had evolved in the Baptist church:

"Long ago many brothers with pain in their hearts noted, and continue to note, that in the activity of the Union of Baptists ... some sort of disorder, some common illness is developing and growing.

"The spiritual life in the congregations has grown cold and no one is concerned about warming up the spirit in them.

"Many enterprises are undertaken with noise, but finish with failure and shame, everywhere there are feuds and disagreements, and, generally speaking, on the whole cause there lies the stamp of some sort of feebleness, some illness....

"We may correctly say that this feeble condition is recognized by all our more or less thoughtful brother Baptists" (Letters 1916: 1).

One "believing brother" noted with anxiety: "Lately in many congregations something new has appeared. I am speaking of the so-called departures." He had in mind people who had broken with Baptism—a member of the congregation who "was sliding downhill, barely stopping short of godlessness", and declared "I am leaving", not waiting to be excommunicated by the church (*B* 1914, No. 1-4, p. 18).

The Russian Orthodox missionary Vortovskii, in a report on the condition of sectarianism in Tavriia Guberniia for 1910, noted concerning "Shtundo-Baptism": "Among the sectarians themselves there is a noticeable decline in interest in their faith"; he even cited the words of one of them that "there is no truth either in Russian Orthodoxy or in sectarianism" (Vortovskii 1911: 11).[...]

Clearly answering the protest from below against the omnipotence of the moneybag in Baptism, V. V. Ivanov in 1910 demagogically called upon believers to "structure their congregations in such a way that among them there would be no needy people, and so that all would be completely and equally materially secure."

V. V. Ivanov demanded "a radical restructuring of our earthly activities". On what basis? "Believers", he declared, "should unite and build public factories or shops and work in them, each according to his ability and occupation, distributing the fruits of their labors equally; or unite in the working of public land" (Ivanov 1910: 266). What Ivanov proposed, essentially, meant replacing bourgeois individual property with bourgeois collective property, supplementing the spiritual brotherhood of the "Cains and Abels" with the economic "concord" of these persons. But Ivanov's plans broke up precisely on those contradictions, for the surmounting of which he had advanced them. Ivanov recognized that there existed "insurmountable difficulties" in the way of economic unification of believers "because of the mental backwardness of the brothers", who did not wish to believe in the efficacy of his plans and (what was most important) "because of insufficient means among ordinary brothers and the lack of desire of rich brothers to give their wealth into common ownership" (Ivanov 1910: 266).

In the atmosphere of ferment existing in the congregations, the open actions of believers against the leaders and increasingly frequent instances of rupture with Baptism, both from religious and in a number of cases from political motives, struggles within the ruling circles of Baptism intensified.

I showed above that in the ruling circles of Baptism there were represented elements personifying various stages of formation of the bourgeois class. On the one hand, these were representatives of agricultural and trading capital, connected in one way or another with the interests of the serf economy, finding means of coexistence with it, borrowing from Molokanism the concept of the unlimited power of "elders" over believers. On the other hand, these were representatives of a bourgeoisie of "average wealth", a second-guild-merchant class, a bourgeois intelligentsia. They belonged to the second generation of Baptists, who had not gone through the school of Molokan social, everyday and religious traditions, in distinction to their fathers who were born as Molokans. They were adherents of "progress", of the bourgeois-democratic structure of the congregations, and of Western-European bourgeois parliamentarianism.

The struggle between the groupings of Dei Mazaev and Vasilii Pavlov, which was unfolding even in the 1870s and 1880s, reflected the inner class contradictions existing in "the highest spheres" of Baptism. The policy of profound isolation of believers from social life, supported by measures of church repression and based on dictatorial forms of rule over believers, was the policy maintained in Baptism by Mazaev's group, and an eloquent example of it was the decision of the Tsaritsyn congress of Baptists in 1903 which I cited above.

Pavlov's group proposed another course. It insisted on a repudiation of the crude forms of leadership of believers, on a rebuilding of the authoritarian structures, on a change of the hierarchical scheme of the structure of the Baptist church in the direction of its democratization, and on the rights of believers to show interest in the events of the surrounding social and political life. This group strove for power in Baptism in order to deflect in good time the growing dissatisfaction of believers, and especially to "nip at the root" the social demands of believers and direct them in the path of class-political interests of the bourgeoisie. Thus, in Baptism a liberal-bourgeois tendency developed and carried on active struggle for its aims (Lialina, ms.).

The struggle between the Pavlov and the Mazaev groupings was conducted in lobbies, in the congregations, at congresses, and in the press, and reached a highly acute state when the most zealous defenders of the Pavlov course broke with the Baptist church, since it was led by the Mazaev group, and defected to the Evangelical Christian church. Polemics between representatives of the hostile groupings and the press primarily concerned the question of the bounds of power of the clergy in the Baptist church.

Representatives of the Pavlov grouping expressed profound conviction that "the administration of the congregation should be in the hands of many experienced brothers, not of one, no matter how experienced"; they expressed "the fear that the presbyter confirmed by the state as 'the preceptor' of the community, depending on this state confirmation, can keep the posterity (i.e. believers—A. K.) at his feet" (Alekhin 1912: 20). Not wishing to be behind the times, the representatives of the liberal-bourgeois tendency trotted out ... Hegel, attempting to justify with his authority their right to the leadership of the Baptist church: "The German philosopher Hegel", wrote one of them, "said that any great idea embodied in the world changes so that its form remains but content evaporates. This evaporation of content must be feared most of all. There will be a preceptor and a council and registers, but there will not be the life-giving spirit of God. Then they will bear supposedly living names, but in fact they will be long dead. Only the forms of church structure will remain, only the title; the spirit of God long ago flew away" (*ibid.*).

The polemics in the press between the representatives of the Mazaev and Pavlov groupings in Baptism do not give a complete idea of the acuteness of the relationships between them: in the last analysis neither side was prepared to wash all its dirty linen in public. Their personal correspondence was another matter, which in 1916 was partially published by Evangelical Christian activists. This correspondence is most interesting not because in the course of mutual squabbles Baptist leaders frankly expressed their opinions of each other, but because the true motives which moved the sides to struggle are laid bare in it. Opponents of Mazaev struggled to preserve the mass base of the Baptist church, and for the policy of "the carrot", since the policy of "the stick" had failed, and to prevent the impending schism in the Baptist church.

In one such letter, addressed to D. I. Mazaev, we read:

"If you stop a minute and follow all your former activity in the Union and in the congregations (of Rostov, etc.) and wish to be honest with yourself, you will see that all your activity was without love, without guardianship and spiritual guidance of the congregations, and was based on 'the scourges' of sharp expressions and 'the scorpion of excommunication'. If you do not see this, we do, having recovered our sight, and soon even the simplest of the simple people from our congregations will see.

"Neither you nor your friends, who call yourselves an organ of a stock company—the Administration—have shown ability to spiritually guide or educate

the congregations, but having advanced the word 'Baptist' and 'Baptism'
... you carry out only one thought, to preserve your power and position in the
Union, zealously supporting it with scourges and scorpions of sharp words and
accusations.... But only one thing can be said, that it will not be surprising if
with this administration we get not two but three, four and even a dozen
Unions. But however many are formed, you, your friends and that administration which is characteristic of you, will be responsible for this ..."
(Letters 1916: 83-84).

In the course of the struggle of the hostile groupings, the publication *Baptist* passed from hand to hand. From the middle of 1907 to 1919, the journal
was in Rostov-on-Don in Mazaev's residence. In 1910, Pavlov had the journal
and transferred its editorship and publication to Odessa. In 1912, Mazaev
again succeeded in taking the publication of *Baptist* into his hands. In 1913,
Pavlov and his co-thinkers Timoshenko, Odintsov and others founded in
Odessa their own publication, called by them *Slovo istiny* [Word of Truth]
(Lialina, ms.).

The repeated manifestation in the Union of Baptists of initiative towards
regularizing relations with the Union of Evangelical Christians was connected
chiefly with the activity of the Pavlov group. To them, Evangelical Christianity,
which had its peculiarities in church structure and its worked-out line in the
fields of social and political questions, was a more or less suitable model by
which the Baptist church should be aligned. A unification of the churches of
Baptists and Evangelical Christians seemed alluring to it, since this would
mean crowding out the Mazaev group from the leadership and a final fixing
of the Baptist church on liberal-bourgeois lines.

On the other hand, a unification of the Baptist and Evangelical Christian
churches could lead to a replacement of the Mazaev leadership by the leadership of Prokhanov and his adherents, in which case the Pavlov group would
be back where they started. In a letter to P. V. Pavlov in June 1916,
M. D. Timoshenko expressed his fears about "joint collaboration" with Prokhanov, predicting that "nothing useful will come of this", and at the same
time insisting on continuing the struggle with the Mazaev group, which he
saw as not adapted to the new circumstances, and as having outlived its time:
"But we, of course, cannot work in agreement with our Molokanizing 'elder-
worshippers'. Honor and glory to them as pioneers in God's cause, but the
plow is heavy for them, and their passion for patronizing workers from among
the Molokans is too noticeable and irritates many ..." (Manuscript division of
MIRA, K. VIII, f. l, s.u. 84, sh. 8-9-v.).

In the struggle with Mazaev, Pavlov's adherents were interested in one
thing: to strengthen their influence on believers by improving the instruments
of influence on them — they wished to replace the "old plow" with a modernized
"plow" of liberal-bourgeois construction. But if the experience of Evangelical
Christianity taught anything, it was that they rejected in one degree or

another even the most modern weapons of bourgeois-ideological influence on believers. Ordinary believers also for the same motives stood out against the leaders of the Evangelical Christian church as they had against the leaders of the Baptist church.

In Evangelical Christianity, in turn, a struggle was taking place which, it is true, did not reach the same dimensions and degree of acuteness as in the Baptist church. This is to be explained partly by the policy of its leaders, more flexible than in Baptism, but chiefly by the fact that in the Evangelical Christian church, which was formed later than the Baptist church, contradictions had not yet had time to show themselves in force. However, even on the eve of World War I, there was taking place the dissillusionment of ordinary believers in Evangelical Christianity, the appearance of schism into groups, and finally, departures from it by believers both as individuals and as entire groups. All this happened although it was carefully covered by a shield of ostentatious democratism.

In August 1908, at a general meeting of the St. Petersburg Evangelical Christian congregation, held under Prokhanov's chairmanship, a resolution was introduced (*Bratskii listok* [Brotherly Leaflet], August 1908; Appendix to *Khristianin* [The Christian], 1908 No. 8, p. 9).:

"1. To introduce and to preserve in the life of the church of God a special equal order....

2. To achieve a more brotherly union, both in action and in life, between educated and uneducated members of the church, and to remove the barriers between them.

3. The general meeting should have primary significance in the life of the church...

4. The brotherly council ... should be an executive institution in relation to the general meeting"

It would seem that everything was not as it was in Baptism.

What occurred in fact? Let us turn to a remarkable account by Ia. Demikhovich, who was for a number of years an enthusiast of Evangelical Christianity. Demikhovich belonged to the Kiev Evangelical Christian congregation. "From the time of weakening of persecution of our congregation", he says, " 'the elder brothers' began to be concerned about its external organization.

"The first transformation in the congregation was the election of a council of 12 persons to whose hands all the affairs of the congregation were entrusted. Thus, all questions were decided by the council, and they then reported to the entire congregation (compare point 4 above—A. K.).

"Since that time, the basis was laid for the division of the congregation into leaders and led, i.e., into bosses and subordinates (compare point 4 above—A.K.)" (Demikhovich 1914: 133).

Further, Demikhovich tells how along with "the council", which ruled the congregation in dictatorial fashion, the presbyter and deacons continued to increase their influence on the affairs of the congregation (*ibid.*). In the congregation "internal mutiny began to grow" (Demikhovich 1914: 134). Demikhovich "clearly understood what enormous changes occurred among the Evangelical Christians. When I entered the congregation, it valued each of its members.... And now they are interested only in submissive sheep" (Demikhovich 1914: 136). In Demikhovich's words, instead of "the spirit of love", "they are occupied with cold dogmatism" (*ibid.*).

The differentiation of the congregations of Evangelical Christians, like that of the Baptist, Molokan, Dukhobor and Khristovover congregations, into ruling clergy and subordinate congregation, was an inevitable consequence of the contradictions of the class make-up of the believers and the deepening class differentiation. The suppression of the "laity" by the "clergy", the action of the laity against the clergy, and the intra-congregational antagonism were an inevitable consequence of the class struggle, expressed in the congregations in religious forms. There were contradictions which it was not given to the clergy to overcome. Mazaev's rule could pass over to Prokhanov's rule, but only in order to return to Mazaev's rule. "Some congregations of Evangelical Christians", Demikhovich wrote, "on the example of the Baptists, also organized a union with a central administration, at the head of which stood the engineer I. S. Prokhanov" (Demikhovich 1914: 137).

It was a vicious circle. "... At the present time", wrote Demikhovich, characterizing the movement of Evangelical Christians contemporaneous with him, "there exist two groups, thanks to which almost everywhere, wherever there are large congregations, they are undergoing schism" (*ibid.*). The congregations breaking away, "wishing to preserve their former autonomy, did not enter the union, thanks to which a hostile relationship exists between these two groups" (*ibid.*). But the development of the group which split away from Prokhanov's union inevitably had to make the same vicious circle. It was only a question of time, and if a comparatively extended period of time was needed for the manifestation of internal contradictions in Khristovoverie or Dukhoborism, the cycle of the development of new religious formations became increasingly shorter as bourgeois contradictions grew in society, and there was ever less distance separating their origin from their death agony.

But let us return once more to Demikhovich's testimony, to its conclusion, for which he used a quotation from a certain "letter of a sectarian to a sectarian": "... every Christian should not only be a believer but have the fullness of the Holy Spirit" (Demikhovich 1914: 140). What did these words mean, which were a kind of summary gleaned by Demikhovich from the experience of disillusionment with Evangelical Christianity? We will return to this somewhat later, but now let me show that the conclusion to which Demikhovich came was shared by some other believers disillusioned with Baptism and Evangelical Christianity.

In February 1908 in the Evangelical Christian journal *Khristianin*, an article was published entitled "On Spiritual Awakenings", in which it was noted that "some believers are very much inclined to consider only the first chapters of the Acts of the Apostles and think that only there are there lessons for spiritual life" (*Khristianin* 1908, No. 2, p. 19). The author of the article thus cautioned the readers of the Acts of the Apostles about superfluous attention, in his opinion, to the so-called descent of the Holy Spirit on the Apostles. Six months later in *Khristianin* there appeared a new article entitled "Can We Expect Another Pentecost?" From the article it appears that "there are so many claimants to the special power among those who declare they have received 'the blessings of the Pentecost', that many Chistians are seriously asking what all this means". It is further explained that "at the prayer-meetings and conferences of preachers the clergy called on all to pray for 'the return of the time of the Pentecost' and for 'the test of the Pentecost' " (*Khristianin* 1908, No. 8, p. 1).

We will not now pose the question of which preachers, which prayer-meetings and conferences the editors of the journal *Khristianin* had in mind. I am interested in the fact that even at the beginning of 1908 among Evangelical Christians (and apparently not only them), the Gospel theme of "the outpouring of the Holy Spirit on the Apostles" (in the Acts of the Apostles) had attracted attention and caused debate. Are not the concluding words of Demikhovich's testimony within this circle of interest: "Each Christian should ... have the fullness of the Holy Spirit"?

In the archives of the Department of Police and the Department of Spiritual Affairs there is preserved information about the activity of a congregation of "Christian Pentecostalists" at the end of 1913 in one of the suburbs of Helsingfors (TsGIAM, div. DP, 1914, No. 166, shs. 1-1 v., 14-14 v., 15; 1916, No. 132, shs. 24-29. TsGIAL, div. 821, f. 133, s.u. 327, shs. 26-27 v.; s.u. 198, shs. 63-64). The congregation's meeting was visited by "sailors, lower officers of the garrison and Russian workers" (TsGIAM, div. DP, 1914, No. 166, sh. 1). At the head of the congregation was a St. Petersburg meshchan, a former Russian Orthodox and later Evangelical Christian, A. I. Ivanov.

When questioned by police authorities in July 1914, Ivanov indicated that the faith professed in the congregation led by him was set forth in a printed brochure, *The Faith of Evangelical Christians*, but was supplemented by "the teaching 'On Awakening as a Consequence of the Descent of the Holy Spirit' and 'On Baptism by Fire and the Spirit' ..." (TsGIAL, div. 821, f. 133, s.u. 327, sh. 34).

In a report of the Department of Police to the Department of Spiritual Affairs, the prayer-meetings of the congregation are described to us: "... during general meetings some of the participants under the influence of Ivanov's sermons, which were distinguished by eloquence and produced a strong impression on the audience, fell into hysterics, shook, cried out and spoke as if they were prophesying in an unknown tongue. All persons who had undergone a similar condition explained these phenomena as the undoubted result of the influence on them of the gift of the Holy Spirit" (TsGIAM, div. DP, 1916, No. 132, sh. 24 v.).

Ivanov, who had gone over to Evangelical Christianity with his family in St. Petersburg, attracted the attention of I. S. Prokhanov by his religious zeal. In 1908, a division of the St. Petersburg Evangelical Christian congregation was started in Helsingfors, headed by Prokhanov who also headed the St. Petersburg congregation. In 1909, Prokhanov named Ivanov preacher of the Helsingfors division of the St. Petersburg congregation. Before his appointment, Ivanov had already been preaching in Vyborg. A schism took place among the Helsingfors Evangelical Christians in 1913, as a result of which Ivanov united the followers of his teaching into an independent congregation.

However, this schism made formal the religious differences which had arisen among Evangelical Christians even before 1913. Ivanov wrote on July 3, 1914: "I have the honor to inform you and answer the questions presented. Question One: 'From what time as the sect founded (by me) existed in the region'. I answer: 'The preaching of the Gospels was begun even before my arrival in Finland by Methodists in 1909 among Russians. From 1910 and to this day, the preaching of the Gospels has been done by me" (TsGIAM, div. DP, 1914, No. 166, sh. 14). Ivanov calls himself the heir of "the preaching of the Gospels", which was done by the Methodists among the Russian population of Finland until Ivanov himself began to do it in 1910.

What Gospel did the Methodists preach in Finland?

From the article by K. Zarnitsyn, "Sekta piatidesiatnikov v Finliandii" [The Pentecostalist Sect in Finland], we learn that "from America the Methodist preacher T. Barrat in 1906 brought the sect to Norway and from there it was soon after brought to Finland. The disseminator of it here was the same T. Barret. For the dissemination of his faith he and his helpers repeatedly traveled into the region, and here in various cities, chiefly in Helsingfors, they set up their religious meetings. The success of their preaching exceeded their expectations. We may boldly say that at the present time in Finland there is not a single city in which there is not a properly organized congregation of Petecostalists" (TsGIAL, div. 821, f. 133, s.u. 327; clipping of Zarnitsyn's article form *Finliandskaia gazeta* [Finnish Newspaper]).

Judging from Ivanov's answer to the question as to the time of founding of his sect, and from the fact that he called himself the heir of the preaching of the Gospels which the Methodists had done in Finland, his world-view was formed as Pentecostalist even before 1910—i.e. approximately at the time when the journal *Khristianin* noted the fact of the attention paid by believers to the teaching about the Pentecost.

Ivanov declared that "we do not recognize the nickname given us of 'the sect of Christians of the Pentecost' ... but we have the honor to call ourselves here in the region Russian Evangelical Christians" (TsGIAM, div. DP, 1914, No. 166, sh. 14). Let us note that after the split from the Evangelical Christians, Ivanov rented in Helsingfors a separate building for use in preaching to a gathering of "free Russian Evangelists" (TsGIAM, div. DP, 1916, No. 132, sh. 25). Ivanov's closest helpers were people who had broken with Evangelical Christianity along with him: F. A. Tuchkov, a retired naval guard, born a peasant in the Rostov-on-Don region; A. K. Chernukhin, a civilian telegrapher and former peasant from Voronezh Guberniia (TsGIAL, div. 821, f. 133, s.u. 327, shs. 29 v. and 30 v.); and a meshchan from Libava, the Lett K. I. Vetsgaver (TsGIAM, div. DP, 1916, No. 132, sh. 28 v.). Maslov, Stepanov, Prokhorov and Khakkarainen, whose social origin and position I did not succeed in learning, were also active members of the congregation founded by Ivanov.

Among Ivanov's followers a significant number were sailors from military ships and lower officers of the garrison in Helsingfors. For this category of Ivanov's followers, apparently, anti-military motifs—which were prominent in his sermons—were most important. During a search of Tuchkov, a brochure was taken away which developed the idea of stopping "squabbles or wars" among peoples (TsGIAM, div. DP, 1916, No. 132, sh. 28).

How well Ivanov's preaching matched the anti-military mood of his sailor audience is evident from the fact that "on June 19, 1915, on the ship 'Slava', several sailors—Ivanov's followers—with whom he had held private conversations, refused to take their places for a military drill, for which they were handed over to a military court. They were deprived by the court of all rights of their position and were sent to prison work for various terms" (TsGIAL, div. 821, f. 133, s.u. 198, sh. 63-63 v.). After the sentencing of the sailors of the ship "Slava", Chernukhin appealed by letter to the sailors of the ship "Sevastopol", asking them to pray for those who were suffering (TsGIAM, div. DP, 1916, No. 132, sh. 28 v.).

Ivanov's anti-militaristic preaching only accompanied his dissemination of the teaching on the Pentecost and on the acquisition by believers of "the fullness of the Holy Spirit". Anti-war motifs were in significant degree a local phenomenon, conditioned by the special surroundings in which Ivanov acted.

In November 1915, Ivanov, Tuchkov, Chernukhin and Vetsgaver were arrested and exiled to Turgai Oblast, and gatherings of their followers were forbidden (TsGIAL, div. 821, f. 133, s.u. 327, sh. 20). However, meetings of

Pentecostalists continued. Thus, in the private house of one Raudsepp, the military authorities of Helsingfors found on January 29, 1917, a gathering led by Stepanov, at which "besides private persons, 20 lower officers took part ..." (TsGIAL, div. DP, 1917, No. 132, sh. 15).

Ivanov, his helpers, and all his followers were subjected to excommunication from the Evangelical Christian church and received from it the nickname of "Shakers".[15] However, the new teaching continued to spread. A group of adherents of Pentecostalism split off from the congregation of Evangelical Christians in Petrograd itself. The same group appeared in Baku (TsGIAL, div. 821, f. 133, s.u. 198, sh. 63 v.). In the newspaper *Utrenniaia zvezda,* published by Prokhanov, in 1914 there was printed a "warning": "in Helsingfors, in Vyborg, and also in St. Petersburg there has appeared a sect of people calling themselves Pentecostalists but who in reality are Shakers. These people are barely discernable from Khlysty and Pryguny. They have nothing in common either with Baptists or with Evangelical Christians. At the present time their 'prophets' Maslov and Stepanov are traveling south. We ask the brothers and sisters to beware of them, as they are bringing another teaching. The same is true of the other preachers — A. I. Ivanov, S. I. Prokhanov, Khakkarainen (an Estonian), and others" (*UZ* 1914, No. 15).

Meanwhile, a Pentecostalist group arose in Tiflis among the local Baptist congregation. The council of the Union of Evangelical Christians, notifying the congregation of this, and at the same time not failing to accuse the Baptist leaders V. V. Ivanov and N. V. Odintsov of Shakerism, noted with alarm in its letter: "We know that abroad the Shaker movement, a terrible whirlwind, has destroyed many congregations. This movement in the beginning does not seem dangerous, but the results are bitter" (Letters 1916: 57).

Pentecostalism arose both in the Baptist and in the Evangelical Christian congregations. Even in 1911 in the journal *Baptist* there was published a "warning" from the Blagoveshchensk Baptist congregation; in it they reported about the Baptist D. M. Chetverikov, "who tended toward Prygunism" (*B* 1911, No. 39; printed on the cover) and departed from Blagoveshchensk in order to preach his doctrine. In the same journal there was published a "warning" coming from Millerovo, where N. P. Smorodin had entered the local Baptist congregation, having directly declared that "he does not belong either to the Baptists or to the Evangelists, but to the Pentecostalists", and after his preaching he left in the congregation "very sad traces" (*B* 1914, No. 13-14, p. 23).

In the journal *Gost',* V. Gedeonov confirmed that "in various places some believers are attracted to the so-called 'Pentecost' movement ..." (*G* 1914,

---

[15] TsGIAL, div, 821, f. 133, s.u, 198, sh. 63; *see* also Letters 1916: 57: "In 1913 in Helsingfors and Vyborg a movement of Shakers appeared. Members of Evangelical Christian congregations who were attracted to Shakerism were excommunicated".

No. 6, p. 155). The Pentecostalist movement had turned into a threat which was impossible to stave off with "warnings". Still the journal *Gost'* published yet another "warning", which I cite not only as testimony to the rapid spread of Pentecostalism, but also in confirmation of the fact that it developed because of the differentiation, contradictions, and internal struggle taking place in the Baptist congregations. "In No. 6 of *Gost'*, in the article by Vasilii Gedeonov about the 'false Pentecostalism', it is said in this 'warning': a serious warning was given to the congregations and to the brothers in general to be very circumspect and attentive, in order not to fall into the snare of the devil. We are now receiving from several places information about sad consequences after visits to the congregations by persons who succeeded in gaining the trust of the brothers. Disturbances, discord, and rebellion against the ruling brothers, etc., has occurred, just as happened in the congregation in M., upon the arrival there of a certain excommunicated S.' (*G* 1914, No. 9, p. 226. The "M" congregation is probably Millerovo where the Pentecostalist Smorodin spoke — A. K.).

Pentecostalism, like the movements of Koval' and Malëvannyi which preceded it, was a religious sect arising out of the Baptist church and in opposition to it, like the religious sects which in their time arose in the midst of the Russian Orthodox Church and against it. In distinction to Khristovoverie, Dukhoborism, Molokanism, Baptism and Evangelical Christianity, it (like Adventism) was not so much an antagonist of the ruling Russian Orthodox Church as its more or less successful competitor.

The criticisms which the opposition which arose in Baptism directed against it recalled in many respects the criticisms directed against the Russian Orthodox Church by the old Russian sects. And like the protest of Russian Orthodox sectarianism (as it is sometimes called), the protest of Baptist sectarianism (by analogy) was fed by no means solely by the contradictions and defects of the church against which it was directed. Pentecostalism attracted many ordinary Baptists and Evangelical Christians, not only by its criticisms of the structure of their church, but by the fact that it commented, in accordance with the prejudices of its followers, on the social life surrounding them.

I do not know the concrete character of Ivanov's preaching when he spoke in Vyborg and Helsingfors to an audience of followers consisting of sailors, artisans, workers and meshchane. The scanty data which I have suggests that Ivanov somehow connected his preaching on the "outpouring of the Spirit" with anti-war moods. I do not have information which would allow me to confirm in what spirit other preachers of Pentecostalism spoke. But it remains a fact that the ideology of Pentecostalism arose due to the powerlessness and disillusionment of "the little man" faced with the contradictions of capitalist reality surrounding him. The Baptist church which he entered disappointed his hopes. Illusions were lost, but reality was as merciless as before, and since "the little man" did not find real paths of struggle to replace broken illusions, there came not sobriety of consciousness but new, still deeper illusions.

To precisely which of man's fears in the face of the present and the future the preaching of Pentecostalism appealed, we can judge for example from the meeting of T. Barrat's followers and helpers which took place on November 3, 1912 in Helsingfors (the place and time of Ivanov's activity). The preacher exclaimed: "Do you not see the signs of the times? Do you not see how strongly the people are preparing? Soon a great, terrible, and exterminating war will be beginning! A time is coming of such misfortunes, as has not been from the creation of the world! Oh, if only people wished to listen to this last warning, the last appeal, the last counsel! The last great conflict is approaching! The evil fire of a great sorrow is ready to burn and then will turn into a great flame" (TsGIAL, div, 821, f. 133, s.u. 327, sh. 13).

Pentecostalism, as happened more than once in the history of religious sectarianism, turned to mysticism, expressed in the teaching of the direct communion of man with the Spirit, and, through its mediation, with the triune God—a concept held by Pentecostalism. But it did not call man to perfect his spiritual forces and to reach, thanks to his will, that fullness of perfection in which he would supposedly become like Christ.

The spirit of man was given no significance whatever, and in this the ideological connection of Pentecostalism with Baptism is especially evident. Man, according to the teaching of Pentecostalism, received the gifts of the Holy Spirit, after which he was moved in his way of life not by his own force, but by that of the Almighty. It is clear that where man was "intimate" with the force of the Most High, there was no place either for senior presbyters or for junior ones, nor for deacons or "fraternal councils". In distinction to the early mystical teachings of Koval', and Malëvannyi after him, which arose in Baptism, Pentecostalism remained one with orthodox Baptism in the recognition of the dogma of predestination. On the other hand, the teaching of orthodox Baptism had mystical origins, which Pentecostalism only subsequently developed.

In fact, Baptist theology distinguishes successive stages of unification with God by man the sinner, in the form firstly of "conversion", and secondly of "rebirth". As concerns "conversion", it is explained as a matter of man's will, which consists in the suppression one after another of worldly interests and desires, in fencing-off the internal world form everything worldly, as a result of which man is turned into a "hollow vessel", ready to accept God. Later, "rebirth" may or may not follow, since this is declared exclusively a matter of divine will, and consists in the installation in man of the spirit of God. This is a purely mystical conception. The act of installation of the spirit of God in man, according to the teaching of the Baptists and the declarations of believers themselves, is accompanied by special spiritual experiences, not accessible to someone who has not been "reborn".

This is really a special feeling in the believer himself, qualified by him as a "birth from above", but essentially it is the result of special long psychic training, called in Baptism "conversion". The Baptist "rebirth" is nothing other than the deluded "spiritual joy" of the Khristovovers, with the sole difference that the ecstatic religious rituals of the Khristovovers have been replaced by more civilized means of artificially over-exciting the psyche. Pentecostalism, with its teaching of the outpouring of the gifts of the Holy Spirit, with its exaltation and its "speaking in tongues", was "flesh of the flesh" of the Baptist belief.

The thunder of Pentecostalism had hardly broken over Baptism before the leaders of the latter found a lightning rod. This was done by the most resourceful of the Baptist leaders—V. Fetler. He founded the society of the Brotherhood of the Acts of the Apostles, raising on its shield "Pentecostalism—the outpouring on the Apostles of the Holy Spirit." At the end of 1910, Fetler made an appeal "for service to the Lord from the whole heart". He did not hide the circumstances which prompted him to call for a new method of "serving of Lord".

"At the present time", Fetler wrote, "our dear Russia is experiencing in all strata of society a very critical period, when unbelief in society and lack of faith in the churches of God are developing with frightening rapidity, where almost everyone has turned onto his own road, and where sin in all forms manifests its deathly activity—it is time to speak" (*G* 1910, No. 2, p. 12).

Fetler appealed for the creation within the Baptist church of a "society of apostles", equivalent in its aims, way of life and method of preaching to that apostolic Christianity described in the Book of Acts. Persons entering the society were expected to renounce property, family and personal interests, and by means of maximal self-limitation and orientation toward the apostolic mission, to become easily flammable material for the activity of the Holy Spirit. This was essentially an attempt to create a monastic order in Baptism. Fetler introduced the giving of Old Testament names to persons who entered his society. The journal *Gost'*, which Fetler edited, became the special organ of the Brotherhood of the Acts of the Apostles (*G* 1910, No. 2, p. 13). Fetler's initiative was supported by some other leaders of Baptism, among them I. V. Kargel' and V. V. Ivanov. This was the means of serving the Lord with the help of which Fetler wished to discharge the tense atmosphere in Baptism. Perhaps Fetler and his associates had in mind the journal *Khristianin*, which expressed dissatisfaction with preachers who were calling in prayer-meetings for a return "to the time of the Pentecost".

Fetler's scheme called forth Prokhanov's displeasure; still less could it be to the taste of Mazaev and Pavlov. In Baptism there had arisen a new organization, but of a kind which used as material for its demagogy the oppositionist moods of ordinary believers. At the time when the Brotherhood of the Acts of the Apostles was being put together, in the circles of the World Congress of Baptists (in 1911) Fetler was spoken of as the leader of the coming reformation in Russia, similar to Luther or Melanchthon. While there was a disdainful attitude (and not without foundation) toward Fetler's enterprise, its realization was impossible.

Although Pentecostalism arose as a form of opposition to the authoritarianism of the Baptist church and the dogmatism of its teaching, it was a profoundly reactionary teaching, narcotizing the consciousness of its followers. Fetler understood this when he created the Brotherhood of the Acts of the Apostles. His initiative, as has already been shown, was condemned by the leading circles of Baptism. However, the upper strata of Baptism based their hopes precisely on the Pentecostalist teaching when, in the course of the Great October Revolution, many ordinary believers began to depart from it. Although this goes beyond the chronological bounds of this work, I will nevertheless cite the statements of Baptist leaders in the first half of 1918, which show to what degree they valued the narcotizing force of the Pentecostalist teaching of the outpouring of the Holy Spirit, and of the fullness with the Holy Spirit, etc. In March 1918, V. V. Ivanov published an article, *Kuda my zashli* [Where We Have Come], in which he wrote in Pentecostalist fashion: "Now we do not hear about the Holy Spirit, and we do not encounter anywhere now such precious words as 'they were filled with the Holy Spirit' and 'the Spirit said'. If once they spoke or wrote of the Holy Spirit, they never heard its voice or saw its action.... Now Christians have to deal with Christ as relatives in Europe do, with those who live overseas, whom they never see and with whom they communicate and have acquaintance only by letters. They do not have telephone lines. Now believers have become like lawyers: everything with them is on the basis of Scripture, on the basis of texts" (Ivanov 1918: 60).

V. G. Pavlov echoed V. V. Ivanov: "Why among you, and not only among you but in Russia in general, is there a low level of spiritual life? We need the fullness of the spirit, the fullness with the Holy Spirit ..." (Pavlov 1918: 82).

It is noteworthy that V. G. Pavlov defined this essentially Pentecostalist preaching as descent from the "first stage" — i.e. the general bases of orthodox Baptism, which already constituted in his words "a pledge, the beginnings of the Holy Spirit". Thus, the teaching of "fullness with the Holy Spirit", so characteristic of Pentecostalism, was, according to a Baptist leader himself, nothing other than the "second stage" in the development of the belief system of Baptism. The Pentecostalist utterances of the most important figures in Russian Baptism were yet another attempt to keep ordinary believers from participating in the struggle for fundamental social transformations, the path toward which was opened by the Great October Revolution.

V. V. Ivanov directly counterposed the preaching of mystical ecstasy to the stormy increase of revolutionary feelings of the workers, including ordinary believers. "And now", he wrote, "in what ecstasy and with what shining faces are many believers — the peasants when the socialization of land occurs, when the landowners and their property-owning brothers have land taken away from them and their estates plundered.... They are swiftly carried away by the violent stream of bloody worldly politics" (Ivanov 1918: 60).

Under conditions where the ordinary preaching of the Baptist faith did not justify the hopes of their preachers, they appealed to the Holy Spirit of the Pentecostalists. They attempted to place this mystical teaching on guard over the interests of the landowners and property-owning brothers, for the preservation of their lands and estates. The Pentecostalist teaching was one of the ideological weapons of bourgeois counter-revolution....

Baptism at the beginning of the 20th century was made up of contradictions. Between its two branches in Russia — the Baptist church and the Evangelical Christian church — a stubborn competitive struggle did not cease. In each of these churches, antagonism between the upper and lower ranks grew, and in the consciousness of the struggling lower classes there began to dawn the idea that their struggle against the upper strata had not a religious but a social and class character.

Cases of participation of ordinary Baptists in the Russian liberation movement occurred, and also cases of their breaking with Baptism and with religion in general. However, in the mass of participants of Baptism, their protest, while it went as far as a direct break with Baptism (the Pentecostalists), was covered with a religio-mystical integument. The struggle between the lower and upper strata in the mutually competing Baptist churches was supplemented by the struggle occurring within their ruling groups, which complicated still more the position of these churches. This was a knot of contradictions reflecting in miniature and in peculiar form the basic contradictions of classes in Russian society at the beginning of the 20th century. Baptism, like any other religious organization, whatever their participants and leaders thought about themselves, was one of the weapons of class-political struggle. In contrast to the groupings of the old Russian sectarianism, whose representatives excelled in searching out and inventing religious concepts in order to cover their social and class interests with them, the leaders of Baptism made very modest use of the religious vocabulary when speaking of their class-political interests.

It is true that Mazaev and the circles which he represented insisted on the apolitical nature of the Baptist church: "My kingdom is not of this world". This also was politics, which had absorbed the "apoliticism" of the Molokan elders, coinciding with monarchism, and matching the mode of thought of Mazaev and his circle of large businessmen — not ideologists, but *practical* bourgeois entrepreneurs and exploiters.

Baptism, in the person of the All-Russian Union of Evangelical Christians and in the person of the Pavlov movement in the Union of Russian Baptists, came out with a political program barely covered with Christian phraseology. This was a program first formulated by Baptism in 1905 and counterposed to the revolution. Baptism carried this program from 1905 to 1917. Among the most important reasons moving ordinary believers to protest against the Baptist church was its political program, which was repulsive in its reactionary nature.

5. Baptism and Evangelical Christianity in the Period of the First Bourgeois-Democratic Revolution (1905-1907)

The history of religious sectarianism shows relations within the sect, each of which proclaims the idea of Christian unity and brotherhood and the mutual relationships of the sects with each other, was characterized by a vicious, irreconcilable struggle, full of hatred.

This was basically a class struggle. As concerns the hostility which marked the mutual relations of the sects, it arose not only from competition in the field of snaring human souls, but from various, and in a number of cases contrary, socio-political interests. Moreover, the sects took a hostile attitude toward the traditions of their own history, renouncing their past like "Ivans who do not know their ancestors". Above, we noted the instance of denial by New Israelites (in 1909) of their connection with the Khristovover movement. This was an attempt by a religious organization which had become reactionary to renounce democratic traditions which existed in its distant past. As Khristovovers at the beginning of the 20th century consigned to oblivion and condemnation the Khristovovers of the 18th century, the Baptist church even at the beginning of its spread in Russia distanced itself from all forms of old Russian sectarianism.

The leaders of the Baptist church acted as conscious representatives of a religious movement setting itself in opposition to any attempts by democratic elements to use religion as an expression of their social protest.

In the 1890s in the pages of *Beseda* [Conversation], a polemic developed between Prokhanov, the head of this Evangelical Christian publication, and the Tolstoyan activist Khilkov. Defending the idea of non-resistance to evil, Khilkov warned the Baptists that "they will turn from a religious sect into a political one", since they did not follow the religious teaching of Tolstoy. Polemicizing with Khilkov, Prokhanov cited history in order to emphasize the complete lack of correspondence between the teachings and the actions of the revolutionary sects during the Reformation and Baptism. "The Anabaptist movement", he wrote," having begun (in Zwickau) with the renunciation of war, military service etc., was transformed into Münzer's violent revolution.

The Baptists in England, however, from the very beginning, not having made a dogma of denial of state service etc., remained all the time the most peaceful of people ..." (Val'kevich 1900: Appendix 3, p. 64).

Prokhanov disassociated himself from the historical traditions and spiritual heritage of the Anabaptists, as from all other forms of old Russian sectarianism. He wrote: "Between the branches called by the government Shtundism (Baptists, child-christeners and Pashkovites), the bases of dogma are common.... But no one can include Dukhobors and Molokans among the Shtundists. They are a separate group of sectarianism" (Val'kevich 1900: Appendix 3, p. 62).

Let us see how the demarcation between the Baptist church and those groups of religious sectarianism, which once arose as phenomena of social protest by democratic elements, was politically realized. We have already had occasion to note the direct and open connection of Baptism with the political interests of bourgeois parties in Russia as one of its distinguishing features (Klibanov 1957: 390-391). In the era of imperialism, with its naked and extremely acute class contradictions, the religious integument was a very poor instrument not ony for covering the protests of the socially lower classes, but also for the expression of the class interests of the bourgeois upper classes. The religious integument of sectarianism was worn thin and was breaking, both for the lower classes affirming their socio-political interests, and for the upper classes, who had abandoned the religious conventions and formulated their interests in congregations, in congresses and in the press, using the political language of the bourgeoisie. This was shown by V. D. Bonch-Bruevich as early as 1902.

To characterize the political views held by the most conscious representatives of Baptism, Bonch-Bruevich cited a letter of one of them written to Khilkov in February 1902: "If we start a revolution and the land remains private property, then of course it is not worth starting it!" The author of the letter, whose name Bonch-Bruevich for quite obvious reasons did not mention, proceeded from the assumption that only the question of the land, and not of a parliamentary system as such, was the basic question of the threatening revolution. He wrote: "Our brothers live abroad in Rumania, and they say there is a consititution there, there is a parliament, but the land is almost entirely in the hands of the landlords, and so what benefit do the people have from this parliament?" (Bonch-Bruevich 1902: 315). It is not impossible that the author of the letter cited belonged to the intelligentsia, although essentially the ideas expressed by him did not go much further than those of the peasant Dukhobor Podovinnikov, whose conversation with the missionary Skvortsov (in 1895) I cited above.

The opinion of the unknown author cited by Bonch-Bruevich lies within the circle of those politically mature utterances of ordinary Baptists which I cited in the correspondence with Tregubov. Using Khilkov's archives, Bonch-Bruevich cites—this time "as an example of the agreement of the ideologists of the large bourgeoisie with *Russkie vedomosty* [Russian News] and *Russkaia mysl'* [Russian Thought] headed by representatives of Old Shtundism (Russian Baptism)"—an excerpt from a letter dated August 22, 1901, by one of the most important, most loyal leaders of the Russian Baptist organization.

Bonch-Bruevich does not mention the name of the author of this letter, written privately to Khilkov. Let us quote a part of this letter: "I think that our people should be enlightened relative to their most important needs, which were expressed, for example, by Count L. N. Tolstoy in his appeal to the tsar. Most important of all is the need for religious freedom. Nevertheless, brochures which deny all authority and law hardly find sympathy in the popular masses. If we wish freedoms in Russia, then 'political figures', even students, should begin by seeking the introduction of a constitution, in order that the people might have their representatives, who could declare their needs, accept or reject projected laws. This would be useful and would sooner lead to tangible results than a denial of any authority" (Bonch-Bruevich 1902: 310-311).

The polemical note in the segment cited relates to the anarchistic views of the state propagandized by the Tolstoyans (in particular by Khilkov, to whom the letter is addressed). Bourgeois constitutional ideals, developed among representatives of the liberal direction in Baptism even in the 1890s, and were formed not without the influence of Western-European bourgeois parliamentarianism. For example, Prokhanov, who visited the British Parliament in 1896, described with enthusiasm how the House of Commons "together with the Lords make all laws and govern the country. The Queen only reigns...." The parliamentary structure of England seemed to Prokhanov the ideal of democratic structure: "Every five years all members of Parliament are elected by people again and of course only the best people are chosen. Any simple worker has a voice in the elections, and thus the people as it were themselves govern the country" etc., etc. (Val'kevich 1900: Appendix 3, pp. 123-124).

Finally, as Bonch-Bruevich notes, "among the Baptists there is also a mature 'right' wing...." For its representatives an ostentatious apoliticism was characteristic—an apprarent devotion "to exclusively religious questions". This was a position which excluded the very possibility of ordinary Baptists having opinions of a political character. The apoliticism of the representatives of the right wing in Baptism consisted in the demand that the autocratic structure be considered not subject to review. One of them wrote in September 1901 to Khilkov: "Personally I attempt to release man from the yoke of the priests, but I do not wish to concern myself with political questions" (Bonch-Bruevich 1902: 311).

The events of class and political struggle in the period of the maturing revolutionary crisis in Russia deepened and made more acute the contradictions within the Baptist milieu. I. P. Kushnerov directly connected the decisions of the Tsaritsyn congress of Baptists in 1903 with the peasant unrest which took place in the second half of 1901-1902 in Khar'kov and Poltava Guberniias, and which spilled over into a mass peasant uprising (Kushnerov 1905: 9-10). Among the peasants in the Khar'kov and Poltava areas there were many followers of Baptism, and it is quite possible that some among them there were sympathetic to the rebels and their cause. Tregubov's archive, which I studied, and which assembled information about the participation of sectarians in the liberation movement, gives reason to deny the immediate participation of Baptists in the uprising. However, we have to remember that Tregubov collected his material with the aim of showing that the mass of ordinary sectarians was hostile to the revolutionary struggle, and that the activity of the Social Democrats directed at the revolutionary enlightenment of sectarians had no foundation.

Indirect data allow us to assume that the famous Rostov strike in November 1902 had the sympathy of some Baptists on its side. In a letter to the Baptist I. D. Liasotskii on May 11, 1903, Tregubov wrote of his supposition that "social revolutionaries have penetrated among the Rostov brothers and they are attempting to sow their seeds ...", and he commissioned Liasotskii to appear "in Rostov at the fraternal meeting" and "without saying anything to anyone earlier, after the service" to read "publicly to all brothers" the Tolstoyan appeal against violent struggle (Tregubov's Letter to Liasotskii, May 11, 1903, ROBIL, Chertkov Collection).

As far as we can judge from subsequent letters by Tregubov to Liasotskii, Tregubov's assignment was not fulfilled by him, and what Liasotskii told Tregubov about the revolutionary struggle of the Rostov workers was profoundly disappointing to the latter. "It was very sad to read", Tregubov answered Liasotskii's communication, "that the Rostov workers, who after all are for the most part Christians, used force and fights with police and soldiers" (Undated Letter by Tregubov to I. D. Liasotskii; see also Tregubov's letters to Liasotskii dated July 3, 5, and 18, 1903, ROBIL, Chertkov Collection).

The leaders of the Baptist church in 1900 and 1904 did everything in their power in order to prevent or at least limit the participation of ordinary Baptists in the revolutionary events which were occurring. The general strike in the south of Russia in 1903, which was distinguished by a combination of economic and political demands; the rise of the peasant movement, which was especially noticeable in the Ukraine; and the Baku and St. Petersburg strikes of December 1904, put the leaders of the Baptist church on their guard, who chose as their basic course in the extraordinary circumstances which were evolving, an open political union with the Autocracy, including support of the ruling Russian Orthodox Church.

The plenipotentiaries of the Kiev and Khar'kov Baptist congregations—
I. P. Kushnerov and V. N. Ivanov—having arrived in St. Petersburg, met
with the plenipotentiary of the St. Petersburg congregation, V. I. Dolgopolov,
in order to work out and present to the authorities a special document—an
oath on the preparedness of the Baptist church to enter into the political
reserves of the Autocracy when faced with the developing revolutionary
events. This document, under the title *Kratkaia zapiska o vozniknovennii,
razvitii i o nastoiashchem polozhenii evangel'skogo dvizheniia v Rossii i o
nuzhdakh evangel'shikh khristian* [A Short Note on the Origin, Development
and Present Position of the Evangelical Movement in Russia and On the
Needs of Evangelical Christians], was composed and signed by Kushnerov,
Ivanov and Dolgopolov in St. Petersburg on January 8, 1905.

The social and political views of Baptism were summed up by the com-
posers of the document thus: "Evangelical Christians profess the bases of the
family and marriage, and also of the state structure with all the obligations of
its citizens, including military obligations in a general Christian sense. It is
superfluous to say that the right of private and public property is recognized
by them in the generally accepted Chistian sense not only in theory but in the
practice of life" (Kushnerov 1905: 9).

The attitude of Baptism toward property and the bases of state structure
hardly called forth great doubt or fear on the part of the Autocracy, in spite
of every sort of false rumor on this account proceedings from ruling church
circles. It was more complicated for the Baptist plenipotentiaries to formulate
their attitude toward Russian Orthodoxy and "freedom of conscience". Attempting to reduce to a minimum everything that could diminish their
significance as a political ally of the Autocracy, the writers of the note
declared that "the views of Evangelical Christians include all the basic principles of the Russian Orthodox Church" (Kushnerov 1905: 10). Even if on
August 22, 1901, a well-meaning Baptist leader wrote to Khilkov: "Most important of all is religious freedom", and considered it necessary to "achieve
the introduction of a constitution" (see above), the Baptist leaders on January
8, 1905 were not considering a constitution or religious freedom. They wrote:
"In respect to the views on freedom and the church, Evangelical Christians
are in full agreement with the best representatives of the Russian Orthodox
Church: Metropolitan Filaret and Khomiakov and Aksakov (Slavophiles) etc.
mentioned above. In this evangelically free Christianity is the salvation of our
dear fatherland from all its weaknesses and diseases: corrupting drunkenness
and decadence and threatening dangers: religious indifferentism to religion
among the middle and upper classes, signs of bitter struggle between classes
and strata, threatening to lead to bloody events. Only in the Gospels is there
reconciliation and renewal" (Kushnerov 1905: 14-15).

How great must have been the Baptist leaders' fear of the revolution if

Filaret, the author of the sadly famous memorandum, *O telesnykh nakazaniiakh s khristianskoi tochki zreniia* [On Corporal Punishment From the Christian Point of View], seemed to them an apostle of freedom! Filaret, whom Lenin called a defender of "serf law based on Holy Scripture"! (*Lenin*: V. 339).

In 1896, Prokhanov disassociated himself from Dukhoborism, Molokanism, Tolstoyism, and "old" religious sectarianism in general, contrasting to it the new Baptist and Evangelical Christian church.

Eight years later the Baptist leaders explained what the novelty distinguishing their church was: "The views of the Evangelical Christians include all the basic principles of the Russian Orthodox Church". There was a share of exaggeration in the words of the Baptist leaders, and a large portion of truth!

The unfolding revolutionary events of the summer of 1905, and the All-Russian political strike in October 1905, forced the Autocracy to make concessions in the form of the Manifesto of October 17. The promise by the Autocracy of freedom, and the calling of a legislative Duma, were considered by the bourgeoisie just and sufficient reward for cooperating with the state structure in the struggle with the revolutionary movement.

Representatives of the various groups of the bourgeoisie, proceeding from the principles of the Manifesto of October 17, united into political parties—the Constitutional-Democratic and "the Union of October 17", the party of large bourgeois businessmen, industrialists and landowners. At the same time there arose a political organization uniting bourgeois elements of the Baptist, Evangelical Christian and Mennonite churches, which called itself "the Union of Freedom, Truth and Peace".

The basic contingent of the members of the Union of Freedom, Truth and Peace consisted of Mennonites, chiefly from the colonies in the Crimea. The Union was headed by M. P. Frizen, who was "a member-supervisor" of the Central Bureau of the Union, which included leaders and important figures of Baptism and Evangelical Christianity, as for example I. S. Prokhanov, N. V. Odintsov, I. M. Staroverov and P. E. Iudin, consisted of 17 active members and one honorary one. In the Central Bureau there were 3 noblemen, 3 peasants, 2 houseowners, 1 kulak, 2 members of the bourgeois intelligentsia, 2 clerical workers, 2 members from a military family and the civil service bureaucracy, and 2 preceptors of congregations (*KV* 1905, No. 298: 3).

From the role which Frizen played in the Union, and the part which Mennonites took in it, this organization received in the press the name of "the Frizen Party". The Union of Freedom, Truth and Peace saw itself as a political party but recruited "some persons who were non-party and not members of the Union, as expert advisors on questions of an industrial and juridical character" (*ibid.*). Sevastopol, whose population included many Baptists, Evangelical Christians and Mennonites, became the Central Bureau's permanent location. N. Vortovskii, describing in 1910 the condition of the eparchy of Tavriia, noted: "... the center of sectarianism in the eparchy of Tavriia, without any doubt, is the city of Sevastopol, and from the role which it has begun to play in recent years in the history of the sectarian movement, we can say that at the present time, Sevastopol occupies one of the first places not only here in the south, but in all of Russia" (Vortovskii 1911: 4).

The Union had as its most immediate task participation in the upcoming Duma elections. The initiators of the Union—Frizen, Prokhanov and Odintsov—issued in October 1905 a pre-election appeal to "brothers, friends and good citizens": "Time is precious and the matter is urgent, therefore let us create out of ourselves one indivisible, holy and large family, bound by freedom, truth and peace, but not by quarrels, theft, arson, blood-letting, destruction and other disorders, to which anarchists and revolutionaries call us" (Manuscript Division, MIRA, K. VIII, f. l, s.u. 3, sh. 1). The appeal concluded with the words: "Let us enter into a good union with each other ... let us peacefully elect our representatives, who will rule from our heart with our tsar and wipe away the long tears of our motherland, for which we call for God's blessing, and may he preserve our sovereign emperor, his house, his good counselors, and us all" (*ibid.*). To the appeal there was appended a document—"The State Platform of the Union of Freedom, Truth and Peace, opponents of any violence, proponents of constant civil, economic, spiritual and moral progress" (*ibid.*, sh. 2).

We can now familiarize ourselves with the character of the constitutional ideas of the Baptist leaders and at the same time evaluate the full justification of the alarm of the Baptist who wrote to Khilkov in 1902 about the constitution and parliament in Rumania, at a time in which the peasants there did not have land. The State Platform of the Mennonite Baptist Party proclaimed:

1. "The stability of the monarchy" under unicameral "popular representation" and with equal granting of legislative initiative to the tsar and to the chamber;

2. "Universal suffrage with equal, direct and secret voting by all adults ...";

3. "The wholeness and indivisibility" of the state with local self-government in the form of regional Dumas, on condition that the activity of these will be "in strict agreement with Empire-wide laws and interests"—i.e., no effective rights for the Duma. It was said of Finland: "The constitution of Finland and its connection with the All-Russian state remains in force";

4. "A firm, incorruptible, humanist government, by appointment from the sovereign, under his control and that of the popular representatives";

5. "A strong state defense" with simultaneous renunciation of "a policy of conquest".

Further, they envisaged a reform of the courts and of penal policy, the introduction of obligatory free education of children, and "the gradual removal of all state protection and subsidization of all faiths. Free competition in preaching of the Gospels and in matters of love", the introduction of ["] freedom of conscience, speech, association and assembly" (*ibid.*, shs. 2-4).

The State Platform was completely subordinate to the desire of its initiators to gather as many votes as possible in the forthcoming Duma elections, counting on the demagogic effect of proposals for renunciation of the policy of conquest, universal free education, universal suffrage, etc., etc. But the "impulse" of the Platform undoubtedly consisted in the principle of the stability of the monarchy; and in fact, everything in the Platform that related to the concept of state power was aimed at the protection of the sovereignty of the Autocracy from the "popular representative". The social legislation in the constitutional Mennonite-Baptist project envisaged the supplying of peasants with allotted and rented land "at just, moderate prices", the extension of credit to "model farms of peasant type", the resettlement of the peasants—in other words, in many respects the program anticipated Stolypin's agrarian policy.

In the heat of constitutional inventiveness, the initiators of the Union hinted at giving "in factual possession to the tillers of the soil a sufficient quantity of land under conditions which would secure a comfortable existence". This is what was said in the State Platform accepted by them in October 1905. But in the published document of November 8, 1905, called "The Political Platform of the Union of Freedom, Truth and Peace", these words were no longer there.

In the new document many beautiful words disappeared: universal suffrage was not extended to the army; the point about wide local self-government was narrowed—the noble impluse of the initiators of the Union cooled earlier than the ink on the State Platform dried, to be replaced by the Political Platform. As concerns the "worker question", it was reduced to payment of "salaries or wages", which would assure "satisfactory food, clothing and housing", to "the obligatory provision of work", the offering of "Sunday rest" and "the legalization of collaboration between workers (white-collar personnel) and employers" (Platform 1905).

The Platform, both in its left (State Platform) and right (Political Platform) versions, left in place the stability of the monarchy and that entire system of social relationships in Russia which the monarchy supported. This was a platform which did not go beyond the bounds of the principles of the Manifesto of October 17. It even preserved the leading position of the Russian Orthodox Church, since it envisaged its separation from the state in the distant future, which could be successfully postponed for any length of time: "... the gradual removal of any state protection...." The proclamation of the principle of "free competition in preaching of Gospels" placed in doubt freedom of preaching for non-Christian religions.

The Kadet Dikii in an article, "Toward the Upcoming Elections", wrote in February 1906: "... if we leave aside some non-essential points of this platform and consider only ... the basic features of it, we immediately note that there is, if not identity, then at least an enormous similarity between this platform and the program of the Constitutional-Democratic Party.

"We will have to say that the 'Frizen Party' essentially is one of the groups of the Constitutional-Democratic Party, and if it is not formally a part of this party (probably chiefly because of a certain religio-moral tinge of this group), then its place is alongside the Constitutional-Democratic Party ..." (*KV* 1906, No. 38: 2).

In December 1905 the Mennonite-Baptist party concluded an agreement with the Kadets about "common future fraternal civil activity in the countryside during the future State Duma" (*KV* 1905, No. 298: 3). The chairman of the Sevastopol committee of the Kadet Party, General Leskevich, was invited by Central Bureau of the Union of Freedom, Truth and Peace to become an honorary member; in their turn the Kadets invited P.M. Frizen to become an honorary member of their party committee in Sevastopol (*ibid.*). The Central Bureau prepared an All-Russian congress of delegates of the Union, which it was proposed to call "in Sevastopol or one of the nearby cities" (*ibid.*).

The Social-Christian party founded by the leaders of the Baptists, Mennonites and Evangelical Christians, was short-lived. The representative of large capitalist landowners and industrialists, the Mennonite Frizen, in February 1906 expressed criticism of both the Kadets and the Octobrists for ... the leftist slant of their political programs (*KV* 1906, No. 44: 4). By this Frizen condemned all platforms which were published by the Central Bureau he headed. Frizen's conflict with the Kadets and the Octobrists was a conflict with the members of the Central Bureau, primarily with the representatives of the liberal-bourgeois tendency in Baptism — with Prokhanov and Odintsov. Frizen had significant influence in the Union thanks to the capital of the Mennonite bourgeoisie, whose will he represented, and thanks to a large circle of his adherents in the Union.

Since the Union was still not in the full sense of the word a "Frizen Party", it fell apart, apparently in 1906. It was not resurrected, but the organized political activity of religious groups represented in the Union continued. Its leadership passed into Prokhanov's hands, who founded the newspaper *Utrenniaia zvezda* "for the expression of the Evangelical point of view on religious, political, social, economic, scientific and literary questions" (*B* 1910, No. 46: 366). In *Utrenniaia zvezda*, "Christians of the Evangelical faiths of various groups: Evangelist, Baptist and Mennonite brothers" participated as once they had in the "Union of Freedom, Truth and Peace" (*ibid.*).

In the period of the first bourgeois-democratic revolution, the political line of the Baptist church was defined basically as a Kadet one. It opposed the class interests of ordinary Baptists and at the same time confused them with its Christian-social demagogy. If deflected ordinary Baptists from participation in the revolutionary struggle, sowing illusions about "constitutional" means of implementing in society "freedom, truth and peace". The policy of the Baptist church bore fruit, in spite of the fact that there were cases in which ordinary Baptists and even whole groups of them acted against the will and policies of their top leadership.[16]

We will show the counter-revolutionary role played by the Baptist church in the period of the first bourgeois-democratic revolution in Russia, from the example of its activity in the Baltic area, where more than 40% of the total number of Baptist churches in Russia were located. In the summer of 1905, Latvia was inflamed by an uprising of poor peasants. In August, tsarism imposed martial law in Kurland Guberniia. In November in Lifland and Kurland Guberniias, revolutionary peasant committees were formed. The Baptist leader Fetler remembered this time with horror: "How many estates of German barons were burned by the Latvians in the Ostsee provinces!" (*G* 1911, No. 7: 151).

The Baptist church helped the Ostsee barons as they did the Ukrainian and Russian landowners to preserve many of their estates from the revolutionary anger of the people. In greater or lesser degree, but with the full measure of its strength, the Baptist church helped the ruling classes to curtail the front of the revolutionary struggle.

Ia. Kurtsit, the chairman of the Latvian Union of Young Baptists, speaking at the All-Russian Congress of Young Baptists in 1909, presented valuable material for describing the political role of Baptism in 1905. He said: "Man without God, without a true living faith, is not fit either for God or for the tsar or for the people. What does the terrible revolution of 1905 in Kurland among the Latvians show? Some university and secondary-school students went among the villages speaking and explaining that there is no God or Holy Scripture, and that the Bible is a book of the dark science, keeping the people over the course of several centuries in darkness and therefore—down with God and the Bible!...

"But this was done not by Baptist young people but by Lutherans and members of the Russian Orthodox Church.... What did the Baptists and their young people do during the revolution? Believing people gathered, prayed to God for the state, the tsar and the people, that the All-Merciful would rule

---

[16] "... At the height of the rebellious events in Odessa in 1905-1906, local authorities had information about the giving by some sectarian congregations of their prayer buildings for gatherings of anti-government organizations and in the buildings mentioned there were political proclamations" (TsGIAL, div. 821, f. 133, s.u. 161, sh. 51).

the hearts of the earthly bosses, make peaceful the heart of the infuriated mob, and establish in the state peace and well-being. Our young Latvian Baptists were prepared to be shot but did not wish to unite with the revolutionaries. The same thing was done by Russian and German believing (i.e. Baptists—A. K.) young people ...; the believers always tried and struggled for freedom of faith and freedom of speech—not with guns and the sword but with the Gospels and love ..." (Baptist Youth 1909: 70).

The zones of influence of the Baptist church served in the period of the revolution of 1905-1907 as the front rank for strengthening the ruling classes. Speaking in 1908 in Berlin, V. G. Pavlov with satisfaction reported to the European Congress of Baptists: "The revolution shook the political and religious foundations of the Russian people, but it clearly showed the falsity of the accusation by the clergy as to the political unreliability of the sectarians; almost all sectarians, with rare exceptions, reacted passively to the terror from both sides" (*B* 1908, No. 11: 38).

The Baptist church, in the persons of Kushnerov, Dolgopolov and Ivanov, on the eve of Bloody Sunday assured the Autocracy of their readiness to increase with their forces its political reserves. The practice of class struggle in 1905-1907 confirmed the counter-revolutionary role of the Baptist church.

6. Baptism and Evangelical Christianity in the Years of Reaction

"The years of reaction (1907-1910). Tsarism won. All revolutionary and opposition parties were destroyed, collapsed, demoralization, schisms, disorders, renegadism, pornography in place of politics. An increased thirst for philosophical idealism; mysticism as a disguise for counter-revolutionary movements" (*Lenin*: XLI, 10).

Parallel to the issuing by the bourgeois-Kadet intelligentsia of *Vekhi* [Landmarks], with its program for narcotizing the working classes with the help of a purified religion, and to the way the Octobrist-Kadet bourgeoisie of the Third Duma based their religious and church policy on the program of *Vekhi*, the Baptist church set out to implement a wide campaign for the moral disarmament of the workers. This was a plan long ago thought up by Prokhanov to draw the socially lower classes into the religious-reformation movement which, according to Prokhanov's way of thinking, was to replace the revolutionary movement of the proletariat and peasantry. Under this slogan, as Kushnerov asserted, Evangelical Christianity developed even at the beginning of its appearance in Russia. But of course, neither under the conditions of maturing revolutionary crisis at the beginning of the 20th century, nor particularly in the years of the first bourgeois-democratic revolution, could Prokhanov hope for any wide success of his reformationist plans.

In 1909, Lenin wrote: "Interest in everything which was connected with religion undoubtedly seized now broad circles of 'society' and penetrated into the ranks of the intelligentsia, close to the workers' movement, and also into well-known workers' circles" (*Lenin, Soch.*: XV, 371). Prokhanov judged the time of reaction as the most suitable for the propagandizing and implementation of a religious reformation in Russia. He was not original. In the political experience of the Western European bourgeoisie, toward which Prokhanov attentively looked, there was also such a weapon as seeming anti-clericalism, used as early as the 1870s by Bismarck with the aim of deflecting the working classes from socialism and the revolutionary struggle (*Lenin, Soch.*: XV, 372). Prokhanov returned to the old plan again in 1906 when the wave of revolutionary struggle began to die down. In August 1906, Prokhanov sent a letter to his co-thinkers in which he proposed to form a Russian Evangelical Union, having the aim of "facilitating ... the spiritual convergence of believing Christians without distinctions of doctrinal shadings" (Vvedenskii 1913: 122).

In 1908, this union was founded with the permission of the tsarist authorities. Since Prokhanov connected his success primarily with the support which he counted on receiving from the ruling classes, he spoke in plain terms of the real aims behind the plan of developing a religious reformation movement in Russia. "The history of Western peoples shows", he wrote, "that in all countries where there was a reformation (renewal of church life), as in Germany, England, Switzerland, etc., a regular political life has been set up, preventing the blood-letting of spontaneous and constant revolutions. And, on the contrary, in countries where there has been no reformation of religious life, and where to this day in the souls of the people there rules the regime (order) of the old formal religion, in many respects not understood by the people — there at the present time there is not the same equilibrium, and in any case not such a many-sided and constant progress, in the life of the people.

"Thus, in spite of the salutary nature of the political and economic reforms, the salvation of our people depends mainly on the renewal of its religious life. This renewal was given in the West the title of 'Reformation' " (Vvedenskii 1913: 124).

That Russia at the begining of the 20th century was not Germany in the 16th century, not England in the 17th century, that reformation is not only Luther but also Münzer, was of course no secret to Prokhanov. "We completely recognize", he wrote, "that the renewal of the Russian church can be accomplished by some other paths, and lead to results somewhat different from those which we see in the West among reformation churches" (*ibid.*).

Attempting to unite in the common stream of a reformation movement the participants of religious groups in opposition to Russian Orthodoxy, and all "believing Christians without doctrinal distinctions", and to place it under the organizational aegis of the Evangelical Union in the person of its governing board (let us note that the chairman of the board was Prince Lieven and the deputy chairman Baron Nikolai), Prokhanov did not exclude figures in the Russian Orthodox Church from participation in the Union. The appeal of Kushnerov and his co-thinkers in January 1905 for a common ground between Russian Orthodoxy and Baptism was not empty words.

The reformation which Prokhanov intended was a reformation from above, directed against the revolutionary movement of the lower classes, and it demanded the consolidation of reactionary forces, including the Russian Orthodox Church. Prokhanov proposed to depend on those circles in Russian Orthodoxy which, beginning with Metropolitan Antonii in 1905, attempted a transformation of the Church, in order to increase its influence on the masses. "We are glad to see", Prokhanov wrote, "that in the most enlightened circles of the Russian Orthodox clergy there is also beginning to be a ferment of thought and a maturing of awareness of the unsatisfactory nature of the present condition of Church affairs". He continued: "The Evangelical movement in Russia is undoubtedly a way of influencing the life of the Russian Orthodox Church by induction". Prokhanov insisted that the Church "awaken, from top to bottom", and "repent before the whole people of time lost, in order that ferment should turn into a movement which seizes everything and everyone: metropolitans, bishops, the whole clergy, black and white, and the whole people" (Prokhanov 1910a. The attempt to draw the Russian Orthodox Church into the Evangelical movement was revived by Prokhanov in 1922; *see* Klibanov 1961: 26). He found a place for everyone in the reformation movement planned by him.

Prokhanov was the initiator, ideologist and *de facto* leader of the Evangelical Union, but his ideas were also shared by the Baptist church leaders represented in the Union administration. Among the responses in the Baptist press sympathizing with the ideas of a reformation movement as represented by Prokhanov, let us cite the article "Khristianstvo i deklaratsiia prav" [Christianity and the Declaration of Rights]. The author of the article, citing as authorities P. B. Struve and the German bourgeois jurist G. Jellinek, contrasted the constitutions operating in the U.S. and England as arising as the result of a religious reformation, to the French constitution as the consequence of political revolution. After this the English and American freedoms were extolled, and the reader was brought to the conclusion that social freedoms would come to Russia not through political revolution, but through religions reformation (*SI* 1914, No. 22: 255).

V. G. Pavlov, who published in 1911 a programmatic article, "The Truth About the Baptists", affirmed the idea of religious reformation in the following expressions: "We should repeat our news about the renewal of humanity by means of acceptance of the Gospels; we should tell people that the new era can begin only through reborn people, that Jesus alone is the just ruler, that all methods of giving us new people without the Gospels are insufficient, that we possess the secret and know the power which will change life, that only a new humanity is twice born; that the only means of making social fruit good is to make a good social tree" (V. P. 1911: 63).

On the basis of these judgments, Pavlov denied in principle the struggle of the workers for the revolutionary transformation of society and scientific socialism: "We do not believe in the betterment of the social system by way of violent overthrow", he wrote. "The method of Christianity in this respect is not the method of the scientific socialists, who mean to take state power in their hands and then to reorganize society.... The trouble is that all these scientific socialists and social revolutionaries forget that moral evil is the root of all social injustice" (V. P. 1911: 63).

The growth of revolutionary moods in various social circles which occurred in the period of reaction, and the significant spread of sectarianism at this time, were interpreted by a number of authors of articles and pamphlets as a portent of religious reformation. M. I. Shaknovich in his important work *Lenin i problemy ateizma* [Lenin and Problems of Atheism] directed the attention of the readers to the notes made by Lenin upon reading the article 'What Is Necessary Now", published in 1909 by an activist of the SR Party. "From this long article," Shaknovich writes, "Lenin marked for criticism the views of the author 'On Religion'. Lenin underlined in this article many phrases which most clearly expressed the hopes of the SRs for the sectarian movement led in the years of reaction by kulaks" (Shaknovich 1961: 440-441). In the article "What Is Necessary Now", the SR author, repeating the hopes of Baptist leaders, wrote of a religion "which could create a broad movement which would serve as the center of attraction, the center of unification for every possible Russian sect ..." (Shaknovich 1961: 440).

The Tolstoyans had also been working concentratedly for a long time on the preparation of a religious reformation as a rebuff to revolution, and they, taking their desires for reality, wrote that supposedly "the ideals of Sten'ka Razin, Pugachev (and Bakunin also) have already outlived their time", that "the new ideals of the Russian people are expressed in sectarianism"; they wrote further: "Keep in mind, Messrs. Revolutionaries, that sectarianism has already spread over the whole face of the Russian land, and sectarianism will transform it and not your violent ideas, foreign to the spirit of the Christ-loving Russian peasant" (Tegubov's Letter to Lazarev, March 7, 1903, ROBIL, Chertkov Collection).

In the years of reaction the *Vekhi* circle also manifested interest in sectarianism. As early as the beginning of the 1890s in Moscow, in a tavern widely known as Iama [The Pit], there functioned a kind of club in which representatives of almost all groups of Russian religious sectarianism gathered and disputed. The God-seeker of the bourgeois-liberal persuasion, A. S. Pankratov, who regularly visited this club, devoted a special sketch to the history of Iama. In particular he wrote: "In general we may say that politics did not catch on at all in Iama. If political protest was expressed in episodic form, as an interpolation in religious speech, or if a political shout burst out of the depths of the spirit of some 'Black-Soil' man—Iama listened in silence.... this lack of desire to deal with politics was sharply emphasized, especially in the later years—in the period of reaction ..." (Pankratov 1910: 40).

Soon after the publication of *Vekhi*, the *Vekhi* pillars Berdiaev and Bulgakov appeared in Iama. The *Vekhi* people sought ideological adherents from among the sectarians. Berdiaev subsequently recalled his attempts to make contact with the sectarian milieu: "In a certain year of my life, which I consider happy, I came into contact with and had dealings with a milieu new to me of God-seekers from the people, and became acquainted with wandering religious Russia. At that time in a Moscow tavern near the Church of Flor and Lavr (not far from Miasnitskaia), there occurred on Sundays public religious conversations between various kinds of religious sectarians. I was very much interested in this.... I took part in religious disputes and became personally acquainted with several sectarians.... Public meetings in the tavern were called by Iama.... Sects of mystical character were more interesting than sects of rationalistic character" (Berdiaev 1949: 212-213).

Summing up his impressions of meetings with sectarians in Moscow and later in Khar'kov Guberniia, Berdiaev wrote: "I remember the years of contact with these people as the best in my life, and these people as the best people that I have met in my life" (Berdiaev 1949: 218-219).

In fact, between the mysticism, God-seeking, and unbounded idealism of the *Vekhi* movement and religious sectarianism contemporary with it, between the profoundly reactionary ideological nature of both, there existed many points of contact.

But Berdiaev preferred meeting sectarians on his native estate rather than at Iama. That way everything would be less dangerous. A. S. Pankratov testified: "In the spring of 1910, S. N. Bulgakov and N. A. Berdiaev descended into Iama with a group of their followers. For two weeks Iama was agitated and arguing. The discussions took on an interesting character. But ... the police learned of it and Messrs. Bulgakov and Berdiaev no longer appeared in Iama" (Pankratov 1910: 44). The police as a rule granted Iama noninterference. This occurred because Iama played the role of a Zubatov club[L] in sectarianism. It allowed the secret police to follow moods in sectarianism, and the activity of every sort of religious teacher operating in it.

Pankratov also noted that "the missionaries used Iama as a missionary testing ground. They went to school in Iama, becoming acquainted here with the sects and their various branches.... A simple idea made them not persecute Iama. It was the only valve in Moscow for Protestant steam. It was more important for the mission to have one such open valve than a dozen secret ones" (Pankratov 1910: 45).

And still, neither the SRs nor the *Vekhi* people, nor even the Tolstoyans, acted so purposefully and firmly in their attempts to call forth a religious reformation movement in Russia as did Prokhanov and his co-thinkers in the Evangelical Union.

With what did Prokhanov and the members of the Evangelical Union connect the prospects for the development of the revolutionary movement in Russia? On what social forces were they placing their bets? To what interests, views and feelings were they appealing? Prokhanov's article "Protestantism i blagosostoianie narodov" [Protestantism and the Well-Being of Peoples] serves as a partial answer to these questions. Citing his recent "flying trip to Germany, Holland and England" and describing the "well-being" of these countries, Prokhanov comes to a conclusion about "the great role which Protestantism played in the lives of these peoples" (Prokhanov 1911:1). The power of Protestanism, according to Prokhanov, consisted in the fact that this "free religion, which removed the fetters from the spiritual world of each individual man, gave room for the development of his capabilities and thereby increased his energy" (Prokhanov 1911: 1); i.e., the force of Protestantism is seen as the force of bourgeois individualism, gumption, cleverness and enterprise.

Gathering together the economic "energy of bourgeois individuals" (for, as we see, he is speaking precisely of it), Prokhanov gets "the well-being of peoples". "Everything taken together", he writes, "when integrated, produced that colossal working ability of peoples which, developing, serves as a source of their wealth and their progress in general" (*ibid.*).

A follower of Prokhanov, a certain A. Ivanov, speaking in 1910 in Novgorod before a gathering of Evangelical Christians, pointed to "the emptiness of spirit of contemporary society", and called for a religious reformation in Russia, "Now look", he wrote, "on the development of all Europe. Her civilization makes us envy her, her order and way of life, her power and wealth, and what is it that gave her this, all these qualities and superiority over us? The Gospels. The reform of the spirit of the European peoples, in the light of the Gospels—that is what gives these peoples priority over us.... Our motherland is also part of Europe, and the biggest part. It is enormous in its population of 150 million, with the enormous territory which it occupies; it is behind the Europe of the West by almost 200 years in its development. What does this mean? It means that the light of the Gospels has not yet shone in our motherland" (Ivanov 1910: 5-6).

The ideologists of the religious reformation called on the spirit of bourgeois individualism, on the instincts of the property-owner, entrepreneurial initiative, the thirst for wealth. They drew a picture for their audience of "well-equipped farms" in Germany, "colossal factories, shops and various industrial enterprises in England", the landscapes of Holland, "where on the green meadows wander uncounted herds of marvelous cattle" (Prokhanov 1911: 1), and declared the Reformation the direct path to a bourgeois El Dorado.

Through the means of religious feelings, the ideologists of the reformation penetrated to the very vibrating strings of the souls of property-owners, and formed in their followers the psychology and ideology of the bourgeois.

In the last analysis, the "spiritual reform" for which the activists of the Evangelical Union called was a spiritual Stolypin reform. And not without reason did the economic aspects of the Stolypin reform find a warm adherent in the person of Prokhanov. In the article "Zamechatel'naia poezdka" [A Remarkable Journey], in which Prokhanov described Stolypin's trip to the Volga region and Siberia, we find the very highest evaluation of the Stolypin agrarian reform: "There is no need to say that the Ministers (Stolypin and Krivoshein — A. K.) saw quite a few good sides in the newly introduced system of isolated farms". In the person of the isolated farmer-kulak, Prokhanov recognized the features dear to him of the "Protestant", in whose name he called for a reformation. "Private farms created in place of the commune", he wrote, "undoubtedly will develop precisely because they, being based on a feeling of direct property-ownership, will attract much more effort, energy and industry on the part of the owner than under the present system, when the peasant could not consider the parcel his own property" (Prokhanov 1910b: 1).

Not without reason did Baptism roll like a wave over the territory covered by the Stolypin agrarian reform. And, of course, not without reason did P. N. Miliukov, from the podium of the Third Duma, proclaim the sectarian operations as cultural oases and recognize in the sectarian type "the symbol of our future". What is being spoken of is nothing but the kulak-peasant with "a feeling of direct ownership, diligent, industrious and energetic".

Let us quote a section of Miliukov's speech, containing its central idea. "I wish to show you", said the orator, "how in this direction, in the direction of struggle with sectarianism, you run up against the same thing, the destruction of cultural values, and you stop Russian life (i.e. capitalism — A. K.). You know what is happening now in the Transcaucasus. You know that there was a whole series of cultural centers which began intensive cultural work precisely in that field which is so dear to you and of which you have thought so much: cotton-growing and horticulture. You know how these oases are being destroyed and how people who are not suitable for Russia, hundreds, thousands, and later perhaps tens of thousands, are moving off and will move to America. The type which is precious to us, which is the symbol of our future, this type is being chased away, thrown out of Russian life, which cannot stand it. I only have to name several names—for instance, the stanitsa of Akstakha, the settlement of Elizavetinskii, completely destroyed after the departure of the New Israelites.... In Kakhetiia, Zelenoe Pole, near it the isolated farm of Privol'nyi. Zelenoe Pole is especially interesting: the Uruguayan consul traveled there and was in raptures over the Russian culture, over the adoption there of machine methods of working the land. The consul wrote to Uruguay, and the Uruguayan government, in accordance with his report, declared readiness to resettle as many people as were willing.... That, sirs, is where our future is, that is how you can ruin and destroy it" (State Duma 1913: 1687-1689).[17]

The line of effort by the counter-revolutionary bourgeoisie directed at the "renovation" and "cleansing" of the state religion, begins with the memorandum by S. Iu. Witte, in which he proposed (in February 1905) that the structure of the ruling church be transformed, and runs up to the Kadet V. A. Karaulov and the Octobrist M. Ia. Kapustin in the Third State Duma. The Evangelical Union made an attempt "on the spur of the moment" to implement what the Kadet and Octobrist bourgeoisie was calling for. However, the success of this attempt was limited, to say the least.

In the years of reaction, the number of followers of Baptism and Evangelical Christianity grew, but the call of the Evangelical Union for a reformation was "a voice crying in the wilderness". The "spiritual reform" of the Kadet-minded Evangelists and Baptists collapsed like the Stolypin agrarian reform. The Evangelical Union eked out a miserable existence. By 1912, it consisted of 90 members, and in 1911 twenty-seven persons had left and 13 been accepted. Behind the commotion of discussions about unifying "all Christians", I. S. Prokhanov put together his own church.

In the years of reaction, the basic efforts of the leaders of the Baptist church were directed toward preaching a reform of the spirit, or, in V. G. Pavlov's expression, "a revolution of the spirit", in contrast to the idea of social revolution. In the area of political tendencies in Baptism, headed in one case by Prokhanov and in the other by Pavlov, they held to principles set down in 1905 on the basis of the platform of the Union of Freedom, Truth and Peace, of which the publication edited by Prokhanov, *Utrenniaia zvezda*, became the ideological heir.

In the years of reaction, as in the years of revolution, the political actions of the Baptist church lay basically in the direction of the Kadet Party.

---

[17] The Kadet defense of sectarianism as "the symbol of our future" helps us to understand the social essence of the theory of liberal researchers, who wrote of sectarianism even at the beginning of the 1880s: "... the Schism as represented by the progressive sects ... is working out the ideal of the future and of relationships in humanity", and saw in it "the great pledge of the development of the Russian people" (Prugavin 1881: 362, 363).

But if the religious policy of the Kadets earned the complete and thankful approval of the leaders of the Baptist church,[18] if the Kadets' program earned the sympathy and support of these figures, the tactical line of the Kadet Party was criticized by them.

In an article called "Nastoiashchii politicheskii moment" [The Present Political Moment], published in February 1910 in the newspaper *Utrenniaia zvezda*, its editors and publishers called themselves "warm adherents of our young representative system, resting on two legislative pillars: the State Duma and the State Council." At the same time, they recognized the inability of the Duma to defend the independent interest of the bourgeoisie. They criticized the election law of June 3, 1907, which secured the rule of the most reactionary elements at the expense of the Kadets, and they demanded changes "in the rights and functions" of the State Council and the responsibilities of ministries to the Duma (*UZ* II/5/1910: 1). They could not forgive the Kadet Party for its cowardice in the first and second State Dumas, its inability to force the Autocracy to consider the class will of the bourgeoisie.

The point was by no means that the Baptist leaders criticized "from the left" the political line of Kadetism, but rather that they criticized the inconsistency of the Kadets in the defense of their political line: "Consisting of the most educated and self-assured figures, this party (the Kadets—A.K.) by the will of the people was twice called upon to play a primary role in state affairs.... The government felt the moral and political force of this party and proposed a compromise to it—i.e., in the first instance a ministry with representatives from the parliamentary majority. At this moment the party should have taken the proper course, and if it had done this, the history of the last three years and our future history would have taken on a completely different character.... But the moment was lost, and hence we have a new election law and a Third Duma, in which the Kadet Party occupies the position of an impotent" (*ibid.*).

What tactic did the Baptist leaders (first of all, of course, Prokhanov) demand from the Kadets? Prokhanov's reaction to the murder of Stolypin serves as an answer to this question. In "an interview on the occasion of the tragic death of P. A. Stolypin", Prokhanov declared that "many excellent features of P. A.'s character did not escape Evangelical Christians, since they were

---

[18] For example, on May 29, 1909, the St. Petersburg congregation of Evangelical Christians directed a statement to Miliukov, in which among other things they said: "Having the view that for a true renovation of Russia, along with fundamental political and economic reforms, there is necessary a moral rebirth of each individual, which is possible only under one condition—that the teaching of Christ, the Gospel teaching, is placed at the base of the life of the individual, of the family, of the school, of society, and of the state— ... the St. Petersburg congregation of Evangelical Christians feels a moral duty to express to you and to the whole Party of Popular Freedom sincere thanks for courageous defense of the laws which must become an embryo of the true renewal of Russia" (TsGAOR, Miliukov Collection, No. 579, f. 1, s.u. 2,561, sh. 1).

reminiscent of the best people of ancient Rus'—his astonishing courage and firmness in implementing his ideas, his directness and honesty. In our neurasthenic century such people are rare" (*UZ* IX/9/1911: 2).

In the article "Stolypina net ..." [Stolypin Is No More ...], published in *Utrenniaia zvezda*, the editor emphasized that Stolypin was distinguished "by unusual firmness in implementing his ideas and unshakable courage in his struggle with his opponents" (*UZ* IX/9/1911: 1).

This was an apologia for the hangman and enforcer Stolypin, and it directly flowed out of the counter-revolutionary course which the ideologists and leaders of Baptism in 1905-1907 implemented. But the articles quoted are interesting for the emphasis of the "qualities of will" of Stolypin, while the Baptist leaders condemned the political "impotence" of the Kadets.

Prokhanov's ideal was a bourgeois statesman who would unite Miliukov's political world-view with Stolypin's Bonapartism. Bonapartism, but not Stolypin's—the Kadets': this was the political course for which Prokhanov called on the bourgeoisie "in our neurasthenic century".

Church and police authorities zealously observed the activity of the Baptist church over the whole course of its existence. The descriptions which the Church gave of Baptism are in general of no interest. The Church harassed its competitors, not being squeamish as to means and resorting to every possible lie and insinuation.

As concerns the police authorities, they, basing themselves on the data of their observations of the Baptist church in localities and in the center, attempted to identify the direction of its activities from the point of view of defense of the state interests of the Autocracy. During the years of revolution and the years of reaction, the Department of Police collected a lot of material on the activity of Baptist leaders, big and small. In the report of the Vice-Director of the Department of Police to the Ministry of Internal Affairs for April 14, 1910, on the Evangelical Christians in Tavriia Guberniia, it was reported: "... there is no connection between revolutionary organizations and Evangelical Christian congregations in Tavriia Guberniia. However, the social ideals of these sectarians ... can in the near future prepare the ground for the formation in Russia of a political party like the so-called Christian Socialists, very numerous in Austria, where they are a strong social force" (TsGIAL, div. 821, f. 133, s.u. 181, sh. 44 v.).

According to the conclusion of the Department of Police, based on the reports of the governor of Kherson, "from information received in the course of 1909, we can come to the conclusion that there is as yet no basis to consider the main leaders of the Baptist sect among persons attached to any revolutionary party" (ORF Institute of History, AS USSR, Sector "Ts", div. VI, s.u. 11, sh. 35).

Especially categorical is the report of the chief of the police administration of Odessa, embracing the period of observation of Baptist church activity from 1903 to 1913, and the conclusion he came to: "Turning to the question of information on the Baptists and other sects, I report that having conducted research for more than ten years in various places of the Empire, and having studied the revolutionary parties from central committees to their peripheral organizations inclusive, I did not once encounter data indicating a connection of the Social Revolutionary, Russian Social-Democratic Workers', and other parties with sectarians, in associations striving for revolutionary goals, let alone as manifesting any activity in collaboration with the revolutionary work of the parties mentioned" (*ibid.*, sh. 6).

The close relationship between the Baptist leaders and the Kadets did not escape the attention of the chief of police: "At the same time, one must mention that leftist social circles, and in particular the members of the 'Popular Freedom Party', constantly mentioned their sympathy with the Baptists" (*ibid.*).

In the report of the Moscow political-police division to the Department of Police in October 1911, it is noted that "Baptism is growing into a strong social force, ready to occupy a definite position in relation to the state ...; among the Baptists one does not see the extreme right, and all their sympathy is on the side of the constitution. According to the declaration of the members of the congress (the congress of Baptists in 1911 — A. K.), the Baptists will hardly vote in the upcoming elections to the State Duma, even for the Octobrists, from whom they do not have support" (ORF Institute of History, AS USSR, Sector "Ts", div. VI, s.u. 8, sh. 35).

There were, in fact, "right-wingers" among the leaders of Baptism, but the greatest political activity was manifested by the liberal bourgeois leaders, who showed political and moral support for the Kadets and prompted their followers to vote for the Kadet election lists (Bonch-Bruevich 1930: 69).

The Baptist church in the years of reaction, as in the years of revolution, came out actively on the side of the counter-revolutionary bourgeoisie.

7. Baptism and Evangelical Christianity in the Years of World War I

Russia's entry into the World War was accompanied by a monarchical demonstration organized by the leaders of the Baptist church. The foundation of it was laid by the St. Petersburg congregation, which appeared with a choir of singers on July 20 at the Winter Palace in order to take part in the expressions of loyalty to Nicholas II (*G* 1914, No. 9: 217). In the capitals and in the provinces, prayer-meetings of Baptists and Evangelical Christians were held "for the state and for the whole motherland".

Attempting to give an organized character to the declaration of monarchist sympathies in their congregations, the Baptist church (the St. Petersburg and Moscow congregations) on September 1, 1914, sent an epistle to the presbyters, to the members of the councils of the congregations, and to all "brothers and sisters" with the appeal: "In all congregations and divisions of the congregations gather members and their children and all parishioners for sincere prayers for the sovereign Emperor, the Empress, the Tsarevich-heir, and for the whole ruling house, and also for His Imperial Highness, the commander-in-chief Grand Duke Nikolai Nikolaevich, and for the blessing by the Lord God of our whole motherland during this world war" (*G* 1914, No. 9: 219).

After prayers for the ruling house, the authors of the epistle proposed that each congregation fill out a prepared form with expressions of loyalist feelings, with the signatures of those gathered, and send it to the office of the Petrograd Baptist congregation for transmittal to its destination (*G* 1914, No. 9: 219-220).

At the same time the Petrograd Baptist congregtion appealed to all Baptists in Russia with the proposal to form a fund "of the Good Samaritan, in order to ease the work of the Red Cross" (Kandidov 1930: 10). On its side, the Evangelical Christian church held analogous prayers in its congregations and organized a collection of monetary contributions for the wounded.

One hundred and thirty congregations took part in the monarchical demonstration of the Evangelical Christians, sending via the Minister of the Palace "a most humble address" to Nicholas II.

The Petrograd, Moscow, Ekaterinoslav, Revel', Simferopol', and most other Evangelial Christian congregations collected funds for the wounded, and the Petrograd congregation donated 11,000 rubles (TsGAOR, div. 579, f. 1, s.u. 2592, sh. 33). The Baptists and Evangelical Christians sent an address to Nicholas II, and Nicholas II sent "imperial thanks" to the Baptists and Evangelical Christians "for loyal feelings expressed on the occasion of military action" (Manuscript Division of MIRA, K. VIII, f. 1, s.u. 5, sh. 1).

A number of Baptist and Evangelical Christian congregations made their buildings into infirmaries. Some congregations, such as the Moscow Baptist congregation, outfitted the infirmaries and paid the salaries of the medical staff which served them. The preceptor of the Moscow Baptist congregation in a letter to the Moscow municipal executive board swore that the wounded would not be subjected to any religious influence, that not one book would be given to them without the permission of the board, etc. (*ibid.*, sh. 3 v.).

Both the Baptists and the Evangelical Christians took part in military action. The preceptor of the Moscow Baptist congregation as early as September 29, 1914 wrote: "... On the basis of our faith, thousands of our members are fighting at the present time on the field of battle ..." (*ibid.*, sh. 3). The preceptor of the Petrograd Baptist congregation in his appeal to the

Ministry of Internal Affairs, May 14, 1916, noted: "... many of the members of our congregation have shed their blood on the field of battle, others have borne severe maiming and wounds, others again have been awarded various marks of distinction including all four degrees of the Order of St. George, and elevation to officer's rank"("The Appeal of the Petrograd Congregation of Evangelical Christian Baptists, May 14, 1916", typescript, pp. 4-5; author's collection).

It would be an oversimplification to explain the military-monarchical demonstrations by the leaders of Baptism and Evangelical Christianity by their servility.

In a letter by Prokhanov, intercepted by the police, dated August 4, 1914, and sent to the rural congregation of Evangelical Christians in the village of Kamen', Tomsk Guberniia, we read: "Our motherland is living through a hard time. Germany moved against Russia, which destroyed the peaceful life of our motherland in general and of each of us in particular.... We are completely convinced that those brothers who were called to the service of the fatherland will bear their cross with patience and if necessary, will sacrifice their lives with joy..." (ORF, Sector "Ts", div. VI, s.u. 8, sh. 6).

The prominent Baptist figure F. Belousov, exiled at the end of 1914 to Ufa Guberniia, wrote on August 26, 1915 to Miliukov: "I wish to be useful and give some material (perhaps you will use it) on the question of provisioning the army with ammunition. From the reports of the Eastern Industrial Congress and Committee, we see that our mobilized industry does not have enough workers, chiefly specialists. And here in Siberia, in Tomsk and Enisei Guberniias, I hear there are 45,000 who have been exiled from various places in Russia, chiefly the southern industrial centers.... Judging from our region, the majority are workers, and I dare say that they are specialists—metalworkers, blacksmiths, lathe-operators, painters—several thousand persons in all.... If only they would take them to those factories and shops, even the provincial ones, where they are making necessary things for the army..." (TsGAOR, div. 579, f. 1, s.u. 3730, shs. 3-3 v.).

Belousov's proposal showed a large unused reserve of skilled workers, the lack of whom was substantially felt on the military provisioning of the army.

However, if Miliukov had used this suggestion, he would have encountered opposition from the Autocracy, which preferred to recruit workers in China and Iran, rather than in Siberia among exiles who had shown themselves to be "unreliable".

I have already shown above that leaders of the Russian Orthodox Church and of the Black Hundred, taking advantage of the flare-up of chauvinism accompanying the developing military events, represented Baptists, Adventists and Evangelical Christians as German agents, traitors, etc., acted as provocateurs, and without great effort achieved the closing of congregations and the court and police repression of "other faiths". But the undercurrent of in-sinuations disseminted by the clergy about the Baptists was completely clear, even to the police authorities.

Let us cite the report of the chief of the Kiev Guberniia police administra-tion, dated April 14, 1915, to the governor of Kiev: "Regarding the agitation (of the Baptist—A. K.) against the war, no one can point to definite cases, and everything rests on some dark rumors and on the fact that sectarians in general are against breaking the commandment "Thou shalt not kill", and in conversations say that war is murder, but as a test and a punishment sent down by God, it should be accepted. In the dissemintion of various rumors directed toward the accusation of Shtundists of anti-state activity, no small role, if not the chief one, is played in many places by the rural clergy, who, being powerless to struggle with the dissemination of the religious teaching of the Shtundists, and at the same time recognizing themselves as responsible for their flock, attempt to use the passing moment for calling down repression in relation to the sectarians, counting on this to paralyze their religious influence on the population" (TsGIAM, div. DP, 1915, s.u. 132, sh. 12 v.).

In 1915, Prokhanov sent the authorities a detailed memorandum "on the persecution of Evangelical Christians and Christians like them in Russia dur-ing the war" (TsGIAL, div, 821, f. 133, s.u. 23, shs. 108-112), in which he refuted the Church-Black Hundred insinuations and convincingly showed the participation of his followers in the World War to be on an equal footing with all other Russian citizens. And in fact, from the beginning of World War I to February 1, 1917, from the total number of Baptists and Evangelical Chris-tians, which was not less than 150,000 persons, only 343, including 103 Bap-tists and 243 Evangelical Christians, were sentenced by military courts for refusal to fight on religious grounds.[19]

Prokhanov wrote in the above-mentioned memorandum: "The history of Russian religious movements has shown that not one of the sectarian movements existing in Russia was a political danger, or was ever harmful to the state order and the public peace" (TsGAOR, div. 579, f. 1, s.u. 2,592, sh. 17).

Of course, the Baptist churches did not abandon their proselytizing aims in the war years. As in 1907 the Baptist figures Baron Ikskul' had called national disasters "a plow", serving to uncover "new hearts", so in 1914 Prokhanov ap-pealed to Evangelical Christians with a reminder that "the present time is the

---

[19] In the summary of data made in the Department of Spiritual Affairs on the basis of information from the procurators of military-district courts, we learn that the 240 Evangelical Christians who refused military service at the beginning of the war were part of 50,000 followers of Evangelical Christianity. These are data as of February 16, 1917 (TsGIAL, div. 821, f. 133, s.u. 198, sh. 102). According to information from the same Department, the number of Evangelical Christians as of January 1, 1912 was 31,000.

most propitious for disseminating the saving Gospel among our agitated Russian people", and he concluded: "In recognition of this the Union Council would like this year to increase even more the number of Evangelists, and therefore the Union Council asks all brothers and sisters not to decrease their contributions, but rather to increase them by at least a third" (ORF Institute of History, AS USSR, Sector "Ts", div. VI, s.u. 8, sh. 7).

A special soldiers' mission was created, propagandizing "the Evangelical news" among lower ranks of the army and navy. The editorial board of the newspapers *Utrenniaia zvezda* as early as August 15, 1914, appealed "for the creation of a special society or circle of people who would take upon themselves the task of collecting funds and sending to each soldier in the army (and especially the wounded and sick) one copy of the Gospels" (*UZ* VIII/15/1914: 1). The attempts at "evangelization" of soldiers and sailors caused alarm in military circles, especially among the military clergy, who feared the penetration of anti-militaristic ideas into the army. There was no basis for this fear, since the evangelization was implemented and controlled by the upper strata of the Baptist church. Whether the evangelization took place in the army or among civilians, it not only did not have an anti-militaristic direction, but on the contrary was designed to lead the "converts" away from the influence of revolutionary ideas, and thereby to turn military and non-military into obedient soldiers of the autocratic regime.

Let us cite "some directions for new converts" published in the journal *Baptist* in August 1914: "Beware of any at all close contact or intimacy with the world. You may not have any activity in common with unbelievers.... Hold yourself apart from lay unions and societies, even when they follow generally useful and political goals, or apparently innocent pleasures and useful exercises ..." (*B* 1914, No. 15-16: 5).

In supporting the imperialistic war with every means available to them, the Baptist churches acted in the name of the class interests of the bourgeoisie. Military provisioning by order of the state brought unheard-of profits to industrial capitalists, and enriched not only large representatives of capital but "middling" capitalists as well. The bourgeoisie staked its hopes for the establishment of class "harmony" and for the deflection of the masses from the revolutionary struggle on the intoxicating effects of military hysteria, and on the extraordinary situation in the country. Under conditions which demanded from the Autocracy the consolidation of all forces and means available to it, the bourgeoisie could allow itself to "raise its voice" and demand a greater share of participation in leadership of state and political life. Finally, the war followed imperialistic aims, hacking out with a sword a path for monopoly capital to new markets of raw material and sale. All this was a source of military inspiration for the Baptist church. Even in the period of the pre-war industrial upsugre, the imagination of Baptist bourgeois ideologists painted a picture of the economic development of Russia similar to the capitalist "prosperity" of the United States of America.

In their thoughts, the Baptist ideologists already saw their class bosses placing in bank safes millions of profits. "In recent years", we read in *Utrenniaia zvezda*, "the condition of agriculture, thanks to good harvests and high prices for all agricultural produce, has significantly improved. There is reason to assume that agricultural industry in future will develop and approach the degree of prosperity which it achieved in the United States.

"The wealth of the farmer is the foundation on which the national wealth of North America and the wealth of American millionaires was based. Perspicacious Americans and other foreigners understand very well that Russia in the near future will become in a commercial and industrial sense a 'New America', a new country of 'unlimited possibilities', and hurry to open their trading and shop enterprises here. We can only welcome all who undertake honest work in Russia, thanks to which our dear fatherland can become a powerful, wealth, and happy country" (*UZ* X/29/1910: 1).

In the course of the imperialistic war, which more and more uncovered the weakness of Russia's economy, the Baptist ideologists called for an end to "backwardness" and the utmost development of the capitalistic exploitation of the country's productive forces. They spoke for the ousting of foreign capital, which occupied advantageous positions in the economy of Russia, and demanded the establishment of the indivisible dominion of the Russian national bourgeoisie.

The Baptist ideologists connected these prospects with the victorious conclusion of the World War. They wrote: "The war which the world, and in particular our fatherland, is now experiencing, opens our eyes to many things." And later on: "Until now, Russia was the tributary of foreign industrialists, who made goods out of Russian materials and sold them to Russia for three times the price.... They took advantage of Russia's backwardness and this conspiracy held back her development even more. Now many inquisitive minds are casting their eyes on various fields and are pointing to sources—rich deposits of various materials—and they are thinking of ways and adopting methods to get at them.... We must study and use our own wealth, and call for the working out a correct plan of exploitation, for the bad management of Russia has already become a proverb... " (*UZ* VII/15/1916: 2-3).

In the call for a planned exploitation of national wealth one cannot help but hear the echoes of the increased activity in 1915-1916 of the autocratic regime, industrial figures and banks in the creation of every kind of organ of economic regulation, stimulated by the war, and which signified the development of a system of state-monopoly capitalism.

For the upper strata of the Baptist church, precisely because of their connections with the bourgeois industrialists and landowners, prospects of possessing the Black Sea straits and the opening of an exit to the Mediterranean were especially attractive — a little less than nine tenths of the grain exports of Russia were sent out through the Dardanelles.

We know what great significance was attributed by the leaders of the Kadet Party (primarily Miliukov) to the Near Eastern question. On October 20, 1914, after the military provocation by the Turkish fleet, Russia declared war on Turkey. The editors of *Utrenniaia zvezda* on October 24 published an article, "Novaia voina" [The New War]: "... Turkey's challenge exceeded everything that was done earlier ... Russia will win. But now the results will apparently be different: an end will be put to the existence of the Turkish empire, the Armenians and other tribes still groaning under the barbarian yoke of this Asiatic tribe will be liberated, and Russia herself will receive free entry to the Black Sea — i.e., the Bosporus and the Dardanelles, and everything which is on them" (*UZ* X/24/1914: 1).

No, it was not servility before the Autocracy, or fear of its "disfavor", that pushed the Baptist church leaders toward military-monarchical demonstrations, toward a whitewashing of the aims of the war and its moral support by every means of oral and written propaganda. They were inspired by the interests of the imperialist bourgeoisie, with whose dominance they associated the turning of Russia into "a new country of unlimited possibilities, into a new America".

On the path of the imperialistic aspirations of the Russian bourgeoisie, as of the bourgeoisie of all the belligerent powers, there was one completely principled, completely firm opponent — the revolutionary proletariat, armed with the Leninist slogan of turning the imperialistic war into a civil war.

Under the conditions of the strike movement, the constantly increasing force of the peasant actions from mid-1915, and the growth of the revolutionary movement in the army and the navy, the bourgeoisie propagandized class peace with every means available to it, implanted all kinds of "workers' groups" as channels for their ideology into the mass of workers, and as "chambers of mediation" for the reconciliation of the interests of the workers and the factory-owners. The religious leaders who created a special organ — the newspaper *Utrenniaia zvezda* — for explaining all socio-economic and political problems from the "Evangelical point of view", made the preaching of class peace their *profession de foi*.

"The Evangelical point of view" on the problem of social relations in Russia in the war years and the post-war period was formulated in the newspaper *Utrenniaia zvezda* immediately after the beginning of the war, and it consisted in the following: "During the war the scales fell from everyone's eyes, and everyone understood that both the town governor and the worker, the general and the soldier, Miliukov and Purishkevich,[M] are equally necessary members of one great family. And it seems to us that this recognition will remain even when the war is over and people are returned to their everyday peaceful occupations" (*UZ* VIII/18/1914: 3).

The Baptist church worked staunchly in the years of the World War in order to accustom the workers to the "Evangelical point of view" toward the Purishkeviches, town governors, and generals, and at the same time placed a moral basis under the vengeance of the Purishkeviches, town governors, and generals on the conscious workers. "... In these hard times of war", Prokhanov wrote in 1916, "strikes are a serious crime" (*UZ* V/6/1916: 1). Prokhanov was indignant: "... now each day is dear for that aim which was set by the threatening attack of the enemy ... how can there be people capable of deciding to participate in any strike now, during this great war?" (*ibid.*).

Prokhanov was a warm supporter of the legislation worked out in 1916 by the Ministry of Trade and Industry of "chambers of mediation". "In this milieu", he wrote, "where one feels class conflict most of all, these chambers will introduce a spirit of reconciliation and will prevent useless clashes with their sad consequences" (*UZ* III/18/1916: 1).

The socio-political role played by the Baptist church in the years of the First World War was reduced to justification and support of its imperialistic aims, and a multiplication with the whole force of its religious influence of the political and ideological resources of imperialism.

8. Baptism and Evangelical Christianity in the Period of the Second Bourgeois-Democratic Revolution

In spite of the fact that the social essence of the Baptist and Evangelical Christian churches was the same (for both were organs of bourgeois reaction), the political face of the Baptist church in some measure remained for a long period in the shade. It is true that the Baptist leaders and preachers, and their press, unceasingly and faithfully served the interests of the counter-revolutionary bourgeoisie, but in the formation of social ideals, political goals and aspirations, the initiative was with the Evangelical Christians, whose head, Prokhanov, could with all justice be called not only a religious but also a political leader of the bourgeoisie. This is explained by the time and the peculiarities of the condition of origin and distribution of Evangelical Christianity, by the peculiarities of its social makeup.

Evangelical Christianity, if we compare it with Baptism, was freer of the "original sin" of old Russian sectarianism—more independent of the burdens of social and everyday traditions of the Molokan elders. As a church it was a pure product of bourgeois society, having arisen at the beginning of the monopolistic stage of its development. Hence the aspiration of the leaders of

Evangelical Christianity for immediate participation in state-political activity, and their connection with bourgeois parties and their leaders.

The bourgeois-liberal grouping in Baptism, more or less analogous to the one in Evangelical Christianity, was forced to reckon with the leading group of "Molokanizing elders", headed by Dei Mazaev. In the pre-war years in Baptism, a certain equilibrium of forces between the two groupings was achieved, the expression of which was the election to the post of chairman of the Union of Baptists of the "neutral" figure Goliaev, who sympathized more with the Pavlovite than with the Mazaevite grouping. But Mazaev, far away on his farm, continued to exert a strong influence on the situation in Baptism. In these conditions, although the development of socio-political events favored the strengthening in Baptism of the position of the Pavlov grouping, the latter gave way to the Prokhanov grouping, in political maneuvering ability, in recognition from the political businessmen of the bourgeois world, and finally in prestige in the international circles of Baptism. Under the circumstances of the second bourgeois-democratic revolution in Russia, the Pavlov grouping secured the leading influence in Baptism.

In the resurrected journal *Slovo istiny* (both the Pavlovite journal *Slovo istiny* and the Mazaevite journal *Baptist* ceased publication at the beginning of the World War), the regime of the bourgeois Provisional Government was welcome. The editorial "K momentu" [On the Moment], published in the first issue of the journal, declared: "No, this is not a dream. Great Russia has really shaken off the burden of the age-old dominion of the Autocracy. The structure of oppression of the spirit and the soul has collapsed, the chains of evil dark forces are broken. And now everything past seems a dream, nightmarish, bloody, delirious and endless. The death agony of decaying reaction, from whose stench our whole country was suffocating, lasted for a long time" (*SI* 1917, No. 1: 1).

This declaration gives no idea of the real attitude toward tsarism of the leaders of the Baptist church. Their ideal was a constitutional monarchy. Along with representatives of Evangelical Christians and Mennonites, they advanced to the forefront of the political platform of 1905 the principle of the stability of the monarchy, and succeeding events in the period 1905-1907 confirmed their principled monarchism. In 1917, the Baptist church made the same attempt at political masquerade as the Kadets, yesterday's constitutional monarchists, who became republicans under conditions in which to defend monarchism meant to share its fate.

The leaders of the Baptist church felt themselves called upon to participate actively in the construction of bourgeois-parliamentary public life: "With good feeling and a profound sense of duty we make our contribution to the cause of the rebirth of the individual and society". They saw their task as that of unifying "both simple and intellectual believers, wishing to assist in the implementation of evangelical ideals and their introduction into the social and political life of the Russian people, which now faces the task of transforming its whole structure on new foundations" (*SI* 1917, No. 1: 16).

The policy of apoliticism, which was unsuitable in conditions of the violent upsurge of revolutionary activity of the masses, was set aside by the Baptist church. In the programmatic article, "The Political Demands of Baptists", published in May 1917, P. V. Pavlov, in the name of the Baptist church, came out with a plan for the political transformation of Russia. The plan completely bypassed social problems and was reduced to obscure (because in no way developed) demands for a unicameral republic, freedom of assembly, association, speech and press, separation of church and state, revocation of the death penalty, inviolability of person and dwelling, and equal rights of citizens without distinction of faith and nationality (*ibid.*: 3).

However, the essence of the political demands of the Baptists was by no means the scheme of formal freedoms of bourgeois democracy enumerated by Pavlov, but a struggle against the development of the bourgeois revolution into a socialist one. Pavlov's article was published after the mass actions of St. Petersburg proletariat on April 21 under the Bolshevik slogan "All power to the Soviets", after the April crisis of the Provisional Government, which was forced to set up a coalition cabinet with the participaton of Mensheviks and SRs.

Pavlov was proceeding from the peculiarities of the time he lived in, when he could not avoid hiding his anti-socialist views with socialist phraseology. He had to respond to the growth of social consciousness of the workers with demagogic assertions that there existed two socialisms—the Christian, which was brought by Christ, "the most terrible revolutionary" (*ibid.*: 2), and the type of socialism based on the expropriation of private property. "Baptists", Pavlov declared, "strive for socialism, but not one of seizure, built on the declaration that other people's property is one's own, but they teach that it is necessary to achieve such moral perfection that nothing earthly is considered one's own, in the sense that one is ready to share everything with one's friend if he needs something" (*ibid.*: 3).

The time was such that Pavlov did not dare openly condemn the growth of an atheistic consciousness among workers. He demagogically proclaimed in his article: "And what is surprising in the fact that there are now people who cannot hear of the Gospels and in general about religion without gritting their teeth, for the extinguishers of light always depended on religion, on the power over souls, in order by fright to continue to hold people in darkness, and fighters for popular freedom came up against religion as the strongest barrier on the path of the movement for progress" (*ibid.*).

The bourgeois extinguisher of light slighted the feudal extinguisher of light and continued to extinguish light. Christ "produced and continues to produce the most terrible revolution, the revolution of spirit", he wrote, and hence: "Socio-economic problems are also near to the heart of Baptists, but the solution of them, according to the evangelical teaching, must pass through a preliminary stage—the revolution of spirit. 'Seek first the kingdom of God, and the rest will be given to you.' In Baptist congregations present-day conflicts are reconciled—poor and rich consider themselves brothers" (*ibid.*: 3).

Rockefeller was an example of a person who had experienced the revolution of the spirit and had become the possessor of a socialist consciousness in Pavlov's view: "The Baptists have nothing against the capital of their American brothers and of the millionaire Rockefeller, for they know that the money was acquired for great causes, which are already known to the whole world, and the latest of his causes is to help entire Polish and Belgian regions. And this money if squandered could never have done so much good" (*ibid.*: 3).

He declared Lloyd George another example of a person transformed by the revolution of the spirit: "We have nothing against the presence in power of followers of the teaching of Christ—and from our whole heart we wish further success to our brother in Christ, the Baptist British Prime Minister Lloyd George, who did so much to heal social wounds, and stands guard over the freedom of the European peoples from the encroachments of German militarism" (*ibid.*).

Pavlov declared that "the Constitution of the United States of America is nothing but an exact copy of the structure of Baptist congregations" and that "for Baptists and other groups like them, different only in name, such as Evangelical Christians, Presbyterians, etc., the slogans of freedom, equality and brotherhood which were suggested have even now been achieved" (*ibid.*).

The sense of Pavlov's political utterance consisted in the assertion that all conceivable possibilities of social creativity are exhausted in the experience of Baptism, which it only remains to adopt on a wide social scale in order forever to establish freedom, equality and brotherhood.

"The political demands of Baptists" set forth by Pavlov are stupid and crude demagogy in comparison with the program advanced in 1917 by Prokhanov. Prokhanov on March 17, 1917 in a gathering of a chosen circle of co-thinkers consisting of 22 persons, which took place in Petrograd, proposed that a political party under the title "Resurrection Christian-Democratic Party" be formed. Prokhanov's suggestion was accepted, elections were held for a temporary Central Committee of the Party, composed of the chairman (Prokhanov), deputy chairman, treasurer, secretary, a secretarial aide and five members. A week later in *Utrenniaia zvezda* the program of the Christian-Democratic Party was announced. In contrast to the Pavlov program which we have considered, the program of Prokhanov's party did not use the phraseology of Christian socialism. It was a variety of "the State Platform" of the Union of Freedom, Truth and Peace, supplemented by political ideas which Prokhanov had developed in 1910-1916 in *Utrenniaia zvezda*, and oriented toward the concrete political situation created at the beginning of the February Revolution.

Prokhanov's program envisaged the points making up the political demands of the Baptists, but was different from the program of the Baptists in that it rejected the short-sighted political approach of the "figures of silence" in the field of questions which were all that the working classes were talking about at that time: peace, land and the eight-hour work day. Prokhanov was an experienced defender of the class interests of the bourgeoisie, and his program was a refined demagogic one. As an example of his bourgeois class insight, let us cite the fact that once, taking part in the chorus of voices which welcomed the Stolypin agrarian reform, he warned that it would give birth to "a landless class", still more threatening, in his words, than the unemployed class, and he demanded a supplementation of the reform by measures which would help alleviate the inevitable further growth of class contradictions (*UZ* IX/24/1910: 1).

Now the program of the Resurrection Party declared "the widest socio-economic legislation on the basis of complete justice for the working classes" (*UZ* 1917, No. 1: 7). The Resurrection Party promised the peasants "the introduction of the principle of allotment, according to labor, of crown, monastery and entailed-estate land for the use of the people", "with compensation", it is true, "as determined by legislative bodies" and (of course) with the preservation of landlord holdings. It promised the workers "freedom to strike, the development of the principle of chambers of medation" (as a means of preventing strikes) and even an eight-hour work day, not, it is true, in the form of a constitutional law, but in the form of good intentions — "the establishment of a eight-hour working day" (*ibid.*).

The Resurrection Party promised the people "a firm international peace", so firm that its establishment required time for the Entente to bring the war "to a victorious end", and also "the direction of all the activity of the Russian state toward the implementation of an international arbitration tribunal, universal disarmament, and the removal of all possibilities of war and a firm international peace" (*ibid.*). And in the meantime, in a note dated March 8, 1917, Prokhanov reported with satisfaction to Miliukov: "The enormous majority of sectarians serve in the ranks of the army with fidelity and devotion ... many of them were wounded in the war and killed, and those who remained alive received marks of distinction, etc." (TsGAOR, div, 579, f. 1, s.u. 2,614, sh. 1).

The program of the Resurrection Party was decorated with demands "for the equality of women, the setting up of a general state pension, universal education" — the boss promised the workers a generous celebration of the preservation of private ownership of the national wealth.

In a large section of the program devoted to the "democratization of the Church", questions of freedom of conscience are interpreted, and also questions of fundamental transformation in the internal life of the Russian Orthodox Church. What was meant was a restructuring of the Church into a religious society based on the principles of bourgeois democracy, with a reformed liturgy (in Russian and with the participation of the believers), with a reduced calendar of holidays (i.e. an increase in the number of work days) etc. In this Prokhanov did not underestimate the role of the Church in the support of the class dominance of the bourgeoisie, and significantly concluded the plan for the democratization of the Church with the words: "All points of the religious program can be implemented only partly by legisltion, but chiefly with the mediation of free religious creativity, by means of conviction and the word of inspired preaching, etc." (*UZ* 1917, No. 1: 8).

Both for Pavlov, and especially for Prokhanov, the ideal of society and the state was exemplified by the United States of America. Prokhanov did not cease propagandizing these ideals over the whole course of the publication of *Utrenniaia zvezda*. In his view, a bourgeois "superstate", whose formation he predicted as the result of a world war, was embedded in the rays of monopolistic capital (*UZ* VII/15/1916: 2). In the program of the Resurrection Party, Prokhanov, in agreement with the ideologists and publicists of the Western European imperialist bourgeoisie, proclaimed: "The unification of all states into one 'World Union of States' with suitable organs for regulating world life ..." (*UZ* 1917, No. 1: 7).

Such was Prokhanov's imperialist utopia.

The establishment of the regime of the bourgeois Provisional Government not only was marked by an outpouring of political enthusiasm from the Baptist and Evangelical Christian churches, but earned the blessing of the World Union of Baptists, which attentively watched the events of politcial life in Russia. For figures in world Baptism, who included Rockefeller and Lloyd George, extolled by Pavlov and his brothers, Russia was the object of highly peculiar alarm: they were afraid of the possibility of a socialist revolution in Russia and its revolutionary withdrawal from the imperialist war. Robert Stuart MacArthur—the president of the World Union of Baptists—on March 30, 1917, sent a letter to Miliukov: "We hope that God will be merciful and give you the power to struggle with the extreme radicals. We unceasingly pray to God to help save great Russia from the danger of internal struggle and in particular from the possibility of internecine war. We all look on you as an enlightened leader of a great people. You know America, you know Russia, you are known to all the world. We believe that you are a reliable channel of great reforms. We believe now that the Baptists will have freedom, and the church will be completely separate from the state in Russia. Now nothing at all is impossible for Russia.... The day of democracy has arrived" (TsGAOR, div. 579, f. 1, s.u. 4,973, shs. 1-2).

The Baptist churches in Russia, and Baptism as an international church, placed their bets on Miliukov as a bourgeois leader capable of dealing with the revolutionary movement which was ever more deeply and widely seizing the masses of Russia. President MacArthur did not wish to leave Miliukov in doubt that his efforts in the struggle with revolution would be evaluated gratefully, and he promised to satisfy the economic and political demands of the Russian bourgeoisie: "We will be happy to see Russia reach Constantinople and the open sea, and this possibility is closer than it has ever been. We hope that God will do everything possible to aid you in the achievement of your great aim" (*ibid.*, sh. 3).

The Baptist and Evangelical Christian churches continued in the period of the second bourgeois-democratic revolution the counter-revolutionary course laid out in their political platform of 1905, enriched by the methods of religious deception of the workers in the years of reaction and world war, and adapted to the circumstances of class struggle which evolved after the overthrow of the Autocracy. In order to hold on the side of the bourgeois Provisional Government tens of thousands of their followers, and to tear them away from participation in the general revolutionary movement of the masses, in order to bring under the ideological dominion of the bourgeoisie thousands and thousands of barely aware workers, the leaders of Baptist congregations in every possible way perverted their political consciousness. Pavlov's Christian-democratic phraseology and the clever Christian-democratic promises of Prokhanov were set in motion. At the same time the religious attack on the consciousness of believers was intensified.

After the July shooting, the leitmotif of Baptist and Evangelical Christian preaching became "brotherly love", class peace, evangelical love "of everyone for everyone". In the congregations and in the pages of the Baptist press there were constant appeals for the unification of hostile classes and parties. Class struggle was declared outside "the evangelical law". "Class or any other kind of struggle ...", we read in the July issue of the journal *Slovo istiny*, "just like war, awakens in its participants one of the vilest of human feelings — hatred. Hatred is diametrically opposed to love. And as love leads to union, so hatred departs from it" (*SI* 1917, No. 4: 50).

Everyone who enters into "modern unions and class organizations" and is a participant of "hatred between various groups of society" becomes an open opponent of Christ: "Everyone who hates his brother is a murderer". Christ taught "love your enemies" (*ibid.*: 51). From July 1917 the journal *Slovo istiny* in issue after issue published articles by members of its editorial board, who in a provocative manner posed the question, "can believers be members of the Social Revolutionary and Social Democratic parties and other political organizations", in order each time to answer that this contradicts "the spirit and the teaching of the word of God" (*ibid.*: 63). In articles appearing in July and August in the journal *Slovo istiny,* one increasingly perceives faint notes of disillusionment in the ability of the ruling bourgeois leaders to prevent the coming socialist revolution.

A. Regnidov, in the article "Spasenie Rossii" [The Salvation of Russia], affirms the decline of the "religio-moral" spirit in tsarist Russia and asks: "Has the situation changed in the new regime of democratically free Russia? The answer must be negative". It is clear to the author of the article that the bourgeoisie did not find a single ideal or a single slogan which could receive a response in, as Regnidov proclaimed it, "the devasted national soul" (*SI* 1917, No. 7: 90). Thus, could not the salvation of Russia come on the wave of a religious reformation? The Baptist leaders returned to the bankrupt idea of a religious reformation which they propagandized after the revolution of 1905-1907.

In an article entitled "Revolutia dukha" [The Revolution of the Spirit], the Baptist figure Vodlinger wrote: "Studying the crooked lines of the Russian revolution, which are reminiscent of the bobbing of a ship being carried along the shoreless ocean without a captain or a helmsman, one comes to the conclusion that the grief of Russia is not in the lack of this or that form of power, but in the lack for the majority of a strong powerful spirit of all-conquering faith...." It lacks "fire from heaven" (*SI* 1917, No. 11: 146). But when the Baptist leaders armed the bourgeoisie with "fire from heaven", the bourgeoisie bristled up against the revolution with the Kornilov conspiracy. And the representative of the upper strata of the Baptist and Evangelical Christian churches, being in equal measure bourgeois, religious and political figures, recognized that the strategy of the struggle against the workers required a combination of fire from heaven and bullets and artillery.

The Provisional Government organized a military conspiracy against the revolution, the implementation of which was entrusted to General Kornilov. With the aim of politically and ideologically guaranteeing the conspiracy and the consolidation of counter-revolutionary forces, a State Conference was called on August 12. This was the political and ideological preparation for a regime of counter-revolutionary terror and military dictatorship.

From the tribune of the State Conference which generals, industrialists and political businessmen mounted and descended, there stood a member of the State Conference, the chairman of the All-Russian Council of Evangelical Christians, Prokhanov: "For the immediate salvation of the motherland, of freedom in this terrible hour from the threat proceeding from the West of Prussian militarism, and of internal dangers of anarchy and counter-revolution," he said, "for the achievement of an integral and undivided country, there is needed, until the Constitutional Assembly and the permanent establishment in Russia of the foundations of popular sovereignty, a firm and strong regime, resting on the moral force of support and trust of all organized vital forces in the country" (*SI* 1917, No. 8: 106).

Prokhanov demanded the "cleaning-up of the army, the firming-up of discipline and order in the country, decisive political and socio-economic measures", but he was not original in this. Kerenskii and others demanded the same thing. But in order for "the afore-mentioned system of measures", as Prokhanov expressed it (the papers were in Kornilov's field bag), to be successful, the leader of Evangelical Christianity proposed "a heavenly fire" — "the psychological factor of faith". Prokhanov considered that "faith, if it inflames every part of the population, can give force to the measures undertaken and open an inexhaustible source of energy, the will to work, the readiness for mutual concessions, for the subordination of the private to the common, to sacrifices and heroic deeds, and can bring about agreement, collaboration, and the unification of all classes into one upsurge for the salvation of the country and of freedom at the present threatening moment" (*ibid.*).

Prokhanov insisted that the State Conference work out in the spirit of his proposal "at least a short common declaration in answer to the Provisional Government from all parties and classes of the population represented in the meeting". Having already left the rostrum, Prokhanov was convinced in personal conversations with Kerenskii, Karaulov and Miliukov of the necessity of adopting such a declaration. Those speaking with Prokhanov agreed with him but "pointed to the impossibility of implementing" such a step, "as a consequence of the too heterogeneous composition of the meeting" (*ibid.*: 107). The bourgeois political leaders had ceased to believe in the effectiveness of any force other than military, and turned aside Prokhanov's desperate attempts to save their dominion with the help of "the psychological factor of faith".

Returning from the state meeting in Petrograd, Prokhanov sent (on August 17) a letter to Kerenskii, attempting to strengthen his will for a struggle with the revolution: "Having returned from the State Conference in Moscow, I cannot forget your last words: 'I will believe less'. I deeply understand the drama you are experiencing and I only wish to tell you one thing: do not lose faith, dear Alexander Fedorovich!... Believe yourself and you will inspire the people with faith and Russia will be saved. They pray for you. Russia needs you" (TsGAOR, div. 3, s.u. 361, sh. 70).

Like Prokhanov, the leaders of the Baptist church held to the political position of the State Conference. In an editorial in the journal *Slovo istiny* we read: "We would like to believe that in fact, as Kerenskii said at the last meeting, 'in the moment of danger all will come and save the country, save the life of the people, who are worthy of a bright better future" ' (*SI* 1917, No. 8: 105).

All statements in the Baptist press in September-October 1917 are filled with motifs of irreconcilable hatred for the revolutionary struggle of the workers. Recognizing their powerlessness to hold back the flow of revolutionary events, organized and directed by the will of the Bolshevik Party, the Baptist and Evangelical Christian churches prepared for a continuation of the struggle by any and all means. And in the first days after the completion of the Great October Socialist Revolution they sent an appeal to their political co-thinkers and to those of their religious co-thinkers whom they for decades held on religious paths: "The Bolshevik Party, using military force, has taken all power from the hands of other parties. Of course, this is not the end of the struggle.... The blood of the killed cries out to the conscience and hearts of us all: enough blood, come to your senses! Let us tumble the idols of party mindlessness and stretch out the hand of brotherly contact to one another on the basis of spiritual unity" (*SI* 1917, No. 12; 162).

The political co-thinkers of the Baptist and Evangelical Christian clergy heard this call. But ordinary believers, Baptists and Evangelical Christians, in the mass turned a deaf ear to it. In the first issues of the journal *Slovo istiny* for 1918 there appeared the mournful admissions of Baptist leaders that believers think only of how to receive land "from the hands of the socialists". But this period of the history of Baptism and Evangelical Christianity lies beyond the chronological bounds of this work.

Editor's Notes

Note A. That is, the land to the west of the Dnepr River, which at various times was under Polish rule.

Note B. "Gray grains" refers to buckwheat, millet and rye.

Note C. Shallow trenches and corresponding mounds were the usual way of marking property lines in rural areas.

Note D. From *The Development of Capitalism in Russia* (1903).

Note E. At this time equivalent to two kopeks.

Note F. From *The Development of Capitalism in Russia* (1903).

Note G. English translation from Karl Marx, Capital, Vol, I: 77.

Note H. From *The Development of Capitalism in Russia* (1903).

Note I. That is, presumably the table in the house of prayer—the altar. In other words, the person in question is being accused, not of embezzling church funds for his personal use, but of a theological deviation.

Note J. That is, a person holding a job requiring higher education, whether humanistic or technical.

Note K. Reference is to the submission of the Holy Roman Emperor, Henry IV, to Pope Gregory VII, at Canossa in the Italian Alps in 1077.

Note L. Zubatov was a tsarist police officer who in the 1890s, operating under cover, became the head of a fairly large and prominent "revolutionary" organization.

Note M. A highly reactionary and anti-Semitic politician of the period.

6

Adventism

1. The Origin of Adventism in the USA and Its Dissemination in Russia

The peculiarities of the ideological formation of American society in the period of industrial revolution in the USA conditioned the peculiarities of Adventism as a form of religious ideology. At the same time there is as yet not a single work in Soviet historiography in which there is any substantial review of the problem of the genesis of Adventism. This compels me to make a brief digression into the history of the birth of Adventism in the USA.

Adventism arose during the industrial revolution in the USA. This was a period of rapid development of the bourgeois entrepreneurial system, of the feverish construction of railroads, and, beginning with the 1830s, of feverish land speculation. The old, customary conditions of life of the workers were scrapped, and rapidly-developing capitalism brought them exploitation, crises, mass unemployment, ruin and poverty, unheard-of before this time. "The older agrarian simplicity of New England", wrote the well-known historian of American social thought, V. L. Parrington, "was being submerged by the industrial revolution" (Parrington 1962: 462) [1927: 397].

During the entire first half of the 19th century the tempo of class differentiation of American society increased. By 1860 in the United States there were already 2.5 million workers, including 1,300,000 industrial workers, 500,000 transport workers, about 700,000 farm laborers, 2,400,000 farmers and 4,000,000 slaves, which "speaks of the presence of antagonistic classes, while on American capitalism there was a 'tumor'—plantation slavery" (Efimov 1958: 223).

In 1818, the American economy suffered a spasm of commercial crisis, which slowed down industrial development for several years, and had a severe effect on the position of the masses. Then there followed the economic crisis of 1825, and especially the severe five-year crisis of 1837-1842, which paralyz-

349

ed industry in the most capitalistically developed states of New England. "By September 1837, nine tenths of all enterprises in New England were closed. Gradually the crisis spread to the agricultural regions. The streets of the cities were filled with tens of thousands of unemployed" (Ocherki 1960: 194). Crises shook the economy of the USA in 1847, 1857 and 1861. With the beginning of the second quarter of the 19th century, they were no longer local. They coincided with the economic crises in the countries of Western Europe, revealing by this the fact of involvement of the USA's economy in the system of the world economy (Efimov 1958: 208-209).

The essayist and public-affairs writer of the 1840s-1850s, Henry David Thoreau, left profound and clear descriptions of the situation of the working masses—the workers and small farmers in the America of his time. "Did you ever think", Thoreau asked, "what those sleepers are that underlie the railroad?" And he answered: "Each one is a man, an Irishman, or a Yankee man. The rails are laid on them, and they are covered with sand, and the cars run smoothly over them. They are sound sleepers, I assure you. And every few years a new lot is laid down and run over; so that, if some have the pleasure of riding on a rail, others have the misfortune to be ridden upon" (Thoreau 1962: 61) [Original English from Airmont edition, 1965: 70-71].

Let us remember that the rail network of the United States, thanks to the labor of hundreds of thousands of workers, grew from 51.2 kilometers in 1830 to 29,398 kilometers in 1885 (Efimov 1958: 218). Thoreau aptly described the situation of workers under capitalism: "... men have become the tools of their tools" (Thoreau 1962: 26) [1965: 33]

The society of his time was a society of sharp social contrasts: "The luxury of one class is counterbalanced by the indigence of another. On the one side is the palace, on the other are the almshouse and 'silent poor'.... It is a mistake to suppose that, in a country where the usual evidences of civilization exist, the condition of a very large body of the inhabitants may not be as degraded as that of savages" (Thoreau 1962: 25) [1965: 32]. Thoreau drew special attention to the ruin of the class of small patriarchal farmers. He wrote that the history of their farmsteads is best known "at the bank where they are mortgaged.... What has been said of the merchants, that a very large majority, even ninety-seven in a hundred, are sure to fail, is equally true of the farmers" (Thoreau 1962: 23) [1965: 30].

The entire first half of the 19th century passed under the banner of intensifying class struggle in the U.S., expressed in the Civil War of 1861-1865. A. V. Efimov makes a compressed summary of the most striking incidents of the class struggle of that time: "The popular uprisings of 1791-1799 in the middle states, the uprising of farmers against the descendants of the patroons in the state of New York in 1839-1842, Dorr's rebellion in Rhode Island in 1840-1842, as a result of which the land qualification for voting was abolished in this state, the Negro uprisings and conspiracies, the armed struggle of the Indians against their inhuman extermination and removal from their land, the mass movement of the farming poor in the southern lands which led more than once to armed clashes with land speculators and the authorities, and finally, the civil war in Kansas in 1854-1856, the uprising of the abolitionists headed by John Brown and the subsequent uprisings of Negroes in a number of southern states. The most important feature of the popular movements of this period, beginning with the 1820s, was the workers' movement" (Efimov 1958: 288-289).

The changes taking place in the situation of the workers in the U.S., conditioned by the heightening of the level of capitalist development of the country, led to profound changes in the social consciousness. This found expression in sharp ideological struggle, in which apologists for the bourgeoisie (Carey and Kriege) issued theories of class harmony, attempting to base it on economic and ethical considerations; progressive ideologists, reacting sensitively to the impoverished situation of the masses, spoke out in criticism of capitalism (Silovis) and propagandized utopian socialism (Godwin and Brisbane); such a distinctive organization as the "Transcendentalist Club" was formed (1836), with its heated discussions on social, philosophical, ethical and religious questions, testifying to a re-evaluation of ideological values taking place in society. Emerson, Ripley, Thoreau—the most important representatives of the "Transcendentalist Club"—for all the contradictions that marked their literary activity, issued accusations against the bourgeois civilization contemporary with them.

One of the peculiarities of the social thought of the USA was that in the course of the first half of the 19th century, most of its representatives expressed their views in religious form. This was a tribute to traditions going back to the 17th century, when ideological disputes were conducted mainly within the ideology of Puritanism. This in turn was a tribute to the theoretical backwardness which was characteristic of the American bourgeoisie, not excluding its intelligentsia.

"... [F]rom good historial reasons", Engels wrote, "the Americans are worlds behind in all theoretical things, and while they did not bring over any medieval institutions from Europe they did bring over masses of medieval traditions, religion, English common (feudal) law, superstition, spiritualism, in short every kind of imbecility which was not directly harmful to business and which is now very serviceable for making the masses stupid" (*Marx and Engels* 1947: 397-398) [1936: 451].

For two centuries, the religious ideology of the ruling classes in America was Calvinism, with its teaching about predestination, and its interpretation of man as a spawn of the devil, as a receptacle of baseness and every possible sin. This conditioned the anti-Calvinist direction of the opposition to the ruling large bourgeoisie and the landed aristocracy.

Unitarianism, taking form around the turn of the 19th century, made the starting-point of its polemic against Calvinism the proposition that in his nature man was from time immemorial free and good. In the words of the prominent ideologist of Unitarianism in the second quarter of the 19th century, William Channing, "[a]n enlightened, disinterested human being, morally strong, and exerting a wide influence by the power of virtue, is the clearest reflection of the divine splendour on earth ..." (quoted in Parrington 1962: 387) [1927: 333].

The ideological uprising against the Calvinist conception of the God-despot, playing at his discretion with people's fates, had completely clear social subcurrents. The dethroning of the heavenly despot served as the dethroning of earthly despots. "It is because I have learned", Channing wrote, "the essential equality of men before the common Father, that I cannot endure to see one man establishing his arbitrary will over another by fraud, or force, or wealth, or rank, or superstitious claims. It is because the human being has moral powers, because he carries a law in his own breast and was made to govern himself, that I cannot endure to see him taken out of his own hands and fashioned into a tool by another's avarice or pride" (Parrington 1962: 388) [1927: 334].

Neither groups specifically religious in their ideological form, such as Unitarianism, which was made up of a number of tendencies, nor philosophical groups, such as the Transcendentalists, bypassed the critiques of Calvinism. "The Unitarians", Parrington writes, "had pronounced human nature to be excellent; the Transcendentalists pronounced it divine. They endowed it with great potentialities; made of it a dwelling place of the Most High ..." (Parrington 1962: 444) [1927: 382]. Unitarianism was not only popular among the exploited classes, but was embraced by some strata of the successful bourgeoisie, which now was also not satisfied with the role of impotent weapon in the hands of God, which Calvinism allotted to people. Of course, bourgeois adherents of Unitarianism did everything in their power to give its ideas a peaceful, inoffensive character.

The changes taking place in the economic and ideological life of American society in the first half of the 19th century put new questions to Baptism, which had at that time a wide circle of supporters among the workers, and had followers among representatives of the bourgeoisie. Not all groups in Baptism held to the Calvinist doctrine of predestination, which had lost its credibility. But the Baptist groups adhering to the Arminian concept of man's free will preached a doctrine of the redemptive sacrifice of Christ, given for all mankind. At the same time, an idea was formed in American social thought, in opposition to Calvinism, of man as being ready to stand on his own, and if necessary to make sacrifices in the struggle for his ideals.

The consistent development of Unitarian ideology could not but reject the dogma of predestination and the dogma of the redemptive sacrifice of Christ, closely connected with the concept of a pitiless, vengeful and frightening God. Delivering a sermon in New York in 1826 against the Calvinists, William Channing said: "Suppose, then, that a teacher should come among you, and should tell you, that the Creator, in order to pardon his own children, had erected a gallows in the centre of the universe, and had publicly executed upon it, in lieu of the offenders, an Infinite Being, the partaker of his own Supreme Deity.... Would you not tell him, that he calumniated his Maker? Would you not say to him, that this central gallows threw gloom over the universe; that the spirit of a government, whose very acts of pardon were written in such blood, was terror, not paternal love; and that the obedience which needed to be upheld by this horrid spectacle, was nothing worth?... [A]nd yet how does this differ from the popular doctrine of atonement?" (quoted in Parrington 1962: 384) [1927: 330-331].

The critique directed by Unitarians and Transcendentalists against Calvinism was at the same time a criticism of Baptism, a group which was more or less close to Calvinism. This criticism could not help but stimulate the development of internal contradictions in Baptism, reflecting in the last analysis the basic contradictions of American society in the period of the industrial revolution.

Of course, the phenomenon of ideological protest, although it took religious form, did not flow in that period only in the channel of Unitarianism. John Noyes, the head and ideological leader of a group of Perfectionists, did not preach the path of individual perfection, but called for a "struggle for universal deliverance from sin", as a result of which a millennial kingdom was to be set up on the territory of the United States. Noyes, in the name of the Holy Spirit which spoke through him, proclaimed Jesus Christ the President of the United States and of the entire world. The titmouse did not set fire to the sea, and in the end Noyes' cause was reduced to the unification of his followers into a religious commune. Still, the idea of the beginning of a millennial kingdom gained popularity among the small farmers and representatives of the lower classes. But it was not so much readiness for collective struggle, as collective expectation of a miracle which was to occur to save God's true sons and daughters—such was the basis of the popularity of the idea of the imminent beginning of the millennial kingdom.

One has only to read the works of American writers in the 1830s-1840s to get the idea of the climate which at that time was forming in the United States for the dissemination of chiliastic and eschatological teachings. In the terrible year of 1837, when the economic crisis broke out, Ralph Emerson wrote in his diary: "Society has played out its last stake; it is checkmated. Young men have no hope. Adults stand like day-laborers idle in the streets. None calleth us to labor.... The present generation is bankrupt of principles and hope, as of property" (quoted in Parrington 1962: 463) [1927: 398]. Henry David Thoreau sensitively noted the mood of his contemporaries among the working classes of the city and the country, characterizing them as moods of hopelessness and despair. He wrote: "The mass of men lead lives of quiet desperation. What is called resignation is confirmed desperation. From the desperate city you go into the desperate country ..." (Thoreau 1962: 8) [1965: 14].

One of the enunciators of these moods was William Miller (1782-1849), like Thoreau and Emerson, a native of the state of Massachusetts in New England — a region ahead of all other parts of the U.S. in the growth of industry and the development of class contradictions.[1] Miller lived on funds gained from trade in lumber. In 1803 he became a farmer in Putney. Miller devoted much time to self-education, manifested great interest in philosophical literature, and openly called himself a deist. Among his readings were the works of Hume, Voltaire, and Thomas Paine. He occupied himself with administrative-judicial activity, being for some time deputy sheriff and justice of the peace. As a captain in the infantry, Miller took part in the War of 1812 with England. Apparently, by the middle of the first decade of the 19th century, Miller's views had undergone a change. This was just the time when America had entered into the grip of a "panic", as the American bourgeoisie called economic crises. In 1816, Miller joined the Baptist church in Lower Hampton, New York State, which belonged to the "true" Baptists, adherents of the Calvinist teaching of predestination.

Without breaking with the doctrine of Baptism, Miller, however, increasingly inclined to the thought that the circumstances and events of the time he was living through testified to the approaching conclusion of the earthly history of mankind: the coming of the end of the world and the second coming of Christ, which would be a visible, personal appearance, like the first appearance of Christ on earth in human form.

The apocalyptic views to which Miller reduced the circumstances of surrounding life, with its howling contrasts of luxury and poverty and its atmosphere of hopelessness, which embraced a wide circle of urban and rural population, were formed by Miller in 1818. However, for a long time he did not openly preach his views. He countinued to read the Apocalypse and the prophecy of Daniel, which unfortunately replaced Voltaire and Thomas Paine for him, a former deist. Behind the symbols of the visions of John the Divine and the prophet Daniel, Miller attempted to discern real historical events, and he attempted to read the numerology found in the prophecies of Daniel as a chronology of these events. However strange it may seem at first

---

[1] "In the 1850s, an approximate relation between the independent population employed in industry and the rest of the population was: 1:8 in New England, 1:15 in the central states, 1:48 in the west, and 1:82 in the south" (Efimov 1958: 210).

glance, Miller attempted to arrive through history and mathematics at an idea about the end of humanity's earthly journey and the approaching coming of Christ.

In the given instance, Miller was taking account of the peculiarities of thought of that milieu to which he himself belonged, and to whose perception of the world he gave religious expression — of the historically conditioned empiricism of thought of his fellow citizens. People of "business", large or small, they believed in the power of fact and concrete proof, and without a share of "sobriety", no theory, even a theological and mystical one, could have in their eyes either value or success. Either consciously or intuitively with his eschatological considerations, Miller was taking account of the character of the world-view of the American large and small bourgeoisie, marked by empiricism, practicality and utilitarianism.

Finally, in 1831, Miller gave public lectures on the end of the world and the second coming of Christ in 1843 (Sekty 1896: 2).

In 1833, Miller published a tract, "A Testimony From the Scriptures and History About the Second Coming of Christ, and About His Personal Rule For a Thousand Years" (*ibid.*). At that time, Miller was still a member of the Baptist church. Moreover, in the year of publication of his essay, he became a preacher in the Baptist congregation in Lower Hampton.

Miller's preaching and the tract published by him were very popular, and numerous adherents collected around him, primarily among Baptists and members of other Protestant sects. The states of Massachusetts, Connecticut, Rhode Island, and New England in general, were made the base of the Millerite movement, which was formally still within the bounds of Baptism. In 1840, at the time of one of the deepest economic crises, most severe in its consequences for the workers — which accounted for their moods — the Millerite newspaper *Sign of the Times* began publication in Boston; after it there followed newspapers with the characteristic titles *Midnight Cry, Trumpet Call* and *Messenger of the Coming* (Sekty 1896: 2-3; Bondar' 1911: 4).[2] In the same year in Boston there was a gathering of Millerites, at which, even though differences appeared over the date of the expected second coming, unanimity was still achieved on the fact that the coming was "especially close, at the door" (Sekty 1896: 2).

[2] Bondar's above-mentioned work was based on documents from the Department of Spiritual Affairs, of the Ministry of Internal Affairs, on extensive direct experience with Adventism in Russia, which was part of Bondar''s duties as an official in the Department of Spiritual Affairs. A spirit of bourgeois liberalism is characteristic of Bondar''s world-view, and his work devoted to sectarianism is distinguished by hidden opposition to the militant clericalism of Russian Orthodoxy. In the words of an Adventist figure, Grigor'ev, contemporaneous with us, S. D. Bondar' "as a result of his study of Adventists compiled ... a very substantial and in many respects just collection under the title 'Seventh Day Adventists' " (Grigor'ev ms.: 4; author's collection).

Essentially a new religious group was formed in Baptism, which had not yet separated out, but which already had its own leadership and press. This was a group which had a mass membership. According to one source, Miller's followers numbered 50,000 persons (Americana 1949: 122), and according to another source, from 50,000 to 100,000 (*EB* 1960: 497).

Meanwhile, 1843, the year for "the end of the world" and "the second coming", approached. The Millerites abandoned all business, all "earthly cares", and demanded from their leaders a definite determination of the time of the event for which they excitedly prepared. Miller declared that the expected events would occur between March 21, 1843 and March 21, 1844. After the general disillusionment which overtook the Millerites after the passing of the time set, Miller admitted the "error" of his computations, but continued to insist on the imminence of the second coming and feared at the same time to name for it any definite period.

This was done by Miller's associate, Snow, who moved back the time of the second coming by only seven months and prophesied it for October 22, 1844.

Miller could no longer deal with the movement aroused by his preaching, which in its own way answered the moods of certain circles of small property-owners and proletarianized elements. As before, yielding to the demands of his followers, he was forced to specify the time of the coming, since now he had to confirm the date of the coming proposed by Snow. However, doubts did not leave Miller, as his declaration shows: "If Christ does not appear on October 22", he, Miller, "will be doubly disappointed" (Bondar' 1911: 5). This "double disappointment" was not long in coming. After October 22, 1844, Miller was left with his disappointment and without many followers. As concerned those who remained true to Miller's teaching, after being twice disappointed in 1843-44, they were not distinguished by a spirit of solidarity, that exalted, elevated condition which, on the threshold, as they thought, of unusual events successfully relieved them of the necessity for any clear external organization.

At the same time there arose opposition to Miller and the ideas asserted by him on the part of a number of his close associates. On the other hand, the Baptist congregations came out with open condemnation of Millerism and the excommunication of those of their members who adhered to this group. In 1845, the Bapitst congregations in Lower Hampton excommunicated Miller himself.

Religious fantasies about the end of the world and the second coming called forth protest among free-thinkers and simply sensible contemporaries of Miller. In a number of leaflets the Millerite movement was subjected to sharp criticism, and against it the traditional weapon of free-thinkers — laughter — was successfully employed. In some leaflets Miller was pictured as rising to heaven with followers hanging onto him, and in others the Millerite ideas about death were ridiculed: a skeleton half-risen from the grave threw his shinbone at a frog croaking at the grave. The ideas of Millerites of the elevation of the just on the Feast of the Purifiction were the subject of a caricature showing angels who draw up the resurrected with hooks (*A* I/1/1958: 8).

Miller's hopes for the founding of an all-embracing religious movement suffered collapse. At the beginning of the 1840s there appeared separate organizations of Millerites—societies of the advent of Christ, which arose in Philadelphia, New York, and many large cities in the northern states (Bondar' 1911: 6). In April 1845 there was a conference of Millerites in Albany (New York State) at which Miller presented a plan for the separation and unifiction of his followers into a new church. At the same time, the conference outlined a number of theological positions which were to play a role as some sort of preliminary creed.

Thus the bases of the Adventist church (Lat. "adventus"—"coming") were laid.

The theological positions of the Adventists approved by the conference in Albany consisted of the following:

1. The visible personal coming of Christ "at a time not definite";
2. The resurrection of the dead—the just and sinners;
3. The beginning of a millennial kingdom after the resurrection of the just. At the same time, the prophecy of the return to Christ by the whole world before his second coming was denied, and also that Christian idea according to which the just immediately after their death received recompense in the form of "the gift of eternal life" (Sekty 1896: 3).

By the time of the conference in Albany, Miller's authority was no longer undisputed among the followers of his doctrine. Along with Miller there appeared new preachers and figures of Adventism who increasingly broadened their influence, among whom in the mid-1840s the most well-known were George Storr, T. Preble, I. Cook, I. Betts, and the married couple James and Ellen White. Miller's proposal for the organizational self-determination of Adventism at the conference in Albany was in agreement with another interpretation of these views, as we have shown.

This interpretation was connected with the dissemination at that time of the teaching of the Millerite George Storr, which was retained in the religious practice of Adventism, that the soul of man was not immortal; dead people were in an unconscious state and sinners would be resurrected in order to be subjected to a final annihilation. Storr's conclusion about the death of the soul seemed to Miller extreme, but insofar as Adventism paid tribute to empiricism, practicality and utilitarianism, and to everything which (in bourgeois consciousness) was honored as common sense, this conclusion found a place in Adventism. One must take account of the success of materialistic natural science in the USA, multiplied in the 1830s-1850s in the works of such scholars as the mathematician Bowley, who translated the *Celestial Mechanics* of Laplace, the geologist Dana, and the follower of the Darwinist teaching, the botanist Gray.

Since Adventism was disseminated not only among farmers but also in the urban population, some of its ideologists had enough foresight to renounce excessivley vulnerable religious conceptions.

Concerning the real motives which led Storr to deny the immortality of the soul, we can only guess, but his later successors in the brochures "The Condition of the Dead", published in Hamburg, frankly wrote:

"Dear reader, we were formerly taught that if our body dies, man—i.e., his soul—does not die, but goes directly to heaven or to hell and there continues to live.

"... Common sense is against such teaching. How can man think without a brain or walk without legs or see without eyes or hear without ears? This contradicts both nature and common sense.

"And the Bible does not teach this in a single text" (TsGIAL, div. 821, f. 133, s.u. 210, sh. 61).

Storr's disagreement with Miller extended to organizational questions. Storr did not agree that the religio-social movement headed by Miller should be given a church character. Less than a year before the conference in Albany he expressed the thought that "any human organization in God's cause is Babylon " (Bondar' 1911: 13). Miller's movement, consisting in the mass of democratic elements, was nevertheless variegated in its social composition. In the ranks there were both farmers of average means and representatives of the bourgeois intelligentsia. Miller's own farm was valued at 2,000 dollars (*A* I/15/1958: 22).

The contradictory nature of the social make-up of the Millerites is explained chiefly by the contradictory tendencies which were already clearly distinguishable in the movement in the first 10-15 years of its existence. In the mid-1840s there arose among the Millerites a group which included in the doctrine laid out by Miller not only Storr's correction about the immortality of the soul, but also the honoring of the Sabbath as "a day of rest". The "theoretician" of Sabbatarianism was Joseph Betts, who published in 1846 a special pamphlet on this theme, but the most important ideologist and figure of this group, which in the second half of the 19th century became basic in Adventism, was Ellen White (1827-1917). Honoring the Sabbath was connected with the general religious world-view of Adventism, in which Old Testament motifs were given an important role. It was also important for the separating out of the Adventist church, which placed Saturday between itself and other religious Protestant organizations, and also Catholicism. In 1858, Sabbatarian Adventists introduced an obligatory tithe, taking from each member a tenth of their income for "the Lord".

In 1860 at a conference in Battle Creek (Michigan) the Sabbatarian Adventists adopted for their church the title "Seventh Day Adventists". Miller's remaining followers continued to celebrate Sunday and constituted a large goup of First Day Adventists. But in the course of the second half of the 1850s and the first half of the 1860s, this group split into differing subsections on one dogmatic question or another, namely: Evangelical Adventists, the Church of Adventist Christians, the Union of Life and the Second Coming, the Church of God in Jesus Christ (they are also Adventists of the Coming Age), and the Church of God.

At the same time, publishing activity, the preparation of qualified theologians in special study institutions, and energetic missionary preaching made it possible around the 1880s-1890s for Adventism, as the Seventh Day Adventist church, not only to be disseminated everywhere in the United States of America, but also to penetrate into the countries of Latin America, into Australia, Africa, Asia (India, Japan, China). In Western Europe, Seventh Day Adventism appeared as early as the 1860s, first in Switzerland, and then in the second half of the 1870s and beginning of the 1880s in Germany, England, Norway, Denmark, and Sweden.

In the 1890s, Seventh Day Adventism was formed into one of the world churches of Protestant type. In 1901, there was created a European general conference of Seventh Day Adventism. The center of European Adventism was set up in Hamburg, where there was a powerful publishing organization, "the International Tract Society of Seventh Day Adventists", publishing Adventist literature in numerous languages, in enormous editions, and having an extremely effective distribution system.

In the first half of the 1880s, Seventh Day Adventism began to spread into Russia. The geography of its original dissemination in Russia in general coincides with that of the dissemination of Baptism and embraces the capitalistically most highly developed territories—Tavriia Guberniia, the Kuban and Don Oblasts, Stavropol', Kiev and Kherson Guberniias (from the late 1880s-early 1890s), and also the Volga area and the guberniias of the Vistula and Baltic (Bondar' 1911: 30-31; Val'kevich 1900: 150-155; Aleksii 1909: 317; Belogorskii 1911: 141).

Among the first disseminators of Adventism in Russia we find German and American preachers such as Laubgan, Perk, Konradi, and also Russian preachers, among whom the meshchanin from the city of Tarashcha, Kiev Guberniia, F. Babienko, a previous adherent of Baptism, was distinguished by his energetic activity. However, growth in numbers of Adventists went relatively slowly. Basically Adventism grew at the expense of followers of Baptism who were disillusioned with the organization and doctrine of their sect.

The scanty data which we possess about the social composition of the Adventists allow us to conclude that these were primarily the rural and urban poor, who connected their hopes for escaping the need and suffering which made their existence unbearable with Adventism's teaching of the second coming and the beginning of the millennial kingdom of the righteous.

Bishop Aleksii, who observed the way of life of the Adventists in Kiev and Kherson Guberniias, wrote:

"In the villages we visited where Adventists live, we were strongly impressed with the difference in the external circumstances of the dwellings of the 'Sabbatarians' from the dwellings of the rest of the peasants: the complete absence of fences, a peeling ramshackle hut, semi-collapsed court-yard buildings, and an abandoned garden overgrown with weeds are characteristic features of the dwellings of followers of the Adventist sect; but at the same time, every time we noticed sectarians sitting next to their huts in white, clean, long shirts with uncovered heads. Everything in them spoke of their profound apathy; both the sluggishness of movement and the slowness of speech, and the gaze of lackluster, lifeless eyes looking into the distance" (Aleksii 1909; 326).

True to his world-view, Bishop Aleksii, in interpreting the reason for that extreme need which struck him on visiting the Adventists, turned the phenomenon upside-down. He derived the improverished position of the Adventists from their eschatological strivings, while, on the contrary, the popularity of the Adventist eschatology was born precisely out of the impoverished position, social oppression and downtrodden state of its followers. Bishop Aleksii admitted that the Adventists "in terms of economics and daily life ... are an extremely unfortunate phenomenon among the simple people", in order immediately after that to give missionary preaching against Adventism the significance of a struggle to ... increase the well-being of the people (Aeksii 1909: 327). Of course, one cannot exclude a reverse influence of the eschatology of Adventism on "disdain for peasant labor", as Aleksii expressed it.

The eschatological views of Adventism themselves, as they were interpreted in the consciousness of those of its ordinary followers whom Aleksii observed in the 1880s in the Kiev and Kherson areas, were marked by the stamp of their social expectations. The eschatology of the Adventists, who lived according to Aleksii in splintered ramshackle huts and experienced extreme material need, was close to the medieval peasant social utopia.

"The pictures", Aleksii writes, "in which the fantasies of the Adventists describe the life of the participants of the millenial kingdom, are a reflection of their ideals of life. In the conceptions of the sectarians there was every imaginable degree of bliss; some imagined a stream of wine, milk and honey, and tables set with the most refined foods, and an uninterrupted feast and entertainment not darkened by anything; others imagined the riches of Croesus, of gold and precious stones. Here there was remarkable fertility of the soil, there idyllic freedom from sin, sadness and disease. A cessation of

war and hatred between people, unanimity, equality and community of property, unity and spirituality in worshipping God ... and with this, as a
necessary addition—eternal spring, with nothing darkening the beauty and
cleanliness of the atmosphere, and general peace in the animal kingdom, supplement the picture of the bliss of the millennial kingdom" (Aleksii 1909:
321).

This is what the poor people whom Aleksii met sitting next to their huts in
white, clean shirts with uncovered heads, eyes looking far into the distance,
were thinking about. Undoubtedly, the religious illusions of the Adventists
lulled their class consciousness and for this reason were profoundly reactionary. But the illusions shutting the eyes of ordinary believers, in this instance the Adventists, had its earthly nucleus.

Adventism achieved relatively wide distribtuion in the cities, including St.
Petersburg, Moscow, Odessa, Sevastopol', Kiev, Stavropol' and Mitava. The
social class which adhered to it, insofar as the data relating to the first decade
of our century allow us to judge, were primarily artisan circles and the urban
poor. Belogorskii writes of the Kiev Adventists that they "sent several of their
members directly to the houses. Having noted for themselves any street or
part of the city settled by workers or artisans, they went from house to
house ..." (Belogorskii 1911: 142).

At the beginning of 1910, in Moscow, Warsaw and Mitava, conferences of
Seventh Day Adventists took place. The official of the Department of
Spiritual Affairs of the Ministry of Internal Affairs, S. D. Bondar', was present. Having studied the social and national composition of the participants
of the conference—the delegates, guests and visitors, Bondar' noted: "The
evening and after-dinner gatherings of the conference (in Moscow—A.K.) attracted few visitors (from 25 to 35). The majority of them were Russians—workers, artisans, small traders, etc. About a third were Germans.
The evening gatherings attracted as many as 120 people. The overwhelming
majority of them were Russians: workers, small shop-owners, artisans, etc."
(Bondar' 1911: 83).

At the conference in Warsaw the majority of the audience were Germans
and Poles. But in social composition they represented the same strata: "the
meetings of the conference", Bondar' wrote, "attracted from 25 to 30 visitors
(in addition to delegates—A.K.). Among them were 3 or 4 Poles, 1 Russian (a
Russian Orthodox), and the rest Germans. Almost all the visitors were
workers or craftsmen. The evening gatherings ... attracted an audience of
110-120. The overwhelming majority of them were Poles. There were not
more than 30 Germans, and 3 or 4 Russians. Almost all belonged to the lower
classes" (Bondar' 1911: 84).

At the conference in Mitava, S. D. Bondar' writes, "the total number of
visitors reached 600 persons. About two thirds of the audience were Letts.

The Germans were next in numerical strength. The Estonian group numbered 25 persons. There were not more than 12 Russians. The overwhelming majority of the audience belonged to the lower classes" (Bondar' 1911: 86).

As follows from Bondar"s information, with all the variety of the national composition of the audience of Adventists' conferences, they were homogeneous in their social position—they belonged to the lower classes.

Adventism was a social phenomenon; its cloudy language equally answered the prejudices of those tormented by work for others, by eternal need, by the lack of rights of the socially lower classes of a capitalist city, whether they consisted of Russians, Germans, Poles, Latvians or Estonians, was all the same. The bourgeois intelligentsia took some part in Adventism too.

I recall the characteristic answer given by the old man Pushilin from the Michurin region of Tambov Oblast to the question of the workers of the Institute of History of the Academy of Sciences about the character of the religious congregation to which he belonged in the 1920s: "... we are not Adventists. Among the Adventists there are only intelligentsia—engineers and doctors. But we have simple peasants, straight from the plow" (Bograd 1961: 138). And in fact, for example, in the report of the chief of the St. Petersburg security force of 1911 about the local congregation of Adventists we find mention of a gathering "in house No. 23, apt. 2 at 4 Rozhdestvenskaia Ulitsa ... at which up to 50 members of the intelligentsia gathered" (Division of Manuscript Collections of the Institute of History, AS USSR, Sector "Ts", div. VI, d. 11, sh. 58).

The number of followers of Adventism continued to grow. Whereas at the end of the 1880s in Russia there were 356 Adventists united into nine congregations, at the end of the 1890s there were already 1,288 Adventists united into 37 congregations (Bondar' 1911: 29, 31).

The dissemination of Adventism caused alarm among leaders of Russian Baptism no less than among those of the Russian Orthodox Church. The point was that Adventism was one of the channels for the expression of the dissatisfaction of ordinary Baptists. At the end of the 19th century, V. G. Pavlov published in the journal *Beseda* an article in which he wrote: "We do not intend here to enumerate all the errors of the Adventists and in general do not wish even to remember them.... Unfortunately, their efforts have not been in vain, and they have succeeded in acquiring followers among our brothers too.... This is why we have found it necessary to acquaint our readers with the chief errors of this sect..." (Val'kevich 1900: Appendix 3, 35).

By 1906, there were already 2,200 Adventists in Russia. After the forced softening of the Autocracy's policy of religious intolerance in 1905-1906, the Adventist mission in Russia had new success. The number of conversions to this sect from Russian Orthodoxy and in part also from Baptist and Lutheranism, grew in the following sequence:

Conversions to Adventism from 1905 to 1911[3]

Years	1905	1906	1907	1908	1909	1910	1911	Total
Number of conversions from Russian Orthodoxy	77	55	139	240	151	259	533	1,454
From Baptism and Lutheranism	31	60	95	125	479	96	175	1,061
Total number of conversions to Adventism	108	115	234	365	630	355	708	2,515

One is struck not only by the increased pace of conversions of believers to Adventism in the period covered by the table, but by the fact that 42% of the transfers to Adventism were former Baptists and Lutherans, and the greatest loss fell upon Baptism.[4] By 1912, there were 5,500 Adventists in Russia, of whom 64% were former Russian Orthodox and 36% were former Baptists and Lutherans (Statistical 1912: 24-26).

It is worth noting that in their struggle against Adventism, the leaders of the Baptist church used not only means of oral and written propaganda, but resorted to forms of political informing of the lowest and vilest kind. Protesting against slanderous accusations of church people that Baptists were a weapon of the "Germanization" of Russia, some Baptist leaders incited the most Black Hundred-chauvinist passions around Adventism, imitating Aivazov, Skvortsov and other Russian Orthodox missionaries like them who personified the nth degree of obscurantism and reaction.

Here is what in June of 1914 one of the patriarchs of Baptism in Russia, V. V. Ivanov, wrote: "... the Adventist sect penetrated into Russia from abroad and has no Russian nature. This sect is ruled by foreigners, Germans, who act and administer it as full masters. They collect the tithes for their own ends. Russian Adventism does not have its own administration and blindly

[3] Compiled from Statistical 1912: 24-26. The data here give only an approximate idea of the growth in numbers of the followers of Adventism. Thus, at the Moscow conference in 1910 it was said that "for the last two years (consequently, from 1909 and 1908 — A. K.) in Russia 1,600 persons accepted Adventism ..." (Bondar' 1911: 94). At the same time, according to the data in our table, we see that for 1908 and 1909 Adventism attracted 995 followers to its ranks.

[4] Let us note the efforts of the Adventist mission among Molokans, which had some success (Zhabin 1914: 30-31).

subordinates itself in everything to foreign agents.... For their tithes, zealously offered, Russian Adventists receive from the foreigners paper 'Olive Trees' (the title of the Adventist journal in Russian which was published in Hamburg—A. K.) and various meaningless tracts" (Ivanov 1914: 15-16).

From all this, contrary to what the priests and missionaries said, it by no means follows, as I have shown, that Baptism and Adventism did not have social roots in the objective conditions of pre-Revolutionary Russian reality.

The Adventist church, from the beginning of its formation and until 1907 inclusive, operated on the bases of organizational dependence and under great ideological influence from the Seventh Day Adventist church in Germany, and from 1901 to 1907 was considered as a component part of "the German union" of Seventh Day Adventists.

In 1907, there took place the first All-Russian congress of Seventh Day Adventists, which laid the foundation of the independent Adventist church in Russia, which from January 1, 1908, was made into a separate "Russian union" of the international church of Seventh Day Adventists (Bondar' 1911: 30-31). The most important figures of the Russian union were Iulii Betkher (chairman of the union), Otto Vil'dgrube (chairman of the "middle Russian field" and the preacher of the Moscow Adventist congregation), and Genrikh Lebsak (chairman of the "west Russian field" and the preacher of the Vilna Adventist congregation). Among prominent figures of Adventism there were also I. A. L'vov (the publisher of the Adventist journal *Blagaia vest'* [Good News], S. S. Efimov (head of the St. Petersburg congregation of Seventh Day Adventists), K. Shamkov (the leader of the Adventist congregation in Odessa). The Adventist conferences which took place in 1910, from among which the conference in Mitava was their second All-Russian congress, were a peculiar review of the forces of this sect. The leaders of the congress were intoxicated at that time by the religious freedom of 1905-1906. Riga was chosen as the center of administration of the Adventist church in Russia (Grigor'ev ms.: 3).

The following years were distinguished by a contemporary Adventist author as the independent "period of 1911-1916" and were called by him "a difficult five years": "Beginning with 1911, the freedom of conscience given earlier was sharply cut back. The years 1912 and 1913 passed with further harassment. And from the beginning of the European war in 1914, the situation still further worsened ... the end of 1916 brought new pressures on our cause ..." (Grigor'ev ms.: 4-5). Nevertheless, Adventism continued to broaden the circle of its adherents, whose numbers grew from 5,500 in 1911 to 6,800 in 1916 (Grigor'ev ms.: 10). The places of greatest concentration of Adventists were the guberniias of Kiev and Lifland; the Kuban Oblast; Podol'sk, Poltava, Stravropol, Kurland and Kherson Guberniias; Terek, Oblast; Tavriia, Samara, Elizavetpol, Irkutsk and Syr-Dar'ia Guberniias.

2. The Social Essence of the Ideology of Adventism

The Seventh Day Adventist church in Russia did not advance its own theologians. In the Adventist periodicals in Russian (the journals *Maslina* [The Olive Tree], *Blagaia vest'*, and *Bibleiskie chteniia* [Bible Readings]), and in non-periodical publications — pamphlets primarily published by the tract society in Hamburg (the journal *Maslina* was published here too) — fragments of the writings of Ellen White and other recognized theological authorities in Adventism were published, paraphrased and commented upon. Along with the writings of Adventist theologians, in these publications one frequently encountered excerpts from the writings of one or another scholar or writer, who were presented to the reader as "natural" Adventists.

The theological views of Adventism were presented in these publictions as agreeing with the facts and conclusions of astronomical, biological and historical sciences. In our sketch of the religious teaching of Adventism we will proceed precisely from those fragments of Adventist theology which had currency in Russian translation and served as an object of commentary for Russian readers. They have currency among Adventists even today.

In the preceding chapter I cited the paradoxical fact noted by Engels that the English "are more concerned about the other world than any other nation, but at the same time live as if there were nothing more for them than earthly existence". The paradoxical nature of this fact increases as soon as we turn to the description of the Adventist movement and teaching. It would seem that there is among religious organizations not a single one which in such degree concentrated its attention on the other world as the Adventists; at the same time Adventism openly declared the necessity that its adherents be devoted to the interests of "earthly existence". How is this paradox to be explained?

In the countries of classical capitalism — the U.S. and England — the bourgeoisie felt itself in the position of Adam and Eve in the Garden of Eden before the Fall: they did not notice their nakedness. They openly gave themselves over to capitalist money-grubbing in all the forms available to them and evaluated this as virtue. They placed highest of all qualities which Parrington describes as "features of the English turn of mind" — "practical, logical, concrete, lucid; loving fact and tireless in its acquisition; master of everyday affairs and competent in dealing with this world" (Parrington 1962: 482) [1927: 414[A]]. For the English and American bourgeoisie no religion was possible which would contradict the interests of business. We will see below how "features of the English turn of mind" were expressed even in the eschatology and chiliasm of Adventism.

One way or another, when the mystical fever of 1843 and 1844 had passed, the ideologists of Adventism became even franker in sending out their followers to arrange affairs in this world. Moreover, they presented earthly cares as a means of increasing the moral capital necessary for acquiring citizenship in the millennial kingdom. The Adventist theologians called on their adherents to work: "Faith in the imminent coming of the Son of Man on the clouds of heaven does not make true Christians indolent and careless in everyday life, but on the contrary, makes them diligent in work. They will work not sloppily but honestly, carefully, soundly. Their uprightness, fidelity, and charity will be tested and glorified in earthly matters. If they are faithful in small things, they will be faithfull in large things" (Bb 1958: 6; manuscript in author's collection).

What was the social content of the labor to which Adventism called its followers?

Adventism asserts the right to private property: "Wealth is not a sin if it is acquired by honest means" (*ibid.*). It denies public ownership. To the question, "what kind of social life did believers lead after the Pentecost", in other words, how should one relate to the so-called communism of the first Christians, an unambiguous answer is given: "Community of property was not forced ... organized, or universal, otherwise the example of an individual would have no meaning ... This support was based only on feelings of love for the needy on the part of some who had property" *(Bibleiskie besedy o deianiiakh apostolov* [Bible Talks on the Acts of the Apostles], p. 15; manuscript in the author's collection).

The proviso about the "honest acquisition" of wealth did not envisage renunciation of exploitation. The appeal for labor, which should not be hindered by the expectation of the second coming, was addressed to exploited workers: "If the worker is not faithful in his everyday obligations, and takes a careless attitude toward work, it will not be unjust for the world to evaluate his religion according to the quality of his work" (Bb 1958: 6).

Here the theology of Adventism plays the role of a factor facilitating an increase in the productivity of labor of workers at capitalist enterprises. But what then determines honesty for those who acquire capital? This is first of all "business honesty": "Children of God should never forget that in all their business enterprises they are being tested on the scales of the sanctuary" (Bb 1956: 70; manuscript in the author's collection).

In the given instance, "the scales of the sanctuary" is not an allegory, but the most prosaic scales, beginning with the spring balance and finishing with improved appliances for weighing large loads: "The inexact weights and crooked scales by which many receive profits for their interests in the world are loathsome before God. However, many who say that they observe the Lord's commandments deal with a crooked scale and false weights" (Bb 1956: 67). To the question, "which commandment preserves the legal right of property?", the answer is given that this is the eighth commandment, which "forbids dishonest enrichment in trade and demands precise payment of debts and also of wages" (*ibid.*, p. 65).

Charity is included in the concept of honesty of capitalists: "Among us today there are many hungry, naked and homeless. The unwillingness to share part of one's wealth, in order to stave off the need of the suffering in some places around us, will be that burden of guilt which will one day frighten us" (*ibid.*, p. 84).

Finally, the "honesty" of the capitalists includes material support of the church: "Some do not wish to dedicate to God even the smallest part of their earthly wealth.... What do they sacrifice for God? Nothing. They say that they believe in the imminent coming of Jesus, but their affairs contradict their faith. Everyone should manifest his faith in life. Treacherous Christian, Jesus knows what you are doing. He hates your belittling contributions, your crippled sacrifices!" (*ibid.*, p. 86).

Thus, in order for wealth and poverty to balance on the scales of the Adventist world-view, it is sufficient to take from the bowl of wealth some crumbs for the bowl of the "hungry", naked and homeless", and a large crumb for the church bowl. In all this the property-owner should not engage in elementary dishonesty in the form of short-weighting and short-measuring his customers. If the property-owner holds to "business honesty" and charity, and sacrifices for the church, he is pure before the Lord: "It is not great or small business enterprises which do good or bad, honest or dishonest things" (*ibid.*, p. 58). The whole question is that of sin, which "is sin, whether done by the possessor of millions or by a begger on the street" (*ibid.*, p. 66).

We have already seen by what simple means the "possessor of millions" can remove sin from his soul. The begger on the street can also remove sin from his soul. For this he must follow the law as Adventism interprets it, and in particular remember his "daily duties" in work and know that "the world evaluates his religion according to the quality of his work." It is true that he must also have work. Recommendations on this score were not given in the material in my possession.

Adventism "removes" class distinctions in society: "In our time there exist in the world only two classes of people, and only two classes will be called to judgment—those who break the law, and those who fulfill it" (Bb 1958: 2).

The social views of Adventism preserve bourgeois property and guard the class dominance of the bourgeoisie. This does not contradict the fact that in the views set forth above, there are hints of the interests of the small bourgeois property-owners, who are asserting, although humbly, opposition to the large capital that was ruining them. All these lamentations about short weights and measures, dishonest dealings, any deceit in trade, introduces us to the world of "those who fail" in bourgeois money-making. They address this to their all-powerful competitors: "If we have offended anyone by dishonest dealings, if we have deceived in trade, even if without crossing the bounds of the law (i.e., not with the help of impermissible means, but with all the "rules of the capitalist game" — A. K.), we should repent of our crimes and make good the loss as far as we can" (Bb 1956: 6).

Let us imagine a case of repentance of a large property-owner ready to return a loss to someone who had suffered it, in order not to be tormented by doubts about whether he will or will not be allowed into the millennial kingdom. The one who has suffered the loss has calculated ahead of time the sum which must be returned. His calculation takes into account the fact that capital is value, which brings surplus value, and proceeding from this, he presents the repentant favorite of fortune a rounded calculation: "And it would be just, in our view, for us to return not only what we have stolen, but that which could be accumulated with these means for the time that it was in our possession" (*ibid.*, p. 68). We have before us the world-view of the petty bourgeois businessman.

It is in the highest degree characteristic that in the center of the social views of Adventism is the problem of the mutual relationships of small and large capital, while the problem of labor and capital is left without attention. The dominance of capital with the limitation of large capital is the basic socio-economic formula which Adventism declares to be the will of God, and which is seen as the key to solving world social problems and contradictions: "If only the principles of God's law were taken into account in the distribution of the world's goods in our time, how much different would the position of people be! The honoring of these principles would avert a terrible evil, which in all ages has provoked the oppession of the poor by the rich, and hatred for the rich on the part of the poor. By restraining the accumulation of enormous wealth, we would facilitate the prevention of an increase in ignorance and of the humiliation of thousands of poorly paid slaves. This could help the peaceful solution of problems which now threaten to fill the world with anarchy and blood-letting" (Bb 1958: 6).

If we turn from the social views of Adventism to its ethical views, we find that the latter are subordinated precisely to what the Adventist author calls "the peaceful solution" of social conflicts between labor and capital.

Appealing to the conscience of the possessors of millions, demanding honesty and charity from them, and threatening them finally with the Last Judgment, Adventism lulled the consciousness of ordinary believers with the hope of achieving harmony of class interests, not to speak of the lulling action of Adventism's eschatological-chiliastic ideas. At the same time, Adventism broke the will of its followers, lowered and trampled in them the knowledge of their own worth — a purpose which was served by its ethical views. In the field of ethical views, Adventism was relatively close to Baptism. Having risen among the followers of Baptism, Adventism adopted the conception of the universal sinfulness of people and of salvation only by faith in the redemptive sacrifice of Christ.

Whereas, according to the Baptists, "having come to the recognition that he is completely bankrupt and cannot mend his affairs, man has only one thing left, to believe 'in the One who justifies the unrighteous', and faith imposes righteousness on him.... But faith is not from us, is not something we earn, but is God's gift, which anyone can receive ..." (Belous 1928: 23), according to the Adventists, "many wander from the true path because they think that they should climb up to heaven themselves, and should do something in order to deserve God's favor. They strive through their own efforts to improve their spiritual nature, but they can never succeed in doing this" (*Conversations on the Book of Job,* manuscript, p. 23; author's collection).

Adventist theologians like some Calvinist theologians in America in the first half of the 18th century (Edwards) and in the first half of the 19th century (Walker), set out to combine the concepts of divine predestination and the free will of man. Of course this could not be anything else than a conditional maneuver. Ellen White's opinion can be evaluated precisely thus:

"Similarly, believers in Christ will be justified in faith in Him, as those who do not believe will automatically be condemned for their unbelief. God has predetermined to save those who will believe and to destroy those who will not. To each is given the choice to believe or not. In this sense, the fate of each believer and each non-believer was predetermined at the beginning on the plane of salvation; however, each person individually was given the right to choose to be a just person or a sinner. The Biblical predestination consists of this" (*Bibleiskie chteniia na 1958 god* [Bible Readings for 1958]: 1; author's collection).

Under conditions in which the Calvinist dogma of predestination was criticized by various religious and philosophical groups in America, this verbal tightrope-walking satisfied those followers of White who were accustomed to thinking in Baptist fashion: the promise of the second coming and the beginning of the millennial kingdom agitated believers incomparably more than theological disputes about the mutual relationship of divine and human will. But the promise of the millennial kingdom was a fiction, fixing the attention of the believers, and for the time being, while waiting for it, believers in their daily activities were really obliged to act with consciousness of their sinful nature, which could not be overcome by any effort of theirs. To what consequences did this lead? Let us cite Ellen White's words:

"All the culture and education that the world can give is not capable of making of a debased child of sin a child of heaven. Renewed energy must come from God. Change can only be made with the strength of the Holy Spirit" (Bb 1959: 1; author's collection).

The following fragment by an Adventist author can serve as a continuation and development of this position of Ellen White:

"In the last days of the history of our earth, the voice speaking on Sinai continues to sound, proclaiming: Thou shalt have no other gods before me. Man can direct his will against the will of God but he cannot silence the voice of the commandment. Human reason cannot escape responsibility before the highest power. Every sort of theory and wisdom can abound; people can attempt to oppose revelation to science and to replace God's law, but the commandment will sound ever stronger: bow to the Lord God and serve Him alone" (*ibid.*, p. 2).

Let us use the quotations given in order to show the fundamentally hostile attitude of Adventism to education, science and culture. This demonstration is especially necessary in connection with the fact that we have noted attempts of Adventist theologians to appeal to the authority of figures in science and culture, citing individual facts borrowed from the field of natural and humanitarian sciences.

An appeal to the data of science and the authority of scientific figures can be combined with the slighting of "all kinds of theory and wisdom" only in the case in which science is reduced to a deposit of facts, and in that form is hired by the theologian as a handmaiden. Returning to the citations adduced, let us emphasize that their content goes beyond the bounds of the question of the attitude of the believer to science and culture. In it the question of the relationship of man to society, to problems which the surrounding reality puts before man, are posed in the citations. Man's consciousness of his sinful nature and powerlessness gives him the guiding rules, "Bow to the Lord God and serve Him alone", and "Thou shalt have no other gods before me".

In other words, the believer can acquire the gift of the kingdom of God on condition that his earthly existence be bound up in the religious capsule of Adventism.

Here it is necessary to remark on the existence in the world-view of Adventism of the concept of "the creation of Christian character in the internal and external man", which we also encounter in Ellen White's writings.

After faith in the imminent advent takes possession of the believer's imagination, and his spiritual forces are concentrated on preparation for the miracle of "investiture with immortality", his personality is destroyed and his individual will is circled by a tight ring of rules which are called in Adventism "the law of God".

By "the law of God" is understood a group of moral rules which are based on God, whom Adventism, as we have already noted, presents as a personal God possessing character. "The law of God", according to Ellen White, "reflects His (God's — A. K.) character" (Bb 1958: 2).

What features are essential to "God's character"? There are two — love and justice. "Many preachers", we read in the Adventist tract, *Conversation About Divine Law,* "adapt to the taste of their audience, and choose mainly themes on Christian love. This is the first and essential feature of the character of our God. But we must not forget about the second feature of God's character—justice" (*Beseda o zakone bozhiem,* [Conversations about the Law of God], ms., p. 18; author's collection). In Adventism this second feature is advanced to the forefront. The God of Adventism is a threatening God requiring iron discipline of subordination, mercilessly punishing those who depart from his "law". The believer preparing for investiture with immortality must give up everything which makes up his individual will and adopt for himself a kind of "divine" standard—the character of God embodied in the law formulated in the ten commandments.

Following the commandments in and of itself is not considered in Adventism the way to "salvation". In this case man would be achieving "salvation" by the efforts of his own will, which contradicts the initial assumption of Adventism about the sinful nature of man. Man's very ability to follow the commandments is declared in Adventism "a gift of God". But after this ability is given, the demand is made on the believer that the ten commandments become for him an internal mechanism leading to control not only of his deeds but of his thoughts. The infallibility and irreproachability of the active mechanism of "divine character" become a criterion of faith, gradually erasing in man his personal character, as a result of which Christ is reflected in man.

The true essence of the psychological process of which I am speaking is the death of individuality, which happens before the death of the person. Nothing less than a spiritual death is the condition anticipating "a character formed according to God's likeness"—what Adventism sees as the "single treasure" which man can "take from this world to another world" (*Molitvennye chteniia na 1958 god,* [Prayer Readings for 1958], p. 1).

The Adventist "ethic" is based on the Old Testament, the significance of which is higher in Adventism than in Baptism; in this respect, Adventism corresponds to the classic traditions of the ideology of American and English Puritanism.

The fostering of "divine character" is implemented in the course of the everyday life of the Adventist congregations through sermons and special studies of this subject,[5] and through systematic control over the believer's

---

[5] Let us cite an example of these studies: among the prayer readings of Adventists there is a reading specially devoted to the theme of "the creation of a Christian character...." Here is its outline: "1. The necessity of fostering character; 2. Incorrect fostering of character; 3. Correct fostering of character; 4. The external appearance of an educated character". The laconic conclusion says: "We will educate our character until we reflect Christ" (*Molitvennye chtenie na 1958 g.* [Prayer Readings for 1958], pp. 1-3).

behavior and entire life, implemented by the leadership of the congregation and its members. The fostering of divine character is transferred to the family, which is seen in Adventism as a micro-congregation. Long before a minor member of an Adventist family receives the right to baptism, the family works to foster in the child the beginnings of divine character.

What are these bases and what are the goals set by this upbringing? First of all, it is affirmed that children owe unquestioning obedience to parental authority, which is elevated to divine authority: "Parents have a right to a degree of love and respect which no other person has. God Himself, who placed on them the obligation to care for the souls entrusted to them, determined that at an early age parents would take the place of God for their children. And he who denies the real authority of parents denies in this way the authority of God" (Bb 1956: 44).

Further it develops that divine character is determined by "obedience", which must replace "judgment" in the believer: "The first thing which must be taught to a child is obedience. Before he becomes capable of judging he must be taught obedience ..." (*ibid.*). Obedience instead of judgment serves as the pedagogical aim, if we may call it so, of the action of Adventism on the child's personality, which is organically connected with the world-view of Adventism, at the center of which is the idea of the fallen nature of man.

Is not the significance of the thesis that obedience precedes judgment (in terms of its influence on the child's personality) private? No, it is not private! The thesis presented is accompanied by the following thought: "Thus those future conflicts between desire and authority which so powerfully promote cooling and bitterness in relations with parents and teachers, and too often work in opposition to human and divine authority, may in large measure be prevented" (*ibid.*, p. 45). And further: "On a cleansed and renewed earth there will be no place for mutinous, insubordinate and ungrateful sons and daughters. If they are not taught to be obedient and submissive here, then they can never learn this; the world of the redeemed will not be darkened by violent, disorderly and recalcitrant children" (*ibid.*, p. 46).

Let us cite an example of what fruits are derived from "the creation of divine character" in man. We have the biography of the Adventist Aleksei Biriulia, who worked until 1909 as a telegraph operator at the Dno Station and then in St. Petersburg. Before setting out on the path of religious searching, Aleksei Biriulia was, in his words, "a complete atheist", denying the existence of God as the creator of the world and "in complete agreement with those scientists who attempted to show that the world (and man) proceeded from the union of chemical particles of nature, and that man subsequently descended from a mentally developed ape" (A. A. Biriulia's Letter of July 2, 1913, p. 21, ms.; author's collection).

Aleksei Biriulia began his conscious life thus; however, let us note that his interests at that time included not only books on astronomy and Darwinism, but, in his words, the works of Renan and Strauss, and the religious writings of Leo Tolstoy. Biriulia also meditated on the social contrasts surrounding him: "I saw poor and hungry people, and saw heaps of produce in the stores. This was hard for me" (A. A. Biriulia's Letter of April 17, 1913, pp. 1-2).

Biriulia led a solitary life, and his attempts to solve independently the philosophical and social questions agitating him led to the atheist in him being conquered by Tolstoyanism, and then by Seventh Day Adventism. Henceforth Biriulia created in himself "divine character". "My faith", he wrote, "consists in fulfilling the ten commandments written on stone tablets, and in faith in Christ as the Son of God, our savior" (A. A. Biriulia's Letter of January 15, 1913, pp. 5-6). For refusing military service Biriulia was placed in a disciplinary battalion, where he was flogged because he refused to work on Saturday, following the Old Testament commandment.

In a letter to the St. Petersburg congregation of Seventh Day Adventists, Biriulia wrote: "Dear brothers and sisters! Don't imagine that here they flog as they would children. No, here they beat so that after the tenth blow the whole skin is made red with great welts, and after the twentieth blow one gets many cut places and the blood stands out in drops and long red bands.... And still, however painful it was, when they finished beating and said stand up, I stood and felt such friendship and such love for my enemies that all fear of their punishment fell away from me. I looked on them with love and began to smile.... Dear brothers and sisters! I inform you that I received immediately after the flogging a great daring and fearlessness. If they had told me at that time: come, we will give you another hundred blows, I would have feared nothing but would have gone and lain under the blows" (*ibid.*).

This was a phenomenon in the life experience of Adventism's demand: "To educate one's character until Christ is reflected in us." The letter of an ordinary Adventist which we have cited is not heroic, as it apparently was pictured by the author and his correspondents, but deeply tragic, since it shows a complete loss of personal dignity, of the will to struggle, which was removed by the infamous "divine character", by the teaching of Adventism which fostered in people "a great daring and fearlessness" in what was nothing but a renunciation of human form, of the demand for a decent human life. If we may allow ourselves a summary image, Adventism educated its followers in a spirit of meek readiness to lie down under the whips of the powers that be.

The so-called sanitary reforms, of which Ellen White wrote much after 1865, was part of the program of fostering divine character in man, and, correspondingly, the suppression in him of individuality. If God, as Adventism teaches, is a "personal" being, (and in the concept of "personal" is included both body and intellect), then this cannot but lead to the thought that God is a personal being who has a definite regime of existence, which in turn must serve man as an example for imitation. According to Ellen White's assertion, "The Lord revealed to me repeatedly ... that He wishes to lead us step by step back to His original plan, according to which man should be fed from the original produce of the earth" ("The False Reformers", pp. 13-14; typescript in author's collection).

Ellen White called for limitation of the use of meat or even renunciation of it, maintaining that people, "weak and exhausted", were especially in need of "nutritious and pleasant" food, consisting of "vegetables, fruits and nuts" (*ibid.*, p. 14). Thus, the Adventists called for a use of food analogous to that which made up the table of the original Adam and Eve. "The sanitary reform" was not reduced to a vegetarian diet, but was accompanied by a great deal of dietetic and in general medical advice, and also by the organization of all kinds of sanitary and "curative" institutions. These institutions conducted active preaching for Adventism.

The Adventist church reproduced special literature devoted to propaganda on the sanitary reform. After 1866, Adventists resorted to a printed periodical, "The Reformer of Heath". The aim which their leaders pursued in this consisted in giving "all the forces of our being, our bodies, or souls, everything that we have, everything that we are" to God. Thus the leaders of Adventism defined the goals of the sanitary reform, which was directed toward a complete subordination of the believer toward the church to which he belonged, toward a seizure by its influence and control not only of his sipiritual but of his everyday physical life.

The goal of the sanitary reform, if we look at it in the system of educational measures for the transformation of human character into a divine one, consisted in the immolation of believers on the altar of the Adventist church. The sanitary reform was in accord with the Adventist conception of God as a personal one. By its appeals to man to feed himself from the fruits of the earth, it answered the patriarchal ideals of the small farmers. Finally, it was impressive as testimony to the concern of the church for the physical well-being of Adventists, who gave extreme significance to their physical well-being, as was charateristic of meshchan circles. Proceeding from all these views, believers agreed to moderate their eating of meat.

The food taboos and limitations were an important element of the system of suppression of the will, which turned Adventists into a disciplined and submissive weapon of the church and supported in them the fire of religious fanaticism. This is well seen in the example of the fostering of divine character in Biriulia. Before being at the disposition of the spirit which allowed him blissfully to lie down under the blows of the floggers, Biriulia not only scourged his will with the help of the divine commandments, but also subjected himself to a severe fast, refusing even the scant prison ration if it consisted of meat.

We have still to characterize the socio-philosophical essence of the religious teaching of Adventism.

Its eschatology and chiliasm are a peculiarity of the religious teaching of Adventism. Another peculiarity of this teaching is the equal status of the Old Testament portion of the Bible with its New Testament part in terms of their significance for believers. These peculiarities distinguish the beliefs of the Adventists from those of the Baptists. Finally, a peculiarity of the Adventist teaching is the observance of the Sabbath on Saturday and the washing of feet, which is not adhered to by the basic groups in Baptism. The doctrine of the total depravity of human nature, and the salvation of man as achieved exclusively by faith in the redemptive sacrifice of Christ and impossible through any kind of effort by man himself, is common to Adventism and Baptism. Such rituals as adult baptism and the Eucharist are also common to Adventism and Baptism.

The eschatological-chiliastic views in Adventism, first formulated by Miller, served as material for subsequent theological reworking. They consisted in the following:

1. The imminent second coming of Christ, the time of which cannot, however, be determined.

2. The resurrection at the second coming of the "just" dead, and "investiture with immortality" for the just, both dead and living.

3. The annihilation of sinners remaining on earth at the time of the second coming.

4. The setting up of a millennial kingdom of Christ with granting of immortality to the just (the location of this kingdom is not determined but it is not earthly).

5. The descent to earth of the kingdom of Christ and the just at the end of a thousand years from the second coming. The resurrection of all sinners who have ever existed on earth. The attack of sinners, led by Satan, on the kingdom of Christ. The final ruin of Satan and the sinners, consumed by heavenly fire.

6. The renewal, from a heavenly model, of the earth as the eternal dwelling-place of the just.

We have seen in what socio-economic conditions the eschatological and chiliastic ideas in Adventism were born: from the despair of the middle strata of American society in the period of the industrial revolution—the patriarchal farmers and the urban petty bourgeoisie, expropriated in the course of capitalist development. The subsequent development of capitalism in the U.S., as in other countries, was inevitably accompanied by calamities, poverty and the repression of the workers, and was the social soil which nourished the eschatological and chiliastic ideas, supported and distributed by a powerful well-organized missionary propaganda, which was conducted and is still being conducted on the widest scale by the Adventist church.

The spread of Adventism, which has adherents in all countries of the world, serves as a clear illustration of Marx's conclusion: "Weakness was always saved by faith in miracles; it considered the enemy conquered if it succeeded in overcoming him in its imagination by the means of spells, and it lost any sense of reality because of the idle raising to heaven of the expected future and of the deeds which it intended to accomplish but about which it considered it at present premature to speak" (*Marx and Engels* VIII [Second Edition]: 123).

Eschatology and chiliasm, of course, were not invented by Miller and his successors. As concerns Christianity, its history from the very beginning was marked by a clear dose of eschatology and chiliasm, registered in the so-called Revelation of John the Divine, which, along with the Book of Daniel, is the basic source from which Adventism gets its fantasies. In antagonistic social orders, eschatology and chiliasm are the inevitable ideological companions of social crises and cataclysms. But precisely because the roots of religion are social, and because religion serves as a fantastic expression of external forces dominating people in their everyday existence, eschatology and chiliasm, even when they come from one literary source (as for example the Revelations of John, which served early Christianity, medieval sectarianism and Adventism), are subjected to historical reworking: the eschatology and chiliasm of the early Christians is different from the corresponding ideas of medieval anti-feudal sectarianism, just as the latter are different from the eschatological and chiliastic ideas of Adventism.

We noted that even Miller attempted to make use in his preaching of the data of science. These attempts acquired a wider and more systematic character among those who continued Miller's theology. There is no doubt of the demagogic significance of this, and above I showed the deeply negative, hostile attitude of Adventism to the scientific world-view, which flows from the basic suppositions of its belief. But behind the demagogic maneuvers of the theologians and preachers of Adventism, one must differentiate the objective conditions thanks to which the demagogy has a definite direction. In other words, we must pose the question not only of the forms in which this or that theological adaptation is wrapped, but also the question of what the theologians are *adapting to,* with *which* ideological currents and with *which* forms of social consciousness they are *forced* to reckon, in order to make sure that their preaching reaches the minds of believers.

Having studied this question in the material of Adventist theology, I came to the conclusion that the eschatological and chiliastic ideas which exist in Adventism were conditioned by forms of bourgeois consciousness which evolved in concrete historical conditions of development of social thought of the American bourgeoisie. But in order to substantiate this conclusion we must turn to the concrete material of eschatological and chiliastic ideas in Adventism. These ideas, if we speak of the most basic of them, are based on the concept of "religious experience", a concept just as unreal as the eschatological ideas of Adventism. It lies at the the base of yet another superstition contemporary with Adventism and widely found in the U.S. — spiritualism.

Spiritualism is a superstition in which "religious experience" is present in its most naked form. Here a kind of experimental base is placed under the phenomena of a supernatural world, and practical criteria for the truth of supernatural phenomena are introduced. These phenomena are "reproduced" in spiritualist circles as in a kind of laboratory of religious experience. Spirits "materialize", and only as "materialized" spirits do they become the objects of superstitious spiritualist worship. In a word, we are dealing with "natural history in the world of spirits", as Engels titled his work devoted to the unmasking of spiritualist superstitions and to the study of their epistemological and historical roots. Adventism, of course, is not spiritualism, although the spectacle which the Millerites presented, when in 1843 and 1844 they gathered in crowds, peering at the heavens, which were ready at any minute to open up in order to reveal "Christ in His glory", a "personal" Christ, visible and "materialized" — this spectacle is reminiscent of a mass seance for summoning spirits.

The religious experience of Adventism differs from the religious experience of spiritualists by the fact that the latter call spirits from heaven to the earth, and the former take the trouble to make the journey themselves. In the pamphlet *Seventh Day Adventists* translated from the English, we read concerning Ellen White that she "often flew to heaven", "to the holy Jerusalem, where she frequently spoke with Jesus, and an angel always accompanied her.... She was also with the angel on the planet Jupiter, where she saw many wonders; people there were very tall, very jolly, and when she asked them 'Why are you happier than those who are on earth?', they answered: 'Because we live in direct obedience to the divine commandments and have never sinned'. Then the angel transported her to another planet — Saturn, which has seven moons. There she saw good old Enoch, who enjoyed great fame and was very well taken care of, as at home. Then she asked him, was this the place to which he had been taken from earth? He said: 'No! I live in the New Jerusalem and have only come here for a visit! And she asked the angel to leave her there but he said: 'Not now, but later. You also will visit all of God's worlds and look at the work of the divine hands' — and he carried her back to earth" (Adventists 1928: 63).

Ellen White was Adventism's unsurpassed medium, but mediumism in the spirit of Ellen White is a permanent element of this sect. A modern follower of the American "clairvoyante", a humble metal-worker in the Lipetsk Office of Grain Procurement, the Adventist P. A. Anokhin, told me in 1960 of his visions, in which he painted the supernatural world in every possible sensual color, "materializing" it like Ellen White (ORF Institute of History, AS, USSR, Collection of the Lipetsk Expedition. A. I. Klibanov's conversation with P. A. Anokhin, manuscript, pp. 17-32).

The teaching of the Seventh Day Adventists defines God as "the eternal father, a spiritual but personal being ..." ("Basic Points of the Faith and Teaching of the Seventh Day Adventists," ms., p. 1; author's collection): Anokhin understands God as a personal being having a physical nature.[6] Has Anokhin made the Adventist idea of God primitive? Among the fragments of White's essays included in the *Textbook on Bible Themes* published by the Seventh Day Adventists, we encounter the following: "When God created man in His image, the human body was perfect in all its parts but had no life. Then the personal eternal God breathed into this body the breath of life.... All parts of the human body began their activity. The heart, the arteries, the veins, the tongue, the hands, the legs, the senses and the direction of thought—all began their work ..." (Textbook 1922: 8).

Like the image of God, the image of Satan was subjected to "materialization" in the Adventist teaching. In the Adventist tract, "To Whom Does This World Belong? To Satan?" (typescript, pp. 6-7; author's collection), we read: "Some people imagine the devil as some mysterious being with horns, hooves and a tail. This idea is really stupid; it denies the existence of the devil. Others consider that the so-called devil in essence is only a bad influence or bad opinions. These opinions play into the devil's hands, for in this case he will not be punished for our sufferings. What is the devil in reality? Jesus says: 'I saw Satan falling from heaven like lightning....' Can some sort of influence or spiritual condition fall? From Jesus' words it is clear that the devil is a person. Besides this in the Gospel of John ... the devil was called a murderer and a liar. One can say this only about a person".

[6] Let us cite a portion of a conversation with the Seventh Day Adventist P. A. Anokhin, which took place in Lipetsk in July 1960:

Anokhin: ... we do not recognize God spiritually as some do. We recognize God in physical form: He has hands, legs, thought, breath, brain—this is God. This is how we understand God. And if it were not so, no physical world could exist at all, for how could it come into being by itself all at once—in physical form?

Klibanov: Then, in your opinion, God is *alive*?

Anokhin: Yes, it seems God is alive.

Klibanov: But can it be that *only you* think so?

Anokhin: No, Adventists think that God has bones and breath, and has as it were mental capabilities. Christ also has flesh, blood and breath. The Holy Spirit does not have flesh and bones, but It senses, understands and breathes...."

The Seventh Day Adventist A. Biriulia wrote in 1912: "I believe and I believe in God and in a living God who created the whole world.... If a living God exists, why then can He not do what is reported there (he has a mind the miracles reported in the Gospels—A. K.)? And before me there was in all its force a decision; if I believe in a living God, then I have to believe in His living deeds, and if I do not believe in His living deeds then it is not worth believing in God Himself, for a God who can do nothing among us is not the living God, but is something doubtful" (A. Biriulia's letter of July 16, 1912, typescript, pp. 4-5; author's collection).

After the supernatural world was "materialized" at its poles — from God to the devil — it was appropriate to expect from Adventism an analogous reworking of the ideas of the supernatural enclosed between the two extreme points. In fact, whether we turn to Adventism's ideas about the last judgment, or the promised land which awaits the just etc. etc. — they all had a materialized naturalistic character.

As Aleksii (Dorodnitsyn) already pointed out, "The process of the last judgment itself among the Adventists is pictured in purely anthropomorphic terms, borrowed from the practice of a legal trial in the okrug courts, with a judge, a lawyer, and a jury. 'Who will be the judge of this (i.e. the last) judgment?' the author of a pamphlet, *The Court,* naively asks ... and he answers that God the father will preside at the court. 'Who will appear as attorney for the just?' is the new question. The answer is given that the attorney will be Jesus Christ. 'Will the court use books?' The answer ... is given in the affirmative. From the further opinions of the author it turns out that the role of jury falls to the Adventists ..." (Aleksii 1909: 319-320).

In the article "On the Beautiful Country" published in the Adventist journal *Blagaia vest',* a description is given of the "renewed land" which the Adventists can expect. We are able to compare this description, made by an Adventist theologian-commentator, with the views of ordinary Adventists in the Kherson and Kiev areas on the same subject. If the views of ordinary Adventists call to mind associations with peasant social utopias, those of the author have nothing in common with them.

"The beautiful country" described by the journal *Blagaia vest'* is prosaically everyday, oriented toward the material considerations of the petty bourgeoisie and advertised in the tone of a carnival come-on: "This country abounds in riches; the streets of the city are paved with pure gold...."[7] "There one does not spend money on dresses and clothes; for the inhabitants of this country clothes are already prepared.... One does not need either to pay taxes for water or gas or electric light; the apartments are given free" (*BV* 1914 No. 6, p. 46). And in addition: "Neighbors there will be only very pleasant and good. Prisons there will not longer be necessary. It is a good place for those who are musical, because musical instruments are given out free.... It is a good country for raising every kind of livestock. The lions will be like oxen and eat straw.... In general there will be no wild animals there.... The owner of this land has already prepared a dwelling for each of its citizens.... It exceeds the best of all the dwellings on earth. To those who wish to build more for themselves, material is given out free" (*ibid.*) etc. etc.

The description of "the beautiful country" follows advertising aims: "Soon a beautiful country will open up, where you can live.... As soon as the

[7] The dots in the text in all cases replace citations to Bible texts which, according to the author of the article, support the description made by him.

required number of believing settlers is filled..., there will be no further opportunity to make arrangements for residence.... Everything has been carefully studied, and there is no doubt that this is the best offer that has ever been made ..." (*ibid*).

Let us note as a characteristic feature of the Adventist teaching the interpretation of the Bible as the universal handbook, embracing not only questions of faith and behavior by believers, but also the historical experience of humanity, culture, science and economic activity. There is an evident tendency to connect the Bible with life, to awaken interest in it, playing not on some metaphysical strings of consciousness, but on its immediate everyday needs.

The Bible in the foreshortened Adventist world-view is a God-inspired book, possessing both metaphysical and physical significance, meaning by the latter its "practical usefulness, its scientific nature". Let us cite typical examples of the Adventist use of the Bible. The preacher Teppone wrote: "In defense of the scientific nature of the Bible, we can cite two instances. The first relates to the fact that people only in the 15th century became certain that the earth was round. Copernicus and others asserted this, but the monks considered their opinions heresy. And only when great sailing ships completed round-the-world journeys were they convinced that the earth was round. But the Bible, through the prophet Isaiah, convinces us that the earth is really round: '... he is the one who sits on the circle of the earth.' This scientific data in the Bible was expressed 700 years before Christ, and if people had looked to the Bible a little more, they would not have argued with Copernicus.

"Still another instance: earlier it was believed that the earth stood on four whales, the whales on turtles, and only the English scientist Newton — the great mathematician — wondered what held the earth up. After his research, he came to the conclusion that the earth was held in the universal force of gravity, which people discovered only in the 17th and 18th centuries. We can read in the Book of Job: '... He hung the world on nothing.' As is said here — on what is the earth hung? — On nothing. Precisely the thought which occurred in the mind of Newton" (Teppone 1926: 6-7).

The quotation allows us to understand the way of thought characteristic of the world-view of Adventism. Let us leave to the conscience of the preacher the semi-literate exposition of the astronomical ideas of Copernicus — for his appeal to the names of the great scientists is nothing more than a forced tribute to "Caesar". I am interested in the mode of thought adopted by the Adventists. What was the mode of thought embracing the mediumism of Ellen White and her pupils, great and small, but the materialization of the supernatural, the attempt to discover in the Bible not only metaphysical but physical truths?

The pragmatist William James in *The Varieties of Religious Experience* defends a special way of religious thought which he calls "piecemeal super-naturalism". James writes: "Piecemeal supernaturalism ... admits miracles and providential leadings, and finds no intellectual difficulty in mixing the ideal and the real worlds together by interpolating influences from the ideal region among the forces that causally determine the real world's details" (James 1910: 512) [1929: 510-511]. James is against the tendency in super-naturalism, which he calls "refined", whose adherents, on the other hand, "think that it [piecemeal supernaturalism] muddles disparate dimensions of existence. For them the world of the ideal has no efficient causality, and never bursts into the world of phenomena at particular points.... It cannot get down upon the flat level of experience and interpolate itself piecemeal bet-ween different portions of nature" (*ibid.*)[1929: 511].

Adventism is a teaching about the supernatural which permits mixing the ideal and the real worlds, the contact of the ideal world with the world of phenomena which in one degree or another allows the ideal world to penetrate into the depths of experience and to distribute in parts the separate fields of nature. Of course, the contact of the ideal world with the real (James avoids the word "material") is exclusively at the expense of the influence of the first on the second.

James' "piecemeal supernaturalism" is the philosophical basis of Adven-tism, in contrast, for example, to Baptism, whose philosophical character James without hesitation would assign to "refined" supernaturalism.

What is the essence of the philosophical direction developed in the religious world-view of Adventism? Let us remember the quotation from Teppone's essay, in which he, among other things, appealed to the great spirit of Newton.

A professional commentator on the Revelation of John the Divine (like any preacher of Adventism), Teppone appealed to Newton's name on the grounds of the same world-view thanks to which, as Engels noted, "Isaac Newton in his old age was much concerned with interpreting the Revelation of John" (*Marx and Engels*: XX, 373).

Let us reproduce the context from which this comment from Engels comes: "There exists an old proposition of the dialectic which has entered the popular consciousness: opposites agree. We will scarcely err, therefore, if we seek the very extreme degree of fantasy, credulity, and superstition not in that natural direction which, like German natural philosophy, attempted to squeeze the objective world into the bounds of its subjective thought, but on the contrary, in that opposite direction which, boasting that it operates only with experience, relates to thought with the profoundest disdain and really has gone farthest of all in the impoverishment of thought. This school dominates in England" (*ibid.*). Further Engels cites the attempts of Francis Bacon to apply his empirical methods for the prolongation of life, rejuvenation, the transformation on one body into another, etc., including proposals for recipes for preparing gold and performing various miracles.

Engels concludes: "In precisely the same way Isaac Newton in his old age was much concerned with interpreting the Revelation of John. Therefore there is nothing surprising in the fact that in recent years English empiricism as represented by some of its spokesmen, who are by no means the worst, has become as it were irrevocably the victim of spirit-tapping and spirit-seeing imported from America" (*ibid.*). And again: "The 'stubbornness' of Yankees, which resurrects even greenback swindles, flows from their theoretical backwardness and Anglo-Saxon disdain for any theory. They pay for this with blind faith in any philosophical and economic nonsense, by religious sectarianism and stupid economic experiments, and some bourgeois cliques warm their hands on this ..." (Marx and Engels 1947: 445).[B]

The world-view of Adventism, including its eschatology and chiliasm, bears the stamp of bourgeois empiricism, which interprets all theory as metaphysical trash and therefore making upon religious metaphysics the demand of experimental proof. Being stubborn in sheer empiricism, the Yankee demands a religion which he can test with his teeth like a coin, in order to be convinced of the worth of the material from which it is made.

Ideas about God and the devil, the second coming, the millennial kingdom, the immortality of the soul, about the entire world of the supernatural, filtered through the prism of the ideology and psychology of bourgeois businessmen, and as a result materialized and naturalized—this is what Adventism is as a religious teaching.

A follower of William James, Rufus M. Jones, writes: "There is nothing essential to salvation or to the spiritual life of man, which cannot be proved and verified as effectively as the facts of the light-spectrum are verified" (quoted in Cohen 1958: 214) [1962: 249-250]. But this is already a contemporary businessman who makes such assertions about religion. Business people of small and middle calibre were content in the period of the Industrial Revolution with that degree of materialization of supernatural phenomena which they found in Adventism and spiritualism. William James, presenting in *The Varieties of Religious Experience* what he called "piecemeal supernaturalism", essentially proposed the discarding of the parts of supernaturalism worn out in the course of historical development in order to save supernaturalism as such.[8]

[8] This was well understood not only by James' kinsmen, who were interested in strengthening the influence of religion, but by his Russian followers, such as S. Kotliarevskii. In an article published in 1910, "James as a Religious Thinker", Kotliarevskii complained: "... in the most important field of contemporary searches—the religious—this fateful inability to separate the eternal from the decrepit form surrounding it, which in any case will be worn away by the herculean stream of things, gives one pause" (Kotliarevskii 1910: 718). Putting the rouge on religion—this is what Kotliarevskii and James concluded was the essence of piecemeal supernaturalism, and its undoubted usefulness for the class interests of the bourgeoisie.

But I wish to draw attention to something else in this connection that interests me: the ideological heritage of religious-mystical groups in the U.S. constituted precisely the material which James used in erecting the theoretical structure of *The Varieties of Relgious Experience.* Spiritualism, Adventism, etc. etc. (James himself was the president of the spiritualist American Society for Psychic Research) served James as building material for his theory of piecemeal supernaturalism, the philosophical axis of which, as James unambiguously declared, was pragmatism. James translated the spontaneous bourgeois empiricism of religious-mystical groups in the U.S. into philosophical pragmatism, receiving in the religious sphere the title of "piecemeal supernaturalism".

Thus, I look on Adventism as one of the religious forms of bourgeois consciousness born in the completely socially contradictory conditions of the period of the industrial revolution in the U.S., expressing the mood of despair and hopelessness of the expropriated patriarchal farmer and urban petty bourgeoisie, and decorated with the flat utilitarian philosophy of empiricism.

3. The Political Role of Adventism

I have characterized above the social views which were adhered to by figures in world Adventism, including figures in its Russian union. Let us remember that in the course of approximately the first 25 years of its existence, the Adventist church in Russia was not only under the ideological influence of, but also organizationally dependent on, the union of Adventists in Germany, and enjoyed significant financal support from this side. In 1906 alone the union of Adventists in Germany spent about 19,000 rubles on the Adventist mission in Russia (Statistical 1912). But even after 1907, when the Adventist church in Russia received the right of union, its internal life was under the observation and influence of figures in German, English and American Adventism. In 1910 the Russian union was visited by the chairmen of the German and British unions; in 1911 the Russian union was inspected by Danielson, the chairman of the general conference of Seventh Day Adventists (Grigor'ev ms.: 4).

Many important figures of the Russian union were foreign citizens, beginning with its chairman, a citizen of the United States, Julius Boettcher. In all these circumstances both the religious teaching and the social views of the leaders of the Russian union were at one with the corresponding views of the leaders and ideologists of the international organization of Seventh Day Adventism.

It would be an error to identify the social and religious views of the upper strata of Adventism with those of the lower. Perhaps not a single other religious organization could bind the consciousness of ordinary believers by such subtle and strong bonds of reactionary bourgeois influence as did the Seventh Day Adventist church. This is what the infamous system of "the creation of divine character" is worth! Adventism's main base was among the rural poor and among artisans, meshchane and small traders. But the preaching of reconciliation which they preached was not rebuffed in any widely organized fashion by the lower ranks of the church.

From this it does not follow that the leaders of Adventism succeeded in liquidating the scial contradictions and internal struggle in its midst. For example, in 1909 from the pulpit of the Odessa congregation of Seventh Day Adventists, words were spoken condemning the bloody terror of the Autocracy: "Where is it evident that Christian powers have built prisons and gallows? Therefore the powers are established by Satan and not by God; all of them are from the anti-Christ. At the present time the devil rules on earth and even in the tsar's palace there is the anti-Christ; Satan has penetrated there also" (TsGIAL, div. 821, s.u. 178, p. 5 v.). The provocative Beilis trial, organized in 1911 by the Autocracy with the aim of inflaming ethnic enmity, called forth protest among the Seventh Day Adventists belonging to the Moscow congregation (*SV* 1913 No. 8-9: 17). But all these were isolated instances at a time when the basic line implemented by the upper strata of the Adventist church was directed toward support for the Autocracy. For ordinary Adventists, the figure of A. Biriulia, inspired by birching to love those who beat him, was more characteristic than the figure of the protester against the tsarist prisons and gallows. The creation of divine character in most cases did its work.

The first open political statement by the leaders of the Seventh Day Adventist church took place in 1905. They declared themselves behind the counter-revolutionary policy of the Autocracy. The Adventist leaders addressed Nicholas II in the name of the conferences in St. Petersburg and Velikoknia-zhesk which took place on October 1 and 9, 1905: "We loyal subjects of Your Imperial Majesty, who belong to the Christian congregations of Seventh Day Adventists, in the person of the undersigned deputized congregation, in view of the serious situation in our dear fatherland, make so bold as humbly to express to Your Imperial Majesty our profound sorrow together with all God-fearing people of our country, praying to the Most High for the complete pacification of our motherland, in which case it can continue its development.... We make so bold as to express our heartfelt wish that the Lord preserve you for our motherland for many more years" (Belogorskii 1911: 145). In exchange for the monarchist feelings expressed in this address, the Adventist leaders petitioned for the extension to their church of the religious freedoms promised by tsarism:

"We are filled with the highest thankfulness to God in His foresight for having predisposed the heart of Your Imperial Majesty to grant to all Christian faiths the long wished-for freedom of conscience, for which we warmly thank Your Imperial Majesty in complete confidence that its blessing will be extended to us also" (*ibid.*).

The Adventist leaders openly accepted the obligation of all the believers led by them to submit to the will of the Autocrat:

"We believe that the government is established by God and we pray for it and on the basis of the Bible assume the obligation to render to Caesar that which is Caesar's, paying to him duties and taxes, fear and honor, and unto God that which is God's observing His commandments" (*ibid.*, p. 146).

The Autocracy looked upon this petition with favor. By a special circular of the Ministry of Internal Affairs, the Seventh Day Adventist church was equated in juridical rights with the Baptist church. However limited were the religious freedoms extended to the Adventist church in 1906, they satisfied its leaders. A contemporary Adventist author describes this time: "With the proclamation in Russia in 1905-1906 of religious freedom, Seventh Day Adventists began to manifest special vitality and the cause began (to go) ahead much more successfully.... The legalization of Seventh Day Adventism as a religious body put the whole cause on a much firmer foundation.... By comparison with the preceding years, this period (1907-1910 — A. K.) was marked by progress for the cause on all sides" (Grigor'ev ms.: 3-4).

Under the protection of tsarism's religious freedoms, Adventists from 1905 to 1911 more than doubled their number. By the beginning of 1908, as we have aleady noted, they separated out into an independent union, and in 1910 held conferences in Moscow, Warsaw and Mitava. The leaders of Adventism were filled with gratitude to tsarism.

S. D. Bondar', summarizing his impressions about attending Adventist conferences in 1910 as a representative of the Ministry of Internal Affairs, wrote (January 1911) in an official report: "... in the conferences which took place under the observation of the Department in February and March of 1910 in Moscow, Warsaw and Mitava, the leaders of the Adventist movement in Russia openly declared: 'We are not enemies of the government but its friends. The true Christian must fulfill God's commandments, and His commandments demand obedience to the ruling powers' " (TsGIAL, div. 821, f. 133, s.u. 209, shs. 121-122).

Moreover, the representative of the Ministry of Internal Affairs confirmed that "to consider these declarations hyprocritical is without foundation", and as proof he cited precisely that element in Adventism which bore the designation of "creation of divine character": "On the contrary", Bondar' concluded, "these declarations have special significance in view of the role which is ascribed by Adventists to fulfilling God's commandments in the cause of saving man. The Adventist leaders constantly and firmly underline this thought in their sermons and in private conversations, and in congresses, inviting those who attend to submit to all the demands of the regime" (TsGIAL, div. 821, f. 133, s.u. 209, sh. 122).

We must note that the years in which Adventism so significantly increased its ranks, when in the words of the Adventist figure Gregor'ev, a contemporary of these years, there was "progress for the cause on all sides", fell basically into the period of the most severe political and ideological reaction following the suppression of the revolution of 1905-1907. The time of the legal activity of the Adventist church was a time of destruction of revolutionary organizations and the indiscriminate dispersal of trade unions. This was a period characterized on the one hand by phenomena of political apathy on the part of the masses and on the other hand by the preaching of the powerlessness of man, mistrust in social ideals, individualism, pessimism, eroticism, which occurred in literary and philosophical circles of the reactionary bourgeois intelligentsia.

Every sort of mystical society and gathering was fashionable. Spiritualist circles were organized and spread. The forces of reaction solidified for proclaiming anathema on all sides in the revolution, socialism, and the class struggle of the masses. Such was the social soil guaranteeing the utmost progress of the cause of Seventh Day Adventism.[9]

The next few years up to the second bourgeois-democratic revolution in Russia were described by the Adventist author as "difficult" (Gregor'ev ms: 4-5). The tsarist "freedoms" in the field of religion, with all their limitations, became still more illusory. Factually they were reduced to nothing. From 1911 to 1916 several Adventist congregations were closed administratively. Both ordinary Adventists and several Adventist preachers were subjected in these years to police and judicial repression. In Grigor'ev's words, at this time "the cause continued to develop, but its tempo slowed down" (*ibid.*).

In fact, whereas during the period 1905-1911 the number of Adventists grew by 250%, in 1912-1916 there was only a 24% increase. But whereas in the first case the growth in the ranks of Adventism was not so much a consequence of its legalization as a result of all the circumstances characterizing the period of reaction, in the second case the sharp slowing-down of the pace of growth of Adventism is explained not so much by the persecution to which it was subject, as by the circumstances characterizing the period of revolutionary upsurge.

We must, however note that the years of the First World War, during which Church and monarchist-Black Hundred organizations by every means

---

[9] The following is indicative: from 1905 to 1911 the number of Adventists grew by 3,300 persons. The Statistics of the Ministry of Internal Affairs contain data on the yearly dynamics of the growth of Adventism for this period of time—2,515 persons. Of this number in 1905-1907, 457 persons were converted to Adventism, and in 1908-1911, 2,058.

fanned chauvinist passions, were especially difficult for churches of Protestant-bourgeois type like the Mennonites, Baptists and Adventists. The Russian Orthodox-Black Hundred circles advanced against the Adventists the accusation of complicity with Germany in sabotaging the military. In Kiev Guberniia, one of the largest centers of Adventism, a case was brought concerning the "anti-state" activity of a group of Adventists living in Uman Uezd of the guberniia. At the same time, from the beginning of the war to September 1916, out of the entire mass of Adventists, whose number was at this time not less than 6,000 persons, only 50 were brought to trial for refusal to serve in the military (TsGIAL, div. 821, f. 133, s.u. 209, sh. 169). For example, the governor of Pskov in June 1916 reported to the Ministry of Internal Affairs: "... at the present time in Pskov there are 14 of these Adventists. Among them there are none who refuse on religious grounds to bear arms and to fulfill their military duty, and neither was there noted among them the manifestation of anti-militaristic and anti-government tendencies" (*ibid.*, sh. 158).

The attempt inspired by the Orthodox churchmen to organize a trial for "anti-state activity" of Adventists from Uman Uezd, Kiev Guberniia, in turn was unfounded. In the report of the chief of the Kiev department of civil order to the governor, he declared: "None of a number of definite witnesses could indicate that the activity of sectarians or their leaders was clearly intended to harm the interests of the state.... Neither was it determined that the Adventists conducted agitation among the population for refusal to go to war, or take up arms against the enemy, calling them brothers. In regard to aid to the population and public institutions for the needs of the war, they were also not peculiar, and readily gave when collections were made of both money and produce, and the Rusanov congregation gave 22 rubles to the Red Cross.... In the activity of the members of this sect, in particular of persons actually corresponding with each other, there is nothing which would threaten the state order and public peace or violate the demands of the law and the authorities or bring harm to the interests of the army ..." (Putintsev 1935: 81-82).

In the article *Kievskie adventisy i voina* [The Kievan Adventists and the War], published in 1914 in the newspaper *Utrenniaia zvezda*, G. I. Lebsak, the preceptor of the Kiev congregation, one of the oldest and most prominent figures of Adventism in Russia, wrote:

"Immediately after the declaration of war with Germany and Austria, the Kievan Seventh Day Adventists through the governor placed at the feet of His Imperial Majesty their loyal feelings and were privileged to receive through the chief of police the following declaration: 'The Minister of Internal Affairs informed the chief of the region that the sovereign Emperor was pleased to thank warmly the Kievan Seventh Day Adventists for their loyal feelings, expressed on the occasion of the opening of military action' ... the Kievan

Adventists with all their strength unite with true sons of our dear motherland to help their friends at the present difficult time and for the glory of the Most High God.

"May the Lord help us in this and in the future too" (*UZ* 1914, No. 45).

World War I interrupted the very close ties between the Adventist churches of Russia and Germany which had been developing for decades and had become traditional. While one of the Adventist church leaders in Russia, G. I. Lebsak, immediately after the declaration of war on Germany, hurried in the name of the Adventists to express loyal feelings to Nicholas II, Adventist church leaders in Germany, in a letter dated August 4, 1914, expressed their loyalty to Wilhelm's government: "Being confirmed on the basis of Holy Scripture and attempting to introduce into life the bases of Christianity ..., we still consider ourselves bound in this serious time to come out in defense of the fatherland and in these circumstances to bear arms also on Saturday ...; we have informed our members of these rules, and besides this we ask all congregations to designate special prayer gatherings and to pray God for the victory of German arms" (Klibanov 1931: 11). Several months later, in March 1915, leaders of the Adventist church in Germany, in a letter to the commander of the 12th Army in Dresden, reported that they "instructed all members obliged to serve in the army in the whole state truly to fulfill their civil responsibilities on the basis of the Holy Scriptures and also on Saturday, as other soldiers do on Sunday ..." (Klibanov 1931: 12). The first among the signators was L. R. Konradi—the same Konradi who in 1886 inspected Adventist groups in Russia and founded the first Adventist congregation in the Crimea; in 1890 he headed the first Adventist conference in Russia and in 1910 delivered inflammatory sermons at the all-Russian congress of Adventists.

The Adventist churches each served the class interest of their national bourgeoisie, their landlords or Junkers, their monarchy, in spite of the painful blows which they—especially the Adventist churches in Russia—received from their ungrateful masters. Of course, they did not like these blows; both the Lebsaks and the L'vovs, and others, secretly envied their Western European and trans-oceanic brothers, who enjoyed the blessings of bourgeois democracy. And yet the tsarist official S. D. Bondar' was right in his assertion that the loyalty of the Adventist leaders was not hypocritical. It was just as sincere as the Adventist leaders' fear of the revolutionary struggle of the masses.

The events of the world war were interpreted by Seventh Day Adventists in Russia as one of the truest signs of the imminent coming of Christ. The clash of armies serving the interest of warring imperialist camps was interpreted by the Adventist church as the fulfillment of the prophecy about Armageddon: "We must recognize that no other race of man like our living one has seen this indisputable fulfillment in which the Western European states are made 'tsars of the whole universe' in the full sense of this word. Their battle before Armageddon is part of the the prophecy whose fulfillment we must still await" (*ibid.*).

Frightening the imagination of its followers with the prophecy about Armageddon, which was supposedly coming true, the Adventist church, remaining true to itself, succeeded this time in comparing "the earthly" with "the heavenly": among other things, it put a theoretical basis, in the form of the Revelation of John, of all things, under the solution of the Near-Eastern question, which corresponded to the interests of tsarism. The Adventist journal published an article, *Blizhevostochnyi vopros v svete Biblii* [The Near-Eastern Question in Light of the Bible], whose author cited a line from Revelation ("... the great river Euphrates: and the water dried up in it'"), in order to propose an immediate solution to the Near-Eastern question on the basis of it: "We find the historical fulfillment of this ("the drying-up of the water" in the Euphrates—A. K.) in the gradual falling-apart of the Ottoman state. We must still expect the loss by Turkey of its European territories, the return to Asia Minor and the destruction of Asiatic Turkey also" (*ibid.*).

The connection of the policy of the Adventist church with the interests of the imperialistic bourgeoisie, whether of the U.S., England, Germany or Russia—a connection which was especially obvious in the years of the First World War, when on both sides of the front Adventists in the active armies annihilated each other, making no exception for Saturdays—sharpened the growing internal contradictions among Adventists. The socially lower ranks of Adventism, who, like the socially lower classes in general, bore the basic burden of military catastrophes, either broke with Adventism or (in the majority of cases) buried their heads in the pit of eschatology, and demanded that their leaders stop procrastinating and name the date of the second coming. In the conceptions of a part of this lower strata, the events of the world war meant not signs of the imminent end of the world, but the first signs of the approach of its demise.

In these very las' days or months of the earthly history of mankind, as they supposed, there ·vere people among Adventists who left behind their cares about earthly matters, preaching severe asceticism and openly accusing their church leaders of betraying the cause of the faith, chiefly in subservience to the bosses of "this world". In their eyes, the Adventist church was just as dissolute and doomed to "Babylon" as Catholicism and Russian Orthodoxy.

On the wave of these oppositionist moods, which were, however, wrapped in deeply eschatological form, the leaders floated, attempting to wrest primacy in the Adventist movement from the hands of the developing Orthodox-Adventist caste. Thus, in 1914, there arose a reformist movement in Adventism, which had adherents in Germany, Romania, the U.S., and later in Russia. This group (in Russia its most important representatives were Netovich, Iantsen, Manzhura, and Unrau) came out with a demand for a "general reform". The basic positions of the general reform, mixed with accusing the ruling Adventist clergy of dissipation and connections with the lay world, came down to a demand for the strictest asceticism, including, along with food taboos, renunciation of marriage and procreation—all this in connection with assertions of the immediate beginning of the end of the world. And this time mysticism went hand in hand with asceticism.

In 1916, the adherents of the new group broke with the Seventh Day Adventist church, and separated out into a new organization called the "Movement of Reform". As was to be expected, this organization had nothing in common with the real interests of ordinary Adventists. On the contrary, it used religious fanaticism as a snare for deflecting the dissatisfaction of ordinary Adventists with the reality surrounding them. By the way, the adherents of the "Movement for Reform" did not appear in the Russian union"; their activity developed after 1917, when they became the most reactionary wing of Adventism, unreconciled to Soviet reality.

Under the conditions of the maturing revolutionary crisis in Russia, the rapid upsurge of the strike movement in 1916, the soldiers' uprising, the growth of the anti-military mood, the Seventh Day Adventist church attempted to block revolutionary propaganda among their charges. In the Adventist publication *Vestnik khristianina* [The Christian's Herald], an article was published in late 1916 containing the admission: "The gospel of social betterment has replaced for many the gospel of salvation from sin...." The author argued that many preferred to follow "the gospel of social betterment instead of doing what was necessary to prepare for life on the new earth." The author declared: "Such a worldly gospel does not guard people from Satan" (*VKh* 1916, No. 11: 151).

The fulfillment of the political strivings of the Seventh Day Adventist church was the power of the bourgeoisie in the person of the Provisional Government which replaced the overthrown Autocracy. Even in the April issue of the journal *Blagaia vest'* a panegyric article was published addressed to the Provisional Government: "A remarkable event has occurred for all the sons of Russia, particularly those who were formerly persecuted for their religious beliefs. The despotism of the old regime hermetically sealed all holes through which a ray of light could penetrate into the darkness. Now by the will of the Most High it is itself buried....

"God's herald, suffering in places of exile and incarceration, deprived of the possibility of accomplishing God's work, heard from God through His angel—the Provisional Government—as an answer to their and our prayers for them: 'You can be free' " (*BV* 1917, No. 4: 78).

The Seventh Day Adventist church prepared to occupy a fitting place in the conditions of political dominance of the bourgeoisie. In 1917 there were congresses of Adventist congregations in Petrograd, Moscow, Kiev, Odessa, Narva, and other cities, which were concluded by an all-Russian congress of Seventh Day Adventists in Saratov, where the most extensive terms were worked out for the "adventization" of the population.

The Adventist church attempted to use conditions favorable for its preaching in order to win over as many souls as possible, and by this to do as much as it could to win away the workers from the revolutionary struggle against the class-political dominance of the bourgeoisie. In June 1917, in circumstances of growing revolutionary dissatisfaction of the masses with the policies of the Provisional Government, it continued to maintain: "The sun of truth is rising in our country and healing is in its rays" (*BV* 1917 No. 6: 106). The Adventist church sowed illusions to the effect that the policy of the Provisional Government corresponded to the policy of Lincoln in the period of the American Civil War (*ibid.*). The year 1917 remained in the memory of a contemporary Adventist author as "a year of complete freedom" (Grigor'ev ms.: 5).

The political ideal of the Adventist church was the state power of the bourgeoisie, which was in complete correspondence with the social views on which it stood, and the basis of which was the immutability of capitalist property.

The Seventh Day Adventist church had fewer members than the Baptist church. But like the latter, it held ordinary believers as much as it could within the bonds of bourgeois-reactionary ideology. Along with the Baptist church, the Seventh Day Adventist church supplemented the political reserves of the counter-revolutionary bourgeoisie.

Editor's Notes

Note A. the Russian translation at this point has been grammatically recast so that the adjectival expressions appear as substantives. The phrase "the English turn of mind" does not appear as such in the original.

Note B. This passage was apparently not included in the English *Selected Correspondence* available to me, which is an earlier edition.

Conclusion

The historical development of religious sectarianism in Russia has peculiar features distinguishing it from forms of "political protest in religious guise" as they developed in the 14th-17th centuries in the countries of Western Europe.

Socio-economic backwardness was the reason why religious sectarianism developed significantly later in Russia than, for example, in Germany and England, and did not play the role of "revolutionary opposition to feudalism" (Engels), as in these countries. It is true that in Russia in the 14th-16th centuries there developed anti-feudal heresies, and among them the heresy of Feodosii Kosoi may with complete justice be called a form of revolutionary opposition to feudalism. However the Russian heresies of the 14th-16th centuries did not flow into a mass movement, bore primarily an urban character, and were suppressed by the united forces of lay and spiritual feudal lords. This is to be explained primarily by the fact that, as distinct from the situation in England and Germany, in Russia at the end of the 15th-16th centuries, the prerequisites of bourgeois relationships had only just come into being.

As we have shown, the sectarian movement attained wide dissemination beginning in the second half of the the 18th century, as the process of the breakdown of the feudal-serf system proceeded. Russian sectarianism, developing in circumstances of a feudal, absolutist monarchy, found a wide response in the peasant milieu, but it could not and did not become a universal form of peasant movement, as occurred, for example, in Germany in the period of the Peasant War of 1525. Sectarianism embraced in relatively small degree the strata of the urban population for whom the religious form of political protest increasingly became a bygone stage.

The basic tendencies of the anti-serfdom struggle in Russia in the 18th century have been shown to be the peasant uprisings and disturbances of the middle of the century, the peasant wars under the leadership of Pugachev in 1773-1775, the popular philosphical writers of the second half of the 18th century, among whom the most prominent, as Iu. Ia. Kogan has shown, were already representatives of *atheistic* thought (Kogan 1962).

At the same time, religious sectarianism in Russia, in its original forms

(Khristovoverie, Dukhoborism, Molokanism) and their derivatives, was significantly more long-lived than early forms of religious sectarianism in Western European countries.

We are comparing those tendencies in religious sectarianism in Russia, Germany, the Netherlands and England, which can be described as "the manifestation of political protest in religious form."

The wide spread of religious sectarianism as a form of class struggle in the late 18th, the 19th, and even the beginning of the 20th century, was in and of itself an expression of Russia's socio-economic backwardness. This expression of political protest in religious guise is a phenomenon characteristic of class struggle in the Middle Ages. Profound survivals of the serf system in the economic and political structure of tsarist Russia up to the beginning of the 20th century nourished and supported in particular strata of the population the most primitive forms of expression of social protest — a medieval form of class struggle.

The development of capitalism in Russia along the "Prussian path"[A] led to a state in which the anti-feudal protest of Russian religious sectarianism, as a rule, did not grow into a revolutionary struggle, being limited to passive resistance to the existing order, which included searching for means of adapting to it.

The history of pre-Reform groups of Russian religious sectarianism, as well as their history in the Reform era, expressed in religious models the tortuous evolution of the patriarchal peasant into a bourgeois property-owner. Khristovoverie, Dukhoborism and Molokanism ideologically reflected the successive stages and parallel forms of this evolution.

In studying on a comparative basis religious sectarianism in 16th-century Germany and 17th-century England, on the one hand, and in 18th- and 19th-century Russia on the other, one is struck by the profound differences in the course of development of these movements. Whereas in Germany and England there was an increase over time in the significance in sectarianism of plebeian elements which stood against the bourgeois elements, having outgrown their influence and taken on an independent role, in Russian sectarianism on the contrary, whether this was Khristovoverie or Dukhoborism or Molokanism, the bourgeois elements became increasingly strong in the role of leaders of sectarianism; they adapted the organizational bases of the movement to the conditions of their dominance, taking away from the ideology of sectarianism everything which could serve the lower ranks for the expression of their independent interests.

The popular sectarian movements in England in the 17th century, starting from Calvinist religious and church doctrine, at the same time broke out of its bonds, speaking against a presbyterial and consistorial, even though democratized, regime, against the division of people into "chosen" and "condemned", against the dogma of predestination as opposed to free will and the activity of people, and against the imposition of a rule of faith, not excluding the cases in which the Bible constituted this rule.

As V. M. Lavrovskii and M. A. Barg, students of the English bourgeois revolution in the 17th century, write: "It would be a profound error to consider Puritanism, which has taken possession of the masses and become the ideological weapon of social agitation, the same 'orthodox Calvinism' as it was in the period of its origin.

"In reality it was as far from that as earth from heaven. The most we can say is that at its base it was undoubtedly the product of Calvinism, but a product so remote and with such significant accidental admixtures ..., that it already had little in common with the doctrine that called it into being" (Lavrovskii and Barg 1958: 164).

In the English popular sectarian movements in the 1630s-1640s, the Calvinist conception of the church and its structure was revised: the "visible" church was contrasted to the "spiritual" church; the conception of man himself as "the temple of God".

The declaration that man was "the temple of God" removed the necessity of all forms of external church organization and at the same time served as an affirmation of the moral and intellectual strength of all peoples, who had equal opportunity to be "living temples", and consequently were not subordinate to blind predestination, nor divided forever into chosen and condemned. In this ideological direction there was a denial by sectarians of "book wisdom", obligatory religious dogma: "If Puritanism advanced to the foreground 'the word of God revealed in the Scriptures', sectarianism, in accordance with the teaching of the mystics, insisted on spiritual acceptance of 'the truth' and consequently placed the inner word over the external word .... In short, truth for the sectarians was not wisdom from reading, but the inner light, of which anyone could become the bearer ..." (Lavrovskii and Barg: 170).

In the popular sectarian movements in England in the 1630s-1640s, there matured with great force at the end of the 1640s a revolutionary opposition to the feudal-absolutist system. The development of sectarian movements in Russia went in the opposite direction.

In Dukhoborism, which appeared after Khristovoverie, and in Molokanism, which appeared after Dukhoborism, the circle of ideas belonging to the creativity of the lower social classes, increasingly narrowed. Even Dukhoborism moderated the mystical fervor of the Khristovovers, and the right to be the mouthpieces of the divine will was monopolized by its leaders. Molokanism in general placed its religious world-view of Old Testament and New Testament booklearning, offering the believers, in the persons of their leaders, a role limited to that of interpreters of the Holy Scriptures. At the same time it covered the Holy Scriptures with the formulas of its ritualists. Khristovoverie and Dukhoborism in those of its forms which co-existed with Molokanism, in turn, ossified into codices of rote prayers worked out by them, and to ceremonial and ritual traditions, at a time when their internal structure was increasingly penetrated by elements of an established church nature.

Sectarianism in all its groups came, although in peculiar form, to that which it had rejected at the beginning of its history: the sects were turned into churches with a hierarchical structure and regime, with religious formalism and external ritual. But these were churches of bourgeois-Protestant type.

The process of becoming churches, through which all the pre-Reform sectarian groups logically passed, led to their being gradually swallowed up in the Reform era by Baptism. In Baptism, Russia sectarianism was included in the system of one of the world bourgeois-Christian churches.

Baptism, although its masses consisted of democratic elements, in general was not an ideology of struggle. It was an ideology of religious comfort for those who were disillusioned with struggle. In this respect, there was no difference in priciple between the religious systems preached by Baptism and by the Russian Orthodox Church. At the base of the religious philosophy of Baptism which was disseminated in Russia lay the dogma of predestination, which came from Calvinism and was modified by time. Bourgeois society cannot, Engels wrote, "either prevent the crisis in general or guard individual capitalists from losses, from hopeless debts and bankruptcy, or save an individual worker from unemployment and poverty. To this day there is still current a proverb: man proposes, but God (i.e., the dominance of capitalist means of production alien to man) disposes" (*Marx and Engels* XX: 329).

Baptism (like Evangelical Christianity and Adventism) was a church competing with the dominant Russian Orthodox Church, but not antagonistic to it.

Thus, after the revolution of 1905-1907, the circle of historical development of sectarianism as a movement of democratic protest in religious guise was completed. Pre-Reform groups of sectarianism were in complete decline, their leaders competed bitterly with one another in searching out means of retaining their followers, and unanimously behaved servilely towards tsarism. At this time in Baptism and Evangelical Christianity there was a marked tendency to set up on the basis of them Christian-political parties with programs akin to the Kadet one.

The democratic lower classes, who participated in sectarian movements and who connected their protest with sectarianism, were faced with a choice in the course of the class struggle: either to break with the religious forms of protest and continue the struggle in political form, or insist on the religious form of their movements, which meant to renounce social protest.

Lenin wrote in 1909: "All modern religions and churches, each and every religious organization, is always seen by Marxism as an organ of bourgeois reaction, serving to defend exploitation and stupefy the working class" (*Lenin* XVII: 416).

Let us now review the internal processes in religious sectarianism which conditioned its political and ideological evolution. Summing up the material set forth in the preceding chapters, we come to the conclusion that religious sectarianism, in its day the result of the creation of bourgeois relationships, in turn facilitated the strengthening and spread of bourgeois relations in Russia.

Lenin wrote: "... the process of formation of a market capitalism has two sides: namely, the development of capitalism in depth, i.e. the further growth of capitalist agriculture and capitalist industry in a given, definite closed territory; and the development of capitalism in breadth—i.e., the spread of the sphere of dominance of capitalism to new territories" (*Lenin* III: 595).[B]

Religious sectarianism, primarily those groups which arose before the Reform, played an especially marked role in the development of capitalism in breadth, in the spread of bourgeois relationships to the southern, Far-Eastern and northern borderlands of Russia. The followers of Khristovoverie, the Skoptsy movement, Dukhoborism and Molokanism were among the pioneers who spread bourgeois forms of economy in Tiflis, Elizavetpol', Baku, Tavriia, and other guberniias of the south, in some regions of Siberia, in the Amur region and Yakutiia. How are we to explain the seemingly remarkable fact that, for example in Yakutiia, among whose population the proportion of sectarians was several dozen percent, it was precisely they who "for the first time in the history of Yakutiia created market agriculture, producing grain for the market with the help of hired labor" (Safronov 1963: 322), and during 1870-1900 dominated the market, beating down both the local competing grain-merchants and those from outside?

At the same time, sectarians who were especially successful in spreading bourgeois forms of economy to the borderlands and in the center acted as bearers of bourgeois relationships. In *The Development of Capitalism in Russia,* Lenin, pointing to "the specially marked examples of complete amalgamation of 'artisan' and factory industry as examples of highly developed (both in depth and in breadth) capitalist manufacture "(*Lenin* III: 402), named "the industrial village of Rasskazovo in Tamov Uezd and Guberniia (in 1897—8,283 residents) the center of both factory (cloth, soap-making, leather-making and distilling) and artisan industry, the latter being closely connected with the former; the crafts—leather-work (as many as 70 owners, and there are enterprises with 20-30 workers), glue-boiling, boot-making, and stocking-making (there is not a household where stockings are not knitted from wool given out by weight by the 'buyers') etc." (*Lenin* III: 406-407).

The population of Rasskazovo was primarily sectarian—Molokan, Subbotnik and Khristovover—and this village had a reputation of being "the sectarian capital". The occupations of the inhabitants of Rasskazovo as described by Lenin were indicative of a great many places inhabited by sectarians in the center of the country.

How are we to explain the fact that, independent of the territory on which the sectarians settled, they were as a rule advanced in terms of crop yields, possession of agricultural technology, method of animal husbandry and horticulture, development of industry, and trade?

How are we to explain the economic zeal of the overwhelming majority of sectarians, which was unanimously noted by students of pre-Revolutionary sectarianism?

This is the same phenomenon which had long ago attracted the attention of numerous students of the history of Protestantism in Western Europe: the Huguenots, the Calvinists, and representatives of other Protestant sects, wherever they were found, showed themselves to be the bearers of bourgeois relationships, which became especially evident in the 17th century.

Thus, by the time of the revocation of the Edict of Nantes (1685), French "Reformists" dominated the iron industry in Sedan, the paper industry in the Auvergne, the leather industry in Turenne, flax-spinning in Normandy, Lyons and Brittany, silk and velvet production in Tours and Lyons, the wool industry in Languedoc, Prosses and Champagne, and the lace-making industry in Paris (Kapeliush 1931: 249). Compelled by persecutions to emigrate from France, the Reformists "introduced everywhere capitalist home industry, especially in the wool and silk industries; other branches obliged in Germany to the refugee Huguenots for their founding or development in a capitalist spirit were the production in stockings, hats, leather, stationery, linseed oil and toilet soap. Through the Huguenots the production of gloves spread into England, Germany and Austria; the Huguenots distributed new forms of tanned leather; chamois and kidskin appeared. It was a highly eloquent picture: a persecuted faith connected with pioneering in industry" (*ibid.*).

The English Puritans played a role analoguous to that of the French Reformists: "The Puritans have the same aspect as the Huguenots and were also pioneers in capitalist industry.... Along with Norfolk and Lancashire, citadels of Puritanism as centers of the textile industry were Yorkshire, Bradford, Leeds, Halifax, Birmingham, Leicester, Gloucester and other centers of English industry" (*ibid.*: 250).

What talisman of economic success did religious sectarians possess, whether they operated in France, England, Germany or North America, where English Calvinism successfully pursued business, and finally, as I have shown, in Russia? We find in Lenin a highly important methodological statement relating to the phenomenon of the genesis of capitalism: "What kind of nonsense is it that intellect and feeling did not take part in the origin of capitalism? Why, what does capitalism consist of if not particular relationships between people? And we know of no people who do not have intellect and feelings.... At that time people built, with sound mind and firm memory, highly refined sluices and dams, chasing the insubordinate peasants into the path of capitalist exploitation; they created extremely clever bypass channels consisting of political and financial measures, along which (channels) capitalist accumulation and capitalist expropriation streamed, and they were not satisfied with the action of economic laws alone" (*Lenin* I: 416).[C]

In the process of establishment of capitalism there occurred changes in the region of superstructural phenomena which in turn influenced the economic bases. Changes occurred in the spiritual outlook of the producers, a re-evaluation began of centuries-old ideological values, behind which stood the Church. Changes occurring in social views of labor were especially marked.

Hegel, studying the ideas which gave birth to the religious reformation, acutely noted: "To live without doing anything also ceased to be considered something holy; it began to be considered more worthy for a dependent person to make himself independent through his own activity, prudence and diligence. It was more honest for the person who had money to buy things, even if for the satisfaction of surplus needs, instead of giving this money to do-nothings and beggars, because he gave this money to the same number of persons and at least fulfilled the condition that they should work actively." Hegel concludes his thought: "From that time industry and craft became moral, and those barriers which the Church had created for them disappeared" (Hegel 1935: 394).

And in fact, Calvinism and Lutheranism declared business success the criterion of the moral way of life of man and even the sign of his free election to eternal salvation, and on the other hand condemned the love of idleness as sin, and were intransigent toward mendicancy. The ideologues of the most diverse groups in Protestantism in the 17th and 18th centuries, as Calvin and Luther once had, paid a notable tribute of attention to the problems of labor, accumulation, mendicancy and idleness.

The Quaker activist John Bellers was the most important English economist in the second half of the 17th and the first half of the 18th century, one of the precursors of the labor theory of value. Marx in *Capital* repeatedly cited Bellers: "John Bellers", he wrote, "a very phenomenon in the history of Political Economy, saw most clearly at the end of the 17th century, the necessity for abolishing the present system of education and division of labour, which beget hypertrophy and atrophy at the two opposite extremes of society" (*Marx and Engels*: XXIII, 499, note) [1967: 488]. Bellers' socio-economic views at the same time were characteristic of Quaker views of labor. Marx wrote: "Amongst other things he says this: 'An idle learning being little better than the learning of idleness.... Bodily labour, it's a primitive institution of God.... Labour being as proper for the body's health as eating is for its living; for what pains a man saves by ease, he will find in disease.... Labour adds oil to the lamp of life, when thinking inflames it ..." (*ibid.*: 499-500, note) [1967: 488].

Followers of Reformationist teaching gave themselves up to earning money with religious zeal, supposing that thus they served the Most High, like the *jongleur* in the well-known medieval tale, who served the Virgin by the fact that he turned somersaults and walked on his hands before her statue.

The activity, prudence and diligence of each individual believer was controlled by the religious congregation which stimulated and corrected it. Similar phenomena were observed in the history of religious sectarianism in Russia. I showed in the first chapter of this book how and in what forms arose concepts of common sense and a feeling of individualism and faith in man's activity, his quick-wittedness and enterprising nature, among the early representatives of sectarianism, combined with the interests of sectarians in earthly matters. As the patriarchal peasant turned into an independent commodity producer, there occurred a restructuring of his spiritual outlook as well.

But among the stimuli which the sectarians had at their disposal, which hastened the action of economic laws, there were not only stimuli of an ideological and psychological character. The religious congregations were at the same time economic organizations, some in greater degree and others in lesser.

P. G. Ryndziunskii's work *Gorodskoe grazhdanstvo doreformennoi Rossii* [Urban Citizenship in Pre-Reform Russia] is an extremely interesting and fresh attempt to study the structure of the Preobrazhenskii priestless Old Believer congregation in Moscow. The author recreates in its basic links the complete uniqueness of the economic "mechanism" thanks to which there occurred in the congregation, "under a highly archaic cover", "the mobilization of monetary resources and financing for industrialists, the proffering of a refuge and initial foothold for peasants liberated from their rural ties, who were passing into the position of small industrialists or workers, and also assistance to them in obtaining civil rights" (Ryndziunskii 1958: 458).

This was one of the "extremely clever bypass channels" along which "capitalist accumulation and capitalist expropriation ..., not satisfied with the action of economic laws, streamed." Structures in part reminiscent of those which existed in the Moscow Preobrazhenskii priestless congregation were also present in the Moscow Kristovover congregations. For example, investigation into the case of the Moscow Kristovovers in 1837 (as many as 150 persons were involved in the case) showed that "girls from infancy were brought up (among the Khristovovers—A. K.) in the greatest dependence.

Primarily the very poorest were chosen; very many were bought from landlord estates. Those pre-selected and greatly favored by the elders are settled into the local meshchan class ... the entire class of women (of 150 Khristovovers brought to court, 130 were women — A. K.) have one primary occupation: they braid silk belts and lace; they help each other very much, and many grow raspberries for sale. They live in communes, 5 to 6 people of various ages in a house ..." (Aivazov 1915: 38).

In this book I did not deal with the history of the Skoptsy movement, inasmuch as this group of religious sectarians had limited distribution, and, being derived from Khristovoverie, is significant mainly in that the ascetic ideals of Khristovoverie had no prospects other than that of degenerating into an ideology of the most monstrous and cruel fanaticism. However, the Skoptsy movement too served as a religiously-camouflaged organization of capitalist accumulation and expropriation.

A Soviet student of this sect, N. N. Volkov, wrote: "Skoptsy cells, or 'ships', having justified themselves as a form of economic organization of part of the peasantry, soon passed over to the city, finding among the merchant class, urban meshchane, and soldiers, their basic source of proselytes. The Skoptsy movement was a no less advantageous form of religio-economic co-fraternity for the merchant class. Spreading throughout the entire empire, the propagandists for the Skoptsy movement were the best agents of and sources of information about trade capital. Earlier than his colleague living 'in the world', the Skopets trader knew the price of goods, and made profitable operations, receiving, when it was required, material support from his fellow believers.... Working in Skoptsy enterprises or trading institutions, the Skoptsy ate moderately, did not drink alcohol, were distinguished by their obedience and diligence, and most important, could not return to the world because of their physical deformity. Over the course of several decades, the leaders of the Skoptsy movement gathered together millions of rubles. The lack of need to divide capital because of the lack of heirs, in addition to mercantile share companies under the flag of the Skoptsy movement, influenced the rapid concentration of capital in the hands of Skoptsy at the end of the 18th and the beginning of the 19th centuries. In case of death, capital went from one Skopets to another" (Volkov 1931: 36).

During the preceding exposition it was shown that other religious sects were at the same time economic units. The most impressive and clearest example in this respect was Dukhoboriia, with its Orphans Home and its entire internal structure. But Baptism too, whose followers were not compactly settled and became increasingly dispersed, also gave birth to the institution of the "church-economic council". The bourgeois economy of the sectarians had one other peculiar feature. They attempted to apply the most direct and crudest forms of exploitation in the first instance to workers who did not belong to the sectarian group. Thus, property-owners from among the Dukhobors and Molokans widely resorted to exploitation of the labor of representatives of the native nationalities of the Transcaucasus. The Amur Molokans especially valued the labor of the peoples who lived next to them. The Skoptsy exploited and ruined the Yakuts, etc. etc. The Dukhobors, Molokans and Khristovovers who lived in other places exploited the labor of Russian Orthodox peasant seasonal migrants. The Mennonites—whom I did not treat specially, since this religious society consisted of people of Duch and German descendants and attracted almost no Russians—in the course of the first decades of their existence in Russia used almost exclusively the hired labor of the Ukrainian and Russian population.

In the period of the formation of bourgeois relationships, those persons advanced who successfully maneuvered, with the help of the "extremely clever bypass channels", among the taboos, harassments, and limitations of serfdom.

As a whole the role of sectarianism in the soico-economic development of Russia consisted primarily in the fact that for the nascent bourgeois elements it served as a bypass with respect to serfdom and its survivals after the Reform of the 1860s. Religious sectarianism played this role regardless of whether it appeared under its mystical-ecstatic form of Khristovoverie, the fanatical form of the Skoptsy movement, or under the respectable forms of Baptism and Evangelical Christianity which were not devoid of worldliness. The fact that religious sectarianism not only found a place among the multiplicity of bypass channels, but having appeared, continued to be used by developing capitalism, is to be explained by the dominance of serfdom, and the force of its survivals in the socio-economic and political structure of tsarist Russia.

Hence, the relationships which developed in the sects could only be relationships of economic dependence and exploitation.

I have shown the phenomena of bourgeois stratification charactristic of all groups of pre-Reform sectarianism. As concerns its Reform-era groups, their peculiarity was that they proceeded from the phenomenon of bourgeois stratification in the peasantry, strengthening it and deepening it in their turn and in their own way. On this basis in all the sects there developed contradictions, and a struggle between democratic, proletarianized elements, who made up the lower ranks of sectarianism, and the elements of the bourgeoisie who made up its upper ranks. In the course of the developing class struggle in sectarianism, a clergy developed and separated out, which in the interests of the bourgeois circles served the function of dominating the "laity". In order to bend the will of ordinary participants of sectarianism and reduce to a minimum the independene of the laity, disciplinary rules were introduced in these sects, and the doctrines were subjected to dogmatic reworking, and in this form were presented as generally binding for believers. The religious practice acquired a ritual, and the institution of preceptors flourished, which replaced the religious inspiration and "living faith" which once existed in the sects.

The process of becoming a church in religious sectarianism, which was the consequence of developing class contradictions in it, not only did not blunt their acuteness, but in turn facilitated the demarcation of forces in sectarianism. As once the origin of religious sectarianism had testified to a crisis of the feudal-Russian Orthodox Church, so new religious formations, as sectarian groups became more like churches, arose in them, which testified to a crises in these groups as one of the forms of the democratic movement.

Following sectarianism on the basis of Russian Orthodoxy, there arose sectarianism on the basis of sectarianism. The participants in the new religious groups in sectarianism acted in the name of the restoration of the original norms of religious life, with which they associated the absence of exploitation by wealthy brothers, and of all forms of dependence on them. But, as was explained, the original forms of sectarianism were adapted precisely to facilitate the maturation of bourgeois elements. History repeated itself.

Only a short time passed until the new religious formations encountered the old, insoluble problems. Then the new formations became like churches and new religious groups separated out from them. And so on indefinitely. "... Within almost all sects", Bonch-Bruevich wrote in his report, *Raskol i sektantstvo v Rossii* [Schism and Sectarianism in Russia], "there was always observed a struggle of various opinions and views. As soon as a doctrine was formed, as soon as it was confined within certain bounds, and became ossified—within the sect there were always new elements maturing who did not agree with the majority, livelier and more sophisticated brothers, who under the pressure of various social reasons began to criticize the orthodoxy of their fellow believers.... Here within the sect, the religious teaching accepted by the majority occupied the place of the teaching of the ruling church in the state. And within it before our eyes a schism takes place, and hostile relationships are created between parts of the sect, a struggle occurs accompanied by 'persecutions' and 'resistance', as the case may be, and so it continues until protesting elements organize and split off completely, forming a new branch on the old root....

"We must seek the basic reason for these schisms within the sect in the developing differentiation of the peasant economy in general, and consequently, in the economies of sectarians also" (Bonch-Bruevich 1959: 166-167).

Such were the peculiar features of the class struggle taking place in sectarianism. Its democratic proletarianized elements most frequently directed their struggle toward the creation of new religious groups, inventing ever new faiths, but this did not enrich the liberation struggle of the working classes of

Russia. However, in both the pre-Reform and Reform-era groups of sectarianism, there were numerous instances of direct protest against exploitation and dictatorial rule by bourgeois property-owners in the congregations, this protest growing in a number of cases into a critique of the system of bourgeois-landowner oppression and violence.

Among the examples which we discussed in this book, let us remember the clear statements of a member of the Dukhobor Large Party, Podovinnikov, and the founder of a group in opposition to Baptism, Kondratti Malëvannyi. We can supplement this by reference to the Siutaevite sect, the founder and ideologist of which was the Tver peasant Vasilii Siutaev, who reasoned: "You come out onto a field; whose land is it?—the state's. Whose forest is it?—the nobles'.... We also were state people, and others the nobles'. The nobles now rule, and we are slaves" (Prugavin 1904: 87). Siutaev declared: "... there are good and evil regimes. Regimes which are not internal and hearts which are not good—these are evil regimes. They act unjustly, because they do not have to obey, since they lead us people astray" (*ibid.*: 112-113). The Subbotnik Timofei Bondarev wrote: "I divide the whole world into two circles: one of them is elevated and honored, and the other is oppressed and outcast. The first is luxuriantly dressed and sits at a luxurious table through the labor of others ... — this is the privilged class. But the second circle is dressed in a shift, worn out by hard labor and dry food, humiliated and with a drooping head, standing at the threshold. This is the poor farmer ..." (Vladimirov 1938: 72). Bondarev came to the conclusions: "The devil fools people at night in the dark, but you, the government, fool people in broad daylight ..." (*ibid.*: 99).

Neiher Podovinnikov nor Malëvannyi nor Siutaev nor Bondarev, nor other sectarians like them, had any real idea of the paths of struggle with social inequality, the nobles' property and power, with a government which deceives the people. In the first instance the agitation and propaganda of the Social-Democratic Party was directed precisely at this kind of democratic element in sectarianism.

The history of all forms of religious sectarianism in Russia is the history of the growth in them of social contradictions and class struggle, frequently dressed in religious form, and leading each individual sect to divide into hostile tendencies, and then (for the same reasons), into new hostile groups. This was, truly, "a war of all against all". As a result there was an uninterrupted flow out of the basic groups of religious sectarianism on the part of the most lively, active, independent and reflective members of the working class, who either broke with sectarianism in general or still tried to seek justice on the basis of newly formed religious groups. Religious sectarianism in its basic groups was steadily maintained by a group composed of the most ignorant, apathetic elements, who had lost themselves or had not yet found themselves. As such it represented a milieu as a whole submissive to the influence of their bourgeois upper strata.

Such were the internal processes in sectarianism leading in their development to its transformation from a movement of democratic protest into a religious organization of bourgeois reaction.

On the basis of the material I collected and studied, it is now possible to raise the questions of building a scientific classifiction of religious sectarianism.

Pre-Revolutionary historiography arranged the multiplicity of forms of religious sectarianism either into two geographical groups—"Eastern sectarianism" and "Western sectarianism"—or into two ideological groups: "mystical sectarianism" and "rationalistic sectarianism". In this case, the group of sects subsumed under the concept of "Eastern sectarianism" more or less corresponded to the makeup of sects subsumed under the concept of "mystical sectarianism". In the same way, the forms of sectarianism described as "Western" more or less corresponded to forms described as "rationalistic".

Khristovovers and Skoptsy were placed in the ranks of the Eastern and mystical sects, while in the ranks of the Western and rationalistic Baptists, Evangelical Christians and Adventists were enumerated. Molokanism was not placed in the ranks of Western sects but was considered rationalistic. As for Dukhobors, they were a source of much concern for the adherents of the above-mentioned classifications: Dukhobors were not placed in either of the schemes, since they combined features which pre-Revolutionary classifiers ascribed to Eastern and mystical sectarianism with characteristics which these classifiers ascribed to Western and rationalistic sectarianism.

Even Miliukov noted that "rationalism and mysticism proceed in parallel fashion in the development of Russian sectarianism and often combine or unite together in one and the same sect" (Miliukov 1931: 159). To replace this he proposed to classify sectarianism into "evangelical" and "spiritual" (*ibid.*). The classification of sectarianism into Eastern and Western, mystical and rationalistic, evangelical and spiritual, is methodologically unacceptable, since it ignores and contradicts the principles of socio-historical study of sectarianism.

The geographical criterion which lies at the base of the division of religious sectarianism into Eastern and Western leads to an explanation of the existence in Russia of sects relating to these two types on the basis of the so-called filiation of ideas. Thus the socio-economic reasons for the origin and development of religious sectarianism in Russian society is avoided.

The Church and the Autocracy used this classification in order to interpret sectarianism as foreign ideological contraband, pursuing disruptive aims. It stands to reason that to deny the classification of sectarianism into Eastern and Western as methodologically unacceptable does not mean to deny the influence on the development of sectarianism of the mystical-gnostic ideas of Eastern sectarianism or the so-called rationalistic ideas of Western sectarianism, or to deny the significance of the activity of preachers of both types.

An ideological criterion lies at the base of the division of sectarianism into mystical and rationalistic, since one or another system of religious ideas is accepted as a definitive feature. Let us add that the Church-missionary literature as a rule equated mysticism with fanaticism, and rationalism with atheism; thus, this classification served tsarism and the Church as the ideological basis for harassing sectarianism and instituting reprisals against its followers. From this it does not follow that in some doctrines of religious sectarianism there do not prevail in some instances elements of mysticism, and in others elements of rationalism.

Whatever the forms of distorted religious consciousness were, they were always formed by relationships of real life. And this is the main point.

The experience of my study showed that in the course of differentiation of sectarianism within the bounds of each of its varieties, there occurred a sequence of so-called mystical and rationalistic forms.

Khristovoverie, in whose religious teaching mystical motifs originally predominated, ended by the separating-out of the New Israelite group, which renounced mysticism and asceticism. Dukhoborism, which began by limiting the mysticism of Khristovoverie and renouncing its ascetic taboos, gave rise to a Postnik group, reviving both asceticism and mysticism. Molokanism, basing its teaching on Biblical "rationally-interpreted" booklearning, gave rise to the Prygun group with ecstatic ritual close to early Khristovoverie, and "speaking in tongues". Bapism, which was viewed by Church and governmental authors as an example of a "rationalistic sect", gave rise to mystical Malëvannism and, somewhat later, Pentecostalism.

The so-called mystical and rationalistic religious forms in sectarianism did not have firm boundaries and succeeded one another in the course of development of each individual form of sectarianism. As a rule, the replacement of the rationalistic integument by the mystical accompanied the rebellion of the lower classes of the sect against its upper classes and the separating-out of the lower classes into a definite group. And on the contrary, as the upper classes succeeded in suppressing the opposition of the lower classes, the rationalistic integument replaced the mystical in sectarianism. Thus, mysticism and rationalism were not specific for this or that form of sectarianism as religious forms, but was a kind of ideological blanket, in which the internal struggle occurring between the upper and lower classes in the sects was wrapped.

The classification proposed by Miliukov is frankly idealistic. Miliukov calls sectarian teachings which are based on the Bible (the Gospels) Evangelical Christianity, while sectarian teachings based on so-called revelation he calls Spiritual Christianity. Essentially this is pure playing with synonyms, since Miliukov equates Spiritual Christianity with mystical and his Evangelical

Christianity with rationalistic. Strangely, Miliukov did not notice that his criticism of the division of sectarianism into mystical and rationalistic can be transferred word for word to the classification he proposes. In fact, do not Evangelical Christianity and Spiritual Christianity "proceed in parallel fashion in the development of Russian sectarianism and often combine or unite together in one and the same sect"?

Let us note, as we have done more than once, that the question of the attitude of this or that doctrine of sectarianism toward the Bible is by no means an idle one, if only we study it in the light of the historical evolution of sectarianism and the development of class struggle in it.

In their turn, the Tolstoyans made an attempt to classify sectarianism.

Deriving sectarianism from the spiritual searches of individuals, and arbitrarily distinguishing in these searches one level at which the desire for spiritual freedom exceeds the force of intellect, another level where this desire weakens, and finally a third level where a person constantly proceeds along the path of spiritual freedom, the Tolstoyans in accordance with this divided sectarians into three groups. In the first they put the Skoptsy and the Prygun movements, in the second Baptism and "moderate groups of Molokans", and in the third Dukhobors, "some branches ... of the Khlysty", and the Malëvannite movement (Biriukov 1905: 5-6. M. V. Muratov [1919: 17-20] expressed an opinion close to Biriukov's). The subjective-idealistic character of these judgments, their arbitrary nature and theoretical poverty, are evident.

The scientific classification of religious sectarianism should proceed first of all from an understanding of the character of sectarianism as a social phenomenon and the paths of its historical development.

I divide sectarianism into two groups: 1. Sects of democratic origin, rising out of the contradictions of serfdom and presenting themselves as "an expression of political protest in religious guise", and 2. Bourgeois sects, rising in the Reform era on the basis of contradictions of capitalism, reactionary in form and content, dissolving in religion the social protest of democratic elements.

Having in mind the basic groups in sectarianism, I place in the first group Khristovoverie, Dukhoborism, and Molokanism, and in the second Baptism, Evangelical Christianity, and Adventism.

I separate out the group of democratic sects primarily because of the fact of its genesis—in other words, taking into account the social significance of its origin—since for the democratic movement which preserves a religious integument, its gradual transformation into a bourgeois one was logical.

Religious sectarianism arose as social protest by the masses. But all the paths experienced in the history of religious sectarianism led away from the struggle for the class interests of the workers, and led the followers of sectarianism to subordinate themselves to the economic and political interests of the ruling classes. On the eve of the Great October Revolution, according to my data, a million workers in village and town were attached to sectarian organizations. Among the upper strata of these organizations were wealthy landowners and owners of enormous capitalist latifundia in the south of Russia, the Transcaucasus, Siberia and the Far East; among them there were also large industrialists and some representatives of monopoly capital. Their programs, carefully worked out in the period 1905-1917, served as the political expression of their interests as bourgeois property-owners. They had something to defend and knew very well what they wanted. From the old world in which the exploiters dominated, they brought out a fund of bourgeois ideas, and worked out a system for the moral disarming of believers, an attempt at organization and propaganda, in order to oppose all this to the world of communism, which was opened by the Great October Revolution.

The paths of evolution of religious sectarianism in Soviet society were complicated. Only with the final victory of socialism in our country was there a break in the political positions of sectarianism. In the face of ever-growing and strengthening moral-political unity of the Soviet people, of the whole people without division into believers and non-believers, the politically loyal line of sectarianism became the condition of the participation in it of the believers themselves.

The Great October Revolution profoundly undermined the social roots of religion.

Whereas in the period preceding the building of the foundation of the socialist economy there had taken place a decline of Molokanism, Dukhoborism and Khristovoverie, and as Baptism, Evangelical Christianity, Pentecostalism and Adventism grew at their expense (as of course also at the expense of Russian Orthodoxy), from the 1930s on there occurred a decline in these sects which did not exclude individual periods of intensification of their activity.

During the existence of Soviet society, the absolute number of followers of sectarianism has markedly declined.

Still more significantly, there has been a decline in the relative number of followers of sectarianism in the population of the Soviet Union in comparison with pre-Revolutionary times. For the ideological development of Soviet society, the departure of the working masses from all forms of religious world-view, including one of the strongest religious survivals—sectarianism, was a natural phenomenon. This increases all the more the significance and influence of the propaganda of social and natural science knowledge, directed toward the spiritual libertion of those Soviet people who are still under the influence of religious survivals of capitalism.

There is a place for the results of historical studies devoted to the social roots, consistent development, and socio-political role of religious sectarianism in the propaganda of scientific knowledge.

Editor's Notes

Note A. Marx distinguished two basic types of capitalist development: the Prussian, which takes places under the direct encouragement and control of the state; and the American, marked by a more or less unfettered growth of free enterprise. Most Soviet historians assign Russian capitalism to the Prussian type.

Note B. From *The Development of Capitalism in Russia*, 1903.

Note C. From *Who Are the Friends of the People?*, 1896.

Appendix

TABLE 1* MOLOKAN FARMS IN AMUR OBLAST BY 1894

| Names of volosts and settlements | Total house-holds | Number of residents | | | Land– |
		Total	Men	Women	Total
Village of Beloiarskaia	16	208	101	107	9,900
Ivanovka Volost					
Village of Andreevka	43	292	150	142	9,850
12 Molokan outlying farms	37	256	140	116	7,620
TOTAL HOLDINGS OF MOLOKANS IN IVANOVKA VOLOST	80	548	290	258	17,470
Gil'chin Volost					
Village of:					
Tolstovka	73	468	235	233	7,700
Tambovka	119	970	474	496	17,500
Gil'chin	66	502	246	256	12,350
Zharikovo	55	360	181	179	10,550
Chuevka	28	130	62	68	5,570
Verkhne-Urtui	10	75	44	31	1,730
Parunova	12	86	47	39	1,300
30 Molokan outlying farms	66	534	331	203	17,440
TOTAL HOLDINGS OF MOLOKANS IN GIL'CHIN VOLOST	429	3,125	1,620	1,505	74,140

*The table is compiled from data published in Grum-Grzhimailo (1894).
All tables were compiled by G. S. Lialina.

TABLE 1 (CONTINUED)

holdings, in des.				Under cultivation, in des.				
Farm-stead	Hay-field	Plowland with fallow	Overgrown by forest	Total	Groats	Spring Wheat	Oats	Barley
15	2,000	2,000	5,885		24	76	58	7
1,700	820	7,080		434	15	185	209	4
150	550	2,560		1,245	68	514	617	4
1,850	1,370	9,640		1,679	83	699	826	8
50	1,000	6,500		1,596	98	710	720	—
5,600	6,600	5,300		2,851	474	1,094	1,200	16
1,350	1,700	9,300		1,650	330	480	746	1
1,300	350	8,600		1,036	60	460	410	16
35	—	5,535		341	76	125	130	—
10	15	1,705		288	66	60	150	—
10	80	1,210		154	20	60	66	1.5
2,284	512	14,644		3,064	270	1,200	1,490	28
10,639	10,257	52,894		10,980	1,394	4,189	4,912	62.5

TABLE 1 (CONTINUED)

Names of volosts and settlements	Millet	Buck-wheat	Peas	Flax	Hemp	Melons
		Under cultivation, in des.				
Village of Beloiarskaia	3/4	1.5	—	0.5	2	—
Ivanovka Volost						
Village of Andreevka	6	—	1	1	1	12
12 Molokan outlying farms	23	1	—	—	—	18
TOTAL HOLDINGS OF MOLOKANS IN IVANOVKA VOLOST	29	1	1	1	1	30
Gil'chin Volost						
Village of:						
Tolstovka	60	—	—	—	—	8
Tambovka	66	1	—	—	—	—
Gil'chin	90	—	—	—	—	3
Zharikovo	90	—	—	—	—	—
Chuevka	10	—	—	—	—	—
Verkhne-Urtui	10	2	—	—	—	—
Parunova	5	1.5	—	—	—	—
30 Molokan outlying farm	46	—	—	—	—	30
TOTAL HOLDINGS OF MOLOKANS IN GIL'CHIN VOLOST	377	4.5	—	—	—	41

TABLE 1 (CONT

				Livestock, head			
			Cattle				
Horses	Cows	Bullocks	Oxen	Yearlings	Total	Sheep	Camels
135	98	22	—	50	170	200	—
257	134	14	—	90	238	—	—
550	223	113		154	490	170	46
807	357	127		244	728	170	46
440	190	50	—	94	334	135	—
700	400	8	—	192	600	600	—
920	328	113	53	311	805	530	—
270	150	5	25	70	250	—	—
95	80	—	—	—	114	—	—
184	80	40	12	38	170	380	—
55	46	11	11	41	109	45	—
1,130	600	160	67	323	1,150	270	75
3,794	1,684	387	168	975	3,198	1,825	75

TABLE 2. PEASANT FARMS OF TAMBOVKA AND GIL'CHIN VOLOSTS IN AMUR OBLAST IN 1917

Names of volosts and settlements	Number of Farms									Number of households with land	Parcels of land, des.		Number of households buying land	Purchased land, des.	
	Total	Hiring workers in a year	With no workers	With non-farming operations	With no cattle	Without working stock	Without cows	Without sown land	Without implements		Plowland	Hayfields		Plowland	Hayfields
Tambovka Volost															
Zharikovo	163	83	14	39	18	6	6	15	24	143	6,104.4	720.9	15	995.5	100.4
Novo-Aleksandrovskoe	160	81	12	26	17	4	8	16	25	131	9,262.2	876.1	—	—	—
Tambovka	274	128	17	43	15	19	14	21	37	251	10,130.7	328.0	34	2,943.1	264.8
Tolstovka	132	70	5	29	9	3	9	13	16	115	6,180.1	233.7	24	1,134.1	116.5
Chuevka	91	57	4	7	7	3	2	9	11	83	3,741.3	305.0	4	126.0	23.0
TOTAL	820	419	52	144	66	35	39	74	113	723	35,418.7	2,463.7	77	5,198.7	504.7
Gil'chin Volost															
Verkhne-Urtui	168	111	10	33	13	9	9	17	21	18	1,536.3	103.0	—	—	—
Gil'chin	26	13	2	14	7	—	—	7	7	144	9,736.5	702.7	—	—	—
TOTAL	194	124	12	47	20	9	9	24	28	162	11,272.8	805.7	—	—	—

*Tables 2-4 are compiled on the basis of data in *Poselennye itogi...*, (1918).

TABLE 2 (CONTINUED)

Names of volosts and settlements	Total Allotted and Purchased Land		Rented — Number of households			Quantity of rented land, in des.		Rented, des				Leased out, des.	
	Plowland	Hayfields	Renting land	Leasing out land	Renting and leasing out land	Plowland	Hayfields	in same community		in other communities		Plowland	Hayfields
								Plowland	Hayfields	Plowland	Hayfields		
Tambovka Volost													
Zharikovo	7,099.9	821.3	92	39	12	4,975.8	366.6	1,876.1	141.8	3,099.7	224.8	1,606.1	226.5
Novo-Aleksandrovskoe	9,262.2	876.1	62	62	4	2,918.6	399.6	2,918.6	389.4	—	10.2	3,911.1	155.0
Tambovka	13,073.8	592.8	160	57	2	6,385.1	339.3	3,605.7	78.6	2,779.4	260.7	1,885.8	10.0
Tolstovka	7,314.2	350.2	69	3	3	3,021.7	123.4	1,261.3	12.4	1,760.4	111.0	2,474.6	2.0
Chuevka	3,867.4	328.0	50	19	1	2,112.5	469.7	1,253.3	56.7	859.2	413.0	756.7	35.5
TOTAL	40,617.4	2,968.4	433	210	22	19,413.7	1,698.6	10,915.0	678.9	8,498.7	1,019.7	10,634.3	429
Gil'chin Volost													
Verkhne-Urtui	1,536.3	103.0	12	3	2	2,313.4	533.9	450.3	20.0	1,863.1	513.9	153.8	7.0
Gil'chin	9,736.5	702.7	89	16	29	7,573.5	1,858.8	2,349.8	294.8	5,223.7	1,564.0	1,120.3	66.4
TOTAL	11,272.8	805.7	101	19	31	9,886.9	2,392.7	2,800.1	314.8	7,086.8	2,077.9	1,278.6	73.4

TABLE 2 (CONTINUED)

Names of volosts and settlements	Sown area, des.				Population			Livestock			
	Under cultivation	Short-term fallow	Long-term fallow	Total Plowland	Men	Women	Including hired workers	Horses	Cattle	Sheep	Goats
Tambovka Volost											
Zharikovo	8,093.1	1,920.7	455.8	10,469.6	852	617	128	1,297	993	1,609	17
Novo-Aleksandrovskoe	6,353.2	1,675.3	241.2	8,269.7	545	425	84	1,038	646	1,362	3
Tambovka	13,278.7	4,167.5	126.9	17,573.1	1,403	1,067	216	2,307	1,396	1,550	19
Tolstovka	5,641.7	2,083.7	135.9	7,861.3	628	485	107	1,117	709	1,125	20
Chuevka	3,711.2	1,503.9	8.0	5,223.1	316	316	51	689	457	1,015	7
TOTAL	37,077.9	11,351.1	967.8	49,396.8	3,826	2,910	586	6,448	4,201	6,661	66
Gil'chin Volost											
Verkhne-Urtui	2,493.0	711.9	486.5	3,691.4	1,063	805	228	430	326	523	27
Gil'chin	10,350.9	4,534.6	1,304.2	16,189.7	173	111	70	1,836	1,727	2,161	133
TOTAL	12,843.9	5,246.5	1,790.7	19,881.1	1,236	916	298	2,266	2,053	2,685	160

TABLE 3*. PRIVATELY OWNED MOLOKAN FARMS OF GIL'CHIN AND TAMBOVKA VOLOSTS IN AMUR OBLAST, 1917

Volosts	Total Farms	Including operating on rented land	Hiring workers or clerical personnel	Lacking				
				Any livestock	Working stock	Cows	Sown land	Tools
Gil'chin	36	5	6	3	—	—	2	3
Tambovka	72	3	22	6	1	2	5	7
TOTAL	108	5	28	9	1	2	7	10

Volosts	Men			Women			Total men and women
	Total	Including work-capable*	Hired laborers	Total	Including work-capable*	Hired laborers	
Gil'chin	494	66	251	222	77	8	716
Tambovka	637	141	166	435	164	16	1,072
TOTAL	1,131	207	417	657	241	24	1,788

*This category includes men 18-60 yrs. of age and women 16-55; people in military service not included.

TABLE 3 (CONTINUED)

Volosts	Number of owners	Land-holding Having, des.		Number of households			Renting-Leasing Rented by them, des.		Leased by them, des.	
		Plowland	Hayfields	Renting land	Leasing out land	Renting and leasing out land	Plowland	Hayfields	Plowland	Hayfields
Gil'chin	34	6,083.5	315.8	26	4	4	4,170.7	841.3	1,055.5	16.7
Tambovka	70	7,809.2	454.1	44	7	11	6,325.5	380.7	749.0	—
TOTAL	104	13,892.5	769.9	70	11	15	10,496.2	1,222	1,804.5	16.7

Volosts	Sown areas, des.				Livestock							
	Sown	Short-term fallow	Long-term fallow	Total plowland	Horses	Cattle Oxen	Bullocks	Cows	Yearlings	Total	Sheep	Pigs
Gil'chin	5,751.6	2,256.8	1,490.4	9,498.7	893	—	25	273	496	794	917	88
Tambovka	8,719.6	2,402.8	2,263.3	13,385.7	1,375	4	39	395	735	1,173	815	63
TOTAL	14,471.1	4,659.6	3,753.7	22,884.4	2,268	4	64	668	1,231	1,967	1,732	151

TABLE 4. TECHNICAL EQUIPMENT OF THE MOLOKAN FARMS OF GIL'CHIN AND TAMBOVKA VOLOSTS IN AMUR OBLAST IN 1917

Volosts	Single-blade plows	Sowers	Reapers	Binders	Threshers	Winnowing machines	Carts on iron wheels	Carts on wooden wheels
Peasant Farms								
Gil'chin	350	115	109	169	62	101	201	792
Tambovka	1,138	513	313	692	213	438	393	2,331
Privately-owned Farms								
Gil'chin	145	38	40	92	19	44	42	337
Tambovka	241 + 1 multi-blade	81	74	146	53	80	107	446

Glossary

Note: We are indebted for some of the definitions in this glosary to *Dictionary of Russian Historical Terms from the Eleventh Century to 1917,* compiled by Sergei G. Pushkarev, edited by George Vernadsky and Ralph T. Fisher, Jr., New Haven and London, Yale University Press, 1970.

Artel'—a traditional form of organization of Russian workers in which the work group is hired and paid collectively and the pay is divided equally (or according to a set formula) among the members. In more modern times the collective farm is referred to officially as an agricultural artel'.

Ataman—the head of a Cossack community (*stanichnyi ataman*) or of an entire Host.

Beguny—"Runners"—a segment of the *bespopovtsy,* who were adherents of a world-rejecting doctrine, similar to *stranniki.*

Bespopovtsy—that segment of the Old Belief which does not recognise a priesthood; their congregations are headed by elected lay preceptors.

Black Hundred—The colloquial name for the Union for the Defense of the Russian People—a super patriotic and anti-Semitic para-military organization of the late 19th and early 20th century.

Chernozem—"Black Earth"—a band of fertile soil running through central Russia approximately east and west, and the territory occupied by this band of soil.

Chetvert'—a dry measure used in the 16th-17th centuries; 4-8 puds.

Commodity-and-money relations—in Marxist theory, relations characterized by the production of goods for sale rather than for personal consumption. The first stage in the development of the capitalist mode of production.

Cossacks—members of a special category of state peasant, settled in border areas (the North Caucasus, the Urals, the Western Ukraine, Eastern Siberia, etc.) who held land on condition of long-term military service, and were governed by their own laws and institutions.

CPSU—Communist Party of the Soviet Union.

Desiatina (pl.-Y)—in this text abbreviated to des.—a measure of area of 2,400 square sagenes, equal to 2.7 acres or 1.0925 hectares.

Edinolichnyi—an unaffiliated peasant, not belonging to a commune or (in modern times) a collective farm.

Edinoverie—a religious group intermediate between the Old Belief and Russian Orthodoxy, which had the right to perform the ritual according to the pre-Nikonian books, but was served by priests ordained in the Russian Orthodox Church.

Emancipation—the decree of Tsar Alexander II in 1861 freeing the serfs; also referred to as the Reform.

Eparchy—an administative division of the Russian Orthodox Church, equivalent to a diocese.

Exarchate—an administrative division of the Russian Orthodox Church operating outside historical Russian territory.

Guberniia—a province in pre-Revolutionary European Russia.

Host—one of the major units into which the Cossack population was divided, both militarily and geographically.

Inogorodyne—non-Cossack peasants living in Cossack communities.

Intelligentsia—generally, the educated part of the population; in modern usage, the term applies to all those holding jobs which call for higher or specialized secondry education.

Iskra—*The Spark,* the organ of the Russian Social Democratic Labor Party.

Izba—the Russian peasant cottage, usually consisting of two rooms separated by a passageway.

Kadetism—the doctrine and program of the Kadet (i.e., Constitutional-Democratic) Party, one of the major pre-Revolutionary political parties, which stood for free enterprise and parliamentary government on the Western European model.

Kholop—bondsman, agricultural slave.

Khutor (pl.-A)—an isolated farmstead, as opposed to one located in a village. Large numbers of these were created as a result of the Stolypin reforms in the early 20th century.

Kulak—a wealthy peasant, particularly one who employs hired labor.

Manufacture—in Marxist terminology, assembly-line production without the use of machines.

Meshchane—in pre-Revolutionary Russia, a catageory of small-scale traders and craftsmen, living in small towns and surburban settlements, and not holding farm land or belonging to peasant communities.

Mir—the Russian peasant community as land-holding entity; also its membership.

Narodnik—a member of a 19th century Russian intellectual-political movement which regarded the Russian peasantry as the source of the future revolution and of healthy Russian values in general.

Oblast—in tsarist Russia, a territorial division corresponding to the guberniia (province); used mainly in the non-European parts of the country.

Obrok—a money payment corresponding to quit-rent in feudal Europe.

Octobrists—the Union of the 17th of October [1907] favored a constitutional monarchy, but on agrarian issues were to the right of the Kadets.

Odnodvortsy—a category of state peasants settled in the borderlands, descended from low ranking service gentry.

Old Belief—Russian: *staroobriadchestvo* or *staroverie,* a conservative religious movement which arose from a rejection of the church reforms introduced by Patriarch Nikon in the 17th century. The movement had great social and political influence and included a large segment of the nascent bourgeoisie.

Otrub—a piece of communal land given to an individual family as private property, mainly as a result of the Stolypin reforms in agriculture.

Popovtsy—those Old Believers whose congregations were served by priests ordained in the Russian Orthodox Church who had defected, or had been ordained abroad.

Posad—urban settlement in Muscovy, inhabited by tradesmen, artisans and some peasants, with service and tax obligations.

Postniki—fasters; a movement within Khristovoverie, and later among the Dukhobors.

Postoiannye—steadfast Molokans, i.e. those who do not jump.

Prikaz—a government department in pre-Catherinian Russia.

Pryguny—Jumpers, a wing of Molokanism.

Pud—a measure of weight equal to 16.38 kilograms.

Reform—see Emancipation; a complex system of social and land-tenure reforms which was implemented only in part.

RSDRP—Russian Social Democratic Labor Party—the ancestral organization of the present-day Communist Party of the Soviet Union.

Sagene—a measure of length equal to approximtely 2.133 meters.

Shkod—the meeting of shareholding (and originally arms-bearing) members of a Russian peasant community, which debates and decides all matters relating to the economic and political life of the community.

Shtunda—a proto-Baptist sectarian movement of German origin, widespread in the southern Ukraine.

Sloboda—a settlement outside the city wall, inhabited by artisans and small tradesmen, usually of the meshchan estate.

Stanitsa (pl.-Y)—a Cossack community.

Starshina (pl.-Y)—the administrative head of a Russian peasant village, usually appointed by the shkod.

Stol'nik—a member of the lower nobility ranking below the members of the Boyar Duma; originally he had the duty of serving the tsar and his guests at the table.

Stranniki—"Wanderers" — a priestless Old Believer group who considered themselves in constant flight from the Antichrist.

Strelets—literally, archer; member of a military artisan group in pre-Petrine Russia.

Strigol'nik—member of an early Russian heretical sect dating from the 14th century.

Uezd—a territorial-administrative division in pre-Revolutionary European Russia subordinate to the guberniia.

Ulozhenie—generally a statute or code of laws, specifically the code promulgated in 1649 regulating the conditions of land ownership, the obligations of peasants etc.

Uniates—a religious group arising from the Union of Brest; essentially Roman Catholics of the Slavonic rite.

Verst—a measure of length usually equal to 0.663 miles.

Volost—a territorial-administrative division in European Russia subordinate to the uezd, usually including one village with its outlying settlements, or two neighboring villages.

Votchina—a hereditary landed estate held in full ownership, as opposed to one held on condition of service.

Zemstvo—a pre-Revolutionary organization charged with representative, administrative, and record-keeping functions on the local level, particularly public health and education.

Abbreviations Used

A—*Der Adventbote* (Herald of the Advent)
B—*Baptist*
Bb—*Bibleiskie Besedy*, na 1956 g., na 1958 g., na 1959 g. (Bible Talks for 1956, 1958, 1959.)
BV—*Blagaia vest'* (The Good News)
d. —dossier
div. —division
DKh—*Dukhovnyi khristianin* (Spirtiual Christian)
EZh—*Ezhemesiachnyi zhurnal literatury, nauki, obshchestvennoi zhizni* (SPb.) [Monthly Journal of Literature, Science and Public Life]
f. —file
G—*Gost'* (Guest)
KV—*Krymskii vestnik* (Crimean Herald)
L. —Leningrad
M. —Moscow
MIRA—Muzei istorii religii i ateizma (Museum of the History of Religion and Atheism)
MO—*Missionerskoe obozrenie* (Missionary Review)
MV—*Molokanskii vestnik* (Molokan Herald)
MZK—Materaily dlia izucheniia ekonomicheskogo byta gosudarstvennykh krest'ian Zakavkazkogo kraia (Materials for the Study of the Economic Life of State Peasants in the Transcaucasian Region), Vol. VII, (Tiflis)
ORF—Otdel rukopisnykh fondov, Instituta istorii Adademii nauk SSSR (Division of Manuscript Collection, Institute of History, Academy of Sciences, USSR)
OZ—*Otechestvennye zapiski* (Notes from the Fatherland)
Pg. —Petrograd
Raion—T-K-E zh.d. —Raion Tiflissko-Karssko-Erivanskoi zheleznoi dorogi v ekonomicheskom i kommercheskom otnosheniiakh (The Region of the Tiflis-Kars-Erevan Railroad from an Economic and Commercial Point of View), Tiflis
ROBIL—*Rukopisnyi otdel gosudarstvennoi biblioteki im. V. I. Lenina* (Manuscript Division of the V. I. Lenin State Library)
RV—*Russkii vestnik* (Russian Herald), Odessa
SI—*Slovo istiny* (Word of Truth)
SPb. —St. Petersburg
s.u. —storage unit
SV—*Sektantskii vestnik* (Sectarian Herald)
TsGADA—Tsentral'nyi Gosudarstvennyi Istoricheskii Arkhiv drevnykh aktov (Central State Archive of Ancient Documents)
TsGAOR—Tsentral'nyi Gosudarstvennyi Istoricheskii Arkhiv Oktiabr'skoi Revoliutsii (Central State Archive of the October Revolution)
TsGIAL—Tsentral'nyi Gosudarstvennyi Istoricheskii Arkhiv Leningrad (Central State Historical Archive Leningrad)
TsGIAM—Tsentral'nyi Gosudarstvennyi Istoricheskii Arkhiv Moskva (Central State Historical Archive Moscow)

UZ—Utrenniaia zvezda (Morning Star)
v. — verso
VIRA—Voprosy istorii religii i ateizma (Problems of the History of Religion and Atheism)
VKh—Vestnik Khristianina (The Christian's Herald)

Literature Cited

ABELOV, N. A. (1887) *Ekonomicheskii byt gosudartsvennykh krest'ian Elizavetpol'skogo uezda Elizavetpol'skoi gubernii* [Economic life of state peasants in Elizavetpol Uezd of Elizavetpol Guberniia], *MZK*, Tiflis, Vol. VII.

ADVENTISTS (1928) *Adventisty sed'mogo dnia (perevod s angl. iaz.)* [Seventh Day Adventists (Translated from English)], Khar'kov.

AFANAS'EV, P. (1915) *Sostoianie sektantstva i raskola-staroobriadchestva i deiatel'nost' pravoslavnoi missii v Ekaterinoslavskoi eparkhii v 1914 godu* [The State of Sectarianism and the Old Believer Schism and the Activity of the Orthodox Mission in the Ekaterinoslav Eparchy in 1914], Ekaterinoslav.

AIVAZOV, I. G. (1915) *Materialy dlia issledovaniia russkikh misticheskikh sekt, vyp. 1. Khristovshchina* [Materials for Study of Russian Mystical Sects, Issue 1, Khristovshchina], Vol. I, Pg.

AKTY (1836) *Akty Arkheograficheskoi ekspeditsii* [Transactions of the Archeographic Expedition], Vol. IV, No. 489 - 490, SPb.

ALEKHIN, A. (1912) Po povodu stat'i "Presviter ili sovet" [About the article "Presbyter or Council"], *B*, No. 12.

ALEKSII, BISHOP (1908) *Materialy dlia istorii religiozno-ratsionalisticheskogo dvizheniia na iuge Rossii vo vtoroi polovine XIX stoletiia* [Materials for the History of the Religio-Rationalistic Movement in the South of Russia in the Second Half of the Nineteenth Century], Kazan.

ALEKSII, BISHOP (1909) *Religiozno-ratsionalisticheskoe dvizhenie na iuge Rossii vo vtoroi polovine XIX stoletiia* [The Religio-Rationalistic Movement in the South of Russia in the Second Half of the Nineteenth Century], Kazan.

AMERICANA (1949) *Encyclopedia Americana*, Vol. 19, New York-Chicago.

ANON. (1914) Ego imperatorskoe velichestvo na Kavkaze [His Imperial Majesty in the Caucasus], *DKh*, No. 10-11.

ARGUTINSKII-DOLGORUKOV, A. M. (1897) Borchalinskii Uezd Tiflisskoi Gubernii. [Borchalinskii Uezd in Tiflis Guberniia], *Raion Tiflissko-Karssko-Erivanskoi zheleznoi dorogi v ekonomicheskom i kommercheskom otnosheniiakh* [The Region of the Tiflis-Kars-Erevan Railroad from an Economic and Commercial Point of View], Tiflis.

ASTYREV, N. (1891) Subbotniki v Rossii i Sibiri [Subbotniki in Russia and Siberia], *Severnyi vestnik* [Northern Herald], No. 6.

BAPTIST (1912) Molodye molokane [Young Molokans], *B*, No. 13.

BAPTIST MISSIONARY (1909) *Otchet baptistskogo missionerskogo obshchestva za 1907-1908 god* [Report of the Baptist Missionary Society for 1907-1908], Odessa.

BAPTIST YOUTH (1909) *Pervyi vserossiiskii s"ezd kruzhkov baptistskoi molodezhi...* [First All-Russian Congress of Baptist Youth Circles...]. Rostov-on-Don.

BARSKOV, Ia. L. (1912) *Pamiatniki pervykh let russkogo staroobriadchestva. Letopis' zaniatii imperatorskoi arkheograficheskoi komissii za 1911 g.* [Monuments of the First Years of the Russian Old Belief. Chronicle of the Transactions of the Imperial Archeographic Commission for 1911], vyp. 24, SPb.

BARSOV, NIKOLAI (1879) *Istoricheskie, kriticheskie i polemicheskie opyty* [Historical, Critical and Polemical Essays], SPb.

BELIAKOV, A. A. (1958) *Iunost' vozhdia. Vospominaniia sovremennika V. I. Lenina* [The Youth of the Leader. Reminiscences of a Contemporary of V. I. Lenin], M.

BELIAVSKAIA, L. B. (1962) Sotsial'no-ekonomicheskie posledstviia pereselencheskoi politiki Stolypina na Dal'nem Vostoke [The Socio-economic Consequences of Stolypin's Resettlement Policy in the Far East]. In *Osobennosti agrarnogo stroia Rossii v period imperializma* [Peculiarities of the Agrarian System in Russia in the Period of Imperialism], M.

BELOGORSKII, V. A. (1911) *Sekta adventistov* [The Adventist Sect], in Kal'nev, ed, 1911.

BELOUS, P. (1928) *Zakon i subbota vo svete sv. pisaniia* [The Law and the Sabbath in the Light of the Holy Scriptures], Khar'kov.

BERDIAEV, N. (1949) *Samopoznanie (opyt filosofskoi avtobiografii)* [Self-Knowledge (An Attempt at a Philosophical Autobiogaphy)], Paris.

BEREZHNIKOV, M. (1898) Obozrenie fabrichno-zavodskoi promyshlennosti Amurskoi Oblasti v 1896 g. [A Review of the Shop and Factory Industry of the Amur Oblast in 1896]. In *Zapiski Priamurskogo otdela imperatorskogo russkogo geograficheskogo obshchestva* [Transactions of the Amur Region Division of the Imperial Russian Geographical Society], Vol. III, vyp. III, Khabarovsk.

BIRIUKOV, P., comp. (1905) Malëvantsy. Istoriia odnoi sekty [The Malëvannites. The History of one Sect]. In *Materialy k istorii russkogo sektantstva* [Materials for the History of Russian Sectarianism], vyp. 9, England.

BIULLETEN' (1924) *Biulleten' Instituta V. I. Lenina* [Bulletin of the V. I. Lenin Institute], No. 2.

BOBRISHCHEV-PUSHKIN, A. M. (1902) *Sud i raskol'niki-sektanty* [The Court and Schismatic-Sectarians], SPb.

BOCHKAREV, V. P. (1897) Karsskaia oblast' [Kars Oblast], *Raion T-K-E zh.d.*

BOGRAD, E. Ia. (1961) Opyt izucheniia sovremennogo sektantstva v Michurinskom raione [A Preliminary Study of Contemporary Sectarianism in Michurinsk Raion], *VIRA*, vol IX.

BOLOTIN, ANDREI (1906) Vpechatlenie posetivshego iubileinoe torzhestvo…[The impression of One Who Attended a Jubilee Celebration], *MV*, No. 4-5.

BONCH-BRUEVICH, V. D. (1901a) Pis'ma dukhoborcheskogo rukovoditelia Petra Vasil'evicha Verigina [The Letters of the Dukhobor Leader Peter Vasil'evich Verigin]. In *Materialy k istorii i izucheniiu russkogo sektantstva* [Materials for the History and Study of Russian Sectarianism], vyp 1, Christchurch, England.

BONCH-BRUEVICH, V. D. (1901b) Rasskaz dukhobortsa Vasi Pozniakova… [Vasia Pozniakov's Narrative…], *Materialy…sektantstva*, vyp. 3, England.

(1902a) Sredi sektantov [Among the Sectarians], *Zhizn'* [Life], No. 2, pp. 280-307; No. 5, pp. 177-198; No. 6, pp. 250-270.

(1902b) Znachenie sektantstva dlia sovremennoi Rossii, [The significance of Sectarianism for Contemporary Russia], *Zhizn'* [Life], London, No. 1, 293-334.

BONCH-BRUEVICH, V. D. [Ol'khovskii, Vladimir] (1905) Obriady dukhobortsev [Rituals of the Dukhobors], *Zhivaia starina* [The Living Past], vyp, III and IV.

(1909) Izlozhenie mirosozertsaniia dukhobortsev [A Description of the World-View of the Dukhobors]. In *Materialy k istorii i izucheniiu russkogo sektantstva i raskola*, vyp. 2, SPb.

(1910) *Materialy k istorii i izucheniiu sovremennogo sektantstva i staroobriadchestva* [Materials Toward the History and the Study of Contemporary Sectarianism and the Old Belief], vyp. IX, SPb.

(1911a) *Materialy k istorii i izucheniiu sovremennogo sektantstva i staroobriadchestva* [Materials Toward the History and the Study of Contemporary Sectarianism and the Old Belief], Vol. III, SPb.

(1911b) Preseledovanie sektantov [Persecution of the Sectarians], *Sovremennyi mir* [The Modern World], No. 7.

(1911c) U zakavkazskikh dukhobortsev [Among the Transcaucasian Dukhobors], *Sovremennyi mir* [The Modern World], No. 6.

(1912a) *Otchet o poezdke v Zakavkaz'e i Predkavkaz'e dlia issledovaniia sektantskikh obshchin sentiabr' 1912 g.* [Report of a Journey to the Transcaucasus and North Caucasus for Study of Sectarian Communities, September 1912], Rukopisnyi otdel gosudarstvennoi bibliotetii im. V. I. Lenina (ROBIL), div. 369, sh 4-7.

(1912b) Polozhenie obiazyvaet [The Situation Obliges Us], *Sovremennyi mir* [The Modern World], February.

(1922) *Krivoe zerkalo sektantstva: Po povodu I Vserossiiskogo s"ezda sektantskikh s.-kh. i proizvodstvennykh ob"edinennii* [The Crooked Mirror of Sectarianism. On the Occasion of the First All-Russian Congress of Sectarian Agricultural and Production Organizations], Moscow.

(1924) *Kak pechatalis' i taino dostavlialis' v Rossiiu zapreshchennye izdaniia nashei partii* [How Our Party's Forbidden Publications Were Printed and Secretly Distributed in Russia], Moscow.

(1930) *Na boevykh postakh Fevral'skoi i Oktiabr'skoi revoliutsii* [At the Battle-Stations of the February and October Revolutions], Moscow.

(1959) *Izbrannye sochineniia* [Selected Works], Moscow, Vol. I.

BONDAR', S. D. (1911a) *Adventizm 7 dnia* [Seventh Day Adventism], SPb.

(1911b) *Sovremennoe sostoianie russkogo baptizma* [The Contemporary Condition of Russian Baptism], SPb.

(1915) *Sekta mennonitov v Rossii* [The Mennonite Sect in Russia], Petrograd.

(1916) *Sekty khlystov, shaloputov, dukhovnykh khristian, staryi novyi Izrail', subbotnikov i iudeistvuiushchikh* [The Sects of Khlysty, Shaloputs, Spiritual Christians, Old and New Israel, Subbotniki and Judaizers], Petrograd.

BOROZDIN, A. K. (1907) *Russkoe religioznoe raznomyslie* [Russian Religious Dissent], SPb.

CHISTOV, K. V. (1962) Legenda o Belovod'e [The Legend of Belovod'e]. In *Trudy Karel'skogo filiala Akademii Nauk SSSR. Voprosy literatury i narodnogo tvorchestva* [Transactions of the Karelian Branch of the Academy of Sciences, USSR. Questions of Literature and Folklore], vyp. 35, pp. 116-181.

COHEN, MORRIS RAPHAEL (1958) *Amerikanskaia mysl'* [American thought] Moscow. [Our source: 1962 *American Thought: A Critical Sketch*, N.Y., Collier].

CONTEMPORARY (1910) *Sovremennoe shtundo-baptistskoe dvizhenie v Severo-Zapadnom krae* [The Contemporary Shtundo-Baptist Movement in the North-West Region], Vil'na.

CPSU (1954) *KPSS v rezoliutsiiakh i resheniiakh s"ezdov, konferentsii i plenumov TsK* [The CPSU in Resolutions, and Decisions of Congresses, Conferences, and Plenums of the Central Committee], Moscow, 7th edition.

DANILOV, V. A. (1914) Ateisty vorob'inogo neba [The Atheists of Sparrows' Heaven], *DKh*, No. 6. (1916) S kem my vedem voniu i kak ee okonchit' [With Whom are We Waging War and How Do We End It?], *DKh*, No. 1-2.

DEMIKHOVICH, Ia. (1014) Chto privelo menia k sektantam i pochemu ia ushel ot nikh [What Brought Me to the Sectarians and Why I Left Them], *EZh* No. 8-9.

DINGEL'SHTEDT, N. (1885) *Zakavkazskie sektanty v ikh semeinom i religioznom bytu* [Transcaucasian Sectarians in Their Family and Religious Life], SPb.

DINGEL'SHTEDT N. D. (1878) Pryguny, *OZ*, No. 10.

DOBROTVORSKII, I. (1869) *Liudi Bozhii. Russkaia sekta tak nazyvaemykh dukhovnykh khristian* [God's People. A Russian Sect of So-Called Spiritual Christians], Kazan.

DRUZHININ, N. M. (1958a) *Gosudarstvennye krest'iane i reforma P. D. Kiseleva* [State Peasants and the Reform of P. D. Kiselev], vol. II, M.

(1958b) Sotsial'no-ekonomicheskie usloviia obrazovaniia russkoi burzhuaznoi natsii [The Socio-Economic Conditions of the Formation of the Russian Bourgeois Nation]. In *Voprosy formirovaniia russkoi narodnosti i natsii* [Questions of the Formation of The Russian People and Nation], M-L.

DUBROVSKII, S. M. (1963) Stolypinskaia zemel'naia reforma [The Stolypin Land Reform], M.

EB (1960) *Encyclopaedia Britannica*, Vol. 15, London-Chicago-Toronto.

EDITORIAL (1914) Otchet izdatel'skogo tovarishchestva dukhovnykh khristian za 1913 g. [The Report of the Publishing Committee of Spiritual Christians for 1913], *DKh*, No. 6.

EFIMOV, A. V. (1958) *Ocherki istorii SShA* [Outline of the History of the USA], M.

EMEL'IANOV, A. S. (1878) Ratsionalizm na iuge Rossii, [Rationalism in the South of Russia]. In *Otechestvennye zapiski* [Notes from the Fatherland], No. 5.

ERITSOV, A. D. (1887) Ekonomicheskii byt gosudarstvennykh krest'ian Borchalinskogo uezda Tiflisskoi gubernii [The Economic Life of State Peasants of Borchalinskii Uezd, Tiflis Guberniia], *MZK*.

EVANGELICAL (1912) *Otchet Russkogo evangel'skogo soiuza za III god* [Report of the Russian Evangelical Union for the Third Year], SPb.

FEDOSEEVETS (1861) Sredi sektantov. (Iz putevykh zametok). [Among the Sectarians. (From Travel Notes)], *Slovo* [The Word], SPb, February, pp. 37-40.

FETLER, V. A. (1910) *Statistika russkikh baptistov za 1909 g.* [Statistics on Russian Baptists for 1909], SPb.

FETLER, V. A. (1911) Tserkvi khristovoi v S.-Peterburge [the Churches of Christ in St. Petersburg], *G*, No. 10.

FEUERBACH, LUDWIG (1955) *Izbrannye filosofskie proizvedeniia, t. I* [Selected Philosophical Works, Vol. I], M.

FILIBERT, ANNA (1870) Predislovie k stat'e 'Neskol'ko slov o molokanakh v Tavricheskoi gubernii' [Preface to the Article 'A Few Works about the Molokans in Tavriia Guberniia'], *OZ*, No. 6.

FUNDUKLEI, I. (1852) *Statisticheskoe opisanie Kievskoi gubernii, ch. II* [A Statistical Description of Kiev Guberniia, Part II], SPb.

GEDEONOV, V. (1914) Svobodoverie [Free Thought], *G.*, No. 11.

GORCHAKOV, M. (1871) *O zemel'nykh vladeniiakh vserossiiskikh mitropolitov, patriarkhov i sv. Sinoda (988-1738 gg.)* [On the Land Hondings of the All-Russian Metropolitans, the Patriarchs, and the Holy Synod (988-1738)], SPb.

GREKULOV, E. F. (1963) Raskhody na religiiu v krest'ianskom biudzhete v kontse XIX – nachale XX v. [Expenditures on Religion in the Peasant Budget at the End of the 19th – Beginning of the 20th Century]. *VIRA*, Vol XII.

GRIGOR'EV (ms) Adventizm sed'mogo dnia v Rossii (Kratkii istoricheskii ocherk) [Seventh Day Adventists in Russia (A Short Historical Sketch)], Klibanov Collection. *ROBIL*, F 648, (A. I. Klibanov).

GRUM-GRZHIMAILO, G. E. (1894) *Opisanie Amurskoi oblasti* [Description of the Amur Oblast], SPb.

HEGEL, G. W. F. (1935) *Filisofiia istorii* [The Philosophy of History], M-L.

HERZEN, A. I. (1919) *Polnoe sobranie sochinenii i pisem* [Complete Works and Letters], Vol III, M-L.

IAKOVLEV, M. S. (1913) Pis'mo [A Letter], *DKh*, No. 6.

IAROSLAVSKII, E. (1925) *Na antireligioznom fronte* [On the Anti-Religious Front], M.

IASEVICH-BORODAEVSKAIA, V. I. (1912) *Bor'ba za veru. Istoriko-bytovye ocherki* [Struggle for Faith. Sketches of History and Daily Life]. SPb.

IATSUNSKII, V. K. (1957) Izmeneniia v razmeshchenii naseleniia v Evropeiskoi Rossii v 1724-1916 gg. [Changes in the Distribution of the Population in European Russia from 1724-1916]. In *Istoriia SSSR*, [History of the USSR], No. 1.

ITENBERG, B. S. (1963) Revoliutsionnye narodniki i voprosy religii [The Revolutionary Narodniks and Questions of Religion], *VIRA*, vol XI, pp. 299-302.

IUZOV, I. (1881) *Russkie dissidentry, starovery i dukhovnye khristiane* [Russian Dissidents, Old Believers and Spiritual Christians]. SPb.

IVANOV, A. (1910) *Otchet o sobranii evangel'skikh khristian 14 marta 1910 g.*, Novgorod.

IVANOV, V. V. (1910) Tsarstvo bozhie [The Kingdom of God], *B*, No. 48.

(1911) Polozhenie baptistov [The situation of the Baptists], *B*, No. 9.

(1914) Subbotnichestvo i adventizm [Sabbatarianism and Adventism), *B*, No. 11-12.

(1918) Kuda my zashli [Where We Have Gone], *SI*, No. 5-6.

IVANOV, V. AND D. MAZAEV (1909) *Vsemirnyi kongress baptistov v Londone* [World Congress of Baptists in London], Rostov-on-Don.

JAMES, WILLIAM (1910) *Mnogoobrazie religioznogo opyta* [The Varieties of Religious Experience], M. [Our source: The Varieties of Religious Experience, N. Y. Modern Library, 1929].

KALMYKOV, M. I. (1906) Otvet A. D. Grachevu [Reply to A. D. Grachev], *MV*, No. 6.

KAL'NEV, M. I., ed. (1911) *Russkie sektanty, ikh uchenie, kul't i sposoby propagandy* [The Russian Sectarians, Their Doctrine, Religous Practice and Means of Propaganda]. Odessa.

KANDIDOV, B. (1930) Sektantsvo i mirovaia voina [Sectarianism and the World War], *Ateist* [The Atheist], No. 51.

KANT, IMMANUEL (1915) *Kritika chistogo razuma* [The Critique of Pure Reason], Pg.

KAPELIUSH, F. (1931) *Religiia rannego kapitalizma* [The Religion of Early Capitalism], M.

KAUFMAN, A. A. (1905) *Po novym mestam (Ocherki i putevye zametki 1901-1903)* [In New Places (Sketches and Travel Notes, 1901-1903)], SPb.

KEL'SIEV, V. I., ed. (1863) *Sobranie postanovlenii po chasti raskola* [Collection of Enactments Concerning the Schism], Vol. I. vyp I, London.

KHARLAMOV, I. (1881) Idealizatory raskola [Idealizers of the Schism], *Delo* [The Cause], No. 9.
(1884a) Dukhobortsy [The Dukhobors], *Russkaia mysl'* [Russian Thought], No. 11-12.
(1884b) Stranniki. Ocherk po istorii raskola [The Wanderers. A sketch of the history of the Schism] *Russkaia mysl'* [Russian Thought], No. 4-6.
(1885) Shtundisty [The Shtundists], *Russkaia mysl'* [Russian Thought], No. 11-12.

KHMYROV, A. I. (1909) Dukhovnye khristiane v s. Mazurka Voron[ezhskoi] gub. [Spiritual Christians in the Village of Mazurka, Voronezh Guberniia], *DKh*, No. 3.

KLIBANOV, A. I. (1928) *Klassovoe litso sovremennogo sektantstva* [The Class Face of Contemporary Sectarianism], L.

KLIBANOV, A. I. (1931a) *Adventisty* [The Adventists], L.
(1931b) *Mennonity* [The Mennonites], M.
(1957) Proiskhozhdenie religioznogo sektantstva Rossii [The Origin of Religious Sectarianism in Russia], *Nauka i religiia (sbornik stenogramm lektsii)*], [Science and Religion (Collection of Lecture transcripts)], M.
(1959) V. D. Bonch-Bruevich i problemy religiozno-obshchestvennykh dvizhenii v Rossii [V. D. Bonch-Bruevich and Problems of Religio-Social Movements in Russia]. In *V. D. Bonch-Bruevich 1959*, pp. 7-28.
(1960) *Reformatsionnye dvizheniia v Rossii v XIV—pervoi polovine XVI vv.* [Reformationist Movements in Russia From the 14th to the Second Half of the 16th Centuries], M.
(1961a) Beseda s postnikom I. V. Selianskim [A Conversation with the Postnik I. V. Selianskii], *VIRA*, vol. IX.
(1961b) Sektantstvo v proshlom i nastoiashchem, *VIRA*, vol. IX. [See translation: The Dissident Denominations in the Past and Today, *Soviet Sociology*, 1965, Vol III, No. 4]
(1963) K khrakteristike novykh iavlenii v russkoi obshchestvennoi mysli vtoroi poloviny XVII—nachala XVIII vv. [Toward a Characterization of New Phenomena in Russian Social Thought in the Second Half of the 17th—Beginning of the 18th Centuries], *Istoriia SSSR* [History of the USSR], No. 6, pp. 85-103.

KOGAN, Iu. Ia. (1962) *Ocherki po istorii russkoi ateisticheskoi mysli XVIII v.* [Essays on the History of Russian Atheistic Thought in the 18th Century]. M.

KONOVALOV, D. (1914) Religioznye dvizheniia. I. Sekta khlystov. [Religious Movements. I. The Sect of Khlysty], *Ezhemesiachnyi zhurnal literatury, nauki i obshchestvennoi zhizni* [Monthly Journal of Literature, Science and Public Life], No. 3.

KOTLIAREVSKII, S. (1910) Dzhems kak religioznyi myslitel' (William James as Religious Thinker), *Voprosy filosofii i psikhologii* [Questions of Philosophy and Psychology], Book 5, M.

KRASIKOV, P.A. (1923) *Na tserkovnom fronte* [On the Church Front], M.

KREMENSKII, P. (1913) Nabolevshii vopros [An Urgent Question], *DKh*, No. 1.

KRYVELEV, I. A. (1960) *Lenin o religii* [Lenin on Religion], M.

KUDINOV, N. F. (1905) *Stoletie molokanstva v Rossii 1805-1906 gg.* [The Centennial of Molokanism in Russia, 1805-1905]. Baku.
(1913) *Dukhovyen khristiane. Molokane. Kratkii istoricheskii ocherk.* [The Spiritual Chrisitans. The Molokans. A Short Historical Sketch], Vladikavkaz.
(1914) O voine [On the War], *DKh.* No. 10-11.

KUNTSEVICH, L. (1912) Neskol'ko slov o 'novykh izrailiakh' [A Few Words on the "New Israels"], *Revnitel'* [The Zealot], No. 7, pp. 33-36.

KUSHNEROV, IVAN PETROVICH (1905) *Kratkaia zapiska o vozniknovenii, razvitii i o nastoiashchem polozhenii evangel'skogo dvizheniia v Rossii i o nuzhdakh russkikh evangel'skikh khristian (izvestnykh v obshchezhitii pod raznymi narodnymi klichkami: pashkovtsev, baptistov, novomolokan i t. p.)* [A Short Note on the Origin, Development and Present Situation of the Evangelical Movement in Russia and on the Needs of Russian Evangelical Christians (Known in Common Parlance under Various Nicknames: Pashkovites, Baptists, Neo-Molokans, Etc.)], SPb.

KUTEPOV, KONSTANTIN (1882) Sekty khlystov i skoptsov [The Sects of Khlysty and Skoptsy], Kazan.

LAVROVSKII, V. M. AND M. A. BARG (1958) Angliiskaia burzhuaznaia revoliutsiia XVII veka [The English Bourgeois Revolution in the 17th Century], M.

LEIKINA-SVIRSKAIA, V. R. (1955) Ateizm petrashevtsev [The Atheism of the Petrashevsky Circle], VIRA, vol. III.

LENIN, V. I. Polnoe sobranie sochinenii [Complete Works], M.

LESHCHENKO, N. N. (1959) Krest'ianskoe dvizhenie na Ukraine v svaizi s provedeniem reformy 1861 [The Peasant Movement in the Ukraine in Connection with the Introduction of the Reform of 1861], Kiev.

LESKOV, N. S. (1877) Velikosvetskii raskol. Lord Redstok i ego posledovateli [The High-Society Schism. Lord Radstock and His Followers], SPb.

LETOPISI (1861) Letopisi russkoi literatury i drevnosti [Chronicles of Russian Literature and Antiquities], vol, IV. M.

LETTERS (1916) Pis'ma k brat'iam evangel'skim khristianam-baptistam [Letters to Evangelical Christian-Baptist Brothers], Tiflis.

LIAISTER, A. F. (1912) Pryguny v Zakavkaz'e [The Pryguny in the Transcaucasus], Erevan.

LIALINA, G. S. (ms) Politicheskaia programma liberal'no-burzhuaznogo techeniia v baptizme (1905-1917 gg.) [The Political Program of the Liberal-Bourgeois Tendency in Baptism (1905-1917)].

LIASHCHENKO, P. I. (1956) Istoriia narodnogo khoziaistva SSSR [History of the Economy of the USSR], Vol. I, M.

LITVINTSEV, KONSTANTIN (1887) Amurskie sektanty: molokane i dukhobory [Amur Sectarians: Molokans and Dukhobors], Khristianskoe chtenie [Christian Readings], November-December.

LIVANOV, F. V. (1872) Raskol'niki i ostrozhniki [Schismatics and Convicts], SPb.

LOKHTEVA, G. N. (1961) Naemnyi trud v monastyrskom khoziaistve XVII v. (po materialam Troitskogo Gledenskogo monastyria) [Hired Labor on Monastery Farms in the 17th Century (From Materials of the Troitskii Gledenskii Monastery)], Russkoe gosudarstvo v XVII v. [The Russian State in the 17th Century], M. pp. 208-230.

LUKACHEVSKII, A. T. (1925) Sekantstvo prezhde i teper' [Sectarianism Then and Now], M.

MAKSIMOV, S. (1867) "Za Kavkaz" [The Transcaucasus], Delo, SPb., No. 6.

MALAKHOVA, I. A. (1961) Religioznoe sektantstvo v Tambovskoi oblasti v posleoktiabr'skii period i v nashi dni [Religious Sectarianism in Tambov Oblast in the post-October Period and In Our Time], VIRA, vol IX.

MALOV, P. N. (1948) Dukhobortsy, ikh istoriia, zhizn' i borba [The Dukhobors, Their History, Life and Struggle], Thrums, British Columbia.

MARFINKA. 1909 Opisnie sela Marfinki Taganr. okr, Donskoi oblasti [A Description of the Village of Marfinka, Taganrog Okrug, Don Oblast], DKh, No. 6.

MARKOV, EVGENII (1887) V glubi narodnoi [In the Depths of the People], Knizhki "Nedeli" [Nedelia Books], October, SPb.

MARX, K. AND F. ENGELS Sochineniia [Works], M.
    (1947) Izbrannye pis'ma [Selected Letters], M.
    [Correspondence] (1846-1895). A Selection with Commentary and Notes, Translated by Dona Torr, New York; International, 1936.

MASALKIN, A. I. (1893a) K istorii zakavkazskikh sektantov. Molokane [Towards the History of the Transcaucasian Sectarians. The Molokans], Kavkaz [The Caucasus], No. 306.
    (1893b) K istorii zakavkazskikh sektantov. Sektanty kak kolonizatory Zakavkaz'ia [Toward the History of the Transcaucasian Sectarians. Sectarians as Colonizers of the Transcaucasus], Kavkaz, [The Caucasus], No. 335.

MATORIN, N. M. (1931) Predislovie [Foreword]. In Klibanov 1931b.

MEL'GUNOV, S. P. (1907-1909) Tserkov' i gosudarstvo v Rossii. (K voprosu o svobode sovesti. Sbornik statei) [Church and State in Russia. (On the Question of Freedom of Conscience. A Collection of Articles)], vyp. 1-2. M.
    (1919) Iz istorii religiozno-obshchestvennykh dvizhenii v Rossii XIX v. [From the History of Religious-Social Movements in Russia in the 19th Century], M.

MEL'NIKOV, P. (1862) Schislenie raskol'nikov, [Counting the Schismatics], *RV*, No. 2.

(1868) Tainye sekty, [Secret Sects], *RV*, No. 5.

(1869) Belye golubi, rasskazy o skoptsakh i khlystakh, [White Doves: Tales of the Skoptsy and Khlysty], *RV*, No. 3-5.

MILIUKOV, P. (1931) *Ocherki po istorii russkoi kul'tury* [Outlines of the History of Russian Culture], Vol. II, Paris.

MINISTRY OF INTERNAL AFFAIRS (1858) *Sobranie postanovlenii po chasti raskola* [Collection of Enactments Concerning the Schism], SPb.

MIRONENKO, A. D. (1910) Zhizn' Alekseia [The Life of Aleksei]. In Bonch-Bruevich 1910.

MISSIONARY (1891) *Vtoroi missionerskii s''ezd v Moskve* [The Second Missionary Congress in Moscow], M.

MOCHALOV, V. D. (1958) *Krest'ianskoe khoziaistvo v Zakavkaz'e k kontsu XIX V.* [The Peasant Economy in the Transcaucasus at the End of the 19th Century], M.

MURATOV, M. V. (1916) Pereselenie novoizrail'tian [The Resettlement of the New Israelites], *EZh*, No. 2.

MURATOV, M. V. (1919) *Russkoe sektantstvo* [Russian Sectarianism], M.

NAGORNOV, A. A. (1910) Vpechatleniia ot Omskogo S''ezda 14 iiunia 1910 g. [Impressions From the Omsk Conference of June 14, 1910], *B*, No. 30.

NECHAEV, V. V. (1889) *Dela sledstvennykh o raskol'nikakh komissii v XVIII v. Opisanie dokumentov i bumag, khraniashchikhsia v Moskovskom arkhive Ministerstva iustitsii, kn. 6* Investigative Cases From the Commission on the Schismatics in the 18th Century. A Description of the Documents and Papers Kept in the Moscow Archives of the Ministry of Justice, Book 6], M.

NIKOL'SKII, N. M. (1930) *Istoriia russkoi tserkvi* [History of the Russian Church], M.

NILOV, NIKOLAI (1904) K voprosu o revoliutsionnoi rabote sredi sektantov [On the Question of Revolutionary Work among Sectarians], *Rassvet* [The Dawn], Geneva, No. 3.

NOVITSKII, OREST (1882) *O dukhoborakh* [On the Dukhobors], 2nd edition, Kiev.

NOVOSEL'SKII, A. A. (1949) *Rospis' krest'ianskikh dvorov, nakhodivshikhsia vo vladenii vysshego dukhovenstva monastyrei i dumnykh liudei, po perepisnym knigam 1678 g.* [A List of Peasant Households in the Possession of the Higher Clergy, Monasteries, and Members of the Boyar Duma, According to the Census Books of 1667], M-L, Vol IV.

OCHERKI (1960) *Ocherki novoi i noveishei istorii SShA* [Outline of the Recent and Current History of the USA], Vol. I, M.

OIDR (1887) *Chteniia Obshchestva istorii i drevnostei Rossiiskikh (OIDR)* [Papers of the Society for Russian History and Antiquities], Book 2.

OSTROUMOV, N. (1912) *Katasono-fedorovtsy* [Katasonovites-Fedorovites], Riazan.

OTCHET (1907) *Otchet o Vserossiiskom s''ezde dukhovnykh khristian (Molokan), sostoiavshemsia 22 iiulia 1905 goda* [Report on the All-Russian Congress of Spiritual Christians (Molokans), July 22, 1905], Tiflis.

PAMIATNIKI (1895) Pamiatniki drevnei pis'mennosti. Otrazitel'noe pisanie o novoizobretennom puti samoubiistvennykh smertei [Ancient Written Sources, A Rebuttal Concerning a New-Found Method of Suicide], CVIII, SPb.

PANKRATOV, A. S. (1910) *Ishchushchie boga. Ocherki sovremennykh religioznykh iskanii i nastroenii* [God Seekers. Sketches of Modern Religious Quests and Moods], M.

PANKRATOV, T. (1906) Vozliublennye i dorogie v gospode brat'ia. [Dear and Beloved Brothers in the Lord], *MV*, No. 6.

PARRINGTON, W. L. (1962) *Osnovnye techeniia amerikanskoi mysli* [Main Currents in American Thought], M. [Vol. II: The Romantic Revolution in America 1800-1860. New York: Harcourt, Brace & Co., 1927].

PAVLOV, PAVEL (1914) Bogatstvo tserkvi [The Wealth of the Church], *SI*, No. 29.

PAVLOV, V. G. (1918) O dukhe sviatom (iz propovedi V. G. Pavlova), [On the Holy Spirit (From a Sermon by V. G. Pavlov)], *SI*, No. 9-12.

PETROV, I. E. (1906) Dukhobory Elisavetpol'skogo uezda [The Dukhobors of Elizavetpol Uezd], Izvestiia Kavkazskogo otdela imperatorskogo Russkogo geograficheskogo obshchestva [Bulletin of the Caucasian Division of the Imperial Russian Geographical Society].

PETROVSKII, G. I. (1958) Vladimir Dmitrievich Bonch-Bruevich. Materialy k bibliografii uchenykh SSSR. *Seriia istoriio*, [Materials for a Bibliography of Scholars in the USSR]. Historical Series vyp 5.

PLATFORM (1905) Politicheskaia platforma Soiuza svobody, pravdy i miroliubiia [The Political Platform of the Union of Freedom, Truth and Love of Peace], *RV*, No. 263.

PLATONOV, A. I. (1905) K voprosu o predstoiashchei tserkovnoi reforme [On the Question of the Forthcoming Church Reform], SPb.

PLEKHANOV, G. V. (1925) *Sochineniia* [Works], M-L.

POKROVSKII, M. N. (1924) *Ocherk istorii russkoi kul'tury* [Outline of the History of Russian Culture], 6th edition, Kursk.

POPOV, I. (1907) Dukhobory. [The Dukhobors], In *Golos stepi* [Voice of the Steppes], Omsk, No. 39.

POSELENNYE (1918) *Poselennye itogi sel'skokhoziaistvennoi perepisi v Amurskoi oblasti v 1917 godu* [Village-by-Village Totals of the Agricultural Census in the Amur Region in 1917], Blagoveshchensk.

POSOSHKOV, I. T. (1895) *Zerkalo ochevidnoe (redaktsiia polnaia)* [The True Mirror (Complete Edition)], vyp. 1 and 2, Kazan.

POZDNIAKOV, V. (1914) Pravda o dukhoborakh. Zhizn' dukhoborov v Zakavkaz'e i v Sibiri [The truth about the Dukhobors. The life of the Dukhobors in the Transcaucasus and in Siberia], *EZh*, No. 8.

PRAVOSLAVNYI SOBESEDNIK (1858) Istoricheskie svedeniia o molokanskoi sekte [Historical Informtion About the Molokan Sect]. In *Pravoslavnyi sobesednik* [The Orthodox Interlocutor], Kazan, Book 3.

PRIAMUR'E (1909) Priamur'e. Fakty, tsifry, nabliudeniia, Sobrany na Dal'nem Vostoke sotrudnikami obshchezemskoi organizatsii [The Amur Area. Facts, Figures, Observations Collected in the Far East by Workers in the All-Zemstvo Organization], M.

PRIBAVLENIIA (1908) Pribavleniia k Tserkovnum vedomostiam 27 sentiabria 1908 g. [Supplement to the Church News of September 27, 1908], No. 39.

PROKHANOV, I. S. (1910a) Religioznoe brozhenie [Religious ferment], *UZ*, May 14, 1910.
(1910b) Zamechatel'naia poezdka [A remarkable journey], *UZ*, September 24, 1910.
(1911) Protestantizm i blagosostoianie narodov [Protestantism and the prosperity of peoples], *UZ*, June 22, 1911.

PRUGAVIN, A. S. (1881) Znachenie sektantstva v russkoi narodnoi zhizni [The Signifance of Sectarianism in the Life of the Russian People], *Russkaia mysl'* [Russian Thought], Book I.
(1887) *Raskol-sektantstvo* [Schism-Sectarianism], Vyp. 1, M.
(1904) *Religioznye otshchepentsy. Ocherki sovremennogo sektanstva* [Religious Dissidents. Sketches of Contemporary Sectarianism], vyp 1-2, SPb.
(1906) *Monastyrskie tiur'my v bor'be s sektanstvom* [Monastery Prisons in the Struggle with Sectarianism], M.
(1907) *Raskol vnizu i raskol vverkhu* [Schism on the Bottom and Schism on the Top], M.

PUTINTSEV, F. M. (1935) *Politicheskaia rol' i taktika sekt* [The Political Role and Tactics of the Sects], M.

RAEVSKII, A. P. (1904) Svidanie s Kondratiem Malëvannym (Iz vospominanii sotsial-demokrata) [A meeting with Kondratii Malëvannyi (From the Reminiscences of a Social-Democrat)], *Rassvet*, No. 1.

RASHIN, A. G. (1956) *Naselenie Rossii za 100 let* [The Population of Russia for 100 Years], M.

RASPREDELENIE (1902) *Raspredelenie staroobriadtsev i sektantov po tolkam i sektam* [Distribution of Old Believers and Sectarians By Groups and Sects], SPb.

RIB (1927) *Russkaia istoricheskaia biblioteka. Pamiatniki istorii staroobriadchestva XVII v.* [Russian Historical Library. Sources for the History of the Old Belief in the 17th Century], Vol. 39, L.

ROSTOVSKII, DIMITRII (1847) *Rozysk o raskol'nicheskoi branskoi vere.* [Investigation of a Schismatic Blasphemous Faith], M.

ROZHDESTVENSKII, ARSENII (1882) Klystovshchina i skopchestvo v Rossii [Khlysty and Skoptsy in Russia]. In *Chteniia v OIDR*, [Papers in OIDR], pp. I-III.

ROZHDESTVENSKII, ARSENII (1889) *Iuzhno-russkii shtundizm* [South-Russian Shtundism], SPb.

ROZHDESTVENSKII, T. (1899) Otkrytoe pis'mo [An Open Letter], *Voronezhskie eparkhial'nye vedomosti* [Voronezh Eparchy News], No. 14.

ROZHDESTVENSKII, T. S. and M. N. USPENSKII, comp. (1912) Pesni russkikh sektantov mistikov [Songs of Russian Mystical Sectarians]. In *Zapiski Imp. Russkogo geograficheskogo obshchestva po otd. etnografii* [Notes of the Imperial Russian Geographical Society Section on Ethnography], Vol. 35.

RYBIN, S. F. (1952) *Trud i mirnaia zhizn'* [Toil and the Peaceful Life], San Francisco.

RYNDZIUNSKII, P. G. (1950) Staroobriadcheskaia organizatsiia v usloviiakh razvitiia promyshlennogo kapitalizma [The Old Believer organization under the conditions of the development of industrial capitalism], *VIRA*, Vol. I.

(1954) Antitserkovnoe dvizhenie v Tambovskom krae v 60-kh godakh XVIII veka [The Anti-Church movement in the Tambov Area in the 1760s], *VIRA*, Vol, II.

(1955) Dvizhenie gosudarstvennykh krest'ian v Tambovskoi gubernii v 1842-1844 gg. [The Movement of State Peasants in Tambov Guberniia in 1842-1844], *Istoricheskie zapiski* [Historical Notes], Vol 54.

(1958) *Gorodskoe grazhdanstvo v doreformennoi Rossii* [The Urban Citizenship in Pre-Reform Russia], M.

SAFRONOV, F. G. (1961) *Russkie krest'iane v Iakutii (XVII—nachalo XX vv.)* [Russian Peasants in Iakutiia (17th—beginning of the 20th Centuries)], Iakutsk.

(1963) *Russkie krest'iane v Iakutiia* [Russian Peasants in Yakutiia], Yakutsk.

SAIAPIN, MIKHAIL (1915) Obshchie [The Obshchie], *EZh*, No. 1, part I, pp. 65-77: No. 2 part II, pp. 60-69.

SAKHAROV, F. (1887-1900) *Literatura istorii i oblicheniia russkogo raskola* [Literature of the History and Denunciation of the Russian Schism], vyp I-III, n.p.

SAMARIN, I. G., ed. (1928) *Dukh i zhizn'* [The Spirit and the Life], Second Edition, Los Angeles.

SAVEL'EV, G. (1912) Brat'ia i znakomye [Brothers and Acquaintances], *B*, No. 20.

S.B. (1910) Po povodu konchiny V. A. Karaulova. [On the Occasion of the death of V. A. Karaulov]. *Molokanin* [The Molokan], No. 8-9.

SBORNIK (1899) *Sbornik statisticheckikh dannykh o zemlevladenii i sposobakh khoziaistva v piati guberniiakh Zakavkazskogo kraia* [Collection of Statistical Data on Land-Holdings and Farming Methods in Five Guberniias of the Transcaucasian Region], Tiflis.

SEGAL', I. L. (1890) Russkie poseliane v Elizavetpol'skoi gubernii [Russian Peasants in Elizavetpol Guberniia], *Kavkaz* [The Causcasus], No. 42.

SEKTY (1896) *Sekty i veroucheniia v Soedinennykh Shtatakh Severnoi Ameriki* [Sects and Denominations in the United States of North America], SPb.

SEMENOV, I. M. (1909) Subbota gospodnia (k svedeniiu brat'ev priniavshikh adventizm). [The Lord's Sabbath (For the Information of Brothers who Have Adopted Adventism)], *DKh*, No. 5.

SHAKHNOVICH, M. I. (1961) *Lenin i problemy ateizma* [Lenin and Problems of Atheism], M-L.

SHAKNOVICH, M. I. (1963) V. D. Bonch-Bruevich—issledovatel' religiozno-obshchestvennykh dvizhenii v Rossii [V. D. Bonch-Bruevich—a Student of Religio-Social Movements in Russia]. In *Ezhegodnik muzeia istorii religii i ateizma* [Yearbook of the Museum for the History of Religion and Atheism], M. Vol VII, pp. 293-300.

SHCHAPOV, A. P. (1906) *Sochineniia* [Works], Vol. I. SPb.

SHELGUNOV, N. V. (n.d.) Sochineniia N. V. Shelgunova [The Essays of N. V. Shelgunov], 3rd edition, Vols. II & III, SPb.

SKVORTSOV, V. (1899) O pereselencheskom dvizhenii v Ameriku sredi zakavkazskikh 'dukhobor-postnikov' [On the resettlement movement to America among the Transcaucasian 'Postnik-Dukhobors'], *MO*, March.

SMIRNOV, A. V. (1896) *Urozhentsy i deiateli Vladimirskoi gubernii, poluchivshie izvestnost' no razlichnykh poprishchakh obshchestvennoi pol'zy* [Natives and Public Figures From Vladimir Guberniia, Who Have Achieved Fame in Various Fields of Public Endeavor]. Vladimir, pp. 144-159.

SMIRNOV, P. S. (1898) Vnytrennie voprosy v raskole v XVII veke [Internal Questions in the Schism in the 17th Century], SPb.

SOKOLOV, D. (1897) *K issledovaniam o sovremennoi khlystovshchine. Ocherk khlystovshchiny v predelakh Tarusskogo uezda Kaluzhskoi gubernii* [A Contribution to Studies of the Modern Khlyst Movement. Sketch of the Movement in the Boundaries of Tarussa Uezd, Kaluga Guberniia], Kaluga.

SREZNEVSKII, V. I. (1900) *Sborniki pisem I. T. Pososhkova k mitropolitu Stefanu Iavorskomu. Soobshchil V. I. Sreznevskii* [Collections of the Letters of I. T. Pososhkov to Metropolitan Stefan Iavorskii. Collected by V. I. Sreznevskii.], SPb.

STATE DUMA (1913) *Gosudarstvennaia Duma. Stenograficheskie otchety* [State Duma. Stenographic Reports], Part II, SPb.

STATISTICAL (1912) *Statisticheskie svedeniia o sektantakh k 1 ianvariia 1912* [Statistical Information on the Sectarians as of January 1, 1912] Spb.

STEPANOV, P. (1882-1883) Zametka o Karsskoi oblasti [A Note on Kars Oblast], *Izvestiia Kavkazkogo otdela imp. Russkogo geograficheskogo obshchestva* [Transactions of the Caucasian Division of the Imperial Russian Geographical Society], Vol. VII, vyp. 1-2.

STOIALOV, A. I. (1870) Svedenie o molokanakh Tavricheskoi gubernii [Informtion on the Molokans of Tavriia Guberniia], *OZ*, No. 6.

SUKHOREV, V. A. (1944) *Istoriia dukhobortsev* [A History of the Dukhobors], Canada.

SYNOD (1910) *Vsepoddanneishii otchet ober-prokurora sv. Sinoda...za 1905-1907 gody* [The Humble Report of the Over-Procurator of the Holy Synod...for 1905-1907], SPb. (1911-1916) In the text, these references are given as, e.g., "see the Reports for 1907-1914." According to Klibanov, Otchety...za 1908-1090 gody was published in St. Petersburg in 1911, that for 1910 was published in 1913, that for 1911-1912 was published in 1915; the Otchet...za 1913 gody appeared in Petrograd in 1915, and the Otchet for 1914 gody was published in Petrograd in 1916.]

TEPPONE, V. (1926) Bibliia — slovo bozhie [The Bible is the Word of God]. *Blagovestnik* [The Evangelist], No. 2.

TERLETSKII, G. (1891) *Sekta pashkovtsev* [The Pashkovite Sect], SPb.

TERLETSKII, G. (1911) Dukhobory [The Dukhobors], in *Kal'nev*, ed. 1911.

TEXTBOOK (1922) *Uchebnik na bibleiskie temy* [Textbook on Biblical Themes], Kharbin.

THOREAU, HENRY DAVID (1962) *Uolden ili zhizn' v lesu* [Walden or Life in the Woods], M. [*Walden.* New York: Airmont Publishing Co., 1965.].

TOLSTOI, V. (1864) O velikorossiiskikh bespopovskikh raskolakh v Zakavkaz'e — Obshchie molokane [On the Great Russian Priestless Schism in the Transcaucasus. Obshchie Molokans.], *Chteniia v OIDR* [Papers Read in OIDR], Vol IV.

TRET'IAKOV, M. I. (1911) Khlysty, in *Kal'nev*, ed. 1911.

TRUDY (1913) *Trudy Amurskoi ekspeditsii* [The Transactions of the Amur Expedition], vyp. II, Vol. III. SPb.

UIMOVICH-PONOMAREV, P. (1886) Zemledel'cheskoe bratstvo kak obychno-pravovoi institut sektantstva [The Agricultural Brotherhood as a Sectarian Institution in Customary Law], *Severnyi vestnik* [Northern Herald], Nos. 9 and 10.

USHINSKII, A. D. (1884) *O prichinakh poiavleniia ratsionalisticheskikh uchenii shtundy...* [On the Reasons for the Appearance of the Rationalistic Teaching of the Shtunda...], Kiev.

USHINSKII, A. D. (1886) *Verouchenie malorusskikh shtundistov* [The Dogma of the Ukrainian Shtundists], Kiev.

USPENSKII, G. I. (1949) *Polnoe sobranie sochinenii* [Complete Works], M, Vol. VIII.

USTIUGOV, N. V. and CHAEV, N. S. (1961) Russkaia tserkov' v XVII v. [The Russian Church in the 17th Century], *Russkoe gosudarstvo v XVII veke* [The Russian State in the 17th Century], M, pp. 295-329.

VAL'KEVICH, V. A. (1900) *Zapiski o propagande protestantsikh sekt v Rossii i osobenno na Kavkaze* [Note on the Propaganda of Protestant Sects in Russia and Especially in the Caucasus], Tiflis.

VARADINOV, N. (1863) *Istoriia Ministerstva vnutrennikh del, kn. 8* [History of the Ministry of Internal Affairs, Book 8], SPb.

VERIGIN, GRIGORII (1935) *Ne v sile bog, a v pravde* [God is Not in Power But In Truth], Paris.

VERMISHEV, Kh. A. (1886) Ekonomicheskii byt gosudarstvennykh krest'ian v Akhaltsisskom i Akhalkalaksskom uezdakh Tiflisskoi gubernii [Economic Life of State Peasants in Akhaltskhe and Akhalkalaki Uezds of Tiflis Guberniia], *MZK*, Vol. III, Tiflis.

VINOGRAD ROSSIISKII (ms) *Vinograd rossiiskii ili opisanie postradavshikh v Rossii za drevnetserkovnoe blagochestie* [The Russian Vineyard or a Description of Those Who Suffered in Russian For Old Church Piety].

VIRA (1961) *Voprosy istorii religii i ateizma* [Problems of the History of Religion and Atheism], vol. IX, M.

VLADIMIROV, V. I. (1938) *Timofei Mikhailovich Bondarev i Lev Nikolaevich Tolstoi* [Timofei Mikhailovich Bondarev and Lev Nikolaevich Tolstoi], Krasnoyarsk.

VOLKOV, N. (1931) *Sekta skoptsov* [The Sect of Skoptsy], Leningrad.

VORTOVSKII, NIKOLAI (1911) *Otchet o sostoianii raskolo-sektantstva v Tavricheskoi eparkhii za 1910 god* [Report on the Condition of the Schismatics and Sectarians in the Tavriia Eparchy for 1910...], n.p.

V.P. (1911) *Pravda o baptistakh* [The Truth About the Baptists], B, No. 46.

VVEDENSKII, ALEKSANDR (1913) *Deisvuiushchie zakonopolozheniia kasatel'no staroobriadtsev i sektantov* [The Legislation in Force Relative to Old Believers and Sectarians], Odessa.

VYSOTSKII, N. G. (1915) Delo o sekte, nazyvaemoi 'khristovshchinoi'. [A Case of the Sect Called 'Khristovchina'], *Russkii arkhiv* [Russian Archive], No. 2.

ZAITSEV, D. V. (1909a) Molodoe sobranie [The Youth Gathering], *DKh*, No. 10-11.

ZAITSEV, D. (1909b) Poezdka v selo Rasskazovo Tambovskoi gubernii [Journey to the Village of Rasskazovo in Tambov Guberniia], *DKh*, No. 5.

ZAITSEV, D. (1914) Idoly i voina [Idols and War], *DKh*, No. 10-11.

ZAVAROV, S. (1899) *Opyt issledovanniia sel'skogo khoziaistva khleborodnogo raiona Erivanskoi gubernii i Karsskoi oblasti* [A Preliminary Study of the Economy of the Grain-Producing Region of Erevan Guberniia and Kars Oblast], Tiflis.

ZERTSALOV, G. V. (1916) *Sel'skokhoziaistvennye kapitaly v seleniakh Tiflisskoi gubernii* [Agricultural Capital in the Villages of Tiflis Guberniia], Tiflis.

ZHABIN, S. (1914) Plevely [Weeds], *DKh*, No. 3.

ZHAROV, IOANN (1912) *Sekta Novyi Izrail v derevniakh Akatove i Piatovskom prikhoda sela Frolova Kaluzhskogo uezda* [The Sect of "New Israel" in the Villages of Akatov and Piatov Parish in Frolov Village of Kaluga Uezd], Kaluga.

ZHIKAREV, N. (1909) Iskateli pravdy (sredi malëvantsev) [Seekers of Truth (Among the Malëvannites)]. In *Poznanie Rossii, kn. II* [Knowledge of Russia, Book II].

ZHURNAL (1906) *Zhurnal zasedanii vtorogo vserossiiskogo s"ezda khristian evangelicheskogo ispovedaniia* [The Journal of Sessions of the Second All-Russian Congress of Christians of the Evangelical Faith], Melitopol.

Name Index

441

Subject Index

447